Psychology of Adjustment

SAGE was founded in 1965 by Sara Miller McCune to support the dissemination of usable knowledge by publishing innovative and high-quality research and teaching content. Today, we publish over 900 journals, including those of more than 400 learned societies, more than 800 new books per year, and a growing range of library products including archives, data, case studies, reports, and video. SAGE remains majority-owned by our founder, and after Sara's lifetime will become owned by a charitable trust that secures our continued independence.

Los Angeles | London | New Delhi | Singapore | Washington DC | Melbourne

Psychology of Adjustment
The Search for Meaningful Balance

John Moritsugu
Pacific Lutheran University

Elizabeth M. Vera
Loyola University Chicago

Jane Harmon Jacobs
Antioch University

Melissa Kennedy
Kennedy Psychological Services, PLLC

**SAGE**

Los Angeles | London | New Delhi
Singapore | Washington DC | Melbourne

FOR INFORMATION:

SAGE Publications, Inc.
2455 Teller Road
Thousand Oaks, California 91320
E-mail: order@sagepub.com

SAGE Publications Ltd.
1 Oliver's Yard
55 City Road
London, EC1Y 1SP
United Kingdom

SAGE Publications India Pvt. Ltd.
B 1/I 1 Mohan Cooperative Industrial Area
Mathura Road, New Delhi 110 044
India

SAGE Publications Asia-Pacific Pte. Ltd.
3 Church Street
#10-04 Samsung Hub
Singapore 049483

Printed in the United States of America

Library of Congress Cataloging-in-Publication Data

Names: Moritsugu, John, author.

Title: Psychology of adjustment : the search for meaningful balance / John Moritsugu, Pacific Lutheran University, United States, Elizabeth M. Vera, Loyola University Chicago, Jane Harmon Jacobs, Antioch University, Seattle, Melissa Kennedy, Kennedy Psychological Services PLLC.

Description: Los Angeles : SAGE, 2017. | Includes bibliographical references and index.

Identifiers: LCCN 2016020238 | ISBN 9781483319285 (pbk. : alk. paper)

Subjects: LCSH: Conduct of life—Psychological aspects. | Life cycle, Human—Psychological aspects. | Psychology.

Classification: LCC BF637.C5 M657 2017 | DDC 150—dc23 LC record available at https://lccn.loc.gov/2016020238

This book is printed on acid-free paper.

Acquisitions Editor: Reid Hester
Editorial Assistant: Alex Helmintoller
Production Editor: Laura Barrett
Copy Editor: Megan Markanich
Typesetter: C&M Digitals (P) Ltd.
Proofreader: Theresa Kay
Indexer: Judy Hunt
Cover Designer: Dally Verghese
Marketing Manager: Katherine Hepburn
Illustrator: Maria Reva

16 17 18 19 20 10 9 8 7 6 5 4 3 2 1

Brief Contents

Preface   xvii

About the Authors   xviii

PART 1   •   **Perspectives and Processes**   **1**

Chapter 1   •   Adjustment: A Life Process   **3**

Chapter 2   •   Purpose in Life   **27**

Chapter 3   •   Community Contexts   **45**

Chapter 4   •   Experience and Learning   **69**

Chapter 5   •   Mindfulness: A Path to Awareness   **89**

Chapter 6   •   Stress, Health, and Well-Being   **111**

PART 2   •   **Applications**   **137**

Chapter 7   •   Social Relationships   **139**

Chapter 8   •   Romance and Intimacy   **159**

Chapter 9   •   School   **179**

Chapter 10   •   Work and Vocation   **203**

Chapter 11   •   Money   **223**

Chapter 12   •   Aging   **243**

Chapter 13   •   Dysfunction and Maladjustment   **269**

Chapter 14   •   The Search for Balance and the Future   **303**

Glossary   331

References   339

Index   373

Contents

Preface   xvii

About the Authors   xviii

PART 1 • Perspectives and Processes   1

Chapter 1 • Adjustment: A Life Process   3

Adjustment   5

  Defining *Adjustment*   5

  Determining Adjustment in Individuals   6

    Goodness of Fit   6

    Lack of Problems   7

    Positive Life Experiences   8

    Mind–Body Health   9

ADJUSTMENT IN PRACTICE: SLEEP MATTERS   11

RESEARCHING ADJUSTMENT: BIOFEEDBACK   12

Types of Change   13

  Change Throughout Human Development   13

RESEARCHING ADJUSTMENT: ERIKSON'S PSYCHOSOCIAL
DEVELOPMENT—COLLEGE TO MIDLIFE   14

RESEARCHING ADJUSTMENT: POSITIVE PSYCHOLOGY   15

  Societal Change   17

Perceptions of Change   18

  Change Can Be Stressful   18

  Positive and Negative Change Events   18

  Planned and Unplanned Change   19

  Comprehensibility of Change   20

Traditions Contributing to Adjustment   20

  Interdisciplinary Approaches   20

  Psychoeducation   21

Organization of This Book   21

Conclusion   23

Chapter 2 • Purpose in Life   27

Existential Psychology   28

  Change, Impermanence, and Awareness of Death   29

  Experimental Existential Psychology   30

The Importance of Purpose and Meaning   31

  Coherence   32

  Purpose in Life   32

  Existential Hardiness   33

RESEARCHING ADJUSTMENT: Academic Hardiness and Grit   34

Spirituality and Religion   35

    Intrinsic and Extrinsic Orientation (Individual and Social)   36

    ASPIRES (Assessment of Spiritual and Religious Sentiments)   36

ADJUSTMENT IN PRACTICE: Five-Factor Theory of Personality   37

    Effects of Religion and Spirituality on Health   38

RESEARCHING ADJUSTMENT: Neurological Effects of Religious Belief   38

    Religion, Spirituality, and Meaning   39

    Note on Our Perspective   40

Autonomy, Choice, and Free Will   40

ADJUSTMENT IN PRACTICE: Creating Choice Conditions   41

Conclusion   41

Chapter 3 • Community Contexts   45

Mentoring   47

Social Support   48

    Types of Social Support   48

    Social Networks   50

      Indegree Centrality and Brokerage   50

      Basic Rules of Networking   51

    Social Capital   52

The Importance of Situation or Context   53

    Person by Situation Interactions   53

    Ecological Psychology and Behavioral Settings   53

RESEARCHING ADJUSTMENT: Context and Identity   54

    Discriminative Setting Stimuli   55

    Two Powerful Social Effects   56

      Conformity   56

      Obedience to Authority   57

ADJUSTMENT IN PRACTICE: In-Group, Out-Group   57

Culture   58

    Collectivist Versus Individualistic Cultures   59

    Cultural Complexes   60

Developmental Psychopathology   60

RESEARCHING ADJUSTMENT: Gene X Environment Interaction   61

    Resilience   63

    The Maturation and Socialization Process   65

Conclusion   66

Chapter 4 • Experience and Learning   69

Pavlovian Conditioning   70

    The Basics of Pavlovian Conditioning   70

    Preparedness in Behavior Acquisition   71

Operant Conditioning   72

    Discriminative Stimulus   73

    Response, Behavior, or Operant   73

RESEARCHING ADJUSTMENT: Hebb's Rule   73

    Consequences: Feedback, Reinforcement, Punishment,
or Nothing   74

ADJUSTMENT IN PRACTICE: Avoidance Learning   75

    Consequences That Are Predictable But Not Always There   75

ADJUSTMENT IN PRACTICE: Premack Principle   77

    Shaping   78

ADJUSTMENT IN PRACTICE: Self-Control   78

    Cognitive Behaviorism   79

Social Learning   80

    Modeling   80

    Perceived Self-Efficacy   81

    Collective Efficacy   81

    Learning Probabilities (Statistical Learning)   82

    Implicit and Explicit Learning   82

Cognitive Development   83

    Jean Piaget   83

    Lev Vygotsky   83

Active Learning   84

Conclusion   85

Chapter 5 • Mindfulness: A Path to Awareness   89

Mindfulness and Meditation   91

    Defining *Mindfulness*   91

    Defining *Meditation*   91

ADJUSTMENT IN PRACTICE: Meditation Exercise   93

History of Psychology and Mindfulness Research and Practice   94

    Origins of Mindfulness Practice   94

    Research on Meditation and Mindfulness   96

    Bridging Science and the Meditation Experience   97

Mindfulness in Practice   98

Mindfulness and Nonjudgmental Awareness ... 98

Mindfulness Promoting Self-Regulation ... 99

ADJUSTMENT IN PRACTICE: A WEEK OF MINDFULNESS ... 100

Mindfulness Promoting Compassion ... 101

ADJUSTMENT IN PRACTICE: CREATE A LOVING-KINDNESS
MEDITATION ... 102

On the Mindful Path: Moving Toward Action ... 103

The Beginning of Action and Change ... 104

The Foundation for Action ... 104

ADJUSTMENT IN PRACTICE: WHAT DO I VALUE? ... 105

The Path to Change ... 106

Moving Toward Commitment and Change ... 107

Conclusion ... 108

Chapter 6 • Stress, Health, and Well-Being ... 111

Stress ... 112

Stressors ... 113

RESEARCHING ADJUSTMENT: MEASURING STRESS ... 114

Stress Processes ... 117

Stress Reactions ... 117

Coping ... 119

Emotion-Focused and Problem Solving–Focused Coping ... 119

Active Coping and Avoidant Coping ... 120

Coping With Controllable Versus Uncontrollable Stressors ... 121

Coping With Culturally Related Stressors ... 122

Microaggressions ... 122

ADJUSTMENT IN PRACTICE: EXAMPLES OF
MICROAGGRESSIONS ... 123

Culturally Relevant Coping ... 123

Healthy Stress Management ... 124

Social Support ... 124

Physical Touch ... 124

Meditation ... 125

Exercise ... 126

Self-Help ... 126

Good Stress Versus Bad Stress ... 126

Bad Stress ... 127

Good Stress ... 127

Growth Through Adversity ... 128

Reframing ... 128

RESEARCHING ADJUSTMENT: STRESS AND TECHNOLOGY 130

    Health and Well-Being 131

    Diet and Nutrition 131

    Physical Activity and Exercise 133

    Avoiding Substance Use 134

Conclusion 135

PART 2 • Applications 137

Chapter 7 • Social Relationships 139

Friendship and Well-Being 140

    First Friendships 141

    Childhood Friendships 141

    Friendship and Diversity 143

    Friendships During Adolescence 143

RESEARCHING ADJUSTMENT: SIMILARITY AND FRIENDSHIPS 144

    Friendships and Social Media 145

    Adult Friendships 147

Friendship Maintenance 148

Building Blocks of Relationships 150

    Empathy and Compassion 150

ADJUSTMENT IN PRACTICE: TEACHING COMPASSION 152

    Altruism and Prosocial Behavior 152

Loneliness 153

Conclusion 155

Chapter 8 • Romance and Intimacy 159

The Seeds of Romance 160

Casual Sexual Arrangements 161

Committed Partnerships 162

    Healthy Intimate Relationships 163

ADJUSTMENT IN PRACTICE: MYTHS ABOUT GOOD RELATIONSHIPS 165

    Sexuality in Intimate Relationships 165

Gay and Lesbian Relationships 166

Intimacy Problems 168

    Infidelity 168

        Online Cheating Versus Off-Line Cheating 168

        To Cheat or Not to Cheat 169

    Relationship Violence 170

Ending Relationships 172

RESEARCHING ADJUSTMENT: PREDICTORS OF DIVORCE 173

Relationship Maintenance 175

Conclusion 176

Chapter 9 • School   179

School's Importance in the Life of a Child   180

     Fundamentals of School Success in Preschool and Kindergarten   181

ADJUSTMENT IN PRACTICE: HEAD START   182

     Individual and Environmental Factors Related to Academic Success   183

         Self-Beliefs   184

         Motivation   184

         School Belonging   185

ADJUSTMENT IN PRACTICE: BULLYING   185

         Teacher Beliefs   186

         Teachers' Encouragement and Praise   187

RESEARCHING ADJUSTMENT: INTELLIGENCE TESTING   188

         School Climate   189

         School Size   190

         School Resources   190

RESEARCHING ADJUSTMENT: SCHOOL DROPOUT   191

The College Experience   192

     First-Generation College Students   193

     Understanding College Success Factors   193

RESEARCHING ADJUSTMENT: TRIO PROGRAMS   194

     Helping College Students Succeed   196

Mentoring   198

ADJUSTMENT IN PRACTICE: HOW TO FIND AND GAIN A MENTOR   199

Conclusion   200

Chapter 10 • Work and Vocation   203

The Psychological Importance of Work   205

Work Across the Life Span   207

     Adolescence   207

     College   207

     Career Indecision   208

     First Job   209

RESEARCHING ADJUSTMENT: INVOLUNTARY JOB LOSS   209

     Midcareer   210

     Retirement   210

Demographic Factors in Vocational Development   211

RESEARCHING ADJUSTMENT: STEM CAREERS   212

Theories of Vocational Decision Making   214

     Theory of Occupational Circumscription and Compromise   214

     Social Cognitive Career Theory   215

     Theory of Person–Environment Fit   216

ADJUSTMENT IN PRACTICE: Holland's Theory 217

Rewards and Risks of Work 218

   Flow 218

   Job Stress 218

      Dealing With Work Stress 219

Conclusion 220

Chapter 11 • Money   223

The History of Money 225

Learning About Money 225

Developmental Aspects of Money 226

RESEARCHING ADJUSTMENT: Social Class 227

Behavioral Economics 228

   Comparisons 228

   Two Decision-Making Processes 229

RESEARCHING ADJUSTMENT: Money's Effect on Us 229

Money Skills 230

   Buying 230

      Seeing Free *Is Tempting* 230

      Slowing Down and Thinking 230

      Shopping When Tired 230

      Anticipating Pleasure 231

      Determining the Worth of Things Bought and Things Lost 231

      Delaying the Pain 232

ADJUSTMENT IN PRACTICE: Credit Cards and Loans 232

   Saving 234

      Parental Influence on Saving 234

      Identification With the Future Self 234

ADJUSTMENT IN PRACTICE: Present–Future Similarity Test 235

      The Powerful Self 236

      Regular and Automatic Savings 236

Money and Happiness 237

Conclusion 239

Chapter 12 • Aging   243

Life Expectancies 244

Age-Related Changes 246

   Physical Changes 246

      Early Adulthood 246

      Middle Adulthood 247

      Older Adulthood 248

RESEARCHING ADJUSTMENT: How Old Is Old?   248

Cognitive Changes   249

    Early Adulthood   249

    Middle Adulthood   250

    Older Adulthood   251

Socioemotional Changes of Aging   251

    Identity Changes   252

    Generativity and Meaning   252

    Sense of Control   253

    Social Support   253

ADJUSTMENT IN PRACTICE: Decreasing Loneliness   254

The Third Age   256

    Retirement   256

    Role Redefinition   257

    Finances   257

    Successful Aging   258

Adjusting to Losses   260

    Grieving   260

Aging in Place   263

RESEARCHING ADJUSTMENT: Retirement Communities and Nursing Homes   264

Conclusion   266

Chapter 13 • Dysfunction and Maladjustment   269

Section One: Mental Illness   271

    Supernatural, Somatogenic, and Psychogenic Explanations   271

    Mental Illness Today   273

Anxiety Disorders   274

    Origins of Anxiety Disorders   276

Mood Disorders   276

    Origins of Mood Disorders   277

Psychotic Disorders   277

    Origins of Psychosis   278

Eating Disorders   278

    Origins of Eating Disorders   279

Substance Abuse Disorders and Addictions   280

    Origins of Addictions   283

RESEARCHING ADJUSTMENT: Suicide—The Most Drastic Choice   284

Neurodevelopmental Disorders   286

    Attention Deficit Disorders   286

    Origins of Attention Deficit Disorders   287

    Autism Spectrum Disorder   287

    Origins of Autism Spectrum Disorder   287

Section Two: Treatment of Mental Illness   288

Early Treatment: Asylums   288

Psychotherapy: A Psychogenic Approach   289

ADJUSTMENT IN PRACTICE: THE EXPERIENCE OF
    SEEKING PROFESSIONAL HELP   291

Psychosurgeries and Psychotropic Medications: Somatogenic Approaches   293

    Psychotropic Surgeries   293

RESEARCHING ADJUSTMENT: BRAIN STIMULATION THERAPIES   294

    Psychotropic Medications   295

ADJUSTMENT IN PRACTICE: MAKING A CHOICE TO TRY MEDICATION   296

The Future of Mental Health   298

Conclusion   299

Chapter 14 • The Search for Balance and the Future   303

Personal Challenges of the Future   305

    The Dynamics of Person and Place   305

    Agency and Communion   307

    Personal Perspectives   308

Societal Challenges of the Future   309

    Diversity   309

      Demographics of Age and Ethnicity   310

      Gender and Sexual Orientation   311

    Effects of Diversity   312

    Reducing Reactivity and Increasing Appreciation   313

      Travel   314

RESEARCHING ADJUSTMENT: MULTICULTURAL EXPERIENCE   314

      Classes   314

      Being Happy   315

      Common Goals   315

      Desire to Change   315

      Contact   316

      Loving Kindness Meditation   316

      Declassification, Reclassification, Individuation   316

Changing Technologies   317

    A Brief History of Technology   317

    Technology Around the Globe   319

    Interpersonal Relationships   320

Negative and Positive Effects of Today's Technologies   322

    Narcissism   322

    Increasing Isolation   323

    Negative Self-Perceptions   323

    Internet Addiction   324

ADJUSTMENT APPLICATION: Steps to Healthy Limits in the
    Use of Technology   324
      Positive Aspects of the Internet   325
Conclusion   327
ADJUSTMENT IN PRACTICE: The Power of the Narrative   327

Glossary   331
References   339
Index   373

Preface

Psychology is a subject of great interest for students. One of the most popular majors in college, it attracts thousands who enroll in psychology courses every year. In answer to the question of why they want to study psychology, many students say that they look forward to a better understanding of themselves and those around them. The psychology of adjustment course is a direct answer to this desire to know more about human behavior.

This text presents answers to student curiosity. The reader will find research on changes in life, on the importance of purpose in life, on the influence of contexts in determining behavior, on how our experiences shape our expectations, on the importance of awareness of our experiences, and on stress as a process and as an outcome. The second half of the text examines what psychology knows about the topics important to the student's life: relationships, sex, school, work, money issues, and aging. There is also a chapter examining serious psychological disorders, along with a section on interventions for these disorders.

Novel to this text is a more explicit exploration of the existential psychological perspective, and how it emphasizes an understanding of life awareness, choice and the importance of purpose in our lives. Meaning and purpose are critical to the interpretation of life events and how we respond to these events.

A second major theme to the text is an emphasis on mindfulness. An entire chapter is dedicated to research and psychological writing on mindfulness and mediation. References to these topics can be found throughout the book. The usefulness of the mindfulness perspective has been demonstrated in studies at the cognitive, behavioral, physiological, and neurological levels. This text incorporates these findings where appropriate.

The authors all have years of teaching experience and apply this experience to their writing, using stories and framing questions to engage the student in exploring the details in each chapter. Psychological applications and research highlights are placed strategically throughout, along with key terms. The text presents diverse perspectives, both in the examples given and in the research cited.

Acknowledgments

We thank the editorial staff from SAGE. It has been a pleasure to work with Reid Hester, who gently shepherded this flock of writers from beginning to end. Development editor Lucy Berbeo helped in refining and sharpening the text and its organization. Leah Mori provided a constructive and critical perspective, helping us through a rewrite, restructuring, and development of chapter details. Megan Markanich helped us all with coordination of moving parts. Morgan Shannon served as our eLearning editor.

We close with a note of thanks to our own inspirational and transformational teachers. Dr. Abe Arkoff at the University of Hawaii provided a lasting framework for empowering and engaging teaching and learning. Dr. Wiley Sypher offered a balance of demanding high standards and providing the personal support to meet those standards. Over many years of teaching and working as psychologists, our students and patients have taught us, inspired us, and transformed our lives as much, if not more, than we have touched theirs. We sincerely thank them for their questions, their sharing, and their gifts of themselves.

SAGE Publishing gratefully acknowledges the contributions of the following reviewers: Rachelle Cohen, Georgia State University; Christopher Davis, Carleton University; Matt Diggs, Collin College; Wendy R. Dragon, Wright State University; Lorraine B. Festa, Arizona State University; Patrick Kubier, University of Central Oklahoma; Bernard H. Levin, Blue Ridge Community College; Sherri McCarthy, Northern Arizona University; Lorren Montou, Brookhaven Community College; and Patricia Taylor, University of La Verne.

About the Authors

John Moritsugu, Ph.D., is a Professor of Psychology at Pacific Lutheran University in Tacoma, Washington. He has taught at the undergraduate and graduate levels for more than forty years. Co-author of *Community Psychology, Fifth Edition* (2013), he has served on the editorial boards of *Cultural Diversity and Ethnic Minority Psychology*, the *Asian American Journal of Psychology*, the *Journal of Community Psychology*, and the *American Journal of Community Psychology*. He is a Fellow of the American Psychological Association, Divisions 1 (General), 27 (Community), and 45 (Culture, Ethnicity and Race).

Elizabeth M. Vera, Ph.D., is a Professor in the School of Education, Loyola University Chicago. Dr. Vera is the co-author of *Community Psychology, Fifth Edition*, the editor of *The Oxford Handbook of Prevention in Counseling Psychology* (2012), and the co-editor of *Social Justice and Culturally Relevant Prevention* (2012). Other publications include articles in *The Counseling Psychologist*, the *Journal of College Student Psychotherapy*, *Professional School Counseling*, and the *Journal of Counseling Psychology*, as well as chapters in *Violence Prevention*, the *Handbook of Racial & Ethnic Minority Psychology*, and the *Handbook of Counseling Psychology*.

Jane Harmon Jacobs, Ph.D., psychologist and educator, holds the position of Academic Dean at Antioch University Seattle. She has taught at the secondary and graduate levels. She has recently been involved in the creation of an interdisciplinary, applied undergraduate program in health counseling and psychology. Past positions have included Clinical Training Director and Dean of the School of Applied Psychology, Counseling and Family Therapy. She has enjoyed over twenty years of clinical experience with children, adolescents, and adults, and continues to be engaged in the study and application of mindfulness to life.

Melissa Kennedy, Ph.D., is a clinical psychologist living and working in Seattle, Washington. A recipient of the Excellence in Teaching Award from the American Psychological Association, as well as local teaching awards, Dr. Kennedy has greatly enjoyed her time teaching psychology at both the college preparatory and graduate levels. Previously on the faculty at Holy Names Academy and Antioch University Seattle, she is currently in private practice providing psychotherapy to adolescents and adults, including couples and families.

Part 1

Perspectives and Processes

Chapter

1

Adjustment

A Life Process

Learning Objectives

1. Explain what adjustment means in psychology and how it is determined in individuals.

2. Identify the different types of internal and external change that humans experience.

3. Describe various ways that individuals perceive change.

4. Discuss the two traditions in psychology that influence the study of adjustment.

5. Summarize the approach of each of the two parts of this text.

Mark had been looking forward to college for a long time. He remembered sitting in elementary school classes and hearing of the great things that awaited him in college. This was reinforced in high school. While most of his friends were not interested in more education, more time away from making money, more reading and writing and studying, Mark had that desire for more. He was not the traditional college student from the right neighborhood, the right high school, the right family. He worked his way into the opportunity, saving his money and living at home until one day he had enough. There were a few years of work between high school and college, but with loans, scholarships, his savings, and his steady job earnings, he went to college.

The college halls did not look like those in high school. The lawns and buildings were more manicured. Mark found course expectations to be different. In high school, attendance was important. In college, many of his professors did not take attendance. He was expected to be there. If he did not come to class, it was his responsibility to master the materials covered. When he asked the teacher for notes, he received a friendly but adamant no. It was up to him to generate the notes. While the professors were happy to help in many ways, the subtle shift in responsibility from teacher to student was clear. And in response, he found that he liked the responsibility. He was an active partner in his education. No more hiding in the back. No more sneaking out of class. It was his education to seek and to gain.

***

Martha assumed she would go to college for as long as she could remember. Her parents were college educated, and their friends were college graduates. She started to collect college banners early in high school (University of Michigan, Yale University, UCLA, University of Hawaii, University of Washington, Arizona State University). She spoke with her parents about what to consider in school selection: size of the student body, geographic location, private or public, and liberal arts-oriented or a research university. By her junior year, she had a list of 20 possibilities and brochures for each school. She visited several campuses at the end of her junior year and into the summer. By the beginning of her senior year, she knew her preferred choices and her second choices. She applied for "early decision" but did not get accepted. When she did get into a university, she did not receive a large financial aid package. And given shifts in her parents' employment, this meant that she would have to work to help pay for her expenses. While possible, this meant that she would have to struggle to include some of the college extracurricular activities on which she had planned or to forgo them if the time did not allow.

Martha went to college but found the experience to be different from what she expected. There were new friends to make. Classes were held at different times. The professor did not always teach the class session. So Martha found herself having to manage her time, balancing studies, work, and social activities. Because she lived on campus, her parents did not oversee her life. Instead, she had roommates her age with whom to relate. Some were neat and some were not. Differences in lifestyle became apparent very quickly. These things made for more changes in her life, and they were not easy.

Throughout life, change and adjusting to change go hand in hand. Mark and Martha both experienced a period of **adjustment** to their new college surroundings. The transition from high school to college represents a normal activity within the range of lifetime events. While this change involves moving from one school setting to another, the differences in physical site characteristics, time schedules, expectations, and behavioral requirements (self-monitoring, appropriate pacing, focus, verbal and mathematical fluency, attention to deadlines) can be challenging. Students are able to adjust to these new settings, while others are not. Success or failure is related to a variety of factors, including skills (interpersonal, self-regulatory, task completion, study, social collaboration), motivation (vocational interests), and resources (general knowledge, technology-related knowledge, access to information helpful to career and educational decisions; American Institutes for Research, 2013; Camara, O'Connor, Mattern, & Hanson, 2015).

This chapter defines *adjustment* and examines the variety of ways adjustment can be achieved through a psychological lens. Adjustment assumes that the world is dynamic and ever changing. These changes may occur within ourselves or in the world around us. Therefore, we will explore how change comes to us throughout our lives and how we perceive these changes. The chapter briefly examines the traditions that have influenced considerations of adjustment. Finally, the book's outline and organization are explained, providing a mental map of what is to follow.

Adjustment

The individual is in a continuous relationship with his or her ever-changing environment. This is a process of seeking balance between internal and external demands, between the needs for continuity and for adaptability to the new, and between the self and others in the larger community. Successful balancing leads to success in adjustment, finding meaning and purpose, learning the necessary skills, and being open to the benefits of compassion and emotion. You will know more about yourself and about others by the end of this book. This information should prove useful in finding balance.

Defining *Adjustment*

Adjustment is defined as coping with the problems of normal, everyday life (Halonen & Santrock, 1997; Weiten, Dunn, & Yost Hammer, 2015). The Latin roots to the term are *ad jure* or "to bring or make right." Our lives are in continuous change, so our adjusting or making it right is a constant process.

Adjustment is like answering the question, how are you? The answer could be a simple "fine," but it could be a lot more complex. The complete answer depends on the depth and breadth of what is meant. For example, a more complete answer could be this: "I am physically fine for now, but I have not slept well for the past few days, my relationship with my significant other is in a delicate position, my job seems overly demanding, I am wondering about the purpose of my life, and my financial position has just taken a very positive advance in the last few days." All of these responses are legitimate and cover different areas of our life. Table 1.1 lists some of the questions addressed in studying adjustment. The questions have a consistent theme: how well we are doing with living a normal life, experiencing everyday challenges, and doing what most people do.

"How are you?" "Do you want the long answer or the short answer?"

©iStockphoto.com/lentolo

Table 1.1	Questions Addressed in Adjustment
What makes us attractive?	
Friends or lovers?	
Does practice make perfect?	
What is really important in life?	
What really makes us happy in life?	
Money: How is it important? How is it unimportant?	
What is the best way to study for a test?	
Does helping others help us?	

Many students study psychology with the expectation that they can find answers to their questions about themselves and their lives. How do humans function? How do relationships work? What in life really matters? These questions are typical to students of psychology. Adjustment attempts to address some of these questions. We will explore some of these questions in this text.

Determining Adjustment in Individuals

Given that adjustment has to do with coping with everyday life, how might an adjusted person look? There are a number of ways we might determine an individual is adjusted. Psychology has provided several models for examining this determination.

Goodness of Fit

The dictionary definition of *adjust* is to "arrange, compose or harmonize; adapt oneself or get used to changed circumstances" ("Adjust," 1993, p. 27). A given situation dictates appropriate and expected behavior. An example using a physical environment is wearing a warm set of clothing in Alaska in the winter. In contrast, a setting like Hawaii or Tahiti would not call for such clothing.

Our behaviors must adapt to our setting or, more specifically, to the environmental conditions. These conditions can be physical, like temperature, or they can be social, like norms and expectations. In a similar way, as clothing choices are dependent on temperature, social behaviors that are acceptable in high school might not be acceptable in college. Examples might include trading notes, skipping class, having meals with teachers, talking with instructors during office hours, volunteering an answer, or initiating a line of questioning in class. Mentioning how much one has been studying may be rewarded in one social **context**, and noting how much one has not been studying may be rewarded in another. This matching context with behaviors is known as **goodness of fit**.

Goodness of fit results when the properties of the environment and its expectations and demands are in accord with the organism's own capacities, characteristics and styles of behaving. When consonance between organism and environment is present optimal development in a progressive direction is possible. (Chess & Thomas, 1999, p. 3)

Studying adjustment provides an opportunity to reflect on life.

This definition speaks to the importance of context as well as personality in determining successful **pathways**. The fit of a person to his or her environment is an **ecological** way of understanding adjustment. An ecological view examines the relationship of an organism to its environment. The context must be understood as well as the individual (Barker, 1965; Bronfenbrenner, 1979, 1993; Kelly, 1966, 2006; see Figure 1.1).

Consider how a new student fits into her college setting. She might read differently, dress differently, or come to think differently. In fact, that is what is expected of her. Or consider what happens when two friends attend different colleges. Meeting over Christmas break, they might find that one refers to the *New York Times* and the other the *Wall Street Journal* or their manner of speaking may be affected—one slower and the other faster, one more animated and the other more level. The assumption is that they have been shaped by their environmental context.

Context shapes our personality, our developmental direction, and the manifestation of any genetic predispositions (Chess & Thomas, 1991; Lerner, 1983; Lerner, Lerner, von Eye, Bowers, & Lewin-Bizan, 2011). The importance of context will be further discussed in Chapter 3. For now, the individual's work for a good fit

What is appropriate for one setting is not for another.

between himself or herself and the environment is important to understanding adjustment and the process of adjustment. In our opening stories, both of the college students had to change. Their situations required them to deal with their college circumstances. Some of these were financial, some were social, and some were academic. In both examples, the students had to acquire new behaviors in order to adjust to their new environments—that is, to fit in.

Lack of Problems

Adjustment is usually assumed when an individual is not experiencing any problems. A lack of problems suggests a level of success in dealing with the environment. Given psychology's historical focus on pathology and problems (Seligman & Csikszentmihalyi, 2000), the lack of mental illness symptoms seems to be a good way to define adjustment.

However, psychopathology is more likely to develop at a particular age. "Half of all lifetime cases start by age 14 years and three fourths by age 24 years" (Kessler et al., 2005, p. 593). The average age of onset of depression is the mid-20s, and the average age for generalized anxiety is 30 (Kessler et al., 2005). If problem pathology is related to age, then one is left to wonder about the biological bases to these problems or to the particular demands of the developmental period.

Problems, or the lack thereof, are dependent on multiple factors and are discussed in Chapter 13. The latest research models support a varying mix of environment and genetics to be factors in psychopathology (Gottesman, 2001; Silberg, Maes, & Eaves, 2010; Sue, Sue, & Sue, 2013). An overview of the genetic studies of depression still cites the interaction of biological vulnerabilities with environmental events (Lohoff, 2010), and there is ample research pointing to the social factors also at play in risk of pathology (Hames, Hagan, & Joiner, 2013).

There are critics of this approach to viewing the human experience. In particular, by definition, problems in living are termed *abnormal*—that is, outside the range of normal. This pathologically based definition also ignores the positive aspects of our

Figure 1.1 Bronfenbrenner's Ecological Model

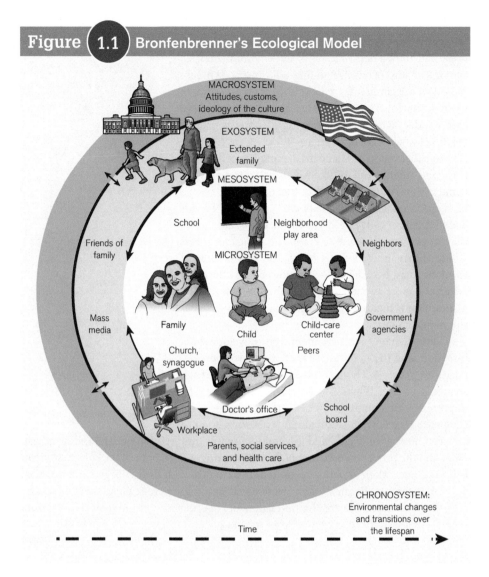

Source: Adapted from Bronfenbrenner and Morris (2006).

lives and the potential for growth and development (Cowen, 1998; Jahoda, 1958; Seligman & Csikszentmihalyi, 2000; Seligman, Steen, Park, & Peterson, 2005).

Adjustment is more than a lack of disease and problems. Though psychology has traditionally focused on the pathological, or the lack of the pathological (Seligman & Csikszentmihalyi, 2000), there is more to life than avoiding problems. The enhancement of life is important, which is what the next definition of adjustment entails.

Positive Life Experiences

Enjoying the company of friends, feeling satisfied with the achievement of some difficult task, or realizing the solution to a problem are examples of positive life experiences. While psychology has been criticized for focusing on people's problems—as far back as 1958—there has been a coherent scholarly argument for an alternative. In 1958, Marie Jahoda first wrote of **positive mental health**. She noted that the lack of pathology was not health. Pathology has to do with what has gone wrong, while health has to do with what is going right.

Jahoda (1958) reviewed the psychological literature and recommended several ways for defining *mental health*. They included an accurate and empathic perception of reality; mastery of skills in love, work, and play; a balanced sense of self; self-regulatory skills; and an investment in living, growth, and actualization. We will discuss many of these topics over the course of this text. These topics provide a good summary of adjustment beyond having no problems.

Cowen (1994), many years later, argued for health-promoting processes to help develop the positive mental health attributes defined by Jahoda (1958). Specifically, Cowen described the pathways to psychological well-being. These conditions included having wholesome attachments, being provided with opportunities to learn appropriate skills and competencies for life tasks and for dealing with stressors, and having settings that encouraged adaptation and fostered a sense of empowerment.

Masten and Tellegen (2012) summarized several decades of work on competency-building communities. They believe such communities are positive and encouraging, nurturing, and competent. In these settings, skills in self-control and good decision making are taught and rewarded. The communities promote hope and the development of a sense of a meaningful life. And lastly, in such communities, one would find helpful friends, partners, and social systems (such as schools and police) to aid the development of competencies. The goal is a **competent individual**, one who has "the ability to be effective, given the situation of one's age and the demands of the setting" (Masten & Coastworth, 1995, p. 724). The competent individual deals with the ever-changing challenges from the environment and continually learns to navigate new territories.

Stepping beyond the traditional, Seligman and Csikszentmihalyi (2000) believed that psychology usually ignored the positive aspects of our psyche. Much research and theory has focused on problems and pathology and ignored the positive aspects of our experience and lives. A solution to this negative orientation was to attend to our virtues. This shift has brought attention to the admirable qualities in human beings. Table 1.2 lists some of the topics in the *Handbook of Positive Psychology* (Snyder & Lopez, 2001) and the *Oxford Handbook of Positive Psychology* (Altmaier & Hansen, 2011). As shown in the table, there are an ample number of topics. Adjustment could be defined as the development of such positive aspects to our existence.

This list is not exhaustive, but it is certainly a good set of examples of the admirable qualities that humans can possess. Psychology is now actively investigating various aspects of this positive psychology. There is even a journal devoted specifically to positive psychology (*Journal of Positive Psychology*). This movement might recommend adjustment to look at how we can be positive, well-functioning, and competent and contribute to the growth of ourselves and those around us. So "being all we can be" in the positive sense might be a way of defining *adjustment* that goes beyond the mere lack of problems.

Mind–Body Health

There is a growing body of research demonstrating the relationship between our psychological well-being and our physical well-being. That leads us to our last way of defining *adjustment*: a holistic definition that argues the integration of mind and body.

Examples of emotional and physical health appear all around us.

Table 1.2 Positive Psychology Topics

Subjective well-being	Authenticity
Resilience	Humility
Flow	Compassion
Positive affect	Forgiveness
Self-esteem	Gratitude
Emotional intelligence	Love
Creativity	Empathy and altruism
Mindfulness	Morality
Optimism	Social support
Hope	Meaningfulness
Curiosity	Humor
Wisdom	Spirituality

Research in psychology and in medicine has found clear evidence of mind–body interaction. Rather than representing two separate parts of one person, there are demonstrable linkages between the physical and the psychological.

In the early 1900s, Walter Cannon's (1915, 1929) research on stress and the fight-or-flight reaction pointed to the influence of the environmental experience (threat detected) and the physical response (body activates, getting ready for fight or flight). Being startled or scared creates body reactions that accompany action (rapid breathing, heart rate acceleration, activation of sweat glands). A **general adaptation syndrome (GAS)** describes the sequence of physiological arousal in response to an environmental stressor (Selye, 1955, 1956). Given this sequence, if the organism is unsuccessful in dealing with the stressor, the body would become exhausted and vulnerable to illness.

Fagundas and Way (2014) reported on the linkages between early childhood stress and later adult vulnerability to inflammation within our bodies. This vulnerability is believed to relate to illnesses such as heart disease, type 2 diabetes, arthritis, and some cancers (Ershler & Keller, 2000).

Epel et al. (2004) found that chronic stress negatively influences the cell's ability to replicate. **Telomeres**, protecting cellular information used in reproduction, were found to be shorter in those suffering chronic stress. This meant that reproduction was less accurate and more distorted over time.

Stress and the mind–body linkages to health will be described in depth in Chapter 6. For the purposes of this definition of adjustment, it may be best to note that prolonged stress decreases our body's ability to fend off infection (Segerstrom & Miller, 2004) and damages the cell's ability to reproduce itself (Epel et al., 2004).

A psychological refinement to stress theory found that the environmental stressor was "in the eye of the beholder"

©iStockphoto.com/Manuel Faba Ortega

Stress can make us vulnerable to illness.

and that it was the appraisal of the event that really mattered (Folkman, Lazarus, Dunkel-Schetter, DeLongis, & Gruen, 1986). Research since the 1980s has continued to reaffirm the importance of our thoughts in the stress process (Gunnar & Quevedo, 2007; Lazarus, 1993). What we think (the psychology) impacts how our body reacts. In turn, our body's reactions influence how we think. Pressman, Gallagher, and Lopez (2013) have found this connection between emotion and health in global data. The relationships were even stronger in other, less economically developed parts of the world.

An excellent example of this linkage at a personal level can be found in sleep and memory. Sleep is necessary to clear biochemical elements that build up during a person's awakened state. Without sleep, the waste of the day remains and interferes with memory functions. This is a case of the body influencing the mind (see Adjustment in Practice: Sleep Matters).

ADJUSTMENT IN PRACTICE
Sleep Matters

We've been told that getting enough sleep is important. Researchers have started to find the reasons why sleep is a physical necessity. Studies on mice have found that while they slept, the space between cells grew as much as 60% allowing for extraneous particles, such as plaque, to be removed from the intercellular spaces. This allows for better brain functioning during the awake state (Xie et al., 2013). Other work has found sleep deprivation and disruption of our sleep cycles decreased metabolism and the ability to handle sugar, increasing diabetes risk and weight control. This disruption took 9 days to correct metabolically (Buxton et al., 2012).

Memory studies underscored sleep serves to facilitate learning before it occurs and after (Walker, 2009a, 2009b). Before, it allows for better apprehension of information in the memory system (called encoding), and after learning, it helps to consolidate our memories, fitting the events of the day into a meaningful framework.

To get a good night's sleep, experts recommend the following:

1. Build a routine into your sleep habits. Your body can then anticipate sleep to come.

2. Start the process of sleeping into a gradual shift, rather than assuming your body will be at your command to instantly do as you want. So that means less excitement, calming signals, and no bright flashing lights. Ideal temperature seems to be around 60 to 67 degrees.

3. Have a place you can readily associate with sleeping—for most, a bed—so that you are signaling sleep behavior to come. For example, sleeping in a given location helps. Some might always sleep on the couch. They have learned the couch is for sleeping.

(Continued)

(Continued)

4. Get physical exercise during the day.

5. Treat sleep as a rhythmic activity. Bright lights signal awake, and dim lights and darkness signal sleep. Try to go to sleep at the same time every night.

6. If you can't sleep, go elsewhere until you feel sleepy again. You want to associate bed with sleep or sex, not with work.

Suggestions adapted from National Sleep Foundation, Healthy Sleep Tips (n.d.).

Reflection Questions

1. When was the last time you had trouble sleeping?

2. Do you remember how you felt the next day? Your thinking? Your mood?

3. How did you feel to get a good night of sleep after that?

4. What were some ways that helped getting to sleep?

In the opposite direction, there are growing numbers of studies showing how we consciously control what were considered **autonomic nervous system** functions (autonomic standing for uncontrolled), which has been demonstrated by decades of research on the practice of biofeedback (see Researching Adjustment: Biofeedback).

RESEARCHING ADJUSTMENT
Biofeedback

Paying attention to our body and the signals it gives us allows us to gain some control over those reactions. Kimmel (1974) and later Miller (1978) described the human ability to gain control over visceral body functions and summarized a growing body of findings to support this. Among the classic types of body responses studied were brain waves (Kamiya, 1969), heart rate (Lang, 1974), muscle tension, and skin conductivity (Prokasky & Raskin, 1973).

Using a simple device, people have learned to relax by paying attention to the amount of moisture on their fingertips. This moisture is measured by a small, undetectable electrical current running between two fingers. Since moisture is a better conductor of electricity, a device signals when the electrical current is weaker or stronger. The participant then consciously tries to bring the signal under his or her control. The latest extension of this biofeedback technology is called neurofeedback (Wyckoff & Birbaumer, 2014). Research indicates the possible effective use of neurofeedback on an issue such as attention deficit disorders (Arns, Heinrich, & Strehl, 2013; Steiner, Frenette, Rene, Brennan, & Perrin, 2014).

Biofeedback gives the individual the power to regulate their very basic physiological reactions. Self-regulation is seen as a part of general self-control, which has been found to be predictive of future health, lack of problems with substance abuse, higher income level, and lower risk of criminal offense (Moffitt et al., 2011). While biofeedback deals with a simple and direct form of self-control, it provides a basis for regulating physical–emotional reactions that are so important in dealing with our environments.

Reflection Questions

1. Can you think of an example of calming down?

2. What are some advantages of responding in a calm and quiet emotional state?

3. When could this skill be helpful?

The ancient Greeks and Chinese may have had it right when they thought that a healthy mind and a healthy body are intricately related. As the saying goes, "A sound mind in a sound body" (attributed to several authors: Juvenal, Thales of Miletus, or John Locke).

Adjustment is dictated by the way we deal with different situations. It can be determined by goodness of fit between the person and the environment, a lack of psychological problems, a developed and healthy life experience, or a combination of physical and psychological well-being. Now, let us consider the situations to which we must adjust.

Types of Change

You can never step into the same river; for new waters are always flowing on to you.

Heraclitus

Change is an inevitable part of life. It occurs personally, throughout our development, and externally, in our surrounding world.

Change Throughout Human Development

Physical aging brings about many physiological and psychological changes. One need only look at typical growth charts to see one of the indicators of this type of change. No one expects us to be the same in kindergarten and then later in high school. Biologically, we typically grow larger in mass; change in muscular development; experience hormonally driven shifts in physiology; and evolve in terms of personality, behavioral tendencies, motivations, and interests. See Researching Adjustment: Erikson's Psychosocial Development—College to Midlife.

RESEARCHING ADJUSTMENT
Erikson's Psychosocial Development–College to Midlife

> Erik Erikson's theory is one of the most influential theories in the field of human development. His stages of development are included in most introductory psychology textbooks and are a central focus of chapters in . . . human development textbooks. (Dunkel & Sefcek, 2009, p. 13)

Erikson believed the important psychological developments in our life were the result of interactions with our external social world (Erikson, 1950). His theory and research looked at *psychosocial development*. The social environment and the individual's psyche moved the individual in a "natural" progression through eight stages related to life tasks (Dunkel & Sefcek, 2009). Successfully dealing with these life tasks laid the foundation for the tasks to come. Notably, these issues were not left behind when new issues arose but continued to be a part of the person's development (Whitbourne, Sneed, & Sayer, 2009).

A study of psychosocial stage development of college students, conducted with two different groups (starting in the mid-1960s and mid-1970s) and then followed for 30/30+ years found changes in the different psychosocial issues as the group grew older (Whitbourne et al., 2009). Industry (learning how to accomplish work tasks) is usually attributed to elementary school years. Yet industry was found to be an issue at age 17 and continued to grow as an issue until people's late 40s. Intimacy (the establishment of close relationships) is an issue that is typically focused on those in their late teens and early 20s. But intimacy progressed from age 17 into the late 30s and leveled off there. Those who were lower on intimacy in their teens usually accelerated through their 20s and caught up with the others by their 30s. A third area of psychosocial development, called *generativity* (making a contribution to society and preparing the next generation for life), has been attributed to those in their 30s or older. Generativity was found in low levels among the teens and showed a slow, steady increase over time. These findings illustrated the continuing nature of the tasks and issues across the lifetime and that development was not always toward more and greater, such as in the leveling off of intimacy and industry.

While many study Erikson's psychosocial stages as a set of eight age-specific stages, this is not as the theorist intended (Erikson, 1950; Whitbourne et al., 2009). Rather, they are issues identified as important to individuals over the course of their life. These issues don't go away but develop over time in ways that correspond to social pressures.

Reflection Questions

1. Why do you think industry continues to be important and grow beyond college?

2. Why might it level off?

3. What about intimacy?

4. What does it mean that those low in intimacy catch up with those who are high in intimacy?

5. And why does intimacy level off in people's late 30s?

A map of these developmental trends is described for us by our society and our culture (Lerner, 1991). Though there is wide variation in these trends, there are the typical stages that most people experience during their development. Erik Erikson (1950) provided the classic description of psychosocial development where both psychological needs and social demands resulted in conflicts and subsequent resolution of those conflicts. The resolution of these issues direct how people perceived their world and how they interacted with that world. Following Erikson's organization, our personal qualities of hope, will, purpose, competence, fidelity, love, care, and wisdom are determined by the resolution of these developmental issues (see Table 1.3). It is not so surprising to note that many of these qualities relate to areas identified as strengths and values under positive psychology (see Researching Adjustment: Positive Psychology).

Table 1.3	Positive Human Qualities From Erikson's Theories of Development
Age	**Virtue Resulting From Successful Resolution of Issues**
0–2	Hope
2–4	Will
4–5	Purpose
5–12	Sense of competence
12–19	Fidelity
19–39	Love
39–65	Care
65–death	Wisdom

RESEARCHING ADJUSTMENT
Positive Psychology

A wave tossed Mihaly Csikszentmihalyi (known for his work on the existential psychology and on "flow") onto the shore of the rocky Kona coast on the Big Island of Hawaii. He was greeted by a sympathetic stranger who

(Continued)

(Continued)

offered to help him get to the infirmary. This stranger turned out to be Martin Seligman (known for his work on *learned helplessness* and on *optimism*; Csikszentmihalyi, personal communication, 2014). From this harrowing chance meeting grew a series of serious discussions on the state of the field of psychology. Their families combined vacations, offering the men an opportunity to discuss mutual concerns over the direction of the field. What emerged from these conversations was an organized response to psychology's illness and pathology focus.

Rather than studying what is wrong with humans, they proposed a "positive psychology," which emphasized the admirable qualities to our humanity. Seligman and Csikszentmihalyi (2000) defined *positive psychology* as the "science of positive subjective experience, positive individual traits and positive institutions. . .(seeking) to articulate a vision of the good life. . . (and) what actions lead to well-being, to positive individuals, and to thriving communities" (p. 5). This eventually led to a special issue in the journal *American Psychologist*, the field's premier publication. Over the next 16 years, specially targeted journals, research centers, grants, and other institutional agencies have come to support this focus on a positive psychology. Research on hope, gratitude, patience, compassion, and wisdom have grown from this repositioning of psychology. Another way to understand adjustment would be to look at the ways in which we develop and use these positive tendencies. You will see ample references to these topics throughout this text.

Reflection Questions

1. What do you see as your positive qualities?

2. How do people react to the expression of these qualities?

3. What are some of the positive qualities you appreciate in others?

4. Do these make it easier to live life?

Research findings support the importance of our social interactions from infancy to early adulthood on our adulthood relationships (Englund, Kuo, Puig, & Collins, 2011). The successful engagement of our social environment brings resources to help us in the present and into the future.

While Erikson (1968/1993) emphasized one critical issue for each of his stages, there are many tasks that must be learned and resolved (McCormick, Kuo, & Masten, 2011). Some of these tasks are common to us all (finding food, drink, and shelter) and some are specific to a culture (table manners, polite conversation, and hunting). While the attainment of the skills may not be set to an exact age, the acquisition of these skills is ultimately important to our success in a society. Hutteman, Hennecke, Orth, Reitz, and Specht (2014) presented a list of some of the tasks of adulthood (see Table 1.4).

In both McCormick et al.'s (2011) and Hutteman et al.'s (2014) life tasks, the commonality is the need for the individual to adjust to the social environment and his or her

Table 1.4 Developmental Tasks of Adulthood

Early Adulthood (18–30)
  Establishing
    Romantic Relationship (Dating, Decisions on Intimacy, Criteria)
    Family Life (Partnership, Marriage, Tasks, Responsibilities, Children)
    Job Life (Career Choice, Internships, First Jobs)
    Social Life (Friendships, Activities, Interests)

Middle Adulthood (30–60)
  Maintaining and developing
    Romantic Relationship (Investment of Time and Emotions)
    Family Life (Partnership, Money, Raising Children, Priorities)
    Job Life (Survival, Advancement, Development)
    Social Life (Deepening of Friendships)
    Adjusting to Physical Changes (Flexibility, Weight)

Old Adulthood (60+)
  Adjusting to further changes in
    Romantic Relationship (Intimacy, Physicality)
    Family Life (Empty Nest, Shift in Family/Work Balance)
    Job Life (New Directions, Retirement)
    Social Life (Deal with New Relationships, Passing of Old Friends)
    Physical Aspects (Changes in Strength and Endurance)

Source: Hutteman et al. (2014).

place in the child to adulthood development. These tasks are continually changing as we continue to age. If these changes in maturation, societal demands, or culture are not successfully dealt with, we will have problems. Notably, the resolution of these task demands may have an even greater impact later in life in what is called the *cascading effect*, in which earlier events impact later events (Masten & Cicchetti, 2010; Sameroff, 2000). To quote Masten and Cicchetti (2010), "developmental cascading refers to the cumulative consequences for development of the many interactions and transactions occurring in developing systems that result in spreading effects" (p. 491).

Societal Change

Change occurs externally as well. For example, our social and cultural worlds can shift demographically. In the United States, Asian and Hispanic populations are increasing proportionally more than the rest of the nation (Colby & Ortman, 2014).

Technologically, cell phones and the Internet have changed our way of communicating. When was the last time you spoke to someone on a landline? Do you still take pictures with a camera? What is this tweeting all about? News comes in newspapers less and less and more over the Internet. We'll explore some of these topics in later chapters.

What societal changes have been most notable over our parents' and grandparents' lifetimes?

What is notable is that change occurs. You might ask your parents or grandparents about the changes they have seen during their lifetimes. You may also note the changes in fashion, music, modes of transportation, and people's attitudes toward sexuality.

Perceptions of Change

While there are various types of change that occur throughout the life span, there are even more perceptions of change. Some individuals welcome change, while others fight against it. Change has the potential to be stressful, particularly in negative or unplanned situations, but with the right outlook and coping mechanisms, it can be a positive, healthy experience.

Change Can Be Stressful

We will describe and discuss change in greater detail in Chapters 2 and 7 when we cover *impermanence* and *stress*, but it is notable that in the early days of human stress event research, change in and of itself was considered stressful (Holmes & Rahe, 1967). The Social Readjustment Rating Scale presented a list of changes in life that were scored according to their impact on one's life. Included in this list were both positive (winning a large amount of money) and negative (sickness in the family) events. Change was believed to be the variable at work. The more change one experienced, the higher the risk of problems. Therefore, change was not seen as healthy for us. While change brings us challenges, research has shown this negative characterization of change to be too broad.

We will explore in the later chapters the work on stress, of which change is but one part. What is of interest to us at this time is that change need not be stressful. It is determined by the individual's interpretation of change and his or her reactions to it.

Positive and Negative Change Events

The positive or negative nature of change makes a difference (Block & Zautra, 1981; Zautra, 2003; Zautra, Affleck, Tennen, Reich, & Davis, 2005). They are different experiences and not just the opposite ends of one feeling dimension with positive at one end and negative at the other. Additionally, the positive or negative evaluation of the change is very subjective and individualized. People differ in how they see life events. For example, one person might like a change of residence and another person might not want to move. When physically compromised individuals (suffering from a variety of medical complaints) were asked to rate interpersonal events as positive or negative, the positive

Figure 1.2 Distributions of Daily Positive Event and Negative Event Scores

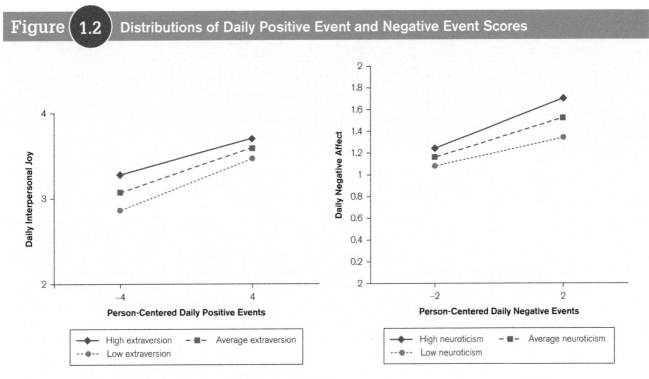

The graph on the left shows that more positive events are related to more joy in life, while the graph on the right shows that more negative events are related to more negative affect.

Source: Wiley; J. Pers. 2005 Dec; 73(6): 1511–1538. doi: 10.1111/j.0022-3506.2005.00357.x. http://www.ncbi.nlm.nih.gov/pmc/articles/PMC2577560/

events were predictive of well-being, while the negative events were predictive of more physical and mental problems (Parrish, Zautra, & Davis, 2008; see Figure 1.2).

These differential effects for positive and negative events occur in small, everyday events in a normal population as well, where the negative events clearly led to problems, while the positive uplifts had more mixed effects (Kanner, Coyne, Schaefer, & Lazarus, 1981). Research on the effects of negative events has been extended to a wide range of topics, including workplace health and problems (Silva & Caetano, 2013), sexual functioning and satisfaction (Hamilton & Julian, 2014), and shifts as a function of aging (Aldwin, Jeong, Igarashi, & Spiro, 2014). Our interpretation of such change events affects our health and well-being.

Planned and Unplanned Change

Researchers in organizational psychology have examined the cognitive and emotional processes in change. In particular, making sense of a change—that is, how people come to understand the change and how it fits with their existing ways of comprehending their world—has been found to be particularly important (Gioia & Chittipeddi, 1991; Maitlis, 2005; Weick, 1995). Some individuals may anticipate the effects of these changes and set up effective coping mechanisms in anticipation of the shifts. This allows them to feel more in control of these events and to make sense of what the events mean.

On the other hand, unplanned changes are, by definition, not anticipated. No forethought can be given to what happens or how to deal with the events as they unfold. Coping must be determined as the changes occur. One can feel out of control and confused by what is happening. In a variation of our considerations of change, we might also consider earlier research on predictable and unpredictable events.

Predictability makes unpleasant events less adverse. When they can be anticipated, the strain of the transition seems to ease (Koolhaas et al., 2011). We can learn new ways to behave, and we can plan. When things are uncertain, we feel anxious (Bordia, Hohman, Jones, & Callan, 2004; Schuler, 1980) because we feel vulnerable and insecure about the situation (DiFonzo & Bordia, 2007).

Comprehensibility of Change

Antonovsky (1987, 1998) reported that a **salutogenic**, or healthy understanding of a situation, helps in dealing with challenging life events. This salutogenic orientation in life is a strong sense of predictability. Antonovsky called this a *sense of coherence*—that is, a feeling that one can comprehend or understand his or her world. While this sense of coherence is explored in detail in the next chapter, it is notable here in determining adjustment. Understanding what is happening buffers the individual from environmental events.

Change may require new ways of understanding our world and coping with it. Yet change is first viewed from our old ways of seeing things, and only gradually do the changes make for new ways of thinking and acting (Balogun & Johnson, 2004). Important to this process is how we understand change in the context of growth and development, which is to be expected in terms of individuals as well as organizations (Weick & Quinn, 1999). Sensemaking at the organizational level converges with the research on coherence in one's personal life.

Traditions Contributing to Adjustment

Where does this area called adjustment come from? Adjustment comes from two traditions in psychology: interdisciplinary approaches and **psychoeducation**.

Interdisciplinary Approaches

The first tradition that contributes to adjustment comes from interdisciplinary approaches to understanding the human experience. Rather than isolated topics in specialty niches, this tradition takes a broad perspective on the factors that affect living. An example comes from Dollard and Miller and their colleagues. Their backgrounds were in sociology (Dollard), laboratory studies of learning (Miller), and psychoanalysis (both). They wrote on aggression (Dollard, Doob, Miller, Mowrer, & Sears, 1939), human learning (Miller & Dollard, 1941), and personality and psychotherapy (Dollard & Miller, 1950). Another example from the more recent literature is the Western writings on compassion in the early 21st century. The disciplines of psychology, philosophy, religion, economics, neuroscience, history, and Buddhist religious perspectives combined to give us a sense of what Buddhist compassion is (Davidson & Harrington, 2001).

Interdisciplinary perspectives help to explain the complexity of our communities and ourselves (Kelly, 2010) and how to intervene in meaningful and effective ways in those communities (Hall, Feng, Moser, Stokols, & Taylor, 2008; Maton et al., 2006; Stokols, 2006; Stokols, Hall, Taylor, & Moser, 2008). This text draws on research, theory, and practices from personality, social psychology, developmental psychology, learning, community, counseling, and clinical psychology as well as aspects of economics and sociology.

Personality contributes existential psychology and the importance of meaning. Social psychology provides research on conformity and social norms. Developmental psychology brings life tasks at various stages in our life, research on aging, and infancy to seniority. Learning describes how we acquire behaviors, thoughts, and emotions from our interactions with the world. Community psychology provides the importance of understanding contexts. Counseling brings descriptions of everyday challenges and the

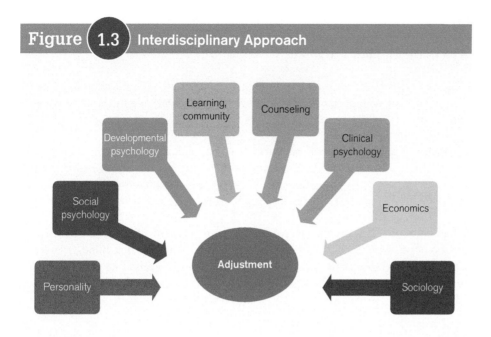

Figure 1.3 Interdisciplinary Approach

understanding of school and education. Clinical psychology adds the work on psychopathology and therapy. Economics brings the work on our understanding of money. And sociology contributes studies of societal level variables' influences on behavior and the experiences of individuals in those societies. These are all to be found in our study of adjustment (see Figure 1.3).

Psychoeducation

The second tradition from which adjustment grows is psychoeducation. Psychoeducation is the provision of useful psychological information to help people understand themselves and how to live their lives. Understanding human emotions, behaviors, thoughts, and physical reactions can help people better control their own lives. It empowers them.

Psychoeducation is a type of prevention program for psychological problems or a promotion program for healthy living. These kinds of programs have a clear history in psychology (Morgan & Vera, 2011). The roots of prevention and promotion programs can be traced to the psychology of Alfred Adler (Ansbacher, 1990; Watts, 2000) or to the traditions of community psychology (Felner, Jason, Moritsugu, & Farber, 1983; Moritsugu, Vera, Wong, & Duffy, 2013; Prilleltensky & Prilleltensky, 2006). Adjustment is a part of that tradition of empowerment, promotion of health, and prevention of disorders.

Organization of This Book

This book focuses on adjustment in terms of the normal experiences with which people contend. Life brings change, and with that change comes the need to learn and grow in order to adapt. Lewin (1936/2008) has argued that understanding a person's behavior requires knowledge of both the person and his or her environment—that is, the forces of our inner and our outer realities. Better control of this adjustment process comes through understanding what it is and how our studies of the human experience relate to that adjustment.

The book is divided into two parts. The first part, called Perspectives and Processes, examines the various areas that influence how adjustment occurs. These topics deal with the general nature of adjustment and the factors that contribute to adjustment.

Chapter 1. This chapter provides an introduction to adjustment and presents the framework of the book. In this chapter, *adjustment* is defined, and change is explained as a part of normal development and growth.

Chapter 2. Here the focus is on how finding meaning in life and understanding that life is impermanent is important to living life. The individual's role in these processes is emphasized.

Chapter 3. The role of the environment in a person's ability to adjust is examined in this chapter. Situations and settings play an important part in determining how we think, feel, and act. Adjustment, by definition, is an effort to cope with the changes in a person's contexts and environmental demands placed on the individual.

Chapter 4. The text examines the role that learning plays in adjustment. The learning process begins with making basic connections between concepts, like honey is sweet, to more complex connections, like on a green light to go, to even more complex things, such as how one successfully argues a point. All of these behaviors are important to adjustment.

Chapter 5. This chapter looks at mindfulness and openness to the present as a part of the adjustment process. Meditation is a method to achieve or heighten this mindfulness and openness. The growing body of research on this topic is explored.

Chapter 6. Stress is described as a normal process in adaptation and adjustment. Knowing what goes into that process provides possible solutions to stress and its outcomes, including both meditation and exercise.

In the second part, called Applications, the text analyzes adjustment topics in life, including relationships and intimacy. It also includes topics like money, school, work and vocation, and the aging process.

Chapter 7. Given humans are social beings, relationships are important. What goes into friendships and how they are maintained? And what of loneliness? These questions are explored in this chapter from a psychological perspective.

Chapter 8. Relationships are explored further. What of intimacy? What of sex? What of love? The research on healthy intimate relationships can help to answer these questions. The chapter also addresses intimacy problems and the ending of relationships since these are potential problem areas in life adjustment.

Chapter 9. School is a major social institution. This chapter examines what goes into successful school adjustment, including the importance of school experiences from early school up to college. Research has found that early successes are the building blocks for later successes. This chapter answers the question as to what is important and why it is important.

Chapter 10. This chapter explores the topic of work and vocation, which are important to being a mature adult in our society. Society assumes adults contribute to the life of the community. Work skills are important to adjustment in this area. Decisions as to why and how we work are important to our sense of well-being.

Chapter 11. Money is a resource for accessing many other experiences. Research has demonstrated that a certain amount is necessary to survive. While the addition of more money improves the quality of life, there is a point at which money does not add to life satisfaction. Here we examine the research on money and its importance in life adjustment and happiness.

Chapter 12. Aging is inevitable. Different phases in aging bring about shifts in thinking and behaving. Some of these shifts are socially directed, while some of these are self-defined. These ways of thinking about aging influence the experiences of aging and the decisions one makes in adjustment. This chapter examines these issues and the research that informs our understanding of these issues.

Chapter 13. This chapter looks at psychopathology and therapy for the problems that can arise in adjustment. The focus is on the major categories of mental illnesses and their impact on a person's life. The chapter ends with a review of effective treatments for psychological disorders.

Chapter 14. The book concludes with an exploration of emergent changes in the world. One of these changes is the demographic shifts in population in the United States. New concepts regarding sexuality and gender call for reconsiderations of their definitions and how they influence our frameworks for dealing with individuals. Finally, the chapter examines how technological advances in communications have changed our understanding of connectedness and the manner in which social relationships are initiated, established, and maintained. These are all seen to be fast-evolving and worldview-shifting developments.

In our daily lives, we face the challenges of dealing with life's tasks. This text provides information from the psychological sciences and allied fields to help understand these tasks. Both practical suggestions and research perspectives are highlighted throughout. The goal is to understand and practice psychology to the betterment of everyday life.

Conclusion

Life is dynamic and full of change. Because of this, individuals must learn to adjust or cope with the problems of everyday life. Evidence of adjustment can include goodness of fit, a lack of problems, a positive outlook, and mind–body health. The way that people perceive change can also affect their reactions to a situation or event. If change is interpreted as stressful or negative or it is unanticipated and incomprehensible, it can have an adverse effect on a person's well-being. However, when a change is anticipated or seen as beneficial and explainable, it can be seen in a positive light. Subsequent chapters will examine ways to adjust to life changes in such areas as relationships, school, work, and aging.

Review Questions

1. What is adjustment? Explain the complexities that may be involved in determining adjustment.

2. Define goodness of fit. How does it relate to the topic of adjustment?

3. What does the positive life experience approach to adjustment contribute to our way of thinking about adjustment and the human experience?

4. Give an example of mind–body health linkage. How have you seen this applied in your life?

5. Discuss two ways to classify and consider change.

6. Describe the various perceptions of change.

7. Think of a major change you experienced in your life. What was your perception of this change? Did it fall into one of the perceptions described in this chapter?

8. What are the advantages of an interdisciplinary approach?

9. Define *psychoeducation*.

10. The end of the chapter describes the rest of the text's chapters. Which two interest you the most? Why?

Key Terms

adjustment 5

autonomic nervous system 12

competent individual 9

context 6

ecological 7

general adaptation syndrome (GAS) 10

goodness of fit 6

pathways 7

positive mental health 8

psychoeducation 20

salutogenic 20

telomeres 10

Sharpen your skills with SAGE edge at **edge.sagepub.com/moritsugu**

SAGE edge for students provides a personalized approach to help you accomplish your coursework goals in an easy-to-use learning environment.

Go to **edge.sagepub.com/moritsugu** for additional exercises and web resources. Select Chapter 1, Adjustment for chapter-specific resources.

Chapter

2

Purpose in Life

Learning Objectives

1. Discuss the basic principles of existential psychology.

2. Summarize findings about the influence of coherence, purpose in life, and existential hardiness on well-being.

3. Explain the role of spirituality and religion in adjustment.

4. Describe the effects of choice and free will on individuals' attitudes and behaviors.

He remembered the discussion quite well. The day had been bright and sunny. His mom had nagged at him about some little detail regarding his college application, but he knew it was her way of handling her nervousness at the prospect of his leaving. So they had an extended discussion regarding his application to an out-of-state school. No, he did not have to go out of state. There were plenty of very good schools near his home. And, yes, the distance to the out-of-state school would put him more than a day's travel away from his family, friends, and his significant other of 2 years. But he had promised his teacher to at least try to get into that out-of-state school. It was something special. He knew it from the way the teacher had spoken of the college. So, he intended to at least try. He knew that it meant leaving his family and friends behind. There would be new friendships and relationships. Even the weather would be different. He would have to find out what to wear and when to wear it—in a more social vein, what was acceptable clothing for classes and what to wear in the dorms. They were small things, but they would punctuate that his life at home had come to an end and a new life in college had begun.

· ·

This story may have been your story. Or it could be one that you are familiar with, secondhand or thirdhand. People make decisions and put a lot of effort into goals and dreams to which they have made some sort of commitment. The importance of our finding those commitments in life and the purpose that drives them are the topic of this chapter. We believe that we seek to find meaning and **purpose in life**. As we shall see, the psychological research in this area is derived from an existential perspective. By that, we mean an important aspect to our life is driven by our awareness of our existence and what that awareness calls us to do (Frankl, 1959/1985; May, 1960).

In this chapter, we will define *existential psychology*, explore what our awareness of the **impermanence** to our life and life circumstances does to us, examine some of the areas that support the importance of meaning in our life, and then consider what that can mean in terms of a broadened worldview, which encompasses **spirituality** and/or **religion**. Psychological studies have demonstrated spiritual and religious factors to be a positive factor in many people's lives. The linkage of spirituality and meaning making is what some propose to be at the core of general findings about the relationship between those who are spiritual or religious and overall health. Finally, the power of choice and free will is explored. Understanding the existential framework, we as humans are aware of being alive and the temporary nature of that life. From this existential perspective comes particular areas of study. One of the most important is the creation of a meaningful life.

Existential Psychology

SAGE edge™

Get the edge on your studies.
edge.sagepub.com/moritsugu

Take a quiz to find out what you've learned. Watch videos that enhance chapter content. Explore web resources and additional exercises.

Existential psychology is a school of thought emphasizing the individual, the realization of being alive, and the results of this awareness of one's life. The power of the individual in forming his or her life is an important element to understanding life and adjustment. Each person has to formulate who he or she is and how he or she fits into that world.

American existential psychology is usually associated with psychologists Viktor Frankl, Rollo May, and Irvin Yalom. Frankl is acknowledged as one of the earliest and best known proponents of the existential approach in the United States. For May (1960) "existentialism involves centering on the existing person and . . . the human being . . . emerging, becoming" (p. 11). Yalom (1980) identified four basic topics for existential psychology:

1. Dealing with our awareness of impermanence, change, and "death"

2. Finding purpose and meaning in life

3. Making choices in our life and taking responsibility for those choices

4. Contending with our ultimate autonomy and aloneness

This chapter follows these four points and the supportive psychological findings related to them. While not necessarily defined as existential in nature, there are several lines of research that highlight these very concerns over change and sense of mortality, the importance of meaning and purpose in life, and our desire to be in control of our lives and make our own decisions. The importance of the individual, their active interpretation of their environment, and their engagement with that environment is emphasized. This is the result of the human capacity for awareness of their existence and of their interactions with their world.

Existential psychology emphasizes the individual, the realization of being alive, and the results of this awareness.

Change, Impermanence, and Awareness of Death

It seems inevitable that life brings change. The first chapter pointed to this inevitability. The research over several decades supports the negative reaction that can come with change (Dohrenwend, 2006). Extending the concept of change to that of *impermanence* (defined as being transient or unenduring, from *The New Shorter Oxford Dictionary* ["Impermanence," 1993]) seems a defendable point, given our language. The Buddhist tenet of impermanence believes change to be a natural part of life (Goldstein, 2002; Rinpoche, 1992). Assuming this impermanence, attempting to hold on to things that will not last is illusory and can lead only to frustration, grief, and suffering. What makes change so hard to accept and live with?

Viktor Frankl (1959/1985) told the story of his life in a concentration camp during World War II. He witnessed daily abuse, murder, and living conditions of the worst kind. Yet he also found acts of compassion, sacrifice, and the expression of human dignity within the dire camp conditions. His insight was that finding meaning to one's existence made all the difference. Even a world gone "crazy" had hope when there was purpose in one's life.

In a second seminal existential psychology text, Rollo May (1960) described the evolution of his own perspective. Following a diagnosis of cancer and facing his own mortality, he engaged his work with renewed effort to describe and understand the process of being in the world.

The realization of our temporal nature and our desire for purpose in life is important to living. Our world is impermanent. It is always changing. Heraclitus, the Roman philosopher, provided us with a concise way to think of it. The river flows and thus is always different. As stated in the first chapter, we are also always changing—physically and psychologically.

Psychological research has found that change brings upset and health risk (Holmes & Rahe, 1967). Reviewing research that spans several decades of work, life change increases the risk of disorders (Dohrenwend, 2006). This link is supported by over 9,000 related articles published between 1967 and 2005. While life changes as a stressor is discussed in a later chapter on stress and coping, for now, note that changes in life have consistently been linked to health or mental health problems. Impermanence and contending with it has proven problematic to human experience. For an example close to your own experience, remember when you first went to college. There were people and places you left behind. You made new friends and had to deal with new demands. These changes brought new challenges to your life. For many, this is not an easy time.

While there is a tendency to think of the self as permanent and unchanging, the psychological reality is that situations influence individuals, and those situations are continuously changing (Baumeister, 1991). As noted in Chapter 1, with maturity comes shifts in physical development and social expectations. Life-changing events, like going to college, meeting a significant other, or getting a job promotion, all have their effects and make life different. These variations can be in everyday matters like energy level, mood, clarity of thought, or sense of direction.

So the world is changing, the person and situations are changing. Change brings "disequilibrium" in contending with the novelty and the resulting shift from a previously calm or balanced state (Hirschberger & Shaham, 2012). Change and unpredictability have effects at the physiological as well as the psychological levels (Burger & Arkin, 1980; Mineka & Henderson, 1985; Mineka & Kihlstrom, 1978; Shors, Foy, Levine, & Thompson, 1990). Change can be perceived as risky. The worries of potential loss typically outweigh the opportunities for gain (Barbaris, 2013; Kahneman & Tversky, 1979). So there is the tendency to believe that all will remain permanently as it always has been, yet naturally, change is inevitable (Hirschberger & Shaham, 2012).

Existential psychologists have researched what happens when this realization of change includes the realization of mortality—that is, death is inevitable (Arndt, Landau, Vail, & Vess, 2013; Burke, Martens, & Faucher, 2010). When reminded that existence can cease, the reaction to this realization or reminder is an assertion of life. This area of research is called experimental existential psychology.

Experimental Existential Psychology

Reminding people of death activates strong reactions. The threat of death raises the themes of meaning and purpose in life. The response to such reminders is to emphatically endorse life in a meaningful, socially connected way (Greenberg, Koole, & Pyszczynski, 2004; Shaver & Mikulincer, 2012). This work has been labeled **terror management theory**. To manage the terror of death, people remind themselves that they are alive and connected to others who carry on their legacy (children or like-minded persons).

Simply being asked to think of our death triggers "terror management" reactions. But this fear of death can also take the form of social and psychological death, such as ostracism or alienation. Studies have measured unconscious reactions to stimuli so subtle that the participant is not aware of the stimuli being presented (Bargh, Gollwitzer, Lee-Chai, Barndollar, & Troetschel, 2001).

For example, students might be asked to think about their own death (called mortality salience) or to think of a neutral topic, like going for a walk or taking a test. Following this exercise, the students who thought of death were more likely to talk about how healthy they were. This was a reaction to the fear of death and illness that the exercise had prompted. When asked for the first word that comes to mind, death-prompt students said things related to death such as grave or cemetery. The nonprompted students might say water or walk. A second type of threat reaction is an increase in defending their worldviews. In one

Cherry blossoms are appreciated all the more for their brief season.

study, this defensiveness took the form of increased national pride (Koole, Greenberg, & Pyszczynski, 2006). If one's ideas or ideals live on, one has overcome death.

One study found that thinking of death increased students' desires to have children (Fritsche et al., 2007). Having children was a way "not to die" but to continue on. Typically, mortality salience would increase people's hostility to out-group members. However, when thinking of children, these negative attitudes are softened. They are a way to "cheat death."

The topic of death did not have to be conscious to the participants. When death or death topics were briefly flashed on a screen for 46 milliseconds, subjects thought more about death and became more defensive of their views of the world (Arndt, Greenberg, Pyszczynski, & Solomon, 1997). Without being aware of it, death affects people. When faced with death, the typical reaction is to assert oneself and "insist" that one is alive and has purpose in that life. This also works when one's group or "culture" is challenged. Holbrook, Sousa, and Hahn-Holbrook (2011) found that hints of uncertainty to worldview led to stronger affirmations of that worldview.

Children provide a sense of continuity to the future.

> Awareness of death represents a formidable challenge in human existence . . . and there is coherence and existential depth to the idea that people, when reminded of their impermanence may cling to meanings and beliefs . . . (Yet, it should be noted that) people typically engage life—that is, they seek challenges, connections, authentic meaning, and significance—not because they are trying to avoid the scent of death, but because they are healthy and alive. (Ryan & Deci, 2004, p. 473)

The Importance of Purpose and Meaning

We are a meaning-making species (Baumeister, 1991; Cacioppo, Hawkley, Rickett, & Masi, 2005), and as such, there is a need to make sense of our world. *Meaning* is defined as a "sense of what is and a sense of why this should be so" (Proulx, Markman, & Lindberg, 2013). Meaning helps us to explain the complexities of the world around us. Given that so much information is available, the ability to find meaning and organize that information is important. This order and structure help to deal with our world. In the face of a changing world, we can find solace in meaning (Baumeister, 1991). As noted by Cacioppo et al. (2005), at the basic neurological level, our brain dedicates 32% and 23% of its mass to those portions that have to do with thinking and dealing with our social interactions, respectively. Whereas other species' brains are dedicated to sensation and action, we biologically "spend" our biological mass and energy on processing and coordinating, ordering and structuring, and generally making sense of the sensations. We are neurologically constructed to think and to interact with others.

Purpose and meaning in life have been extensively researched over several decades. The conclusion from this research seems clear: Purpose and meaning are related to well-being (Heintzelman & King, 2014; Ryff & Singer, 1998; Steger, 2012).

This relationship is so compelling, the question was raised: Are happiness and meaning the same thing (Baumeister, Vohs, Aaker, & Garbinsky, 2013)? Baumeister et al. (2013) found that while meaning and happiness are highly related—they were different. Happiness is present focused—that is, I like where I am now. Meaning is an integration of past, present, and future—that is, I understand what has happened, is happening, and what will happen. Happiness appears to be a response to need fulfillment—for example, I am enjoying my meal. Meaning is not related to need fulfillment, so having a meal has no effect on understanding my world. Happiness seems based on an individual focus, such as how one feels, and meaning is other-focused, or how one can contribute to the well-being of all. Therefore, while there is a strong relationship between meaning and happiness, the two are different.

Meaningfulness has been studied in a number of forms. While the terms regarding *meaningfulness* have varied, they all refer to the same concept and its definition—meaning intention or purpose (*The New Shorter Oxford English Dictionary*, 1993). Research has confirmed the power of meaning in life, through such concepts as coherence, purpose in life, and existential hardiness.

Coherence

Antonovsky (1979, 1993) found that a **sense of coherence** to one's world was related to health, or what he called salutogenesis. Those who believed their world was "coherent" were both physically and psychologically healthier. A coherent world is one that is understandable and psychologically manageable. This concept has proved powerful in looking at long-term health in the face of everyday adversity (Eriksson & Lindstrom, 2005). Coherence has been related to the positive qualities of life, such as physical and psychological well-being, relationships with others, and feelings of empowerment and fulfillment (Eriksson & Lindstrom, 2007). Coherence was also found to increase with age and experience (Eriksson & Lindstrom, 2005, 2007).

A sense of coherence was the best predictor of health outcomes over a 10-year period (Cedarblad & Hansson, 1995). Coherence was a better predictor than intelligence, feelings of self-mastery, and locus of control. In a follow-up, done after a second 10-year interval, the original sense of coherence continued as a good predictor of successful and healthy development (Dahlin & Cedarblad, 2009).

In a second longitudinal study over a 20-year period, sense of coherence was again found to predict lower rates of mental disorders. This methodology, known as a prospective study, is an especially powerful one at examining factors that can then later predict behavior (Kouvonen et al., 2010).

While the use of sense of coherence as a protective factor has been around for several decades and the test has been translated into several languages, researchers continue to find it a significant factor in predicting health.

Purpose in Life

Crumbaugh and Maholick (1964) devised a test of purpose in life to try to measure meaning and purpose in one's life. Purpose in life has been found to be related to a person's satisfaction with his or her life in general (Bronk, Hill, Lapsley, Talib, & Finch, 2009). It has also been found to have protective properties in regard to physical reactivity to life circumstances and to be predictive of lower death rates (Hill & Turiano, 2014). Additionally, purpose in life has been found to be related to lower social anxiety (Kashdan & McKnight, 2013).

Machell, Disabato, and Kashdan (2015) found purpose in life to be related to prosocial behaviors in teenagers. Teens high in purpose were more willing to help others, share, and empathize with others. They volunteered more and provided services for those in the community. Generally, having purpose in life predicted the extent to which adolescents contributed to their communities. They found purpose in life to mediate the negative impact of low income as well as to consistently lower the tendency for antisocial behaviors in teenagers (see Figure 2.1).

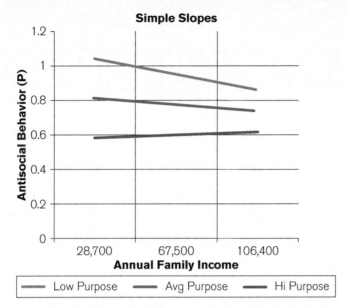

Figure 2.1 The Moderating Effect of Purpose in Life on Antisocial Tendencies in Teens

While there is a relationship between family income and antisocial behaviors in teens, this effect is not found in those with high purpose in life. Note that there is no family income effect for those with high purpose in life.

Source: Figure 2 from Buffering the negative impact of poverty on youth: The power of purpose in life. Kyla A. Machell, David J. Disabato, Todd B. Kashdan. *Social Indicators Research.* March 2016, Volume 126, Issue 2, pp. 845–861. Used with permission from Springer Science+Business Media.

Among the other positive aspects that purpose in life brings is increased willingness to be in ethnically diverse situations and less perception of threat from these contexts (Burrow, Stanley, Sumner, & Hill, 2014). Additionally, feeling that one had a purpose in life decreased distress over contact with ethnically diverse populations encountered in a real-life situation (Burrow & Hill, 2013). It seems that having a purposeful orientation may open individuals to the world of possibilities and assure them of their own abilities to cope with novelty and change.

Purpose in life and a belief that one can make a difference in his or her world are important to new college students (DeWitz, Woolsey, & Walsh, 2009). Students who have a purpose in life also feel they can be effective, have support, and stay in college. When the work or tasks seem boring, those with goals that reach beyond themselves persist longer and did better (Yeager et al., 2014). Others have found socially oriented goals in young adults (early 20s) were related to later life interest in growth, continued feelings of purpose, and interest in helping the next generation (Hill, Burrow, Brandenberger, Lapsley, & Quaranto, 2010). Working solely for achievement–recognition and artistic and financial goals, which are more individualistically focused, did not have the same linkages to a later sense of purpose or altruistic motives. Hill et al. (2010) noted that it matters what our purpose is. Heintzelman and King (2014) reported that most individuals (80% to 90%) feel they have found a sense of purpose to their life. Oishi and Diener (2013) looked at data from 132 countries, finding and affirming that this number averages around 90%.

Existential Hardiness

Those who face change and difficulty yet are able to survive and thrive are called **hardy individuals** (Kobasa, 1979, 1982; Kobasa, Maddi, & Courington, 1981; Kobasa, Maddi, & Kahn, 1982; Kobasa, Maddi, & Puccetti, 1982; Maddi, 2006). Among workers who faced

©iStockphoto.com/pixdeluxe

Commitment and hardiness influence effort and grades.

job loss or major job changes over the course of a few years, some recovered well and others did not. In dealing with conditions that Maddi (2002) called cataclysmic, researchers found that those who were committed, challenged, and perceived themselves as in control did better.

Kobasa (1979) defined these qualities as follows:

- Committed: having a sense of purpose and drawing meaning from their experiences
- Challenged: seeing new and different situations as opportunities for growth and advancement
- In control: believing one could do things to effect their lives and change what could be difficulties into successes

In a 12-year follow-up study of these same workers, those who experienced job changes were helped by these personal ways of seeing themselves and their world (Maddi, 2002). Additional qualities they added to the list (of being committed, challenged, and in control) were social support and physical exercise (Maddi, 2002).

In a review of research on hardiness, Maddi (2002, 2006) concluded that hardiness related to how both people and organizations dealt with change and uncertainty. The hardy personal qualities helped to dampen the negative effects of change. In addition to the attitudinal qualities of challenge, control, and commitment, specific coping behaviors added to the individual's hardiness (Maddi, 2002). These coping behaviors included building a supportive social environment that was encouraging and helpful, being open to opportunities, and taking decisive action when necessary. A second review of the literature confirmed that people who had hardiness characteristics assembled better support from those around them, were more actively engaged in their world, and were less likely to fall into non-productive ways of responding to life changes and stressors (Eschleman, Bowling, & Alarcon, 2010). Hardy individuals were less likely to be distressed, burned out, frustrated, and acting in destructive ways. They were more likely to be engaged in life, focused on growth, and generally happy and satisfied. Maddi (2002) characterized this hardy personality as having the existential courage to live life (Root, 2016).

Hardy individuals do not react negatively to new situations and appreciate innovation (Maddi et al., 2006). In a study of physiological reactivity, Sandvik et al. (2013) found negative hormonal reactions to stressful conditions when there was a lack of balance among control, commitment, and challenge. High control and commitment without a sense of challenge resulted in these biological responses, placing individuals at risk. See Researching Adjustment: Academic Hardiness and Grit.

RESEARCHING ADJUSTMENT
Academic Hardiness and Grit

Academically, commitment and overall hardiness were found to be positively related to undergraduate grades and final year research projects (Sheard & Golby, 2007). Having long-term goals seemed especially important to good grades and what could be called capstone projects. Yeager et al. (2014) found the power of purpose to be based on goals beyond the individual self (for my neighborhood, for society, for the greater good), which they termed *self-transcendent*. When prompted to consider such self-transcendent motives, college students persisted on tasks and attempted to learn material more deeply. Notably, Yeager and colleagues (2014) also found that such motives were positively related with college graduation. Thinking beyond oneself can be helpful to completion of tasks, especially long-range tasks like completing college.

Duckworth, Peterson, Matthews, and Kelly (2007) called this passion for long-term goals and task perseverance—grit. They defined this quality as "working strenuously toward challenges, maintaining effort and interest over years despite failure, adversity, and plateaus in progress" (pp. 1087–1088). Where others get bored, tired, or discouraged, those with grit stayed the course, continued to work, and found the "finish line." Those with grit would be those who spent the extra time studying, practiced longer or harder, or saw a bad grade as a signal to study harder and not give up. The researchers found this quality to be related to college grade point average, West Point Academy retention, levels of educational attainment (associate's, bachelor's, post graduate degrees), and spelling bee finalists.

These qualities of hardiness and grit increase our chances of success in adjustment to the world at large but especially in situations that are challenging or competitive.

Reflection Questions

1. Can you think of a time that your grades or a project benefited from personal extra effort? What motivated you to continue your efforts? In what situations would this be helpful? Not helpful?

2. How might you suggest increasing commitment and hardiness in an individual?

The link between meaning in life and well-being seems clear. Individuals who are able to establish coherence, purpose in life, and existential hardiness have meaningful, well-balanced lives. How do so many of us come to have such meaningful lives?

Spirituality and Religion

One of the ways by which we derive meaning and purpose is through spiritual and religious beliefs and activities (Steger & Frazier, 2005). Religion and spirituality have been a part of psychological considerations for a long time. William James, thought by many to be the "father of American psychology," was involved with religious considerations and gave a series of lectures in 1901 and 1902, which were compiled into a book. The book, titled *The Varieties of Religious Experience: A Study in Human Nature* (James, 1902), explored and considered what religion did for us as humans.

In his work, James made the distinction between **institutional and personal religion**, the first having to do with the many established formal religions that can be found in the world (Buddhism, Christianity, Hinduism, Islam, Judaism). He deferred on the institutional religions so as not to become engaged in the debate over who is right or wrong. Rather, he dealt with personal religion and personal experience. In the same way, psychology as a science does not take on the theological debates but addresses the human experiences to which spirituality and religion relate.

Religion and spirituality are different concepts in psychology (Pargament, Mahoney, Exline, Jones, & Shafranske, 2013; Schlehofer, Omoto, & Adelman, 2008; Wulff, 1997; Zinnbauer et al., 1997). Religion is related to a given set of institutionally

Spirituality reflects a sense of awe and wonder.

based codes of conduct, values, and ceremonies, which emphasize the symbols and beliefs of a given group. *Spirituality* is, in the broadest sense of the term, a personal worldview that brings appreciation, compassion, caring, a sense of interdependence to our work, and a perspective that reaches beyond the individual (Cacioppo et al., 2005; Wolff, 2010). Pargament, Exline, and Jones (2013) stated succinctly, in spirituality, "There is more to life than meets the eye" (p. 266).

While the distinction between religion and spirituality appears to be one that grew during the end of the 20th century, the trend is clear that such a distinction is firmly in our psychological studies (Pargament, Mahoney, et al., 2013). Where at one time the overlap of the two terms made for one to be seen as the other, there is now a growing acknowledgment that one does not necessarily mean the other. There are a variety of ways in which to find the spiritual in life. Besides the institutional versus personal distinction used by William James, intrinsic versus extrinsic religious orientations defined by Gordon Allport have been found to be helpful in marking the differences within religion.

Intrinsic and Extrinsic Orientation (Individual and Social)

Among the classic distinctions made in the psychological study of religion and spirituality is that of **intrinsic and extrinsic orientations** (Allport, 1950). The intrinsically oriented person is involved with religion and spirituality in search of personal meaning. The extrinsically oriented person is involved because of the social aspects of religion, such as the norms, expectations, and advantages that religion fulfills. This leads to very different kinds of religious experiences with very different kinds of outcomes (Bergin, 1991). Reviewing years of research, Bergin (1991) reported on the varying outcomes for the varying religious orientations. Psychologically, the intrinsic religious person appears to be more internally directed and looks psychologically healthier. These individuals find religious or spiritual experiences to be personally fulfilling. The extrinsically oriented are looking for external validation and are driven by outside forces. These individuals look quite different from the intrinsic individuals. They are more dogmatic and seem to be helped less by religious or spiritual involvement and show higher anxiety. The intrinsic, religious-oriented individuals have good grades and academic success. The extrinsic have lower grades and are academically challenged.

Newer considerations of personality variables acknowledge the historical contributions of this internal versus external orientation research to our exploration of the religious experience. For example, Ryan, Rigby, and King (1993) found that those who saw their religious beliefs as a matter of personal choice and not the result of external pressure (they called this **internalization**) were mentally healthy. On the other hand, if the beliefs were conflicted and the result of social pressure (incomplete or **introjected beliefs**), religion and health were negatively related.

One of the newer areas of study is the possibility of religion and spirituality as a basic personality variable in itself. We will consider this area of study next.

ASPIRES (Assessment of Spiritual and Religious Sentiments)

Piedmont and Wilkins (2013) described work examining personality and religion and spirituality. The current five-factor model (FFM) of personality (openness to experience, conscientiousness, extraversion, agreeableness, and neuroticism) was related to religious and spiritual tendencies. In longitudinal studies of the FFM and these tendencies, agreeableness and conscientiousness seem the best predictors of developing religiosity and spirituality (McCullough, Enders, Brion, & Jain, 2005; Wink, Ciciolla, Dillon, & Tracy, 2007). Piedmont and Wilkins (2013) saw these predictions as reasonable, since agreeableness relates to a social focus and conscientiousness means guided by an internal value to do well. Please see Adjustment in Practice: Five-Factor Theory of Personality.

ADJUSTMENT IN PRACTICE
Five-Factor Theory of Personality

Looking at the various ways in which personality can be described, researchers have statistically come to the decision that there are five basic personality dimensions (Digman, 1990; McCrae & Costa, 1987). They have argued that these five dimensions cover all of the variations that occur in human personality—or at least best summarize personality. Factor analysis is the statistical procedure used to come to these five. Therefore, it is called five-factor theory. These factors are made up of the following:

- Openness to experience: Curious, cultured, intelligent

- Conscientiousness: Self-disciplined, hardworking

- Extraversion: Outgoing, enthusiastic, stimulation seeking

- Agreeableness: Nice, socially oriented, in search of harmony with others

- Neuroticism: Anxious, nervous, emotionally unstable

Reflection Questions

1. Do these factors seem to summarize your sense of your own and your friends' personalities?

2. Are there any factors that you feel are missing? If so, explain them and justify your reasoning. If not, explain why you feel these factors are acceptable on their own.

However, they also believed a more thorough explanation of their findings could be obtained by adding a sixth factor to the FFM. Piedmont (2012) derived an Assessment of Spiritual and Religious Sentiments (ASPIRES) scale from which a sixth factor might be identified. This additional factor was focused on our spiritual and religious aspirations. The components of such a factor would include fulfillment, prayer and meditation (experiencing contentment from prayer and meditative behaviors), transcendence and universality (unity of purpose in life), connectedness (linkage to others), involvement (rituals and other activities), and crises focus (dealing with problems or conflicts with the external forces). There is a growing body of research to support such a sixth factor (Piedmont, Ciarrocchi, Dy-Liacco, & Williams, 2009; Piedmont & Leach, 2002; Rican & Janosova, 2010).

This research area attempts to place our religious and spiritual tendencies within the psychological framework of personality. The advantages to this placement are that spirituality and religiousness might be framed within our basic psychological tendencies. Of course, the most basic question is whether this added personality dimension is justifiable from a psychometric viewpoint. Those who have argued for the FFM of personality might point to possible redundancies. Yet research has presented a convincing body of evidence to support the existence of ASPIRES (Piedmont, 2012; Piedmont & Wilkins, 2013). Now we will turn to the effects of religion and spirituality on our mental and physical health.

Effects of Religion and Spirituality on Health

Do religion and spirituality relate to well-being? The simple answer is yes. Being religious and spiritual can have positive effects on one's health (George, Ellison, & Larson, 2002; Koenig, 2001; Pargament, 1997, 2002; Powell, Shahabi, & Thoresen, 2003). There have been findings of a clear reduction of risk of physical illness for churchgoers (Powell et al., 2003), as well as better self-reports on physical health (Boswell, Kahana, & Dilworth-Anderson, 2006). There are positive research findings on efficacy of religious coping when dealing with stress (Ano & Vasconcelles, 2005; Arévalo, Prado, & Amaro, 2008; Tix & Frazier, 1998) and with depression (Braxton, Lang, Sales, Wingood, & DiClemente, 2007; Lee, 2007). Religious and spiritual coping are also found to be related to well-being and happiness (Gillium & Ingram, 2006; Lee, 2007).

However, there are two answers to the question of the effects of religion and spirituality on our overall well-being. Kenneth Pargament (2008) stated it best: "It depends" (p. xx). As noted by reviews of studies on religiousness and health (Bergin, 1991; George et al., 2002), the results are mixed: While religion and health can be related, this relationship depends on the specifics of the religion and spirituality within a person's life and his or her ways of

RESEARCHING ADJUSTMENT
Neurological Effects of Religious Belief

In a study of neurological correlates to religious belief, researchers (Inzlicht, McGregor, Hirsh, & Nash, 2009) found differences between religious and non-religious subjects in the reactivity of the brain area that serves as an alarm bell to signal danger. This area of the brain is called the anterior cingulate cortex (ACC). The ACC is implicated in both anxiety and self-regulation. When presented with uncertainty or error, the religious were less reactive, meaning they were calmer when faced with challenging conditions.

Reflection Questions

1. Do you find that reflections of a spiritual (here defined as a perspective beyond yourself) or religious nature help to calm you down? Please explain your reasoning.

2. Find a partner, and discuss if he or she feels that spiritual or religious reflection is helpful to him or her. Describe his or her experiences.

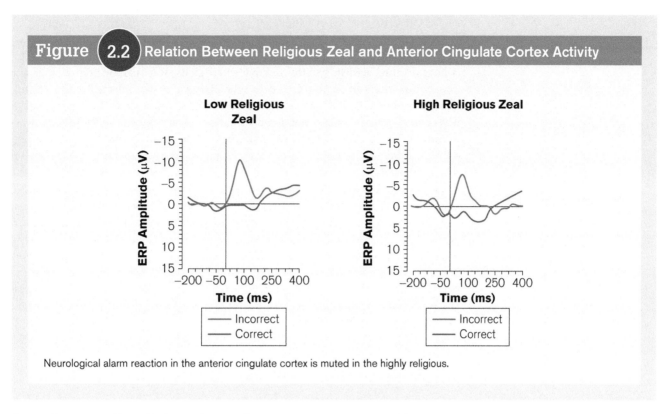

Figure 2.2   Relation Between Religious Zeal and Anterior Cingulate Cortex Activity

Neurological alarm reaction in the anterior cingulate cortex is muted in the highly religious.

Source: Figure 1 from Neural Markers of Religious Conviction. Michael Inzlicht, Ian McGregor, Jacob B. Hirsh, and Kyle Nash. doi:10.1111/j.1467-9280.2009.02305.x Psychological Science March 2009 vol. 20 no. 3 385–392.

coping (Pargament, 2008). There is no simple answer to the question of whether religion and spirituality are helpful or harmful, and we are left to wonder what the right answer is. See Researching Adjustment: Neurological Effects on Religious Belief.

Religion, Spirituality, and Meaning

Religion and spirituality can provide a "framework" for life (Pargament, 1997). While Steger and Frazier (2005) found that religiousness and life satisfaction related to each other, it was meaning that mediated over 90% of this relationship. This mediating effect was found for the relationship between religion and optimism and between religion and self-esteem. In a second study, Steger and Frazier (2005) found that religious activity and meaning in life were highly correlated. They believed the effects of religion on well-being could best be explained by religion's leading to a higher sense of meaning in life.

Such a model fits with others' findings of religion's role in meaning making (Park, Edmondson, & Hale-Smith, 2013). Religious and spiritual frameworks have been found particularly able to withstand events that challenge them (Inzlicht et al., 2009; Park, 2005). This robustness would make such meaning making especially desirable, since explanatory and organizational aids are helpful and play such a vital role in living effectively (Heine, Proulx, & Vohs, 2006; Park, 2005, 2010).

Korotkov (1998) noted the advantages of spiritual and religious systems in that they are comprehensive in nature. In many cases, added to this cognitive appeal are supportive cultural norms and social support networks for such explanatory systems (Krause, 2008). We will explore and discuss the power of such cultural and social contexts in a later chapter. Religion and spirituality are a major meaning-making system around the world and across cultures (Silberman, 2005).

Note on Our Perspective

Our consideration of religion and spirituality is at the level of scientific analysis. This is not meant to be disrespectful to anyone: religious, spiritual, or nonreligious and nonspiritual. Rather, as MacKenzie and Baumeister (2014) reflected on the usefulness of meaning in life, the usefulness of ways to understand life experience is well-demonstrated. What is not demonstrable are assumptions that go into the ways of constructing meaning. This examination of religion and spirituality does not take on the validity of the frameworks or their empirical basis. Rather, what is reported is that in a psychological sense, a spiritual or religious orientation may be helpful. These researchers take William James's position of not engaging in discussions of institutional religion but rather examine the impact of a personal religion on our lives. We are psychologists, not theologians (or at least none of the authors of this text are). What is useful to consider is why religion and spirituality may serve such an important role in the lives of many. The examination of this phenomenon helps to understand the importance of meaning and purpose and of cognitive frameworks to help us, who are thinking beings given the advantage of neural capacities to process large amounts of information from our sensory and social worlds. How we make meaning of the world is a matter of choice.

Autonomy, Choice, and Free Will

Humans like to make their own decisions independent from outside pressures (Ryan & Deci, 2006). There is a research basis to the assertion of the importance of autonomy, free will, and choice, demonstrated in the self-determination theory (SDT).

Engaging in activities that the individual has determined to be reinforcing (intrinsic reinforcement or motivation) leads to more enjoyment and greater persistence (Deci & Ryan, 1985; Vansteenkiste, Simons, Lens, Sheldon, & Deci, 2004). In turn, the imposition of externally imposed reinforcers and motivators to an activity can lead to a decrease in the enjoyableness and persistence of that activity. The emphasis in SDT is on the actor feeling free and in control of his or her destiny (Deci & Ryan, 2008). The difference between autonomous (self) motivation and externally controlled motivation is at the basis of their research. Their research has found that when the decision and control of behavior lies with the individual autonomously, performance is superior, persistence is longer, feelings are more positive (fun?), relationships are better, and people report being healthier. Examining the list of advantages, one might surmise that the human being is predisposed to autonomy and the exercise of free choice.

Studies have found that choice feels good (Nix, Ryan, Manly, & Deci, 1999), is not mentally taxing (Moller, Deci, & Ryan, 2006), adds a sense of energy or vitality to a person's life (Kasser & Ryan, 1999; Ryan & Frederick, 1997), and is related to feelings of well-being (Reis, Sheldon, Gable, Roscoe, & Ryan, 2000). When people worked for intrinsic rewards, they did better than when they work for extrinsically imposed rewards (Cerasoli, Nicklin, & Ford, 2014; Vansteenkiste et al., 2004). Cerasoli and Ford (2014) found that self-mastery goals (to make oneself better) added to self-motivation in producing better performances. When engaged in the pursuit of self-defined goals within self-defined tasks, time seems to go quickly and the completion of tasks can seem effortless, in what Csikszentmihalyi (1997) has called the "flow" of life.

Self-determination (choice) versus external pressures determining our actions makes a great difference in the experience of our lives. The importance of our autonomy, our self, and our exercise of free will have been demonstrated in these psychological findings (Ryan & Deci, 2006). See Adjustment in Practice: Creating Choice Conditions.

ADJUSTMENT IN PRACTICE
Creating Choice Conditions

Experimenters have created "choice" conditions and "controlled" conditions though a careful use of language. In choice conditions, participants hear words like *may*, *could*, or *can*. In control conditions, the words are *should*, *must*, and *have to*. The phrasing for choice emphasizes the participants deciding to take part: "we ask you to . . ." or "if you choose . . ." versus the more directive control condition phrasing, "you have to . . ." or "you must . . ." or "you had better . . . ." Given these shifts in phrasing, significant differences were found in participants' effort, engagement, and final performances (Vansteenkiste et al., 2004). Try these differences in language with others.

Reflection Questions

1. How do people react when you vary the emphasis on choice or control? Why do you think they react that way?

2. Which emphasis do you prefer and why?

Conclusion

In this chapter, we examined the issues impermanence raise for us. To better deal with these issues, meaning and purpose in one's life can help to assure us of an organized way to deal with the incoming information. A sense of purpose, a coherent worldview, and a sense of commitment are all positive factors in dealing with life.

Religion and spirituality can serve as an effective organizational framework to generate meaning in life. This does not mean it is the only framework, but it is one that is found commonly around the world. Whatever the manner for deriving meaning in our life, from the existential perspective, this is an important step in readying oneself for the challenges to come. And finally, importance of autonomy and choice in the human experience is demonstrated by the "flow" that comes from the exercise of these human qualities. This chapter centers on embracing life and the realization of the human capacities of awareness, creation of meaning, autonomy, and free will.

Review Questions

1. What is existential psychology?

2. What are some of the findings in experimental existential psychology research? How do the findings apply to meaningfulness in life?

3. What is the difference between happiness and meaningfulness?

4. Give an example of purpose in life.

5. What are the components of existential hardiness?

6. What is the importance of spirituality and religion to our considerations of adjustment?

7. Distinguish between extrinsic and intrinsic religious orientations. What are the differences in their effects on well-being?

8. What is ASPIRES?

9. Provide an example that is either personal (yourself or someone you know) or in the news regarding the effects of religion and spirituality on health.

10. What research supports the importance of choices in life? How does this fit into the existential framework?

Key Terms

existential psychology 28

hardy individuals 33

impermanence 28

institutional and personal religion 35

internalization 36

intrinsic and extrinsic orientations 36

introjected beliefs 36

purpose in life 28

religion 28

sense of coherence 32

spiritual and religious aspirations 37

spirituality 28

terror management theory 30

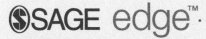

Sharpen your skills with SAGE edge at edge.sagepub.com/moritsugu

SAGE edge for students provides a personalized approach to help you accomplish your coursework goals in an easy-to-use learning environment.

Go to edge.sagepub.com/moritsugu for additional exercises and web resources. Select Chapter 2, Purpose in Life for chapter-specific resources.

Chapter

3

Community Contexts

Learning Objectives

1. Describe methods and advantages of mentoring in the context of community.

2. Describe the roles of social support, social networking, and social capital in adjustment.

3. Discuss the importance of settings and contexts in adjustment.

4. Explain how culture provides a framework for understanding and reacting to the world.

5. Discuss ways that developmental psychopathology influences the adjustment process.

Patricia and Mary were the best of friends as little girls. They met in preschool and went to the same swim lessons. They were playmates, and their parents planned to send them to the same elementary school.

Then Patricia's family moved to another city. Over time, the two girls lost touch. It was not until 20 years later, quite by accident, that the two women met each other on the street. After all the years apart, they still remembered the physical features of their "best friend."

What they found was that the course of life for the two of them had taken very different paths. Patricia was an attorney at one of the city law firms, well on her way to partnership. She worked hard but found life to be interesting and full. Mary had struggled in high school and dropped out after running into academic trouble. She had felt there was nothing for her there, and she saw no direction to her life. She held irregular jobs, making enough to survive, but it was a struggle. To look at the two women, one would think of them as very different.

Yet, looking back, the two were so much alike as young girls. Was Mary that much different from Patricia with regards to intelligence, motivation, and the ability to focus and work hard? Note that problems in these areas are what many would point out. However, closer scrutiny would show differences in opportunities, social support, and peer groups. Do these discrepant backgrounds really relate to adult outcomes? Are we that susceptible to environmental forces?

***

People comment that George is like two people. In the classroom, he is quiet, studious, reflective, and serious. On Saturday night at a party, George can be found at its center, hooting and hollering at the top of his lungs, dancing and singing to the music. There are some who don't even recognize him at the party. Who is the real George? In fact, he never does these things in class. How might we explain his behavior?

. . . .

The previous stories provide indicators of environmental influences. The first story hints at the cumulative impact of external forces and changes in life direction that these external forces may have brought. The second is more explicit in detailing the effects of changes in settings. How are these stories important to our consideration of life adjustments?

The individual is at the center of Western considerations of accomplishments and failures (Markus & Kitayama, 1991). Psychology tends to ignore the situation or context that surrounds the person (Shinn & Toohey, 2003).

Patricia and Mary's story provides an example of how changes in circumstances can lead to differences in life outcomes. Psychological research has demonstrated that this is not an accident. Knowing the "where" or the succession of "wheres" helps to understand a person's behaviors.

George's story provides an example of varying behaviors in varying situations. One set of behaviors appears in the classroom, and another totally different set of behaviors emerges at the party. These changes in environmental location produce quite divergent sets of actions. This too is an example of the power of the "where." The preceding chapter focused on the power of the individual in the making of meaning and the choices that are made. This chapter provides a perspective on the impact of the world around us. We do not exist in a vacuum. We are not alone. We are social creatures attuned to the circumstances around us. These environments or contexts can help bring positive or negative behaviors. What are some of the ways in which this occurs? What are the processes that are in play? We look at the answers to these questions in this chapter.

Mentoring

At a very personal level, mentoring provides an excellent example of a positive, productive relationship in which an individual can grow. The term *mentor* comes from the Greek stories of Odysseus and the Trojan War. Mentor was Ulysses' adviser. (Athena, goddess of wisdom, would take his form in order to offer advice.) Mentors offer "guidance and new learning opportunities" to the mentee (Eby et al., 2013).

The mentor–mentee relationship is a personal one and requires a fit between the parties involved (American Psychological Association, 2006; Straus, Johnson, Marquez, & Feldman, 2013). Reviewing youth mentoring programs, Dubois, Portillo, Rhodes, Silverthorn, and Valentine (2011) found the best mentors had a good relationship with their charges and advocated for them. Mentors and mentees did better when matched for their interests. The mentor's skills and knowledge in the areas of mentee's interest was helpful. Mentors could offer knowledge about jobs when work was the focus or about academic skills when school was the focus.

Dubois et al. (2011) described a model of mentoring growing from mutual empathy and trust. Length of time in the mentoring relationship helped in building the relationship and the overall success of the youth mentees. Outcome measures on the mentoring programs included social and emotional areas as well as academic and work behaviors.

In a second review of mentoring programs, Eby et al. (2013) found similar positive results. Again, factors that reinforced the relationship were important to the outcomes. They noted that things like the length of the relationship and the mentor–mentee similarity in attitudes, values, and personality affected a mentee's perception of the mentor's emotional and practical support as well as the quality of the relationship. In turn, these perceptions of mentor support were related to a variety of behavioral, attitudinal, and health outcomes. For occupational mentoring, the effects were better work advancement, more satisfaction with one's position, and greater commitment to the organization (Allen, Eby, Poteet, Lentz, & Lima, 2004). For academic mentoring, the mentee usually enjoyed greater success in his or her field of study (Clark, Harden, & Johnson, 2000; Johnson, 2007). For youth programs, better adult life adjustment was found (Dubois et al., 2011). In studies of at-risk youth (Kogan, Brody, & Chen, 2011; Zimmerman, Bingenheimer, & Notaro, 2002), the presence of supportive, naturally occurring mentors were found to decrease acting-out behaviors. Kogan et al. (2011) found that these mentors helped when the youth experienced high levels of stress. Youth with mentors were more likely to have hope and an orientation to the future. They also exhibited better self-control.

The conclusions from these studies support the importance of mentoring. The mentor is the personal vehicle by which we may gain the

In the Odyssey, Mentor was a teacher and overseer to Odysseus' son, Telemachus.

"wisdom" of society (remember Ulysses' story of Mentor and Athena), which can help us in planning for our future and developing the necessary skills to attain our goals. Studies of mentoring define the details of this contextual variable.

In general, mentoring that occurs naturally and informally is seen to be more helpful and meaningful (Eby et al., 2013; Johnson, 2002). This finding underscores the personal nature of this relationship. It cannot be forced. It is best when the persons can relate to each other. Obstacles to developing such relationships include the lack of time, the requirement of effort, the lack of formal support, and the need to address ethical concerns of boundaries and power imbalance (American Psychological Association, 2006; Johnson, 2002). Yet, the recognition of the clear advantages of this contextual opportunity has contributed to the growing encouragement of mentoring efforts at the formal and informal levels (American Psychological Association, 2006).

The role of mentoring to adjustment is that the mentored has access to the experiences and resources of the mentor. While we can learn everything we need through trial and error, the mentor can provide hard-won information. Among the information that can be provided are the social networks and **social capital**, which are a discussed later in this chapter.

Mentoring is one very powerful way in which access to useful information and support occurs. Mentoring has been advocated across multiple settings, including business, school, and social groups. Social support is, in a manner of speaking, an expansion of the mentoring concept.

Social Support

Individuals with good social support are healthier and are better able to contend with stress (Cohen & Wills, 1985; Lin, Simeone, Ensel, & Kuo, 1979; Thoits, 1995; Uchino, Cacioppo, & Kiecolt-Glaser, 1996). Early studies examined how social support helps people. Did it make us happier and healthier for having this support (i.e., positive effects)? Did it help us to deal with problems (buffering effects)? It seems that social support does both (Cohen, 2004; Cohen & Wills, 1985; Procidano, 1992; Taylor, 2011). Social support relates to positive feelings when it measures integration into the community but serves to lessen the impact of stress (a buffer) when it measures access to resources.

Studies of social support continue to show a positive relationship to (a) physical health (Eng, Rimm, Fitzmaurice, & Kawachi, 2002; Holt-Lunstad, Smith, & Layton, 2010; Uchino, Bowen, Carlisle, & Birmingham, 2012; Uchino et al., 1996) and (b) psychological health (Cohen & Wills, 1985; Gottlieb, 1981; Leavy, 1983; Maulik, Eaton, & Bradshaw, 2010). Whether the measure is illness, blood pressure, depression, or anxiety, social support promotes well-being. Social support has been found to reduce risk and increase health indicators for longevity across the life span (see Figure 3.1). Adolescent social support influences physical reactions in midlife, which then affect longevity in old age (Yang et al., 2016).

Types of Social Support

Social support comes to us in a variety of ways (Barrera, 1986). While there are several ways of describing how support comes to us, an early measure of perceived social support devised by Cohen, Mermelstein, Kamarck, and Hoberman (1985) separated it into four types: **tangible support** (I feel like I can get help when I need it), **informational support** (I can get good advice when I need it), **emotional or self-esteem support** (I am valued and respected), and **belonging** (I feel like I have friends). Another formulation of social support measurement also found four factors: informational, emotional, social–companionate, and instrumental (Timmerman, Emanuels-Zuurveen, & Emmelkamp, 2000).

Figure 3.1 Associations of Social Support With Biomarkers of Functioning Over the Life Course

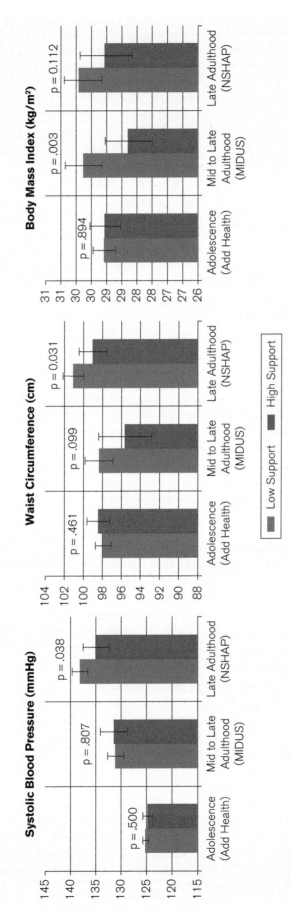

Source: Social relationships and physiological determinants of longevity across the human life span. Claire Yang, Courtney Boen, Karen Gerken, Ting Li, Kristen Schorpp, and Kathleen Mullan Harris. Published online before print January 4, 2016, doi: 10.1073/pnas.1511085112. PNAS January 19, 2016 vol. 113 no. 3 578–583.

Bowen et al. (2014) found that emotional and tangible support buffered the impact of an acute stressor on participants' blood pressure (a physiological measure of stress). However, the best stress buffer for blood pressure effects was informational support. In a study of cardiovascular reactivity to acute stress in women, emotional help provided by a positive, supportive friend helped reduce increases in blood pressure and other measures of cardiac strain (Uno, Uchino, & Smith, 2002). On the other hand, an ambivalent (both positive and negative feelings) relationship with a female supporter led to increases in strain. They concluded that in their study, the quality of the relationship was a critical variable in social support effects.

In general, women are usually more involved in providing and receiving social support (Taylor et al., 2000; Thoits, 1995). In a study of Spanish youth, mothers were perceived to provide the most support of all the available people (Hombrados-Mendieta, Gomez-Jacinto, Dominguez-Fuentes, Garcia-Leiva, & Castro-Travé, 2012).

Social support provides an important contextual element that aids in dealing with the stressors in life and raises our overall sense of well-being. Social support serves as a measure of embeddedness in our community as well as an indicator of access to social resources. These aspects of our context contribute to our overall sense of well-being (Cohen, 2004).

Social Networks

The concept of social networks describes and explains our linkage or connectedness to others. This provides a sense of the people who surround us and their association to others. As will be described in this section, the nature and extent of one's social networks provide access to opportunities to interact with others. These opportunities provide advantages in dealing with life tasks. Whether it be when the library opens, or what this professor is like, or what should be focused on in an interview, these networks can help us to deal with the demands of the world around us (see Figure 3.2). How well we meet these demands is directly related to our abilities to adjust to the environment. The better the networks, the better the context for realizing our individual potential.

To begin analyzing a social network, one can ask a group who speaks with whom. These social interaction patterns illustrate the network. From this data, we can see who has the most contact and who has the least contact with group members. We can derive a sense of the different subgroups within the larger group and how we might get messages between groups—that is, who served as a bridge from one group to another.

Indegree Centrality and Brokerage

Two important characteristics in terms of social networks are **indegree centrality** (Wasserman & Faust, 1994) and **brokerage** (Stovel & Shaw, 2012). Indegree centrality is the number of contacts one person has. The more contacts one has, the better placed one is in the network. Brokerage is the degree to which an individual connects different networks.

The advantages of being within a group network and having a high indegree centrality position are access to that group's information and resources, increased ease in obtaining help from the group, greater mutual sense of loyalty to members, and the advantages of being an in-group member (more likely to be seen as positive and less likely to be seen as negative, despite one's behaviors). Those with indegree centrality are more likely to receive social support in general (Baldwin, Bedell, & Johnson, 1997; Fang et al., 2015; Gibbons, 2004).

Figure 3.2 Examples of Networks

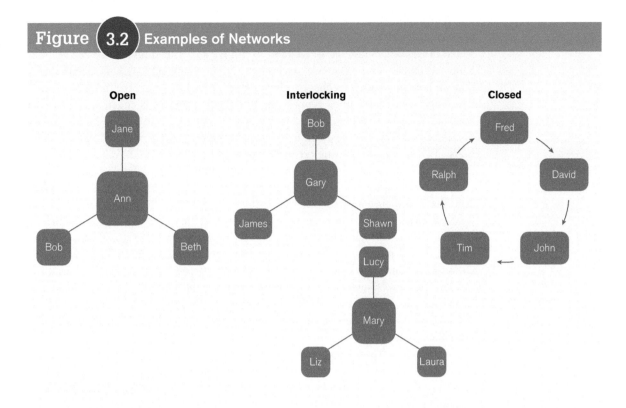

The brokerage position provides the individual with access to information and resources not available to others. People in this position also gain power by serving as negotiators among the various parties who want linkages and the information and resources they provide (Burt, Kilduff, & Tasselli, 2013).

If the group is not open to links to other groups, it can be exclusionary and limit access to resources outside of the group (Granovetter, 1973, 1974). Weaker ties give members the ability to access connections outside of the in-group (Granovetter, 1973, 1983). This larger, looser network produces "strength in weak ties" (Granovetter, 1973). Granovetter (1983) found that using acquaintance contacts (people who are known but are not close friends) was important for the college-educated and for those in higher organizational positions. This was not the case for lower level jobs.

Basic Rules of Networking

Christakis and Fowler (2009) found three basic rules to govern our networking. First, we choose who we have in the network (usually those like us in some way), how many we have in the network (few to many), if our friends know each other (dense or loose ties), and our location in the network (central or peripheral). We play an active role in creating the network. Secondly, our networks influence us. We tend to observe and copy those around us. This might come through learning from others (we'll discuss this more in Chapter 4) or feeling socially pressured to conform to a norm (as described later in this chapter, under Conformity).

The third rule is that the network influence goes out three degrees. Our "friends' friends' friends effect us" (Christakis & Fowler, 2009, p. 22). Christakis and Fowler (2009) reported this ripple effect works for both happiness and loneliness. That is, we can see the impact of happiness on friends and friends of friends. Happy people tend to have happy people around them, and they, in turn, have happy people around them.

Neurologically, our positive emotion centers respond when we hear the sounds of positive emotions from others (Warren et al., 2006). We mirror the emotions around us. When others are smiling at us, we tend to smile back. And smiling back can make us happy. As far back as the Harvard psychologist William James (1884), it has been believed that we take our body's feedback to help determine what we are feeling. The modern neurological literature finds support for this theory of what is called somatovisceral feedback (Berntson, Sarter, & Cacioppio, 2003). When we want to feel happy, placing ourselves in a happy context can make us more emotionally positive. Smiling is infectious and can influence our mood and the mood of those around us.

This also works for a network of loneliness. There may be a kind of "lonely hearts club." Lonely people have fewer interactions with others and may communicate negative moods across their networks.

Beyond these basic rules, there are also rules specific to given groups. One example is from a study of high school sexual partnering (Bearman, Moody, & Stovel, 2004). The rule they found was that the teens did not sleep with their "ex-lover's lover's ex-lover" or "don't date your old partner's current partner's old partner" (Christakis & Fowler, 2009, pp. 97–98). This rule within the group influenced the sexual contact network that was found in their study. There could be other rules that emerge to influence the structures and processes within networks particular to that group, neighborhood, region, or **culture**.

Social networking is a powerful and useful way to understand some of the reasons for people's behavior. These reasons reside outside of the individual and yet help determine how the person thinks, feels, and behaves. We will now consider an area of growing interest in the study of social and community groups, called social capital.

Social Capital

An early definition of social capital is the "goodwill, fellowship, mutual sympathy and social intercourse among a group of individuals" (Hanifan, 1916, p. 130). It is more broadly seen to be the resources (capital) that come from social relationships (Neal, 2015; Poortinga, 2006; Portes, 1998; Vyncke, Peersman, Maeseneer, & Willems, 2012). Putnam (1995) highlighted social capital as a community characteristic. Others have noted social capital at the individual level—the personal gains or access to resources resulting from membership in the community (Portes, 1998). Neal (2015) accepted that social capital is both. In a review of the various definitions, the sociologist Portes (1998) noted social capital was simply that "involvement and participation in groups can have a positive consequence for the individual and the community" (p. 2).

There are costs and benefits to community membership. Social capital is the benefits. With social capital, one can gain information, ask favors, understand the social situation, and have the necessary skills to negotiate problems.

Among the advantageous of social capital are **bonding** and **bridging** functions (Putnam, 1995). Bonding has to do with the attraction we have for those within our group. This is sometimes called **homophily** (*homo* meaning same; *phily* meaning friends). Bridging is the connection to other groups. As Neal (2015) pointed out, these two functions reside in tension to each other. Bonding focuses us inward and bridging focuses us outward. We need both of these to realize the advantages of social capital.

While social capital provides us with access to information, physical help, and positive perception within the group, there are negative aspects to social capital as well. Within an established group there is a tendency to exclude others, to provide pressure to conform to group rules, and a sense of obligation to the group and member needs that may tax the group member's time and energy (Portes, 1998).

Putnam (1995) wrote of the decline in engagement with established formal civic and social organizations from the 1940s to the 1980s and 1990s. Trends in joining, participating, and volunteering were declining. Participation in political discussions decreased. These were signs of social disengagement. However, an article by Sander and Putnam (2010) reported a rebound in political interest in the 2000s among younger middle-class adults.

Students of adjustment can understand social contexts in terms of social capital. Social capital can be earned, accumulated, and used. It resides in the groups with which one associates and can be accumulated by an individual. It conveys, to those who have it, the power to do things and access things better than others who do not have social capital. This adds to our understanding of the social nature of our world and the advantages that can come from that social nature. Social capital adds to our understanding of our contexts and their influence on individuals.

The Importance of Situation or Context

The importance of situational or contextual influences are many times overlooked when considering why people are the way they are (Shinn & Toohey, 2003; Trickett, 2009). How an individual adjusts may be directly related to the situations or contexts in which they are placed. While the individual was the focus of the last chapter, this chapter examines ways in which our environment is an important factor in determining our life and the adjustments to that life.

Person by Situation Interactions

Kurt Lewin was among those psychologists who emphasized the importance of the environmental context on behavior. His formula for determining behavior was this:

$$B = f(P, E)$$

A behavior (B) is the result (function) of both the person (P) and the environment (E). To understand the likelihood of a behavior, we need to know about the individual *and* the environmental context. In a study illustrative of this point, anxious students were found not to be anxious all the time. They were anxious in specific situations, like tests or meeting other people (Endler, 1975; Kendall, 1978; Spielberger, 1972). Neurological research supports the existence of a specific neurological site for situational anxiety (Satpute, Mumford, Naliboff, & Poldrack, 2012).

Ecological Psychology and Behavioral Settings

The importance of behavioral settings has been studied a great detail in the **ecological psychology** of Roger Barker (1968). Barker's study of human ecology highlighted the importance of behavioral settings, which were places and times in a community where specific and predictable behaviors occurred. He believed these place–behavior links were socially based. An example of a behavior setting is the classroom, where classroom-like behaviors are expected. Screaming, yelling, or dancing are not classroom behaviors. Most students understand that in the classroom they should sit and talk in a quiet manner. If asked to stand up and walk around the room, many hesitate since this is not appropriate behavior. Also note that time is important. Before class begins, students talk with each other and ignore the front of the classroom. When

Why do we behave differently when in church than when in a sports stadium?

class time arrives, they look for instruction from the instructor. What should they do? What is expected of them? Students watch others or ask what to do during the first days in class. The power of the setting shapes and enforces particular behaviors. See Researching Adjustment: Context and Identity.

RESEARCHING ADJUSTMENT
Context and Identity

Swanson et al. (2003) pointed out the importance of identity to overall adjustment: "Identity lays the foundation for . . . perception, self-appraisal, and behavior, yielding adverse or productive life-stage, specific coping outcomes" (p. 749).

In the Swanson et al. (2003) model, the individual's perception of his or her environment is an important determinant in the creation of an identity. Identity is dynamic—that is, it interacts with the environment. From a sense of identity comes the perception of the relevancy of the environment—that is, is it an important part of his or her working world? This sense also provides an understanding of their place in that world. Is her or she a member? Does he or she have importance? Is he or she able to influence events? In turn, identity influences how the individual behaves. Does he or she try to engage in that world? Does he or she work to support it? Does he or she endeavor to succeed in it? This model of identity and context is an interactive ecological model, with the outside world influencing the individual's perception of that world, and in turn, those perceptions bringing positive or negative reactions from the individual.

Connell, Spencer, and Aber (1994) demonstrated the effects of this interactive ecological model in a study of high school students followed over a number of years. They found that a student's perception of parental involvement predicted positive student outcomes: sense of self as competent, self-awareness, and a feeling of belonging within his or her school community. These, in turn, were related to better student academic performance over the years. The data for this study came from three different communities and used African American high school samples. The authors concluded that the parent involvement was the contextual first step. This made a difference in the students' perceptions of themselves—that is, their identity as well as their family and their school.

In a second study, of immigrant children, Kumar, Seay, and Karabenick (2015) found identity-affirming school settings to lead to positive perceptions of the experience and support of cultural identity. In contrast to this, challenges to traditional values and practices contributed to identity confusion and conflict and perception of school as a negative place.

Both of these studies support the interactive nature of context and identity, the model proposed by Swanson et al. (2003).

Reflection Questions

1. What of your experiences growing up?

2. Did your family, neighborhood, and school contribute to your sense of identity? In what ways? If it did not, then what happened?

3. What was the effect on how you thought of yourself and those around you?

Source: Adapted from Swanson et al. (2003).

As another example, one might think of a handsha 54'ke. Who shakes hands (people in general, though in certain areas of the United States, males in particular), when do they shake (on meeting), what is the handshake procedure (soft or firm, full or partial grip, lasting for a second or two)? This has changed over time. People may give a fist bump, a wave, a slight bow, or a hug in place of the handshake. These variations are socially determined and are of social significance. One would not shake hands in the middle of a meeting for no reason. Therefore, time and place determine this ritual behavior. Barker explored behaviors that occurred in the natural environment outside of the laboratory, studying in great detail a small Midwestern town setting for many years. From his work, we have good examples of the power of the setting.

Discriminative Setting Stimuli

B. F. Skinner's (1965) study of behaviorism focused on controlled laboratory conditions. Reducing environmental variations to a bare minimum, he observed and manipulated laboratory animals, noting how they learned to behave in a particular way at a given signal. The typical sequence would be a light on (discriminative setting signal) means that a lever press (behavior) would be followed by a desirable consequence (reinforce). The discriminative setting signal was much simpler than the complex social signals within Barker's human community, but the results were similar. The setting or signals influenced the displays of specific behaviors. When the signal was present, the conditions were set for behavior reward. When absent, behaviors would not be rewarded. This distinction was learned quickly and the signal could control when a behavior was displayed. The Skinnerian example is further elaborated in Chapter 4.

In real life, contextual signals can be socially based, such as a team shirt, a school tie, or a uniform (based on group memberships or allegiances), or physical, like the entrance

Conformity is the tendency to agree with members of a group.

to a church, a playing field, a beach, or bar (characteristics of the physical world). They direct the individual as to appropriate behaviors.

In other ways, we may think of ourselves as rural or urban and take for granted that this rural–urban distinction stands for a whole set of beliefs and behaviors shaped by our contextual experiences. Note that these contexts can be in the present, the here and now, or they can be from our past (e.g., ancestry, regional origin, social–political status). You might think about what you assume when someone says they are from New York City or Los Angeles or Texas or Hawaii. Toward that end, one's history is an important part of their "context" (Kelly, 2006; Kelly & Chang, 2008). While the present is important, one's past is as well. People are trying to figure out others' prior contexts when they ask where someone is from and where he or she has been.

In many ways, who we are at the moment is the result of a variety of individual choices but also forces from the world around us. The importance of the setting influencing our behaviors can be found in social situations and cultures. We will now consider some social psychology and cultural psychology principles that influence these contexts.

Two Powerful Social Effects

We are social creatures by nature. Given this, the power of social situations on influencing our behavior is especially important. **Conformity** and obedience to authority are among the many strong socially driven tendencies that we have. This section explores the findings on these tendencies and what influences them.

Conformity

Asch (1951) conducted a series of experiments to determine if conformity, or the tendency to agree with members of a group, is present in groups. He found that students asked to make a judgment call would agree with others in their group, which happened even when the group decisions were wrong. People did not always agree with obviously wrong answers, but a majority of people agreed with incorrect decisions at least once. Among the reasons for such conformity has included our desire to be an accepted member of the group, the power of social pressure to act like others in the group, and not to be punished or expelled from the group. This is called normative influence. The second reason for this to occur is that in uncertain circumstances, the tendency is to depend on the group for information. The group is perceived as a reliable source of direction, which is information influence.

Western and Asian leaders give different smiles to the public.

Studies on conformity found variations in this tendency in different time periods (1960s, 1970s, 1980s, 1990s) and in different cultures (Bond & Smith, 1996). Less conformity has been found in recent times. More conformity has been found in cultures that emphasize a group membership. In the original Asch study (1956), when one person disagreed with the incorrect group answer, the group pressure to conform was lessened. Therefore, while group pressure to conform is strong, it can be broken or lessened.

Conformity comes in many forms. It can be seen in clothing styles (Rose, Shoham, Kahle, & Batra, 1994), political opinions (Bolsen, 2013; Suhay, 2015), or prejudices (Allport, 1949/1979; Crandall & Stangor, 2005).

Obedience to Authority

When individuals are perceived to be authorities, we tend to obey them, despite misgivings about the consequences of our obedience (Milgram, 1963, 1974/2009; Miller, 2014). One very powerful manipulation to obtain obedience is to gradually increase the level of the demands (Cialdini &

"Birds of a feather flock together."

Goldstein, 2004; Cialdini, Kallgren, & Reno, 1991) also pointed to the ambiguity of the situation and the power of social norms under these conditions.

In Milgram's studies, obedience to authority was found to be a normal reaction and environmental circumstances could strengthen or weaken this tendency. Obedience was greater when there were (a) clear displays of authority (lab coats), (b) the setting was a prestigious university, or (c) when responsibility was shared (two people followed the orders). However, obedience dropped (a) when others disobeyed, (b) when obedience resulted in negative effects to someone the participant knew, or (c) when there was physical contact with those suffering negative consequences (Rochat & Blass, 2014). Therefore, while obedience to authority could be strengthened, it could also be weakened by situational contexts.

Replication of the Milgram study, with minor modifications, has been conducted into the 21st century (Burger, 2009). Burger found the tendency to obey continues to be strong, and the tendency was as strong in women as in men.

The social setting is a powerful influence on an individual's behavior. While it can be used for both good (promoting healthy behaviors) or bad (encouraging unhealthy tendencies), the effects are clear. In either case, the social context is important to understanding behavior. As a further example of social context influences, Adjustment in Practice: In-Group, Out-Group describes the psychological advantages of group membership and the disadvantages of not being a group member.

ADJUSTMENT IN PRACTICE
In-Group, Out-Group

Our desire to be a member of a group may be based in part on the advantages of group membership (Brewer, 1999). There are clear, positive gains to be made by such membership. In looking at "in-group" versus "out-group" identification, those seen to be "in" are immediately seen more positively and are given the

(Continued)

(Continued)

benefit of the doubt when mistakes are made. Research indicates these biases are fairly automatic and may be the result of maintaining "in" group advantages, since that advantage applies to the "in" group member as well (Allport, 1949/1979; Brewer, 1999).

What is also interesting about this in-group and out-group advantage is that it is based on self-identification—that is, who we see as part of our in-group. The identification criteria are diverse and dependent on what the individual believes to be important. Criteria for group membership could be racial identification, class identification, school identification, regional identification, common friends, or common activities in sports or school. This list is not exhaustive but serves as an example of the many different ways we can identify with others, which is interesting when we consider culture and gender as possible contextual variables influencing our behaviors.

Reflection Questions

1. How might in-group advantages help to motivate conformity?

2. Who do you consider to be part of your in-group? How do you identify with the individuals in this group?

3. Watch a group of individuals interact together. Can you tell who is part of the in-group and out-group? What criterion or criteria for group membership applies here?

These diverse findings suggest we are social beings, with predispositions to seek others and attend to them. Now let us look at another manifestation of our social nature: culture.

Culture

In the broadest sense of the term, *culture* is anything that is "human made" (Triandis, 2002, p. 3). There are material aspects of culture, which include objects, buildings, and physical products, and there are the "subjective" components, which include our values, roles, and cognitive and emotional styles (Triandis, 1996). Culture is where we find shared memories (Kluckhohn, 1954) that help us to adapt and survive in the world (Berry, 2004). It provides both the setting to which the individual must adjust and the answers to coping with the setting.

Culture provides a framework for understanding and reacting to the world. Sometimes reactions may be so automatic that an individual is unaware of the influences (Devine, 1989, 2001; Dovidio, Kawakami, Johnson, Johnson, & Howard, 1997). Researchers have examined how American culture has produced automatic reactions to members of different ethnic or cultural groups (Greenwald & Banaji, 1995; Jones, 1996). This cultural influence affects people's attitudes and behaviors to others as well as how we think of ourselves and our relationship to others.

How we shake hands and greet each other differs across cultures.

Collectivist Versus Individualist Cultures

Cultures emphasize the "self" as separate from others or embedded in their social group (Markus & Kitayama, 1991, 2010; Triandis, 1995). The group-oriented culture, termed *collectivist*, emphasizes interdependence, group identity, and the importance of roles and respect for members' positions. This contrasts with more individualist cultures where the accomplishments of the person are emphasized along with the importance of freedom of choice and of living in the present moment (Bond & Smith, 1996; Markus & Kitayama, 1991).

This creates very different sets of values; behaviors; and, at a psychological level, ways of defining who we are—that is, our sense of self (Markus & Kitayama, 2010). The tendency to see one's self as independent from one's environment or to see one's self as dependent on that environment influences how we might answer this question: Who am I? Some traditions emphasize the individual, while others emphasize their communities. See Table 3.1 for examples of individualist versus collectivist behaviors. These cultural differences serve as a larger environment that guides our actions. For example, people from collectivist cultures are more likely to conform to their social group (Bond & Smith, 1996).

These cultural tendencies are found in childhood stories (Tsai, Louie, Chen, & Uchida, 2007). Western–individualist children see joy and excitement at the end of their tales. Asian–collectivist children stories end with calm and peace. This cultural difference is also found in the way politicians smile (Tsai et al., 2016). Western

Table 3.1 Collectivist Versus Individualist Tendencies

Collectivist	Individualist
"We"	"I"
"Our"	"Mine"
Group outcomes	Personal empowerment
Community progress	Personal achievement
Being quiet	Speaking up
Patient	In the moment
Conformity	Independence
Calm	Excited

leaders give broad, toothy grins, and Asian leaders show closed mouth looks, suggesting contentment.

It is no surprise that people from different cultures have difficulty in "reading" each other. Culture leads to different communication codes. Behaviors can mean different things. Those from similar cultural backgrounds are better able to read and understand spontaneous emotions (Kang & Lau, 2013). While sharing a language makes for easier communication, the nonverbal behaviors, such as smiling, are also important to that communication. Sometimes a nod means yes, and sometimes it means "I heard you but don't necessarily agree."

Culture Complexes

Sets of behaviors with symbolic meaning are called cultural complexes. These complexes dictate given collections of behaviors in sequence. They capture what Elliott (2002) called "socially constructed networks of meaning that divide one human group from another" (p. xi). These behaviors fulfill particular values and are interpreted. For example, the way in which we eat meals says something about what we think of food and its place in our lives. Are meals eaten together? Does anyone serve? Is anyone served? What is the sequence to the meal? Where is it eaten? How is it concluded? The answers to these questions provide us with an understanding of what the meal is intended to convey. The meaning can go beyond the mere ingestion of food. Some families have rules about sitting down when eating, such as no cell phones at the table or talking in turn. Some people argue about this topic. Others make a distinction between formal and informal meals.

Shweder (2003) asked this question: "Why do men barbecue?" When cooking occurs in the United States, where it occurs influences who does the cooking. Men typically cook outdoors, while women cook indoors. Why is that?

What other cultural sources to our behavior and attitudes might there be? Men in dresses? Men in kilts? Women walking ahead of men? Men walking ahead of women? Men and women walking together? Who pays for a date? Who initiates social contact? And how is that contact made? (The final chapter to this text examines the impact of technology.) Who stays home to care for the children? These are all good examples of the influence of culture complexes.

Culture is acknowledged to influence our everyday behaviors, emotions, and thoughts in ways that are "spontaneous and unselfconscious" (Geertz, 1984, p. 125). It has been shown to systematically affect different groups' moral evaluations, school learning styles, physical and emotional responses to stress, and understanding of one's self (Shweder & Sullivan, 1993). It influences our perception of time and how time is used (Levine, 1998). (One might think about what time to arrive at a party that starts at 9:00 p.m.) Culture impacts our psychological world in so many ways that any serious consideration of human phenomena is considered incomplete without some description of the cultural context (Leong, Comas-Díaz, Nagayama Hall, McLoyd, & Trimble, 2014; Shweder & Sullivan, 1993).

Developmental Psychopathology

Developmental psychopathology examines the outcome of Lewin's (1936/2015) person X situation interactions. Successful or unsuccessful adjustment to developmental demands involves the "interplay among the biological, psychological, and social-contextual aspects of normal and abnormal development across the life course" (Cicchetti & Toth, 2009, p. 16). By developmental demands, they meant the changing social expectations of the infant, then child, then teenager, then adult. At each of these stages, the behaviors and duties of the individual shift in relation to the assumption of greater cognitive and behavioral skills.

While genetics and biology are a part of the human equation, there are many possible outcomes in the human maturation process, called **multifinality**. The interplay of genetics with personal and social variables influence the adjustment process (Moffitt, Caspi, & Rutter, 2006). See Researching Adjustment: Gene X Environment Interaction for an example. Therefore, while two people may start from the same place (e.g., from the same neighborhood, family situation, or genetics), they may arrive at very different places in life. There are a variety of factors that influence outcomes, such as a supportive family friend or an increase in pay to a parent.

RESEARCHING ADJUSTMENT
Gene X Environment Interaction

In a child study that tracked children over a 6-year period, researchers found that children with hyperreactive nervous systems who came from risky, stressful family environments were likely to become impulsive problem children. The hyperreactivity alone did not predict this, nor did the risky, stressful family environment. It took the combination of both to bring about the negative changes. This supports the idea that there may be a biological tendency (hyperreactivity) that can but does not necessarily lead to problems. Only in the circumstance of high-risk stress environments does this tendency contribute to the development of problems.

Sameroff (2010) noted that in the discussions of nature or nurture, the most contemporary and sophisticated theories now acknowledge the influence of both. It is like a dialectic, where the interactions between nature and nurture influence each other. The biological sciences now look at what is called epigenetics, where the environment influences the expression of the genetic potential. While we are looking at biology, we have to look at the influences of the contexts for the organism. Therefore, even in genetics, there is an understanding of the influence of the environment.

Reflection Questions

1. How might this understanding of genetics change your thinking about people's behaviors?

2. What is your stance in the nature versus nurture argument? Did this information change your opinion?

In a similar vein, there may be many ways to achieve the same outcome (called **equifinality**). There are many pathways to the same outcome, given the possible interplay of genetics, developmental tasks, resources and skills, and opportunities to learn and gain support. Consider a classroom full of students. They have all come to that place through different routes. In a typical college class, students have had a wide variety of life experiences. Some could have been homeless, some come directly to college from upper-middle-class homes, some have been in the military, some are single and some are married with children, and yet all arrived in the class as students.

To this mix of various influences on our life, developmental psychopathology adds a developmental framework (Cicchetti & Toth, 1998; Masten, 2001; Masten & Cicchetti, 2010). Mental and physical changes occur over time, and with these changes come shifts in expectations and duties. Beyond growth in height, weight, strength, coordination, and ability to reproduce, our brain grows and matures. These increasing capabilities to consider our world and make thoughtful decisions bring new life tasks (Johnson, Blum, & Giedd, 2009). Researchers have found that our brain does not fully mature until our mid-20s (Galvin, 2014; Sowell, Thomspon, Holmes, Jernigan, & Toga, 1999). At the same time, the individual's neurological capabilities to deal with emotional demands appear to be influenced by culturally based demands (Galvin, 2014).

Developmental psychopathology principles place the individual as an active and participating member of the world around them (Masten, 2006; Masten & Ciccehtti, 2010). That means the settings influence a person, but the person also influences the setting. Therefore, a child is shaped by her or his parent and by her or his school, friends, and neighbors. In turn, the child has an impact on all of those people. This type of mutual influence is increasingly recognized in psychology. For example, social learning psychologist Albert Bandura (2001) wrote of "transactions" between the environment and the person, with both being changed in the process. See Figure 3.3.

Finally, the developmental psychopathology field reminds us that early experiences influence later experiences. In what is called the **cascading effect**, it has been found that early critical events can have larger and broader impacts later on in our lifetime (Masten & Cicchetti, 2010). For example, not learning to read has a profound impact on our lives, since reading is crucial to accessing information and mastering later skills in school and life in general. Another example might be learning to think through our behavioral options and to see the outcomes of each option. Those who do not have these reflective skills could be perceived as impulsive and those who do have the skills seen as reflective and wise. The acquisition of self-regulatory skills is important to our progress in our social groups (Mischel et al., 2011; Shields, Cicchetti, & Ryan, 1994; Shoda, Mischel, & Peake, 1990). These skills are important in the cascade of consequences that come from the successes or failures they bring.

One way to acquire these skills is through a mentor. Finding and keeping a mentor has good implications for the future in many ways. Beyond teaching specific problem-solving

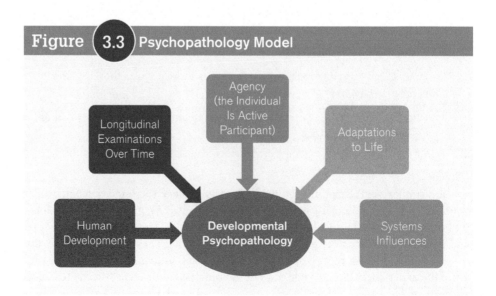

Figure 3.3 Psychopathology Model

skills, the mentor can provide information, provide an objective perspective, and lend support when needed (Dubois et al., 2011). In contrast, the absence of a mentor means that impulsive behaviors may go unchecked and actions can go uninformed as well as there being a lack of perspective and no one to listen (review the discussion of mentoring from earlier in this chapter).

Developmental psychopathology reminds us that in looking at an individual, we must take into account his or her resources and opportunities as well as his or her age and capabilities. Problems and/or solutions are embedded in the person's environment. There is also an understanding that actions or events can have a later and greater impact on lives "downstream."

Early critical events can have a cascading effect on our lives.

Resilience

Developmental psychopathology helps us to understand the evolving nature of our life course and the necessity to master the different tasks that come as a natural part of maturing. The emphasis is on the potential long-term negative or positive outcomes from early experiences. Psychology research has explored these outcomes and found we are surprisingly robust in our response to adversity, which is known as resilience. Luthar, Cicchetti, and Becker (2000) defined *resilience* as "a dynamic process encompassing positive adaptation within the context of significant adversity" (p. 543). From these studies of resilience, psychologists have learned that the individual is adept at getting what is needed from the environment and good at learning what needs to be learned. This provides evidence that humans are good at adjustment.

The concept of resilience grew from studies of high-risk children (Bleuler, 1974; Rutter, 1978, 1987, 2012). Psychologists wanted to find what placed people at risk (see Table 3.2).

Rather than risk leading to problems, researchers found many individuals with healthy outcomes despite the risk factors (Masten, Best, & Garmezy, 1990; Rutter, 2012). This tendency to survive and thrive has been found in studies that followed at-risk children into their teens, 20s, and later adulthood. The studies were across cultures: Rutter (1976) studied two English communities, Werner and Smith (2001) examined an island population in Hawaii, and Garmezy's work (Garmezy, 1987; Garmezy & Streitman, 1974) was based in Minnesota. All reported similar results. To

Table 3.2 Typical Risk Factors
Poverty
Parent with diagnosis of major mental disorder, alcohol or drug abuse
Family discord
High stress level
Pre-birth complications
Mother with less than eighth-grade education
History of abuse

counter the risky situations, communities could provide help and support and, in many cases, successfully override these risky situations. Parents, grandparents, uncles, aunts, neighbors, extended relatives, teachers, or other community members within the risky settings often gave the support needed to the individual at risk. In a listing of qualities related to resiliency, Masten (2001) provided an insightful list of positive factors (see Table 3.3). These resiliency factors were a combination of personal attributes and positive social settings.

Personal qualities interacted, or transacted, with the environment (Sameroff, 2010; Sameroff & Chandler, 1975). In a longitudinal study, Hart, Eisenberg, and Vallente (2007) found that highly reactive children in multiple risk family situations were more likely to develop problem behaviors. The combination of reactivity and risk seemed to work together.

Note that despite risk factors Masten (2001) found the tendency for healthy development and successful adjustment was quite strong. The reasons for this resided in the larger community providing what was needed to the individuals at risk (Masten, 2001; Werner & Smith, 2001). In essence, the community stepped in to help the at-risk individuals learn what was needed to thrive and to grow. Table 3.4 shows a number of qualities that resilient individuals have at different stages in life.

A kind of additive or multiplicative growth of abilities occurs over time. Masten and Cicchetti (2010) described the positive developmental cascades as "competence begets competence" (p. 492). Werner and Smith's (2001) list of personal qualities (intelligence, emotional, and social skills, a combination of tendencies to independence yet openness to learning) were illustrative of other studies that compiled similar lists. Werner and Smith (2001) described the transaction of person and environment, where personal qualities helped those at risk to attract positive attention, learn what was needed from those who knew the required skills, and then provide opportunities for these skills to be exhibited and reinforced (see Table 3.4). These personal qualities changed as the infant grew into adulthood, but success in the earlier stages provided opportunities to

Table 3.3	Resiliency Factors
Child	• Social and adaptable • Positive outlook on life • Sense of meaning in life • Sense of humor • Self-confident
Family	• Harmonious • Positive and supportive extended family • Parents have same characteristics as listed for child • Parents involved with child education
Community	• Safe neighborhood • Recreational opportunities • Stable • Caring mentors and prosocial peers • Access to police, fire, and medical services
Schools	• Trained, effective, and well-paid teachers • After-school programs

Source: Copyright © 2001 by the American Psychological Association. Reproduced with permission from Masten, A. S. (2001). Ordinary magic: Resilience processes in development. American Psychologist, 56(3), 227–238. The use of APA information does not imply endorsement by APA.

Table 3.4 Qualities of Resilient Individuals

Toddlerhoood	• Alert, positive social orientation, communication skills, self-help
Middle Childhood	• Gets along with others, good reading and reasoning, engaged
Adolescence	• Positive self-concept, nurturing, responsible, achievement oriented
Early Adulthood	• Educated; employed; values parenthood; if married, values in-law relationships • Women at work: cooperative; men at work: competitive • Women: married; men: once committed, work to resolve any issues
Middle Adulthood	• Compassionate, committed to family and community

Source: Adapted from the work of Werner and Smith (2001, pp. 56–79).

continue this trend in later stages. There was a cascading effect of positive bringing more positive versus negative bringing more negative. Consider the qualities that were listed in Table 3.4. Would they not be the type of characteristics that would bring positive attention to the individual at that stage in life? Might they make an adult consider investing time and resources into the child's development?

The argument could be made that the phenomena of resilience is an excellent illustration of the importance of the context to individual adaptation. Certainly there are personal qualities that relate to resilience. But these qualities are to make the person better able to take advantage of the contexts in which he or she might find himself or herself. The context must be supportive and provide the requisite information and skills. Luthar and colleagues (2000) emphasized the importance of the individual, the family, and the community in the resiliency model.

The Maturation and Socialization Process

The human baby is born helpless and immature. By some measures, over two decades are required to attain full adulthood (Arnett, 2000, 2014), as the human brain does not reach full maturity for about 20 years (Galvin, 2014; Sowell et al., 1999). This long period of time enables "caregivers" to teach the individual how to behave in an "adult" manner (Erikson, 1968/1993; McCormick, Kuo, & Masten, 2011). These influences come from both informal and formal sources, like extended family, friends, and neighbors as well as school and church. These social influences have an impact on the individual's development and life course.

Linguistically, there are signs that human infants are especially sensitive to parental input. Babies show neurological reactivity to their mother's voice (Therien, Worwa, Mattia, & deRegnier, 2004). Newborns have a preference for their mother's speech (Fifer & Moon, 1989), and they favor their "mother tongue"—that is, the language their mother speaks (Moon, Cooper, & Fifer, 1993). Through these mechanisms, human infants attend to and learn from their mother and those sharing their mother's language—that is, the mother's culture.

Among our basic needs are those for physical contact (Harlow, 1958) and for interacting with and pleasing others, also called affiliation (McClelland, 1987). The importance of social contact may be so integrated into the human experience that the neural mechanisms for social warmth are related to the sensation of warmth (IJzerman & Semin, 2009; Inagaki & Eisenberger, 2013).

These diverse findings demonstrate the power of our contexts. Support for the importance of social contexts comes from our social nature. We are predisposed to attend to important others, to follow their lead and be a part of the social group. The extended period of our maturation process increases this influence on our development into mature adults.

Conclusion

Our community contexts influence who we are. From mentors to social support systems, we are aided by those around us. Social networks provide the linkages to others, and social capital is accumulated and used in a way very similar to money. Models for understanding behavior take into account both the person and the environment. In human ecology, the variability of behavior settings helps to explain the variability in behaviors exhibited. At a very basic level, stimuli can help direct expectations of what is reinforced.

Social psychology contributes findings of tendencies to conform to others and to obey the recognized authorities. Culture also provides guidelines and values as to how to behave, think, and feel. It is the framework for deriving meaning in our communities. Developmental psychopathology adds the insight that our life tasks change as we age, and the successful completion of these tasks provides the foundation for later success. In the face of adversity, the human capacity for resilience is strong. This resilience is a combination of both personal and community factors. The most important individual qualities have to do with the ability to attract community resources.

In evolutionary terms, we as a species have the advantage of a long period of time in which to learn from the social environment around us. With preference for parental input, the infant matures over many years under the guidance of adults. This underscores the importance of social contextual influences in shaping the individual.

Review Questions

1. Analyze the role of a mentor. How does he or she help an individual with life or adjustment?

2. What is a social support system? Explain the various kinds of support that can be provided.

3. Describe social networks, and explain the basic rules of networking.

4. How might a person use social capital?

5. Describe a person by situation interaction.

6. What is a behavior setting in ecological psychology? Provide an example of a behavioral setting.

7. Provide a personal example of conformity.

8. What is culture? Give an example of culture at work.

9. What roles do equifinality and multifinality play in developmental psychopathology? How do you think they affect adjustment throughout the life span?

10. What role does the community play in resilience? How does this differ from the role that personal qualities play in resilience?

Key Terms

behaviorism 55
belonging 48
bonding 52
bridging 52
brokerage 50
cascading effect 62

conformity 56
culture 52
ecological psychology 53
emotional or self-esteem support 48
equifinality 61
homophily 52

indegree centrality 50
informational support 48
multifinality 61
social capital 48
tangible support 48

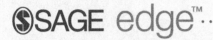

Sharpen your skills with SAGE edge at **edge.sagepub.com/moritsugu**

SAGE edge for students provides a personalized approach to help you accomplish your coursework goals in an easy-to-use learning environment.

Go to **edge.sagepub.com/moritsugu** for additional exercises and web resources. Select Chapter 3, Community Contexts for chapter-specific resources.

Chapter 4

Experience and Learning

1. Identify the principles and techniques of classical and operant conditioning.

2. Discuss ways that individuals experience social learning and its advantages.

3. Explain the principles of Piaget's and Vygotsky's theories of cognitive development.

4. Explain what active learning is, how it can be achieved, and how it impacts adjustment.

It had been only a few months—less than half a year really—and the young college student returned to his familiar haunts from high school. What he found was comfortable and known. The businesses in his hometown were the same, and the people who walked the streets and interacted with each other were friendly. Yet the student noted that they saw him as different. The student spoke at a different pace, used new words, thought of and discussed different ideas. References were also changed. The *New York Times* and the *Wall Street Journal* defined news for him. People heard these things and saw these things. Both the student and the community knew there had been a transformation with his going to college.

· ·

Our experiences shape us. Psychology has contributed much to understanding how these experiences influence life from feelings and emotional reactions to how one behaves in given situations, to what is thought and remembered. We become what we practice. Experience and adaptions to the world create change down to the neurological level.

This chapter first examines the work of the 19th-century Russian physiologist Ivan Pavlov. Pavlov defined and described what has come to be known as classical conditioning. Next, the principles of operant learning derived from the work of B. F. Skinner are described as they apply to voluntary behaviors. These Skinnerian principles are then extended to cognitions, which lead into the work of Albert Bandura and **social learning theory**. Beyond cognitions, the work on learning probabilities is then explored in an area called statistical learning, as well as **implicit learning** and **explicit learning**. The way in which our experiences help to shape our cognitive development is then discussed, and the chapter concludes with consideration of **active learning** versus passive learning. The impact of experience on our lives can be better understood from the examination of all these works. We interact with our contexts, experience them, and are influenced by them.

Pavlovian Conditioning

When speaking of experiences, the most basic learning is in Pavlovian conditioning. This deals with the association between two stimuli. This basic association learning contributes to our ability to adjust to the world. For example, snarling dogs may lead to the pain of a bite, so stay away from snarling dogs. Pavlov was a Russian physiologist in the early 20th century who discovered and refined what is now called Pavlovian conditioning.

The Basics of Pavlovian Conditioning

The basics of Pavlovian conditioning, also known as classical conditioning, are fairly straightforward (Pavlov, 1923/1928; see Figure 4.1). Stimuli come to be associated with each other, and in the association, reactions become similar. To begin with, one stimulus may bring a given reaction. This is called the **unconditioned stimulus (UCS)**, which elicits an **unconditioned response (UCR)**. Another stimulus does not elicit that response; this is known as a neutral stimulus (NS), which provides no response. Given the appropriate pairing of the unconditioned and neutral stimuli, in time both stimuli will elicit the same response. At this point, the NS is no longer neutral but a **conditioned stimulus (CS)**. The CS is described as eliciting a **conditioned response (CR)**.

The classic example of this type of learning from experience is a bell (CS) followed by food (UCS). In time, the bell will bring about salivation (CR)—that is,

Figure 4.1 Pavlov's Dog

Source: Wikimedia Commons.

our mouths will water when the bell is rung. Another example might be going to a particular restaurant (NS) that does not cause salivation until several delicious meals (UCS) have been paired with the location. After that, just thinking of that restaurant (CS) brings about salivation (CR).

In technical terms, a UCS brings about a UCR. The second stimulus, once learned, is a CS, which then brings about the CR. Research has shown that the pairing of the two stimuli is best when the CS is followed by the UCS. This is called forward conditioning.

What does this have to do with humans? Consider the story of Michael, who once dated Marnie. It turns out that Marnie had a favorite shampoo that smelled like jasmine. Michael had smelled jasmine all his life but did not think much of it. However, over the course of their dating, he came to learn that the smell of jasmine usually preceded the appearance of Marnie, who set Michael's heart to beating. She excited him. In time, the mere smell of jasmine got Michael excited. He could associate that smell with Marnie's presence. Michael had learned about his world in a Pavlovian way.

These associations can also be made between categories. For example, Devine (1989) found that responses to categories of people (e.g., Black Americans, Asian Americans) could be influenced by their association with certain qualities (e.g., athletic, hardworking, studious). These categories could then influence decision making about people in these categories unconsciously and nearly instantaneously (Greenwald, Poehlman, Uhlmann, & Banaji, 2009).

Preparedness in Behavior Acquisition

Research has shown that there can be biological predispositions to certain stimulus pairings (Brcland & Breland, 1961; Garcia, Kimeldorf, & Koelling, 1955; Ohman & Mineka, 2001). Garcia et al. (1955) found their animal subjects learned somc things easily but not others. The associations made between stimuli varied. They reasoned that this ease of learning was linked to biological predisposition (Garcia & Koelling, 1966; Garcia, Lasiter, Bermudez, & Deems, 1985).

The Brelands (Breland & Breland, 1961) described patterns of behavior acquisition that also appeared to follow a line of species-specific tendencies, which made sense in an

PAVLOV'S PARADIGM

UNCONDITIONED STIMULUS

UNCONDITIONED RESPONSE

SCENT OF SHAMPOO

(NO RESPONSE)

CONDITIONED STIMULUS

CONDITIONED RESPONSE

maria reva

We learn to associate stimuli, such as perfume and a person.

ecological manner—that is, the learning tendencies seemed to make sense when considering where and how the species survived in their environment.

Seligman (1970, 1971) coined the term *preparedness* to describe these and other findings of biologically based predispositions to certain learning sequences. Where there appears a clear tendency to learn certain things, we are considered prepared. For those things we are less prepared to learn, we are unprepared. And for learning that runs in opposition to what a species has typically learned, we are contraprepared. In these cases, learning is nearly impossible.

Extensions of classical learning and its impact on our everyday lives may be seen in human reactions to symbols or to groups of people. We might think about our emotional reaction to a favorite team. The automatic emotional response is probably related to good feelings or excitement related to that team. We might be biologically programmed to prefer to be a part of a winning team (Cialdini et al., 1976).

Classical conditioning can be seen in more complex social behaviors. Hein, Engelmann, Vollberg, and Tobler (2016) found that when a member of a disfavored group provided help, participants who received the help changed their feelings toward that disfavored group. On both self-report measures and on neurological measures, those who had received the help were more empathic to the disfavored group members. This feeling was not just for the individual who had helped them—the empathic reaction extended to other members of the disfavored group. The pairing of help and the disfavored group membership changed the way in which the participants felt about that group. These findings followed newer conceptions of Pavlovian or classical conditioning, in which the importance of the stimulus pairing had to do with predictability (out-group member and help) and not just physical stimuli and reactions (Rescorla & Wagner, 1972).

Pavlovian or classical conditioning is seen as one of the basic learning frameworks that addresses experience. The second—**operant conditioning**—follows.

Operant Conditioning

Experiences come in various forms. Skinner distinguished between Pavlovian **respondent conditioning** and his own Skinnerian operant conditioning (Skinner, 1938). Operant conditioning involves stimulus signs and voluntary behaviors acting on the environment.

There are three elements to **operant conditioning**: (1) a stimulus signal, called a **discriminative stimuli**; (2) a behavior "operating" on the environment (called an **operant**); and (3) consequences for that action.

Discriminative Stimulus

There are stimuli in our environment that signal us that a behavior is appropriate. When we see a friend, we usually nod and say hello. Seeing him or her signals in us that the nod and hello are appropriate to the situation and will probably lead to something we want—a returned nod and hello. Think of a person walking down the hall where there is no person present but who says hello. A hello to no one would not seem appropriate, since there is no one to return the hello.

Sometimes this stimulus is called the setting or the situation, which guides or directs behavior. The situation determines the appropriate behavior to exhibit. The male author of this text once went to a party and wore a bow tie. Someone walked up to him and asked why he was wearing a tie. They believed it was not appropriate to wear a tie at the party. He responded that he had worn ties to similar parties and been complimented on tie wearing. Others had thought the tie was appropriate and good. In particular, the host and hostess felt the tie was good for the occasion. He had worn ties to concerts, to weddings, and to certain celebrations. He thought the party was such an occasion, so the tie was "called for." The person who had asked the question had not been to situations where ties were worn so had not learned to wear them. The situation, the signaling stimulus, the discriminative stimulus directs us as to what behaviors to display. (Note that ties at the beach are probably not going to be applauded.)

Response, Behavior, or Operant

The discriminative stimulus is the first part in the sequence. The response, behavior, or operant on the environment is the second part. When signaled, the behavior occurs. A green traffic light signals a person to go; a walk signal means to walk across the street. Behaviors can vary based on the discriminative stimulus. If playing football, playing does not commence until the snap of the ball. If playing soccer, playing occurs when the ball is kicked inbounds.

The behavior that is appropriate at a particular time is dictated by the discriminative stimulus, or the signal for a behavior. In some sports, a whistle is the stimulus signal to start; in others, it means to stop. In learning the sport, players learn what behavior is expected at the signal. In life, there are discriminative stimuli that indicate what behavior to exhibit. When that behavior is exhibited, feedback is provided on that behavior—for example, "Please wait to be called on before speaking." Therefore, people speak only when they are called to speak. To complete the sequence, we would need to have appropriate feedback for speaking when called on. See Researching Adjustment: Hebb's Rule.

RESEARCHING ADJUSTMENT
Hebb's Rule

By practicing what we learn, we strengthen the neural connections governing the behavior. This is known as Hebb's rule, often paraphrased as, "Neurons that fire together, wire together" (Hebb, 1949). We literally change our neurology

(Continued)

(Continued)

by refining the connections related to the behavior. Any accomplished athlete knows to repeat the desired behavior sequence over and over. Musicians also say that once a piece is mastered, it should be repeated. When learning something new, repetition increases the ease to which it can be performed.

Reflection Questions

1. Can you think of an example where this has worked in your life?

2. Where might it be useful to you?

Consequences: Feedback, Reinforcement, Punishment, or Nothing

When a behavior has been initiated, there are consequences or feedback to that behavior. Feedback that increases the likelihood, or strengthens a behavior tendency, is called a **reinforcer**. Reinforcement by definition strengthens a behavior. For example, if a thank-you following a behavior increased the behavior coming again, that thank-you is a reinforcer. It could also be a smile, or "well done." Consequences that decrease the likelihood of behavior tendency are called **punishers**. Here, a behavior followed by something not liked, such as "No!" stops that behavior appearing again. It could also be something physical, such as a slap. There are also times when a behavior brings no consequence, which then leaves the person with no feedback for an action. This usually leaves people confused. Were they supposed to do something or not? The reinforcer tells them they are supposed to do something, and the punisher tells them they are not to do something.

Behaviors are best affected when a consequence comes soon after the action. The passage of time between behavior and consequences can make it harder to associate the action to the consequence or outcome. It is easiest to learn when the consequences are obvious, which typically means a short time sequence of behavior to consequence.

Exceptions to this time rule come when other aspects of the learning sequence make better sense. A common example is eating and stomach nausea. The usual association is between the eating and the later nausea, since they involve the digestive system. What is important is the cognitive linkage between behavior and consequence (Rescorla, 1988; Rescorla & Wagner, 1972). Expecting certain behaviors to be reinforced or punished leads to increases (expecting reinforcement) or decreases (expecting punishment) in the probability of our behaviors (Bandura, 1977b, 2006).

In research on expectancies, students who believed academic performances could be influenced by hard work worked harder (Hong, Chiu, Dweck, Lin, & Wan, 1999). This emphasis on effort and practice for knowledge acquisition led to more studying. Since effort counted, students believed their effort would be rewarded. And so what we believe about how success is achieved can influence our behaviors to achieve that success. When faced with problems that were described as set by biological ability and no amount of work would help, people did not work as hard.

©iStockphoto.com/apomares

Students work harder when they believe their efforts will be rewarded.

Given the two options, which do you think will lead to more studying?

1. "Sure, I know how hard I work is related to my success."

2. "What's the use, the smartest students always get the best grades, and I know I'm not that smart."

In an interesting combination of classical and operant conditioning, the use of punishments can lead to classical conditioning of the punisher, leading to avoidance learning. See Adjustment in Practice: Avoidance Learning for elaboration on this topic. It is a cautionary tale on the use of punishers.

ADJUSTMENT IN PRACTICE
Avoidance Learning

In a variation on expectancies, learning to anticipate negative consequences occurs quickly. In anticipation of negative events, subjects try not to be in situations that have led to unpleasantness. Staying away from or rather avoiding situations means that there is no possibility of reexperiencing the disliked experiences. For example, following negative interactions with a person, the tendency is to avoid that person. Another example of this is when we read a particularly boring textbook and then find it hard to read that text again. In this case, pairing the text with pleasant experiences (classical conditioning) or giving oneself a reward for reading the text (operant conditioning) may help.

One of the problems with the use of punishment to suppress behaviors is that the punisher may then be avoided. The punishment will be associated with the punisher, so by avoiding the punisher, there is no likelihood of punishment to arise again.

Reflection Questions

1. What do you think of the negative effects of punishment if a punisher is ultimately avoided?

2. How have you participated in an avoidance learning situation? How could you have used reinforcement of new behaviors instead?

Consequences That Are Predictable But Not Always There

Learning occurs when specific behaviors lead to predictable results in certain settings. Can someone depend on two stimuli occurring together? Or can someone depend on a stimulus, behavior, consequence sequence? Then these are predictable (Rescorla & Wagner, 1972). When the probability of the outcome is random, we learn that the behaviors do not seem to matter—that is, the outcome is random. When the probabilities of events occurring together are high, they are said to be predictable. In classical conditioning, the link between the CS and UCS needs to be predictable (Balsam, Fairhurst, & Gallistel, 2006; Rescorla, 1968; Rescorla & Wagner, 1972). The same is the case for operant conditioning (Ferster & Skinner, 1957). In another variation on the association between doing things and the consequences of doing things, there are times when the predictable outcomes require more than one action (Ferster & Skinner, 1957).

Someone playing a song on a guitar knows that one correct note does not make a complete song. A poet knows that one word does not make for a complete verse. There are times when we must complete several of the same behaviors or a prescribed set of behaviors before we accomplish our task, like playing a song or writing a verse. **Chaining** occurs when a sequence of behaviors is required to finish a task. Each behavior in the sequence needs to occur in that same order, like links in a chain.

The number of behaviors or the timing of behaviors can be set or varied. If a certain number of the same behaviors or certain timing to the behaviors is required, it is called a **schedule to the reinforcement**. If a fixed number of behaviors is required to receive reinforcement, it becomes predictable and behaviors respond to this predictability. When the number of behaviors required for reinforcement is changeable, or variable, then responses are more difficult to predict. Behaviors will then shift in anticipation of the predictably variable reinforcement. Responses to a variable reinforcement pattern are usually steady and unrelenting behaviors, since the very next behavior may lead to reinforcement.

In an informal experiment, a friend of one of the text's authors once found that people would typically say hello regardless of knowing her, on average, about once in every three times. She would say hello to many people, anticipating that at least one third of them would say hello in return. This number could increase if she smiled and made eye contact. She learned that smiling and making eye contact brought many hellos from those walking by, regardless of her knowing anyone. The smile and eye contact were discriminative stimuli for others, signaling them to say hello. This made for a very friendly feeling in her

Figure 4.2   Fixed Interval and Variable Interval Schedules

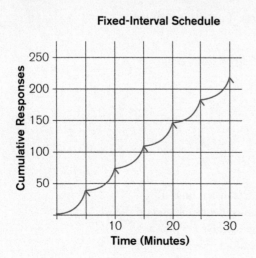

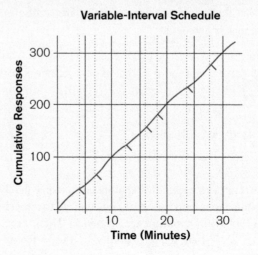

world. While this ratio likely varies across different regions and cultures, it makes for an interesting application of learning schedules to her world. See Figure 4.2.

Sometimes the timing of the behavior is critical to reinforcement. This is called an interval schedule. When reinforcement occurs at variable times, a slow and steady pace is needed—not exerting too much effort but doing just enough so that the needed action is taken when required. If an employee never knows when his or her boss is coming by, except that she walks by about every 10 minutes, a slow and steady work pace seems in order. In another example, if students know that their teacher gives a quiz every other day, they should make sure that they are studying every other day. When that teacher changes quiz days so it is on average every third or fifth class, students are left to guess when to study. The safest bet is to keep up with the class, since the timing of the quiz is uncertain.

Regularity in consequences results in regularities to behavior. When feedback is less regular but still predictable, the subject responds in certain ways (Estes, 1950, 1964,1976; Ferster & Skinner, 1957). We respond to variations in consequences by matching probabilities (Estes, 1950) and by developing cognitive strategies to deal with these consequences (Erev & Barron, 2005).

The consequences to behavior can be learned and influence that behavior. The consequences can strengthen or reinforce a behavior, increasing the probability of its happening again, or it can weaken or "punish" a behavior, decreasing the probability of its happening again. When reinforced with an "attaboy" or "well done," the motivation is to do more. When punished with "that's awful" or "you have to be kidding me," the tendency is to stop doing what had been done. These consequences influence behaviors.

Think of a parent's smile or frown, a coach's nod or shake of her head. Remember, according to psychology, to increase a behavior, reinforce it. To decrease a behavior, punish it.

Note that if a behavior is decreased by punishment, one cannot be certain of what will replace the suppressed behavior unless a preferred behavior is reinforced. Therefore, if punishing undesirable behaviors, desirable behaviors must be reinforced.

ADJUSTMENT IN PRACTICE
Premack Principle

Looking for a reinforcer can sometimes be difficult. Premack (1959) discovered that things we already do often can serve as reinforcers. He believed the more frequent behavior can serve as a reinforcer for the behaviors that are less frequent. For example, if one often reads the newspaper in the morning, then he or she can use reading the newspaper as a reinforcer for another behavior (i.e., I can't read the paper until I have done what I want to increase).

Reflection Questions

1. So where could you use such a principle?

2. What are some of the things that you do a lot? Would you "work" to get to do them?

Shaping

Refinement of behavior is called shaping. Like a piece of clay, behavior can be shaped toward what is desired. Successive approximations can be reinforced until the desired behavior is obtained.

For example, if public speaking is targeted, an individual would practice what is to be said in private until the desired behavior (smooth, confident, comprehensible) is obtained. Then he or she would practice more to increase neural connections, and once well practiced, he or she would take the behavior to a small group, slowly building the group in size.

In a similar manner, how to behave in social situations is shaped from childhood, such as when to say something, what to say, and how to say it. In new situations, the person might try variations of what is said until the feedback indicates it is right. Parents or peers may provide feedback on the effectiveness of what is said.

Social norms play a role in determining appropriate behavior or, rather, behavior that is reinforced. It can be subtle like standing in an elevator. Have you ever stood "facing the wrong way" in an elevator? People become nervous and give nonverbal feedback for the strange behavior. The same happens in many social groups. What was the last thing you did where you received feedback? When was the last time you gave someone feedback (verbal or nonverbal)? What was it for? In that moment, you were in the midst of operant conditioning. See Adjustment in Practice: Self-Control.

ADJUSTMENT IN PRACTICE
Self-Control

In this Adjustment in Practice feature, we provide the basic steps for running a self-control program. You will see the use of discriminative stimuli and reinforcers. If you do this self-control program, note if it works and why. If it does not work, also learn from it by asking yourself what was effective and what was not. Were the principles from classical and operant learning useful? Start with something simple. The biggest hint is to make sure you have something that you can reinforce. If you don't have a chance to reinforce the behavior, you cannot increase it. It may seem like cheating, but start with easy goals.

We can use the learning principles around stimulus control and reinforcement to increase or decrease behaviors in our life. The process follows these steps:

1. Define the behavior that you want to control. The behavior should be clearly described and observable (examples may include studying for two hours, saying hello to five strangers today, walking 2 miles each day, or writing five pages in a journal).

2. Count and record the behavior to establish what is presently done (i.e., how many hours we presently study each day, how many pages we read, how many push-ups we do, how many times we say hello to those in our dorm).

3. Look for an effective reinforcer to strengthen the desired behavior, or look for a punisher to weaken the behavior not desired (for a reinforcer, something one would clearly work for, like food or money or time with

friends; for a punisher, something not desired, like giving away money, a rubber band snap on the wrist, doing a boring task; see Adjustment in Practice: Premack Principle). Our recommendation is to do a project that uses reinforcement first. Leave punishment for later, or do that in consultation with the instructor.

4. Also look at where you are more likely to do a desired behavior (if studying is more likely in your library and less likely in your room, then go to the library; if exercise is more likely with a friend, then seek out a friend). If you want to decrease a behavior, see where you are less likely to partake in the behavior (if it is harder to procrastinate when you study with others, then study with others; if it is harder to eat excessive amounts with some people over others, then seek out those people).

5. Put together the two pieces of information you have from Steps 3 and 4. If seeking to increase behaviors, put yourself in situations where the behavior is likely to occur, and then reinforce yourself for doing it. If you want to decrease behaviors, place yourself in settings where the behavior is less likely to occur, punish yourself if the behavior occurs, and reinforce yourself for doing healthier alternatives to the behavior you want to do less of. Note that in decreasing behaviors, it is helpful to reinforce the alternative behaviors one wants to increase.

6. Keep track of your behavior with the program, and adjust as the data suggests, keeping things the same if it works and making adjustments if it does not. If you continue to have trouble getting control of your behavior, you may want to consult a psychologist.

Reflection Questions

1. What do you think will be easiest for you to do?

2. What do you think will be difficult to do? Why?

3. How could you deal with the difficulty?

4. Do you think a systematic examination of behavior can help to show patterns to your behaviors?

Cognitive Behaviorism

The basic principles governing our behaviors extend to our thoughts. Following theoretical models described by Hull (1943) and later translated into human personality theory by Dollard and Miller (1950), psychologists have treated cognitions as behaviors, as signals for behaviors, and as consequences for behaviors. These signals can be used to control and direct internal and external behaviors. When controlling our impulse to act by reminding ourselves to think first, this reminder and the act of thinking itself are signals and behaviors that can be used to help deal with a situation. If this skill is not present, it can be learned by using the same principles described by Pavlov (associations) or Skinner (behavior increases or decreases based on feedback for the behaviors). When thinking is rewarded, thinking increases. When thinking is not rewarded, thinking decreases.

A regimen of increasing constructive thinking and decreasing unconstructive thinking using Skinnerian principles with people dealing with problems in life has been found to be highly effective (Beck, 1975; Meichenbaum, 1977). It is recognized as a major form of evidence-based therapy (Butler, Chapman, Forman, & Beck, 2006). This cognitive behavioral technique will be explored in greater depth in Chapter 13. Thoughts can be treated as behaviors and changed as behaviors. Specifically, thought-controlling behaviors have been found to be useful. Treating our thoughts as behaviors leads to changes in predictable directions.

Social Learning

Learning goes beyond linking stimuli or learning behaviors through reinforcement and punishment. Social learning theory provides a cognitive model to explain how observations of others' experiences influences our own behaviors (Bandura, 1977b, 2011). The stimuli don't have to be physically placed together as in Pavlovian conditioning, nor do the stimulus, behavior, and consequence sequences have to be experienced by the individual. Expectations regarding associations, or the cognitive representations of stimuli and behavior consequences, are important (Bandura, 1986).

These learning capabilities provide an advantage in acquiring new behaviors in problematic situations. This is a clear advantage in adjustment. We do not have to experience everything ourselves; we can learn from the experiences of others. In this way, our family, our social groups, and our cultures can exert an influence on us more easily.

Modeling

Observation changes the knowledge about behaviors and consequences (Bandura, 1976). New behaviors and new anticipations of outcomes for such behaviors can be acquired without concrete practice. Modeling occurs when the observed person demonstrates a behavior. Imitation occurs when the modeled behavior is copied.

Note that there are two different pieces of information that can be learned: (1) the behavior and (2) the outcome. Learning can be conceptualized as a series of steps where the learner has to first attend to the teacher–model. This is usually someone who the student admires, feels connected to, or controls the student's reinforcers (Bandura, 2001). Then the student has to adequately store and retrieve the information when needed. Putting this to use is limited by the individual's physical capacity to reproduce the behaviors.

When watching a soccer player score a goal, one might note how she maneuvers the ball through a gauntlet of opposing players. While appreciating the motor control and executive functions that allow for such a performance, reproducing these skills is limited to individual performance capabilities. One might recall these skills and relate them to friends. However, the ability to replicate the moves is limited to specific mental and physical skills. Just because one sees Hope Solo block or Amy Rodriguez kick a soccer ball does not mean the capacity to replicate their moves is present without a lot of practice, if ever at all (Bandura, 2006).

The following steps make up observational learning:

1. Attend to the model.

2. Remember the model.

3. Be able to reproduce the modeled behavior.

4. Be motivated to reproduce the modeled behavior.

©iStockphoto.com/spotmatik

"Watch me!" Much of our learning happens through modeling.

©iStockphoto.com/ariwasabi

What is termed *vicarious learning* happens through model observations. For example, the latest fashions are copied by many individuals. Seasonal color trends are picked up and duplicated by the masses. Loose jeans are everywhere, then tight jeans are popular.

While the examples given have to do with clothing and sports, this kind of vicarious learning can be found in social attitudes. For a while the French are good, then not good, then good again. Religion is an important topic of discussion or not. Dating is a good thing, then not dating is a good thing, then dating is back. Note that attitudes toward drinking are influenced in the same way. Vicarious learning is dictated by asking such questions as follows: Who do you attend to? Who do you admire? What do you expect to gain as a reward from learning their behaviors?

Perceived Self-Efficacy

Among the more important learned expectations are the ones of the self. Perceived self-efficacy deals with what is expected of our efforts (Bandura, 1977a, 1982, 1993, 2001a). Individuals who believe their efficacy is high are able to see the probability of successful outcomes. They are more likely to take on challenges, work harder, persist at tasks, and ultimately succeed (Zimmerman, 2000). There is evidence that those high in perceived self-efficacy are more likely to do well in college (Chemers, Hu, & Garcia, 2001; Torres & Solberg, 2001; Zajacova, Lynch, & Espenshade, 2005). Given this expectation, they are less likely to be afraid or act in a fearful manner, making them less likely to be victimized. Therefore, the perception of self-efficacy is an important variable in promoting life success.

Self-efficacy affects our ability to respond to stress. Our immune functions are strengthened in a variety of ways (Wiedenfeld et al., 1990). In very clear terms, our psychology has a positive impact on our physical health.

Collective Efficacy

The concept of efficacy or effectiveness is extended to groups (Bandura, 2001a, 2001b). In perceived collective efficacy, individuals expect their collective efforts will be successful. These groups take on the qualities of the self-efficacious individual. The collective, or group, tries harder and longer, takes on more challenges, and in the end is more successful. Group perceived efficacy has been increased by media. In a particular example, women in underdeveloped parts of the world were empowered by watching popular soap operas with healthy and productive women models. The exposure to efficacious models leads to increased efforts to gain an education and to start up businesses (Bandura, 2006).

Learning Probabilities (Statistical Learning)

Beyond simple behaviors and cognitions, there is evidence that rules and probabilities can also be learned. In studies of language acquisition, researchers have found that infants can learn to discern what to expect next in a sentence (Aslin & Newport, 2012; Romberg & Saffron, 2010). Given an understanding of the regularities governing the probability of events in the sentence sequence, they come to anticipate what comes next. It is a kind of "statistical" learning, or a discovery of patterns in verbal stimuli (Romberg & Saffron, 2010). Aslin and Newport (2012) called this **rule learning**. The capability to learn the complexities of language using rules makes language learning easier. Sometimes learning seems to occur without much effort. Language is an example of particular stimuli having the natural capacity to gain our attention. With this attention, learning is easier (Aslin & Newport, 2012).

There also seems to be a predisposition to learning particular common language patterns (Fedzechkina, Jaeger, & Newport, 2011; Hudson Kam & Newport, 2005). Humans may be naturally programmed to note certain rules, which can be acquired without much effort. This readiness to learn seemingly complex patterns serves to aid in learning how to communicate. It could be said that humans are "prepared" to acquire language. While rule learning has been focused on language, humans may be naturally prepared to acquire rules in other areas of life. The next section examines a way to understand the quick acquisition of complex social behaviors.

Implicit and Explicit Learning

Psychology now considers there may be two types of learning: implicit and explicit learning (Frensch & Runger, 2003). In implicit learning, acquisition is automatic and without effort. In explicit learning, there is a conscious decision to learn and a clear awareness of the learning effort. This has challenged the adequacy of Hebb's very basic neurological rule regarding learning as a simple neural connection (Gallistel & Matzel, 2013). This simple neural connection type may describe what happens when learning is automatic and without conscious purpose. The other, more effortful learning brings change through the use of intention, focus, and strategizing. Since more neurological activity seems required for decision-based learning (weighing options, noting various outcomes), new neurological models for explicit learning are being proposed. These models use a more elaborate information-processing **schema** as opposed to the simpler direct model of association strengthening of a neural connection. For effortful learning, there are a network of decision linkages that need to be made across a variety of brain sites. This poses new ways of understanding what may be happening in learning and helps in efforts to build better learning experiences. This distinction lends support to the cognitive or information models in higher learning.

Examples of implicit learning are learning to ride a bicycle or "absorbing" a language. These are hard to explain, but somehow the learning occurs. For more explicit learning, think about studying a difficult subject. The effort to learn may require several attempts, and conscious practice is necessary to ensure some retention.

In explicit learning, the student is very much aware of the attempt to influence thinking. As cognition is moved to a central place in the understanding of our processing of experiences, we now turn to the possible ways in which the human cognitive capacity develops and grows more capable in understanding and dealing with the world, its complexities, and the abstractions humans have created to better describe them.

Cognitive Development

The chapter has moved from basic mechanistic ways of understanding the effects of experience to the use of cognition in the learning process. This captures the psychological perspectives of experience and learning (Shanks, 2010). What of experience affecting cognitive development to deal with complexity? In psychology, there are two major theorists most referenced in considerations of this question: Jean Piaget and Lev Vygotsky.

Jean Piaget

The Piagetian theory of experience and cognitive change proposes two ways of adapting to world observations. The manner in which these world observations are organized and understood is called a schema. The first way of adapting to new information fits it into the person's existing ways of understanding, which is called **assimilation**. In assimilation, what is learned is fitted into our view of the world. If it is not expected, or somehow does not make sense, it is not accepted or it is seen as an exception to what is normal. In the second way of taking in information, new data causes a change in the schema or the way we think about the world, which is called **accommodation**.

Assimilation and accommodation explain how we cognitively adapt to experiences, creating more sophisticated structures from which to comprehend our world (Flavell, 1996). As Piaget proposed, the individual uses both assimilation and accommodation to adapt his or her cognitive framework, or schema, to the world he or she experiences. This adaptation process builds more abstract and sophisticated ways of comprehending the world.

Lev Vygotsky

The second major contributor to our understanding of cognitive development is the Russian psychologist Lev Vygotsky. He proposed that humans internalize their social–cultural world, developing their worldviews from what they had been taught through their social interactions (Vygotsky, 1934/1978, 2012). The acquisition of language in particular provides a way to think about the world that goes beyond the immediate and concrete world. The acquisition of language creates the capacity to think abstractly and to plan beyond the immediate future.

Thought and language are seen to be in a **dialectic**. Language and thought depend on each other and interact with each other; language produces ways of thinking and thinking produces language. They "climb on top of each other," upward. In this way, humans develop more sophisticated frameworks to understand their experiences.

Vygotsky believed that the learning process works best when the progression is gradual. He believed teaching the more sophisticated ways of thinking occurred only when the appropriate structural guides were in place. He called these guides

scaffolding. With appropriate scaffolding, or supports, the student moves forward in using more advanced cognitive frameworks.

Both Piaget's and Vygotsky's work have influenced educational practices. In school, there are discovery projects, gradual progressions from simple to more complex issues, discussion of teaching, or pedagogical supports for students. All of these are the result of the two theorists. In the next section, you will see elements of both when we discuss the topic of active learning.

Active Learning

There is a growing movement in education for use of active learning. Active learning requires people to construct meaning from their experience. Rather than hearing information in classroom lectures, students are asked to respond to questions, discuss information, write, or work on projects—either individually or in groups. The student is engaged in considering what is important, memorable, and useful. They must put effort into the learning task.

As one example of active learning, Bertsch and Pesta (2014) reported on the impact of the *generation effect*. In this procedure, students create, or "generate," the material they have to learn. Findings show this leads to superior memory for the information. Among the most effective techniques for generating material, writing questions and answers from the course material led to high retention. One problem with this technique was that students did not always know what was important information—that is, the information on which teachers would test.

In a comparison of active learning versus passive learning in science, technology, engineering, and mathematics (STEM) classes, the active learning condition provided superior student performance (Freeman et al., 2014). Grouping a number of studies on the effects of active learning, the researchers found students in active learning classes had higher grades and failed less (see Figure 4.3).

Supportive of such active learning findings, research on learning and memory found superior retention for material that was elaborately rehearsed (the meaning of the item was emphasized; Craik & Lockhart, 1972). Reviewing the cognitive and learning literatures, Brown, Roediger, and McDaniel (2014) advised the following for success in learning:

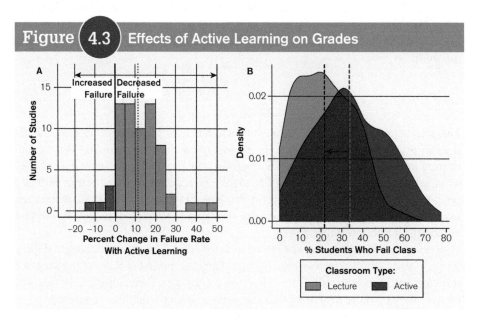

Figure 4.3 Effects of Active Learning on Grades

Source: Freeman, S., Eddy, S., McDonough, M., Smith, M, Okoroafor, N., Jordt, H., & Wenderoth, M. (2014). Active learning increases student performance in science, engineering, and mathematics. Proceedings of the National Academy of Science, 111, 8410–8415.

1. Practice asking questions and finding the answers. This provides practice in recall, which is a separate skill.

2. Study material again when your memory has started to fade so you have to relearn the material. Relearning strengthens the memory.

3. Put things in your own words, not the words of others. This moves the material into consolidation and integration, a deeper level of processing and learning.

Notable in this advice is the emphasis on actively working with the material to be learned. The techniques create meaning and make the information personal. This helps students to scaffold the material and integrate their learning into their personal schemas.

Discussing and exploring with others helps us to be engaged in our learning.

Conclusion

We have reviewed some of the ways in which our experiences shape and change us. At a very basic level, we come to associate stimuli (person and perfume; restaurant and food) as well as stimuli, behaviors, and consequences (a friend, a hello, and a smile back; a person, a gesture, and a kiss). Realizing the human, cognitive dimensions to our lives, what we think influences these basic paradigms. We learn to expect sequences, and these interpretations of our world become powerful. What happens matters, but how we interpret what happens matters as well.

This brings us to the complexities of how those cognition schema are developed. The two predominant theories on the development of cognitive frameworks emphasize the importance of interaction between the person and his or her environments. These adaptations to the incoming information bring more advanced ways of thinking. Finally, in looking at effective learning, we see that the more active we are in creating and processing of material, the better our retention. In making the experience our own, we incorporate those experiences into lasting memories. We are not so much passive observers to our experiences as we are active creators of our world.

Review Questions

1. What happens in classical conditioning? Provide a personal example of when this has occurred in your life.

2. How does preparedness affect conditioning?

3. What is Skinnerian conditioning? Name and describe its components.

4. Name two types of feedback and their effects in Skinnerian conditioning.

5. How does cognitive behaviorism work?

6. Describe what happens in modeling.

7. What is statistical learning?

8. What is perceived self-efficacy?

9. What are Piaget's two different ways of adapting to environmental input?

10. Provide three examples of active learning.

Key Terms

accommodation 83

active learning 70

assimilation 83

chaining 76

conditioned response (CR) 70

conditioned stimulus (CS) 70

dialectic 83

discriminative stimuli 72

explicit learning 70

implicit learning 70

operant 72

operant conditioning 72

punishers 74

reinforcer 74

respondent conditioning 72

rule learning 82

scaffolding 84

schedule to the reinforcement 76

schema 82

social learning theory 70

unconditioned
    response (UCR) 70

unconditioned
    stimulus (UCS) 70

vicarious learning 81

Sharpen your skills with SAGE edge at **edge.sagepub.com/moritsugu**

SAGE edge for students provides a personalized approach to help you accomplish your coursework goals in an easy-to-use learning environment.

Go to edge.**sagepub.com/moritsugu** for additional exercises and web resources. Select Chapter 4, Experience and Learning for chapter-specific resources.

Mindfulness

A Path to Awareness

Michael's coach addressed the team on the benefits of mindfulness meditation. The coach was a student of sports psychology and used knowledge from psychological research to motivate and educate the players to improve their performance. Michael was uncertain how this activity could benefit him, let alone affect his performance on the field. He had read about meditation but never imagined that it could be relevant to his life. The coach provided an introduction to mindfulness meditation at practice the next day. It seemed so simple: Just breathe and pay attention to the breath. At the end of the exercise, Michael noted that he felt more relaxed. After several days of this new practice, he observed other effects: His concentration seemed better and his focus was sharper. Some days, he had a harder time focusing on his breathing. When he complained about the difficulty staying focused on breathing to his coach, he chuckled and said, "Don't fight it. Let it be. Just go back to breathing." Something interesting was happening to Michael, but it was too early to understand. The coach's instruction to the team was "just continue to practice and remain curious."

· ·

Adjustment is a process of adaptation to the changes and challenges of life. Life changes and challenges come in different forms and arise both within the individual and from the environment. For example, navigating the physical changes of adolescence requires adaptation to a changing body and a developing identity. Throughout life, physical changes associated with growth and aging require adaptation to changing physical realities. Other changes and challenges come from the relationship between the individual and the external world. For example, the breakup of a romantic relationship forces an individual to come to terms with loss and a changed social reality: The change in status from being part of a couple to being single brings a set of challenges to navigate.

The topic of mindfulness has been selected as a focus for this chapter for the purpose of providing fresh perspectives and possibilities, derived from wisdom traditions, to enhance the process of adjustment to life's inevitable changes and challenges. In the story of Michael's introduction to mindfulness meditation, Michael's coach identified a strategy to assist his players to improve their performance. The challenge of athletic competition is as much about mental preparedness as it is about physical conditioning and skill. A practice of mindfulness meditation could assist in the development of habits of mind, which could influence Michael's performance. However, mindfulness is more than a set of tools, techniques, or strategies for improving performance to reach specific goals. Mindfulness involves many aspects of discipline, practice, and the development of habits of mind, which can contribute to healthy adjustment.

The previous chapter described how the regular, predictable patterns in our world are incorporated into our understanding of that world. Learning about externalities and their predictability provides insight into the influence of experience and thoughts on human behavior. But there is more to living than regularities, cognitions, and behaviors. A growing body of research and practice in psychology supports the notion that how we think of our world is important. This importance can be linked to health and a sense of well-being (Shapiro, 2009). This body of research also points to the ways in which humans have the capacity to change their relationship to experiences. By investigating the mechanisms, processes, and effects of **mindfulness** practices derived from ancient wisdom traditions, current scientific research points to the value of understanding how the application of mindfulness can contribute to the search for meaningful balance in life (Dimidjian & Segal, 2015).

Mindfulness and Meditation

The terms *mindfulness* and *meditation* have become increasingly common as interest has grown in strategies to manage the pace and pressure of modern life. These terms occur frequently in the context of self-help articles and books. A whole industry has developed around products and services designed for meditators and to promote mindful living. From meditation cushions to mindfulness-based meditation tapes, the marketplace for items and services associated with mindfulness and meditation represents a recognition of the possibilities of mindfulness and meditation to enhance well-being. For the purpose of this chapter, definitions of *mindfulness* and *meditation* have meanings that are directly related to adjustment. As these terms are defined and understood, the relationship of mindfulness and meditation to positive adaptation to the challenges of life will begin to emerge. To understand the meaning of these terms is a step toward linking knowledge to practice and action in the service of psychological and physical health.

Defining *Mindfulness*

A simple definition of mindfulness is the act of paying attention, moment to moment, to lived experience. Sensations, feelings, and thoughts are the fundamental ingredients. Most people have the occasional experience of "being in the moment," when it seems that our senses are sharp, our mind is focused, and we may be aware of a sense of connectedness to ourselves and the world. We may be highly involved in an activity or we may be in a state of alert relaxation. The experience of being aware in the moment is the basic experience of mindfulness.

The opposite of mindfulness is mindlessness, or lack of attention to experiences. Most people can easily relate to the idea of being on automatic pilot as they engage in life activities. Some common examples include worrying about an upcoming test while driving to school, thinking about paying bills while preparing lunch, or daydreaming about vacation while mowing the lawn. There is nothing wrong with the mental activities of thinking, worrying, or daydreaming. However, engaging in these mental activities means that we are less attentive to the activities of driving, preparing lunch, or mowing the lawn. To the extent that these mental activities occur, we are not fully engaged in the activities and may be functioning on automatic pilot.

In this chapter, we will explore the development and practice of mindfulness and the effects on increased awareness of our present experience. The effects and potential benefits of mindfulness will be identified: changes in brain biology and cognitive functioning, improved ability to deal with life stress, ability to prevent recurrence of depression and to better manage anxiety, increased capacity for creativity, and the development of compassion for oneself and others. Activities to learn and practice mindfulness approaches will provide the opportunity to experience the challenges and potential benefits of developing mindfulness as a kind of mental muscle. Through training and practice, the ability to bring a mindful attitude to the present is cultivated and strengthened. To begin, we will explore the role of meditation.

Meditation can lead to inner stillness.

Defining *Meditation*

Meditation is a disciplined approach to experiencing our world. The word *meditation* has been initially associated with religious practices from the wisdom traditions of the world. Each of these traditions has developed practices that provide the practitioner with a unique way to cultivate the habits of mind valued by the traditions and cultures from which the practices arose. Across the world's wisdom traditions, there are commonalities of goals or aspirations that meditative practices aim to develop: selflessness, compassion, a way to deal with the struggles and challenges of life, a way to make meaning of human experience, and a way to live in harmony and balance with oneself and the community. One useful definition offers clarity for our further discussion: "Meditation refers to a family of techniques which have in common a conscious attempt to focus attention in a non-analytical way, and an attempt not to dwell on discursive, ruminating thought" (Shapiro, 1980, p. 14).

The major forms of meditation practice that have emerged as techniques of interest to Western scientists are zen, Transcendental Meditation, and vipassana or insight meditation. Examples of other major forms of meditation include the following:

- Mantra-based meditation
- Yoga
- Loving-kindness (metta) meditation
- Contemplative prayer
- Sufi meditation
- Tibetan meditation practices

Meditation practices can be grouped along two dimensions. The first dimension addresses whether the practice involves being physically still or being in movement. An example of this dimension is a sitting meditation versus a series of yoga practices. The second dimension addresses the cognitive focus of the meditation. **Focused attention (FA) meditation** instructs the meditator to focus on a word, phrase, or object that he or she continually returns to when the mind wanders. The effort to return attention to the chosen word, phrase, or object provides the opportunity to develop an awareness of distractions and reorient to the chosen focus. **Open-monitoring (OM) meditation** directs the meditator to pay attention to all cognitions that arise but doesn't direct focus to anything in particular. The intention is to observe one's inner experience and the constant flow of sensations, feelings, and thoughts as they arise in one's awareness. This approach favors paying attention to all the thoughts, feelings, and sensations that occur during meditation while learning how to avoid becoming absorbed by them or continually judging them. The development of an inner observer of experience is cultivated with this type of practice. The FA approach, when practiced over time, can lead to an increase in awareness, also cultivated with the OM approach so it is important to see these approaches as not mutually exclusive (Lutz, Jha, Dunne, & Saron, 2015).

While the practices associated with meditation may have their origins in the diversity of the world's spiritual traditions, there appear to be common elements to these practices that are open to study and application. Through the regular practice of **mindfulness meditation**, an openness to all aspects of the present experience can develop. Mindfulness meditation can be described as specific meditation practices that cultivate awareness through the focus of attention on the basic fundamentals of experience: breath, sensations (i.e., sight, sound, smell, taste), emotions, and thoughts. This openness to experience includes awareness of what is going on around us, along with awareness of thoughts, feelings, and physical sensations. The practice of meditation allows us to live more fully in the present moment.

Meditation practices refer to the disciplined practices that are thought to promote the development of increased mindfulness in daily life. While different types of meditation practices have found their way into the mainstream culture and the psychological literature, the most frequent term that currently describes the use of meditation is *mindfulness-based practices.* Mindfulness-based practices and their application to physical and psychological health deserve attention as potential contributors to the topics and themes of this book. During the past four decades, a proliferation of scientific research on mindfulness-based practices has emerged, which addresses physical and mental health issues and promotes health and wellness (Sedlmeier et al., 2012). Contributions from research on mindfulness in psychology, medicine, and neuroscience inform the application of mindfulness to the theme of the search for meaningful balance. We provide one example of this in the Adjustment in Practice: Meditation Exercise.

ADJUSTMENT IN PRACTICE
Meditation Exercise

Sitting meditation: Bringing the breath into focus

Find a quiet, comfortable place where you will be undistracted for 10 minutes. It is helpful to have a clock or gentle alarm to remind you when 10 minutes is complete.

Sit in a chair, with both feet on the ground, back straight, arms resting comfortably at your side, hands resting on your lap.

Close your eyes or, if you prefer, focus your eyes on a point about 3 feet in the distance.

Become aware of your breathing, and begin to focus on a point where you notice your breath when you exhale. People generally focus on the tip of the nostrils or on their abdomen.

You may notice that your mind frequently wanders. As soon as you become aware of your mind wandering, bring your attention back to the point you have chosen to observe your exhalation—your nostrils or your abdomen. Each time you notice your thoughts, bring your attention back to your point of exhalation.

You may notice sensations in your body: an itch you want to scratch; an uncomfortable feeling in your back or neck; or a sensation of sleepiness, irritability, or pain. You may notice that your breaths are shallow or deep. There is no need to change anything; just try to observe the sensation without acting to change it. Bring your attention back to your breath.

When you hear the alarm, bring your attention back to the room you are in with fully open eyes. Finish your practice with a thought of appreciation for the time that you have taken to meditate.

Reflection Questions

1. What sensations and thoughts did you notice?

2. How was this experience different from "just relaxing" or sitting quietly without any specific direction?

History of Psychology and Mindfulness Research and Practice

An understanding of the historical background out of which the current interest in the scientific applications of meditation and other mindfulness-based practices emerged will provide context for the relevance of this recent development in psychology. We trace the origins of modern Western psychology to the works of Wundt and Fechner (perception studies) and Husserl and Wertheimer (Gestalt and phenomenology). These European-based theorists and researchers focused on laboratory work. Early American scientists and psychologists visited and worked in these first psychology laboratories in the 1800s and returned to the United States with practices and theories that were based in the work of their teachers and mentors. These pioneers were interested in the studies of perception, sensation and learning that could be accomplished in controlled laboratory settings (Boring, 1950; Wertheimer, 2012).

A pioneering psychologist of this time, William James (1842–1910), had different interests. James was known for contributions to psychology that combined psychological work with philosophy and more broadly defined interests. James's (1902) classic book *The Varieties of Religious Experience* represents the inquiry of early psychologists in the area of philosophy. Indeed, the history of psychology in Europe was initially identified with the study of philosophy.

As the field of psychology developed in the United States, the emphasis on the laboratory and experimental method became the prevailing orientation (Boring, 1950; Wertheimer, 2012). Researchers in this stage of development focused theory and research on areas with practical applications like public education and the measurement of individual abilities. One example is the work of John Dewey, who wrote on educational philosophy and practices to develop an educated citizenry. Dewey is also known for the development of the decimal coding system for books.

World War II brought further developments in American clinical psychology as psychologists in increasing numbers assisted the U.S. military in addressing workforce issues related to the war effort of the time (Benjamin, 2004). Psychologists were being recognized for their contributions along with other medical personnel. The field of clinical psychology grew as a discipline during this time. From an overview of the historical context, Western traditions in psychology came to be identified as laboratory and experimentally focused or clinically focused.

While mainstream Western psychology developed a foundation based on experimental and laboratory-based research, some psychological scholars followed a path associated more closely with the philosophical origins of European psychology. Schools of theory and practice, such as humanistic, gestalt, existential, and transpersonal, associated with the philosophical orientation of European psychology (Benjamin, 2004) continued to find expression around the time that clinical psychology was becoming predominant as a field. A Western orientation to either experimental or European philosophical approaches dominated the traditions of psychology, with contributions from other cultures unexplored. This limited the range of psychology's work. Some students of psychology looked elsewhere for different models. One such model is derived from the psychology of **Buddhism**, a study of the mind that has very different cultural roots than the European or American origins of Western psychology.

Origins of Mindfulness Practice

Buddhism has been described as "a blend of religion, spirituality, and psychology" (Kristeller & Ragpay, 2013, p. 635). Tracing roots to 486 BCE, Buddhism took its name from the historical figure Siddhartha Gautama, a wealthy Hindu prince from Northern

India. Living a privileged life as a young man, Siddhartha was sheltered from the realities of poverty, illness, and death. He gave up a life of comfort and undertook a journey outside the walls of his privileged royal existence to understand life, especially the suffering to which humans seemed destined.

In experiencing the suffering of human beings he encountered, as well as his own suffering, Siddhartha came to the realization that human beings can develop themselves through an understanding of how the human mind creates the conditions in which people suffer. Through practice, humans can free themselves from the suffering that defines human existence. Based on his own experience of the universality of human suffering, he devoted his life to teaching the ideas and practices through which this freedom can be gained. These ideas and practices came to be known as Buddhism.

A basic idea in the philosophy associated with Buddhism is that every human being has the capacity to free himself or herself from the ordinary ways in which our minds (i.e., thoughts or cognitions) create mental unease, dissatisfaction, or "suffering." The word *suffering* has a special meaning since it refers not only to the inevitable pains and losses that humans experience but also to how the human mind creates its own special form of

The flower of compassion can arise from mindfulness.

suffering. Buddha was, in a sense, an early scientist and empiricist who studied the human mind, created a system of psychology based upon this study, and developed a systematic way to apply what he learned from his own experience to better the lives of others (Kristeller & Ragpay, 2013). The teachings derived from the experience of the Buddha spread throughout the East: Variations of Buddhism arose in regions of the world we know today as India, Thailand, Myanmar, Japan, and China. Each culture absorbed the influence of Buddhist teachings according to its own cultural **values**, beliefs, attitudes, and expectations.

How did this influence find its way into mainstream Western psychology? Beyond some early academic interest, as evidenced in the writings of William James, the most influential opportunity for the transmission of these ideas to the West came at a time during the 1960s when youth of Western countries took up an interest in Eastern philosophy and meditation as an alternative to drugs as a route to altered states of consciousness (Harrington & Dunne, 2015). After their experiences in the cultures of the East, some went on to study psychology and realized that their studies and immersion in Buddhist cultures could contribute to Western culture and specifically to Western psychology. The ideas from ancient spiritual practices came to be seen as relevant to the 20th-century world to which these volunteers and explorers returned. While not all of the interest and influence came from students of psychology, ideas and practices found their way into the study of psychology through the work of psychologists who had an early interest in bringing the practices into their clinical work. See Figure 5.1.

Figure 5.1 Historical Development of Mindfulness Practice

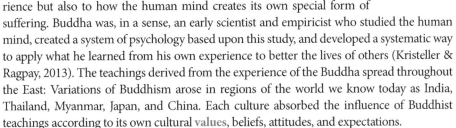

Source: Figure 1 from 10.1177/1363461514562061. The contemporary mindfulness movement and the question of nonself. Geoffrey Samuel. Transcultural Psychiatry, August 2015; vol. 52, 4: pp. 485–500., first published on December 5, 2014.

Research on Meditation and Mindfulness

In the late 20th century, interest in the effects of meditation practice became the subject of scientific research. Jon Kabat-Zinn (1990), a researcher in the area of stress, began to teach mindfulness meditation practices in a program for patients at a major medical center. With a goal of assisting patients in dealing with the stress of being in chronic pain, Kabat-Zinn led groups of patients in an 8-week course that came to be called Mindfulness-Based Stress Reduction (MBSR). Patients learned mindfulness meditation, which focuses on training attention through observation of one's breath, sensations, emotions, and thoughts. In the early days of this research, participant self-report was the main assessment tool. Valid (measures what it says it does) and reliable (it can be depended on; it holds up over time) measures of mindfulness were not yet developed. The results of the early studies suggested that participants benefited from their participation in the training, reporting greater ability to cope with pain (Kabat-Zinn, Lipworth, & Burney, 1985). See Figure 5.2.

This work was the beginning of the application of mindfulness-based stress management practices in the treatment of physical and psychological disorders. To date, thousands of studies have investigated the effects of mindfulness-based practices and a strong body of research now supports its efficacy in reducing stress and increasing psychological wellness.

What was happening inside the people who developed a regular meditation practice? Technology has developed tools to look within the human body and provide a way to see changes at levels of detail previously unimaginable. With the growing focus on neuroscience and the development of technology to observe physical states and changes in the brain, research was beginning to look at the brains of meditators. Through the images generated by functional magnetic resonance imaging (fMRI) and

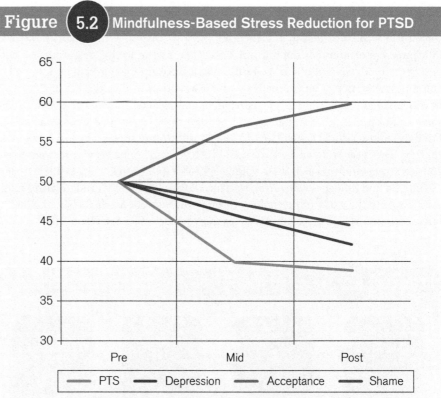

Figure 5.2 Mindfulness-Based Stress Reduction for PTSD

PTS — Depression — Acceptance — Shame

Acceptance increases, while depression, shame, and post-traumatic stress symptoms decrease following mindfulness-stress reduction treatment.

Source: Figure 1 from 10.1177/2156587214533703. Mindfulness-based stress reduction for PTSD. Published online before print May 7, 2014.

positron-emission tomography, it became possible to infer through data which parts of the human brain were activated or deactivated during meditation. Observations of changes in blood flow or electrical activity made possible the study of the brain changes that could be associated with meditation practice (Davidson & Kaszniak, 2015; Davidson & Lutz, 2008).

Studies of the brains of long-term, experienced meditators provided interesting results. In one study (Davidson et al., 2003), long-term meditators were found to have more activity in the part of the brain associated with positive emotions and mental health. Another study (Lutz, Greischar, Rawlings, Ricard, & Davidson, 2004) showed similar findings in the increased activity in the part of the brain associated with positive emotions when the meditators were engaged in an activity that focused on the cultivation of compassion. A growing body of research suggests that meditation practice is associated with changes in neural structures in the brain (Tang & Posner, 2014).

Can Stock Photo Inc./PixelsAway

Other studies suggest that meditation can support improved academic performance (Hall, 1999) and improvement of cognitive flexibility (i.e., the ability to use different strategies to solve problems) in elderly adults (Alexander, Langer, Newman, Chandler, & Davies, 1989). The training of attention through mindfulness-based meditation practices can potentially have positive effects on learning, emotional self-regulation, and prosocial behavior. Research is beginning to study the effects of meditation on the development of empathy and compassion (Shapiro, 2009). Such effects can contribute to an enhanced sense of well-being and a sense of being more connected with other people, society, and the natural environment.

As methods for studying the effects of meditation become more refined, the underlying mechanisms that contribute to the changes attributable to meditation will be better understood. Future directions may uncover the mechanisms through which meditation practices may be useful to whom and under what conditions. In the meantime, what we have learned to date can provide us with a basic knowledge and tools to apply to our understanding of ourselves and to our search for meaningful balance.

Bridging Science and the Meditation Experience

From the previous discussion of the contribution of mindfulness to the psychology of adjustment, the focus shifts to understanding the experience of mindfulness, as understood by current research. The measurement of blood flow and electrical activity in the brains of long-term meditators offers one scientific method of study: physiological changes that can be observed through tools that measure basic biological processes.

Websites and Resources for Research Around Mindfulness

http://www.mindfulnesscds.com

http://marc.ucla.edu/body.cfm?id=22

https://www.fammed.wisc.edu/aware-medicine/mindfulness

http://greatergood.berkeley.edu

http://www.chopra.com/ccl/5-types-of-meditation-decoded

The other major method of study is the subjective report of individuals using self-report measures to gather data to understand the internal experiences of mindfulness practice.

In the past 25 years, a number of assessment tools designed to measure the experiences of meditators have been devised. While the study of the effects of meditation practices—both mindfulness and spiritually based—has advanced to the point where the effects of these practices can be observed, current research is at the stage where questions related to the ways in which the effects of the practices can be accurately measured and understood remain. What practices work for whom and under what conditions will continue to be areas of research and contribute to the understanding and application of these approaches.

The body in a traditional position for meditation.

Mindfulness in Practice

What are the key concepts that a Buddhist psychology of mind can contribute to the psychology of adjustment? Positive mental states are known contributors to adjustment. Research in the diverse areas of emotional regulation, self-efficacy, social and emotional intelligence, and commitment to the well-being of self and others point to these factors as hallmarks of psychological health. Through the examination of different Buddhist schools of thought, several concepts emerge that fit with these desired outcomes. There is emerging evidence that a mindfulness practice can support and enhance the development of positive mental states and more adaptive, positive habits of mind.

Mindfulness and Nonjudgmental Awareness

Monkey mind is a term that can be used to define the basic condition of the human mind: thoughts actively jumping from topic to topic, unless an intentional effort to discipline one's focus is used. Have you had the experience of sitting in a class or riding on a bus, slightly bored (no cell phone available to distract you), and noticing that your mind is wandering from anxious thoughts about an upcoming test to thoughts about what to eat for dinner that evening to thoughts of excitement about a visit from a friend to thoughts about reminding yourself to make a dentist appointment? You may be replaying an experience from the previous day where one of your class instructors praised your work on a project that you had completed. Some of these thoughts are positive, some are neutral, and some may be considered negative.

As much as a group of monkeys may chatter, scatter, and otherwise be constantly in motion, our minds can be similarly active and unfocused. The situation becomes even more complicated when we start to react to our own thoughts: Thoughts about the upcoming test may make us nervous and our breathing becomes slightly more rapid; thoughts about our friend's visit bring up a pleasant feeling of excitement. Thoughts of self-judgment or self-evaluation complicate our distress even further ("I'm not going to do as well on the test as my classmates"). Our emotions become activated by our thinking. At times, our thoughts contribute to a sense of internal tension, disease, and what Buddhist psychologists of mind refer to as "dukka" or suffering. Western psychological theories and models suggest that we can have control over our thoughts and can change them in more positive directions by modifying the content of our thoughts to make them more realistic. Worry about not passing the upcoming test could be replaced with an alternative, balanced thought: "When I study for the test, I will feel prepared and when I am prepared, my chances of passing the test will be much greater."

The Buddhist view offers an alternative proposition. Rather than change the content of our thoughts, we can train our minds through a disciplined practice to become aware of our thoughts and, most importantly, become aware of the ways we judge or evaluate our thoughts. If we learn to recognize our thoughts and indeed all of our experience and bring an attitude of acceptance and **nonjudgmental awareness** to our experience, we can use this nonjudgmental awareness in many aspects of our lives. Nonjudgmental awareness, experienced and reinforced by an activity that promotes mindfulness, can provide the groundwork for developing positive mental habits of mind. These habits of mind can enhance our sense of well-being and potentially influence our mental and physical health.

© Can Stock Photo Inc. / rml

Rather than deny and ignore, we can choose to be aware and accept.

Mindfulness Promoting Self-Regulation

Self-regulation refers to the ability to manage emotions, thoughts, and behaviors in ways that support individual values and goals. An important component of self-regulation is the manner in which we deal with our emotions. The complex role of emotion has been a long-standing focus of inquiry in psychology and is an important component in the concept of self-regulation. In the 19th-century world of Western European psychology, Sigmund Freud developed a theory of psychological functioning in which the ego, the rational part of the self, engaged in an ongoing struggle to tame unbridled emotions (i.e., rage, extreme fear) that exist within individuals. The id represented the potentially wilder, unfettered manifestations of emotions that were generally harnessed in adaptive ways for most individuals (Hall, Lindzey, & Campbell, 1998). An unrestricted, unbridled id would result in chaos for the individual and society. The well-functioning ego represented mastery over and taming of the id. A healthy ego allowed for productive behavior that manifested in work and relationships.

Freud developed his theories through work with individuals who showed symptoms of mental illness. These theories were viewed through the lens of his culture and time in history. As an early pioneer in psychology, his method of research was based upon close observation and analysis of individuals from 19th-century European society. As the field of psychology matured, the emphasis on empirical methods of research and the advancements in technology allowed the study of human emotion to move beyond observation and description to new ways of measurement and understanding. As the methods and tools for investigating human emotion have become increasingly sophisticated, science offers the means to understand human emotion as a complex interaction of human biology and our environment. Emotion brings an important factor to the equation that defines self-regulation, which refers to self-regulation of emotion, thought, and action.

What does mindfulness offer to strengthen this ability to self-regulate? Let's begin with an example from daily life. Mindful Molly is a student approaching the end of the school term. Several tests and important assignments are scheduled in the upcoming week. She has been staying up late to work on assignments and getting less sleep than usual. She is so busy that she hasn't had time to think about healthy food choices so finds herself eating the quickest but not the healthiest meals. In addition to school deadlines, Molly's family is expecting her to participate in a family event in the upcoming weekend. She wants to attend but feels as though it would be better to stay home and work on her assignments. She is looking forward to going out with friends over the weekend as well but wonders if it is a good idea. Most of us can relate to this scenario or a variation of it and are faced with the challenge of managing the feelings and thoughts that can add additional stress to our life situation in this moment.

In the example of Mindful Molly, self-regulation refers to more than just the ability to make choices and solve problems, although those actions are important components of self-regulation. Self-regulation applies to managing the stress that can take the form of anxiety, difficulty making decisions, and poor self-care that Molly was experiencing. Self-regulation relates to the awareness of thoughts, feelings, and sensations that can promote proactive problem solving and positive choices.

How can a mindfulness practice contribute to an outcome that fits with our values and goals? Let's return to Molly's situation and investigate her internal experience of the anticipated tasks, deadlines, and events. With a mindfulness practice in which the focus of attention is directed on moment to moment experience, Molly has become aware of tension in specific parts of her body, anxious thoughts of not having enough time, being behind in class readings, excitement about seeing friends, and guilt about the thought of choosing to study rather than see her family. These may be among the thoughts and feelings that pass through Molly's awareness. As she becomes mindful of these thoughts and feelings, she experiences them as an observer, noting each thought or feeling with curiosity, and seeing the sensation, thought, or feeling arise and pass.

With a mindfulness practice, Molly reports that she noticed a decrease in the negative symptoms of stress when faced with competing demands and priorities in her life. By noting and accepting feelings and thoughts through a mindfulness practice, the ability to see the available choices may increase. More options for action may appear. We are in a better position to respond to our situation rather than react to it and to make choices based upon our values and our goals. This is the way in which mindfulness can support self-regulation of our thoughts and emotions. See Adjustment in Practice: A Week of Mindfulness.

ADJUSTMENT IN PRACTICE
A Week of Mindfulness

Approach this exercise with an attitude of curiosity and discovery. You are in the role of explorer and observer of your own experience. This exercise combines a brief mindfulness practice (see Adjustment in Practice: Meditation Exercise) with a follow-up reflection activity.

Step 1: Conduct the meditation exercise for 10 minutes a day for 7 days with a paper and pen at hand.

Step 2: At the end of each day's exercise, reflect and write the answers to the following questions:

- Did I notice or observe any sensations in my body? What were they?

- Did I notice or observe any feelings or emotions? What were they?

- What thoughts came up during the practice?

Step 3: At the end of the 7 days of mindfulness practice, reread your observations and answer the following questions:

- What have I learned about myself as a result of the 7 days of mindfulness?

- In what ways have the 7 days of practice affected me in my daily life?

There are no right or wrong answers to these questions. The point is to begin to observe and become aware of your experiences, moment to moment, both in mindfulness practice and in your daily life.

Reflection Questions

1. How might the activity of mindfulness meditation paired with self-reflection be a strategy for managing stress?

2. If you found the practice helpful, would you recommend it to others? If so, why?

3. If you were going to change the exercise in any way to improve it, what changes would you recommend and why?

What does scientific research contribute to the understanding of the effectiveness of mindfulness practices for self-regulation in managing the challenges and stress of daily life? We can look to the studies that have examined the outcomes of meditation practices on stress, immunological function, heart disease, and reduction of anxiety (Dimidjian & Segal, 2015). These studies give support and evidence to the potential of mindfulness practices to develop or improve self-regulation strategies.

Mindfulness Promoting Compassion

Research over four decades suggests that mindfulness practices can contribute to the development of other positive individual outcomes: sense of happiness and optimism; improvements in memory, information processing, creativity, and relationships; prevention of future episodes of depression; and growth in empathy, self-compassion, and spirituality (Shapiro, 2009).

From this list, two areas have special relevance to the contribution of a Buddhist perspective on mindfulness to adjustment: self-compassion and empathy. One definition of empathy is the capacity to understand or feel what another person is experiencing from within the other person's frame of reference—that is, the capacity to place oneself in another's position. A child falling off a bicycle elicits an empathic response from another child who has observed the accident: "I am sorry that you fell. That must hurt." Photographs of a family stuck on a rooftop in the aftermath of a hurricane elicit feelings of empathy that may lead to the compassionate action of donating money to disaster relief efforts. The demonstration of empathy has important consequences for the individual and society.

Caring and compassion create basic human connections.

We learn to be kind.

Neuroscience research appears to suggest the possibility that the human capacity for empathy is based on our biological inheritance. Working with monkeys, researchers discovered a type of neuron, or brain cell, which they named **mirror neurons** (Rizzolatti & Craighero, 2004). A mirror neuron is a neuron that fires both when an animal acts and when the animal observes the act. This means that when an action is performed and the same action is observed by an individual, the mirror neurons are activated by the act of doing and the act of observation. The child who observed the bicycle accident may have responded to witnessing the accident with an empathic response based upon imagining the effects of the accident as if it had happened to her. The discovery of mirror neurons has led to theoretical speculation that the presence of mirror neurons are the biological underpinnings of the capacity for empathy in human beings.

Yet there is evidence that the practice of meditation brings about notable shifts in brain activity (Lutz, Brefczynski-Lewis, Johnstone, & Davidson, 2008). Meditative experience changes the brain activity of the meditators, increasing the sensitivity and the consideration of emotion. Those circuitries related to empathy were best activated in those with meditation practice.

Related to the concept of empathy is the Buddhist perspective that holds that compassion for all living beings (including oneself) is both a state of mind (cognitive) and a state of heart (affective) that promotes well-being for self and others. Compassion for self and others is an intention and desire that other beings be free from suffering. In traditional Buddhist teachings, compassion is considered an antidote to cruelty, which intentionally inflicts suffering on others. Along with compassion, other habits of mind and heart are desirable and can be developed: empathetic joy (experiencing pleasure or happiness at the fortunate circumstances of another person; an antidote to jealousy), loving-kindness (goodwill and wishes to others; an antidote to anger and hatred; see Adjustment in Practice: Create a Loving-Kindness Meditation), and equanimity (a balanced, calm attitude regardless of circumstances; an antidote to being overly attached to or rejecting of circumstances).

ADJUSTMENT IN PRACTICE
Create a Loving-Kindness Meditation

A loving-kindness meditation is a set of phrases that extend good wishes and kindness. The phrases express positive thoughts for the welfare and happiness of ourselves and others. These phrases begin with the words: May I be . . . or May you be . . .

Note the following examples:

- May I be (calm and peaceful)

- May I be free of (confusion, doubt, pain, and suffering)

- May I be (happy, liberated and free)

In creating a personal loving-kindness meditation, choose one or two words that express your intention of loving-kindness for the benefit of yourself and others. Once you have created these phrases, you can close a mindfulness meditation practice with a silent repetition of the phrases. It is good to begin the practice using the phrases that send loving-kindness thoughts to yourself; you can progress to sending thoughts of loving-kindness to others. For a more complete description of this practice, see *Lovingkindness: The Revolutionary Art of Happiness* by Sharon Salzberg (1995).

Reflection Questions

1. How might this practice influence your attitude toward people with whom you may have experienced discomfort or even conflict?

2. What benefits do you see in using this practice in your life?

3. How might a regular practice of loving-kindness toward self and others contribute to adjustment?

Self-compassion is an aspect of compassion that Western cultures do not readily recognize. In the face of failure or pain, self-compassion includes acceptance of the experience as it is and avoidance of self-blame. Another component of self-compassion is an attitude of kindness toward oneself. Just as you express thoughts to comfort a friend in a similar situation, you extend to yourself thoughts of acceptance, comfort, and kindness. This is the opposite of the harsh, self-critical thinking that frequently accompanies these experiences. Self-compassion consists of being mindful of the feelings and self-critical thoughts that may arise in the context of pain or failure and practicing an attitude of nonjudgment toward them. Research (Neff, Rude, & Kirkpatrick, 2007) has shown that self-compassion can predict other indicators of positive psychological well-being such as happiness, optimism, and personal initiative.

On the Mindful Path: Moving Toward Action

The previous sections of the chapter focused on developing an understanding of mindfulness and related concepts of self-regulation, self-compassion, and empathy. The next part of the chapter will explore how mindfulness can further contribute to adjustment. To the degree that mindfulness can be integrated into one's life in a systematic way, it can offer a foundation to make personal choices and actions in alignment with personal values and life goals. Choices and actions that are directed toward enhancing physical and mental health can contribute to positive outcomes in dealing with specific life challenges. For example, an elder faced with a decision to stay in her home at a time of decreased mobility and increased risk of falling could be knowledgeable of the residential options available to her. She could also be dealing with a fear of losing independence and a parallel fear of becoming dependent upon family members. How could mindfulness assist her in making a decision that fits with her values? This section of the chapter provides a perspective on aspects of mindfulness that can enhance her decision making.

Hayes, Strosahl, and Wilson (2012) have provided a model in which mindfulness is combined with an exploration of personal values and commitment to actions in harmony with those values. This model of psychotherapy teaches people to embrace and accept all parts of their experience, even those parts that are difficult, painful, and problematic. Although this treatment program was developed to help individuals suffering from mental health disorders, the study of the mechanisms of the mind and pathways to change can be beneficial to anyone looking for strategies to take charge of one's life.

The Beginning of Action and Change

Mindfulness practice promotes the acceptance of experience, without judging. As previously described, being mindful means developing an internal observer who passes no judgment on the stream of moment to moment sensations, feelings, and thoughts that form the constantly changing flow of our human experiences. *Radical acceptance* is a term that is similar to the idea of nonjudgmental awareness. It refers to the capacity to accept all of human experience—pleasure, as well as pain. As human beings, we tend to attach ourselves to experiences that are positive and stimulate feelings of satisfaction and pleasure. We have brain centers that orient us to pleasurable experiences. When life goes well, it is easy to accept our experiences.

Painful, difficult experiences present a different challenge. To make space for and accept those experiences without judgment and with compassion is a radical act that goes against the grain of our biology. As human beings, we avoid physical and emotional pain and tend to avoid situations that are associated with painful sensations, feelings, and thoughts. We avoid situations that pose a real threat to our safety since our survival as individuals and as a species depends upon that adaptive avoidance. Sometimes we can overestimate the actual danger in a situation, and our thoughts can trick us into believing that a threat is real. If we are primed to react to misperceived danger by fleeing a situation as if our lives depended on it, we can develop patterns of avoidance that interfere with engaging with our life and interfere with pursuing and accomplishing our goals. As we develop the mindfulness muscle, we can begin to observe how our thoughts about painful, distressing life experiences might be contributing to our distress and develop other ways to respond.

Through mindfulness practice we can begin to accept the full range of our human experience. Instead of rejecting or denying aspects of ourselves and our experiences, we can learn to acknowledge and accept them in different ways. The moment to moment awareness of changing experience and the acceptance of the totality of experience provides a different vantage point and sets the stage for evaluating choices and taking action. Before moving to action, however, we need to take into account the importance of our values and goals.

The Foundation for Action

If mindfulness and acceptance provide access to the full range of experiences, clarification of personal values provides landmarks on the road map for actions. A value can be described best in the form of a question: What do you want your life to stand for? Hayes and Smith (2005) have defined values as "chosen life directions" (p. 154) and have identified 10 domains: marriage/couple/intimate relationships; parenting; other family relations; friendship/social relations; career/employment; education/training/personal growth; recreation/leisure; spirituality; citizenship; and health/physical well-being. Values arise out of the family, neighborhood, community, country, and culture in which we are embedded. Reflection on values in life domains can provide a flashlight to illuminate the mindful path. As self-knowledge of values becomes more apparent, we can choose goals that fit with our values; goals can be landmarks along the way. Going to college, getting a job, getting married, and having children can be considered goals that are in service to personal values. When combined with a mindful awareness of experiences, clarification of values and deliberative choice of goals can set the stage for right action (see Adjustment in Practice: What Do I Value?).

ADJUSTMENT IN PRACTICE
What Do I Value?

In this exercise, you and a partner will focus on your values and clarify their meaning in your lives. Since this is a shared experience, find a person who is interested in participating in a values clarification exercise.

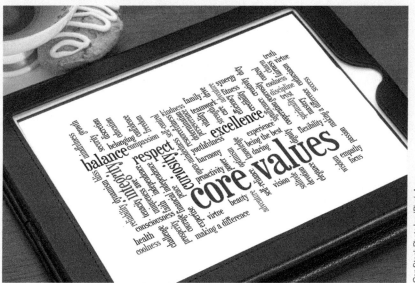

Can Stock Photo Inc./PixelsAway

You will need three things to complete this activity: a partner to share the experience with; access to photos you will incorporate into a collage; and writing materials, scissors, and glue.

Step 1: On a piece of paper, write down each of the valued life domains on the left-hand side of the page. To the right of each domain, answer the question that follows the domain.

- Intimate relationships: What kind of person do I want to be in an intimate relationship?

- Parenting: What kind of person do I want to be as a parent?

- Other family relations: What kind of person do I want to be in relationship to other family members?

- Friendship: What kind of friend do I want to be to others?

- Work: What do I want to stand for in my work? What kind of worker do I want to be?

- Education: What kind of learner do I want to be? How do I want to be involved in all forms of education and growth?

(Continued)

(Continued)

- Recreation: What are the activities that are important to me in my leisure time? How would I like to have those areas be represented in my life?

- Spirituality: How do I want to be engaged in the area of life in which I feel connected to something larger than myself?

- Citizenship: How do I want to participate as a member of my community?

- Health: What areas related to my physical health and wellness do I want to emphasize?

Step 2: Choose two or three domains that are especially important to you at this time in your life. On a large piece of paper, create a collage of pictures and words that illustrate the domains you have chosen. A collage is a combination of pictures, images, words, and phrases that have a theme. For this exercise, the theme is the life domains from the list in Step 1. Glue the pictures to a piece of paper, and add any words or phrases that you wish to illustrate that domain.

Step 3: Taking turns with your partner, share the collage you have created, explaining the meaning of the pictures, images, and words as they relate to the valued life domains you have chosen.

Step 4: Consider the following questions as you reflect on this exercise: What have I learned about myself that is new from doing this exercise? How can mindfulness of my values be a support in living my life?

Reflection Questions

1. What did you learn about how your partner's values differed from yours?

2. What did you learn about how your partner's values were similar to yours?

3. What does this say about you?

The Path to Change

One outcome of mindfulness is contained in the Sanskrit word *vipassana,* a type of mindfulness practice known in the West as insight meditation. The definition of vipassana is "seeing things the way they are." Strengthened by mindfulness, we can develop the awareness to see our experiences not as we wish them to be but as they really are. The practice of experiencing and accepting experiences without judgment (i.e., criticism or blame of ourselves or others) is akin to "seeing things as they are."

With a regular practice of mindfulness, awareness develops, which allows observation of the full range of the content of experiences (i.e., sensations, emotions, thoughts). Developing awareness is strengthened by bringing an attitude of nonjudgment (i.e., acceptance) to the range of experiences. As previously stated, acceptance is an important concept as we learn to apply what we have learned in our mindfulness practices to our lives. Acceptance of all aspects of experience, along with an attitude of compassion to self and others, is a basic requirement for changes to occur. This statement may seem counterintuitive or against common sense. How is it that we have to accept something in order for it to change?

The normal human response to dealing with a difficult situation is to turn away, reject, or avoid that situation. Few people rush headlong into difficult situations, and if they do, they may not do so in a mindful, skillful manner. For example, a difficult emotion like anger may evoke such unpleasant feelings that avoidance of the angry feelings through distraction or denial may be the visible response. The consequence of avoidance is that the feelings are never fully acknowledged and accepted. Without acceptance, the anger may not be addressed in a skillful, compassionate manner. Mindfulness of anger involves seeing angry feelings and thoughts clearly: its expression in body and in thoughts.

Like chrysalis to butterfly, mindfulness can promote change and transformation.

Nonjudgmental awareness means acceptance of anger— not criticizing oneself for being angry ("I shouldn't be angry"). Once anger is acknowledged and accepted, the path has alternatives and choices for action: self-soothing statements like "I can handle my anger. It's not going to kill me"; self-calming actions like listening to music, talking to a friend, or going for a walk; or even extending a compassionate thought to a person who is the recipient of angry feelings: "I feel compassion for the driver who cut me off; he must be having a really difficult day." In this example, the acceptance of anger is the necessary condition for skillful action. With acceptance, the possibilities for different and creative solutions increase. We can respond skillfully to a situation rather than react.

Along with the possibility for skillful responses, personal values play an important role in determining actions. If the value of showing respect for other people is considered important, a response that aligns with that value can be chosen. In the case of the angry driver, the choice of response could be not reacting back in anger but letting go of the anger and wishing the other driver a more relaxed and peaceful drive. Values are important guides to choices and commitments.

Moving Toward Commitment and Change

With a foundation of mindfulness and an understanding of personal values, we have some of the tools needed to create positive changes in our behaviors. With additional tools derived from cognitive and behavioral psychology, goals can be set and steps can be taken to make positive changes in habits and behaviors. A pattern of behaviors that is established and occurs over time can be described as a habit. Habits can be harmful to physical and psychological well-being, or they can enhance wellness and sense of fulfillment.

Most people can identify habits that support their well-being and others that detract from their well-being. Common examples of positive habits are regularly following health regimens like flossing one's teeth daily, exercising moderately at least 30 minutes daily, and eating six to eight servings of fruits and vegetables daily. On the other hand, harmful habits are all too common: overconsumption of food, lack of regular exercise, lack of moderation in use of alcohol, etc. The commitment to developing a new habit takes us in the direction of mindful action or the application of mindfulness in the choices and actions of our lives.

Commitment to positive behavior change involves committing to a deeply held value. Identification of a goal that is consistent with a deeply held value is the first step. For example, the goal for taking up a regular exercise regimen could be related to a number of motivations: preparing to run a marathon, losing weight, or finding an activity to socialize with a friend. While all of these motivations have importance, they may not be as important as serving the personal value of health and well-being. Commitment to a deeply held value like health and physical well-being will be the strongest motivator to following through on the goal.

Beyond commitment to a goal that fulfills an important value, commitment to specific actions is critical to creating a new positive pattern of behavior. A clear plan of the specific actions that you are willing to commit to will increase the likelihood of achieving the goal. What are you going to do? How are you going to do it? When are you going to do it? The more specific the plan, the greater the chances you will be successful. Anticipation of obstacles is an important component of constructing a specific behavioral plan for success. Knowing that there will be obstacles to following through and creating a plan to overcome those obstacles is an important step in the process to successfully achieving the goal.

With an awareness of the specific strategies and understanding of the obstacles that can arise, the use of the strategy of **visualization** can support success in creating a new habit. Visualization refers to the creation of a focused mental picture, both of the plan for change and the strategies that will be used to overcome obstacles on the path toward achieving a new set of behaviors or a positive, durable habit.

Conclusion

After four decades of study, scientific research into mindfulness is still evolving. The consensus within the scientific community is that mindfulness works (Sedlmeier et al., 2012). However, there are still many questions to be addressed, such as the following: How best can the effects be studied? How effective are the interventions? What are the psychological and neurocognitive mechanisms that produce the effects that people report? How do we reconcile the wisdom tradition roots of mindfulness with a Western cultural orientation to science based on inquiry, observation, measurement, and theory building?

Using the tools of research, investigators can study the different dimensions of mindfulness that have been commonly observed, such as whether a practice focuses on an object or whether a practice is more open to observing all the contents of experience (Lutz et al., 2015). As scientific findings accumulate, we can translate the research into applications that have beneficial relevance to our individual lives and circumstances as well as making contributions to the health of our communities.

As mentioned previously in the chapter, *mindfulness* has become a common term in popular culture. It is applied to a variety of endeavors, from enhanced athletic performance to improved workplace climate and worker productivity. Mindfulness training can be a tool for the reduction of stress, improvement of performance, alleviation of human suffering in both physical and psychological ways, enhancement of cognitive skills, improvement in emotional and self-regulation, and a gateway to a greater sense of connectedness to one's experience and world.

While research will continue to refine our understanding of the mechanisms, processes, and outcomes of mindfulness training, the accumulation of current scientific findings provides a foundation of support to apply mindfulness-based practices to health, wellness, and a range of physical and psychological issues. With this knowledge, we may choose to explore this topic further through study and practice of a mindfulness-based approach. This can be accomplished through an extended class, workshop, or meditation retreat. The direct experience of learning mindfulness in a structured format is the most reliable way to personally evaluate the benefits of mindfulness training. Through discipline, practice, and effort, mindfulness can be a source of strength, support, and resilience. Mindfulness, developed as a healthy habit of mind, can further the goal of finding meaningful balance amid life's changes and challenges.

Review Questions

1. Define *mindfulness*.

2. Define *meditation*. Discuss the differences between FA meditation and OM meditation.

3. Describe and discuss the historical roots of mindfulness.

4. Identify and discuss two of the studies done on mindfulness and meditation.

5. Explain the role that acceptance plays in mindfulness practice.

6. Discuss the connections between mindfulness and self-regulation.

7. Explain the connections between mindfulness and compassion.

8. What types of challenges arise when a person experiences painful or difficult experiences, and why?

9. Discuss the connections between mindfulness and values.

10. Define *the strategy of visualization*, and explain how it can help a person create a new habit.

Key Terms

Buddhism 94
cognitive flexibility 97
focused attention (FA) meditation 92
meditation 91

mindfulness 90
mindfulness meditation 92
mirror neurons 102
nonjudgmental awareness 99

open-monitoring (OM)
     meditation 92
values 95
visualization 108

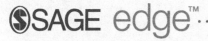

Sharpen your skills with SAGE edge at **edge.sagepub.com/moritsugu**

SAGE edge for students provides a personalized approach to help you accomplish your coursework goals in an easy-to-use learning environment.

Go to **edge.sagepub.com/moritsugu** for additional exercises and web resources. Select Chapter 5, Mindfulness: A Path to Awareness for chapter-specific resources.

Stress, Health, and Well-Being

Lance is a White male who comes from a working-class family. Lance has not always been interested in school, and his grades have fluctuated throughout the years. Now that he is about to graduate from high school, Lance has been thinking about what is next for him. Lance's father suffered a stroke a month ago, which has left him unable to work and in need of extensive rehabilitation and 24-hour care. Lance's mother works as a waitress and has been struggling to keep her job while tending to her husband's needs. While extended family has been helping out financially and also providing care for Lance's father, Lance realizes that he must find a way to contribute to the needs of his family, particularly because his father's recovery will be a long one. As he thinks about his current and future life, he is stressed, is constantly worried, and sleeps poorly.

***

Diana is an African American female who comes from a middle-class family. Diana graduated near the top of her high school class and was accepted into every college she applied to. She has chosen to attend a prestigious university three hours away from home. She is not the first to attend college in her family; her parents are college graduates and her sister is in her junior year of college, but she is still nervous about the upcoming experience. She has always done well in school, but she is about to start a pre-med program that will be very challenging. She is also nervous about living away from home and not having the day-to-day support of her family. She worries if she will find friends and if she will meet her parents' and her own academic expectations. As she shops with her mom to purchase things she will need for her dorm, she feels stressed, finds herself worrying a lot more, and is sleeping poorly.

. . . .

Lance and Diana are at important transitions in their lives. While reading the details of their stories, the reasons that they both are experiencing **stress** are apparent. But are their experiences of stress the same? Will they cope with their stressors in similar ways? What short- and long-term outcomes will each person experience?

An important aspect of adjustment is coping with stress. Lance's and Diana's stories illustrate important details about how we conceptualize stress in the field of psychology. Not all stress is equal. The circumstances that bring about stress are important, as well as their predictability and regularity. Furthermore, in understanding the toll that stress takes on people, it is important to understand the concept of **coping**. No two people have the same response to a stressful situation largely because circumstances often dictate how they tend to react in such situations. In the course of this chapter, we will review definitions of stress, explain the stress reaction, explore different types of stressors, and unpack the concept of coping. Furthermore, we will explore different types of coping styles, along with their advantages and disadvantages, and try to answer the question of whether stress is ever a good thing. Finally, we will tie together the relationships among stress, coping, health, and well-being with the aim of identifying how we can best promote optimal growth.

Stress

Most of us utter the phrase "I am so stressed out" multiple times a week, especially when working on assignments or preparing for final exams. Technically, however, the term *stress* refers to the occurrence of three separate things: a stimulus event (e.g., Lance's father having a stroke), a process (e.g., the aftermath of realizing what the consequences of the stroke are), and a reaction (e.g., attempts to cope, actions taken to help the family recover). Each component of this chain is important in understanding what stress is and what it means in the lives of people. We will begin exploring these components one at a time, starting with the stimulus event, also known as a stressor.

Stressors

As a personal exercise, take 60 seconds and write down everything you can remember that caused stress in your life this week. Now look at that list. You will notice that some of the items might be big deals (e.g., midterm exams week), while others may be smaller deals (e.g., your roommate

Upcoming exams can be a significant source of stress for college students.

snored last night, and you woke up multiple times). You also might note that some of the things on your list are regularly occurring events (e.g., your roommate left her wet towel on your bed again), while others are atypical (e.g., you lost your cell phone).

Psychologists have studied how the magnitude of a stressor or its predictability in our lives impact our reaction to these events as well as the ease with which we can adjust to such an event. While early studies of stress focused on the "life events" that caused stress for all people, such as the death of a parent or getting fired from a job (Rahe, Meyer, Smith, Kjaer, & Holmes, 1964), as the field has evolved, psychologists also began studying what we might consider to be more everyday stressors or **hassles**.

In the 1980s, researchers began studying daily hassles (DeLongis, Coyne, Dakof, Folkman, & Lazarus, 1982; Kanner, Coyne, Shaefer, & Lazarus, 1981). Hassles are more minor in scope but more frequent in how often they occur, like a roommate who constantly leaves dirty dishes in the sink, a friend who always texts in the middle of the night, or all your professors giving homework on a given day. Interestingly, when researchers started looking at which types of stressors—major life events versus hassles—caused more distress, they found that hassles were more problematic because of their cumulative effect.

Psychologists have categorized some stressors as *acute*, time-limited problems that can arise irregularly, or *chronic*, persistent situations that tax people's reserves (Gottlieb, 1997; Wheaton, 1997). Wheaton (1997) defined the **acute stressor** as a "discrete, observable event . . . possessing a clear onset and offset" (pp. 52–53). He defined **chronic stressors** as "less self-limiting in nature . . . typically open ended, using up our resources in coping but not promising resolution" (p. 53). Different types of stressors can lead to different stress processes and reactions (Gottlieb, 1997) as well as differing physiological consequences. For example, an acute stressor (e.g., having your cell phone stolen) causes heightened levels of adrenaline and cortisol to be released in our bodies. These changes arm the individual's physical system to be ready for fight or flight.

However, chronic stress, like living in poverty, from which a person does not find relief and cannot necessarily adjust, can result in more catastrophic neurological breakdowns (Compas, 2006; Romeo & McEwan, 2006). Chronic stress has even been demonstrated to have destructive effects on DNA and contribute to premature aging (Epel et al., 2004). In fact, in examining exposure to chronic racism in African Americans, researchers found that the presence of this stressor could be a significant contributor to heightened levels of physical disorders like heart disease (Clark, Anderson, Clark, & Williams, 1999). We will revisit the topic of culturally related stressors later in this chapter, but they are a powerful example of how chronic stressors can really be more damaging than acute stressors. See Researching Adjustment: Measuring Stress.

RESEARCHING ADJUSTMENT
Measuring Stress

Psychologists interested in studying stress and its impact needed to develop ways to measure people's perceptions of stress in the research they have conducted. Two major ways of assessing stress exist: objective and subjective. Objective stress measures such as the Schedule of Recent Experience (Holmes & Rahe, 1967) or the Social Readjustment Rating Scale (Scully, Tosi, & Banning, 2000; see Table 6.1) often list presumably stressful events and then add up the number of times people have experienced such circumstances. The higher the score on these measures, the more stressful events an individual has encountered in an objective way.

Table 6.1   Social Readjustment Rating Scale

Life Event	Weight	Rank
Death of a spouse	100	1
Divorce	73	2
Marital separation	65	4
Jail term	63	5
Death of close family member	63	8
Personal injury or illness	53	3
Marriage	50	6
Fired at work	47	13
Marital reconciliation	45	15
Retirement	45	29
Change in health of family member	44	7
Pregnancy	40	16
Sex difficulties	39	10
Gain of new family member	39	23
Business readjustment	39	40
Change in financial state	38	9
Death of close friend	37	12
Change to different line of work	36	14
Change in number of arguments with spouse	35	17
Mortgage more than $51,000	31	30
Foreclosure of mortgage or loan	30	11
Change in responsibilities at work	29	24
Son or daughter leaving home	29	31
Trouble with in-laws	29	42

Life Event	Weight	Rank
Outstanding personal achievement	28	21
Spouse begin or stop work	26	19
Begin or end school	26	25
Change in living conditions	25	18
Revision of personal habits	24	37
Trouble with boss	23	22
Change in work hours/conditions	20	20
Change in residence	20	28
Change in schools	20	32
Change in recreation	19	33
Change in church activities	19	36
Change in social activities	18	26
Mortgage or loan less than $51,000	17	41
Change in sleeping habits	16	34
Change in number of family get-togethers	15	27
Change in eating habits	15	38
Vacation	13	39
Christmas	12	43
Minor violations of the law	11	35

Source: Life Event Checklists: Revisiting the Social Readjustment Rating Scale after 30 Years. *Educational and Psychological Measurement.* December 2000, vol. 60, no. 6, 864–876. doi: 10.1177/00131640021970952

Subjective measures of stress such as the Global Measure of Perceived Stress (Cohen, Kamarck, & Mermelstein, 1983; see below), however, do not assume that individual stressors have a cumulative effect (i.e., the greater the number of individual stressors, the more stressed out we feel). Rather, subjective measures often focus on how a person perceives the severity of any particular stress as opposed to what specifically the event is. For example, two people may face a similar stressor, such as a serious illness, and have very different perceptions of how severe a stressor illness will be for them.

Global Measure of Perceived Stress

The questions in this scale ask you about your feelings and thoughts during the last month. In each case, you will be asked to indicate how often you felt or thought a certain way. Although some of the questions are similar, there are differences between them and you should treat each one as a separate question. The best approach is to answer each question fairly quickly. That is, don't try to count up the number of times

(Continued)

(Continued)

you felt a particular way, but rather indicate the alternative that seems like a reasonable estimate. For each question choose from the following alternatives:

0. never

1. almost never

2. sometimes

3. fairly often

4. very often

1. In the last month, how often have you been upset because of something that happened unexpectedly?

2. In the last month, how often have you felt that you were unable to control the important things in your life?

3. In the last month, how often have you felt nervous and "stressed"?

4. In the last month, how often have you dealt successfully with irritating life hassles?

5. In the last month, how often have you felt that you were effectively coping with important changes that were occurring in your life?

6. In the last month, how often have you felt confident about your ability to handle your personal problems?

7. In the last month, how often have you felt that things were going your way?

8. In the last month, how often have you found that you could not cope with all the things that you had to do?

9. In the last month, how often have you been able to control irritations in your life?

10. In the last month, how often have you felt that you were on top of things?

11. In the last month, how often have you been angered because of things that happened that were outside of your control?

12. In the last month, how often have you found yourself thinking about things that you have to accomplish?

13. In the last month, how often have you been able to control the way you spend your time?

14. In the last month, how often have you felt difficulties were piling up so high that you could not overcome them?

Reflection Questions

1. Which approach do you think is better?

2. Can you think of any situations where one approach might be more accurate than the other?

Stress Processes

Lazarus and Folkman (1984) described stress as a process that is influenced by multiple steps and emphasized that the appraisal of any given situation (i.e., stressor) was the first step in this process. Appraisal is an assessment of the situation, which has two parts. The first part, **primary appraisal**, determines whether the event represents a threatening situation. For example, a computer malfunction could be very threatening in the middle of an assignment but less so if it occurs over the semester break. The second step is called **secondary appraisal**, which factors in the person's expectations of handling the situation.

In this secondary appraisal stage, the individual's coping skills and other resources are taken into account and viewed as being either sufficient or insufficient in responding to the situation. For example, if the computer is fixable and the student has the money to fix it, the threat may be less severe than if it is a catastrophic meltdown requiring a new computer. Thus, the stress process is influenced by a person's ability to deal with the environmental demands of the situation. The resulting level of distress experienced would be influenced by how successful we are in using our available resources. In this model, it is possible for one person to experience extreme levels of stress in response to an event and another person to be relatively unaffected by the same event, depending on their appraisal of the situation and their resourcefulness in responding to the event. Figure 6.1 depicts the relationship between stressors as well as primary and secondary appraisal strategies.

Stress Reactions

Reactions to stress often influence the adjustment process. Psychologists have examined the ways that people respond in the face of stressful events for many decades. Hans Selye (1956) was the first to note a particular set of physiological reactions to a variety of harmful or noxious stimuli that he called the general adaptation syndrome (GAS). Since then, stress reaction has been measured more precisely in both physiological terms, such as illness or changes in cortisol levels, or in psychological terms, such as symptoms of depression or anxiety (Derogatis & Coons, 1993).

While there are some patterns of reactions that have been observed between certain stressors and certain reactions in people, many individual differences exist that make stress reactions less predictable. For example, Gaylord-Harden, Elmore, Campbell, and Wethington (2011) studied the relationship between stressors, anxiety, and depression symptoms in African American youths. The authors found that peer relationship stressors (e.g., not getting along with friends) were positively associated with depression in African American girls, but the same stressor was associated with anxiety in African American boys. This study suggests that gender may be an important factor that determines how stress affects an individual. Gender is also a determinant of what kind of stressors a person most frequently experiences, a topic that we will revisit shortly.

In reality, perceived stress tends to have a stronger correlation with mental health outcomes than does objective measures of stress (Cohen et al., 1983). However, it is arguable that both types of measures have value. For example, it might be relevant to know that a person who experiences the death of a parent perceived that event as minimally stressful. Likewise, it might be relevant, especially to a counselor, if a person perceives an event like an argument with a friend as critically stressful. Hence, studies have utilized both types of assessment of stress, objective and subjective, depending on the focus of the study. In Table 6.2, you will find an illustration of objective versus subjective ways of measuring stress. With the objective approach, you will note that specific types of stressors have predetermined values, and regardless of how an individual experiences the stressor, it is assumed to have an inherent magnitude of impact. For example, in Table 6.2,

Figure 6.1 Stress Processes

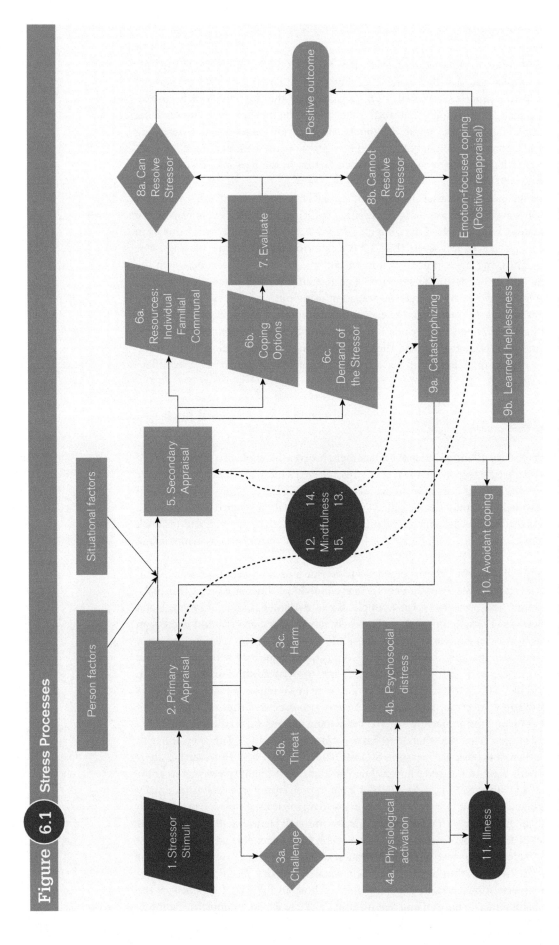

Source: Figure 1 from doi: 10.1177/1533210107301740. The Meaning of Mindfulness: A Second-Order Cybernetics of Stress, Metacognition, and Coping. Eric L. Garland. *Complementary Health Practice Review*, January 2007; vol. 12, 1: pp. 15–30.

Table 6.2	Objective Versus Subjective Ways to Assess Stressful Events
Objective Evaluation of Stressful Events*	**Points Assigned to the Stressor**
1. Car breaks down	10 points
2. Parents fight	30 points
3. Computer stops working	50 points
Subjective Evaluation of Stressful Events	**Range of Stress to Be Determined by Rater**
1. Parents are coming for a visit	Stressful 10 Neutral 5 Not at all 1
2. Argument with best friend	Stressful 10 Neutral 5 Not at all 1
3. Car breaks down	Stressful 10 Neutral 5 Not at all 1

* Note that events have a range of values depending on how much stress the individual attributes to the event.

Source: Cohen, S., Kamarck, T., Mermelstein, R. A global measure of perceived stress. *Journal of Health & Social Behavior*. 1983 Dec; 24(4): 385–96.

your computer breaking down is assumed to have a more serious impact than your car breaking down, but you might imagine that for someone who is very computer-savvy and capable of repairing a computer but not a car, just the opposite could be true. The subjective approach to assessing stress allows the respondent to decide and rate accordingly how serious of an impact any given stressor might have.

Coping

Compas (2006) described *coping* as a voluntary response to stressors that involves "regulation of emotion, cognition, behavior, physiology and the environment in response to stressful events or circumstances" (Compas, Connor-Smith, Saltzman, Thomsen, & Wadsworth, 2001, p. 89). As such, coping is a part of a self-regulatory process that individuals use in dealing with environmental demands or the adjustment process. Studies of coping have found a variety of ways that people frequently attempt to deal with stress. It is important to note that although people typically have more than one way to cope with any given stressful situation, it is often the case that not all coping strategies will work the same in every situation.

It is also important to remember that not all coping strategies are helpful or healthy to use. For example, some people might cope with stress by ignoring what is happening, while others will want to problem solve as a coping mechanism. Drugs and alcohol are also commonly used to cope with stressors but often hurt the person and make problems even worse. On the other hand, some people may reach out to others for support in the midst of a stressor, which is likely to be a good strategy in most cases. There are a number of effective and ineffective coping strategies, which we will examine in greater detail.

Emotion-Focused and Problem Solving–Focused Coping

Lazarus and Folkman (1984) identified two categories of coping styles that are helpful in understanding how coping works for people. **Emotion-focused coping** styles

Breakups can cause emotional distress and elicit the need for a coping response.

usually work by modifying the emotional impact of an event. For example, if a person experiences the breakup of a romantic relationship, the emotional response is typically quite intense.

A person might not feel like it is healthy to be constantly immersed in this intense emotion and as a result chooses to do things to relieve the intensity. A common emotion-focused coping style is called self-distraction, or doing something else to avoid feeling the intense emotion or minimizing negative feelings. The "something else" could include watching television, going to the gym, going out with friends, or doing any other activity that takes a person's mind off the breakup. Another emotion-focused coping style is called venting. Venting is exactly like it sounds: letting off steam and giving the intense emotions an outlet. A person who is venting might journal about his or her feelings or talk to friends about sadness and loss. While venting may feel good in the short run, it is not necessarily a good strategy to use repeatedly because it often makes people feel worse over time (Vera et al., 2012).

Problem solving–focused coping is not intended to modify emotions per se, but rather it is intended to make changes to a person's environment in response to the stressor. Individuals try to deal with what is bothering them by examining the situation, weighing options as to possible changes to make (e.g., finding a new boyfriend or girlfriend; joining a club to meet new people), and then acting on those plans. Problem-solving coping is considered to be more strategic, requires more planning, and often appeals to people who like to "do something" in response to problems and stressors, rather than merely process how they are feeling. However, there are certain stressful situations that problem-solving coping is more appropriate for and others where it would be less appropriate.

Lazarus and Folkman (1984) reported that problem-solving coping is more attractive in situations where a person thinks that his or her environment can be changed, whereas emotion-focused coping styles typically might be more attractive when there is a feeling that nothing can be done to modify the environment.

Active Coping and Avoidant Coping

Carver, Scheier, and Weintraub (1989) presented a second way to differentiate coping styles. They divided coping strategies into two categories: active coping, where the individual does something to try to solve the stressful situation, and avoidant coping, "where responses potentially impede or interfere with active coping" (Carver et al., 1989, p. 280). Examples of active coping include planning, seeking social support, turning to religion, or making changes in one's life. Avoidant coping is typified by using self-distraction, being in denial, using alcohol, and withdrawing from the situation. The emphasis on this manner of categorizing coping styles is slightly different than what Lazarus and Folkman (1984) originally presented. In this system, coping styles are defined by whether they are more likely to help people resolve stressful situations (i.e., taking action of some sort) versus delay or impede a resolution (i.e., not dealing with the situation).

Research has examined whether or not there is a practical difference in active versus avoidant coping or whether one is better than the other. The majority of findings suggest that active coping leads to better results than avoidant coping (Compas et al., 2001). However, active coping may not always be the best coping strategy. For example, Rasmussen, Aber, and Bhana (2004) investigated how African American and Latina/o adolescents coped with stressors related to living in a low-income urban environment

Table 6.3 Examples of Different Coping Styles

Coping Style	Stressor	Examples
Emotion-focused	Failing a class	Talking to your friends about being overwhelmed with the workload
		Going to see a movie to lift your spirits
Problem-focused	Failing a test	Speaking with the teacher about changing the grade
		Working with a tutor to improve your understanding of the content
Active	Romantic breakup	Talking with your ex to try and work things out
		Seeing other people in an attempt to find a new relationship
Avoidant	Incompatible dates	Starting up a new hobby to avoid dating
		Going to a bar and drinking away your sorrows

and whether any particular coping styles were associated with more positive mental health outcomes. Results showed that active coping styles were associated with increased perceptions of safety but also increased exposure to further violence in neighborhoods in some circumstances. In other words, active coping (e.g., carrying a weapon) as a response to violence in one's neighborhood, for example, could make people feel safer but may actually lead to them to become involved in potentially violent situations. Thus, it is not always obvious which type of coping is "best." Discussions of this distinction have argued that the situation or context is an important factor that should be considered in determining what is best. See Table 6.3.

Coping With Controllable Versus Uncontrollable Stressors

The type of stressor that one needs to cope with can be an important consideration in choosing effective coping strategies. Clarke (2006) argued that it is important to take into account whether or not a stressor is *controllable* before determining which coping style might be more advantageous. At times where there is a controllable situation, active coping may make sense. However, in cases where stressors are uncontrollable, avoidance strategies may be more appropriate.

What determines whether a stressor is controllable versus uncontrollable? There are certainly some, if not many, realities of life that are out of our control and unavoidable, like having to complete final exams at the end of every semester. However, those types of stressors—exams—are also predictable. There are other uncontrollable stressors that are more unpredictable and, in the absence of healthy coping, could take a serious toll on an individual. As mentioned in the previous example, stressors that come from living in an urban environment (e.g., more crime, more noise, fewer safe recreation spots) can be examples of uncontrollable stressors that vary in their predictability. The type of coping that people use to deal with these stressors may determine how big of an impact they have on individuals' mental health.

To illustrate this point, consider the following study. Vera et al. (2011) found that self-distraction (i.e., an avoidant coping strategy) was a significant buffer on the impact of exposure to urban stressors and negative emotion in a sample of urban adolescents of color. In other words, the more that adolescents used self-distraction as a coping style, the less likely it was that their exposure to urban stressors would lead to negative emotional consequences. The lesson to be learned from these studies is that different problems require different solutions and that both the stressor and the context in which one experiences the stressor can be important in determining what coping style is needed.

Coping With Culturally Related Stressors

Another example of uncontrollable and unpredictable stressors is found in the study of racism, sexism, and homophobia. Psychologists have studied the link between experiences with perceived racism and lower mental health among Asians and Asian Americans (Lee & Ahn, 2011), Latina/o/s (Lopez, 2005), and African Americans (Pieterse, Todd, Neville, & Carter, 2012). From academic achievement to physical health problems, people from these ethnic groups are at greater risk for poorer health outcomes due to chronic exposure to the stressor of racism. Mays, Cochran, and Barnes (2007) reported data from physiological measures of stress, which supported the contention that perception of racism serves as a chronic social stressor for ethnic minorities. Studies of racism, however, have revealed that culturally related stressors come in many different forms.

Microaggressions

Dovidio and his colleagues (i.e., Gómez, Dovidio, Huici, Gaertner, & Cuadrado, 2008) have found that while overtly racist events still plague our communities, there is also a subtler, more covert form of racism that may be just as harmful. Sue, Bucceri, Lin, Nadal, and Torino (2007) are among scholars that have described these more subtle forms of racism known as **microaggressions**. Microaggressions are "brief, commonplace, daily . . . indignities . . . that communicate negative or derogatory slights" (p. 271). Examples of microaggressions include telling Asian Americans that they speak English well or crossing the street when a Black man is walking in a person's direction. These events can be stressful, even if they are less overt forms of racism because they are perceived as offensive and bigoted. Microaggressions may also be unconscious and unintentional, which means that confronting a person about their remark or actions may be met with surprise or denial. See Adjustment in Practice: Examples of Microaggressions.

Microaggressions are not limited to expressions of racism. Recent research has documented the existence of gender and sexual orientation microaggressions (Sue, 2010). Gender microaggressions could come in the form of insulting comments ("You throw like a girl") or stereotypes ("Women in college are really looking for their *Mrs.* degree"). Homophobic microaggressions often come in the form of assumptions people make (e.g., asking a girl if she has a boyfriend) or the derogatory slurs that people use (e.g., "That's so gay"). While people who make these remarks often defend themselves by saying they are joking, it is the cumulative effects of these incidents that eventually takes a negative toll on individuals.

Researchers have categorized microaggressions into three types. Microassaults are explicit belittling remarks or actions (e.g., displaying a swastika or telling a racist joke). Microinsults are insulting assumptions or remarks (e.g., saying that a person of color or woman got a job because of affirmative action). Finally, microinvalidations occur when the offended person's experiences are denied (e.g., "I do not believe racism exists today"—saying that someone's report of racism is not true).

ADJUSTMENT IN PRACTICE
Examples of Microaggressions

You assume a student of color was admitted to college on scholarship and with lower entrance scores.

You assume a woman health care professional must be a nurse.

You assume a male health care professional must be a doctor.

You assume someone speaking Spanish must be an immigrant.

You assume an African American male student is a college athlete.

As a person of color, you are followed by store security guards.

You assume a male friend has a girlfriend and refer to his significant other as "she."

You tease a friend by saying, "Stop acting so gay."

Reflection Questions

1. What are the underlying biases indicated in these assumptions or actions?

2. How might a person who is confronted by these microaggressions respond to correct these biases?

Psychologists and other social scientists are studying how people cope with microaggressions to see if specific styles are more effective than others. As an example of the variety of ways that people might respond to a microaggression such as a sexist comment, some people may ignore the remark, chalk it up to someone being a jerk, and move on, while others may feel compelled to confront the offender. Further research is needed to determine what coping style will work best.

Culturally Relevant Coping

Hobfoil and Vaux (1993) argued the importance of cultural and community or social contributions to coping in the research literature on active versus avoidant and problem-solving versus emotional styles. Gaylord-Harden and Cunningham's (2009) research on culturally relevant coping has found that African American adolescents benefit from utilizing culturally sanctioned coping mechanisms such as religiosity in the face of race-related stress. Other researchers have examined culturally relevant coping strategies outside of the United States. Based on research conducted in Taiwan, Heppner et al. (2006) described culturally relevant coping that reflects Eastern philosophy and Asian cultural influences that they called collectivist coping styles. Examples of these collectivist coping styles include the following: "I tried to accept the trauma for what it offered me." "I believed that I would grow from surviving." "I shared my feelings with my family." "I saved face by not telling anyone."

Similarly, in the study of Chinese adolescents, Hamid, Yue, and Leung (2003) identified coping styles that reflect Chinese values. Examples of these styles are *shui-chi tzu-an* (let nature take its course) and *kan-kai* (to see a thing through), each of which are derivatives of a Taoist philosophy where nonaction is not seen as avoidance but rather the understanding and acknowledgment of the nature of things. These studies illustrate that how we see the world (under our control, predictable, determined by fate) can often impact how we cope with stressful events. Thus, adjustment can have strong cultural influences.

Healthy Stress Management

There are several strategies that scientists have discovered that have a positive effect on adjustment, hence reducing the negative impact of stress. Ironically, these magic bullets are things that are usually available to us in our daily lives and are often free of charge. Let's examine them in greater detail.

Social Support

With respect to stress, reaching out to others is known as the "tend and befriend" stress reaction that yields positive results (Azar, 2011; Hays, 2014). Social connection has the effect of releasing oxytocin, a hormone that ultimately reduces stress and makes us feel good. The benefits of social support have been documented for decades in the psychology field, explained by the "buffering" theory (Barrera, 2000; Dean & Lin, 1977; Wilcox, 1981).

According to this theory, the potential damage of stress is minimized when social support is in place, and when it is absent, people are much more vulnerable to the toxic effect that stress can have.

One study that illustrates this effect is by Brissette, Scheier, and Carver (2002), who explored the reasons social support and optimism were associated with good psychological adjustment in college freshmen. The researchers found that social support was directly related to lower stress levels and fewer symptoms of depression. Furthermore, the number of friends a person had was also related to optimism and the ability to use problem-focused coping. Therefore, it appears that having others in one's life for support when things are difficult is critical to the use of effective coping measures, the likelihood of experiencing depression, and the reduction of one's stress levels.

It is also important to note that social support is a strong predictor of good health regardless of one's level of stressors. Richmond, Ross, and Egeland (2007), for example, found that for Canadian First Nation (indigenous) people, women reporting high levels of positive interaction, emotional support, and tangible support from others were more likely to report thriving health. For men, emotional support was also related to thriving health. In Chapter 12, we will revisit the issue of social support since it is a predictor of longevity and good health for the elderly. It is clear that having close family, friends, and confidants in your life is one way to help immunize yourself to the potentially toxic effects of stress. Even when those people cannot eliminate the presence of a stressor, their presence and the knowledge that we are not alone and that people care and want to help can be enough to restore our health and well-being when times are tough.

Physical Touch

Scientists like Dacher Keltner and his colleagues have been behind the "science of touch" movement (Hertenstein, Keltner, App, Bulleit, & Jaskolka, 2006), which posits that touch is one of the simplest and most effective ways to manage our stress levels. Proponents of this idea note that touch soothes us; it calms our cardiovascular stress response by activating the vagus nerve, which triggers a release of oxytocin. In a study by Coan, Schaefer, and Davidson (2006), participants obtain a functional magnetic resonance imaging (fMRI) brain scan. Those participants anticipating a painful blast of white noise showed heightened brain activity in regions associated with threat and stress. However, participants whose romantic partner stroked their arm while they waited didn't show this reaction at all. They concluded that touch had "turned off" the threat switch, which prevented the hardwired stress response from occurring.

Similarly, research by Francis, Diorio, Liu, and Meaney (1999) has found that rats whose mothers licked and groomed them a lot when they were infants grew up to be calmer and more resilient to stress, with stronger immune systems. This research sheds light on why, historically, an overwhelming percentage of human babies in orphanages where caretakers starved them of touch failed to grow to their expected height or weight and also showed behavioral problems. In turn, research is finding that prematurely born infants seem to better thrive if they have regular schedules of soft stroking following birth (Feldman, Weller, Sirota, & Eidelman, 2002).

Physical touch has been shown to lower the cardiovascular stress response.

In response to research such as these studies, a new form of touch therapy has arisen to provide people with hugs that work as "stress busters." Touch therapy, or "professional hugging" (see http://www.professionalhugger.com), notes that hugs and hand-holding, even as little as 10 minutes, can greatly reduce cortisol levels, lower blood pressure, and create surges of feel-good brain chemicals. While not everyone may be in the market for a touch therapist or a professional hugger, this ideal is certainly replicable in romantic and familial relationships. In the absence of such relationships, massage therapy is another form of touch therapy (perhaps more conventional) that boasts similar effects. Not only does a massage help us if we are experiencing aches and pains but it releases hormones that combat stress, lowers our blood pressure, reenergizes our immune systems, and essentially is a good way to manage our stress and stay healthy (Field, 1998; Field, Hernandez-Reif, Diego, Schanberg, & Kuhn, 2005).

Meditation

Meditation has been a commonly practiced form of self-care and reflection for hundreds and hundreds of years throughout the world. While it may be a relatively more recent practice within the United States, science is revealing the health benefits, both physical and mental, of regular use of meditation as a stress management tool (Grossman, Niemann, Schmidt, & Walach, 2004). In fact, research has found meditation to be so effective in improving well-being that some have argued it is superior to other formal types of stress reduction such as psychotherapy (Simon, 2011). Hays (2014) argued that both meditation and talk therapy have their benefits and recommended their integration as part of an overall stress management and wellness life plan.

Meditation has been discussed in Chapter 5, so for the purposes of this chapter, we will summarize its function as a stress management technique. Meditation involves focusing on breathing in an intentional way that allows us to observe our thoughts and feelings in a calm, nonjudgmental way (Kabat-Zinn, 1994). Most meditation starts with deep breathing exercises that force the body into a relaxed state, preventing tension and strain in the muscles, which are often associated with stress. Additionally, when we focus in on our breathing, the brain is quieted from its vigilant scanning for threats or its prolonged stress reaction that we discussed earlier in this chapter. When we meditate, we allow ourselves to become outside observers of our experience rather than being immersed within the experience, and it changes our relationship to stressors and stress (Hays, 2014).

The regular practice of meditation can also make us more in tune with our body's signals of stress and tension. These signals often include pain and tension in our head,

Exercise not only helps us to manage stress but may make us less vulnerable to future physiological effects of stress.

neck, shoulders, or stomach and indicate that we are holding on to toxic stress that is taking its toll on us physically, if not also psychologically. As little as 15 minutes of meditation per day can make a significant difference in our ability to manage stress. In fact, celebrities such as Russell Simmons and Dan Harris have written books about how regular meditation has not only significantly reduced stress for them but also has allowed them to eliminate substance abuse problems and panic attacks, respectively.

Exercise

Many of us have been raised to understand that exercise is good for our bodies. But not everyone knows that exercise is equally good for our minds, particularly when it comes to stress management. With respect to the stress-reducing physical benefits of exercise, research has found that exercise relieves chronic muscle tension that forms as a result of the prolonged stress reaction. It also releases endorphins in the body that reduce pain, decrease depression and anxiety, make us more alert, and help us to feel better (Walsh, 2011).

In studies that have specifically looked at the ability that exercise has to decrease stress, anxiety, and depression (Blumenthal et al., 2007; Smits & Otto, 2011; Weir, 2011), in comparison to medication, for example, exercise consistently outperforms psychopharmaceuticals. What is most impressive about these studies is not only does exercise have an immediate effect but it appears to be able to immunize us against the effects of future stress (Hays, 2014). For example, 20 minutes of running or 45 minutes of walking can provide a stress "inoculation" that lasts up to 2 hours (Jayson, 2012). Thus, exercise, when done regularly, has the ability to not only help us manage current stress reactions but also may allow us to be less vulnerable physiologically to the effects of future stress exposure.

Self-Help

Ironically, many of us tend to give up activities like exercise when we have too much to do or during a particularly busy time period. Thus, our experience of stress sometimes results in us eliminating an activity that would have enormous benefits on our ability to manage stress. The lesson here is simple. Even when we feel too busy and stressed to be able to fit in exercise, it is precisely the best time to make a point to exercise.

What is true about the stress management activities that we have reviewed is that all are free (or relatively low cost), and each is effective even with a small time commitment: 20 minutes of running, 10 minutes of hand-holding, 15 minutes of meditation, or 1 hour spent having coffee with a good friend. The key to implementing these effective stress management techniques is that we make an effort to practice them consistently not only when we have free time or when our to-do lists are smaller. It may help to schedule these stress management activities into your daily planner, as the cost of not doing so may be a very high price to pay.

Good Stress Versus Bad Stress

So far in this chapter we have defined what *stress* is, defined different types of coping, explored some of the subtleties of understanding how people interpret stressful events, and discussed healthy ways to manage stress. Yet at a practical level, it is valid to wonder if stress is something that we should avoid altogether or if some experience of stress (or some stressors) can be good for us.

The short answer to this question is, in fact, that some stress is good for us, and some stressors can be beneficial and represent opportunities for growth. However, distinguishing bad stress from good stress is largely a function of how we think about a situation and the actions we take as a result of those thoughts.

Bad Stress

As has been mentioned previously in this chapter, human beings are physiologically hardwired to be alert to stressors in our world as a survival mechanism (Selye, 1956). Evolutionarily speaking, if we didn't have the fight-or-flight instinct, we would probably be eaten by lions (if we lived near lions). A big part of our physiological reaction to stress is what makes stress such a significant factor to our health and well-being. Specifically, our hardwired stress response involves the release of cortisol from our adrenal glands, which sets off reactions that allow us to make quick reactions (e.g., our heart rate accelerates, blood vessels dilate to increase blood flow to our muscles) that are necessary in fight-or-flight moments. However, the physiological reactions to a stressor are intended to be temporary, and our bodies should return to normal as soon as the stressful event is over. This is where things can become complicated.

Unlike animals, whose physiological stress response quickly returns to normal after a threat is gone, people have the ability to recall memories of past stressors and to worry about the potential for future stressors (Hays, 2014). Unfortunately, such thinking can trick our bodies into staying in a prolonged, heightened physiological stress state, even if the immediate and real threat is no longer there.

If our bodies remain in an aroused state with heightened cortisol levels, our immune system begins to pay a price. Among the many things that prolonged cortisol levels can do to us are a decreased resistance to infections and illness, high blood pressure, heart disease, insomnia, and exaggerated pain to existing medical conditions (MedlinePlus, 2016). This is why stress is identified as a risk factor for practically every illness—mental or physical—that we know of.

In addition to these physical and illness-related costs of stress, Hays (2014) identified three other areas that stress can impact in a negative way. Stress can manifest itself mentally in the form of obsessive, intrusive, and ruminating thoughts. It can show up emotionally in the form of anxiety, depression, anger, or irritability. It can also influence our behaviors, in particular the self-defeating ones like substance abuse, as we attempt to numb our feelings and make the negative thoughts and feelings stop. While all of this information may lead us to conclude that stress is a very bad thing, it is important to note that while stressors and stress reactions may represent a real danger, the ultimate toll they take on us is determined by how we attempt to lower stress levels once they are elevated. Scientists have unlocked many of the secrets to effectively reducing the negative effects of stress, which is good news, and this information is enormously helpful to managing our mental health. It is also helpful to counselors and therapists and other health professionals who work with people to recover from stressful, traumatic events.

Good Stress

As we have seen throughout the chapter discussion, not all stress is bad stress. In fact, some stress is good because of what it represents, like getting accepted into college and moving away from home (think about the example of Diana at the beginning of

Many people would say that having a child is both the most stressful and most rewarding event they will experience.

this chapter). It is also the case that while prolonged stress reactions that expose our bodies to too much cortisol are not good for us, small activations of our adrenal gland's release of cortisol can actually enhance our performance. What is it that defines good stress?

Eustress refers to the positive responses we have to stress (Simmons, 2000), which is often a result of stressors that are good for us or are things we want, like having a baby or getting married. A good way to think of eustress is the experience we have when confronted with a positive event, yet an event that represents enormous upheaval in our lives and thus elicits a response from us. When we respond in an adaptive way, the outcome can be very positive (O'Sullivan, 2011).

One of the first scientists to introduce the idea of eustress was Selye (1974), who described the notion that some stress can result in good changes for people, bringing them outcomes that would not happen without the presence of the stress. Having a child is a commonly used example. Most new parents will say that having a baby was the most stressful thing that they have had to deal with, yet it is the best thing that has ever happened to them. If we consider the life satisfaction and fulfillment that comes from having a child, a parent might say that life is dramatically better *because* of having the child than it could have been without having become a parent.

What is critical about understanding eustress is that it is not a function of the event itself but rather how the event is perceived and the reactions that follow. For example, for most people, getting married is a positive stressor. But if a person gets cold feet and decides to abandon his or her partner as a response, it would hardly be considered a positive outcome. When we see the event as an opportunity for positive change, in which we work through the necessary adjustments, it can result in overall well-being. O'Sullivan (2011) demonstrated the relationship of eustress to life satisfaction in a study of college students. Those who reported greater eustress experiences also reported higher life satisfaction and hope. Thus, not all stress is bad for us, and when we can tailor our response in ways that are healthy, we can actually benefit from some stress experiences.

Growth Through Adversity

What doesn't kill you makes you stronger. When one door closes, another opens. These adages illustrate that it is our perspective that often determines whether adversities—or for our purposes, negative stressors—are viewed as misfortunes or as opportunities for change and growth. While eustress is often viewed as an opportunity for growth, it is also possible to grow in the face of negative events, like the breakup of a romantic relationship or getting fired from a job. The key to coming away from these events as a stronger person is the way in which we think about and explain these events.

Reframing

Reframing is a tool that we can use to modify our thinking about a stressful event or stressor. Reframing provides a new way of seeing a situation by suggesting alternative perspectives on a given event. It is based on the work of Gregory Bateson (2000) and Virginia Satir (1983), who believed our understanding of events was influenced by these different perspectives. Hence, the context or frame for our experiences is extremely important. In general, reframing allows us to see potential benefits that could arise in the aftermath of adversity.

For example, imagine that you are a competitive runner and you receive an injury that will take you out of competition for at least 6 months. For many athletes, this could be a crushing event that overwhelms the system with anxiety and stress. Rather than focusing on the diagnosis as a loss and feeling angry (e.g., "Why did this happen to me? I am in great shape. Life is so unfair"), it might be possible to see a variety of "upsides" of having this situation occur. Consider the following ways that this event could be reframed more positively:

1. "I am disappointed that this happened, but maybe it is sign that I need to take a break from the hectic schedule of training and competition and focus on my studies."

2. "I am shocked that this injury happened to me, but perhaps it gives me an opportunity to slow down and think about how much I want competitive running to be a part of my future, especially now that I am out of school and starting my career."

3. "I wish this hadn't happened, but it will allow me to spend more time at home with my family—something I had been missing when I was so busy with training."

These ways of reframing the situation acknowledge the emotion that is connected to the injury, but they also shift the person's thinking away from the negative consequences that could result in a prolonged stress response and toward a more adaptive, optimistic viewpoint that could result in growth. Having a more positive viewpoint may not only help a person feel less stress about the event but it may also facilitate the physical recovery process since high levels of cortisol would interfere with a person's immune system.

Importantly, reframing is not just a matter of looking at the glass half full versus half empty, but rather, it is a reflective process that allows us to take stock of our life experiences, ask ourselves what we can learn from them, explore how we can grow as a result of unexpected events, and deepen our understanding of ourselves and what we want from life (Hays, 2014). Reframing also acknowledges that obstacles are a normal part of life, so we expect them to happen from time to time, and when they do, we try to handle the adversity with compassion and optimism. People who consistently use reframing give themselves a gift that can protect them from the potentially negative effects of stress, which can facilitate the kind of ongoing development that makes them stronger, happier people over the course of their lives.

Finally, it should be noted that reframing is a restructuring of our cognitions, which is one of the tenets of cognitive behavioral therapy (Beck, 1997). Oftentimes when people are depressed or have diagnosable emotional disorders, their brains become stuck in unhealthy patterns of thinking that can prolong their depressive moods. Therapists often use reframing as a way to help their clients view their life in a more adaptive way that facilitates recovery. Eventually, therapists want clients to implement this type of thinking on their own so that in the face of future stressors, they are less debilitated and will be more resistant to the prolonged stress reaction that exacerbates their depressive symptoms.

Finally, with respect to understanding the connection between health and stress as it appears in our world today, it is worth considering to what extent our reliance on technology has made us vulnerable to problems such as poorer sleep or anxiety from trying to keep up with social media demands. Researching Adjustment: Stress and Technology explores this issue.

RESEARCHING ADJUSTMENT
Stress and Technology

How much time per day do you spend on your phone or in front of a computer? For most of us, today's technology allows us to stay in almost constant contact with friends and family via Facebook and Instagram as well as texting, facilitating multitasking. Overall, media use among youth has increased by 20% during the past decade, but multitasking—simultaneously accessing two or more forms of media—has increased by more than 119% (Rideout, Foehr, & Roberts, 2010) in the same period. While this may be the new normal, is it healthy?

A study conducted by psychologist Mark Becker, Reem Alzahabi, and Christopher Hopwood (2013) found a 70% increase in self-reported depressive symptoms in people who spent the most time multitasking in comparison to those who spent the least time multitasking. When it came to social anxiety, there was a 42% increase between the groups. What is the reason for these differences? Some have speculated that there is an inherent stress associated with several aspects of social media multitasking. First, we spend the majority of our waking hours listening for and being interrupted by texts, tweets, and other communications that come to us instantaneously. Second, we feel compelled to respond to those communications instantly, which distracts us from other things we might be doing (e.g., sleeping, studying). Third, anxiety is produced by worrying about the feedback we receive about ourselves via social media (e.g., how many likes you receive on a post). The constant stress from trying to project an image of perfection—a perfect career, perfect relationship, or perfect everything—leads to the constant release of the stress hormone, cortisol, and ultimately can lead to depression and anxiety.

What can be done to manage the stress associated with living life online? Permanently unplugging oneself is not realistic. However, it may be wise to consider setting limits on social media use. Consider a social media detox, eliminating social media usage completely for a week or two, to determine if social media is causing depression anxiety. If it is, it may be advisable to turn off your devices completely for blocks of time during the day when you are engaged in important activities like sleeping, studying, and spending time with loved ones. Not only will it allow for more concentrated attention in these activities but it gives your body a rest from the constant vigilance needed to be accessible to others via technology. We will explore other implications of our technological advances in our last chapter on future issues.

Reflection Questions

1. Have you found that your use of technology and social media decreases or increases your stress level? How easy do you find it to unplug from technology?

2. Find a peer-reviewed research article about technology and stress. What were the results of the study? Do you agree with the results? Explain your reasoning.

Health and Well-Being

While much of this chapter's coverage concerns the impact of stress on our well-being, it is also important to discuss how individuals can live lifestyles that are compatible with optimal growth and development, regardless of what types of stressors they encounter along the road of life. In this section of the chapter, we will explore issues related to health promotion. Namely, we will discuss issues related to diet and nutrition, exercise, and avoiding substance use.

Diet and Nutrition

Most of us have heard the saying "you are what you eat." This saying refers to the fact that nutrition is a building block of our health: If you eat healthy foods, you increase the odds of having a healthy body. The U.S. government has historically developed guidelines for what is believed to be healthy eating. The *2015–2020 Dietary Guidelines for Americans* (U.S. Department of Health and Human Services & U.S. Department of Agriculture, 2015; see Figure 6.2) emphasized three major goals for Americans:

1. Balance calories with physical activity to manage weight.

2. Consume more of certain foods and nutrients such as fruits, vegetables, whole grains, fat-free and low-fat dairy products, and seafood.

3. Consume fewer foods with sodium (salt), saturated fats, trans fats, cholesterol, added sugars, and refined grains.

What we eat is oftentimes determined by factors such as what we can afford, what food has been a part of our cultural and familial rituals, and what is most readily available. Beginning in early childhood, all human beings need a well-balanced diet to fuel healthy physical development. Children's diets are dependent on what parents provide and what schools offer them. That being said, in the United States, there are some large disparities in terms of who eats healthy food and what the consequences of those inequities are. For example, according to a national health and nutrition survey (Foltz et al., 2011), fewer than 10% of our nation's adolescents meet the federal guideline of eating five or more servings of fruit and vegetables per day. Instead, the majority (56%) have only one serving of fruit or vegetables every day. Since our nutritional habits as children often are strong predictors of our habits as adults (Mazzeo, Gow, & Bulik, 2012), it is important to understand the current state of affairs with respect to childhood nutrition and health outcomes.

Many children in the United States are eating low-cost, high-calorie snacks and meals; as a result, obesity rates are increasing astronomically. For example, 21% of U.S. preschoolers are overweight, and that figure increases to 33% for school-aged children between the ages of 6 and 19 (Ogden, Carroll, Kit, & Flegal, 2014). This is not a problem restricted to the United States. The trend is being observed in many industrialized nations (World Health Organization [WHO], 2013b). For example, with the past 25 years alone, China has observed a fivefold increase in the percentage of its children who are overweight and obese (Ji, Chen, & Working Group on Obesity in China, 2013). Establishing a poor diet in early childhood increases the likelihood for a person's diet to remain poor based on the percentage of children, adolescents, and adults who meet the criteria for being overweight (Berk, 2014b).

Across all racial and ethnic groups, the prevalence of children ages 6 to 19 being overweight appears roughly equivalent in boys and girls. However, some noteworthy gender disparities exist within specific racial groups. Forty-three percent of African

Figure **6.2** **Federal Dietary Guidelines**

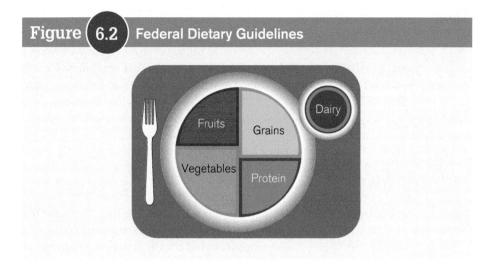

Source: ChooseMyPlate.gov.

American girls were overweight, compared with 34.4% of African American boys (Mazzeo et al., 2012). As is the case with other health problems, socioeconomic status (SES) is negatively associated with childhood obesity (Shrewsbury & Wardle, 2008). This finding is explained by the fact that oftentimes foods that are part of a well-balanced diet (e.g., fruits, vegetables, proteins, whole grains) cost families more to purchase. Additionally, some of the chain grocery stores that are most well-known for their healthy food choices can be some of the most expensive places to buy groceries.

Being overweight is a big problem in terms of health consequences. High blood pressure, insulin resistance, type 2 diabetes, sleep, and digestive disorders are all highly related to being overweight (Krishnamoorthy, Hart, & Jelalian, 2006) in children and adults. Since overweight children ages 10 to 17 are over 20 times more likely to be obese in adulthood compared to their nonoverweight peers (U.S. Department of Health and Human Services, 2011b), it is important to examine what can help children to access well-balanced diets. In an effort to show that access to good food is a critical component of decreasing childhood weight problems, researchers have begun to evaluate the efforts of programs that limit access to the traditional foods that kids most readily crave.

For example, Foster et al. (2008) investigated the effects of a school nutrition policy intervention (School Nutrition Policy Initiative, or SNPI) on fourth- to sixth-grade children from 10 schools with a high proportion of low-income students. As part of the SNPI, intervention program schools removed sodas, other sugar-sweetened beverages, and snacks of low nutritional value from vending machines and cafeteria service.

Water, low-fat milk, and non–artificially sweetened juice were the only beverages available in intervention program schools during the course of the project. In addition, school staff in the intervention program schools participated in nutrition education, and students were provided with 50 hours of nutrition education each school year. Students in intervention program schools were offered incentives (e.g., raffle tickets for prizes) for purchasing healthy foods.

Two years after the initiation of the SNPI, significantly fewer children in the intervention group had become overweight or obese compared with the control group (Foster et al., 2008). Specifically, 15% of children in control schools became overweight during the study period compared with 7.5% of children in the intervention schools. Moreover, the intervention was particularly effective for African American children, who were 41% less likely to be overweight at a 2-year follow-up than their African American peers in control schools. One of the other factors found to be involved in controlling weight issues is physical activity, which we will examine next.

Physical Activity and Exercise

In a similar trend to diet and nutrition, children and adolescents' physical activity levels have been shown to be decreasing, which has resulted in very few children meeting the national recommended levels of physical activity. Furthermore, children appear to become less physically active as they move from childhood to adolescence (Gortmaker et al., 2012). One study by Troiano et al. (2008) found that only 8% of adolescents engage in 60 minutes of moderate to vigorous exercise per day. As was true for diet, children need opportunities for regular physical activity whether it is in school, a part of recreational time, or as part of sports involvement.

Among adults, it would appear that the picture is grim as well. Over half of U.S. adults are inactive, with no regular or even light activity in their lives (U.S. Department of Health and Human Services, 2011b). More women than men are inactive, and inactivity rates are inversely related to SES (Berk, 2014b). In adults, physical activity fosters resistance to diseases that tend to become more frequent in young adulthood. For example, physically active adults are less likely to develop diabetes and cardiovascular disease (Bassuk & Manson, 1985). Regular exercise promotes cardiovascular functioning and decreases problems with being overweight and obese, which creates risk for a host of medical conditions. While the recommendation is for children and adolescents, who require more time devoted to exercise and recreation because they are still growing physically, adults can meet national recommendations by being active at a moderate to intense level for as little as 30 minutes per day (Garber et al., 2011).

What might compromise adults' ability to be physically active? It is not a lack of awareness. According to the U.S. Department of Health and Human Services (2011b), almost all adults are aware of the benefits of physical activity. Rather, it is likely to be competing demands for their time and energy. Think about the daily life of most adults who are no longer in school and have full-time jobs. If those same adults have families, much of their waking time is devoted to their jobs and spouses or children as well as maintaining households. Oftentimes there may not be enough hours in the day for a trip to the gym on top of those other obligations. This problem is further compounded for adults who live in low-income neighborhoods where there may not be community gyms or facilities and exercising in parks or going for a run outside may not be safe (Berk, 2014b).

How can people learn to become healthier in terms of physical activity? There is no shortage of businesses that have attempted to answer this question. Diet businesses, gyms, and home exercise equipment companies make many promises of a "new you." But are there any types of programs that appear to be effective at changing the behaviors of people who have poor diets and low levels of physical activity? Researchers are trying to identify successful programs that involve families as a system to change the tide of overall health of our nation's communities.

For example, PACE (Patient Centered Assessment and Counseling for Exercise and Nutrition) is a family-based program that uses computerized assessments of diet and both physical and sedentary behavior in participants (Patrick et al., 2006). The program starts out by using these assessments to help participants set goals and offer tools to help monitor goals. Parents also have goals and try to be good role models for their children by being actively supportive and involved in making changes for themselves. Program staff (such as physicians and nurses) provide support by making regular phone calls to help adjust the plans and to monitor progress.

Compared to families who were not involved in programs to help them change their diet and exercise routines, participants in PACE reduced sedentary behaviors by an average of 1 hour per day, and boys in the program increased the number of days that they were active every week. Girls experienced dietary gains by reducing the amount of unhealthy saturated fats that they ate. Programs such as PACE, which attempt to change the dietary and exercise norms of families, help participants to set and monitor goals, and provide active support from experts, may be successful due to their comprehensive nature. Since most overweight and inactive kids have overweight and inactive parents, it is important to address families as systems when trying to make changes to the lifestyles of individual members.

Avoiding Substance Use

A major challenge to the health and well-being of adolescents and young adults in particular is substance use. Whether the substance is tobacco, alcohol, or other drugs, there is unequivocal evidence that putting any toxins into the body is not compatible with health promotion and optimal growth. Not only are substances such as the ones listed here damaging to human bodies but many of them have addictive potentials that transform use into abuse.

Researchers have determined that substance use is influenced by a powerful mix of factors that include the drug-related attitudes and behaviors of those around us (e.g., friends, significant others, family members), popular culture and media portrayals of substance use, and individuals' own genetic makeup and self-regulation abilities (Berk, 2014b). In other words, while evidence suggests that some people have a family history that predisposes them to substance use and abuse, it is equally important to understand that glorifying substance use (e.g., most beer and alcohol commercials), being around friends that encourage substance use, and potentially using substances to regulate emotions are involved in explaining why substance use is so popular.

In terms of current use patterns, there are some promising findings emerging from a recent longitudinal examination (Lanza, Valisenko, Dziak, & Butera, 2015). For example, teenagers' use of alcohol has decreased since the 1970s. Likewise, fewer adolescents are taking up smoking cigarettes. However, trends do not necessarily tell the entire story of where substance use rates are with adolescents and young adults. For example, even though cigarette rates are down compared to previous years, in 2013, approximately 10% of African American teens smoked cigarettes and 19% of White teens did as well. Perhaps even more disturbing is that smoking rates for marijuana have now outpaced those of cigarettes for both groups (25% of African American teens and 22% of White teens). Similarly, while rates of alcohol use may be lower than they were in previous generations, there is still a concern about how many adolescents drink alcohol and how many use it in heavy amounts.

The dangers of using alcohol are not merely restricted to its immediate effects as a drug, but it is often involved in other health-compromising behaviors such as unprotected sexual activity. Alcohol use before or during sex is a major risk for unprotected sex (Cooper, 2002), which might result in unwanted pregnancy and acquisition of sexually transmitted diseases (STDs; including HIV). According to the 2009 Youth Risk Behavioral Surveillance Data (Centers for Disease Control and Prevention [CDC], 2010b), nearly one fifth (21.6%) of all students had used alcohol or drugs before their most recent sexual intercourse. Given that having most substances in our bodies can impair our ability to make good decisions and to consent to activities like sex, it is important to think about the short-term and long-term consequences of uncontrolled substance use.

Finally, while trends indicate that traditional substance use in many instances is improving generation by generation, there are new substances that are becoming popular in terms of their potential for abuse. For example, data have documented that 10 million individuals, or 7% of the U.S. population, reported nonmedical use of prescription drugs (Substance Abuse and Mental Health Services Administration, 2007), and this trend seems to be increasing over time. Given that prescription drugs can range in their effects, many abusers of these drugs are risking their lives by using these substances recreationally. Many public awareness campaigns have been implemented to educate parents about the dangers of drug abuse from the medication that they have in their medicine cabinets.

Is there any healthy amount of substance use? According to the 2015–2020 *Dietary Guidelines for Americans* (U.S. Department of Health and Human Services & U.S. Department of Agriculture, 2015), the only drug addressed is alcohol and the recommendations are clear. When alcohol is consumed (by adults of legal age), no more than one beverage per day for women and no more than two drinks per day for men are recommended. That provision does not encourage the use of alcohol but rather provides limits for its use when it is consumed. However, no studies exist that have found any health benefits of smoking (cigarettes or marijuana), using illegal drugs, or consuming prescription drugs that are not prescribed by a physician. Thus, in terms of optimizing health and well-being, substance use is not part of the plan.

Conclusion

In this chapter, we examined the relationship between stress and adjustment. Stress refers to the occurrence of a stimulus event (stressor), a process, and a reaction. A person's reaction to stress often influences the adjustment process. Coping with stress is a voluntary response to stressors, which can be defined in various ways, such as being emotion-focused versus problem-focused or active versus avoidant. It is not possible to conclusively determine which types of coping, if any, are the best or most effective because the effectiveness of coping is dependent on the context. In other words, depending on the type of stressor and the circumstances in which it occurs, some types of coping may be beneficial some of the time while other types of coping can be helpful in other situations. It is most helpful to have an arsenal of coping styles at one's disposal so that one has different tools to cope with the situation depending on the kind of a stressor that is being faced.

This chapter also explored the physiological and psychological costs of stress, as well as some of the most effective ways of managing stress. While not all stress is negative (e.g., eustress), we make choices about how we view and respond in the face of stressors that will determine whether we suffer from the experience or whether we grow from it and become better off or stronger for having gone through it.

Finally, we are coming to understand more clearly the linkages between mind and body. "A healthy mind in a healthy body" might be a maxim for a more holistic approach to well being. Toward that end, we explored our understanding of diet, exercise, and substance use on our health. This follows an increasing emphasis on integrated health that has grown in medicine and in psychology (DeGruy & Etz, 2010; Levey, Miller, & deGruy, 2012).

Review Questions

1. What is the difference between an acute stressor and a chronic stressor? What strategies can people use to avoid becoming overwhelmed by these stressors?

2. Think of a stressful situation that you have experienced. Describe this situation in terms of primary and secondary appraisal.

3. Define *coping*, and provide examples of two coping strategies that people may use.

4. Explain what microaggression is, and discuss its three types of categories.

5. Identify two strategies that you would use to manage stress, and discuss their benefits.

6. Analyze why physical touch is an effective way to manage stress levels. Have you experienced this in the past? Explain.

7. Compare and contrast good and bad stress. Do you feel that stress is positive or negative? Explain your reasoning.

8. Provide a personal example of eustress that was not used in the chapter.

9. Describe a negative stress event, and reframe it in a positive way.

10. Choose one aspect of health and well-being, and analyze how it can help decrease stress in people's lives.

Key Terms

active coping 120
acute stressor 113
avoidant coping 120
chronic stressors 113
coping 112

emotion-focused coping 119
eustress 128
hassles 113
microaggresions 122
primary appraisal 117

problem solving–focused
    coping 120
reframing 128
secondary appraisal 117
stress 112

Sharpen your skills with SAGE edge at **edge.sagepub.com/moritsugu**

SAGE edge for students provides a personalized approach to help you accomplish your coursework goals in an easy-to-use learning environment.

Go to **edge.sagepub.com/moritsugu** for additional exercises and web resources. Select Chapter 6, Stress, Health, and Well-Being for chapter-specific resources.

Part 2
Applications

Chapter 7

Social Relationships

Learning Objectives

1. Explain how childhood and adolescent experiences influence adult relationships.

2. Describe the ways that friendships can change over the life span, both in quality and quantity.

3. Identify friendship maintenance behaviors and outcomes.

4. Explain how empathy and compassion, altruism, and prosocial behavior promote adjustment.

5. Discuss the impact of loneliness and how it may be reduced through intervention.

After her divorce, Caila moved back to the neighborhood where she had been raised. Adjusting to being a single parent would be easier if she lived near her parents in a familiar setting. However, after a few months of adjusting to her new home environment, Caila realized that few of her old friends from high school still lived in the neighborhood, and she found that most of her "social life" consisted of taking care of her kids and spending time with her parents when she wasn't at work. She had people in her life—very important people in fact—but she felt lonely. After having spent so many years involved in her marriage, she was now craving companionship. She wasn't ready to date but was in dire need of friendship and support. It was only now that Caila was gaining an understanding that "starting over" would involve rebuilding her life in ways she hadn't anticipated.

. . . .

No man (or woman) is an island. That may be literally true, but the metaphor suggests that relationships are vital to the survival of human beings. This is obvious in the case of infants and children. From the day a child is born, the availability of a caretaker to whom the child can bond is essential to survival. Since children are unable to survive alone or care for themselves, the caregiver relationship is considered crucial to healthy development (Ainsworth, Blehar, Waters, & Wall, 1978; Bowlby, 1969) both physically and emotionally. For these reasons, examining relationships between children and parents has been an important area of study for psychologists.

After infancy, during childhood, relationships other than the one with a child's caregiver become critical to healthy development as well. The relationships that children form with other children, whether with siblings or playmates, have enormous importance for the development of social skills that are not only valuable in and of themselves but are predictive of later academic success (Berk, 2009). For example, learning how to share, listen to others, take turns, and cooperate sets the groundwork for school-based learning (Ladd, Birch, & Buhs, 1999; Li-Grining, Votruba-Drzal, Maldonado-Carreno, & Haas, 2010).

In addition to the range of survival needs and skill development opportunities that relationships help nurture in the first years of life, relationships also provide human beings with many important resources such as companionship, intimacy, and validation. This was the realization Caila had in our opening vignette. Some would argue that our abilities to develop and foster relationships are as important as any other aspect of our life.

In this chapter, we will explore the importance of relationships across the life span beginning with friendships as they function across childhood and adulthood. In addition, we will look at the complexities of using technology and social media to maintain relationships. We also introduce suggestions for maintaining friendships. We will examine some of the so-called building blocks of friendships such as **empathy** and compassion, and we will conclude by examining the consequences of not having meaningful friendships—namely loneliness.

Friendship and Well-Being

Friendships are incredibly important to adjustment at every point throughout the life span (Graham, Munniksma, & Juvonen, 2014). In fact, they are considered to be assets in people's lives that facilitate healthier functioning. For example, there is clear evidence that children who have at least one mutual friend, as opposed to children who have no friends, are less lonely, have higher self-esteem, and are less vulnerable to stressors in their lives (Bukowski, Motzoi, & Meyer, 2009). While there are aspects of friendship that need to be studied in order to understand the significance of friendships in the current generation of children, such as the impact of exclusively social media initiated friendships (e.g., Instagram followers), as opposed to friends whom we meet and interact with in person, it is universally accepted that friendships matter a lot and they are key ingredients of psychological health.

First Friendships

For decades, psychologists have studied the relevance of friendships during childhood, adolescence, and adulthood. For example, peer interactions among toddlers have been studied by psychologists since the early 1930s (Parten, 1932). Early research suggested that young children (e.g., toddlers) start out primarily engaging in nonsocial activities when it comes to other children. However,

Learning how to share, listen to others, and take turns happens early in life and has profound effects on our later relationships.

their interactions quickly shift to what is called *parallel play*, where children play near one another with similar objects (e.g., two children each play with blocks) but do not try to influence each other's behavior (Berk, 2009). This is a child's first attempt to engage another peer in a shared activity. Truly interactive play—namely **associative play** and **cooperative play**—does not happen until after the first two types of interaction are established, which typically is observed by the time children are preschool age.

Associative play is a more mutual type of parallel play where children are focused on separate activities but comment on each other's play and exchange toys. Cooperative play is a type of peer interaction where there is a common goal such as playing make-believe or working on a puzzle together. Research has supported Parten's (1932) identification of these distinctive types of interactions in young children as well as the fact that various types of play develop in the order she had specified (Rubin, Bukowski, & Parker, 2006). Over the past decades, we have learned a lot more about children's first friendships.

Childhood Friendships

Children's first peer relationships often arise from opportunities to play together (e.g., playdates). These "first friendships" are often based on a combination of utilitarian concepts of relationships as well as emotional features. For example, preschoolers often describe friendships as the relationships we have with people we like and with whom we can spend time playing (Hartup, 2006). However, during middle childhood, friendships become more mutual in nature, and the social interactions that are experienced between friends contribute greatly to an individual's emotional and social development. Thus, rather than identifying a friend based solely on his or her shared enjoyment of an activity, children move toward defining friends as people who can be trusted based on personal qualities (e.g., kindness, generosity; Berk, 2009). These changes in friendship criteria correspond with socioemotional changes that are occurring during middle childhood, namely with the emergence of **perspective taking** (i.e., the recognition that one's own viewpoint may not be shared by others) and empathy (i.e., the ability to relate to others at an emotional level; Selman, 1980).

As children develop throughout childhood, they increasingly pay attention to how they are treated and how their peers treat others. Thus, children are more interested in being friends with children they observe as being altruistic, kind, and generous than they are with kids who are bullies or who treat them (and others) poorly. This shift reflects their newly acquired sense of empathy and the ability to see the perspectives of

Our early friendships are often based on who we spend time with and shared play experiences.

other children (Selman, 1980), which makes them more careful monitors of how their own behavior impacts others. Hence, friendships become much more selective as children get older, as opposed to the more random nature of friendships in early childhood. In other words, older children (i.e., around age 8) choose their friends more carefully and may reject others as friends based on how they see them behave toward others (Hartup, 2006). For example, a child who is kind to or helps other kids or has a good sense of humor becomes more attractive as a potential friend than a child who perhaps shares a common interest—for example, soccer—but lacks these other qualities.

In addition to the more sophisticated criteria for friendship that comes during middle childhood, the sheer number of people one considers to be friends with begins to decline around age 8 and continues to decline as children move through adolescence and into adulthood. For example, Markovits, Benenson, and Dolenszky (2001)

Table 7.1   How Children's Friendships Change Over Time

Level	Description	Approximate Age Range	Criteria
0	Momentary Playmates	3-7 years	• Friendship is about o having fun together o proximity o shared activities • Children are intolerant of disagreements and differing opinions
1	One-Way Assistance	4-9 years	• Friendship is o based on utilitarianism o used as a commodity • Children value having friends, even friends who do not treat them well
2	Two-Way, Fair Weather Cooperation	6-12 years	• Friendship o is based on fairness and reciprocity o can become very rule-based (for example, creating a secret handshake)
3	Intimate, Mutually Shared Relationships	11-15 years	• Friendship is based on closeness and trust • Best friends are highly valued • Being a good friend is as important as having a good friend
4	Mature Friendship	12 years and up	• Friendship based on emotional connection • Differences within friendships are understood and tolerated • No longer possessive of friends • Different kinds of friendships exist, casual and close

Source: Adapted from Kennedy-Moore (2012); based on Selman's 1980 model.

found that by age 8, children will only name a handful of individuals when asked to list their friends, as opposed to preschoolers who will list many more people as friends. In particular, girls appear to become even more selective about who they consider a friend at this age, which is attributed to the greater demand for closeness that girls have as compared to boys at this age. During preschool, friendships tend to be more mixed in gender but become more gender segregated as children get older (Maccoby, 2002).

Friendship and Diversity

In addition to gender influences on friendships, there are also some studies that suggest race and ethnicity play a role in friendship formation in kids. Children tend to select friends who are similar to them racially and ethnically

Cross-ethnic friendships may play a role in decreasing the intergroup peer conflict.

(Graham, Taylor, & Ho, 2009); however, this may be influenced by the degree to which children attend racially and ethnically diverse schools and whether their classrooms at school reflect this diversity. If children attend schools that are racially or ethnically homogenous, they would only be able to select friends with similar cultural backgrounds.

In one study, researchers provided opportunities for African American and Latino middle school students to form cross-ethnic friendships (Graham et al., 2014). They then compared children who established cross-ethnic friendships with those who did not on a number of factors such as sense of safety, peer victimization experiences, loneliness, ethnic identity, and quality of friendships. Students who had befriended kids from their same ethnic group looked similar to the cross-ethnic friendships group in terms of quality of friendships and loneliness. The same-ethnicity friendships, however, were more strongly related to ethnic identity scores, suggesting that having friends who share ethnic backgrounds may be helpful in processing issues related to unique cultural group experiences.

However, the cross-ethnic friendships also predicted some unique outcomes in this same study. Cross-ethnic friendships (but not same ethnic friendships) were uniquely related to feelings of safety and lower levels of peer victimization. Thus, it may be the case that cross-ethnic friendships play a unique role in decreasing the likelihood of peer conflict between members of various cultural groups. The findings of this study suggest that having friends who are similar to us have certain value and serve certain purposes such as allowing for the exploration of identity (e.g., what it means to be African American or figuring out what is acceptable behavior for girls). On the other hand, the findings also suggest that having friends who are different from us is valuable and serves other purposes, such as helping us to see different perspectives or appreciate cultural differences.

Friendships During Adolescence

A point in human development that impacts many things, including the significance of friendships, is the life stage of adolescence. During adolescence, friendships increase in importance relative to the other relationships that people have at that age (e.g., relationships with siblings or parents). This results in part because of what is happening developmentally at this stage of life, namely the search for identity and the initial attempts we make at establishing intimacy with non–family members (Graham et al., 2009). The search for identity, or the need to explore various possible selves and who a person might become, is greatly facilitated by spending time with friends and peers, as is experimenting with new behaviors and opportunities. While theorists like Erikson believed that these opportunities to explore possible identities and new behaviors were a necessary part of healthy development, not all exploring may be viewed as positive. In fact, friendships during adolescence often give parents a great deal of distress due to their fear of peer pressure.

There is a saying that birds of a feather flock together. As it turns out, research supports the accuracy of this saying, which may suggest that parents cannot fairly blame their children's friends for the decisions that their kids make. For example, Hamm (2000) conducted a study of the similarities between friends in a sample of African American, Asian American, and White adolescents. The dimensions of similarity that were included in the study were academic orientation, ethnic identity, and substance use levels. The results suggested that for all groups of adolescents, similarities existed among friends on levels of academic orientation and substance use. Compared with Asian American and White adolescents, African American adolescents chose friends who were less similar with respect to academic orientation or substance use but more similar with respect to ethnic identity. The important point of this study is that adolescents' existing behaviors and senses of self were what caused them to gravitate toward peers who were similar, not that the friends became more similar over time. This suggests that similarity in friendships is relative rather than absolute and that friends are not identical in all possible ways but may be similar to one another in the ways that are most valued by adolescents at that particular point in their lives (see Researching Adjustment: Similarity and Friendships).

RESEARCHING ADJUSTMENT
Similarity and Friendships

While existing research suggests that we are drawn to people who are similar to us, researchers in the United Kingdom have started a longitudinal study to see if people who live in environments where there is more diversity have more friends who are different from them. The project "Children's and Adult's Friendships Across Social Class and Ethnic Difference" is a multiyear project where people who live in socially mixed or "super diverse" urban settings are being interviewed about their friendship patterns. Some preliminary findings were released (Neal & Vincent, 2013) that suggest that even when people choose to live in diverse communities, it is not merely shared geography that is necessary to create cross-cultural friendships. Specifically, they found in their interview data with adults that while residents in diverse communities share public spaces such as libraries or parks, their social networks do not necessarily reflect that diversity. While many of their participants did socialize with ethnically different people, there were fewer connections across social class. The authors discuss that structural barriers such as economic restrictions often serve as impediments to friendships across social class lines. For example, if an individual is middle class and can afford to go to a fund-raising event in the community, it is likely that only other individuals of a similar social class will be present at the event, which limits opportunities for socializing across groups.

In a report that focused on children's friendships, the authors found that sharing contexts such as school in a diverse neighborhood makes it more likely that children will have friends who are different ethnically and on social class lines (Iqbal, Neal, & Vincent, 2016). The authors found that almost all the students they interviewed had at least one cross-ethnic friend in their list of top five friends. However, friendships across social class lines were less common. Furthermore, they found that children's social interactions were influenced by parents to a large degree and that the friendships that existed in school were not always extended into their home environments. Studies such as these suggest that forming and maintaining diverse relationships requires a reexamination of the societal barriers that contribute to social segregation, not just the formation of neighborhoods that are heterogeneous.

Reflection Questions

1. Can you identify any social class or other cultural barriers that restricted who people socialized with where you were raised?

2. In a college or university setting, do you feel that opportunities for cross-cultural friendships are more ample?

Friendships and Social Media

Technology is a major mechanism for initiating and maintaining friendships, but it also is a significant factor in adolescents' self-esteem and well-being. For example, Kalpidou, Costin, and Morris (2011) studied the relationship between college adjustment, self-esteem, and Facebook use. Their findings reveal a mixed picture of how technology relates to these important factors. In their study, they found that a high number of Facebook friends potentially hinders academic and social adjustment for freshmen, and spending a lot of time on Facebook is related to low self-esteem early in one's college experience. However, the picture is quite different for more advanced students, where their results indicate that the number of Facebook friends is positively related to social adjustment and attachment to the college or university. The results suggest that later in college life, when students use Facebook effectively to connect socially with their peers on campus, it becomes a positive resource. However, early in one's college experience, spending too much time with Facebook friends may prevent new students from participating in campus events where they meet people face-to-face, which is important to becoming socially and academically integrated into the campus environment.

Researchers have been very interested in not only how many people we connect with using social media but also what type of feedback we get from doing so. For example, Valkenburg, Peter, and Schouten (2006) found that receiving positive feedback on their profiles enhanced adolescents' social self-esteem and well-being, whereas receiving negative feedback decreased their self-esteem and well-being. This study's findings suggest that using social media is not only a way to stay in touch with one's friends but is a powerful way that we give and receive feedback about and from the friends in our lives. Given findings like these, should we be concerned with the role of social media in determining adjustment? Since social media is now a permanent vehicle in our lives, let's take a closer look at the relationship between friendships and technology.

When a person has 500 Twitter followers, does this mean that he or she has meaningful connections with all 500 people? Understanding the role of technology in human relationships is undergoing serious investigation at this point in time. While social scientists

Research suggests that the Internet does not replace in-person and telephone communication with friends; rather, it adds to such communication.

©iStockphoto.com/lovro77

were once concerned that our media-obsessed society was going to produce a generation of people who were more comfortable in front of their computers than they were in face-to-face interactions (van Dijk, 2006), there has been more evidence suggesting that there may be a positive connection between Internet use and contact with friends. Wang and Wellman (2010) summarized some of the following research findings on the relationship between social media use and friendships:

1. The time that people in general spend with friends since they started using the Internet has either increased or stayed the same (Center for the Digital Future, 2009).

2. The more time that people use the Internet, the more social contact they have with their friends (Hampton, Sessions, Her, & Rainie, 2009).

3. The Internet does not replace in-person and telephone communication with friends; it adds to such communication and helps people to stay connected in between the times when they see or speak with one another (Mok, Wellman, & Carrasco, 2010).

4. The Internet appears to provide expanded opportunities for people to develop new friendships that often continue in person or by phone (Hampton et al., 2009).

5. Compared to people who do not use the Internet, those who do have more total friends and a more diverse set of friends (Hampton et al., 2009).

Interestingly, Wang and Wellman's (2010) research (see Figure 7.1) found that only 20% of Internet users report having one or more friends who are exclusive to their online social life. In other words, the vast majority (80%) of Internet users have no "strictly virtual" friends, which suggests that the Internet does not take the place of face-to-face friendships.

Scholars like Boyd (2014) have also argued the merits of social media by noting that many young people access social media when they are in the physical presence of their

Figure 7.1 Internet Usage and Offline Friends

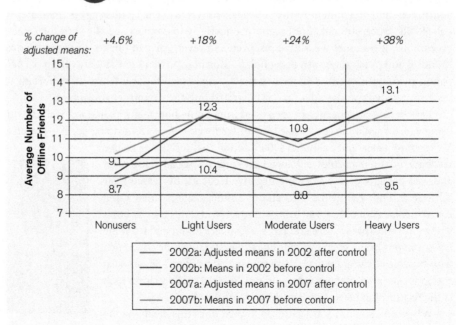

Source: Figure 2 from Wang, H., & Wellman, B. (2010). Social connectivity in America: Changes in adult friendship network size from 2002 to 2007. *American Behavioral Scientist.*

friends (e.g., watching a YouTube video together). Additionally, she argued that for some adolescents who are unable to "hang out" with their friends in person, sometimes due to geographical obstacles or even because their parents want them at home, social media provides a relatively safe place to recreate and feel connected. Even adults who have concerns about Internet use by their kids understand that the need to recreate with one's friends is a healthy impulse (even if in their youth they used to do so by hanging out in malls).

Social media is a major tool through which we access and maintain friendships. However, one of the other purposes that friendships begin to serve in adolescence is the opportunity to develop the skills that result in more intimate personal relationships. Thanks to puberty, intimacy and romance are very much on the radar of most adolescents, and in fact, intimate romantic relationships will begin to take priority in the lives of late adolescents. During emerging or early adulthood (e.g., college years), friendships are still important, but they begin to take a backseat to the desire to establish intimate relationships (Arnett, 2000). However, nonromantic relationships still play an important role in our lives as adults.

Adult Friendships

Friendships continue to play an important role in our well-being during all phases of adulthood. Even though many young adults begin to spend proportionately more time with significant romantic others and, in the case of adults who ultimately start families, with their children and extended families, friendships still provide us with social opportunities, support, and affirmation (Collins & Masden, 2006). Due to the competing demands for our time, however, adult friendships may not share some of the same characteristics of friendships we have earlier in life.

A main difference between friendships we have in adulthood versus earlier periods of our life is numerical. In a survey conducted by Gillespie, Frederick, Harari, and Grov (2015; see Figure 7.2), adults who ranged in age from 18 to 75 (with a mean age of 42) were asked a variety of questions about their close friendships. To estimate the typical size of adults' friendship circles, they asked participants to tell them how many friends would likely celebrate their birthdays, how many they felt they could call to discuss their sex life, and the number of friends they could contact at an unusual hour if they were in trouble.

As participants' age increased, the numbers they gave in answers to these questions decreased. For example, adults in their 20s said that between 8 and 10 people would likely celebrate their birthdays, but adults in their 30s said that they would celebrate their birthdays with between five and seven friends. Similar trends existed for the answers to the other questions.

Additionally, for answers to the other questions, the average numbers that participants gave in response were even smaller. For example, on average, participants said they would only feel comfortable discussing their sex lives with or calling late at night for help from only four to seven friends. Few demographic differences were found with respect to factors like the participants' gender or sexual orientation. This led the researchers to conclude that as we get older, most of us only have a handful or so of intimate friends.

In this same study (Gillespie et al., 2015), it was found that heterosexual adults have more same-gender than cross-gender friendships (which was also found for lesbian women but not gay men). This may be because of trends that are established in childhood (we find more similarities with those of the same gender) or it could be in some cases an effort to minimize sexual issues for heterosexual cross-gender friends. However, men have greater numbers of cross-gender friendships than do women (especially in college), and women tend to evaluate their same-gender friendships more positively than men evaluate their same-gender friendships (Blieszner & Roberto, 2012). One important finding that emerges from much of this research (Berk, 2014b; Gillespie et al., 2015) is that being satisfied with our friendships is highly related to our overall life

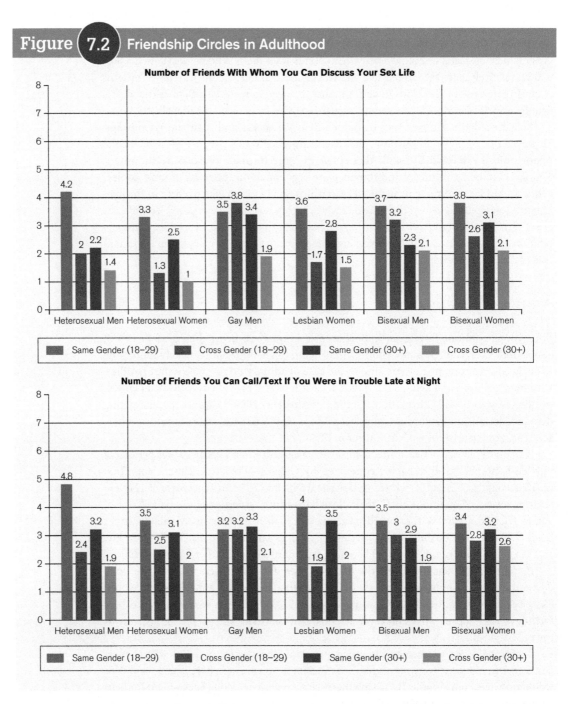

Figure 7.2 Friendship Circles in Adulthood

Source: Figures 1 & 2 from Gillespie, B.J., Frederick, D., Harari, L., & Grov, C. (2015). Homophily, close friendship, and life satisfaction among gay, lesbian, heterosexual, and bisexual men and women. PLoS ONE 10(6): e0128900. doi:10.1371/journal.pone.0128900.

satisfaction. Thus, it would appear that making and developing important relationships during adulthood is just as important as it is in earlier parts of our lives.

Friendship Maintenance

Similar to our romantic relationships, friendships require a certain amount of care and maintenance. In other words, while making friends may be easy, keeping friends requires some work on our part. Oswald, Clark, and Kelly (2004); McEwan and Guerrero (2012); and other scholars (Hays, 1984) have discussed the elements of successfully maintaining friendships in college students. Think about maintenance behaviors as regular actions that are taken in a relationship to keep it satisfying for both parties.

The first friendship maintenance behavior identified by McEwan and Guerrero (2012; based on previous scholarship in the area) is **positivity,** or actions that make spending time with a friend enjoyable and interesting. For example, planning an event that is mutually enjoyed by a friend, such as seeing a foreign film, would be an example of an action that both friends would find pleasant and interesting. While friends are also there for one another in difficult times, this friendship maintenance behavior speaks to the need to plan "good times" with those we call friends.

The second friendship maintenance behavior is **assurance.** Assurance behavior refers to affirming statements made about the friendship (Wettersten, Schreurs, Munch, Faith, & Sell, 2015). Examples of this type of behavior might be when you tag someone your "BFF" or verbally express appreciation for the friend's importance in your life. Assurance behaviors may be most valued in times of transition. For example, leaving your hometown friends and moving to college may create some feelings of vulnerability for childhood friends who worry they will be replaced by new college friends. Assurances can help remind those who are not a daily part of one's college life that they still matter and cannot be replaced.

The third friendship maintenance behavior is **social networking** behaviors. This type of behavior refers to involving others in one's friendship. For example, two best friends may be part of a larger circle of friends. While the best friends may spend some of their time as a twosome, it is important to also stay connected with the larger group. This type of maintenance behavior is not necessarily difficult for most young adults who may prefer to socialize in larger groups, but it is still related to the overall health of the friendship (Wettersten et al., 2015).

The fourth friendship maintenance behavior is called **task sharing.** Task sharing simply refers to the tangible help that we can give to our friends when they are in need and vice versa. Examples could run from helping to study for a test, checking the hours of the tutoring center if a friend needs some extra help on an assignment, or even helping a friend unpack his or her belongings in a new dorm room.

The fifth friendship maintenance behavior is scheduling **routine contact** or actual time together. We have explored how friendships are being transformed by new technology. No matter how common it is to stay in touch with friends via texting and social media, this maintenance behavior speaks to the importance of remembering that face time is important and scheduling regular times to see our important friends is beneficial to the relationship. This may require some extra effort for friends who are not within our immediate proximity (e.g., friends who live in our hometown versus friends we see all the time at school).

The sixth friendship maintenance behavior is **computer-mediated communication.** Particularly for this and future generations of young adults, staying in touch with friends electronically is a highly valued maintenance behavior. Imagine how it feels when a good friend does not respond to a text message. It is not uncommon for most people to expect fairly instantaneous communication on our devices. Thus, being a good friend can involve staying on top of online communication as well as paying attention to our use of face-to-face opportunities to maintain friendships.

Finally, the last friendship maintenance behavior is referred to as **banter.** This is the private jokes or stories that exist between us and the close friends in our life. This shared history works like a glue and gives friends a unique life history that isn't shared with others. Being able to reflect and remember those moments in history not only brings back pleasant memories but often serves to remind us of how important special friends have been throughout periods of our lives.

Research on friendship maintenance behaviors has found different patterns in people's use of these behaviors in comparison to scholars who study romantic relationship

| Table 7.2 | Friendship Maintenance Behaviors |

Behavior	Examples
Positivity	Doing things you enjoy together
Assurance	Reminding each other of how much you value the relationship
Social Networking	Hanging out with common friends
Task Sharing	Helping out in a crisis
Routine Contact	Staying connected on a regular basis
Computer Mediated Communication	Responding to each other's Facebook pages
Banter	Sharing a private joke

maintenance behaviors (reviewed in the following chapter on romantic relationships). First, close friends tend to engage in higher levels of friendship maintenance behaviors than do casual acquaintances (although having both types of friends contributed to perceptions of being adequately supported), and second, men and women use friendship maintenance behaviors at similar levels (McEwan & Guerrero, 2012). Also, it has been found that positivity, task sharing, and routine contact were the best predictors of close friendships in college students in comparison to casual friendships. See Table 7.2.

Building Blocks of Relationships

In this chapter, we have looked at a variety of statistics and trends about friendships. We have also examined how friendships may change throughout the life span. But regardless of how friendships transform over time, there are some basic building blocks of healthy relationships that make us able to be a friend or a significant other. It is arguable that having these abilities is key to healthy adjustment in a social world. In this section, we will explore what is known about empathy and compassion as well as altruism and prosocial behavior and how these factors are related to relationship formation and maintenance.

Empathy and Compassion

Empathy and compassion are two closely related building blocks of relationships. Empathy is the ability to understand another's emotional state and, importantly, to really feel with that person (Berk, 2014b). As mentioned earlier in this chapter, empathy is related to the concept of perspective taking (Selman, 1980) or the ability to recognize that others have experiences of events that are similar to what we have experienced, but others' interpretations may not align with our perspectives. A toddler, for example, has to have the ability to recognize that other children have experiences that they can understand at some level, in order to respond appropriately. For example, if a toddler hears another child crying, the toddler might go over to the child and offer her a blanket or teddy bear because it is something they find comforting (Moreno, Klute, & Robinson,

2008). While many toddlers might also find the blanket comforting, some toddlers might reject the blanket and look for their parent to soothe them. This example illustrates that even young children express the first signs of empathy. Our capacity for empathy grows as we develop cognitively, emotionally, and socially.

It is also likely, however, that our capacity for empathy is hardwired within our nervous systems. Scientists identified very specialized cells within the cerebral cortexes of primates that are called mirror neurons. Mirror neurons fire identically regardless of whether we observe an action or if we are engaged in an action (Ferrari & Coude, 2011). In human beings, we have a very elaborate set of mirror neurons that are thought to be the biological basis for empathy, imitation, and other complex social abilities (Iacoboni, 2009). These neurons allow us to observe another person having an experience (e.g., laughing at a funny movie) and simulate the same behavior in our own brain (e.g., our brains register as if we are laughing), and in some cases, we spontaneously imitate the behavior (i.e., we begin laughing too). Clearly having the neural capacity to empathize with others must have an evolutionary purpose. Being able to empathize and imitate others may be keys to social connections, which, in return, are needed for the survival of our species.

Compassion, which is related to but not the same concept as empathy, refers to our ability to take an empathic response an extra step, namely to feel moved to help another person. For example, let's say you are on campus and you observe another student stumble while walking and drop their books. Your initial empathic reaction may be to feel bad for that person, perhaps remembering a time when that happened to you, and remember how embarrassed you were and perhaps wonder if the student is equally embarrassed. If you felt moved to go over to the person, ask if he or she is all right, and help pick up his or her books, then you have also felt compassion for the person. Clearly if you have seen a scenario like this unfold, you know that not everyone feels moved to be so compassionate. In fact, many onlookers might feel empathy for the person who has fallen but continue walking to class without giving the situation much thought at all.

While not everyone responds compassionately all the time, compassion is thought to have a very important evolutionary purpose, similar to what we believe the function of mirror neurons to be. It turns out that being compassionate is closely tied to fostering and maintaining relationships between friends, spouses, and family members—all of which allow our species to survive (Keltner, Haidt, & Shiota, 2006). So how is it that some people are more compassionate than others?

This question is not easy to answer. However, studies being conducted on compassion reveal two exciting things: Compassion is contagious, and compassion can be taught. Compassion, along with many types of behaviors, both positive and negative, tends to be learned and imitated from the people in our environment. If we see our neighbors picking up garbage off the streets in front of their houses, we are more likely to pick up garbage ourselves. With respect to compassion, researchers have found that it is more common when it has become a social norm (Christakis & Fowler, 2009). This means that much of our ability to become compassionate people can be learned though role modeling. Simply put, if you see examples of people who are compassionate, you are more likely to become a compassionate person yourself. This is good news for parents who are trying to raise compassionate, caring children. There is great power in their own behavior and role modeling.

What happens if children are raised in environments where there is not a great deal of compassion available? This could be the case for kids who are raised in neighborhoods that lack community bonding and good deeds. In other words, some kids are raised in environments where they may not know or trust their neighbors and the social norm involves keeping to oneself (and leaving other people to handle things on their own). Can compassion be taught? In fact it can. Adjustment in Practice: Teaching Compassion contains ideas for promoting compassion.

ADJUSTMENT IN PRACTICE
Teaching Compassion

Compassion can be taught, and many programs are popping up with that goal in mind. Some of the elements of compassion training programs include the following:

1. Look for commonalities between yourself and other people. While we are simultaneously similar to and different from the people in our lives, if we focus on aspects that we share, we automatically feel more compassionate.

2. See people as individuals, not objects. When we hear people's stories or testimonials, we have much stronger compassionate reactions in comparison to when we hear statistics about people. Reducing people to numbers, which statistics often do, can have the unintended consequence of objectifying people and making us less compassionate.

3. Resist the urge to blame the victim. Even though we live in a society where we assume that good things happen to good people (which conversely suggests that bad things happen to bad people), it is important to remember that bad things also happen to good people, and when we remember this, we are much more likely to respond compassionately to their hardships.

4. Remember that being compassionate is just as good for us as it is for others. Studies have shown that helping out others (e.g., mentoring) has just as much benefit for the helper as the helpee. Bringing good things into other people's lives makes us feel good.

    a. What experiences have you had that allowed you to hone your compassion skills?

    b. What do you think is the impact of being compassionate on the helper?

Source: Adapted from Greater Good (n.d.).

Altruism and Prosocial Behavior

Altruism and prosocial behavior are terms we use to refer to selfless behavior that is typically prompted by feelings of compassion. Altruistic or prosocial behaviors include actions that benefit another person without any expected reward for oneself (Spinrad & Eisenberg, 2009). An example of a prosocial or altruistic behavior would be to interrupt a bullying situation among acquaintances, even though the bully might turn his or her attention to us instead. However, in this example, interrupting the bullying episode would have to be motivated by the desire to help prevent distress for the victim, not to impress others. What is it that moves some people to act altruistically while others, even those who feel compassion, chose to refrain from these actions?

Two factors may be predictive of whether people ultimately gravitate toward prosocial behaviors. The first factor is related to a person's disposition. Specifically, children who are assertive, sociable, and good at regulating their own emotions are more likely to assist others and act selflessly (Bengtsson, 2005; Eisenberg et al., 1998). This suggests that to some extent, people who have more outgoing personalities and those who do not get overwhelmed by their own feelings in a help-inducing situation are more likely to behave altruistically. To illustrate the point, let's return to our bullying example. If a child who observes a peer being bullied becomes flooded with feelings from previous personal experiences of being bullied, that child may become emotionally paralyzed and unable to help his or her peer.

However, it is not solely personality or dispositional factors that predict altruistic behavior. Similar to what researchers have discovered about compassion, altruistic behaviors can be learned and are accurately predicted by children's exposure to role modeling (Eisenberg, 2003). Studies done with children as young as 3 and 4 have shown that parents' sensitivity and empathic responses to their preschoolers' emotions predict how altruistic their children are toward other children who are in distress (Michalik et al., 2007). Longitudinal research such as this shows that these altruistic patterns of behavior are not short lived. Rather, they persist into early adulthood. Therefore, it would appear that parents role model behaviors related to altruism very early in the lives of their children, and this vicarious learning sets in motion tendencies that define their behavior as adults. In addition to parental role models, community role models may be important for teaching altruism, which can occur through involvement in organized religion. For kids who belong to religious organizations and who participate in sponsored activities, prosocial behavior levels tend to be higher than they are for kids who do not have such affiliations (Berk, 2014b).

Social-emotional learning programs taught in schools can be an important vehicle for teaching empathy and altruism.

In another similarity to the literature on compassion, it has also been shown that prosocial behavior can be taught (Eisenberg, 2003), and teaching altruism is a component of many social–emotional learning programs (SEL) that are offered in schools (Greenberg et al., 2003). The emphasis of many SEL programs is teaching children and adolescents what types of behaviors we want to see from them instead of solely punishing them for behaviors we don't want to see. Furthermore, SEL programs operate from the assumption that just as we assume that our children need to be taught academic skills, they also need to be taught social and emotional competencies. Thus, while much of the past research on altruism has focused on the dispositional and parenting practices that lead to prosocial behavior in kids, increasingly the focus is shifting to studies that identify effective ways to teach kindness in thought and action.

It is worth noting that despite the fact that most children, adolescents, and adults successfully obtain and maintain relationships with friends throughout their lifetimes, there remains a subset of people who truly struggle to have or keep meaningful friendships. For some of these individuals, SEL programs might be very necessary interventions, along with counseling, to help them improve their skills and interpersonal sensitivities. For individuals who lack the presence of significant friends, life can be very painful.

Loneliness

Many of us remember the kids in elementary school who were so-called loners, who ate lunch alone, and who did not seem to have many friends. Oftentimes these kids are easy to spot and stand out like sore thumbs in comparison to the popular kids who seem to have

Lonely children are often the recipients of peer rejection.

an abundance of friends and who are well regarded by almost everyone. Adults often wonder if these more isolated kids have adjustment problems. Psychologists have studied issues of peer acceptance and rejection for decades. The people who are most lonely are oftentimes also the ones who experienced high levels of peer rejection as children (Berk, 2014b). However, understanding the causes of rejection and loneliness can be a question of which comes first, the chicken or egg.

Rejected children who do not have friends fall into one of two categories: **rejected aggressive** or **rejected withdrawn**. Rejected aggressive children tend to be impulsive, hyperactive, and inattentive as well as have a high level of conflict in their lives (Berk, 2014b). Not surprisingly, these kids also appear to have deficiencies in perspective-taking abilities and social skills (Dodge, Coie, & Lynam, 2006). Rejected aggressive children typically turn off their peers and find it hard to avoid conflict when they interact with others.

Rejected withdrawn children are socially awkward and more avoidant of people. Sometimes these kids have social phobias or feel very anxious around other people. Rejected withdrawn children are much more avoidant. In both cases, however, these rejected kids experience increasing rejection and exclusion, which makes them more lonely and more worried about being scorned or attacked (Rubin, Bowker, & Gazelle, 2010).

This information should help to explain this cause and effect question that arises when trying to explain loneliness. There have been some studies that reveal that in many cases being lonely alters our ability to change circumstances that might relieve social isolation. Masi, Chen, Hawkley, and Cacioppo (2011) are leading scholars on loneliness, and they have found that when people feel isolated, their brains become preoccupied with their own welfare, not others', which may make these children less empathic, compassionate, and prosocial. Even though the tendency to want to protect ourselves from the potential harm of others may seem to be linked to self-preservation (i.e., to be hyper-prepared for attacks, teasing, or other types of scorn), that very reaction appears to harm their physical and mental health as well as well-being and makes us more likely to see everything in a negative light. It can also make us seem cold, unfriendly, and socially awkward. This reaction, in other words, starts a self-fulfilling prophecy and cycle that brings about more isolation and loneliness.

The impact of loneliness on physical health is perhaps most startling. Cole, Hawkley, Arevalo, and Cacioppo (2011) analyzed the gene expression profiles of chronically lonely people and found that genes expressed within two subtypes of white blood cells are uniquely responsive to feelings of loneliness. The cells are associated with diseases such as atherosclerosis and cancer, as well as "first line of defense" immune responses. This research suggests that the more time we spend feeling lonely and worried about social dangers in our midst, our stress response becomes hyperstimulated, which makes us more likely to be ill as well as more likely to experience psychological pain.

In a review of interventions to reduce loneliness, Masi et al. (2011) found that counselors who encouraged participants to challenge their own negative thought processes—for example, by sharing a positive part of their day with someone else—were more effective than interventions seeking to improve social skills, enhance social support, or increase opportunities for social contact. In other words, for lonely individuals, forcing themselves to be positive and to reflect that positivity outward to another person may help to reset the brain to move out of its hyperprotective mode and, depending on the response of the person to whom they share, it may begin to erode their assumptions that all people are threatening.

In the information age when technology is a large supporter of people's relationships, is it possible that social media could be used as an intervention against loneliness? There is mixed evidence here. On one hand, some studies have found that positive experiences with social media are most common among people who are already well connected (Sheldon, Abad, & Hinsch, 2011). These researchers posited that this may be the case because Facebook and other social media supports relationships among those who are already highly socially connected but might make those who are isolated feel even more so.

Other studies, however, have indicated that social media can be useful in teaching kids social skills and helping them to connect with peers who are outside of their immediate environment (Berk, 2014b). As researchers continue to examine the potential benefits of SEL programs, technological and face-to-face interventions for lonely individuals, we will hopefully be able to unlock some of the keys to helping lonely people become more connected to others.

Conclusion

In this chapter, we have explored the importance of relationships throughout the life span as a key aspect of healthy adjustment. It is clear that our capacity to form social relationships has an evolutionary purpose. Without those abilities, infants and young children would be unable to survive, and their parents and caretakers would not be able to provide for their needs. But even after physical survival no longer depends on social relationships, our mental and physical health is very much affected by their presence in our lives.

People's criteria for friends change as they grow up, and the purpose and benefit of social relationships changes as we become adults. We have discovered that in many ways, technology has become a tool for establishing and maintaining friendships. However, we have also found that technology does not substitute for actual face time with friends. In fact, there are many aspects of maintaining friendships that happen entirely off-line.

We also have reviewed scholarship on what might be considered the building blocks of friendships and social relationships: empathy, compassion, and prosocial behaviors. We have discovered that these building blocks can be taught to people who were not successful at obtaining them early in life. These discoveries are important in designing programs or interventions for people to help enhance their adjustment potential. Not having the skills to establish and maintain social relationships turns out to be a large determinant of quality of life for lonely and rejected individuals. Science is now identifying some of the interventions that may make it possible for people to recover from social deficits, which allow them to lead more productive, healthy lives.

Review Questions

1. What early childhood experiences contribute to successful relationships in adulthood?

2. What type of trends have been observed with respect to the changing nature of friendships from childhood to adulthood? Have you noticed these trends in your own friendships?

3. Explain why friendships increase in importance to adolescents.

4. How does social media play a role in establishing and maintaining friendships?

5. What is the main difference between friendships in adulthood and earlier in life? Why do you think this is the case?

6. What are three examples of friendship maintenance behaviors? Do you practice these behaviors in your own friendships? Why or why not?

7. Explain the difference between compassion and empathy.

8. Describe the two factors that are predictive of whether an individual will demonstrate altruistic and prosocial behavior.

9. Describe one of the categories of rejected children. Imagine you are trying to help a child in this category. What would you suggest he or she do to establish friendships?

10. Given the negative effects of loneliness, what are several strategies that can help people feel less alone?

Key Terms

altruism 150

associative play 141

assurance 149

banter 149

computer-mediated
   communication 149

cooperative play 141

empathy 140

perspective taking 141

positivity 149

prosocial behavior 140

rejected aggressive 154

rejected withdrawn 154

routine contact 149

social networking 149

task sharing 149

Sharpen your skills with SAGE edge at **edge.sagepub.com/moritsugu**

SAGE edge for students provides a personalized approach to help you accomplish your coursework goals in an easy-to-use learning environment.

Go to **edge.sagepub.com/moritsugu** for additional exercises and web resources. Select Chapter 7, Social Relationships for chapter-specific resources.

Chapter

8

Romance
and Intimacy

1. Describe the characteristics of early romantic attraction and casual sexual arrangements.

2. Describe the characteristics of committed partnerships, including the role of sexuality.

3. Discuss ways in which gay and lesbian relationships are similar to and different from relationships among heterosexual couples.

4. Discuss reasons for infidelity and methods of recovery.

5. Discuss trends in intimate partner violence (IPV).

6. Identify relationship maintenance behaviors and outcomes.

Teresa was a 25-year-old who had spent the past 7 years of her life working a full-time job and putting herself through school. After receiving her associate's degree, she transferred to a 4-year university to receive her bachelor's degree in accounting. Working full-time and going to school part-time left very little time for a social life, much less dating. While Teresa was confident that her commitment to staying in school was worth all the sacrifice, her parents told her that she would never really be happy unless she found her soul mate and got married. Teresa explained away most of her parents' nagging as a function of their "old school" values and stereotypical thinking that women would be most fulfilled in the roles of wife and mother. However, there was a small part of her that wondered if they were right. She wondered if by spending all her time in school and at work if she was missing out on opportunities to find a partner and if being "in love" was necessary to being a happy, adjusted adult.

. . . .

Love makes the world go 'round. All you need is love. Adages such as these remind us of the central place that romantic relationships have for most people. Love was thought to be a necessary element of adjustment according to scholars like Freud. People who are not in love, like Teresa, may question whether they are truly missing out on a necessary part of life. Yet is it true that romantic relationships are always a source of well-being? One might certainly assume this given that so many people spend significant amounts of time pursuing relationships, being in relationships, or transitioning out of relationships.

In this chapter, we will explore the elements of healthy romantic relationships and discuss how much well-being is linked to being in such relationships. First, we will explore what is known about the origin of romantic feelings and interests. Next, we will discuss different forms of romantic relationships (some traditional, some less traditional). Then we examine what is known about healthy relationships (for both heterosexual and gay or lesbian couples) and explore the role of sex in relationships. We will also cover some of what is known about relationship problems such as infidelity and violence and offer some insight on whether recovery and a return to healthy adjustment in these situations is possible. Finally, we will describe some of the consequences of breaking up and offer some hope for maintaining and promoting health in relationships.

The Seeds of Romance

For most people, there is a moment in life when relationships begin to signify the potential for intimacy and closeness beyond mere friendship. This new potential, romance, often becomes salient during puberty, when people pass through the stage in life that results in sexual maturity. This is not to say that much younger children do not have crushes on their peers, but it is not until adolescence that most youths have an interest in acting on these feelings. What is the age by which most people report having a girlfriend or a boyfriend? The answer to this question depends on a variety of factors, but in particular, it may depend on one's developing sexual orientation.

Children of all sexual orientations report first awareness of sexual desires and attractions as early as age 9 (Savin-Williams, 2005). Thus, sexuality and sexual orientation do not suddenly emerge during adolescence but rather gradually develop over the course of childhood and adolescence (Diamond & Savin-Williams, 2009). What is unique to the experience of children and adolescents with same-sex attractions, versus those with opposite-sex attractions, is the existence of heterosexism

and homophobia that results in strong prejudices against gay, lesbian, and bisexual identifying individuals. This strong bias usually delays the emergence of same-sex romantic experiences in gay, lesbian, bisexual, or questioning adolescents.

According to data from the National Survey of Family Growth (Chandra, Mosher, Copen, & Sionean, 2011), approximately 9% of adolescents report same-sex sexual experiences, and adolescents who identify as lesbian, gay, or bisexual experience their first same-sex sexual encounters from ages 17 for boys and 19 for girls (Grov, Bimbi, Nanin, & Parsons, 2006), with girls tending to have their first experiences within the contexts of romantic relationships, whereas boys tended to report first experiences with passing acquaintances (Savin-Williams, 2007). It is important to note that these youth almost always experience intense pressure to date members of the opposite sex during adolescence, which accounts for the fact that over 50% of gay men and over 80% of lesbian women reported opposite-sex dating experiences during adolescence (Diamond & Savin-Williams, 2009).

Heterosexual adolescents, however, have fewer societal pressures that would result in delaying one's quest to find a boyfriend or girlfriend. In fact, for many adolescents there is a status that comes with being in a dating relationship (Berk, 2009), which results in a pressure to date sooner rather than later. An analysis of dating behavior revealed that by age 12, about 25% of heterosexual adolescents say that they have been involved in a romantic relationship within the past 18 months. By age 18, that number jumps to 75% (Carver, Joyner, & Udry, 2003). While in some instances, especially in early adolescence, romantic relationships are short-lived, on average adolescents report dating the same person for approximately two years (Carver et al., 2003).

Casual Sexual Arrangements

In many cases, romantic relationships provide adolescents with companionship, affection, support, emotional intimacy, and physical intimacy. However, results are mixed in terms of whether dating relationships are the primary context in which adolescents explore sexual intimacy. For example, findings from the ADDHealth study show that among 15- to 18-year-olds who report any type of sexual activity, 35% of them had more than one sexual partner (Kelley, Borawski, Flocke, & Keen, 2003). Furthermore, research suggests that increasing percentages of adolescents are pursuing sexual relationships outside of conventional dating relationships. Two examples of these arrangements—*hooking up* and *friends with benefits*—appear to be increasingly popular (Vrangalova & Savin-Williams, 2008).

Manning, Giordano, and Longmore (2006) studied adolescents who reported hooking up to find out more about who they hooked up with and what their expectations were around this type of activity. They find that adolescents having sex outside of the dating context are choosing partners who are friends or ex-girlfriends and/or ex-boyfriends. Moreover, one third of these nondating sexual partnerships are associated with hopes or expectations that the relationship will lead to more conventional dating relationships.

Grello, Welsh, Harper, and Dickson (2003) found that adolescents whose first sexual experiences took place in one of these more casual arrangements rather than with a formal boyfriend or girlfriend were more likely to report being depressed and more likely to abuse substances. However, the authors found that these tendencies were true for these adolescents both before and after they participated in

Romantic relationships can provide adolescents with companionship, affection, support, and opportunities to explore intimacy.

hooking up. This then creates a sort of chicken and egg question. Are kids who are depressed and abusing substances more likely to pursue casual sex, or is it the casual sex that makes them more depressed and likely to use substances? It is probably the case that both hypotheses could be supported. Interestingly, there is a gender difference we must point out. Girls who engage in casual sex tend to report the most depressive symptoms while boys tend to report the fewest depressive symptoms (Grello, Welsh, & Harper, 2006). Furthermore, girls who engaged in casual sex versus those who did not tended to also have lower self-esteem, feelings of guilt, and feeling out of control (Grello et al., 2003). No similar patterns emerged for boys.

However, a case could be made for the benefits of avoiding serious dating relationships as one explores sexuality. Manning et al. (2006) found that friends with benefits arrangements where the sexual partner is an existing friend allow youth to seek sexual gratification within familiar, stable, safe relationships that allow them to avoid the potential power differentials that might exist in heterosexual romantic relationships. In other words, it may be freeing on some level to be able to explore one's sexuality in a low-stakes environment. This possibility is further supported by research that has examined casual sexual behavior in adults, which, on average, has failed to find a consistent connection between casual sex and mental health problems (Weeden & Sabini, 2007). Thus, it is probably impossible to say whether hooking up and friends with benefits arrangements are good or bad as a rule. Like most things, it depends on the people who are participating in these arrangements.

Committed Partnerships

Regardless of one's preference for traditional dating relationships or nontraditional casual sex partnerships, at some point during early adulthood (e.g., after high school, during college), most young adults seek out a steady romantic partner, and while the average age for formal commitments is changing, many pursue marriage or monogamous partnerships. However, while it is still the norm that most people pursue marriage, what we know about marriage changes constantly.

For example, the age at which people who do marry will marry for the first time has changed over the past century. The age at which people marry for the first time is older than it has ever been (see Figure 8.1). According to a study conducted by the National Center for Family and Marriage Research (Cruz, 2013), the median age at first marriage is 27 for women and 29 for men. Furthermore, the percentage of people *not* in marital relationships (due to choice, divorce, or death) is increasing. For example, the proportion of people who have never married is increasing in comparison to past decades. In 2011, approximately 29% of women and 31% of men were never married. Also, the number of people who are divorced has increased. Fifteen percent of men and women are divorced as opposed to a single digit rate that existed in 1920.

There are some interesting demographic differences that exist, however, in marriage rates. For example, a woman's odds of never marrying increase with her level of formal education. This statistic may reflect the gender difference in men's and women's rates of higher education. Since the 1980s, women have been attending college at higher rates than men, and this has led to a demographic mismatch of people who want to marry others with the same educational level. Specifically, for college-educated people in their 30s, the dating pool has five women for every four men (Birger, 2015). This gender difference is even more pronounced for African Americans, which highlights a variety of cultural differences in marriage statistics. For example, more African American people are

©iStockphoto.com/tororo

The majority of people will seek out a committed relationship such as marriage.

Figure 8.1 U.S. Median Age at First Marriage, 1890 to 2014

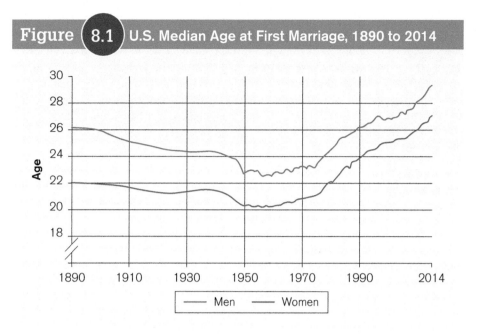

Source: U.S. Census Bureau.

unmarried, and more Asian American people are married as compared to the national average (Cruz, 2013). Hence, it is important to note that while romantic relationships are a critical part of many people's lives, there are a significant number of people in the United States who will never formalize those relationships or may choose to stay unmarried.

Healthy Intimate Relationships

Psychologists are among the many mental health professionals who have studied relationship satisfaction trying to determine whether there are "secrets" to a fulfilling, happy, intimate relationship. John Gottman is perhaps one of the most well-known researchers who has examined marital relationships, both successful and unsuccessful, for decades. Gottman's (1999) work has been very influential in the practice of couples counseling but also has applicability in other types of relationships, such as friendships.

Gottman has found that we can tell a lot about a relationship by looking at *interactive behavior* and what percentage of that behavior is characterized by positive and negative emotions (Gottman & Driver, 2005). On average, spouses are engaged in negative emotional states about 25% of the time with their partner. This statistic suggests that a certain amount of bickering, arguing, and being frustrated is typical of most relationships, and furthermore, it is not a sign of a bad relationship. However, what Gottman found to be more important than the frequency of negative emotion is how a partner responds to a negative feeling from his or her partner. How we respond to our spouse's negative emotionality is called **negative affect reciprocity**. When the negative emotionality increases to, say, a statement of frustration, an escalation of negativity in conflict situations can result, which can be harmful to the relationship. However, understanding how legitimate complaints can turn into dangerous escalations requires an examination of both partners' statements and behaviors.

For example, let's say that a partner has a negative complaint that is appropriate and necessary to share (e.g., "It did not feel good to me that you did not ask me anything about my day over dinner tonight"). In this case, the complaint is contained to one event and does not make any assumptions about the partner's intent or motivation in having failed to

How we respond to our partner's negative emotions can either repair the situation or be harmful to the relationship.

ask how the day went. A complaint turns into a **criticism** when it becomes a generalization about the partner (e.g., "You never ask me how my day was"). Not surprisingly, criticism is more likely to lead to a defensive response (e.g., "That's not true. I remember asking you how your day was last week") and, consequently, a negative escalation.

According to Gottman's (1999) research, there are four types of negative affect behavior that are damaging to relationships and highly predictive of relationship dissatisfaction: criticism, **defensiveness**, **stonewalling**, and **contempt**. We have described how complaints can be transformed into criticism by making generalizations about a person (e.g., "You never . . . ," "You always . . ."). Defensiveness, as was also discussed, is essentially a type of denial, often accompanied by some sarcasm, where one partner attempts to blame the other (e.g., "You make me say these things").

Stonewalling is where a person physically leaves a conversation or emotionally shuts down in the middle of a discussion. When someone storms away from a conflict with a significant other or hangs up the phone on that person out of anger, that is stonewalling. Gottman has found that stonewallers are more likely to be men about 85% of the time (Gottman & Driver, 2005). Finally, contempt is any behavior that belittles a partner or suggests to a spouse that one is better than he or she is. Examples of contemptuous behavior are mockery, insults, eye rolling, and other dismissive or disrespectful statements.

So what does Gottman's (1999) research find about successful relationships? Essentially, couples who can interrupt negative affect reciprocity and attempt to repair the interaction are much more likely to stay together and feel satisfied in their relationships. The antidote to negative emotionality appears to be positive emotionality. The presence of positive feelings, which can range from affectionate gestures such as a smile, a hug, or a kind word (e.g., "Look, I love you and don't want to waste time fighting with you about this"), to the use of humor, can be an effective repair mechanism if used sincerely. The key is knowing when a negative interaction needs to be stopped to prevent the escalation from getting any worse and then knowing what type of positive affect works in the relationship.

Gottman spends a great deal of time studying conflict in relationships, as opposed to other characteristics that predict satisfying marriages (e.g., how much compatibility there is in goals or interests). However, this may be the case because of the importance of conflict within relationships. In fact, Gottman has found that most conflict within relationships is not solvable. Approximately 65% of conflict involves what he calls **perpetual problems** (Gottman, 1999). Perpetual problems are problems that are chronic and reoccurring, such as how a couple may try to resolve the fact that they have different preferences for how clean the house should be. Establishing a dialogue about perpetual problems is key in stable marriages, and it should be dialogue that minimizes negative escalations. Perpetual problems are analogous to coping with a chronic illness in that the symptoms must be managed, the reoccurrences should be kept to a minimum, and partners should try not to provoke the condition. Gottman (1999) offered a helpful way to understand this: Choosing a partner is choosing a set of problems. In other words, no relationship is problem free, so it is important to figure out what kinds of problems can be tolerated and which ones cannot.

Probably what is most impressive about Gottman's decades of research is that there are different types of successful relationships. For example, there are some successful couples that would appear to be quite volatile to outsiders, where there is a high level of emotionality and passion and lots of disagreements. There are also successful couples that look very conflict-avoidant to others where there is infrequent disagreement, low emotionality, and perhaps a more low-keyed atmosphere in the relationship. It is not how these relationships appear that is predictive of success but rather what happens within these relationships, in particular, in response to negative affect that appears to be more important. See Adjustment in Practice: Myths About Good Relationships.

ADJUSTMENT IN PRACTICE
Myths About Good Relationships

Gottman (1999; Gottman, Driver, & Tabares, 2002) has identified some myths of good relationships that may be popularly accepted but in reality are not supported by any evidence. Determine which of these relationship statements are true and which are a myth.

1. Active listening is essential to a healthy marriage.

2. Anger is dangerous in a marriage.

3. Quid pro quo (giving to get) is an essential ingredient of a healthy marriage.

4. Noncontingent positivity (i.e., the opposite of quid pro quo) is an important ingredient of a happy marriage.

5. Harmonious marriages cannot include bickering or conflict avoidance.

6. Problem-solving skills are critical elements of a good marriage.

7. Clarity of communication is an important predictor of good relationships.

8. Similarity between spouses is a predictor of stability.

Answers: All of these statements are relationship myths! None are true.

Reflection Questions

1. How many of these statements did you think were true? Do you recall where you learned this information?

2. Which of these do you think should not be a myth and why?

The evidence that we have about healthy intimate relationships has been used widely in couples counseling. It also reveals to us that love is complex. Robert Sternberg (2006) described three components of love that shift in emphasis as romantic relationships develop over time: intimacy, commitment, and passion. Intimacy, the emotional component of love, stems from the desire that human beings have to connect with others and to be truly understood. Commitment is the choice component of love, which leads people to want to maintain love and seek longevity in a relationship. Passion, which is the desire for sexual activity and romance, is the more physical component of love. It is also the "spark" that oftentimes attracts people to one another. Over time, passion declines in most relationships in favor of greater intimacy and commitment, but each is important to sustaining long-term relationships (Hendrick & Hendrick, 2002).

Sexuality in Intimate Relationships

How important is sex in a relationship? This is likely to be a question that depends on who is being asked, at what age the question is being asked, and how long one has been in a relationship. Earlier in this chapter we discussed the exploratory nature of sex in

Figure 8.2 Sternberg's Triangular Theory of Love

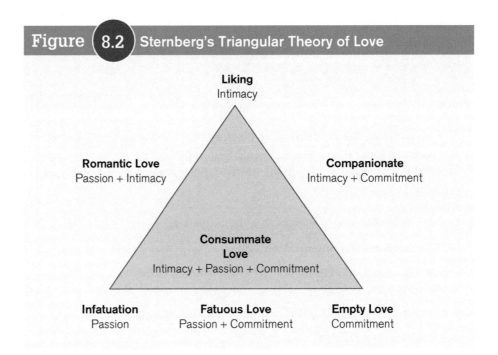

relationships early in life. When we are focused on long-term, monogamous relationships such as life partnerships or marriages, the meaning of sex changes over the course of the relationship.

In general, it seems to be the case that sexual problems are more significantly related to overall relationship dissatisfaction than is having a positive sex life related to relationship satisfaction. Healthy sexuality is thought to contribute 15% to 20% to marital satisfaction (McCarthy, 2002)—probably because of the role it plays in the relationship (e.g., shared pleasure, intimacy reinforcer, stress reducer). However, when sex is a problem, it plays a more inordinately powerful role in impacting the satisfaction one feels with the relationship in general (i.e., bad sex plays a more powerful negative role than good sex plays a positive role).

The overall frequency of sexual activity tends to decline among married couples during middle adulthood, but it does not tend to be a dramatic change. In other words, couples who had frequent sex in early adulthood are much more likely to continue to do so in middle adulthood (Walsh & Berman, 2004). However, it is not only frequency of sex that changes during adulthood. The intensity of sexual responses due to biological changes in our bodies occurs as well. For example, it takes both men and women longer to get aroused and to have orgasms. However, despite these facts, most married people who are over the age of 50 report that their sex life is still an important part of their relationship and that they find ways to overcome any difficulties that either partner may have (Gott & Hinchliff, 2003).

Gay and Lesbian Relationships

Many of the ideas presented by Gottman are applicable to relationships in general whether they are marriages, lifelong partnerships, dating relationships, or familial relationships (Gottman et al., 2003). The field has less information about the unique challenges that gay and lesbian couples face, because for many decades, researchers failed to include gay and lesbian couples in their studies. However, there are scholars who have explored these relationships, and as a result, more information is available on the ways that gay and lesbian relationships are both like and unlike other intimate relationships.

It is important to preface our discussion with a statement: Being gay or lesbian and in a same sex-relationship is not a risk factor. Living in a homophobic society is a risk factor, however. Homophobia is the belief that enduring love relationships between same-sex partners are wrong or impossible to achieve (Green & Mitchell, 2002). When a gay or lesbian person internalizes homophobic beliefs, an unconscious sabotage of the relationship can occur. Living under such conditions results in minority stress (e.g., fear of discovery, discrimination; DiPlacido, 1998). These fears are realistic ones for many people and can result in partners concealing their relationship status. Examples of this may be not expressing affection in public, self-monitoring statements in the workplace (e.g., never saying whether your partner is male or female, removing pronouns), or not having pictures of your partner in your office.

Gay and lesbian couples may experience unique stressors compared to straight couples, but in most ways, the characteristics of healthy relationships are similar.

Gay and lesbian individuals are more likely to live in a world that is not as supportive of their relationships, despite the fact that gay and lesbian marriage is legal in every state, but in terms of the relationships themselves, researchers are interested in determining if there are differences between homosexual versus heterosexual relationships. What is unique about LGBT (lesbian, gay, bisexual, and transgender) couples? Spitalnick and McNair (2005) addressed this question and came up with the following list:

1. Sex roles in the relationship are much more flexible in same-sex couples. Without normative traditions about "who does what," lesbian and gay couples are freer to invent their own relational configurations. But there are also complexities that come from dual gender role competition. For example, both women might try to please each other too much and fail to communicate their own needs, neither man will relocate for the other's job offer, men act competitively with one another in work domains, or a woman who makes more money than her partner may disempower herself in other ways in the relationship.

2. There is a lack of role models for same-sex couples, which means fewer opportunities to see "good relationships" as well as bad ones. Most lesbians and gay men are raised by heterosexual parents who do not share their minority status, do not face the same discrimination, cannot recount the history of the gay community, and would not be able to prepare their children to deal with homophobia even if they knew their child's sexual orientation. In contrast to other minority families, parents of gays and lesbians do not necessarily side with their children against society and in extreme cases may sympathize with or become the oppressors. Thus, it is very difficult for even the most accepting heterosexual parent to identify with the experience of their child.

3. There is lack of clarity about how to define couplehood to themselves and others. Ambiguous commitment can exist in some same-sex couples because prior to 2015 there was no formal courtship or engagement process for gay and lesbian couples, and sometimes couples encounter a lack of acceptance by one's family. Also, this ambiguity may be reinforced from family members who treat their son's or daughter's partner as a "friend of the family" rather than a family member.

4. There may be coming out issues for the couple (and differences in perceptions of safety in doing so). It is important not to overemphasize being out as a sign of self-acceptance because in many communities being open with one's sexual orientation may have negative consequences. Additionally, studies suggest that being out to one's family of origin is not related to relationship satisfaction, staying together as a couple, or any other marker of relationship happiness (Green, Bettinger, & Zacks, 1996).

Thus, while there are some distinct differences between heterosexual and homosexual romantic relationships, it is probably fair to say that there are also a great number of similarities. In the next section, we explore some of the more serious problems that exist in some relationships, both gay and straight in nature.

Intimacy Problems

Romantic relationships are dynamic and subject to highs and lows. There are, however, some problems that are challenging to resolve and often threaten the viability of the relationship. In this next section, we will review several of these problems.

Infidelity

Infidelity is viewed as one of the most damaging problems that couples encounter and a problem that can be difficult to treat (Atkins, Yi, Baucom, & Christensen, 2005). Many behaviors are considered under the umbrella of infidelity. Glass (2002) defined extramarital involvement as sexual intimacies, with or without intercourse, and may or may not include emotional involvement. Additionally, she identified subtypes of infidelity: primarily sexual, primarily emotional, and combined sexual–emotional affairs.

Affairs differ from friendships in that they entail a level of emotional intimacy combined with secrecy and sexual chemistry. Many therapists view infidelity as a trauma that creates a loss of innocence in a relationship that was considered loving and safe (DiBlasio, 2000). For many couples who want to remain in their relationship following an infidelity, some type of therapy or repair work is required. We will discuss some potentially necessary elements of healing from infidelity later in this section.

Infidelity may be more common than we assume it to be. Atkins et al. (2005) estimated that 20% to 25% of Americans report at least one extramarital sexual encounter during their lives. It is a common issue for couples who seek out couples counseling. Approximately 30% of couples initiate therapy because of an affair, and an additional 30% disclose an affair during therapy (Glass, 2002). Glass (2002) also noted that of couples who seek therapy because of an affair, 45% of husbands and 23% of wives were the adulterers. While men may be more frequently involved in affairs, there are also important gender differences in the circumstances that surround situations of infidelity (Glass, 2002). Women tend to become involved in affairs for different reasons than men—primarily emotional ones versus sexual ones—and the incidence of women being unfaithful in their relationships has risen dramatically over the past decades due to opportunities increasing in particular as more and more women have full-time employment. This may be because the workplace has become the most common context for affairs. Finally, regarding gender differences, women are also more likely to report being in love with their extramarital partners than are men.

Many therapists argue that experiencing infidelity is a trauma and recovery requires extensive work.

Online Cheating Versus Off-Line Cheating

Psychologists have been studying how social media and changes in the technology landscape have affected intimate relationships. It is tempting to think that searching for sex behind the safety of a computer or smartphone screen might increase the number of people tempted to cheat on their partners. However, research suggests that there are no differences between the number of people who are likely to cheat in online forums and those who are likely to cheat in real life or off-line situations (Wysocki & Childers, 2011).

In their study, Wysocki and Childers (2011) also found that men and women were equally likely to cheat online and in real life when in a serious relationship. The only individual differences found in this study were that women were more likely to use sexting in their relationship pursuits and that older men were more likely to cheat in real life than were younger males. They also found that people who considered having affairs had a high degree of anxiety about getting caught, whether online or off-line.

Perhaps it is the case that online vehicles like chat rooms create new opportunities for exploring possible extramarital relationships or affairs that were once limited to meeting people in bars or other social settings. A factor that seems to impact the perception of harm associated with online hookups is whether or not the cyberrelationship becomes physical in nature. Whitty (2003), for example, found that online relationships were considered betrayals by men if their female partners ultimately became physically involved with their cybermates but were less likely to consider an online relationship that was only emotional in nature to be a betrayal. Women, on the other hand, were more likely to see emotional infidelity as an act of betrayal. It is possible that men and women view the purpose and ultimate goals of online relationships differently and thus define online cheating in different ways. There is no doubt that the use of technology will be a permanent factor in how people navigate their relationships, both primary and elicit ones, for generations to come.

To Cheat or Not to Cheat

Why do people cheat? Addiction and feelings of entitlement are the two most common explanations (Glass, 2002). Infidelity addicts seek the passion and idealization of new relationships and in many ways are addicted to the excitement that comes from an affair in a way that makes their behavior look compulsive. On the other hand, entitlement-motivated affairs are not compulsive. Rather, the person takes advantage of an opportunity but is not driven to seek out such opportunities. Thus, these individuals seek affairs because the opportunity presented itself and they decided to capitalize on it. Hence, someone who is compulsive about affairs may end up having multiple infidelities or have chronic problems with monogamous relationships, whereas a person who has affairs based on a feeling of entitlement may be less ritualistic about infidelities.

Recovery of trust is the key to healing after an affair (DiBlasio, 2000; Glass, 2002). It is impaired by staggering disclosure of significant facts (e.g., how many affairs, with whom, when; Glass, 2002). Thus, honesty about the extent of the situation should be encouraged from the beginning. However, discussion of explicit details should be deferred until significant progress has been made in repairing the loss of trust in the relationship. Many couples turn to counseling when dealing with the aftermath of an affair. There have been recommendations made about what elements are necessary to address in recovering from infidelity. According to Glass (2002), therapy must involve the following:

1. Establishing safety and hope (stop and share openly; information that is obtained via interrogation or detective work erodes trust). Recovery cannot truly begin until the extramarital relationship is no longer a threat.

2. Fostering care and goodwill (although relapses in the form of distancing and conflict are common after particularly loving interactions).

3. Managing affect and posttraumatic symptoms. Obsessive rumination will decrease with the eventual disclosure of all the details of the affair (the betrayed partner is encouraged to write down all questions and bring them to therapy to be used in the next stage; journaling is also helpful; flashbacks will occur for a prolonged period and are triggered by many things; hypervigilance will decrease as trust and security increase).

4. Telling the story of the affair. This is essential. It must account for all the secrets, unanswered questions, and contrasting interpretations. Early on, this may be more adversarial, but it will gradually shift to a more neutral process. The therapist takes an active role and often asks most of the questions about the affair or at least helps the process begin.

5. Understanding the vulnerabilities. This is important and cannot become a blame game. Although marital dissatisfaction contributes to affairs, personal and moral values act as deterrents in couples that remain unhappy but faithful. Rather, transgenerational patterns of infidelity, social norms, and cultural double standards should be accounted for.

6. Mastering meaning and terminating successfully. This stage incorporates the lessons learned and establishes the meaning of the affair. Rituals of forgiveness and recommitment can be useful here. A common request is for the involved partner to write a letter to the affair partner that makes it clear that the decision to stay in the marriage is by choice and based on love, not duty.

It is important not to give up prematurely for couples who are struggling to recover from infidelity. It takes months and sometimes years for the healing process to be complete (DiBlasio, 2000). Staying together is not necessarily a sign of successful healing and recovery, nor is separation a sign of failure. Recovery is also most commonly a series of steps forward and backward on an uphill slope. Not every relationship can survive the betrayal of trust that comes from an affair. Predictors of failure include a partner who is unwilling to end the affair, the existence of combined (emotional and sexual) type affairs, situations where both partners are unfaithful, when men are involved in primarily emotional affairs, and when there is a low commitment to the marriage by one or both parties (Glass, 2002). Infidelity is a huge challenge to overcome for most couples, even when these signs are not present.

Relationship Violence

According to the Centers for Disease Control and Prevention (CDC; 2010a), **intimate partner violence (IPV)** describes physical, sexual, or psychological harm by a current or former partner or spouse. This type of violence can occur among heterosexual or same-sex couples and does not require sexual intimacy to be a part of the romantic relationship. The most common type of IPV that is experienced not only in the United States but around the world is violence toward women. While there are instances of men being abused by women, they are in the minority of total reported cases. For example, the Bureau of Justice reported that in 2007, IPV resulted in 2,340 deaths. Of these deaths, 70% were females and 30% were males (Bureau of Justice Statistics, 2009). Lifetime estimates are that 28% to 30% of heterosexual married couples experience physical aggression once in their marriage, and one out of eight husbands engage in physical aggression against his wife each year, statistics that have remained relatively stable over the past 15 years (Feldman & Moreno-John, 2014; Holtzworth-Munroe, Meehan, Rehman, & Marshall, 2002).

Some studies have found that women engage in the same level of physical aggression (mild, not battering) with their male partners (Archer, 2000; Machado & Matos, 2014) but are more likely to be psychologically abusive than physically abusive. However, male-perpetrated violence typically has more severe consequences because of the more common size differential between men and women (i.e., they are much more likely to injure their partners).

Despite the fact that the vast majority of studies have examined women victims and male perpetrators of IPV, statistics reveal that men who have sex with men, as well as bisexual and lesbian women, should be included in research efforts. For example, Stults et al. (2015) surveyed a sample of men who have sex with men about their IPV experiences and found that 39% reported IPV victimization, 31% reported perpetration, and 25% reported mutual IPV. Their definition of IPV included physical, sexual, and emotional types of abuse. This study also found that various types of gay-related stigma were associated with being victimized by and perpetrating IPV. In analyzing studies conducted with self-identified lesbians, Badenes-Ribera, Frias-Navarro, Bonilla-Campos, Pons-Salvador, and Monterde-Bort (2015) concluded that the average rate of IPV victimization over one's lifetime was 48%, and the prevalence of IPV in a current relationship was 15%. They

Not all fighting becomes physical, but 28% to 30% of heterosexual married couples deal with violence in their relationship.

further found that the prevalence of psychological or emotional violence over one's lifetime was 43%, and the prevalence of physical IPV over one's lifetime was 18%.

In terms of consequences to individuals who are survivors of IPV, there are some obvious physical costs of being in a relationship with an abusive partner (e.g., bruises, broken bones, concussions; Breiding, Black, & Ryan, 2008). However, research has also revealed that there are significant health consequences of IPV to the endocrine and immune systems, including the emergence of conditions like fibromyalgia, irritable bowel syndrome, gynecological disorders, central nervous system disorders, gastrointestinal disorders, and heart and/or circulatory conditions (Crofford, 2007; Leserman & Drossman, 2007).

Equally upsetting to the physical and health consequences of IPV are the emotional and psychological consequences of IPV. The emotional costs of being involved in a violent relationship include reduced self-esteem, feelings of helplessness, depression, fear, and psychological numbing (Moradi & Yoder, 2011). While some of the aforementioned physical and health consequences either heal in time or can be medically treated, the extent to which a survivor of IPV ever completely recovers from the psychological wounds varies from person to person. Additionally, for children who are raised in a home where a parent is being abused, the impact of such role modeling can greatly increase the likelihood that they will be in an abusive relationship as an adult (Olds, 2010). Thus, preventing incidents of IPV is of paramount importance to the entire family.

In the psychological literature, there are typically two types of IPV: characterological violence (severe, persistent violence used as a means of inducing fear) and situational violence (mutual, low-level violence that may occur as a means of conflict management and is more bidirectional in nature; Friend, Cleary Bradley, Thatcher, & Gottman, 2011). While more couples may experience the second kind of violence when violence is present, it is important to note that more mild physical aggression (e.g., pushing, throwing objects) can escalate into the first type, which may have more life-threatening consequences. Thus, *any* and *all* types of reported violence and aggression in a relationship must be taken seriously.

IPV is a problem that is difficult to change. Among spouses in their first year of marriage, 60% to 76% of those who were violent in their first year went on to be violent in second and third years (Babcock, Green, & Robie, 2004; Holtzworth-Munroe et al., 2002). This statistic increases to 86% for severely violent men. The effects of violence in a relationship are quite literally a matter of life and death in some situations, but even in nonlethal cases, the physical and psychological damage done is very serious for battered women and their children.

Many studies (see Holtzworth-Munroe et al., 2002) have revealed the following predictors of violent behavior in partners: age (less than 30); socioeconomic status (SES; lower); exposure to violence in the home as a child; head injury (frontal lobe); misattributions of partners behavior; belief in aggression as a means of problem solving; stressful life events; association with violent peers; alcohol use; jealousy; and psychological problems such as depression, anxiety, bipolar disorder, and borderline or antisocial personality disorder. In their study of men who have sex with men, Stults et al. (2015) found that childhood trauma and the degree of public gay-related stigma were associated with IPV perpetration. Thus, it may be for gay and bisexual men, the stress and discrimination associated with being gay or bisexual add an extra dimension to understanding aggressive impulses and behaviors.

IPV is difficult to detect in most cases because of the shame associated with revealing its existence. For example, in counseling, only 6% of women report having experienced violence (Lawson, 2003; O'Leary, Vivian, & Malone, 1992). However, if a checklist is used in which a therapist asks about specific behaviors such as having been pushed or shoved, 53% report having experienced violence.

Therapeutically, violence is treated typically in couples counseling or in gender-specific individual treatment (GSIT; e.g., batterer treatment and survivor treatment; Holtzworth-Munroe et al., 2002). Women may also be referred to a shelter to develop individualized safety plans and to obtain community resources. Most GSITs are group based and are influenced by feminist and cognitive-behavioral techniques. Few studies have examined the benefit of either couples counseling treatment or GSIT or compared them, but in general, it appears that either treatment is better than no treatment, but neither is highly effective (recidivism rates are +70% in most studies; Holtzworth-Munroe et al., 2002). However, in couples therapy, the cessation of violence has to be a primary treatment goal, and it has to be the first topic (a no violence contract should be obtained). Anger management should be the focus until the couple is in a safer position to address other presenting problems.

IPV is not a normal part of most relationships, and it has no place in a loving relationship. Nonetheless, it can become a life or death aspect of dating or committed relationships, and it is important to review what is known about its prevalence and treatment.

Ending Relationships

Even in relationships between loving, well-intentioned people, there can come a time when one or both partners decide it is time to move on. Sometimes parting ways is necessary to an individual's own happiness, but ending relationships requires a great deal of adjustment even if it is something both parties desire. The statistics on divorce among U.S. couples have remained largely steady in the past few decades, with 45% of all marriages ending most typically within the first seven years (U.S. Census Bureau, 2013; see Researching Adjustment: Predictors of Divorce). Because divorce is so common, children of divorced parents often struggle in their own relationships as adults—typically because of the ripple effect that divorce can have on the entire family. Not only is separation from a parent—the most obvious consequence of divorce—difficult for children to adjust to, but typically divorce can change the financial stability of the family as well (Clark-Stewart & Brentano, 2006). The impact of parents' divorce on children appears to elevate the risk of divorce for two succeeding generations (Amato & Cheadle, 2005). Thus, given how divorce impacts all members of a family, it may not be a surprise that history finds a way to repeat itself in many cases, thus keeping the divorce rate relatively stable.

RESEARCHING ADJUSTMENT
Predictors of Divorce

Given that divorce has a series of negative effects on not just the spouses but the entire family, researchers such as Gottman (1999) have tried to identify the most important factors in predicting which couples stay married versus get divorced. In fact, six predictors have been identified as being strong indications of a relationship that is not destined for eternity.

1. Harsh "start-ups" or approaching conflictual conversations with accusations or criticism (e.g., "You are so thoughtless" instead of " "Even though I know you didn't mean to upset me, I feel disappointed that you forgot to make a reservation for dinner to celebrate my birthday")

2. Common appearances of the "Four Horsemen of the Apocalypse" or the omnipresence of defensiveness, criticism, contempt, and stonewalling

3. Emotional shutdowns and detachment that flood the other partner with negativity

4. Frequent physiological states incompatible with conflict resolution such as increased blood pressure or heart rate, which are often connected with being flooded with negativity

5. Failed attempts to repair conflict. An inability to "start over" in the aftermath of fights is a very strong predictor of divorce. For example, saying to your partner, "I know that things got out of hand, and I said things that I didn't mean. I feel badly and would like to try and start over. I know I can do better this time" would likely help to repair conflict in the relationship.

6. Bad memories of times past and present. Even when couples go through rough patches, they can often reflect back on better times, in particular, early in the relationship. When couples have an inability to remember anything good, this is a sign that they may be at the end of the road of their relationship.

Reflection Questions

1. Of these six signs of divorce, which do you think are most amenable to change?

2. What are some ways that partners can develop the skills that help their marriages last in relationships they have earlier in life (e.g., family relationships, friendships)?

While a lot of research has been directed at tracking the effects of divorce on children, for the purposes of this chapter, we will explore how breakups impact the main players, the partners, regardless of whether they were married or not. What are the most important consequences of breakups and divorce for the participants? Some answers to this question vary based on the gender of the partners, while others are more universally applicable.

The end of a relationship, especially one that has been relatively long term in nature, results in a disruption in social relationships and, for many people, an increase in symptoms of anxiety, depression, and sometimes impulsive behavior (Amato, 2000). For example, imagine that you have been in a serious long-term relationship with someone for several years. You may have merged many social circles and enjoyed many common friends. When the relationship ends, it may require a reorganizing of those social relationships and a loss of friends and acquaintances could be a consequence of the breakup. The loss of social support received from both the romantic partner and the friends that are no longer part of one's social circle could be part of the reason people have such strong emotional reactions to breakups. The good news is that these reactions are often temporary, and even in cases where the breakup is a divorce, the symptoms rarely last more than 2 years (Berk, 2014b).

While intuitively it may seem that psychological responses are the most common consequences of breakups, there may be more to the story. There are some indications that our bodies may experience romantic or emotional pain in a similar way to physical pain (Eisenberger, 2012; Eisenberger, Lieberman, & Williams, 2003; Kross, Berman, Mischel, Smith, & Wager, 2011). For example, Kross et al. (2011) conducted a study where they hooked up their participants to a brain imaging machine and had them complete two tasks. One task involved looking at pictures of their ex-romantic partners while thinking about the breakup, then viewing pictures of a good friend. The other task was completely physical in nature and involved receiving a very hot stimulation on their forearms, then receiving another stimulation that was just warm. The brain imaging revealed a finding that was similar to past studies: brain activity in areas associated with emotional pain increased during both of the more intense tasks (seeing the "ex" and feeling the strong heat). But activity in areas of the brain linked with physical pain also increased during these tasks. The results suggested that social and physical pain have more in common than merely causing distress: They share sensory brain regions too.

Thus, broken hearts may actually "hurt" us in more ways than one. The good news is that while severed relationships can do damage, new or renewed relationships can be quite healing. Finding a new partner has been found to bring the greatest degree of life satisfaction to adults who experienced divorce (Forste & Heaton, 2004), in particular for men. Women appear to bounce back from breakups better than men, with some exceptions (Berk, 2014b), and the reason for this may be similar to the reason that women adjust better to becoming widows than do men (which is discussed in Chapter 12). Women may be better able to access support in times of crisis than do men and often experience less disruption in their day-to-day functioning than men, who in traditional gender-role conforming, heterosexual relationships often depend on their female partners to manage their daily rituals (Berk, 2014b).

With respect to physical pain, relationships have a similar healing quality. Master et al. (2009) did an experiment with women who had been in relationships for at least 6 months and brought them into the lab with their romantic partner. They determined each woman's pain threshold, then subjected her to heat stimulations. Half of the stimulations were given at the woman's threshold pain level; half were given one degree higher. Meanwhile, the women took part in a series of tasks to see what might reduce their perceptions of the pain. Some tasks involved direct contact (e.g., holding their partner's hand, a stranger's hand, or an object), while other tasks involved visual contact (e.g., viewing their partner's photo, a stranger's photo, or an object). Results indicated that contact involving a romantic partner—both direct and visual—led to significantly lower pain ratings compared to the other tasks. In fact, looking at a partner's picture led to slightly lower pain ratings than actually holding his hand. This study provides compelling evidence that our emotional and physical experiences of pain may be interconnected in important ways.

Relationship Maintenance

When owning a car, there are certain actions that must be done routinely if it is to function properly. For example, every several thousand miles, an oil change is due. Tire pressure must be checked and adjusted to avoid blowouts and flats. Fluids must be refilled, tires should be rotated, and the list goes on and on. While these automotive maintenance behaviors are frequently time consuming and require a certain level of planning to make sure they happen, they are critical to the health of the car. Similarly, researchers have found that the implementation of maintenance behaviors in our romantic relationships yields similar results.

Researchers began writing about relationship maintenance behaviors in the 1980s, and in 1991, Stafford and Canary identified seven dimensions of relationship maintenance behavior that were predictive of relationship satisfaction in young adults (see Table 8.1). The first is called positivity, and it refers to behaviors that bring about pleasant experiences. For example, one or both partners may really enjoy horror movies or amusement parks. Making plans to engage in either of those activities would be considered an injection of positivity in the relationship. While some couples are very good at scheduling "fun," it is not hard to imagine that at certain points of time—for example, during a hectic semester—fun experiences as a couple may not happen as readily as they should.

The next relationship maintenance behavior identified by Stafford (2011) is called self-disclosure. Self-disclosure behaviors involve sharing one's feelings and experiences and sometimes require a willingness to be vulnerable. For example, it might be relatively easy to share some emotions, in particular positive emotions, or to talk about lower-stakes events such as how we feel about a friend's decision to study abroad for a year. Yet it may be increasingly more difficult to share emotions like sadness or disappointment or to disclose past events that were painful to experience. In fact, disclosing some very personal information about who we are can feel risky. Social penetration theory (Altman & Taylor, 1973) suggests that it is actually taking these kinds of risks that bonds us closer to people.

Another maintenance behavior identified by Stafford and Canary (1991) is relationship talks. Relationship talks involve active processing of the relationship and should occur routinely. These types of talks can be thought of as "check-ins" where we ask our partner questions such as the following: "How do you think we are doing right now?" or "How are you feeling about this relationship?" or "Is there anything that is bothering you about our relationship at the moment?" While some people might avoid such conversations because of fear that there might be a complaint registered in response to the

Table 8.1 Relationship Maintenance Behaviors

Positivity: Planning activities that bring you and your partner happiness

Self-disclosure: Sharing your thoughts and feelings; a willingness to be vulnerable

Relationship talks: Checking in with your partner to see if everything is okay

Assuring behavior: Reminding your partner how much you value him or her

Networking: Connecting with the significant others (i.e., family, friends) in your lives

Understanding: Using words and actions that convey your empathy and compassion for what your partner is experiencing

Task behavior: Taking the time to be helpful in tangible ways to your partner questions, it is actually a very effective way to show a partner that we care about the relationship and value his or her opinions. It also is a great way to remind each other that regular communication about the relationship itself is welcome.

The fourth relationship maintenance behavior is called **assuring behavior**. Assurances can be issued as reminders of how we see and value our partner. Assurances that we commonly use are expressions of love and affection. They can also be moments where we share appreciation of or commitment to the relationship such as by saying, "I am so lucky to have you in my life. Your support means everything to me." While in long-term relationships, we might wish to take a lot of these sentiments for granted, putting in the extra effort to verbalize these thoughts on a regular basis can be much appreciated and serve as a powerful way to tend to the fire of a relationship.

The fifth relationship maintenance behavior is called **networking**, where partners interact with other important relationships they have developed. This could include making sure that they make time to do things with other couples that they have befriended. It would also include behaviors that keep them connected to the important family members in each other's lives. Attending holiday rituals of our partner's family or including our partner on a trip home for the weekend from college are examples of networking. These behaviors not only help our partners know the many contexts of our lives but they are good ways to promote support for the relationship itself and to make public statements about being together.

The sixth relationship maintenance behavior (Stafford, 2011) is **understanding behaviors** or behaviors that demonstrate to our partner that we understand what is happening in their lives, can empathize with what he or she may need, and can cooperate to help meet changing needs. For example, let's say that your partner has just received a call from home that his grandmother is ill. You know that your partner is very close to his grandmother and that the news is very upsetting. You also know that your partner oftentimes needs some alone time to process difficult information before he is able to talk about how he feels or what he needs. Hence, an example of understanding behavior in this scenario would be to say to your partner, "I am so very sorry to hear this news. I want to give you some time to wrap your head around this but as soon as you are ready to talk or figure out next steps, I am here."

The final relationship maintenance behavior identified by Stafford (2011) is called **task behavior**. Task behavior refers to actions that assist our partner with obligations in their lives. These types of behaviors can range from accompanying our partner to an event that she really does not want to attend but is obligated to make an appearance or helping to get the apartment ready for an impromptu visit by the parents as well as more substantial offerings of help like packing up to go home for the summer. These kinds of behaviors demonstrate to our partner an "I've got your back" mentality that can foster interdependence and mutual reliability.

As we mentioned previously, the regular use of relationship maintenance behaviors is highly predictive of relationship satisfaction in both dating college student couples and married spouses (Stafford, 2011). Women tend to use more relationship maintenance behavior strategies than men, but this might be attributed to the gender socialization that women sometimes receive to be attentive to the needs of others (Stafford, Dainton, & Haas, 2000). It seems clear that if we wish to participate in well-adjusted, problem-free relationships, being proactive in the area of relationship maintenance behaviors is important.

Conclusion

In this chapter, we explored many facets of romantic relationships. We established that romantic feelings and a curiosity about sex develop in childhood even though adolescence and early adulthood may be the times in life when we first act on our attractions. We also discussed the variety of relationship opportunities that we may encounter throughout our lifetimes ranging from friends with benefits to committed partnerships to formal marriages.

The field is full of valuable information about what makes relationships work and what to do when things go wrong. Gottman's (1999) groundbreaking research on the components of sound relationships has helped thousands of couples repair and strengthen their relationships. We also examined the role that sex plays in relationships across the life span.

We also know that issues such as infidelity and violence can infiltrate relationships, and our review of these issues contains suggestions for how couples can work through these difficulties. Even in relationships that are not characterized by significant traumas, many relationships do eventually end, and we have reviewed some of the science on the consequences of breakups. Finally, we examined ways to proactively protect relationships—namely relationship maintenance behaviors—and how practicing these behaviors can lead to greater relationship satisfaction. Relationships are an important part of the human experience. Being able to understand how to successfully nurture and, when necessary, repair relationships with significant others is a life skill that can benefit us all throughout our lifetime.

Review Questions

1. When in life do most people experience their first romantic attraction? At what age do you remember having your first romantic attraction?

2. What does research tell us about the reasons that people might sexually experiment with people who are friends?

3. Based on Gottman's work, what are the most important predictors of successful relationships?

4. Of the issues that create problems in relationships, which do you think are the most difficult to overcome and why?

5. What unique issues might gay and lesbian couples face?

6. Can technology have a negative impact on the quality of our romantic relationships, and if so, in what ways?

7. What are important steps for couples recovering from infidelity?

8. What do we know about trends in IPV among couples?

9. What are the ways that broken hearts hurt us? Have you experienced physical pain after a breakup?

10. What are three examples of relationship maintenance behavior?

Key Terms

assuring behavior 176
contempt 164
criticism 164
defensiveness 164
intimate partner violence (IPV) 170

negative affect reciprocity 163
networking 176
perpetual problems 164
positivity 175
relationship talks 175

self-disclosure 175
stonewalling 164
task behavior 176
understanding behaviors 176

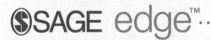

Sharpen your skills with SAGE edge at **edge.sagepub.com/moritsugu**

SAGE edge for students provides a personalized approach to help you accomplish your coursework goals in an easy-to-use learning environment.

Go to **edge.sagepub.com/moritsugu** for additional exercises and web resources. Select Chapter 8, Romance and Intimacy for chapter-specific resources.

School

Learning Objectives

1. Identify the social and emotional skills needed to participate in a school environment.

2. Identify individual and environmental factors that contribute to school success.

3. Discuss college success factors, challenges, and strategies.

4. Describe methods and advantages of mentoring in the context of school.

Jessie was the son of immigrant parents who moved him and his siblings to the United States as young children. Jessie's parents stayed in school in Mexico until they were in sixth grade, after which time they went to work to help contribute income to their poor families. Jessie knew his parents' greatest dream for him was to graduate high school and go on to college. They were thrilled when he applied and was accepted to the local community college. But as high school graduation loomed and Jessie thought about starting his first day at college, he was struck with a mixture of hope and fear. What if he wasn't smart enough to learn college-level material? What if he wasn't organized enough to keep up with his assignments? Would his parents be able to give him the support he needed while he continued to live at home with them? Would he find new friends at school and keep his friends from high school? His greatest fear was disappointing his parents who had sacrificed so much for him, but he felt that this extra pressure might actually make it harder for him to adjust to his new world.

. . . .

All I Really Need to Know I Learned in Kindergarten is a well-known book by Robert Fulghum (1993). Among the nuggets of wisdom he offered to readers is to share everything, play fair, don't hit people, put things back where you found them, clean up your own mess, don't take things that aren't yours, and say you're sorry when you hurt somebody. These basic guidelines for living are truly things that kids begin learning when they are in kindergarten. But how important are early childhood experiences to later school success? Are more academically accomplished people really better off than those with less education? If education is that important, then how do we determine the key ingredients to ensuring success? Can these ingredients be taught? Do all people have an equal chance at being academically successful? Students like Jessie may wonder if there are things he should be doing to ensure his future success.

The answers to these questions and more will be the focus of this chapter. First, we will examine what is known about the importance of school in the overall development of children. Next, we will look at personal and environmental factors that are related to school success. Then, we will look at what is known about differences in academic experiences based on gender, race or ethnicity, and socioeconomic status (SES). Finally, we will explore the college experience and what factors are related to success in college.

School's Importance in the Life of a Child

Most college students have spent the majority of their lives in school settings and needed to make adjustments to new schools, new teachers, and new expectations along the way. School plays a critical role in the life of children, which is why there are laws in most parts of the world requiring children to enroll in school. Children spend an enormous percentage of their daily life in school settings.

During the school year, children spend just as many waking hours in school as they do at home, and given the legal obligation that parents have to send their children to school, it becomes an unrivaled force in children's social, emotional, and intellectual development. School teaches us many skills that we use in every part of our lives as well as core information that we need to be literate, functioning adults. It could be argued that the academic and nonacademic things we learn in school are equally valuable. For example, learning how to listen to instructions, how to work with others in small groups, and how to wait one's turn are

$SAGE edge™

Get the edge on your studies.
edge.sagepub.com/moritsugu

Take a quiz to find out what you've learned. Watch videos that enhance chapter content. Explore web resources and additional exercises.

just as valuable as learning how to count and read. The two types of "knowledge" used in this example are actually related to one another. Kids who cannot listen to the teacher cannot take full advantage of opportunities to learn to read. Hence, much of the emphasis of early childhood education is on teaching fundamental social skills that are related to academic success.

Fundamentals of School Success in Preschool and Kindergarten

During the school year, children spend as much of their waking time in school as they do at home.

The majority of U.S. families enroll their children in preschool and/or kindergarten in an effort to make sure that they begin first grade as well prepared as possible. Preschools offer planned educational experiences aimed at enhancing overall development of 2- to 5-year-olds (Berk, 2014a). Some preschools are designed to be "child centered," while others emphasize academic training. Child-centered programs provide a variety of activities for children to use in their play, and children are allowed to select how they want to spend their time. More academically focused programs are directed by teachers to emphasize the formal learning of letters, numbers, words, and other academic tools. Both types of preschool programs have their advantages. But since parents often have to choose between one type of program or the other, it is important to understand if one produces better outcomes.

As counterintuitive as it may seem, it is actually child-centered programs that yield stronger academic results (Hart, Newell, & Olsen, 2003). To illustrate this, let's consider a well-known type of child-centered preschool, **Montessori preschool**. Montessori preschool, named after its creator, an Italian physician named Maria Montessori, is designed to promote exploration and discovery, child-selected activities, and the equal promotion of social development and cognitive development (Lillard, 2007). Controlled experiments, where kids are randomly assigned to 2 years of preschool in the Montessori program versus non–child-centered preschool programs, have revealed that Montessori "graduates" outperform their peers in literacy and math, problem solving, and cooperative play with classmates by age 5 (Lillard & Else-Quest, 2006). Follow-up studies find that these results last into elementary school and are most pronounced for kids from low-income families (Hart et al., 2003).

Based on these studies, it appears that play is the key to helping kids prepare for formal school environments. However, it is important to qualify this conclusion by saying that not all play is equal. The play that kids are exposed to in Montessori and other child-centered types of preschool environments is not random. Rather, children are provided with developmentally appropriate stimulation, they are involved with other children, and adults prompt the children in ways that help them learn critical social skills. In summary, sustained play, rich with stimulating materials and activities, that involves other children and adult supervision is critical to helping develop children's **self-regulation** (Whitebread, Coltman, Jameson, & Lander, 2009). Self-regulation describes the skills that allow us to inhibit our impulses and redirect our attention so that we don't get distracted and off task. It involves a number of cognitive skills that are critical to learning: namely, being able to sustain attention, to exercise impulse control, and to delay gratification.

Let's consider an example of how these skills are helpful to young children in a classroom setting. Imagine a classroom filled with 20 bubbly, energetic first graders. They are attending their first day of school with a new teacher in a new environment. Children in that situation have a lot to learn quickly. They have to learn a new routine, which classroom is theirs, where to put their coat and book bag, which desk to sit in, and the names of their new classmates. They have to learn what time lunch will be and the process for being escorted to the cafeteria. If a first-grade teacher has students who lack self-regulation skills, she will probably face a greater degree of chaos on that first day. Children without good self-regulation skills will likely burst out expressions of confusion or frustration with not getting to sit where they want. They may push to the front of the lunch line because they are impatient. They may forget to raise their hand if they have a question to ask, and they may be less likely to share materials with their peers, which may make them less attractive classmates. All of these potential frustrations will also make it more difficult for these kids to absorb what is being taught and to block out distractions during instruction time. Hence, these kids will be less equipped for formal learning and may begin to have early behavioral problems that follow them as they progress through school.

This example should make us reconsider the building blocks of learning. While it is easy to understand the value of coming to school ready to learn to read or being familiar with actual academic material, such as knowing numbers, letters, colors, and shapes, it is perhaps more important to begin school with the social and emotional skills necessary to properly participate in a school environment. These different types of building blocks are thought to be so fundamental to the long-term academic success of children that the U.S. government started a program called Head Start in the 1960s to create opportunities for low-income children whose parents may not be able to afford preschool. You can read more about Head Start in Adjustment in Practice: Head Start.

ADJUSTMENT IN PRACTICE
Head Start

In the 1960s, the U.S. government started a program that was intended to help young children from poor families be better prepared for school. For these kids, unlike their middle- and upper-class counterparts, there was more involvement in making that happen than just providing free preschool programs. Thus, Head Start was created as part of the War on Poverty. Head Start began in 1965 by providing poor children with 1 or 2 years of no-cost preschool along with health services (Head Start Bureau, 2008). In addition to providing preschool and health care, parents of children in Head Start received parenting classes and participated in the program, sometimes by being on planning committees or by being in the classrooms with the children. Head Start was then more than just a preschool program—it was designed to care for the whole child and the child's parents by emphasizing parental involvement in the education of their child.

Many researchers have examined the effectiveness of Head Start over the years, and while there have been some criticisms of the program, most studies have found that compared to low-income children who did not receive high-quality preschool education, Head Start kids have greater academic skills and, in the long-term, have higher rates of high school graduation, college enrollment, and lower rates of social problems such as juvenile delinquency or drug abuse as young adults (Garces, Thomas, & Currie, 2000; Love, Tarullo, Raikes, & Chazan-Cohen, 2006; Mashburn, 2008).

In terms of criticism, one consistent finding in most of the research that has been conducted is that the educational benefits in terms of achievement test scores of Head Start kids dissolve over time (Berk, 2014a). However, after children graduate from Head Start programs, they often begin school in low-income neighborhoods that often lack the resources, both in school and in the community, that middle- and upper-class neighborhoods have. It is likely that these factors explain the finding that the initial gains that kids receive from participating in Head Start don't translate into lasting academic superiority in the short run (Brooks-Gunn, 2003). Nonetheless, when factoring such things as higher high school graduation rates, college enrollment, and less tendency to be involved in the legal system (Garces et al., 2000), there are obvious benefits to the program. Many advocates of Head Start have pointed out the fact that it is a cost-effective program when compared to the alternative costs of special education, incarceration, or support of unemployed adults (Heckman & Masterov, 2004).

Reflection Questions

1. Do you think that Head Start is accomplishing its goals?

2. What are other types of resources that may be tied to improving school readiness in low-income children?

Individual and Environmental Factors Related to Academic Success

Moving away from preschool and considering kids' formal educational experiences, there is great interest in knowing what the ingredients of a successful education might be. Educational researchers have studied the personal and environmental factors that are related to school success for decades. A good way to define personal factors is to think about the individual qualities or skills that kids bring to the school environment. For example, if a person has good listening skills and is an organized person, those qualities will help him or her whether he or she is a third grader or a sophomore in college. However, possessing particular individual abilities might not be enough for some students to be successful.

Environmental factors are those qualities or characteristics of the school setting that are related to academic success. For example, the effectiveness of an instructor or the resources (e.g., library holdings, technology) of the university can be important in promoting student success. If a university has professors who are experts in their fields and are great lecturers as well as accessible to their students, this undoubtedly contributes to student success. On the other hand, if a high school has poor technology in the classrooms or it is difficult to access current reference materials to write papers, these factors will undoubtedly make it harder for students to succeed to their full potential. Given that not all universities or high schools are comparable on these types of factors, it is important to determine what might need to change to level the playing field so that everyone has access to a high-quality education. We will take a closer look at how our beliefs about ourselves, our connection to the school, the way teachers view us as students, and characteristics of the school itself play a role in predicting academic success (see Table 9.1).

Table 9.1 Factors Influencing Academic Success

Individual Factors	Environmental Factors
Self-beliefs (e.g., academic self-efficacy)	Teacher beliefs about student (e.g., stereotypes)
Academic motivation	Teacher encouragement
School belonging	School climate
Study skills	School size and resources

Self-Beliefs

Self-beliefs are individual ideas that we have about ourselves within a particular setting. Among the most frequently researched self-belief within the academic context is **academic self-efficacy** (Valentine, DuBois, & Cooper, 2004). Bandura's (2001) research has demonstrated that academic self-efficacy, or confidence in one's ability to be successful, is a strong predictor of actual behavior. Academic self-efficacy is not a broad, generalizable self-belief (e.g., having confidence in getting straight As in every subject), but rather it is domain specific (e.g., students may have confidence in their ability to do well in math but not art).

According to Bandura's (2001) social cognitive theory (see Chapter 4), self-efficacy may be enhanced through both direct and vicarious experiences. Specifically, a student gains a sense of efficacy by having individual success experiences (direct) or by viewing other relevant individuals enjoy success experiences (vicarious). Thus, a student may have confidence in his or her own academic abilities because he or she has done well in a particular subject throughout his or her entire academic career (direct experience) or because in a new subject, he or she knows that people who are similar to him or hcr have done well (e.g., "If she can do well, why can't I"). Research has found that students' sense of self-efficacy is a strong predictor of their actual performance as well as their future persistence in school (Schunk & Pajares, 2005). Later in this chapter, we will revisit the issue of how to help students at risk of school failure feel more self-efficacious.

Motivation

Another popular area of inquiry in the school literature is the role of **academic motivation** (Eccles & Roeser, 2009). Academic motivation is the "intrinsic value, interest, and importance that students attribute to academic schoolwork" (Goodenow & Grady, 1993, p. 63). This conceptualization of motivation is derived from the expectancy-value theory of motivation (Eccles et al., 1983), where motivation to engage in achievement-related behavior is influenced by a combination of one's expectations that the behavior will be successful and the value one attributes to that success. Hence, academic motivation is enhanced when one both expects to be successful and places value on such success.

Conversely, academic motivation would be compromised when one does not value success in an academic arena or does not believe that such success is possible. Students can be motivated by a love of learning and focus on mastering the material for their own benefit (i.e., mastery-oriented goals) or by a competitiveness to do better than other students or "being the best" (i.e., performance-oriented goals). The former type of motivation is known to sustain engagement in school and academic achievement more so than does a performance-oriented motivation. However, both types of motivation can lead to good grades (Berk, 2014a).

School Belonging

Researchers have also found that the school context can also have a significant relationship to academic success through a factor called perceived **school belonging** (Goodenow & Grady, 1993). School belonging is defined as students' perceptions that others in the school are on their side and that they matter in the school community (Wehlage, 1989). School belonging can be affected by transitions such as the move from elementary to secondary school (Eccles & Roeser, 2009) in which students may feel less nurtured or recognized as individuals, and it can also be impacted by whether one feels that the school has respect and investment in people "like them" (Goodenow & Grady, 1993). Thus, school belonging can be impacted by the relationship that teachers have with their students, but it also can be affected by students' overall ability to participate in the larger school community via extracurricular activities (Eccles & Roeser, 2009). This is why it may be harder for students who attend large schools to have a strong sense of school belonging and why small schools—where there are opportunities for the majority of students to be involved and have good relationships with their teachers—are advantageous (Elder & Conger, 2000). See Adjustment in Practice: Bullying to see how some students experience a negative sense of school belonging.

ADJUSTMENT IN PRACTICE
Bullying

We have explored how a sense of school belonging is related to school success. Yet there are some kids for whom a negative sense of school belonging becomes a chronic problem. Oftentimes these kids are rejected by a majority of others and become the target of ridicule or harassment. When ridicule is accompanied by a power differential of some kind, this is referred to as bullying. School bullying exists as a societal epidemic that affects millions of school-aged students (Espelage & Holt, 2012). Rigby (2007) defined *bullying* as the repeated oppression—psychological or physical—of a less powerful person by a more powerful individual or group of persons. Kids from historically marginalized groups such as children who have a disability or gay, lesbian, or bisexual students receive proportionally more bullying attacks than do children who are part of the cultural majority (Kosciw, Greytak, Diaz, & Bartkiewicz, 2010; Rose, Monda-Amaya, & Espelage, 2010).

The emotional damage that results from repeated bullying exacerbates the damage that such experiences do to kids' school success, including increasing the likelihood that these kids will drop out of school (Polanin & Vera, 2013). Research also suggests that the effects of bullying linger into adulthood. For example, bullying victims were 4 times as likely to develop an anxiety disorder in adulthood compared with kids who were uninvolved in bullying. Both bullies and their victims also had a 5 times greater risk of depression than uninvolved kids, as well as 10 times the likelihood of suicidal thoughts or actions and 15 times the likelihood of developing a panic disorder in adulthood (Copeland, Wolke, Angold, & Costello, 2013).

(Continued)

(Continued)

The damage that kids experience from being bullied includes mental health problems and dropping out of school.

iStock/Highwaystarz

What can schools do to prevent bullying? First, it is important that school leaders educate all adults and students about what defines bullying and that policies are developed that make bullying a school offense. Second, consequences have to be consistently enforced against students who bully, and counseling needs to be given to children who are victimized. Third, careful adult monitoring needs to take place in areas where bullying is frequent (Polanin & Vera, 2013), such as lunchrooms, playgrounds, bathrooms, and hallways. Fourth, bystanders (or the kids who see bullying happening but do not try to stop it) need to be held accountable and trained to intervene when they witness bullying. Eliminating bullying requires a team effort. Many schools are now instating antibullying policies to create safer school environments for all students.

Not all bullying is contained to middle school or high school years. There are adult bullies in the world (Lutgen-Sandvik, Namie, & Namie, 2009). While bullying is not necessarily a serious concern in college because of the wider variety of social options that students have, bullies do reemerge in more confined settings in adulthood, such as the workplace. In fact, 25% of American employees report experiencing some form of bullying at work. The damage that bullies do to adults, especially when their victims are in subordinate roles, is just as damaging. It is important to note that harassment in workplace settings is illegal, so the first part of dealing with a bully as an adult is to make sure that the behavior is reported to the appropriate authority.

The following additional tips come from the Project for Wellness and Work–Life's report *How to Bust the Office Bully* (Tracy, Alberts, & Rivera, 2007). First, document your story, highlighting actual examples of bullying. Remain calm in telling your story, be consistent with details and facts, and finally be understanding of others' points of views when relating your experiences. The goal of these steps is to get the bullying to stop.

Reflection Questions

1. Why are some kids more vulnerable to being bullied than others?

2. What do you think explains the unwillingness of many bystanders to intervene when they see bullying?

Teacher Beliefs

When teachers hold high expectations of their students and hold them accountable for meeting those expectations, students learn more, feel more competent, and feel more engaged in the learning process (Wigfield, Byrnes, & Eccles, 2006). Alternatively, when teachers have low expectations of some students, students quickly become aware of those beliefs, and it often leads to disengagement from school. When these negative expectations are based on stereotypes (e.g., girls can't do well in math), a phenomenon known as **stereotype threat** can develop.

Stereotype threat, or the knowledge that a stereotype is held about a group to which you belong, creates anxiety that interferes with performance on tests and can create a misidentification with the subject matter or school in general (Aronson & Steele, 2005). Hence, teacher beliefs, when negative, can, in some ways, create a self-fulfilling prophecy for students. They are expected to do poorly and therefore do poorly. Even though teachers are aware of the power they have to shape their students' own expectations, they are still human beings who are vulnerable to stereotypes that exist in our society. Thus, while we would like to believe that all students are viewed as equally capable of learning, it may not be the case that teachers actually believe this or treat their students the same (Aguado, Ballesteros, & Malik, 2003).

While this research has focused on the beliefs of teachers of younger individuals, it is also likely that teacher beliefs continue to influence us in college settings. For example, Umbach and Wawrzynski (2005) found that college students are more engaged in classes where professors use active and collaborative learning techniques, engage students in experiences, interact with students, challenge students academically, and value enriching educational experiences. Challenging students academically is a function of a professor's belief that the students are up for the challenge. Therefore, even in college, professors' attitudes about their students and the subsequent in-class expectations and activities will impact students' experiences.

Teachers' Encouragement and Praise

Psychologist Carol Dweck and her colleagues have conducted many studies that have shown the effects of teachers' encouragement and praise on students' persistence and, ultimately, academic success (Dweck, 2002, 2006, 2007). In fact, many of their experiments have been based on teaching kids that their brain is a muscle that can be "worked out" and that the harder they work that muscle, the better able they are to learn things. When teachers encourage students' efforts and persistence, they learn the value of not giving up. This realization actually results in changing students' study habits and improving their grades.

On the other hand, when teachers praise students for being smart, students learn that intelligence is a trait (i.e., they are either born smart or dumb), and such praise fails to result in academic gains. The other interesting finding in Dweck's (2007) research is that when children are praised for their intelligence versus effort, they start to avoid challenging themselves over time, in particular when it is possible that they will not succeed at a task. In other words, students who are praised by their teachers for being smart will begin to think of themselves as smart and will stick with subjects and tasks that confirm that belief. They will avoid subjects or tasks that might be too challenging and disconfirm their belief that they are naturally smart.

This research has interesting implications for classroom teaching. Children should be praised for persistence and effort and when they fail must be encouraged to keep trying. For example, instead of telling a child, "You are good at math," Dweck (2007) would recommend saying, "I like how you are really trying to solve that math problem." Likewise, when a student's performance is less than he or she expected, Dweck (2007) would recommend saying, "If you keep working at this, I know you will eventually figure it out" instead of something like, "It's okay. Not everyone is good at math." This is a simple difference with potentially profound results.

Returning to the discussion of self-beliefs, this finding also has implications for how students start to think about themselves as learners. Students who have good early experiences in school may begin to think of themselves as smart and expect success. Students who struggle early on may begin to think of themselves as not being smart and will expect to struggle in school. Without adults like parents or teachers around to encourage students to struggle and overcome these difficulties, students may give up on the idea of being successful in school. Thus, the encouragement and support we receive from others is critically tied to our academic adjustment. In college, parent and teacher influence is complicated by a new social network of professors and peers.

Rather than minimize the importance of intelligence, this research attempts to put our understanding of intelligence into context. In other words, intelligence might best be seen as a quality that can be developed rather than a fixed trait and in addition, qualities like perseverance and motivation to meet goals are equally important in predicting success (Duckworth, Peterson, Matthews, & Kelly, 2007). For more information on the debate on intelligence and intelligence testing, see Researching Adjustment: Intelligence Testing.

RESEARCHING ADJUSTMENT
Intelligence Testing

Intelligence testing has a rocky history in the field of psychology. Early on, psychologists developed intelligence tests that were used to determine whether or not immigrants should be admitted into the United States and to make claims of genetic inferiority for ethnic minority groups. While intelligence tests are no longer misused, there is still a question of whether they are good predictors of people's actual potential. The answer to this question depends on when they are administered and whether or not they predict success equally well across gender, race, and social class groups.

The first issue is a question of the developmental appropriateness of giving intelligence tests. Let's consider the example of parents who believe that the key to their child's ultimate success in school begins with a prestigious preschool. Such preschools do exist in the United States, and in almost all cases, decisions about who to admit are made based on so-called intelligence tests for pre-K kids.

These intelligence tests are not valid and are unable to pick out kids who are gifted versus average. In fact, these early childhood intelligence tests misclassify kids over 70% of the time (Kim & Hoi, 2003). In other words, preschools that use these tests would deny admission to kids who would have benefited from their program and would admit kids who it turns out are really not gifted at all. The good news is that intelligence tests have become better, although not perfect, predictors of academic success when they are given later in life, specifically any time after third grade. Intelligence seems to become more consistent and predictable at that point in children's development. Therefore, giving kids an intelligence test in third or fifth grade is actually a useful tool in determining what their achievement will look like in high school (Laidra, Pullmann, & Allik, 2007).

Finally, there have been experts in the field who have argued that there is cultural bias in intelligence testing that disadvantages non-White, non–middle-class children. In some cases, it may be because there are linguistic differences that are not taken into account by the test developers (e.g., interpreting the word *wrapping* to mean "rapping"; Champion, 2003). In other cases, it may be that in lower SES families, the environments are more social than object oriented, which makes some of the nonverbal tasks of the test (e.g., manipulating patterns on blocks) more challenging for kids who do not have blocks in their home. To correct for these potential biases, experts recommend using intelligence tests with equally valuable information to make academic decisions. For example, using a child's grade point average in school or observational data of what they are capable of doing in and out of school is a more reliable way to measure a child's actual abilities versus relying solely on a test score.

The following are examples of test items:

Why do we need police officers?

Tell me what carpet means.

How are ships and trains alike?

Repeat these numbers in this order and then in the reverse order: 3, 7, 1, 9, 4, 2.

Reflection Questions

1. Can you think of why some children may have a harder time answering these questions?

2. Why do you think that our society is so focused on measuring intelligence in our children?

3. What other abilities do you think we should be trying to measure?

School Climate

School climate or culture refers to the values, policies, practices, and general expectations that schools have. For example, schools that use class rankings, have different tracks of classes (e.g., Advanced Placement [AP] versus general classes), and have few nonacademic extracurricular opportunities (e.g., drama, art) may set a climate where academic excellence and competition are valued. Schools that have inconsistent discipline codes that tolerate bullying and other inappropriate behavior may set a climate where students do not feel safe or treated fairly.

Studies have shown that school climate factors can be directly related to delinquency rates, grades, and truancy in students (Eccles & Roeser, 2009). School climate is also related to factors such as sense of school belonging and teacher beliefs. Kids who feel like their school is not a safe place or it is a place that marginalizes certain students may feel less engaged in school or that their teachers don't really care about them. Hence, school climate, even though it may be harder to measure than some of the other factors we have discussed, can play a very powerful role in shaping students' success or failure. School climate plays an important role at the university level as well. In fact, for first-generation college students and underrepresented populations of students

Going to college can be one of the most transformative experiences in a person's life.

(e.g., veterans, ethnic minority students), special programs have been put in place to help make the school climate more inclusive.

School Size

For most of us, school and class sizes have increased as we have advanced our way through the educational system. In elementary school, class and school sizes are likely at their smallest, whereas in some public high schools, enrollment could be as high as several thousand students at any given time, with class sizes that average around 40. While that sounds big, it pales in comparison to the size of some universities where an introductory lecture class might enroll up to 300 people.

Most of the research on school size and its relationship to student success points to the advantage of attending smaller schools with smaller student to teacher ratios (Elder & Conger, 2000). Of course, school size is determined by factors that are largely out of the control of most individuals, such as the number of school buildings relative to the population of students in any given community. Class size is often determined by school funding and how many teachers can be afforded within the school budget. With respect to college, some similar conclusions can be drawn. Attending a large university with 30,000 other students creates some difficulties in terms of connecting with others and utilizing the resources that universities offer students. This topic will be discussed further in the section on college students. Thus, one final factor, **school resources**, is an important topic related to school success and academic adjustment.

School Resources

School resources include a wide variety of environmental factors such as the quality of the school building itself, the amount of money spent per pupil, teachers' salaries, the technology and books available, etc. It has been found that there is a positive relationship between these resources and academic success (United Way, 2008). Students who have the best of everything are not only more motivated to perform well but they tend to learn more and have fewer behavior problems than do students who attend poorly resourced schools (Clark et al., 2006; Eccles & Roeser, 2009). They may also have the easiest time with academic adjustments because they have access to all the resources they need.

Policies like property taxes determining the funding level of schools can give an advantage to kids whose families can afford to live in expensive neighborhoods. Those kids' parents pay more in taxes, and the schools receive more resources as a result. The impact of resources persists even at the college level. While most colleges should provide state-of-the-art resources for their students, university and college tuitions vary greatly, and parents who pay for their child to attend the most expensive university in the country expect their child to "get more" than would parents who can afford a more modest institution. It is easy to see that these same issues could apply beyond high school in terms of higher educational settings (e.g., community colleges and 4-year universities). However, the connection may be less direct. There are many college students who attend very expensive schools who do not take advantage of the resources available to them and struggle. There are also students who attend more modest institutions who do very well. Thus the research that has looked at the link between institutional resources and undergraduate education outcomes is inconclusive (Umbach & Wawrzynski, 2005).

In summary, there are many factors that influence academic success. Some factors are directly related to the school environment, and others are related to the students themselves. For some students, a combination of any of these factors leads to diplomas

RESEARCHING ADJUSTMENT
School Dropout

As of 2011, approximately 7% of young adults (16–24 years of age) were not enrolled in school and had not earned their high school diploma (National Center for Education Statistics, 2013). The average freshman graduation rate for high school graduation is 78.2%, with some states having rates below 60% (Stillwell & Sable, 2013). Regardless of which statistic paints a more accurate picture of the dropout rate, it is an important challenge facing educators throughout the United States.

Why do some kids stay in school while others drop out? There is no single reason. There are a host of factors that put kids at risk for dropping out. One useful way of categorizing these factors is the distinction between push factors and pull factors. Push factors are aspects of the school environment that cause students to become academically disengaged, while pull factors are events and circumstances outside of school that compel students to disengage (Lehr, Johnson, Bremer, Cosio, & Thompson, 2004). Students at greatest risk for dropping out may experience both push and pull factors. Imagine, for example, a student whose teacher has underestimated his intelligence, is being bullied by peers, and feels unsafe in school. This same student might be vulnerable to the recruitment of a neighborhood gang who offers a sense of importance, protection, and a source of income. This combination of push and pull factors might be enough to result in the student dropping out of school.

Research has found that not all students are equally likely to drop out of school. Inner-city youth, especially those living in poverty (Pong & Ju, 2000; Roscigno, Tomaskovic-Devey, & Crowley, 2006); students who are chronically absent (Sheldon & Epstein, 2004); students who repeat a grade (Entwisle, Alexander, & Olson, 2005; Stearns, Moller, Blau, & Potochnick, 2007); those who attend large urban schools (Christenson & Thurlow, 2004); and adolescents who switch schools multiple times (South, Haynie, & Bose, 2007) are at particular risk for dropping out.

The costs of dropping out of school are immense. High school dropouts experience more unemployment during their work careers, have lower earnings when employed (see Figure 9.1), are more likely to be on public assistance, and are more likely to use illegal substances or commit crimes than those who complete high school or college (Christenson & Thurlow, 2004; Christie, Jolivette, & Nelson, 2007). Young women who drop out of school are more likely to become pregnant at young ages and are more likely to become single parents living in poverty (Freudenberg & Ruglis, 2007). Thus, finding preventions and interventions for those at risk of dropping out are extremely important.

(Continued)

(Continued)

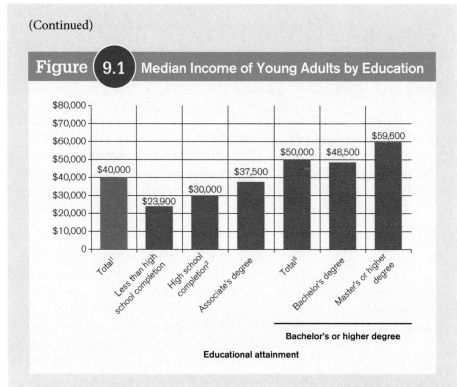

Figure 9.1 Median Income of Young Adults by Education

¹ Represents median annual earnings of all full-time year-round workers ages 25–34.

² Includes equivalency credentials, such as the General Educational Development (GED).

³ Represents median annual earnings of full-time year-round workers ages 25–34 with a bachelor's or higher.

Source: National Center for Education Statistics. (2015, May). *Annual earnings of young adults* (Figure 2). Washington, DC: Author. Retrieved from http://nces.ed.gov/programs/coe/indicator_cba.asp

Reflection Questions

1. What types of support do you think would reduce "pull" factors that students at risk for dropout might experience?

2. What type of programs could schools offer to reduce the number of students who leave school each year?

and degrees while for others, their academic journeys end prematurely. To take a closer look at the research that has been done on school dropout, see the Researching Adjustment: School Dropout box.

The College Experience

Most college students view this period in their lives as one of the most transformative. Whether they live on campus or commute from home, they must deal with new responsibilities and expectations and are learning to juggle multiple important, competing demands in their lives. According to the U.S. Department of Education (2013), about two thirds of high school graduates enroll in some institution of higher education. While not all will graduate with degrees, it is likely that the transition to the college experience will represent some form of culture shock (Berk, 2006). This may be more pronounced for students who are the first members of their family to go to college. These students are referred to as first-generation college students.

First-Generation College Students

First-generation college students have been identified as one group of students with the most difficulty accessing higher education (e.g., Choy, 2001; Martinez & Klopott, 2005). Despite these difficulties, as a group, first-generation college students are gaining in their presence on college campuses. For example, data from the National Center for Education Statistics' Beginning Postsecondary Longitudinal Study demonstrated that first-generation students comprised 34% of all students entering 4-year institutions and 53% of all students entering 2-year institutions (Provasnik & Planty, 2008).

First-generation college students face challenges that their counterparts, whose parents or other relatives have attended college, do not have. For example, they have less knowledge regarding the admissions process, often have more limited financial support, and have less emotional support related to academic success from their parents and families than their peers (e.g., Ceja, 2006; Choy, 2001; Thompson & Phillips, 2013). First-generation college students are also more likely to have limited access to role models who can offer insider information on the college experience or the culture of universities (Martin Lohfink & Paulsen, 2005). Since their parents do not have experience in college environments, they might also be less likely to encourage their children to pursue more rigorous courses or become involved in extracurricular activities in high school, which may, in turn, lead to the student being less prepared academically when he or she arrives at college (e.g., Martinez & Klopott, 2005; Thompson & Phillips, 2013). Fortunately, colleges and universities have invested a lot of time and resources into supporting students with these types of backgrounds, which we will review later in this section.

Understanding College Success Factors

Perhaps the best measure of success in college is obtaining a diploma. However, 45% of U.S. college students at 2-year institutions and 30% of students at 4-year institutions drop out of college, most within the first year (ACT, 2008). Ethnic minority students from low-income families have even higher rates of college dropout (Montgomery & Cote, 2003), perhaps due to their overrepresentation in the category of first-generation college students. People with college degrees will earn more money than their peers who do not have such degrees and most high school graduates, as compared to college graduates, will hold lower paying, unskilled jobs with less room for advancement (U.S. Department of Education, 2009). Thus, because of the value of graduating from college, it is important to understand what factors influence success in college.

Tinto's (1987) theory of student departure is a very well-documented theory of college success and failure that applies to first-generation college students as well as college students in general. The theory emphasizes the influence of precollege characteristics with which students enter college (e.g., gender, race, skills, parental education level, educational achievements) on the students' level of commitment, intention, expectation, and motivation toward the goal of graduation. Academic and social integration, or the fit between a student's norms, values, and behaviors and the culture of the institution, is a critical factor in a student's willingness to remain enrolled in college. Specifically, Tinto proposed that students who are integrated socially (e.g., they become involved in student organizations, develop friendships with other students) and integrated academically (e.g., they have positive relationships with faculty, take advantage of academic resources) are more likely to stay in school than are students who fail to do so (Tinto, 1987).

However, as critics of this theory have speculated, while this integration may happen easily for some students, for others, assimilating into the university environment may be more difficult, in particular when students feel isolated and different from the majority of students or if they are living at home as opposed to living on campus (Guiffrida, 2006). Thus, universities have been forced to examine the types of efforts they make to reach out to students, like first-generation college students, for whom social and academic integration might not come as easily. TRIO programs are examples of initiatives that have come out of these self-examinations (see Researching Adjustment: TRIO Programs).

RESEARCHING ADJUSTMENT
TRIO Programs

Programs such as Upward Bound are designed for at-risk students.

TRIO programs represent one large-scale effort designed to help students overcome the social and cultural barriers to higher education. TRIO programs were born out of legislation in the 1960s designed to increase economic and educational opportunities for low-income young people in middle school, high school, or college. The TRIO programs currently encompass a range of initiatives on college campuses that have evolved since their inception (Thompson & Phillips, 2013). Upward Bound and Talent Search were the original TRIO programs, followed by others that targeted more specific groups of students who may have trouble integrating into the university environment (e.g., Veterans Upward Bound). The Ronald E. McNair Post-baccalaureate Achievement Program for mentoring underrepresented students into doctoral programs (U.S. Department of Education, Office of Postsecondary Education, 2008) is another TRIO program aimed at keeping ethnic minority (first-generation) students engaged in higher education from the bachelor's level into graduate school programs. Figure 9.2 illustrates one ethnic breakdown of college enrollment trends and graduation between White and Black students.

TRIO programs are designed to offer program participants the social and cultural connections and support that they might not have received from their families and peers. These programs typically begin as early as junior high school, when students can become involved in educational enrichment activities on the weekends, after school, and during the summer (Engle, Bermeo, & O'Brien, 2006).

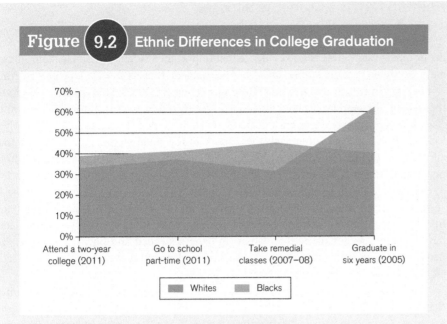

Figure 9.2 Ethnic Differences in College Graduation

Source: Data from National Center for Education Statistics.

Students and their parents also receive information, guidance, and counseling about topics such as the college admissions process, academic requirements for a college-bound student, study skills needed to perform effectively in college, informational material regarding financing college, and career exploration (Engle et al., 2006). These programs are designed to enhance students' academic self-efficacy and to increase their sense of belongingness on campus (e.g., via spending time on campus, being familiarized with prospective fellow students, and learning about available campus resources; Thompson & Phillips, 2013).

Researchers have examined the success of TRIO programs (Myers, Olsen, Seftor, Young, & Tuttle, 2004), and findings suggest that Upward Bound programs, for example, were effective in promoting student engagement, college retention, and graduation for certain at-risk populations, including low-income first-generation college students. Findings also indicated that students who were enrolled in the programs for longer periods of time received the most benefits (Myers et al., 2004). Thus, it appears that TRIO programs are an effective way of promoting retention and facilitating social and academic integration for college students who may be at risk for not graduating. This research emphasizes the importance of social and academic integration in the success of college students. It is important to talk to academic advisers and campus student life staff who can help students to find any academic opportunities (e.g., faculty research, mentoring) that they would benefit from receiving as well as social opportunities to connect with other students (e.g., clubs and organizations).

Reflection Questions

1. On your campus, how easy is it to access academic advisers and become involved in academic opportunities?

2. Are you aware of efforts that your college or university make to reach out to underrepresented students?

Helping College Students Succeed

In addition to the many contextual and environmental factors that are related to academic adjustment, there is also evidence that important academic skills facilitate adjustment. **Study skills** are examples of "academic enablers" that are associated with academic competence in college in particular (Gettinger & Seibert, 2002). Study skills are tricks of the trade in the world of academics and are recognized to be critical tools for learning. Capable students may experience difficulty in their academic careers not because they lack ability but because they lack these tools. Study skills include competencies that allow for acquiring, recording, organizing, synthesizing, remembering, and using information (Gettinger & Seibert, 2002). The problem is that although students are expected to use study skills to complete homework or study for tests, very little, if any, time is spent explicitly teaching these skills. To make matters even more complicated, studying in college is an intentional act. It is not a required part of college courses, so students have to figure out for themselves when studying is needed and how to best do it. To determine which study skills appear to be connected to college success, researchers studied the habits of good studiers.

Good studiers use strategies that are efficient and planful, and they carefully monitor their progress toward a goal, whether it is completing homework or preparing for a test. For example, in Pressley and Afflerbach's (1995) research they found that high-achieving students (with good study skills) did the following:

1. Looked for important information and paid greater attention to it when they studied

2. Related important points to one another

3. Used their prior knowledge to understand new ideas

4. Changed their strategies when their understanding was unclear

5. Corrected inaccuracies in their comprehension

Conversely, low-achieving students assumed a passive role as learners and overrelied on others like teachers to regulate their studying and learning. Additionally, their studying was haphazard and disorganized and also had trouble keeping track of materials and assignments, following directions, and completing work on time. Low-achieving students also do not allow enough time to study and complete projects, and the time they did allot was often interrupted by friends, music, or poor concentration. This research then allowed for the identification of study habits and skills that are related to academic success in college.

Interestingly, this research also revealed that there is a relationship between one's sense of control, self-efficacy, and study strategy use (Zimmerman, 2002). Good studiers see themselves as in control of their academic performance (as opposed to being a function of luck or if the teacher likes them) and capable of doing good work. As a result, they are more motivated to devote time and effort to their studying. In contrast, less successful students may have lower self-efficacy, doubt their ability to succeed, and thus lack motivation to do well or improve their performance. See Figure 9.3.

Some have argued that study skills, although they were developed to facilitate independent learning in college settings, have more "real-world" value than it might seem on the surface. Scholars such as Wingate (2006) have suggested that study skills would be better integrated into a wider life skills framework in which they would be seen as part of students' overall personal, academic, and professional development. This approach would recognize the complexity of the learning involved and the relevance of the skills beyond the university setting. Accordingly, Wingate (2006) referred

Figure 9.3 Sample Items From MARSI

To get a sense of some study skill strategies associated with reading and retaining information, consider the items that are included in the Metacognitive Awareness of Reading Strategies Inventory (MARSI; Mokhtari & Reichard, 2002).

1. I have a purpose in mind when I read.

2. I take notes while reading to help me understand what I'm reading.

3. I think about what I know to help me understand what I'm reading.

4. I preview the text to see what it's about before reading it.

5. When text becomes difficult, I read aloud to help me understand what I'm reading.

6. I write summaries to reflect on key ideas in the text.

7. I think about whether the content of the text fits my purpose.

8. I read slowly but carefully to be sure I understand what I'm reading.

9. I discuss my reading with others to check my understanding.

10. I skim the text first by noting characteristics like length and organization.

11. I try to get back on track when I lose concentration.

12. I underline or circle information in the text to help me remember it.

13. I adjust my reading speed according to what I'm reading.

14. I decide what to read closely and what to ignore.

15. I use reference materials such as dictionaries to help me understand what I'm reading.

16. When text becomes difficult, I begin to pay closer attention to what I'm reading.

17. I use tables, figures, and pictures in text to increase my understanding.

18. I stop from time to time to think about what I'm reading.

19. I use context clues to help me better understand what I'm reading.

20. I paraphrase (restate ideas in my own words) to better understand what I'm reading.

21. I try to picture or visualize information to help me remember what I'm reading.

22. I use typographical aids like boldface type and italics to identify key information.

23. I critically analyze and evaluate the information presented in the text.

24. I go back and forth in the text to find relationships among ideas in it.

25. I check my understanding when I come across conflicting information.

26. I try to guess what the text is about when reading.

27. When text becomes difficult, I reread to increase my understanding.

28. I ask myself questions I like to have answered in the text.

29. I check to see if my guesses about the text are right or wrong.

30. I try to guess the meaning of unknown words or phrases.

This MARSI list includes examples of study skill techniques that facilitate learning that comes from reading texts, which is a common activity of college studying. The reader may see that it is a more elaborated list of behaviors first noted in Chapter 4.

Having a mentor can be a key asset to success in school and work settings.

to these skills as communication (both written and oral), information technology (or the ability to use technology to gather relevant information), problem solving (planning and conducting projects), numeracy (using statistics to solve problems and represent solutions), working with others, and self-management (which includes time management and self-learning).

We can teach study skills to students who did not acquire them earlier in life. Teaching study skills is typically done via social cognitive learning approaches as described by Gettinger and Seibert (2002). First, students observe models using the skills, and then they begin to imitate what they are seeing while being coached by an expert. Next, they begin to use the skills independently while being monitored. Finally, they engage in self-regulation by using the skills independently. Given the involved process that seems to best teach study skills to students who need to learn them, it may not be practical for study skills to be taught one on one, which is why more often, study skills are taught in a group format. Overall, training students to use study skills has been shown to improve academic performance, strategic knowledge, and effective responses among students with learning problems (Harvey & Goudvis, 2000; see Table 9.2).

Mentoring

Recall from our earlier discussions of social learning theory that self-efficacy can be increased by seeing someone we identify with be successful. A natural extension of this theory has been the study of role models and mentors. A role model might be someone we look up to, maybe a family member or a friend, who helps us to believe, "I could be like that." Even better is when we have a close relationship with that person, and he or she takes us under their wing. This person might be labeled a **mentor**. A mentor is usually a person with advanced experience and knowledge who is emotionally invested in someone else's development (Ramaswami & Dreher, 2007).

As we have discussed previously in this chapter, for some students, role models and mentors appear naturally in their environments, and students benefit from the vicarious learning and nurturing that they receive from these people. For other students, however, in particular underrepresented minority students, role models and mentors may need to be identified and made available to the students. This is an important aspect of the

Table 9.2   Helpful Hints for Effective Studying
Complete difficult work at times when you are most alert and least distracted.
Divide long assignments into shorter, manageable units.
Vary the type of study tasks (alternate reading and writing).
Be flexible in scheduling breaks and rescheduling study time if conflicts arise.
Use your own words and examples to summarize information because it will build on what you already understand.

TRIO program discussed earlier and the STEM (science, technology, engineering, and mathematics) intervention programs discussed in Chapter 10.

Mentoring programs can provide students with opportunities not only for exposure to role models but also to problem solve how to deal with challenges of, for example, being a first-generation college student or being a commuter student (see Adjustment in Practice: How to Find and Gain a Mentor). Scholars such as Gloria and Rodriguez (2000) have posited that students of color often have unique self-beliefs (e.g., imposter syndrome or the belief that they don't deserve to be in college), varying levels of social support (e.g., from family if they are first-generation college students), and less comfort in the university environment (i.e., in particular on predominantly White campuses) than do their White counterparts.

ADJUSTMENT IN PRACTICE
How to Find and Gain a Mentor

1. Be clear on why you want a mentor. Based on your personality and goals, decide what kind of person would be a good mentor to you. For example, you could choose someone very similar or very different from yourself depending on what you are trying to learn.

2. When asking someone to be a mentor, explain why you are seeking the relationship, and be open to different forms of mentoring (e.g., face-to-face meetings, phone or e-mail correspondence).

3. Look for someone who has the kind of life and work you'd like to have. Also, choose a mentor you truly respect. Don't just go for the biggest name you can find.

4. When looking for a mentor, think about former bosses and professors, older family members or friends, neighbors, spiritual leaders, community leaders, the networks of your friends and colleagues, or officials of professional or trade associations you belong to. Avoid asking your direct supervisor at work.

5. Don't become too dependent on your mentor. A mentor should help you become the best version of yourself, not a clone of him or her. In fact, you may not take every bit of advice your mentor offers. Continue to think for yourself.

Reflection Questions

1. Do you have a mentor? If so, how has that person helped you get to where you are today? If not, who are the types of people that you could contact to receive mentoring in your life right now?

2. Talk to someone who has had a mentor. Find out about his or her experience. What was the most valuable thing he or she learned from that mentor?

Source: Adapted from Burns (2009).

Another practical extension of the literature on mentoring is the practice of developing peer mentors. Peer mentors are not necessarily more senior in age or experience than typical mentors, but they can serve an important function in supporting the educational success of students who may be at risk for dropping out. One comprehensive initiative that has utilized this approach with students of color (and first-generation college students) is the use of learning communities (Thompson & Phillips, 2013). Learning communities are groups of students who have a common interest or identity status who take classes together; engage in extracurricular activities; and, in some cases, reside together. The support that is provided to these students is intended to offset some of the social isolation that can negatively impact them.

Inkelas and Weisman's (2003) evaluation of a learning community intervention at one university found that African American and Latina/o students who participated in an academic honors learning community felt more confident in their first-year transition to college in comparison to their counterparts who did not participate in the learning community. Thus, mentors and mentoring programs appear to be important resources related to the academic adjustment and success of underrepresented student groups. Fortunately, many colleges and universities have invested in these programs, which is a good sign, since having an educated population is important for the success and well-being of nations around the globe.

Conclusion

In this chapter, we have explored a variety of topics related to schools and academic success. Parents, educators, and our society as a whole are invested in having children who grow up to be intelligent, literate, productive members of society. We have also seen that academic success is a result of a lifetime of learning and opportunities. We have also seen that not everyone has the same opportunities to be academically successful, but there are programs and supports that have been created to try to level the playing field.

Students can improve their academic success by strengthening their study skills, establishing social networks that will encourage their educational efforts, and seeking out mentors and models who are helpful in skill building and emotional support. Such efforts are rewarded by higher grades, increased likelihood of staying in college, and advancement in students' field of interest. While a complex situation with many factors at work, the acquisition of skills and support systems have significant impacts on students' lives. While it is not always easy to utilize the resources and tap into the self-regulation that is necessary to stay focused on academic success at every point in the educational pipeline, there are legitimate reasons to persevere and to seek out additional help when it is needed.

Review Questions

1. Describe a Montessori preschool. Do some research, and create a list of advantages and disadvantages to this type of school.

2. Why is self-regulation important in preschool and kindergarten?

3. Discuss two of the factors that predict academic success.

4. What is school belonging? How is it impacted?

5. What is a stereotype threat? What do you think teachers can do to avoid this phenomenon?

6. How do school factors like size and resources affect the day-to-day experiences of students?

7. What factors contribute to school dropout?

8. What are first-generation college students, and why are they in need of specific types of support?

9. What competencies are included in study skills?

10. How would you define a mentor, and what can mentors help us to accomplish?

Key Terms

academic motivation 184

academic self-efficacy 184

first-generation college students 189

mentor 198

Montessori preschool 181

school belonging 185

school climate 189

school resources 190

self-beliefs 184

self-regulation 181

stereotype threat 187

study skills 196

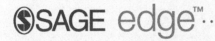

Sharpen your skills with SAGE edge at **edge.sagepub.com/moritsugu**

SAGE edge for students provides a personalized approach to help you accomplish your coursework goals in an easy-to-use learning environment.

Go to **edge.sagepub.com/moritsugu** for additional exercises and web resources. Select Chapter 9, School for chapter-specific resources.

Chapter
10

Work and Vocation

Learning Objectives

1. Explain how work fulfills basic human needs.

2. Identify work-related milestones across the human life span.

3. Explain how contextual factors such as gender, race, and SES impact vocational development.

4. Discuss the major theories of vocational decision making.

5. Describe rewards and risks associated with work.

Angie is a 17-year-old high school junior. She is Mexican American, born in a large Midwestern city to parents who emigrated from Mexico when they were in their 20s. Angie's parents often talk about their dream of seeing her go to college and have a successful life. In fact, the American Dream was their motivation for coming to the United States. As a member of an immigrant family, Angie's life has been challenging. Her parents both work multiple low-wage jobs to make ends meet, and the apartment that she lives in is modest in size and located in a low-income, urban neighborhood.

At school, Angie hears a lot about college and is encouraged to become a lawyer or a doctor. In fact, she receives very good grades and would probably be accepted into many universities. However, Angie has no idea how she would afford a college education, and her parents, having never been to college themselves, are unable to give her any advice about the college experience. Angie also looks around her high school and sees that about only 50% of the students graduate, and far fewer go to college. Most of the kids she knows who have graduated high school end up in a trade school or in a vocational training program such as the cosmetology institute a few blocks from where she lives. Angie dreams about having a career that would allow her and her family to move out of their cramped apartment and into a nicer neighborhood. However, she thinks that it is an unrealistic goal and instead is setting her sights on a career as a hairstylist.

***

Michael is an 18-year-old third-generation Chinese American whose parents are both surgeons. Michael and his brothers were raised in a very wealthy community in the Pacific Northwest and attended private school their entire lives. Michael is beginning his first year at a prestigious, private university in the premed program—the first step in becoming the doctor his parents expect him to be. Michael is an excellent student who is doing well in his biology and other science courses, but he finds himself unenthusiastic about this career path. His passions are music and poetry, and in his heart, he would love to become a songwriter. However, Michael knows that being a doctor is his parents' dream for him, and he does not want to disappoint them and set a bad example for his younger brothers. His friends have encouraged him to take a few courses in the performing arts and consider talking to his parents about not declaring a major until he has explored a variety of options. However, Michael fears that this would be a sign of disrespect to his parents and is willing to commit to a career in medicine to keep the peace.

Angie's and Michael's stories have several things in common. First, both of these young people may end up never exploring their interests and dreams because of what they perceive to be barriers. In Angie's case, the barriers may be her family's economic situation and the norms that exist in her community for kids who graduate high school. In Michael's case, the barrier may be his parents' expectations for him to carry on the family tradition in medicine. Second, without a change in the current plan, both of these individuals may end up in unsatisfying careers that do not reflect their true interests and life goals.

Do you think that Angie's and Michael's decisions about their careers are mistakes? If so, what would you suggest should happen to help them reconsider their options? If not, what might these decisions tell us about the priorities they both have in making choices about their future careers? Do you believe that their decisions will result in a good person–environment fit, one of the hallmarks of adjustment?

Sigmund Freud believed that the two most important aspects of life are love and **work** not only because relationships and careers consume so much of our time on a daily basis but because they also help define who we are as individuals. Meaningful relationships and careers are also related to healthy adjustment. Having previously examined some of the challenges of making relationships successful, we now turn our attention to the world of work. To begin this process, take a moment and reflect on these questions:

Regardless of one's occupation, work is an important component of psychological health and adjustment.

- What was your first **job**?
- How did you get that job?
- What type of career do you hope to have in the future?
- How did you decide that this particular **occupation** was the best choice for you?

If you were able to answer these questions, you might have already identified some of the factors that impact the meaningfulness of work. For example, if you found yourself answering the first two questions (i.e., your first job and how you got it) with descriptions of low-paying, entry-level positions that you secured because they were the only options available to a young person in your community, then you are like most young adults in the United States. Environmental *opportunities* to find work and the *qualifications* a person has to successfully perform certain jobs dramatically impact the type of work that is obtainable.

On the other hand, you probably had a much more elaborate story to tell regarding the last two questions (i.e., your future career and the process involved in deciding on that path). Your future career aspirations likely reflect your *interests*, *abilities*, and the *future opportunities* you perceive as being available to you. *Vocational development*, as opposed to finding a first job, is a complex pathway that is an interaction of individual and environmental factors, and in an ideal world, vocations can be an important source of happiness and adjustment over a lifetime.

In this chapter, we will review definitions of work as well as present what is known about vocational development across the life span and how cultural group memberships (e.g., gender, social class) impact the decisions that people make about work. We will also discuss what is known about how people find meaningful, fulfilling work, which is related to adjustment and well-being. We will also consider what can be done to help people who may not have an optimistic view of their future work lives. Finally, we will discuss the risks of occupational stress in work settings and how handling such stress is critical not only to adjustment but also to having satisfying work lives and avoiding burnout.

The Psychological Importance of Work

While the terms *job, work, occupation,* and *career or vocation* are often used interchangeably, they have different meanings in different contexts. A job is frequently seen as a means to an end or a way to pay the bills (e.g., the "McJob"). An occupation is what a person might be trained to do (e.g., an engineer), and he or she may have many jobs or positions related to his or her training during a career, but technically an occupation requires a specific type of education or preparation. *Work* is a more all-encompassing term that describes both jobs and occupations. Finally, a career or vocation reflects a person's lifelong pursuit and ideally represents our "calling" or what we think we are meant to do with our life.

Scholars within the field of psychology have argued that working is important to a person's psychological health and adjustment (Blustein, 2008). Specifically, researchers have found that working connects people to the broader world, provides a source of accomplishment, and enhances feelings of well-being (Blustein, 2006; Brown & Lent, 2005). Furthermore, according to researchers such as Lucas, Clark, Georgellis, and Diener (2004), when people lose their jobs, mental health problems such as substance abuse and/or depression often result and even when these people find new jobs, their mental health does not return to its previous level. Thus, it is arguable that finding and maintaining steady, meaningful work is a powerful predictor of individuals' well-being across the life span.

In communities where there are disproportionately high levels of job loss (e.g., the disappearance of the manufacturing industry in Detroit), not only are there serious mental health consequences to the individuals who lose their jobs but there are dramatic effects on the quality of neighborhoods, family relationships, and a general disintegration of safety and trust (Wilson, 1996). For example, imagine a community where masses of people were all laid off at the same time, resulting in people losing their homes, their ability to send their kids to college, and their dreams for the future. The collective impact of such a situation could create circumstances where everyone feels a sense of despair and hopelessness.

Blustein's (2006) "psychology of working" perspective suggests that work has the unique potential to fulfill three fundamental human needs: the need for survival, the need for self-determination, and the need for relatedness. Let's consider each of these needs.

First, as scholars such as Maslow (1943) have argued, human beings' need to survive is their primal motivating factor. Without access to food, water, shelter, and safety, humans are unable to engage in higher order activities such as becoming self-actualized or engaging in civic activities. Thus, work uniquely provides people with access to money that secures their survival needs.

Second, self-determination refers to the notion that a person is fully in charge of the direction that his or her life is taking. In other words, a person who is self-determined is an active agent guided by intrinsic interests or abilities in pursuing goals. If a person ends up taking a job out of desperation, where the job is more of a means to an end than an expression of what they love or are good at doing, such a person may feel a very low level of self-determination. On the other hand, if someone is able to explore who he or she is, know what it is that they love, and pursue the opportunities necessary to find meaningful work in that area, it is arguable that a great deal of self-determination is present.

Third, the need for relatedness refers to the idea that working provides people with access to social support and significant relationships. Granted, there is wide variation in the extent to which jobs require us to work with others. For computer programmers, it is possible that their main social interaction occurs during breaks or during company meetings. On the other hand, emergency room nurses' days are spent collaborating with

In communities where factories have closed and many people have become jobless, the sense of despair can be collective.

their colleagues to treat a large volume of people. Regardless of whether a person works in a highly interactive or highly solitary work setting, the role that work plays in connecting with other people cannot be underestimated. This idea is illustrated by the fact that many people who retire find it difficult to give up the social importance of work in their lives, even if they are tired of doing the job itself.

Thus, not only is it important to understand how people go about finding the kind of careers that they pursue but it is also important to understand why work is so psychologically important in people's lives. The significance of work changes over the course of our lives. For example, for college students, career choice may be a major focus right now. Forty years from now, retirement may be their major focus. Next we will explore how psychologists have viewed work across the life span and work's relationship to adjustment and well-being.

Work Across the Life Span

As was illustrated in the questions raised at the beginning of the chapter, the meaning of work and the processes involved in obtaining and maintaining it change across a person's life. Scholars such as Fouad and Bynner (2008) have maintained that the salience of work is present at every episode in the life span, including early childhood when young kids are often asked what they want to be when they grow up. In addition to its salience across the life span, they also argue that work and/or career can be understood as the culmination of a series of choices that people make over their lifetime, choices that are often constrained by access to resources, economic opportunities, and other important contextual factors.

Adolescence

Developmental theorists such as Erikson introduced the notion that adolescence was a critical period in which identity exploration would begin, which would ultimately lead to career decisions. Research has suggested that aspects of this process, such as interest development, probably occur earlier, during childhood, and that some occupational narrowing occurs sometime prior to high school. In fact, research suggests that middle adolescence is the time of life when the development and crystallization of educational and vocational perceptions occurs (Super, Savickas, & Super, 2006).

College

One important vocational transition takes place after high school, or if we were in a different country in the world, the equivalent of the last mandatory period of education. For students who successfully graduate high school, a decision must be made about whether to seek work or continue one's education (Fouad & Bynner, 2008). Currently, about 60% of high school graduates enroll in college (Arnett, 2000; Berk, 2009). The college experience itself is another transition (Arnett, 2000) that is critical in helping students to determine their future careers. Even though the hope is that students are making important decisions related to their careers while in college, career indecision is common at this stage of life. In fact, 80% of students in the United States end up changing their major at least once, according to the National Center for Education Statistics (Gordon, 2007). On average, college students change their major at least three times over the course of their college career.

Career Indecision

As we have seen throughout the chapter, **career indecisiveness** is a common theme that affects many individuals throughout the life span. In some ways, the college experience is designed to help students explore many career options and professional fields, which is why students have a required core of classes from varying disciplines regardless of their major. However, at some point, students must choose not only what major to pursue but also what jobs to prepare for as they think about launching their career. For some students, the decision is an easy one. For other students, there is a high degree of anxiety around making a decision. These students might suffer from what is called career indecisiveness.

Researchers have identified two subtypes of career indecision. One is being indecisive due to insufficient information, and the other is chronic indecision regardless of information received (Chartrand et al., 1994). In the former case, it may simply be helpful for a student to seek out more information about various careers, and such a process will facilitate making a decision. In the second case, however, it may be more difficult to help a student commit to a decision and, as a result, more intensive intervention may be required.

Some of the contextual factors that were discussed earlier in the chapter may indirectly affect career indecision by impacting the type of information and knowledge that students have about careers and the factors they weigh in what to pursue. For example, lower socioeconomic status (SES) and ethnicity were the strongest predictors of occupational knowledge in children (Jordan & Pope, 2001). Thus, kids from poorer families have less career knowledge than do their more affluent counterparts. Furthermore, girls' awareness of work–family demands seems to impact the choices they make about careers. Girls appear to consider fewer career options than boys and worry about the need to balance multiple life roles sooner than do boys (McMahon & Patton, 1997), which suggests that they may make career decisions more prematurely.

Career counselors are often tasked with helping students to make decisions about majors or their careers in general. They often do so by utilizing a combination of individual, group, and technology-driven interventions. Many of the interventions used by career counselors are derived from some of the vocational decision making theories discussed in this chapter. For example, one set of individual interventions related to Holland's (1997) theory is used in which students explore their interests and career personalities by taking inventories such as the Strong Interest Inventory.

Other interventions might be done in groups divided by gender to help students explore stereotypes of certain careers or to help them analyze perceived barriers or supports that may be related to SES or cultural expectations. There are several online resources that can be accessed independently by students, even those not in career counseling. The Occupational Information Network (O*Net) is the nation's primary source of occupational information and provides comprehensive information on characteristics of workers and occupations. The Strong Interest Inventory is typically used only in formal counseling relationships, but similar assessments can be found online (http://personality-testing.info/tests/RIASEC) and may be a good starting point for students who are interested in learning more about themselves and their vocational personalities.

Additionally, the National Career Development Association (see http://association database.com/aws/NCDA/pt/sp/resources#list_resources_all-R140-NCDA) sponsors a website that contains a plethora of career development resources that range from self-assessment inventories to discovering vocational personality, occupational information, salary information, educational information, job banks, and job search instructions. Students seeking information about various occupations as well as seeking clarity about their own vocational personalities would benefit from using these resources. The additional assistance of career counselors at either the high school or college level can be a great supplement to these resources.

First Job

Another transition point is graduating from college and securing a first job. While this should be a time of great excitement and anticipation for many college graduates, it is worth noting that the health of the economy, which dictates the availability of jobs, is a major determinant to whether this time of transition goes smoothly. While the first job a graduate finds should ideally be a good person–environment fit and a first step in a career, these positions may not be available in the job market. When the economy is not thriving, which has been the case in the United States since the Great Recession in 2007, students graduating from college may experience heightened anxiety and insecurity about their futures. Because economic instability can lead to unexpected job loss, we present the findings of research on involuntary job loss in Researching Adjustment: Involuntary Job Loss.

RESEARCHING ADJUSTMENT
Involuntary Job Loss

Anticipated, voluntary work transitions are typically planned in advance and, in theory, allow individuals to access resources that make them smooth and successful. Fouad and Bynner (2008) noted that voluntary work transitions, like taking a new job, changing careers, leaving work to raise a family, or to retire, are dramatically different than involuntary transitions such as being laid off from a job, being forced to retire, or being forced to enter the labor force due to various circumstances.

For example, a college student who aspires to be an engineer may be forced to leave school due to a financial change in the family's resources, like a father losing his job due to corporate downsizing. In the case of both the father, who has lost his job, and the college student, who must quit school and find a way to support himself, both are dealing with involuntary work transitions. These types of transitions are often accompanied by a great deal of disappointment and anger and may also force people into making decisions about what to do next that are riddled with obstacles (Fouad & Bynner, 2008).

The father in this example may seek work that he is overqualified to do just to provide for his family. The son in this example may end up taking a job he is not invested in for the long term because of the lack of having a college degree, a slow economy, or the sudden need to contribute to the family income. The fact that involuntary work transitions typically do not give people sufficient time to prepare for the change creates significant psychological distress and can tax a person's inner resources.

Is there an optimal way to adjust to involuntary job loss? Scholars such as Maddi and Khoshaba (2005), who have studied people's reactions to involuntary job

(Continued)

(Continued)

loss, noted that being resilient in the face of such stress requires three qualities: **commitment, control**, and **challenge**. Commitment refers to the attitude that it is best to stay involved with the people and events around us rather than to withdraw. Control refers to making efforts to influence the outcomes (e.g., like going through retraining programs) rather than to give up. Finally, challenge refers to a perspective where we try to discover how the job loss might be an opportunity to grow rather than to bemoan our fate.

Reflection Questions

1. How do individual qualities affect a person's sense of commitment, control, and challenge in the face of job loss?

2. What environmental factors may contribute to a person's sense of commitment, control, and challenge?

Midcareer

If we consider the best case scenario, where a person can have a fulfilling career in one or more jobs, there will be a period of time where relative stability and/or advancement occurs. Thus, in midcareer, relative to other times across the work life span, there may be a stabilization period, where barring involuntary job loss, there are relatively fewer transitions. Depending on the career and one's age, retirement is then the next important transition time that has been studied extensively.

Retirement

Retirement is not a requirement in some occupations, and for some people, it is not a realistic option. However, for many people, there is a dream of retirement that might include travel, more leisure time, and the ability to spend more time with family. However, for as much as there is a sense of excitement that may accompany retirement for some people, there are also considerable losses associated with retirement. If we revisit the three needs that work fulfills (Blustein, 2008), it is important to consider how leaving work may impact these areas.

First, the need for survival may not necessarily be impacted by retirement if a person has saved their money sufficiently or has a pension available, along with other income from social security, that allows their standard of living to remain the same. However, it is possible to imagine a situation where retirement brings about a considerable decrease in income and the need to live within a tight budget due to a fixed income. Some retirees end up securing part-time work as a result of changes in their anticipated financial status.

The second need, the need for self-fulfillment, may also be impacted by retirement. While there are other ways that individuals can feel self-fulfilled, such as through being a parent, being engaged in the community, or other ways of giving back, the absence of a formal work role can sometimes force retirees to be much more planful in how they express their self-fulfillment. Volunteer mentoring programs for retirees are examples of ways in which the need for self-fulfillment can be transitioned into a new setting. However, it is possible that without the existence of a plan for how one will spend their retirement, a sense of self-fulfillment could be lacking for some retirees. This lack of focus has been found to be one of the vulnerabilities of older adulthood, and it has been found to predict mental health problems such as depression in this age group (Friedman & Martin, 2011).

Finally, the need for relatedness is often impacted by retirement (Blustein, 2008), especially for people who worked in positions that had a high level of social interaction. There are many ways that this need to relate to others can be supplemented for retirees, such as through being involved in senior groups, volunteer activities, or leisure activities (such as a golf or bowling league). However, this also assumes that individuals have access to these opportunities, which is much more likely to be the case for middle- or upper-class retirees.

Research has examined vocational development as a lifelong endeavor, and there are several critical transition points during which perceived opportunities and choices have implications for the future. While there may be some universality to vocational development across the life span, there are some important contextual influences that must be considered as well, which is the focus of the next section.

Demographic Factors in Vocational Development

Many complexities impact the development of work over the course of one's life; however, the degree to which contextual factors such as gender, race, and SES influence career paths are profoundly important (Fouad & Byars-Winston, 2005). Let's take an example, such as the case of Angie, presented earlier in this chapter. The SES of Angie's family may determine where the family lives and what schools their children will attend. The resources of the school may determine what kinds of academic and extracurricular opportunities are available to the children who attend the school, which can influence not only the level of preparation that students have for future educational and career opportunities but even the levels of aspirations and dreams the children have (Fouad & Bynner, 2008). Angie's decision to pursue a career as a hairstylist may be greatly influenced by how she perceives her environment, her opportunities, and even her level of confidence in herself.

In addition to the impact of socioeconomic influences, which is a key factor in the example of Angie, children also learn a great deal about their perceived opportunities for work in their immediate and extended family contexts (Hendry & Kloep, 2002). This is where gender and ethnicity play a role in shaping work aspirations and expectations. Fouad and Byars-Winston (2005) found that while aspirations do not vary by race or ethnicity per se, expectations of work availability differ significantly. In other words, when making decisions about the future, kids often consider what kind of work "people like me" are likely to do.

Furthermore, gender shapes the work expectations of children. For example, the division of housework between parents or the employment status of mothers have been found to influence adolescent gender role beliefs (Cunningham, 2001; Davis & Greenstein, 2009). Specifically, employed mothers hold more egalitarian gender attitudes, as do parents who have less stereotypical division of household labor practices. Girls who see fewer gender stereotypes in their families may see a greater range of career opportunities compared to their counterparts who have a more stereotypical gender role socialization experience and hence, might see far fewer career options for girls. Careers in science and math are examples of vocational areas where the greatest gender discrepancies are seen. Researching Adjustment: STEM Careers presents research on how interests in such careers might be shaped.

Many factors influence our career choices, including our views of the occupation itself.

RESEARCHING ADJUSTMENT
STEM Careers

Career decisions are influenced by a variety of factors, including perceived prestige level, gender stereotypes, perceived accessibility, etc. Thus, in some occupations, there can be an underrepresentation of people who fall into a number of cultural groups. This is an issue that affects careers in science, technology, engineering, and math (STEM) careers. According to the National Science Foundation and the U.S. Census Bureau, underrepresented minorities earned only 25% of the degrees in STEM fields, as compared to 75% of the degrees being earned by their White counterparts. The statistics on women are a bit more hopeful, as women constitute the majority of undergraduate STEM degree recipients, but at the graduate level, 75% of all STEM field graduate degrees go to men (Myers & Pavel, 2011). However, as depicted in Figure 10.1, males' interests in fields such as math continue to outpace females' interests. Thus, psychologists try to change this state of affairs so that more women and people of color will serve as role models for future generations of students who are interested in STEM careers.

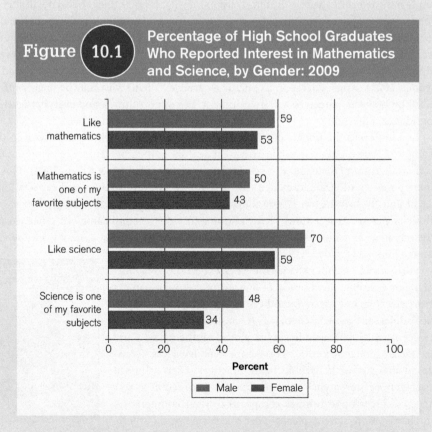

Figure 10.1 Percentage of High School Graduates Who Reported Interest in Mathematics and Science, by Gender: 2009

Sources: U.S. Department of Education, Institute of Education Sciences, National Center for Education Statistics, High School Transcript Study (HSTS), 2009; National Assessment of Educational Progress (NAEP), 2009 Mathematics and Science Assessments. http://nces.ed.gov/pubs2015/2015075.pdf

According to scholars who have studied the issue (Hernandez, Schultz, Estrada, Woodcock, & Chance, 2013; Myers & Pavel, 2011; Wai, Lubinski, Benbow, & Steiger, 2010) the following practices appear to promote STEM degree pursuit by underrepresented groups:

1. Intensive curriculum exposure, in particular for students who show early aptitude in math and science (e.g., Advanced Placement classes)

2. Hands-on research opportunities with faculty members

3. Faculty and peer tutoring and mentoring

4. Financial support for college

5. Promotion of educational aspirations through career guidance

Thus, based on this research, it is possible to not only predict which individuals may be most vulnerable to the effects of career stereotypes but also to design programs that help to provide opportunities to increase interest in STEM careers.

Reflection Questions

1. While you were a student in elementary school, did you have any preconceptions about your ability to be successful in science or math?

2. What kind of career guidance or mentoring opportunities were available to you as a student?

While contextual factors such as gender and social class influence the perceptions of appropriate and available work and often predict what type of work is most commonly secured for people, they may influence the perceptions of work and its meaning. Chaves et al. (2004) studied the work perceptions of urban adolescents of color who were in ninth grade, the majority of whom came from poor neighborhoods. The authors of this study found that this group experienced significant challenges, such as racism and discrimination, that hindered their vocational development and created barriers for them to finding stable and meaningful employment.

As a result of being exposed to high levels of community underemployment or unemployment, racial minority youth who are from low-income families may never view work as an expression of one's interests or talents but rather an elusive goal that is not directly under their individual control at all. With these types of findings in mind, researchers have sought to explain the mechanisms that might be able to change the future orientations of low-income, urban youth of color with the hopes that in doing so, educators and counselors might be able to develop programs that can make these kids more hopeful about their careers. While one might correctly assume that a significant change in the financial resources and employment status of the communities in which these kids reside is key in making long-term changes, there is also evidence to suggest that even for kids who do not have a wealth of opportunity, adolescents with positive future outlooks are more resilient, able to overcome obstacles, less likely to exhibit risky behaviors, and more likely to complete school than are kids who have negative future outlooks (Brown, Lamp, Telander, & Hacker, 2013).

The field of vocational psychology has made important efforts to design career development and guidance programs that help adolescents to feel more hopeful about their futures. For example, Lapan, Gysbers, and Petroski (2001) found that students who participate in career guidance programs (e.g., exploring their interests through interest inventories, researching the world of work in areas that match their expressed interests) showed greater life satisfaction after high school and, in the short run, generated ideas about what careers reflect good person–environment fit (or adjustment) and had a positive impact on kids' academic performance in comparison to kids who did not participate in career guidance. Presumably, giving kids the time and opportunity to explore future possibilities as well as learn more about themselves pays off both in the short and long term.

The field is now in the process of trying to determine the key ingredients of successful interventions and also attempting to make these programs relevant to the issues that individuals facing challenges in vocational development, particularly urban adolescents of color, confront on a regular basis. The concept of **vocational hope** has been suggested as one of the key characteristics of successful programs. Brown and his colleagues (2013) defined *vocational hope* as "a positive motivational state associated with envisioning a future in which meaningful work is attainable" (p. 383).

Brown et al. (2013) emphasized that because vocational hope is a state (as opposed to a trait), it is something that can be changed. In other words, even if a person does not currently possess a positive view of the future, he or she could come to have a different view on the matter. Furthermore, this vision of the future is not necessarily determined by one's past or present circumstances. Finally, they state that because the emphasis is on finding meaningful work, it has the potential to reflect any definition of meaningfulness to an individual, rather than only objective measures of being "successful," such as the amount of money that can be earned.

Theories of Vocational Decision Making

While much of the scholarship in the area of work and vocation has examined the significance of work and what factors predict work outcomes, there are several psychology scholars who have developed and tested theories that attempt to explain how people make decisions about work. These theories are relevant in understanding to what extent such decisions reflect a "good fit" for the individual and lead to greater adjustment. No single theory adequately describes the processes of work decision making, satisfaction, or the contexts that impact individuals' experiences of work. However, there are a number of theories that attempt to explain certain aspects of career decision making, several of which we will highlight along with the research that has supported the theories.

Theory of Occupational Circumscription and Compromise

Gottfredson (2005) developed the theory of **circumscription** and **compromise**, which describes the factors involved in how people narrow down options based on how they view themselves and how they view specific occupations. Key elements in this theory are a person's self-concept (both public and private view of self), images of occupations (and in particular, stereotypes associated with those occupations), ideas people have about the prestige level of various occupations, the accessibility of occupations, a person's aspirations, and how far one is willing to push boundaries related to the conceptions that have been formed about certain occupations.

In this theory, circumscription is a narrowing process where occupations are eliminated based on the aforementioned factors. Compromise is the process of giving up the most preferred choices for less compatible choices that are perceived as more accessible (Gottfredson, 2005). This theory helps explain why people may eliminate various occupations from their list of options based not on interests but on whether an individual's characteristics are consistent or inconsistent with beliefs or stereotypes that are held about various occupations. There have been several studies that support this theory. For example, one investigation found that socialization and stereotyping seem to influence occupations that kids prefer (Oppenheimer, 1991)—in particular if those preferences are gender conforming.

An example can illustrate how the narrowing down process plays out in real life. Let's take our example of Michael from the beginning of the chapter. Michael may have a positive view of himself as a well-rounded individual, and as an Asian American male from a successful family, he may be aware that people also see him as a successful person with a lot of potential (his private and public view of self). He may see his fantasy profession of songwriter as one that is associated with artsy, free-flowing types of individuals and his chosen profession of medicine as one that is associated with intelligent, focused, successful people (images of occupations).

Girls who see fewer gender stereotypes in their families may see a greater range of career opportunities, including gender-nonconforming careers.

In terms of ideas about prestige level, he may see becoming a physician as much more prestigious and financially superior to being a songwriter (prestige ideas). He may also see that the pathway to becoming a physician is accessible through his college studies whereas a songwriting career may be more risky and less proscribed (accessibility). Finally, in terms of aspirations, he may feel that while his heart of hearts tells him to do what he loves, he knows that meeting his parents' expectations is a more important motivation. Thus, his willingness to push boundaries may be limited. This theory would predict that Michael will pursue medicine over songwriting. Note that this theory does not address whether such a decision would result in a satisfying work life for Michael, only how he might arrive at that decision.

Social Cognitive Career Theory

A second theory of career decision making is the social cognitive career theory (SCCT; Lent, Brown, & Hackett, 1994), which is based on Bandura's (2001) social cognitive theory (see Chapter 4) and gives self-efficacy primary importance as the driving force behind occupational decisions, interests, performance, and persistence. Self-efficacy is a type of confidence that we have in our ability to accomplish something; it is domain specific rather than a general feeling. For example, a person might have high math self-efficacy but low artistic self-efficacy.

Another important element of this theory is a construct called outcome expectations (tangible outcomes, social outcomes, self-evaluative outcomes). Outcome expectations refer to what a person expects will happen if he or she pursues a specific path; these expectations can be both positive and negative. Goals or the determination a person has to engage in a particular activity to produce a particular outcome (Brown et al., 2013) are also an element of this theory. Finally, supports and barriers that impact specific decision making are thought to be influential as contextual factors. For example, making a decision that goes against the wishes of one's family or making a decision that requires extensive resources (e.g., medical school) may be met with barriers that decrease the likelihood of success. Pursuing a vocation that one's friends admire might be viewed as a support factor.

In Michael's case, he likely has specific ideas about what outcome expectations surround a decision to pursue medicine (e.g., his parents will be happy, he will be encouraged by his extended family, he will make a lot of money) versus a career as a songwriter. One of Michael's goals may be to uphold his family's reputation (goal), and he may know that he is capable of doing well in medical school (self-efficacy). Using this theory, a person's beliefs, whether or not they reflect reality, play a large role in the career they pursue.

Research supports this theory as explaining a variety of elements of the career decision-making process. Rottinghaus, Larson, and Borgen's (2003) meta-analysis revealed that self-efficacy correlates strongly with interests in academic context, and Lent et al. (1994) found that outcome expectancies predict intentions. In particular, Brown et al. (2013) found that this theory is a robust predictor of vocational choices and vocational satisfaction and, presumably, adjustment.

Theory of Person–Environment Fit

The final theory is Holland's (1997) theory of person–environment fit, which speaks directly to issues of person–environment match. This theory posits that people search for work environments that let them express their interests and abilities. When there is a good fit between the person and the work environment, people are better adjusted. The theory is predicated on the notion that we all have career personalities that are a combination of the following types (see Figure 10.2):

- Realistic Type: refers to people who thrive working outdoors, working with their hands, and are interested in mechanical fields
- Investigative: refers to people interested in sciences, analyzing and solving problems
- Artistic: refers to people who are creative, musical, and artistic
- Social: refers to people who like to work with and help others
- Enterprising: refers to people who like to manage, initiate, and lead others in a work setting
- Conventional: refers to people who like to organize, work with data or numbers

These vocational personality traits are typically measured with tools such as the Strong Interest Inventory (Donnay, Morris, Schaubhut, & Thompson, 2005), and every person is thought to be characterized by a three-letter code that represents their three strongest traits. Each three-letter code is then used to describe work environments based on what activities are commonly done in that job and what types of people gravitate toward that work. Hence, a psychologist may be a combination of social, investigative, and artistic traits and being a therapist may map onto the same combination of traits. A person whose personality code closely resembles the code of

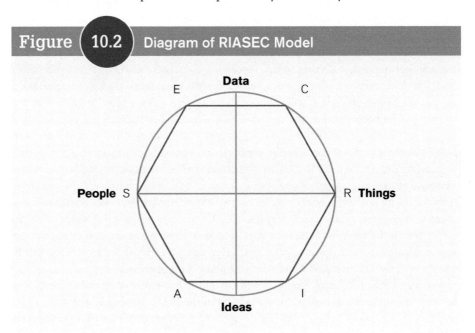

Figure 10.2 Diagram of RIASEC Model

Source: Figure 1, *Psychological Science*, January 1998, vol. 9, no. 1, 40–44.

their job are thought to be better adjusted than those whose personality and job code are mismatched.

To illustrate this theory, we can revisit Michael and Angie. Michael has a passion for poetry and art, which would suggest that he would thrive in a work environment where there are opportunities for creativity and artistry (artistic type). Will a career in medicine (investigative type) be a good person–environment fit? Would songwriting be a better fit? According to this theory, if Michael pursues medicine, he may not have the kind of fit that fosters career satisfaction and success.

Angie, who is an excellent student and loves learning, may have a work personality that thrives in settings where she can continue to learn new things and investigate what she doesn't know (investigative type). Would being a hairstylist (realistic type) be a good fit for Angie? This theory would say that the environment of hairstyling careers may be an insufficient challenge and intellectually understimulating for someone like Angie.

Research has supported the utility of Holland's theory (see Adjustment in Practice: Holland's Theory). Many studies have found that work personalities exist and apply to diverse populations of people (Day & Rounds, 1998). Also, support has been found for the fact that congruence between the person and environment do lead to better adjustment (Spokane & Cruza-Guet, 2005). However, it is not always the case that such congruency leads to higher job satisfaction (Tsabari, Tziner, & Meier, 2005). However, the popularity of this theory has led to the development of many online tools for the assessment of vocational personality and the three letter codes associated with various occupations. This type of resource will be discussed later in the chapter.

ADJUSTMENT IN PRACTICE
Holland's Theory

The following are examples of careers as categorized by Holland's (1997) theory.

Realistic careers: Forest ranger, auto mechanic, carpenter, chef, firefighter

Social careers: Counselor, community organizer, minister, day care provider

Enterprising careers: Small business owner, salesperson, manager

Investigative careers: Physician, researcher, private investigator

Artistic careers: Dancer, actor, musician, clothing designer

Conventional careers: Accountant, bank teller, office manager, file clerk

Once you have reviewed these careers, take an online version of the test at the following URL: http://personality-testing.info/tests/RIASEC

Reflection Questions

1. What types of careers are you drawn to? Do you feel that there are any gender stereotypes associated with certain categories of careers?

2. After taking the Holland (1997) assessment, are you surprised by how you were categorized? What career(s) would you best be suited for?

Rewards and Risks of Work

Work can be a source of great reward and risk. Both of these premises will be explored in this section. In terms of the reward, work can be a powerful way to express one's interests and abilities, and it can also be an expression of one's identity, ideas that we have explored throughout this chapter.

Flow

In an ideal world, the work that people commit to should be a source of invigoration, which is a reward indeed. This concept has been described by psychologists such as Csikszentmihalyi (2008) as **flow**. Flow is the state of being in which a person performing an activity is fully immersed in what is happening. It is characterized by a feeling of energized focus, full involvement, and enjoyment in the process. In other words, flow is characterized by complete absorption in what one is doing.

According to Csikszentmihalyi (2008), flow is a state where one is completely focused, in an almost single-minded way where one might lose a sense of self and awareness of bodily needs (e.g., forgetting it is meal time); one might forget about the time, where 5 hours feel like 15 minutes; or one might make sacrifices to stay involved in the activity (e.g., forgoing a planned event to spend more time on the activity; Hays, 2014). Furthermore, activities that are characterized by a flow state should involve continuous learning where one always feels challenged to learn more. Thus, the true hallmark of flow is a feeling of spontaneous delight and complete absorption. Creating a state of flow in one's occupation is a wonderful thing, even if it may not be commonplace.

However, flow is not limited to the world of work. Many people have hobbies or other types of involvement where they experience flow, independent of whether income is being earned. For example, someone who works as a grocery clerk may choose to reside in Hawaii so that his or her real passion, surfing, can be a daily part of his or her routine. Surfing would represent the state of flow in this example, not working as a grocery clerk.

Job Stress

While a state of flow may represent one end of the spectrum, where work represents an expression of a person's true passion, we also know that work can be a source of great risk and negativity to some people. Specifically, there are many people who find work to be a significant source of stress in their lives. In fact, the CareerCast (see http://www.career-cast.com/jobs-rated/most-stressful-jobs-2014) annual list of the most stressful jobs for 2014 contains some of the jobs that most people would predict create enormous stress for workers.

Each year, CareerCast analyzes stress levels for 200 careers based on the following factors: amount of travel (the less travel, the better), growth potential (e.g., dead-end jobs tend to create more stress), deadlines, work in the public eye, competitiveness within the workplace, physical demands, environmental conditions, how often one's life is at risk, how often *other* lives are at risk, hazards, and contact with the public. Here is a list of careers that were named "most stressful":

©iStockphoto.com/Joel Carillet

Careers in the military are among the most stressful.

- Enlisted military personnel
- Military general
- Firefighter
- Airline pilot
- Event coordinator
- Public relations executive
- Senior corporate executive
- Newspaper reporter
- Police officer
- Taxi driver

When looking at this list, what are some common denominators of these occupations? Stress and safety factors may be associated with many of these positions, and high levels of responsibility and physical demandingness may be other characteristics of these fields.

However, one might argue that even within these occupations, stress levels may vary depending on the traits of the person in the position as well as the extent to which the employer makes an effort to create a positive working environment for their employees. For example, not every police officer would say that the job is a source of unmanageable stress or experience the symptoms of stress-related illnesses as a result. A veteran police officer may have found effective ways to cope with the stresses of the job, or a police officer who works in a school may find the work rewarding and only occasionally stressful. The impact of job-related stress on one's life can be enormous (see Chapter 6), so it is important to be able to adjust and cope with such stresses.

The field of occupational health is dedicated to understanding factors that contribute to workers' well-being; therefore, understanding the impact of stress is a high priority within this discipline. The National Institute for Occupational Safety and Health (NIOSH; 2009) placed work stress–related disorders among its main priorities. The NIOSH position is that work stress results when there is a poor match between job demands and capabilities, resources, or needs of workers. The problem of job stress impacts many workers, with an estimated one third of all workers reporting high levels of job stress. Work-related stress has a significant correlation with cardiovascular disease, depression, anxiety, cognitive impairments, and substance abuse (Azaroff, Champagne, Nobrega, Shetty, & Punnett, 2010). It also has direct negative effects for the employer, since occupational stress is also associated with absenteeism and worker productivity (von Freymann, 2002) as well as an association with accidents (Chima, 2004). Therefore, it is mutually beneficial to both workers and employers to attend to work-related stress issues.

Dealing With Work Stress

Employee assistance programs (EAPs) are often tasked with addressing issues of employee stress, and they typically approach the problem from one of two standpoints. The first approach involves individual interventions such as counseling and teaching coping strategies, anger management, or other techniques related to efficiency on the job. The second approach involves making changes to the workplace itself. Examples of this may include having a flextime program where workers do not have to put in all their required time between the hours of 8:00 and 5:00 during the week. Another example could be telecommuting, where employees work from home and have contact with the employer via the Internet or phone conferences. A third example would be having onsite child care opportunities to reduce the commute time that parents spend having to transport their children to outside day care providers.

Employee assistance programs can help workers deal with occupational stress.

A study by Awa, Plaumann, and Walter (2010) examined the effectiveness of programs in the workplace to reduce stress and prevent burnout. A total of 25 primary intervention studies were reviewed that had been evaluated for their effectiveness. Eighty percent of all programs led to a reduction in burnout. Person-directed interventions reduced burnout in the short term (6 months or less), while a combination of both person- and organization-directed interventions had longer lasting positive effects (12 months or more). In all cases, positive intervention effects diminished in the course of time, which suggests that workers may not consistently utilize new skills that they acquire or support programs that companies make available as time goes by.

What then can we conclude about reducing stress in the work environment? First, a combination of both person-centered and organizational-focused qualities appear to be associated with being resilient in the face of stress. Having good personal coping skills and the ability to problem solve, for example, might be key ingredients to overcoming job stress. Additionally, working in an environment where there are supports in place to help workers minimize their exposure to stress (e.g., on-site child care, the ability to work from home) is also beneficial.

These findings may be useful to keep in mind when considering jobs to pursue and the type of companies that have good reputations for taking care of their employees. For example, large corporations such as Google are now integrating stress reduction practices into their workplace due to the fact that information technology companies typically expect their employees to work long hours and often to meet deadlines, which creates stress in the workplace. The program, called Search Inside Yourself, has been taught to Google employees since 2007. More than 1,000 Google employees have been through Search Inside Yourself training, which include classes such as Neural Self-Hacking and Managing Your Energy. They also have a bimonthly series of "mindful lunches," conducted in complete silence except for the ringing of prayer bells. Using mindfulness as a basis for stress reduction is discussed in Chapter 5, so it should not be a surprise that successful companies wishing to sustain their success are searching for ways to keep their employees happy and productive and to create work environments where collaboration thrives.

Conclusion

Work is a critical element of people's lives. It has the ability to create a sense of meaningfulness and purpose for some, while it may merely be a way to pay the bills for others. Although there are theories of vocational development that attempt to explain how people make career decisions, it is clear from our review of the literature that contextual factors such as gender, social class, and race or ethnicity have an impact on work-related outcomes.

While work can be a great source of life fulfillment and a major determinant of overall adjustment, it is also a source of stress for many. Because employers are aware of the impact of stress on not only employees but their bottom line, there seems to be a need for more employers to actively create work environments that promote health and well-being (as well as productivity) in their employees. Career counselors are a great resource to people who wrestle with career indecisiveness, which often can be effectively remedied with exposure to career information. Clearly understanding the psychology of work is complex, but its availability or unavailability, as well as its ability to provide satisfaction to people, has dramatic impacts on overall health and well-being. Hence, it remains a vitally important topic in the field of psychology.

Review Questions

1. What is the difference between a job and a career?

2. What are the three needs that work fulfills for most people?

3. Describe two vocational transitions that occur over the life span.

4. What are specific ways that cultural group memberships such as gender or social class impact vocational development?

5. Describe the two core processes of Gottfredson's (2005) theory of circumscription and compromise.

6. What are the main predictors of vocational choice in SCCT?

7. What are the six types of personality referred to in Holland's (1997) theory of person–environment fit?

8. What factors contribute to career indecisiveness?

9. What are examples of important rewards and risks associated with work?

10. What workplace programs have been established to reduce stress and prevent burnout? Which do you think would be most helpful to employees?

Key Terms

career indecisiveness 208
career or vocation 205
challenge 210
circumscription 214

commitment 210
compromise 214
control 210
flow 218

job 205
occupation 205
vocational hope 214
work 205

Sharpen your skills with SAGE edge at **edge.sagepub.com/moritsugu**

SAGE edge for students provides a personalized approach to help you accomplish your coursework goals in an easy-to-use learning environment.

Go to **edge.sagepub.com/moritsugu** for additional exercises and web resources. Select Chapter 10, Work and Vocation for chapter-specific resources.

Chapter

11

Money

Learning Objectives

1. Discuss the historical, learning, and developmental aspects of money.

2. Explain how and why behavioral economics works.

3. Identify variables that influence individuals' choices about buying and saving.

4. Summarize scientific findings about money and happiness.

She was an attractive woman. Her accomplishments were known. When they met, she was the wittiest conversationalist, with a low "smoky" laugh. The back-and-forth was not only funny but intelligent and—what was best—sensitive. Explaining her point of view, she had thought of most matters yet was open to hearing others' perspectives. When she talked, she listened as much as she spoke. And the sense was that there was a mutual attraction. So asking her out seemed the natural thing to do. Knowing she liked the theater, a neighborhood play was proposed. Between dinner and the play, the cost of the date was a little over $100 by the end of the evening. It was money well spent. There would have to be a few extra shifts to make that back. But that did not matter.

· ·

In Chapter 1, *adjustment* was defined as learning to adapt to everyday demands in life. These demands change as we grow. The ability to deal with money has been included here as among the important skills of the mature individual. Considerations of the role of money has not been traditionally considered as a separate topic in the psychology of adjustment. Yet this topic has implications for life choices and decisions. This chapter explores the psychology of money and how this knowledge can inform financial decision making. The life tasks around money relate to our adjustment in practical ways. An understanding of how psychology influences these tasks can lead to better management of this area of life.

What is money? Why is it so important? In what ways is it important? How do we think of it and treat it? What have we found to be helpful in considering it and dealing with it? These are some of the questions that this chapter explores. In our opening story, money was secondary to the events of the evening. A first date is important.

Money has a different meaning to different people. Money is more than money. Total sums and absolute values are almost irrelevant. Yet we know that money is an important area to our overall lives.

In informal polls of students in the authors' classes, money is consistently reported as one of the most important topics concerning stress in their lives. Money issues have been found to be stressful to over 40% of students in a large national survey ("Money Matters on Campus," 2015). This percentage increases to 50% for community college students, about 55% for female respondents, and over 60% for Latina/o students. When asked about their preparedness to deal with college matters, students feel least prepared to manage their money (58% felt prepared in 4-year colleges, 71% in 2-year colleges). As a comparison point, 70% to 80% felt prepared in academic matters.

This chapter explores money—what it means and how it is used. Money is relevant to our everyday adjustments in life. As we can see from the opening story, money's worth is psychologically determined. We review the history of money, followed by the conceptions of money and its use, which have been profoundly influenced by the psychological research in **behavioral economics**; how multiple factors go into our determination of worth and our willingness to pay for something; how contexts influence our perceptions of money; and how and why we save. We will finally examine the work on how money is related to happiness. Having more money can be helpful but not in a manner we might expect.

Note that this chapter does not discuss making more money. There are many other books that advise on that subject. It does not deal with our working. Our focus is on money, what it is, what it means to us, how we deal with it, and how it affects our well-being.

The History of Money

Authorities on the subject of money have traced its origins to the shift away from direct bartering for goods and services. Prior to currency, we might have traded salt for wheat or a day's labor in the fields for food and shelter. Those bartering exchanges were clearly linked to observable objects or activities. However, at some point, this type of trade was not practical or convenient. Around 9000 BC, cattle and other livestock of value came into use as mediums for exchange, and in agricultural societies, grains or other crops were used as markers of recognized worth. The cattle or crops served as a medium for exchange. One's fields being plowed might cost two cows or one might trade a certain amount of crops for labor.

Around 1000 BC, the first metal coins were used in China. Around 600 to 500 BC, coinage began to appear in Persia, Turkey, Greece, and Rome. At this time, the coins might be made of precious metals. Around 100 BC, decorated leather pieces were served as bank notes or money in China. This later evolved into paper currency around 800 AD. Paper was not used as money in Europe until the 1600s. The first use of paper money came in Europe's colonies, where coinage was difficult to transport. In the early 1800s, England established gold as a standard of value, a "gold standard" to which bank notes could be linked. This gold standard was relinquished in the 20th century, and we have currency and coinage as found today, backed by various national governments. As we move to debit and credit cards for exchange, our money is now "electronic" (Connors & Davies, 2015; NOVA, 1996).

Note that the pieces of money did not hold value in and of themselves. The accepted money medium varied from cattle or wheat to leather or, in some places, shells to coins made of base metals (copper, iron etc.) or precious metals (gold and silver) to paper currency (with fancy printing but still paper). The importance of money is its acceptance as a medium of exchange (cattle, coins, paper money) with a standardized and commonly accepted value (dollars, euros, pesos, francs). There is even something called a bitcoin, which some are trying to establish as a computer-based method of payment. Money is human made. How we understand and use it is also very human.

Learning About Money

Money is an excellent example of a learned "reinforcer." In itself, paper money and coins do not hold intrinsic value. Paper is paper. Their meaning is learned. In Pavlovian learning terms, money is conditioned or learned through its pairing with stimuli that elicit natural reactions (e.g., money and food, money and drink, money and attention, money and hugs or praise). Skinner (1965) might call this a kind of conditioned or a **secondary reinforcer**. That would make it something that acquires reinforcement capacities, given its pairing with primary or intrinsic reinforcers, like food or drink (Skinner, 1965).

Learning can also occur by observing others. Seeing the value others place on money, we learn how to think of it and use it (Bandura, 1977b). Such ideas on learning about money are supported by studies of parents' behaviors and their children's knowledge of money matters (Gudmunson & Danes, 2011). It has been found that parents not only serve as models but are also the source of information in money matters (Danes &

"Do you take foreign currency?"

Haberman, 2007). Parents teach their children how to think of money. For example, Marshall and Magruder (1960) found that children's understanding of money (various coins and the cost of toys and candy) was related to parents' money education practices.

A particularly interesting distinction is between parents as educators and as **protectors or regulators** (Furnham, 1993; Gunter & Furnham, 1998). Parent educators consciously and actively teach their children about money matters. Protectors or regulators, on the other hand, do not want to burden the child with adult matters like money and see their parental role to be that of a money source. Differences in parental approaches lead to differences in child learning, with the educators producing children who know more about money matters (Furnham, 2008). Beyond specific parenting practices, it appears that "good experiences with money and appropriate guidance" within the child's social–economic situation are helpful. Parental encouragement of thinking about money matters is the determinant of adult monetary behaviors (Beutler & Dickson, 2008; Webley & Nyhaus, 2006).

Developmental Aspects of Money

There is a predictable progression in our understanding of money, based on cognitive maturity. The developmental nature of monetary meaning in children has been demonstrated (Strauss, 1952). Younger children have a simpler understanding of money, its meaning, and usage. Leiser, Sevon, and Levy (1990) documented such a progression across several cultures. The younger children saw prices as absolute and nonnegotiable. There was only one possible price for an object. Older children added new considerations into price, such as cost, wages of workers, and the need for profit. Money, in this case, was placed within a larger context.

Researchers (Beutler & Dickson, 2008; Gudmunson & Danes, 2011; John, 1999) have acknowledged the developmental progression in our understanding of money from simpler, single dimension concrete ways of thinking (around age 3) to more analytical, dual factor concrete conceptualizations (around age 7), and then to more complex, hypothetical, and strategic ways of thinking about money and its uses (around age 11). These progressions are directed by the experiences and the environments (such as social class) in which children and adults find themselves.

Childhood social class experiences have been found to affect adult responses to economically stressful situations (Griskevicus et al., 2013). When faced with economic scarcity, those with low social class backgrounds were less likely to delay reinforcement, even though the delay would result in larger rewards. On the other hand, those from wealthier childhood conditions were willing to delay reward with the promise of later higher payouts.

Read Researching Adjustment: Social Class for an extended definition and discussion of the term *social class*. Those from lower social class backgrounds are more likely to take greater risks in return for higher payouts. These differences in social class background did not appear under normal conditions—only under economic stress. This demonstrates how childhood experiences lead to different approaches to money. These distinctions remained hidden until the right conditions emerged. All this leads us to believe the concepts of money and its use are learned. Money matters are not dispassionate and rational; there is a psychological dimension to it, known as behavioral economics.

RESEARCHING ADJUSTMENT
Social Class

Social class is a significant variable in people's well-being across the life span. Understanding the meaning and impact of social class is important in considerations of adjustment and health (Saegert et al., 2006).

In "egalitarian" America, the distinctions among people's backgrounds are supposedly ignored. The class system relates back to the days where the ruling class was determined by heredity. One was born in a ruling class or a serving class. There is also the middle class, which fell in the middle. They were the owners of businesses and merchants—neither the ruling class nor the servant class.

In America and other democratic societies, social class is determined by social variables, not birthright. The variables that determine social class usually include education and occupation (the two-factor method of determining class). Education levels are based on one's highest level of education: high school, college (bachelor's degree), postbachelor's degree (master's degree), and doctorate. Occupation is based on prestige attached to the work, which runs from unemployed to manual labor to office worker to business owner and professional (doctor, lawyer, professor). Note that this listing is based on what people think is prestigious.

In the three-factor method of determining class, income is added to the first two factors (Diemer, Mistry, Wadsworth, López, & Reimes, 2013; Oakes & Rossi, 2003). The levels for the class differences are negotiable and open to change. For example, DeNavas-Walt, Proctor, and Smith (2011) provided the following categories according to income:

- Top 1%: $500,000 or higher

- Upper income (top 4%): $200,000 or higher

- Middle income: $50,000–$199,999 (with distinctions between upper-middle: $150,000–$199,999 and lower-middle: $30,000–$75,000)

- Lower income: Below $50,000

Rank, Hirschl, and Foster (2014) argued that it is the accumulated wealth that really counts. They noted that this better describes the individual's or the family's access to resources. The access to resources is what best describes social class.

Some researchers have argued that class is a complex cultural phenomenon, with upper classes having multigenerational placement in powerful families, schooling at elite institutions, placement in prestigious jobs, and membership in social clubs and organizations that signify privilege and provide access to other powerful families, social influence, and the advantageous networking opportunities (Coleman & Rainwater, 1978; Gilbert, 2010).

(Continued)

Reflection Questions

1. What do you think of social class?

2. Do you think social class should include how much money is made?

3. Do you think someone's social class background is helpful in understanding their approach to money?

Behavioral Economics

Money and how we determine its worth is highly subjective and can be irrational (Ariely, 2010; Kahneman, 2013). How we evaluate money and money decisions are influenced by the situational variables affecting our perceptions of reality. This is the field of behavioral economics.

Daniel Kahneman and Vernon Smith shared a Nobel Prize in Economics in 2002. Kahneman received his award for "integrated insights from psychological research into economic science, especially concerning human judgment and decision making under uncertainty" (Royal Swedish Academy of Sciences, 2002).

Our considerations of money are influenced on its "framing"—that is, how the money question draws on cognitive tendencies (Kahneman & Tversky, 1984; Tversky & Kahneman, 1981) and the "mental accounting" of gains and losses that determine value (Thaler, 2008). These ways of looking at money recognized the psychological creation of money's meaning at any given point in time, which is dependent on a number of psychologically determined variables (Kahneman & Tversky, 1979; Thaler, 1980). Our understanding and use of money are not necessarily rational but influenced by how we think of it and the variables that influence how we think of it.

Ariely, Loewenstein, and Prelec (2006) suggested that money decisions are like the Tom Sawyer story of painting his fence. Tom found it hard work. But when his friends came by, Tom displayed great pleasure in the painting task and convinced one of his friends that much fun could be derived from painting. His friend came to believe painting was pleasurable and so was willing to pay to participate in such an enjoyable activity. The demand for painting was psychologically created.

Among the contributions of behavioral economics to our understanding of cognitive determinants to money related matters are the use of comparisons in judgments and the description of two decision-making processes. These are examples of how economics is a human activity and can be influenced by subjective decisions.

Comparisons

We make monetary decisions based on situational and behavioral cues. Value is open to negotiation and input from our social circles or our own behaviors. We look to our situation and try to draw coherence from the past to the present. For example, if we have put effort into something, then it must be worth it. When examining the use of money, the comparison is with the other things that the money could buy. Should we buy ice cream or vegetables? Which has more value in comparison to the other? The answer depends on the occasion and the intended use. Therefore, the value of money, objects, or activities is relative (Buechel & Morewedge, 2014).

We evaluate worth by comparisons to standards. These standards can be external and abundantly clear, or they could be subtle and unconsciously communicated (Adaval & Wyer, 2011). If the ice cream versus vegetables example is used, is the standard in favor of nutrition or to satisfy a craving for sweets? Does one make comparisons of success based on income? Or does one decide on success based on level of happiness?

Our standards can also vary, depending on given situations. For instance, Kassam, Morewedge, Gilbert, and Wilson (2011) found differences in how we evaluate winning. The comparisons are dependent on if we win or lose. When gamblers win in Las Vegas, they like to consider their winnings. When they lose, they like to think of all the other fun things they have done, such as dine, see shows, and enjoy the desert air. Therefore, while standards are applied, those standards can vary, depending on the situation.

Two Decision-Making Processes

Kahneman (2003, 2013) wrote of two different decision-making processes that seem to govern our choice making. One decision-making system is fast and intuitive. It is based on quick impressions—that is, choosing by liking. The second system is slower, deliberative, and rational (Kahneman, 2003, 2013), based on thoughtful judgments of the separate pieces of information presented (Kahneman, 1994).

Kahneman (2003, 2013) argued that sometimes quick judgments are mistakenly thought to be deliberative. Among those factors influencing our decision making is how the question is framed or presented for solution (what we should consider important, such as winning or losing).

Context influences how information is perceived (the difference of $0.10 to a $1.00 transaction or $0.10 to a $100 transaction). It has also been noted that high emotional states increase high emotional thoughts and immediate needs, which block otherwise more reasoned processes (Fiske, 1998; Loewenstein, 1996).

When in decision-making situations in the immediate-intuitive mode, the tendency is to focus on the obvious information that is easily accessible and to ignore the information that is most important. The decision maker may believe they have given serious consideration to all information when they have not. Money decisions can be driven by immediate, emotional reactions to the situation or problem. The sense of urgency is always a clue that the first thought system is being invoked. Any time one is placed in such an "urgent" situation, there is good reason to slow down. See Researching Adjustment: Money's Effect on Us.

RESEARCHING ADJUSTMENT
Money's Effect on Us

We influence the perception of money and money issues, and in turn, money influences us. In a series of studies, Vohs, Mead, and Goode (2006) demonstrated how money seemed to shift us away from an others-focused orientation. After reading a story about money and wealth, subjects worked longer before asking for help (greater self-sufficiency) and were less likely to help others. Even the mention of money increased self-sufficiency tendencies. It was found that just looking at money led to increased choice of solitude in work and in play. Money led to a shift into "I want to be alone" mode.

Reflection Questions

1. Can you think of an example from your life where this happened?

2. How do discussions of money effect you or the conversations you are having?

Money Skills

Given the psychology that has been discussed to this point and the realization of the psychological research that has focused on our personal economic behaviors, how might this translate into specific behaviors and skills? The following section looks at research addressing everyday behaviors involving our interactions with money.

Buying

Ariely (2010) wrote of the ways we were not rational in money matters. There are many times that we make buying decisions that are not to our advantage, because we make mistakes in the calculations that go into our deliberations on buying. We make these decisions by making comparisons. In turn, these comparisons regularly fool us, given our cognitive tendencies to perceive things in particular ways. The following are examples of these tendencies.

Seeing *Free* Is Tempting

One example of this irrational behavior is the power of the word *free* in our decisions (Ariely, 2010). When Amazon offered shipping for $0.20 on purchases, sales were not affected. When Amazon changed the offer to free shipping, sales increased dramatically. Free versus $0.20 is an insignificant difference objectively. Yet that difference was a sufficient incentive to increase buying. The free shipping served as a release for the consumer to go on a spending spree.

Make a note the next time you see an Internet sale offer of free shipping. Is your first impulse to take advantage of the offer? Even when other decisions make better sense, free is a powerful incentive (Shampanier, Mazar, & Ariely, 2007). The next time you are offered a free anything, stop and calculate. Awareness of the automatic response makes it easier to control.

Slowing Down and Thinking

As noted previously, Kahneman (2013) found two decision systems: one fast and impulsive and one slow and deliberative. He believes our buying behaviors are influenced by both of these systems. When faced with what appears to be emotionally obvious, or well-practiced decisions, the fast system works. When confronted with complex or strange situations, the tendency is to slow down, grow more self-controlled, use restraint, and carefully consider options.

One way of making this change into the slower, deliberative mode is to anticipate the good feelings (or pride) that result from judicious self-restraint (Patrick, Chun, & Macinnis, 2009). This self-rewarding method of motivating self-control appears to be more effective than using self-shaming to resist temptation to be impulsive. Therefore when shopping, speak of the advantages of considering the purchase, as opposed to mocking other shoppers and oneself for the tendency to engage in impulse buying.

Shopping When Tired

Self-control or self-regulation is the primary mechanism that allows us to have restraint in buying (Vohs & Faber, 2007). However, self-regulation is tiring. Schmeichel, Vohs, and Baumeister (2003) found that when a person is tired, self-regulation decreases, abilities to reason declined, and decision making capabilities worsened. It is hard to be restrained when tired. Impulsive buying increases as the day wears on and weariness sets in. This situation is called ego depletion. Gailliot and Baumeister (2007) found that ego depletion was related to the

When Amazon offered free shipping, sales increased dramatically.

Anticipating pleasure influences our purchasing decisions.

lowering of blood glucose levels, the energy source for the brain. Vohs and Faber (2007) found students were more willing to spend money and spend a higher amount in these conditions. While we have complex decision-making capabilities, they take effort to use, and we tire when using them. Therefore, buying when tired is less deliberative (Baumeister, Sparks, Stillman, & Vohs, 2008).

Anticipating Pleasure

Another consideration in making purchases is the person's anticipation of how much pleasure the purchase can provide (Wood & Bettman, 2007). The ability to accurately forecast the amount of pleasure (or pain) to be experienced is not very good. Called the **durability bias**, expectations are usually that pleasure is long lasting (Wilson, Gilbert, & Centerbar, 2003). These emotional expectations are easily influenced by social norms (Eid & Diener, 2001; Robinson & Clore, 2002). Who we are shopping with or the store we are in impact our thinking in regard to the purchase. We might think of how our friend's encouragement of a purchase serves as information to feed our own anticipation.

Determining the Worth of Things Bought and Things Lost

Worth can be expressed as the specific amount of money that is attached to an object or service. However, as seen in the earlier section on developmental monetary concepts, the complexity of determining cost grows with a more mature understanding of costs and expenses of delivering the object or service and the need to turn a profit in transactions (Leiser et al., 1990).

Beyond these researched quantifiable factors, there is research that suggests that we are more reluctant to lose an object to which we have an emotional attachment. The emotional attachment is possibly based on our hedonic (affect-rich) experience of that which is being sold, versus a utilitarian (affect-poor) experience of the object (Dhar & Wertenbroch, 2000). This is the difference between what it means versus what it does.

Emotionally, we weigh the differences between the pain of loss (avoiding the pain of paying for something) versus the pleasure of gain (wanting to approach that which we are buying). Buyers were likely to be focused on the gain (of the object) and ignore the loss (of their money). Savers were more likely to be focused on the loss of money and

Our family photos grow more precious with time.

ignore the potential gain from the purchase (Higgins, 1997; Prelec & Loewenstein, 1998; Rick, Cryder, & Loewenstein, 2008). Labeling the price as "small" helps a reluctant buyer, the "tightwad," to pay (Rick et al., 2008). Sometimes making a choice and buying something can cause pain over the loss of other options that the money could have purchased (Carmon, Wertenbroch, & Zeelenberg, 2003). We sometimes mourn the loss of what we cannot purchase because of what has been spent. We can't buy the shirt because we bought the pants.

We tend to value that which is already owned (Strahilevitz & Loewenstein, 1998). The longer the object is owned, the more value it accrues. The loss is not just in terms of absolute monetary value but also in regard to the memories that accompany the object. You might think of a favorite coffee mug, a school T-shirt, or something given to you by a significant other. When the object is sold (lost), some of the affective memories are also lost. Ariely, Huber, and Wertenbroch (2005) believe these feelings are involved in attachment to things and justifiably added to our considerations of cost and loss as well as benefit and gain. They add to our understanding of the economic exchange process. Some things are worth more than their utilitarian function, and we are willing to pay for them.

Delaying the Pain

The use of credit cards seems to be linked to an increased willingness to spend (Roberts, 1998). The obvious reason is that credit cards delay the pain of payment for up to a month and a half. The gain is the immediate purchase and the loss is a payment in the distant future.

Lyons (2004) found that college students were more likely to have financial difficulties with credit cards they obtained independently through mailers or campus tables. Of course, this may also be the result of differences in family economic status, with parent-bestowed cards coming from families with more resources and the independent cards coming from families with less money. We further explore credit card issues and the application of psychology in Adjustment in Practice: Credit Cards and Loans.

ADJUSTMENT IN PRACTICE
Credit Cards and Loans

At a practical, everyday life level, most people have to deal with credit cards, loans, and checking or debit cards, all of which relate back to banking behaviors. They are life skills necessary to living in a modern economy. If you are like most students, you will receive offers for all of these "services" soon after you arrive at college. The banks, credit unions, and other financial institutions are practicing a type of applied psychology. We'll describe the basics here but recommend you look at other informational sites if you need more details (see "Money Matters on Campus," 2015).

First of all, you may be wondering why credit card companies are interested in giving us all these services. It is probably because they understand that we learn through experience and we develop habits. If they can get us to learn to look to them for money matters, then we will look to them in the future. If we have positive experiences now, we anticipate there to be positive experiences later. As well, they learn about us—that is, they get to track our financial behaviors. This will be used later to help them determine our behavioral tendencies and our risk.

If we are responsible in our money behaviors, paying our bills to them on time, then we will probably do that in the future. Therefore, we are developing a track record that will determine our credit risk score for our adult life. This is important for our finances in the future. A credit score is a way to quantify our desirability for having a banking relationship. We are creating this score based on our financial behaviors in college.

Credit cards are tempting because they delay the pain of paying until a later date. We have noted in this chapter that we all tend to spend more when we use a credit card. Therefore, by delaying payment, the financial institutions and the businesses that sell us things benefit by our buying more. Note that the businesses have to pay the financial institutions a fee for the charging, so no matter if you pay on time or not, the institutions get paid. In the meantime, if we miss a payment, we are charged a fairly high percentage for use of credit. This is usually several percentage points higher than the rate the institutions are being charged. Say, as an example, the banks have to pay 1% for the money. They charge 9% if your credit rating is good. They may charge 20% if it is not. Making 8% to 19% is excellent! Therefore, while they may not say so, the financial institutions issuing credit cards are indeed offering you credit up front. They make money whenever you use your credit card. And if you delay paying the card charges in full each month, they make a lot more money from us on interest. This is not because they are being mean. They are doing what they do, which is to make money. Note what happens if we pay the minimum due each month on a charge of $1,000 and are charged 20% interest each month (time to pay off the credit card = 26.25 years, amount paid = $4,083.81 [calculated at http://www.1728.org/credcard.htm]). The lessons here might include paying off credit card charges each month and therefore only charging what can be paid off at the end of each month.

Loans are a third way in which we are involved in money issues. Note that credit cards are loans amplified. But we take out loans for our education, housing, and living expenses. We usually "guarantee" our loans with something that matches the amount of the loan. Note that the money we borrow for our automobile or for our home uses the automobile or the home for the guarantee. If we do not repay the loan as agreed, we can lose the guarantee. People have lost their homes or cars when they fall behind on payments. It sounds drastic, but that is how it works. So when we take out an educational loan, what are we putting up as a guarantee? It is our lifetime of earnings that we use to guarantee the loan. As the laws are currently written in the United States, our educational loans are the only loan that we cannot get out of through "default" or "bankruptcy." In essence, you are bound to repay the loan no matter what happens to you.

(Continued)

(Continued)

Reflection Questions

1. How many credit cards do you have?

2. How did you get them and what are their interest rates?

3. What of loans and their terms?

4. What typical banking behaviors do you have? Are there things you can do to develop better banking habits?

Saving

Thaler (1990) created the "simple, elegant, and rational" life cycle theory of savings. In this theory, there are three phases to our saving behaviors based on our age. For the young, who do not make much, savings is low and borrowing is high. For the middle-aged, savings grows in anticipation of future retirement needs. In old age, there is spending of what has been saved. According to Thaler (1990), this is the simple, obvious, but inaccurate description of saving. The model makes several assumptions: that people live within their means, that there is rainy day fund put aside, and that saving for retirement is automatic. Yet according to Thaler, research has shown these assumptions are incorrect. For example, in looking at individuals with increases in income, Flavin (1981) found that increases in spending went up in an unreasonable manner. People did not consider what the increase meant to their total lifetime income, they just spent. They spent for the moment without planning for the future.

Parental Influence on Saving

Parents influence their children's thoughts about money. Webley and Nyhus (2006) found that adolescent savings and future orientations were related to their parents' savings and future orientations. Parents' discussions of financial matters also influenced adolescent behaviors. **Economic socialization** is evident in a number of parent practices that help the child learn about money. These socialization effects can be found in children's thoughts and behaviors as they become adults (Webley & Nyhus, 2013). Adolescent (ages 12–17) savings patterns are related to their savings patterns as young adults (ages 17–25; Friedline, Elliott, & Nam, 2011).

How the parent saves, the education level of the head of household, and race are all related to young adult savings. Friedline et al. (2011) found that social structure variables such as social class also influenced savings behavior. The middle class were savers. Bernheim, Garrett, and Maki (2001) found a relationship between parental savings and their children's savings into middle adulthood (ages 30–40). The finds support a strong socialization effect lasting long into adulthood.

Identification With the Future Self

Saving is influenced by identification with the future self. Ersner-Hershfield, Garton, Ballard, Samanez-Larkin, and Knutson (2009) found that the greater the continuity between the present and the future self, the more people saved money. If there is no identification with the future self, why sacrifice? If there is identification, then savings for self-gain makes sense. Ersner-Hershfield, Wimmer, and Knutson (2009) found this present-future **self-matching** to be related to the willingness to delay gratification and to larger financial assets. In a neuro-imaging study, subjects with brain activity signaling treatment of their future self as another person were more likely to deny greater future gains in favor of immediate but lesser gains (see Figure 11.1). Saving is a similar proposition in which we forgo immediate rewards in favor of future security and gain.

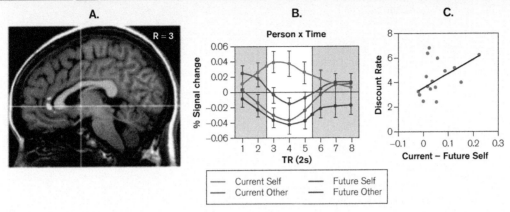

A. Activation sites for self vs. other, and for current self and future self

B. Activation pattern for current self differs from future self, current other and future other

C. Differences between current and future self (seeing future self as another person) are related to discounting the future (taking immediate gains rather than future gains).

Source: Ersner-Hershfield, H., Wimmer, G.E., & Knutson, B. (2009). Saving for the future self: Neural measures of future self-continuity predict temporal discounting, *Social Cognition and Affective Neuroscience*, 4, 85–92. doi:10.1093/scan/nsn042

Take the present–future similarity test provided in Adjustment in Practice: Present–Future Similarity Test. It is an example of how one might determine how much they see themselves to be constant. The findings have suggested that this relates to saving for the future.

ADJUSTMENT IN PRACTICE
Present–Future Similarity Test

The following is an example of the present–future similarity test used in research, examining how this affects savings (Ersner-Hershfield, Garton, Ballard, Samanez-Larking, & Knutson, 2009). If we change physically over time, do we also change our sense of self? Or do we consider our "self" constant?

Complete the following test twice.

Instructions for taking the test the first time:

Check off those words that describe you as you are today.

Instructions for taking the test the second time:

Now return to the list of words, and check off those words that describe you in 10 years' time.

(Continued)

(Continued)

Compare the two tests for similarities, noting the overlap from the first and second taking.

_____Accepting

_____Adventurous

_____Bold

_____Calm

_____Determined

_____Eager

_____Friendly

_____Generous

_____Hard-Working

_____Messy

Reflection Questions

1. Note how you see yourself now versus in the future. The more alike the present and future self is, the more likely a person is to save. What do you think of this finding?

2. Can you think of reasons why this might happen?

3. How might this help us to help people to save more?

The Powerful Self

Savings are related to feelings of power (Garbinsky, Klesse, & Aaker, 2014). Those who are made to feel powerful were more likely to think of saving and to save in comparison to those made to feel less powerful or left alone. Saving money was a means to power and ceased when power was attained.

Joshi and Fast (2013) demonstrated a link between power experiences and increases in future-self connections. This future-self connection leads to a willingness to delay immediate gratification for greater rewards in the future—that is, more saving behavior.

Regular and Automatic Savings

Another strategy to address the tendency to take immediate, smaller rewards was tested by Tam and Dholakia (2014). Subjects who were told to think in terms of important habits as repeating cycles planned to save more and then did save more. In one of their series of studies, planned savings estimation was 70% higher and actual savings were over 80% greater. Thinking of time along a straight line leads to perceiving the future as distant from the present. When thinking of time in cycles, specific behaviors can be built into life as a routine. Saving can become a regular habit.

This accumulation of money can be for a variety of purposes. As noted earlier, money buys us necessities in life like food and shelter. Beyond these survival basics, money is seen by many to be related to happiness, which we will examine next.

Money and Happiness

We need money or its equivalents to survive in our civilization and understand the desire for a certain level of resources to live comfortably. Yet it is not a simple relationship between money and happiness, where the more money one has, the happier one is. Rather, what has been found is that the relationship between happiness and money is a curvilinear function; the relationship is not a straight line but a curved one (Kahneman & Deaton, 2010). At some point, the amount of money we have contributes less to the amount of everyday happiness.

Based on a U.S. study, Kahneman and Deaton (2010) found the relationship between income and everyday happiness levels off at $75,000. Less predicts lower levels of emotional well-being but more does not predict more well-being. This is interpreted as the estimated household income to live "comfortably." Others have adjusted these figures for various cities, arguing that cost of living varies by region (see Figure 11.3).

Money buys necessities and relief from worry. The relationship between money and sense of well-being is well-established (Diener, Ng, Harter, & Arora, 2010; Diener, Tay, & Oishi, 2013). However, this relationship is more complex than we might think.

The relationship between income and everyday happiness is based on comparisons to previous income levels (Kahneman & Deaton, 2010). Perception of differences are based on the starting point, with higher starting points requiring more change to be noticed. For example, think of adding 5 pounds to a 10-pound weight, versus adding 5 pounds to a 100-pound weight. Shifting from 10 pounds to 15 pounds will be noticed more than going from 100 pounds to 105 pounds. In the same way, Kahneman and Deaton (2010) described the way in which differences in income are noticed.

Beyond this relativity, income loss is felt more than income gain (Boyce, Wood, Banks, Clark, & Brown, 2013). As humans, we hate losses. In a two-nation (Germany and Great Britain) sample, sense of well-being was related to increases in income, but that sense of well-being was more markedly decreased when there was a decline in income.

Figure 11.2   Money and Happiness

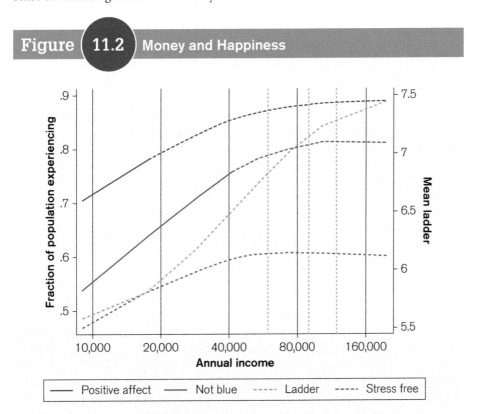

Source: Kahneman, D., & Deaton, A. High income improves evaluation of life but not emotional well-being. PNAS, September 21, 2010, vol. 107, no. 38.

Figure 11.3 The Ten Richest Cities in America* With Cost of Living Calculations**

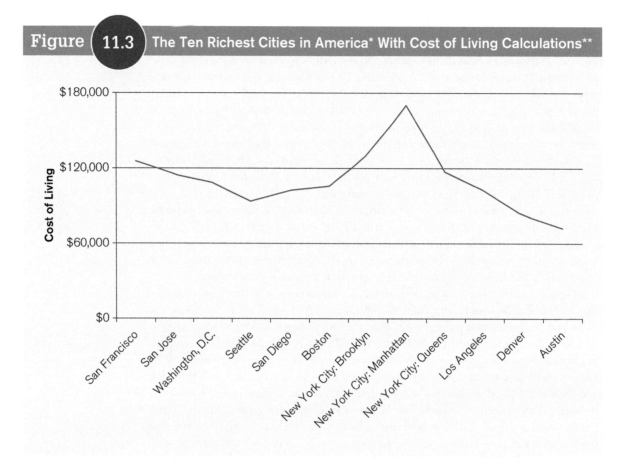

*Populations over 500,000 with the highest percentage of households making $150,000 or more.
** National estimate is $75,000 "to be comfortable."
Source: Rawes (2015).

Level of income influences a sense of well-being, but this relationship declines with increases around $75,000 (Kahneman & Deaton, 2010); what seems to have a greater impact is the direction or trajectory of our income, with modest gains for increases and larger declines for decreases (Boyce et al., 2013). Of course, this $75,000 figure was based on data collected in 2009 and assumed an average household size of approximately 2.5 people.

Easterlin (2003) approached the question of money and well-being from another viewpoint. Looking at national survey data, he noted that what contributed to happiness did not necessarily relate to more money. He found that nonmonetary factors such as health and marriage were good indicators of well-being. Better education led to higher levels of happiness. But increases in income and the accumulation of material goods had less of an impact on happiness indicators.

In another study, Easterlin, McVey, Switek, Sawangfa, and Smith Zweig (2010) reported seemingly contradictory national survey findings: Individuals with higher incomes were generally happier. On the other hand, national increases in income over a 10-year period did not yield increases in population happiness. These results held in U.S., European, Latin American, and Asian samples. These findings were present both in established and in developing nations. Easterlin (2003) believed the lack of relationship between national income and national levels of happiness could be caused by changes in the social norms for income. As everyone makes more money, the expectations for income grow. Given these national sample findings, it appears that money concerns should be balanced with attention to health and relationships.

Diener et al. (2013) refined the measurement of well-being into three different dimensions: life satisfaction, positive feelings, and the lack of negative feelings. Their research found that household income was consistently related to all three dimensions of well-being. Income could enable the acquisition of material goods and services and raise expectations for the future. When a national indicator of wealth (gross domestic product, or GDP) was correlated with the three indicators, only life satisfaction was found to be related, meaning that while the nation's wealth related to people's overall sense of life being, it was not related to their feelings.

Dunn and Norton (2014) examined the psychology literature and concluded that happiness was not solely dependent on the amount of money we had but how that money was used. They described five principles relating money to overall happiness.

1. Focus on experiences over material goods (Carter & Gilovich, 2010, 2012) since we are what we do, not what we have.

2. Pay for experiences ahead of time so we can enjoy what we gain (experience) and not worry about what we lose (cost; Carter, 2014; Higgins, 1997).

3. Time is valuable; when we feel we have time to do things, we tend to feel good about our life (Kasser & Sheldon, 2009).

4. Anticipation and waiting can help prolong the appreciation of the moment (Wood & Bettman, 2007); the length of time we will experience a feeling is increased by expectations of positive emotions due to the "durability bias" (Baumeister, Vohs, DeWall, & Zhang, 2007).

5. Doing things for others makes us feel good. For example, donating to a worthy cause activates the reward centers in the brain (Harbaugh, Mayr, & Burghart, 2007) and seems to universally lead to increased feelings of happiness (Aknin, Barrington-Leigh, et al., 2013).

Greater benefits come from spending money on others (Dunn, Aknin, & Norton, 2014). This is especially true when there is a connection to those being helped (Aknin, Sandstrom, Dunn, & Norton, 2011). The benefit may also come from improved connection to others (Aknin, Dunn, Sandstrom, & Norton, 2013). This connection between giving and well-being has been found around the world. Acting charitably has been found to activate reward centers in the brain (Harbaugh et al., 2007; Moll et al., 2006).

This list makes clear that while money is important to survival, it is only a means to an end. And as social beings with existential concerns, the direction of our ways to happiness are aligned with these orientations.

Conclusion

Money is a human invention. We can follow the development of money through history, noting that in all cases, it is the human who gives it meaning. We learn and teach others about money and its uses. The combination of cognitive psychology and microeconomics has led to improved understanding of how we view money and use it. Our conceptions of money are influenced by the contexts for money. We compare and evaluate. We feel as well as count our money. We make decisions on buying and on how much to pay based on estimations of value. To buy or not to buy is dependent on cognitive interpretations. Saving also depends on conceptions of self and the future.

We explored the relationship between money and happiness, which is complex. What we find is that it is not the money but how we think of and use it that counts. There is a base level of income that provides the basics: food, drink, and shelter. Beyond these levels, the relationship between money and happiness decreases in strength. Money can strengthen our relationships with others, expand our experience of our world, and give ourselves time. This fits with the existential and cognitive orientations to explaining behavior.

Review Questions

1. When and where was the first paper money used?

2. How do we learn about the meaning of money?

3. What is the developmental progression in our understanding what goes into the price of things?

4. Define *behavioral economics*.

5. How do we estimate the worth of an object or experience?

6. What are the two decision-making processes discussed by Kahneman?

7. Discuss the implications of "free" on our buying habits.

8. Discuss what happens when we buy with credit.

9. How does the feeling of power influence savings?

10. Someone asks you about money and happiness. What advice might you give them?

Key Terms

behavioral economics 224
cognitive psychology 239
durability bias 231

economic socialization 234
protectors or
   regulators 226

secondary reinforcer 225
self-matching 234

Sharpen your skills with SAGE edge at **edge.sagepub.com/moritsugu**

SAGE edge for students provides a personalized approach to help you accomplish your coursework goals in an easy-to-use learning environment.

Go to **edge.sagepub.com/moritsugu** for additional exercises and web resources. Select Chapter 11, Money for chapter-specific resources.

Chapter

12

Aging

Learning Objectives

1. Discuss how life expectancy has changed worldwide over the past century.

2. Describe the age-related physical and cognitive changes of early, middle, and older adulthood.

3. Describe the major socioemotional changes associated with aging.

4. Identify behaviors associated with aging positively.

5. Identify factors that contribute to the ability to cope with loss.

6. Summarize findings about optimal living situations for aging adults.

Terrell was close to his grandfather throughout all of his childhood and adolescence. Not only did they share a home in which Terrell's mother, father, and younger sister also lived but they shared a love of cars and basketball. When Terrell was a senior in high school, his beloved grandfather had a stroke, and as a result, he lost many of his physical abilities and some of his cognitive abilities. The stroke was a serious scare for the entire family, but the adaptation that Terrell's grandfather and parents (as his primary caretakers) made was truly life changing. His parents had to provide round-the-clock care for his grandfather. His grandfather had to learn to depend on Terrell's parents in ways he had never expected. Terrell was grateful to still have his grandfather around, but he was worried about his ability to get used to his new normal. Terrell also started to worry about the well-being of his parents. This was the first time he had ever really seen the challenges of adapting to unexpected aspects of aging, and it was not easy to witness.

. . . .

What did George Bernard Shaw mean when he quipped, "Youth is wasted on the young"? One possibility is that when we are young, we don't truly appreciate what it means to be at a point in our lives when we are healthy, developing dreams for the future, and very much at the beginning of a long journey. Sometimes it takes an aha moment like the one Terrell experienced to help us understand that change is inevitable. As people age, some aspects of their health inevitably decline, dreams may be realized or abandoned, and the preciousness of time becomes more and more apparent. Thus, aging transforms us in both positive and negative ways. We gain perspective and wisdom. We also lose certain abilities or life options. This requires great adjustment and adaptation, which is why we will discuss aging as a key context of life span adjustment.

It is important to note that not all people experience the aging process in the same way. Some people feel that their later years are their golden years. Others feel anxious about the possibility that they might become seriously ill or disabled, while others fear that their lives may soon end.

In this chapter, we will discuss some of the challenges that accompany the aging process, along with opportunities that come with getting older. Additionally, we will talk about healthy aging and why some people are able to maintain a high quality of life while aging and others have great difficulties throughout the process. We will also examine what we know about adjusting to some of the hallmarks of later life, namely retirement, the loss of loved ones, and making decisions about where to live. First, let's consider some statistics about life expectancy.

Life Expectancies

In the United States, the **average life expectancy**, or age to which we can expect to live, increases every year. In fact, life expectancies for Americans have changed dramatically over the past century. For example, in 1900, life expectancy was approximately 50 years of age (Berk, 2014b). Data from the Centers for Disease Control and Prevention (CDC) in 2014 tell us that the average life expectancy is now 78.8 years for people in the United States, with men living to age 76 on average and women living to age 81 on average. Furthermore, because of population fluctuations, there are now more older adults within the larger population than there have ever been (Hill, 2015). For example, in 1950, people 65 years of age and older constituted only 8% of the entire population. In 2030, it is expected that 20% of the population will be 65 years of age or older (Shrestha & Heiser, 2011).

Figure 12.1 Life Expectancies

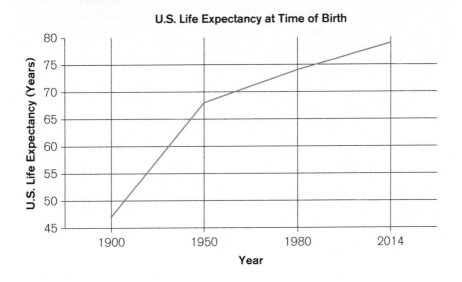

U.S. Life Expectancy at Time of Birth

Source: Based on data from Centers for Disease Control.

Another related statistic is that the number of "very old" people is increasing, such that there are now more than 10 million people who are over the age of 85 residing in the United States (Hill, 2015). To give us some perspective, this is not just an American phenomenon. The United States ranks 26th in terms of life expectancy worldwide (World Health Organization [WHO], 2014d). This means that the population on our planet is increasingly older, and the proportion of people who are considered to be elderly is growing daily.

Another global trend that is significant is that women as a group outlive men on average 2 to 3 years, although the U.S. statistics indicate that it is closer to 5 years (WHO, 2014d). There are also racial and socioeconomic differences in life expectancies. For example, according to the U.S. Department of Health and Human Services (2011a), a White child born in 2010 is likely to live 3 years longer than an African American child born that same year. However, when we look at statistics of people over the age of 85, we find that in this "very old" age group, low-income ethnic minority individuals live longer than their White, better resourced peers (Masters, 2012). Researchers have speculated that the overall racial and socioeconomic differences in life expectancy may be explained by different rates of infant mortality, accidental deaths, stress, and poverty between White versus ethnic minority individuals (Berk, 2014b). However, the tendency for White people to be less well represented in over-85 age groups may be due to the resiliency of lower income people of color, who in order to survive to age 85 in spite of exposure to the risks mentioned previously, must be biologically and psychologically strong (Berk, 2014b).

Why is it that people are living so much longer in this century versus previous centuries? There are important individual differences that must be examined when answering this question, which we will explore in the remainder of this chapter. However, length of life of people in countries around the world can be accurately predicted by a nation's health care (access and quality), its quality of housing for older adults, and its available

Among people over age 85, ethnic-minority individuals tend to outlive their White counterparts.

©Can Stock Photo Inc. / zurijeta

social services (Berk, 2014b). In other words, without knowing anything about an individual's biology, psychological health, or disposition, if a person lives in a part of the world with widely accessible, high-quality health care; is living in housing that meets his or her needs; and is able to access social services such as transportation or recreational programs, the person will likely live to his or her maximum life span. This kind of information has important implications for what the United States and other countries must be able to provide for its citizens to help protect their quality of life as they age.

All of us are aging every day of our lives. While it is easy to assume that the issues and concerns of aging are not relevant for younger adults, as we will discover in this chapter, the decisions we make early in life about our health, lifestyles, and money have serious effects on the quality of life we experience when we are older and our ability to adjust to age-related changes.

Age-Related Changes

There are many different ways that we know we are aging. Some of the most prominent changes have to do with our physical state, our cognitive abilities, and our social–emotional well-being. It is important to again note that not everyone experiences the various changes that come with aging in the same way. For example, most people experience graying or losing hair as they get older. Some men will opt to wear hairpieces to conceal their balding, some women will choose to color their gray hair. Others will accept their new appearances with little thought. As we explore the changes that are associated with aging, we will also explore some of the factors that influence how people's well-being is affected by such changes. Adaptation to changes and one's ability to make meaning of such changes can greatly determine whether one wears the signs of aging as a badge of honor or something to hide.

Physical Changes

Our bodies are often the initial harbingers of changes associated with aging. Our body structures reach our maximum capacity and efficiency in our teens and early adulthood years (Berk, 2014b). Biological aging, which begins in early adulthood, is the effect of our DNA being damaged over time, which leads to less efficient cell repair and the release of free radicals (Stohs, 2011). Also, due to telomere shortening, genetically determined biological changes may begin to emerge (Epel et al., 2009; e.g., if one is predisposed to certain types of diseases such as heart disease, arthritis; see Table 12.1).

Early Adulthood
Some of the first physical signs of aging occur in early adulthood. Declines in heart and lung performance take place, which may lessen our endurance and impact our motor performance (Wilkie, Guenette, Dominelli, & Scheel, 2012). The immune response declines after age 20 (Berk, 2014b). Women's reproductive capacity begins to decline with age due to the reduced quantity and quality of their eggs (Balasch, 2010). For men, reproductive capacity is less compromised with age, but sperm quality does decrease after age 35 (Lambert, Masson, & Fisch, 2006). Relatively speaking, early adulthood is the point in time in which our body begins to lose its full capacity, so many of the changes we see in early adulthood are very subtle (e.g., it may become increasingly more challenging to conceive a child, but it is still quite possible). Typically, the more obvious signs of aging begin to emerge in middle adulthood.

Table 12.1	Physical Changes With Aging
Change	**Nature of change**
Immune response	Decreases after age 20
Reproductive ability	Decreases during middle adulthood
Physical appearance	Most notable changes begin in middle adulthood continuing through older adulthood
Vision	First changes begin in middle adulthood continuing through older adulthood
Hearing	First changes begin in middle adulthood continuing through older adulthood
Susceptibility to disease	First changes begin in middle adulthood continuing through older adulthood
Temperature sensitivity	Most notable changes in older adulthood
Sleep patterns	Most notable changes in older adulthood

Middle Adulthood

In middle adulthood, physical signs of aging are often more obvious to both aging individuals and important people in their lives. There is a series of changes we can see. For example, our skin begins to wrinkle, loosen, and dry out; also, muscle mass begins to decline.

Hair begins to gray more profoundly and become thinner as hair follicles begin to die (Berk, 2014b).

Some changes cannot be seen as readily but have noticeable effects on our lives. For example, bone density declines, which can make us more susceptible to height loss and bone fractures (Berk, 2014b). Vision is likely to decline, in dim light conditions in particular, and after age 40, there is an increasing risk of glaucoma, which is a buildup of pressure in the eye that can damage the optic nerve (Owsley, 2011). Some people who have had perfect vision their entire lives now need reading glasses or find themselves to be more nervous driving at night. In addition to vision changes, there are hearing changes that come with age. Age-related hearing loss, or presbycusis, initially is characterized by a decline in the detection of high-pitched frequencies and then over time spreads to other frequencies (Center for Hearing and Communication, 2012).

In addition to these physical changes, in middle adulthood, major changes occur in reproductive abilities and susceptibility to disease. Women gradually produce less estrogen, which ultimately concludes with menopause (Berk, 2014b). Men continue to produce sperm throughout the life span, but the quantity of semen diminishes and erections become harder to attain and maintain (Shaeer & Shaeer, 2012). Thus, the sex lives of many adults begin to change in response to the aging process. In middle adulthood, the diagnosis of life-threatening diseases also becomes more commonplace. The death rate from cardiovascular disease and cancer spikes dramatically during this time (U.S. Census Bureau, 2012).

Changes to one's appearance begin as early as middle adulthood and continue through later adulthood.

©iStockphoto.com/shapecharge

Older Adulthood

After age 65, physical declines become more apparent, and more of our systems begin to decline. The number of individuals with cataracts, which results in foggy vision, increases tenfold from middle adulthood to later adulthood (Owsley, 2011). Macular degeneration, which also results in blurred vision and ultimately blindness, is also a sign of aging more common in later adulthood (Berk, 2014b). Both cataracts and macular degeneration are treatable with surgery if diagnosed early but can impact the confidence of older adults to see properly and drive a car (Berk, 2014b).

Hearing loss also becomes more profound and common in later adulthood (U.S. Department of Health and Human Services, 2011a). While most loss of hearing is not great enough to impact daily living until after age 85, many older adults have to turn up the volume on their televisions or phones, and many become uncomfortable in social settings like parties where listening to a conversation in the presence of background noise becomes challenging (Kidd & Bao, 2012). Hearing aids are common, albeit expensive, ways in which this decline in hearing can be adapted. However, older adults can sometimes be self-conscious about wearing hearing aids.

Other common physical changes associated with aging in older adults are temperature sensitivity and the loss of ability to regulate one's temperature and reduced oxygenation (less efficient breathing), which results in less endurance and feeling out of breath (Berk, 2014b). Changes are also detected in sleep patterns due to brain changes: Older adults have a harder time falling and staying asleep, and the tendency to go to bed and awaken earlier are also common (Edwards et al., 2010; see Researching Adjustment: How Old Is Old?).

RESEARCHING ADJUSTMENT
How Old Is Old?

When do we technically become old? Is it at a particular age? Is it a state of being? There are a few different ways to answer this question. If we look at the models of human development that have been discussed by psychologists like Erikson (1950), we could divide up the aging process into stages such as early adulthood, middle adulthood, and late adulthood. Late adulthood, which we most typically associate with "becoming old," is thought to describe people ages 60 or 65 and older. On the other hand, there are some 65-year-olds who do not look or act old. Therefore, some scholars have described the process of aging by differentiating young-old people from old-old people as a function of their health status (Berk, 2014b). If a person is 65 or older but healthy and capable of living independently, they might best be considered a young-old person. However, if a 60-year-old has serious health problems or disabilities and is very dependent on others for daily care, that person might be considered an old-old person. It is easy to imagine that adjusting to the aging process in later adulthood is greatly facilitated when one feels good physically and has the ability to function independently. Having serious health problems or disabilities can require more radical types of adaptation and, hence, more challenging adjustment.

When physical changes become unavoidable, the need to adapt and adjust arises for most people. For those who are anxious about aging and death, concerns about one's appearance are exaggerated (Montepare, 2006) and investing in strategies to reduce the outward signs of aging is more common (e.g., wigs, toupees, plastic surgery, injectables, hair dye). While it is debatable how healthy these attempts to adjust to aging are, there are certainly less controversial methods that people use in an effort to maintain their quality of life and functioning. For example, there is a great deal of technology available to help older adults who are experiencing physical changes to maintain their routines. Voice commands allow people to use phones for calling and texting without the dexterity of their fingers or ability to see small icons being an issue. Computers that enlarge text size or can read messages aloud help with vision declines. Hearing aids, as previously mentioned, can be enormously helpful for those experiencing hearing problems.

However, one factor that underlies these adjustments is the ability to acknowledge that one needs assistance. Being open to help can be difficult for many older adults who do not wish to admit any decrease in their ability to function independently. This can cause significant stress and conflict in families where younger generations may see such changes more objectively than their older relatives do. Sometimes it can take a number of years for all family members to be on the same page with what adaptations need to take place to preserve the quality of life of an older relative. While younger family members may see such changes earlier than do their aging relatives, oftentimes efforts to be proactive (e.g., telling your grandfather that you are worried about his ability to drive at night) can be misinterpreted as attempts to take away an older relative's control.

Cognitive Changes

While many of the aforementioned changes that accompany aging impact minor types of adjustment like adapting to a new physical appearance as well as major types of adjustment such as living with a disability, there are also changes that happen to our brains and thinking that are a part of the aging process. Some of the changes in our thinking or cognitive abilities are welcome and actually improve our functioning. Others—especially those that occur later in life—can be much less welcome and require more serious adaptations.

Early Adulthood

In the early part of our adult lives, our brains are still maturing in some important ways. Scientists now estimate that some of the newer cognitive abilities that first begin to appear in adolescence (around puberty), such as abstract thinking and the ability to plan, are not fully matured until age 23 (Paus, 2009). Therefore, to begin our discussion of cognitive changes of aging, we will outline some of the major ways that thinking changes in young adults.

The area of greatest change in the brains of adolescents and young adults is in the prefrontal cortex, which is the part of the brain in charge of our executive functioning. The types of activities that are included in executive functioning are monitoring, organizing, planning, and strategizing (Kuhn, 2009). While in early adolescence, the prefrontal cortex blossoms with connections that allow for these new abilities, but what happens later in adolescence and into early adulthood is considered more of a pruning of these new abilities. In other words, we become more efficient at these newly acquired abilities as our established neural connections become better insulated and smoother (Giedd et al., 1999). This process of fine-tuning in many ways accounts for the paradox that is seen in adolescents: namely both immature and mature types of thinking (i.e., problem solving), which sometimes results in negative consequences. Young adults, while not completely immune from making a bad decision every now and then, are much more likely to consistently use their executive functioning in ways that are beneficial to them.

Processing speed also increases beginning in adolescence and throughout early adulthood (Kuhn, 2009). This means that adolescents pay better attention, remember more and remember more efficiently, and are capable of learning things often in less time than it took in childhood. Another important cognitive change is in the area of response inhibition (Paus, 2009). Response inhibition is helpful in two ways. The first is that it allows us to pay more selective attention (e.g., being able to tune out your friends who are trying to distract you during a lecture in class), and the second is that it helps us be less impulsive. We can resist temptations much easier when we can inhibit our responses. Again, these skills are not necessarily mastered in early adulthood, or even middle adulthood, but these cognitive skills are important aspects of development in early adults.

Middle Adulthood

Cognitive changes associated with middle adulthood are explained by various theories of cognitive development such as Labouvie-Vief's (1985) theory of adult cognition and Schaie's (1994) model of adult intellectual development. Both theories suggest that middle adulthood is the time when cognitive abilities are peaking, not declining, and that the stereotype that 50-year-olds are "over the hill" is grossly inaccurate when it comes to intellectual abilities. Labouvie-Vief (1985) highlighted the increase in **pragmatic problem solving** and **cognitive–affective complexity** that occurs in middle adulthood. Pragmatic problem solving, which involves using logic to solve real-world problems, is a function of cognitive skills and, importantly, experience in the real world, which younger adults lack in comparison to their older counterparts. Cognitive–affective complexity is reflected in older adults' ability to have self-awareness and a greater sensitivity to others' perspectives, which can make us less emotionally reactive when people have different opinions than we do, and that ability can assist in thinking rationally about real-world problems.

Another cognitive gain associated with middle adulthood is the acquisition of expertise, or extensive knowledge in a particular field or context (Berk, 2014b). Again, older adults typically have years to master particular abilities, for example, multitasking, if one is in charge of a household or is a corporate executive, or generating creative concepts by identifying questions that haven't yet been asked in one's field (e.g., product development). It makes sense that life experience both in general and in specific fields promotes cognitive gains such as these. Therefore, if a great deal of cognitive change in aging is positive and does not require much adaptation, is there anything that is vulnerable to decline in our older years?

Older Adulthood

Many of us are familiar with the phrase, "I'm having a senior moment." This phrase reflects a widespread stereotype associated with aging: We become senile and forgetful as we age. While there is some validity to the idea that our cognitive abilities change as we age, not all these changes involve a loss of cognitive abilities. Rather, some cognitive changes of aging reflect mastery and expertise that we gain as we get older. But indeed, there are some normal declines in abilities that are part of the aging process.

Cognitive tasks that require us to quickly process information are the areas of cognition most vulnerable to decline during the aging process (Schaie, 1994). This type of intelligence, known as fluid intelligence, begins to decline as early as our 20s. For example, perceptual speed, or our ability to quickly detect similarities between two photos, is affected by the speed with which we can process information.

Working memory, another feature of fluid intelligence, is also impacted negatively during the aging process (Berk, 2014b). An example of working memory skills is the ability to try and remember a new phone number after hearing it once. Thus, working memory is the ability to form new memories, some of which ultimately get rehearsed and embedded into our **long-term memory**, but many of these memories do not. Working memory is different from long-term memory, or the fund of knowledge we acquire throughout our lifetime, which is a type of intelligence that is less impacted by aging (Schaie, 1994). This is demonstrated by the fact that many elderly people have exquisite recollections of their early life experiences but have a hard time remembering the name of a person they just met.

Furthermore, a certain amount of "forgetfulness" is common in aging adults (Alzheimer's Association, 2015). However, normal forgetfulness can be remedied by taking extra time to remember or having someone prompt us (e.g., we forget the name of a neighbor but eventually remember or answer a question about the person's name correctly). This type of forgetfulness often indicates a delay in being able to retrieve memories that are still in existence. Many of us, regardless of age, have had the experience of going into a room to retrieve something and upon our arrival forgetting what we were trying to retrieve. Typically, if we return to the place where we first had the idea or take a moment to review the most immediate history in our mind, we can remember what we were looking for. Thus, there are ways we can adjust to changes in our short-term memory that work for most people.

Because the speed with which information is processed declines throughout adulthood, many adults try to adapt to these changes in a variety of ways. Mentally active people are more likely to maintain their cognitive abilities than are inactive people (Alzheimer's Association, 2015). Staying involved in work or regular hobbies can be a key to staying mentally active. For people who are no longer working, there are a number of ways that they can continue to stay active. Taking courses or being involved in community or travel programs can be effective ways of staying active and learning new things. In fact, some universities offer specialized educational programs for retired adults, which makes some college towns desirable retirement destinations. However, taking advantage of these ideas requires opportunity and resources, luxuries that not all older people have, which is why many residential or retirement communities advertise their recreational activities and opportunities.

Socioemotional Changes of Aging

In addition to cognitive changes, socioemotional changes accompany the aging process, namely in terms of how we see ourselves, our life goals, and transformations in our

During middle adulthood most people are at their prime cognitively, as noted by their presence in leadership positions.

©iStockphoto.com/Steve Debenport

Decreasing personal control is a major socioemotional change associated with older adulthood.

relationships. Some of these changes impact our social lives and others our inner emotions. Like cognitive and physical changes, all of the following socioemotional changes require important adaptation as part of the process of healthy adjustment to aging.

Identity Changes

In early adulthood, we spend time establishing ourselves in new careers and relationships—or as Freud identified, the worlds of love and work. The process of establishing ourselves in relationships and work is discussed in detail in Chapters 8 and 10. Without doubt, the process of seeing ourselves as professional members of particular careers (e.g., counselors, teachers, bankers, accountants) and as partners, spouses, and parents are major aspects of early adulthood for many (Berk, 2014b). During the bulk of our adulthood, it is easy to feel a sense of stability associated with our careers and families. However, as we enter later phases of adulthood, we often experience another major transition with respect to our identities.

Changes to one's identity are common and occur throughout the middle to later parts of adulthood. For example, major changes take place during the process of retirement, when children grow up and move away (aka empty nest syndrome) and, eventually, due to the loss of spouses and family members through death (Berk, 2014b). There tend to be several gender differences associated with how people adapt to these changes. For example, men have a much harder time adapting to retirement than do women (Osbourne, 2012). Conversely, women have a much harder time adapting to empty nest syndrome than do men (Berk, 2014b). While losing a spouse to death is difficult for both men and women, women tend to have an easier time adapting to life as a widow than do men who become widowers (we will discuss this in more detail in upcoming sections of this chapter). Some of the explanations for these differences are found in the main ways that men and women define themselves as individuals throughout the life span.

Generativity and Meaning

Psychologist Erik Erikson (1950) was one of the most prominent scholars to discuss the social and emotional developmental hallmarks of older adulthood. He outlined two important milestones that occur in middle and late adulthood: **generativity** and **ego integrity**. Generativity refers to the need that Erikson believed we all have to leave a legacy or make a contribution to subsequent generations. For some adults, raising children is a concrete way to literally contribute to future generations. Given that raising a family can consume almost 50% of our adult lives, this task in and of itself could make a person feel generative. On the other hand, having children is not the only way people leave legacies. Artists create works of art that live long after they have died. Thus, one of the socioemotional changes of aging is the need for generativity, or the need to make a contribution to the world. Erikson thought that if a person was unsuccessful in being generative in their adult years, a feeling of stagnation would set in. Thus, he would argue that successful adjustment to aging in later life necessitates having a sense of generativity.

Another later socioemotional need of older adulthood is ego integrity, or the capacity to view one's life in the context of larger humanity, which involves coming to terms with the life one has lived. This is an existential exercise in many ways and requires a great deal of reviewing and reflecting on one's life. Am I happy with the decisions I made, the paths that I chose, and those that I did not? Do I have any regrets? Do I feel that my life had meaning to others? In many ways, this is a solitary activity, but it can be informed by those around us. In societies such as ours, older people are not often valued for their wisdom and life experience, which can make achieving ego integrity a challenge.

However, regardless of whether an older person receives feedback from important others that his or her life has been meaningful, each of us must answer the question for ourselves. For example, if you have been a generous, philanthropic person during your life but you were never able to maintain a lasting relationship or become a parent, would you consider your life to have been meaningful? If you lived life as a loving parent but had to sacrifice many of your own personal goals as a consequence, would you feel satisfied in the end? Questions such as these have to be asked and answered in a process of life review in order to achieve ego integrity, according to Erikson (1950). The ability to engage in this process is thought to be related to successful adjustment in later life.

Support from one's immediate family is often more welcome than support or companionship from strangers.

Sense of Control

Decreasing personal control is another socioemotional change that we face in later life (Hill, 2015). As we have discussed, there are a significant number of ways that our bodies show signs of aging that over time require us to make accommodations. One accommodation that many older adults face is whether or not they can truly live independently or whether they need some assistance. This assistance could come in the form of a housekeeper, home health care worker, or an adult child spend time helping with chores or basic self-care. In more extreme cases, the assistance might need to be in the form of more around-the-clock care or moving into a retirement community or nursing home.

Social Support

Declines in social support and loneliness are other major socioemotional changes associated with aging in later life. As we have mentioned earlier in this book, social support is a major way that stress is reduced throughout the life span, and later life is no exception. In fact, social support might be even more important in later life given that it is not necessarily built into our daily lives (e.g., if we are not working or living alone). Furthermore, for older adults, social support and companionship can be a major safety factor. If an older relative is living with his or her spouse or partner or resides with adult children, social support may be built into their daily routine. Even if not residing with family members, older adults can maintain social support through nearby family relationships, but more and more, families may not be residing in close enough proximity to make this a regular event. Thus, formal support, which might come from agency-provided services or paid home helpers, may be another way that older adults can receive companionship and the tangible support they need.

One source of support that appears to be most welcome in particular from ethnic minority elders is help that is offered in connection with a known, respected organization such as a church (Berk, 2014b). Support from members of one's church is welcome by most older adults in part because they are not strangers and the recipients often feel that the help is being offered due to genuine care, not just obligation (Krause, 2012). It is important to note that welcomed, more formal help such as from a church member can often supplement family-based help nicely. Family members who provide regular care for aging parents or relatives appreciate a break, and the care recipient often appreciates a new person to connect with.

The question then becomes this: Do all older adults need companionship, or might there be some elders who are fine on their own? This is a question that researcher John Cacioppo and his colleagues (Luo, Hawkely, Waite, & Cacioppo, 2012) sought to answer in a study on loneliness in older adults. Specifically, the researchers tested the possibility that a person's subjective sense of feeling alone (e.g., isolated, left out) may be a determinant of healthy aging. In this study, they found that it matters whether one "felt lonely": The seniors with the best health outcomes, both medically and psychologically speaking (e.g., depression), were the ones who had regular social contact in their lives and who felt less alone. It did not matter whether the participants lived alone or with others; their subjective sense of feeling alone was a risk factor for many health outcomes.

Furthermore, they found that loneliness contributed to one's mortality. In other words, lonely people die sooner than do people who are not lonely. Their conclusion is that loneliness alters our physiology at a more fundamental level. This is an important reminder that if elderly relatives say that they don't want visitors (which may be because they don't wish to make anyone feel obligated or burdened to visit), it is far better for their well-being if we ignore their wishes and visit them anyway. See Adjustment in Practice: Decreasing Loneliness for ways to combat loneliness.

ADJUSTMENT IN PRACTICE
Decreasing Loneliness

Up to 32% of adults over the age of 55 report feeling lonely, and as people age and retire from work or lose loved ones and friends to death and disability, their vulnerability to loneliness can increase (Masi, Chen, Hawkley, & Cacioppo, 2011). How do we help people feel less lonely? There have generally been four ways that loneliness has been confronted by health care professionals: improving social skills of the individual, enhancing social support available to the individual, increasing opportunities for social interaction in the environment, and addressing maladaptive social cognitions (i.e., dysfunctional thoughts). In a recent meta-analysis, researchers examined the effectiveness of these strategies to successfully combat loneliness (Masi et al., 2011). What they found is that while all the strategies had some benefit in reducing feelings of loneliness, working with individuals to address their maladaptive social cognitions was the most effective approach. Cognitive behavioral therapy, which we discuss elsewhere in this book, is particularly effective in reducing loneliness in older adults. For example, if a person feels that the reason he or she is lonely is because no one is interested in his or her life anymore or that a person feels that life has little value anymore, a therapist would work to replace these cognitions with more realistic and optimistic thoughts. This research suggests that it is not merely changes in one's social environment that lead to loneliness being a chronic problem for older adults, but rather, it is what those situations may do to their thinking over time that creates more serious problems. Simply creating opportunities for people to socialize with others is not enough if the person's thoughts are contributing to the feeling of isolation (see Table 12.2).

Reflection Questions

1. What might this research suggest for settings like retirement homes or nursing homes that attempt to help older adults adjust to new living situations?

2. What are ways that older people can continue to think positively about their lives, even in the midst of losses?

Table 12.2	Cognitive and Socioemotional Changes With Aging	

Cognitive changes		
Change	**Example**	**Nature of change**
Executive functioning	Multi-tasking, problem solving	Increases in early adulthood Peaks in middle adulthood
Processing speed	Reaction time	Increases in early adulthood Peaks in middle adulthood Declines in older adulthood
Response inhibition	Selective attention	Increases in early adulthood Peaks in middle adulthood
Pragmatic problem solving	Logical decision making	Increases in early adulthood Peaks in middle adulthood
Cognitive-affect complexity	Self-awareness	Increases in early adulthood Peaks in middle adulthood
Working memory	Ability to form memories	Declines in older adulthood
Long-term memories	Ability remember the past	Rarely declines in older adulthood
Socio-emotional changes		
Change	**Example**	**Nature of change**
Identity	Roles played in life	Increases in early-middle adulthood Decreases in older adulthood
Generativity	Need to leave a legacy	Emerges in middle-older adulthood
Sense of control	Self-determination	Increases in early adulthood Peaks in middle adulthood Declines in older adulthood
Social support	Sense of connection	Increases in early-middle adulthood Declines in older adulthood

The Third Age

Within the literature on aging, a new term has emerged to describe the opportunities to reinvent oneself associated with older adulthood: the *third age*. The third age describes the period of time after middle adulthood (which typically involves work and family obligations), usually around ages 65 to 79, which is a time of personal fulfillment (James & Wink, 2007). Given life expectancies of today's older adults, many see old age as something they will need to confront around age 80. Thus, they see this third age as a time of self-realization and high life satisfaction (Berk, 2014b). From a societal perspective, this is not only an opportunity for aging adults but one for the nation as a whole. The large pool of energetic, generativity-minded third agers could make enormous social and economic contributions to our society if given the opportunities to do so (Berk, 2014b). Retirement is often an important transition of the third age.

Retirement

Participation in the labor force by older adults (i.e., age 65 and older) has been increasing in the past 25 years and will likely continue to increase (U.S. Bureau of Labor Statistics, 2013). In some professions like teaching, the minimum age of retirement is actually rising in many states as a way to delay pension income. In other cases, people are choosing to stay in the workforce later in life due to economic need (McQuown & Sterns, 2015). Hence, for some people, the notion of retirement is more fantasy than fact. The stereotype many of us have of retirement of moving to Florida or Arizona and playing 18 holes of golf every day is a middle-class fantasy that fewer and fewer people are able to achieve.

Since we discuss the potential psychological consequences of retirement in Chapter 10, we will limit our discussion here to one of positive retirement adjustment. It is also important to note that our discussion of successful retirement is limited to individuals who voluntarily retire as opposed to those who face involuntary retirement or job loss (e.g., reduction in force [RIF] programs). Being forced to retire by an employer before one is ready can be a significant barrier to successful retirement transitions. We discuss some of the successful ways of coping with job loss in Chapter 10.

There are several factors that appear to be related to successful retirement for individuals who are in the position to retire. Having a plan is considered a crucial element of retirement (Berk, 2014b). For some future retirees, the plan can begin with the decision to retire. For many, a successful plan for retirement is one that involves the gradual shift from full-time to part-time work. This is sometimes referred to as bridge retirement (Benz, Sedensky, Tompson, & Agiesta, 2013) or phased retirement that occurs over a number of years. The advantage of this type of retirement is that one does not make a clean break from the many advantages associated with a career (see Chapter 10), and it allows a person to more slowly develop a plan for how time outside of work will be spent. While some people may have a fantasy that sleeping late and living spontaneously is a sufficient retirement plan, this "honeymoon phase" of retirement is short-lived for most people (Berk, 2014b).

There are many things that bring people fulfillment during retirement that can be part of a successful plan. Volunteering, being active in the community, traveling, taking classes, or even finding a different type of part-time employment are possible components of a plan that gives people a meaningful way to spend their time. However, whatever specific components of the retirement plan are developed, the key to successful retirement planning is the ability to update and alter plans according to changing circumstances (Hill, 2015). For example, imagine that someone develops a retirement plan that involves traveling with his or her spouse. This plan will work only if his or her spouse is also able to retire and if both people's health status is stable enough to endure travel. Imagine that his or her spouse is unable to retire as planned; becomes ill or disabled; or in a worst-case scenario, dies. While the odds of any of these events happening may be slim, successful retirement would warrant the ability to modify one's plan in response to these realities.

Another facet of adjusting to retirement is the importance of considering significant others in one's retirement plan. The ability to coordinate retirement with one's spouse might be an important aspect of the plan. While not all couples can or want to retire together, significant thought should be given to what life will be like if one partner is still employed full-time while the other is retired. There may also be gender differences in how couples feel about retirement planning. For example, women tend to be overrepresented in lower skill jobs that pay less (Taylor & Geldhauser, 2007). This means that for women as a group, it may make it necessary to stay in the workforce longer to be able to retire successfully (i.e., have the financial means to do so). If one partner's work affords retirement opportunities earlier than the other,

Being open to help from others can be challenging to older adults who want to preserve their independence.

the couple must decide if a premature departure by the other partner is feasible. As we mentioned in Chapter 10, men also have a more difficult time adjusting to retirement than do women, potentially because men's identity is more connected to work (Osbourne, 2012). This brings us to the next aspect of successful retirement—role redefinition.

Role Redefinition

The aging process involves a great deal of role redefinition. For example, a parent may have to adjust the role that he or she plays in the life of his or her adult children over the life span (e.g., empty nest syndrome or becoming a grandparent). But retirement is also a poignant time when people have an opportunity to reexamine their roles in life. Bratter and Dennis (2008) offered a vision of retirement where the emphasis is not on the ending of work and one's career but rather the redefinition of one's roles and an opportunity to find new ways to experience meaning in one's later years.

Hill (2015) noted that retirement can be an important opportunity for renewal and a time in life when people can enter into "new endeavors for fulfilling spiritual, relational, and interest goals which may or may not result in continuance of pay but merely pleasure" (p. 395). What implications does this have for healthy adjustment? For some people, becoming involved in leadership within their church or community can be a way to fulfill their need for generativity and use leadership skills that were honed within the business world. For other people, taking a former hobby and developing those talents into a new enterprise could be a way of redefining their roles (e.g., making and selling handmade furniture or quilts). For others, recommitting to a role such as a grandparent by being involved in more day-to-day activities (e.g., child care, coordinating family events) may be a successful way to redefine their role. However, inherent in all these examples is the will and ability to see retirement not as an end but as a new beginning.

Finances

It may go without saying that being able to retire is based on the assumption that a person has been successful with financial planning throughout their adult life. An important element of successful retirement is having sufficient resources to take care of oneself. Being able to retire comfortably with respect to a retirement income requires that we save more money than we may want to for a longer period of time beginning in our adult years. Thirty-one percent of U.S. adults have no retirement savings, and those who do

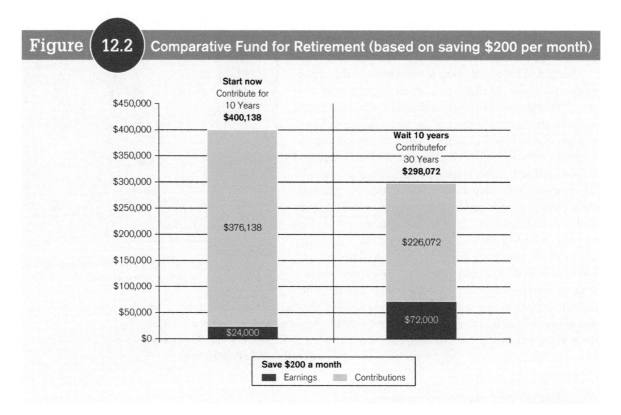

Figure 12.2 Comparative Fund for Retirement (based on saving $200 per month)

Source: Augelli, C. (2012). Navigating the Changing Landscape of Retirement: What Plan Sponsors and Employees Need to Do to Achieve Retirement Security. *Compensation & Benefits Review, 44*(6), 340–344. doi:10.1177/0886368713477812.

save are well below the yearly amount needed to retire comfortably (Board of Governors of the Federal Reserve System, 2013). These numbers indicate that the majority of us have not done a good job with our financial planning, oftentimes for legitimate reasons such as economic recessions, divorces, unexpected illnesses, or other expenses. To see how important saving at a young age is to meet one's retirement goals, consider Figure 12.2.

Not only is financial insolvency a concern for retirees and society as a whole, but the psychological reactions of depression and anxiety are all conditions that are perhaps preventable (Fretz, Kluge, Ossana, Jones, & Merikangas, 1989). Formal retirement programs are one way that companies, organizations, and community groups (e.g., AARP) can provide aging adults with supported opportunities to become knowledgeable about the retirement process and its options and also increase the likelihood that a plan will be developed prior to retiring (Willett, 2008). Dennis and Fike (2012) showed that those who plan for retirement show greater satisfaction in their actual retirement.

Taylor-Carter, Cook, and Weinberg (1997) found evidence that formal and informal retirement preparation programs help to increase confidence in one's ability to make a successful transition to retirement. In other words, the evidence is clear that helping today's workers *in their active working years* in realistic planning and support for their retirement goals could prevent possible psychological and financial crises later on (Hill, 2015). Successful retirement demonstrates a point made earlier in this chapter: Many of the decisions that we make in early and middle adulthood impact our quality of life as we age.

Successful Aging

Given all that we know about the aging process and its vulnerabilities, is it possible to conclude anything about what is necessary to promote successful aging? Due to the fact that age expectancies in the United States continue to rise and the number of older adults is growing exponentially, there is a great interest in identifying strategies for **positive aging.**

What is successful aging? In the 1990s, findings emerged from a study that explored the aging process longitudinally (Berkman et al., 1993), which enabled scholars to generate a definition of successful aging:

1. Active engagement with life

2. Absence or avoidance of disease risk factors

3. Maintenance of high levels of physical and cognitive functioning

Two ideas emerge from this definition that are related to healthy adjustment in later life: staying active and being proactive. Staying active might refer to both the process of staying physically active (through exercise and recreation) and staying socially active (being in contact with friends and community). Being proactive may involve determining what risk factors one faces (e.g., having a medical condition such as prediabetes) and having a plan to either reduce risk (e.g., monitoring diet) or to optimally manage chronic diseases.

Another term, *positive aging*, is often discussed in the literature. The definition of positive aging (Hill, 2011) contains behaviors thought to protect a person from the potentially negative effects of aging:

1. The ability to mobilize dormant social or psychological potentialities

2. **Flexibility** in thinking and behaving

3. A decision-making style that affirms well-being even in the face of irreversible loss

4. An optimistic viewpoint about age-related functional decline

Mobilizing dormant social or psychological potentialities refers to the importance of having a plan to utilize resources that may have not been as necessary in the past to preserve one's well-being and psychological health. For example, an older person may be experiencing physical or sensory problems that make it difficult to drive to the store alone to pick up a prescription. That older person might have a neighbor who has offered to help with transportation in the past. Despite the fact that such help might not have been necessary in the past, a person with a positive aging profile would call that neighbor to ask for a ride. This example would also be relevant to demonstrate flexibility in thinking and behaving. While the older person in our example might have been a fiercely independent person for most of his or her life, flexible thinking would allow this person to know that making a decision to relieve the anxiety of driving to the store alone does not diminish a person's sense of control, it merely shows adaptation.

A decision-making style that affirms well-being and an optimistic viewpoint about age-related decline refer to psychological aspects of aging. For example, choosing at some point to live with an adult child might be seen as an opportunity to spend one's final years having a closer relationship with children and grandchildren rather than being seen as a concession of one's self-control. Seeing one's old age as a sign of resilience and a source of wisdom are examples of being optimistic about age-related decline. Again, while not all people view the aging process so positively, the definitions of successful and positive aging (and successful adjustment) suggest that we can make choices about how we view our later years. In the next section of this chapter, we will examine strategies that can optimize a major life change—adjusting to retirement.

Adjusting to Losses

One unavoidable aspect of aging is ultimately dealing with death and dying. Not only do people have to face the reality of their own death, but they also must learn to cope with losses of significant people in their lives such as spouses and partners. Elders who have lost a spouse comprise one third of all older adults in industrialized nations (Berk, 2014b). Because of important gender differences in life expectancy (which we discussed at the beginning of this chapter), there are many more women who must learn to adjust to the loss of their male partners than there are men who must learn to adjust to the loss of their female partners. Forty percent of U.S. women age 65 and older are widows compared to only 13% of men (U.S. Census Bureau, 2012). In this section, we will discuss what is known about adjusting to the loss of a loved one.

Grieving

Before we begin this discussion, it is important to note that grief, or the emotional response we often have to death, is expressed in many different ways, and there are not obvious recommendations for a *best* way to grieve. Rather, it is important to think about grieving as a highly individualized experience that changes over time. There are two commonly acknowledged approaches to grieving, both of which can be quite adaptive. **Intuitive grievers** have strong emotional responses to loss and experience significant relief from being able to express those feelings through crying or talking to others (Doka & Martin, 2010). **Instrumental grievers**, in contrast, experience loss less emotionally and more cognitively; thus, they are less likely to feel any catharsis from crying or talking about their feelings (Doka & Martin, 2010; Hill, 2015). These individuals prefer to act out their grief by creating rituals or memorials such as putting together family events where their loved one can be remembered or by starting foundations in the name of their loved ones to keep their spirits alive and well. It is important to note the differences in the way people grieve so that when we make recommendations about ways to success-fully deal with loss, we can be sensitive to those differences.

To begin our discussion of adjusting to loss, it must be said that the loss of a spouse or partner is considered to be the single most stressful event in a person's life (Lund & Caserta, 2004). The loss of other significant others such as siblings, friends, or other relatives are also extremely stressful and often involve the loss of major life roles (e.g., spouse, brother, best friend) and represent the loss of major sources of support (Lund & Caserta, 2004). The period of adjusting to loss can last months or years and, for many people, require the creation of a new normal.

The two most immediate effects of losing a loved one are loneliness and the need to reorganize one's life to go on without the involvement of the deceased individual (Berk, 2014b; Connidis, 2010). While future companionship can be provided by friends and family, there is still a normal feeling by those who grieve that the person who died can-not ever truly be replaced. For example, when a spouse dies, the shared life history and experiences that were unique to the couple cannot be replaced, and even if one compen-sates by spending time with adult children, the uniqueness of that relationship is still missed and can be the source of great loneliness and sadness.

There are some important gender differences in how men and women react to becoming widows. Men show more health problems, both physically and psycholog-ically, and have a greater risk of dying themselves after the loss of their spouses (Bennett, Smith, & Hughes, 2005). The explanation of this finding may involve two components. First, because of gender role differences that exist in many heterosex-ual marriages, men have a harder time taking care of themselves, attending to their emotional needs, and becoming responsible for household and daily living tasks that they may not have fully taken part in previously (e.g., meal preparation, house cleaning; Bennett, 2007). Additionally, men may have a harder time expressing their grief and asking for the additional support that they may need in transitioning to widowhood (Lund & Caserta, 2004).

Another gender difference that exists before the experience of widowhood but ends up being a factor in adjusting to loss is the fact that men tend to be less involved in religious activities than women. Having a sense of spirituality and/or religiosity, which we will discuss momentarily, is a major asset to adjusting to loss. A caveat to this gender difference is that in at least one study (Elwert & Chistakis, 2006), African American men, in comparison to White men, do *not* show an elevated risk for dying in response to spousal loss, and they show less depression than their White counterparts. It is thought that African American men's greater involvement in and support from church may explain this difference.

Because men struggle more overall with the loss of their spouses than women, men are far more likely than women to remarry after the loss of their spouse (Berk, 2014b). It is possible that women are more easily able to find and connect with other widows, given gender differences in life expectancies, which may help them grieve and feel less lonely and ultimately may result in them feeling less urgency to remarry or find a new mate. Women may also have an easier time adjusting to the new daily routines of being widows since they were more likely to have been in charge of the household management throughout their marriages, hence their need for help is less pronounced.

Several resources can greatly facilitate adjusting to loss for both men and women. The first is having a developed sense of *spirituality and religiosity*. Having a mature sense of spirituality and/or religiosity is an important asset in learning to accept loss and represents a rich opportunity for older adults to receive social support (Berk, 2014b). According to the Gallup News Service (Newport, 2012), 70% of adults over the age of 65 say that religion is a very important part of their lives, which is the highest of any age group. People of color and women tend to have higher rates of involvement in organized religion than do White males (Wink & Dillon, 2002).

There are enormous potential benefits that come with having a mature sense of spirituality and/or religiosity when adjusting to losing loved ones. First, many people find existential meaning in death from their religious or spiritual beliefs that helps them better accept loss. Such beliefs may provide an explanatory framework (Rando, 1993) for understanding death. For example, they may see death as a transition or have beliefs about what happens to us after we die that bring comfort during the grieving process. Additionally, active involvement with organized religion or faith groups can relieve loneliness and offer opportunities for new relationships, meaningful roles within the group, and both tangible and emotional support (Berk, 2014b). Gamino, Easterling, and Sewell (2003) found that grieving persons who have high levels of intrinsic spirituality and who practice their beliefs within a community of other believers have lower levels of distress involved in adjusting to major losses than do those with lower levels of spirituality and no involvement within such communities.

The second resource that can be important to coping with loss is having *regular involvement of friends and family* to not only assist with the immediate adjustment to loss but to provide sustained support as one defines a "new normal." Oftentimes people are better at responding in the immediate aftermath of loss (e.g., calling frequently, dropping by with food, offering to help run errands) than they are weeks and months after the loss. Communities can provide important resources to older individuals who are adjusting to loss through senior centers, churches, synagogues, or mosques. For example, participating in communal meals or other social activities allows older adults to relieve their sense of loneliness and find comfort in people who have experienced similar circumstances (Berk, 2014b). Staying involved with people who knew and loved the person who has died can also be comforting, which is why support from family can be so crucial to successful adjustment to loss.

The third element of adjusting to loss of a loved one is *having rituals and opportunities to remember the importance of the loved one.* For intuitive grievers, having regular opportunities to talk about their deceased loved ones is cathartic. This could happen in informal contexts where a person is able to share stories and recollections of the person who has died. It could also be beneficial to some people to participate in grief or bereavement support groups that are offered through senior centers, hospitals, or mental health organizations. Such formal groups could help by putting the survivor in touch with professionals who are training in grief reactions and fellow group participants who share their experience of adjusting to the loss of a loved one. Another benefit of having professional support is that if there are any signs or symptoms of serious distress, anxiety, or depression, they can be detected and treated immediately.

For instrumental grievers (those who prefer to act), regular activities that help keep them connected to their deceased loved ones are important ways to keep their memories alive. Rather than emote in group settings, such individuals may feel comforted by tending to a garden that their loved one planted or continuing volunteer work that they previously participated in with their loved one. They may also find comfort and adjust to their loss by participating in activities that allow them share the skills they acquired through the loss experience to be of help to others (e.g., volunteering at a hospice center or working at the American Cancer Society). The actions that instrumental grievers take after their loss can be just as cathartic to them as participating in a grief support group at a hospital to an intuitive griever (those who prefer to emote). For both types of grievers, finding avenues to channel their experiences of loss are important components of adjustment.

Adjusting to the loss of a loved one is a serious part of the aging process for many (see Table 12.3). While it is an inherently stressful experience, there are individual, gender, and ethnic differences in people's experiences relating to loss of a loved one. Fortunately, there are many ways that people's adjustment to loss of loved ones can be made easier and less painful.

Table 12.3	Overview of Adjusting to Grief
Sense of spirituality and religiosity	• Helps provide existential explanations of death and the afterlife • Religious involvement provides communal support during grieving process and during widowhood
Regular involvement of friends and family	• Provides immediate, tangible support in the immediacy of death • Helps to stay connected with deceased loved one, provides new opportunities for socialization during widowhood
Having rituals and opportunities to remember the importance of the loved one	• For intuitive grievers, finding opportunities to talk about deceased loved one and cry over loss can be cathartic • For instrumental grievers, finding rituals to keep the memory of the deceased loved one alive can be comforting (having family outings in the memory of the deceased or raising awareness of a disease that was the cause of death)

Aging in Place

One of the most discussed concerns of aging centers on which type of living situation is optimal for people as they become older and their needs change. Some older adults live in their homes and prefer to do so indefinitely. However, others may decide to move into retirement communities or assisted living facilities in anticipation of impending declines associated with aging. Still, other older adults might at some point find themselves living in highly restricted environments such as nursing homes, potentially against their will or because no other options exist. In this section, we will discuss what is known about the concept of aging in place and discuss the pros and cons of various housing arrangements for older adults.

Aging in place refers to older adults' strong preference to grow old in communities and settings that are familiar to them, where they have control over their daily routines (Berk, 2014b). Over 90% of older adults wish to remain in or near their own homes, and statistics show that only 4% ever relocate to other communities (U.S. Department of Health and Human Services, 2011a). Even when relocation does occur (e.g., due to a desire to downsize into a smaller home), most older adults move within the same community (Sergeant, Ekerdt, & Chapin, 2008). For the majority of older adults who are not significantly physically impaired, staying within their family home affords the most control over their day-to-day activities and routines, and the familiarity with their environment brings a great deal of comfort to these individuals.

However, at some point, some older adults begin to have physical declines that make independent living more risky. Most U.S. homes are not accessible for people with disabilities, and even when homes are more friendly to people with impairments (e.g., ranch-style homes with no stairs to major rooms), the physical abilities needed to keep daily routines can become daunting. For example, imagine an older person with worsening arthritis who may not easily be able to get to the washer and dryer in the basement. Or that same individual may struggle to take the long walk down the driveway to get the mail. Research suggests that older adults with physical disabilities who also live on their own are more vulnerable to social isolation and loneliness (Adams, Sanders, & Auth, 2004), and they may also be more vulnerable to physical injuries due to falls.

For older adults who are married or have partners, continuing to cohabitate in one's familial home could be feasible provided that at least the partner is able to assist the other who has a physical disability. For senior citizens who are widowed or single, family members such as adult children often wish to have them move into their homes—particularly in immigrant and ethnic minority families (Berk, 2014b). However, statistics show that fewer and fewer older adults prefer to live with their grown children not only in the United States but in other countries around the world (Tagaki, Silverstein, & Crimmins, 2007).

This shift in trends could be because more and more children live in communities that are not close to where they grew up, and aging parents who live with their adult children are forced to give up their familiarity with their community and surroundings, which is highly undesirable. Another reason aging parents may not wish to live with their adult children could be due to the possibility of role reversal, where the parent will have to fit into the routines established by their children. Since aging adults value their independence and privacy, it is easy to see why these situations may not be ideal to many older adults (Berk, 2014b). For more information on how where one lives may impact adjustment and quality of life, see the Researching Adjustment: Retirement Communities and Nursing Homes for what research has found about older adults who live in retirement communities and nursing homes.

RESEARCHING ADJUSTMENT
Retirement Communities and Nursing Homes

As an alternative to living with family members, another option for older adults who cannot or choose not to live on their own are residential (i.e., retirement) communities. Approximately 7% of older adults 65 years old and 22% of older adults 85 years old live in residential communities, which can be either single-family homes or apartment units. The attractiveness of these communities is that they are often exclusively for people 65 years of age or older and provide many accommodations both within the residences and the community itself that make it easier for these adults to continue living independently.

For example, in residential apartment complexes, there may be elevators and bars on the walls, staff who will do laundry for residents, and common rooms for eating meals with other residents. Oftentimes residential communities give their residents options for living that run from complete independence to greater dependence on others. Residential communities will also sometimes arrange for outings to malls or other destinations that allow residents to let someone else drive or to receive assistance with getting their purchases home.

On the surface, residential communities seem to represent a viable alternative to our aging population of older adults and in many cases, having an environment that accommodates one's needs reduces stress (Lawrence & Schigelone, 2002). There are two major issues that must be considered with this type of a living arrangement, however. First, residential communities are not regulated the way that hospitals and nursing homes are, which means that the quality of these communities can vary considerably (Berk, 2014b). Some studies have shown that living in lower quality residential communities can actually create more stress for older adults (Ball, Perkins, Hollingsworth, Whittington, & King, 2009) than they would experience living independently. Lower income adults may be at higher risk for ending up in lower quality residential communities.

The other issue with this type of living situation is that not all communities provide medical support for residents, and if residents become too incapacitated, they are asked to leave (Hernandez & Newcomer, 2007). For example, if a resident develops a medical condition that needs monitoring and frequent medical interventions (e.g., dialysis), the resident may be forced to leave and find a situation that can more appropriately handle their medical needs. These situations often require older adults to consider living in nursing homes either temporarily or indefinitely. Given the significant cost that is associated with some residential communities (e.g., some require a large initial payment and then monthly fees), a person may have exhausted their savings when unexpectedly faced with the need to find a new place to live.

Nursing homes are the least common places that older adults choose to reside, with statistics suggesting that 5% or fewer seniors call such places home. In part, this may be because nursing homes impose the highest degree of restrictions on older adults in being in control of their daily routines and being able to determine how and when they have access to other residents. Ironically, while there are often a plethora of potential companions for older adults living in nursing homes, the social interaction there is lowest in comparison to residential communities or seniors who are aging in place. This may be because nursing homes are often overcrowded, and staff are often in complete control of where residents are at any given time so they are able to manage the number of people needing various supports throughout the day.

When residents do have "free" time, they may be in their rooms alone or placed in large recreation spaces with crowds of other residents. Social withdrawal is a common response to these highly restricted settings where people have little to no control over their daily routines. Many studies have found that nursing home residents are far more depressed, anxious, and lonely than their counterparts who live in residential communities or on their own (Gueldner at al., 2001). Perhaps even more troublesome are the statistics of mortality associated with nursing home living. The average time that people live in nursing homes before dying is 6 months (Kelly et al., 2010). While it could be argued that this statistic is a reflection of the fact that most people who live in nursing homes have a poorer health status than older adults who live residentially or in place, it is also arguable that the psychological effects of such living can make life a lot less worth living.

Reflection Questions

1. How can families that must move their loved ones into retirement or nursing homes increase their quality of life?

2. What can families do to protect the well-being of their aging relatives?

What can be concluded about the optimal living situations for aging adults? For those who can physically do so, aging in place is the best option. Many communities have senior centers or departments of aging that provide a wide variety of in-home services to seniors that make it possible for them to live as long as possible in a familiar setting. Services provided, often at no or low cost, include home health care, transportation, meals-on-wheels, bathing and grooming assistance, housecleaning, and lawn care. Communities also provide recreation and companion services to seniors who may not have social access due to the loss of loved ones or restricted opportunities. Adjusting to some of the changes that come with aging can be efficiently managed by accessing these services.

Residential communities, especially those with high-quality environments and services, can be another option for seniors who cannot or choose not to live alone, but the selection of such communities must be done very carefully. Living with relatives may be a more attractive option for older adults who lack the means to afford high-quality residential community living. Nursing homes would appear to be the least desirable option due to the fact that people are robbed of their independence, privacy, and choices. Given the increasing number of older people who will need care for longer periods of their lives given increasing life expectancies, creative ways of meeting the needs of aging adults with compassion and dignity are a high priority in this country.

Conclusion

Given what we know about increasing life expectancies for adults in the United States (and globally) and the increasing percentages of adults who are considered "old," issues of aging are of critical importance to our entire society. In this chapter, we have considered some of the issues involved in defining who is "old," and reviewed many of the age-related changes that appear in our bodies, minds, and social–emotional functioning. While many of the changes associated with aging are not always positive or welcome, there are ways in which aging represents opportunities for peak performance (e.g., cognitive functioning) and renewed opportunities (e.g., retirement).

Models of successful or positive aging help us to understand how we can maximize well-being during the aging process while adapting to unavoidable transformations. We also have discussed specific ideas for how to best adjust to many of the hallmarks of aging, namely retirement, loss of loved ones, and decisions about where to live as we get older. While aging may be an idea that younger adults may think of in the hypothetical, there are clear ways in which the decisions we make as younger individuals can impact the ways in which we experience growing old.

Review Questions

1. Describe some of the main physical changes that are associated with aging.

2. How would you describe the main cognitive changes that occur in adulthood?

3. What are two main socioemotional changes that occur as we age?

4. Of all the age-related changes reviewed in this chapter, which do you think are the most stressful for people to experience and why?

5. A major theme of the chapter is healthy aging. What types of behaviors associated with earlier stages of life might ultimately increase the likelihood of someone aging more positively?

6. What do you think are the major influences on why some people adapt to aging with relative ease whereas other people have a very hard time adjusting?

7. Explain what the third age is.

8. What are some keys to successful retirement?

9. What are factors that contribute to people's ability to cope with loss?

10. What are some of the options for housing arrangements for older adults?

Key Terms

aging in place 263
average life expectancy 244
cognitive–affective complexity 250
ego integrity 252
flexibility 259

generativity 252
instrumental grievers 260
intuitive grievers 260
long-term memory 251
old-old 248

positive aging 259
pragmatic problem solving 250
third age 256
working memory 251
young-old 248

Sharpen your skills with SAGE edge at **edge.sagepub.com/moritsugu**

SAGE edge for students provides a personalized approach to help you accomplish your coursework goals in an easy-to-use learning environment.

Go to **edge.sagepub.com/moritsugu** for additional exercises and web resources. Select Chapter 12, Aging for chapter-specific resources.

Chapter 13

Dysfunction and Maladjustment

Learning Objectives

SECTION ONE: MENTAL ILLNESS

1. Identify the criteria for diagnosis of mental illness.

2. Explain the main ideas of supernatural, somatogenic, and psychogenic explanations for mental illness.

3. Synthesize explanations of mental illness into a biopsychosocial perspective.

4. Summarize the cognitive, emotional, physical, and behavioral aspects of the major mental illnesses.

5. Describe potential etiologies, or causes, of the major mental illnesses.

SECTION TWO: TREATMENT

6. Explain the impact of stigma and the costs of mental illness in the United States today.

7. Summarize early treatment methods for mental illness.

8. Identify reasons why a person should seek professional help for symptoms of mental illness, and identify the types of clinicians providing services.

9. Compare the basic concepts of the four major types of psychotherapy.

10. Describe psychosurgeries and the major types of psychotropic medications.

Mary, a bright and energetic 19-year-old college student, experiences a racing heart and can't catch her breath. Her hand is shaking, and she can't seem to think clearly as she sits in the classroom to take her final exam. She sits, quaking in her seat, as the clock ticks by. She looks around at all of the other students diligently writing and answering questions at their desks. Her breathing continues too fast, and she is feeling nauseated. All she can think of is failing the exam and failing the course. Though she studied for hours, the answers seem to have permanently vanished from her mind.

***

The alarm goes off. Jake reaches out and turns it off. It is time to get up for work. But Jake lies in bed, now awake, feeling as if he can't move. He pulls up the covers and sinks down into his bed. Jake hasn't gotten out of bed, except to go to the bathroom, for four days. He has ignored phone calls and texts. He has heard his friend pounding on the door to try and rouse him, but he ignores all of these attempts. Jake doesn't have the energy to go to work, to go to his evening classes, or to talk with his girlfriend. Jake can't seem to remember not feeling this way, even though a few days ago, before life was this terrible, his friend tried to remind him of other things and told him everything would be all right. He knows he needs to get with it, but life is futile and he believes wholeheartedly that he is worthless. There is no point to anything.

. . . .

What is happening with Mary and Jake? What happens when life becomes simply too overwhelming for a person to get through their normal day?

We have been talking throughout this textbook about adjusting or coping with problems of normal, everyday life. Unfortunately, sometimes, problems are simply too overwhelming; they are psychological or physical or both and are beyond everyday hassles. At times like these, mental illness overwhelms mental health, and additional steps need to be taken for an individual to manage and function in everyday life. One of the major signs that someone meets the criterion to be diagnosed with a mental illness is the interference in everyday life at work, school, or in their social life. In other words, a **mental disorder** occurs when adjustment and coping simply fall short of meeting overwhelming psychological, physiological, and social challenges in life. The term *mental disorder* is used interchangeably throughout the chapter with psychiatric illnesses or mental illnesses.

Both Mary and Jake are struggling with two of the most common forms of mental illness—anxiety and depression. Highly stigmatized, mental illness affects millions of Americans of all ages, genders, races, and income levels every day. Multiple, interrelated factors cause someone to slip into the dysfunction of mental illness. Sufferers struggle with compromised thinking, physical symptoms, and problematic behavioral issues. No two individuals share the same experience of depression or anxiety or psychosis; each person experiences their world being torn asunder in their unique way. The field of clinical psychology has nearly 300 terms to categorize mental illness. The impact on the lives of individuals struggling with mental illness and their families and friends, however, cannot be categorized or quantified.

This chapter will explore what happens when an individual is unable to adjust to the challenges of life and slips into dysfunctional ways of coping. The discussion is framed by first exploring the ways in which societies have explained dysfunction over time and talk about mental illness today. The basic concepts regarding the most common types of mental illness, anxiety and depression, will be explained, along with theories regarding their origins. Similar explanations of well-known mental illnesses including psychosis, eating disorders, substance abuse disorders, attention deficit disorders, and autism spectrum disorder (ASD) will follow. What happens to a person whose methods of coping are dysfunctional? From the dark days of asylums, through the advent of psychotherapy and psychotropic medications, the second section of the chapter will discuss the treatment of mental illness.

Section One: Mental Illness

Why do some people struggle with mental illness? How do we understand the causes of these struggles? As your text has discussed, adjustment to the many challenges of life requires determination, grit, imagination, and perseverance. Yet for some people, no method of coping seems to be enough to fight back the shadows of depression, anxiety, or the loss of touch with reality. Instead of managing, individuals struggling with mental illness find themselves feeling overwhelmed, often isolated and stigmatized. Sadness or fear, often both, can distort thinking, causing logic and reason to vanish. Emotions can be tumultuous and overpowering. Behaviors can be reckless, withdrawn, and confusing. The opposite of adjustment or functioning is maladjustment or dysfunction, and unfortunately for millions of individuals, mental illness is a reality that must be faced.

Supernatural, Somatogenic, and Psychogenic Explanations

Throughout history, explanations for mental illness have fallen into three main etiologies, or causal explanations: supernatural, somatogenic, and psychogenic. Overlapping with one another across time and cultures, these theoretical foundations have guided the course of treatments and interventions. Medications and talk therapy, the treatment of our time, was preceded by treatments ranging from prayers, incantations, bloodletting, to literally chaining people to stone walls. Treatment has been driven by the beliefs surrounding the origins and causes of mental illness, or times in one's life when adjustment and coping fail.

Supernatural, or explanations beyond scientific knowledge or the laws of nature, attribute mental illness to demonic possession, the wrath of gods, the alignment of planets, curses, and the wages of sin. Belief in supernatural causes for mental illness appear in cultural traditions across the globe, including perceptions of madness as punishment by the gods and belief in repentance as a cure. Attendance at religious healing ceremonies has been long believed to facilitate healing. In some ways, supernatural explanations have been the most social or relationally based explanations, with their focus on the relationships between people and their communities.

Somatogenic explanations focus on the body as the causal agent and include physical illness, genetics, brain damage, and chemical imbalances. Some early examples of somatogenic explanations can be found in the writings of the Greek physician Hippocrates (460–370 BC), who believed that the body created humors, or bodily fluids, including blood, yellow bile, black bile, and phlegm. Imbalances in these humors created conditions such as epilepsy, mania, melancholia, and brain fever. Treatment required the realignment of humors through interventions such as bloodletting and ingestion of substances to counteract the imbalances. Current types of somatogenic explanation and treatment include the biological approach of neuroscience, genetics, epigenetics, and psychotropic medications, which we will discuss in greater detail in the treatment section.

Psychogenic explanations focus on environmental factors such as stress and trauma, as well as dysfunctional, learned associations established as early as childhood, and distorted perceptions. These explanations grew through the advent of psychoanalytic theory and continued into the behavioral and cognitive principles of the mid-20th century. Treatment for mental illness stemming from psychogenic etiologies involves talk therapy, cognitively based interventions designed to change the way an individual thinks and manages emotion. Learning-based interventions referred to as behavior modification are included in psychogenic treatment.

Another key component to the understanding of mental illness can be seen in the *social constructivism movement*. Originating with the continental philosophers of the mid-20th century, this theory suggests that an individual jointly constructs meaning and explanation through interactions with other people and the society they live in. The social constructivism movement resulted in the new theories of explanations beyond the somatogenic or psychogenic. One example is a revisionist view of explanations for witchcraft as manifestations of mental illness (Schoeneman, 1984). Previously, many abnormal psychology textbooks explained witch hunts and trials in the 15th through the 17th centuries as persecution of the mentally ill. A more constructivist view explains the deaths of more than 100,000 people by the early 18th century as the intersection of societal expectations, cultural change, human conflict, and prejudice.

Through inclusion of the role of society in understanding the etiology of mental illness, we arrive at the current approach. Today's predominant etiology for most clinicians, or people who diagnose and treat mental illness, is the **biopsychosocial model** (see Figure 13.1). In 1980, a physician named George Engel (1913–1999) proposed to expand the traditional somatogenic, biomedical model to include an understanding of the person as part of a system involving the community and environment in which they live. To fully treat any type of disorder, Engel proposed that each of three components—somatogenic (biological), psychogenic (psychological), and social—should be considered in understanding etiology and treatment. This biopsychosocial model grew in popularity, and the majority of clinicians attempt to grasp all of these factors when evaluating the development of mental illness and the direction for treatment.

Wikimedia Commons

Seventeenth-century witch trials: The intersection of societal expectations, cultural change, human conflict, and prejudice.

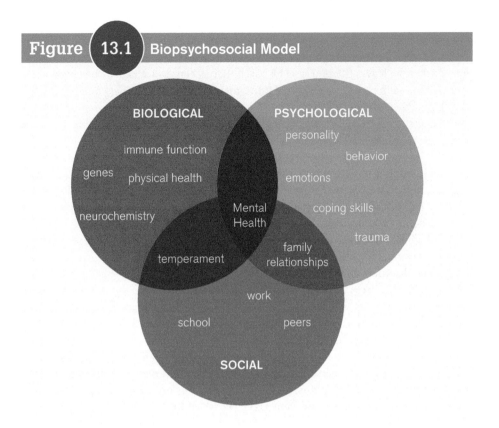

Figure 13.1   Biopsychosocial Model

BIOLOGICAL
immune function
genes   physical health
neurochemistry

PSYCHOLOGICAL
personality
behavior
emotions
coping skills
trauma

Mental Health

temperament

family relationships

work
school   peers

SOCIAL

Mental Illness Today

Who is affected by mental illness in America today? And throughout the world? The National Institute of Mental Health (NIMH), a department of the National Institutes of Health (NIH), is the federal agency for research on mental illnesses. The most recent data from the NIMH gives a best estimate of the number of adults with any diagnosable mental disorder over the past 12 months as 43 million Americans, or about one in five adults (Insel, 2015). Of these individuals struggling with mental illness, nearly 10 million, or 1 adult in 25, have serious functional impairment. This means that about 10 million Americans cannot work or go to school or otherwise function in their daily lives because of the impact of their anxiety, depression, psychosis, or other serious mental illness. Similarly, the World Health Organization (WHO; 2001) has estimated that mental disorders affect one in four people worldwide, or about 27% (2009). While there are some cultural differences in the perception of what constitutes mental illness in different cultures, the WHO and the *International Classification of Mental and Behavioural Disorders, Tenth Revision* (*ICD-10*; WHO, 2014a), clearly identifies the types of mental illness we will be discussing as occurring globally.

In discussing any type of illness, understanding a few terms might be helpful. When we talk about how many people have a disorder and giving statistics, we are most often describing the *prevalence*, or how often a disease appears in the population. *Twelve-month prevalence* refers to the percentage of individuals who had symptoms in the 12 months prior to reporting the illness. *Lifetime prevalence* refers to the percentage of people who have ever had the illness in their lifetimes. While our discussion of disorders creates the appearance of discrete separate conditions, these disorders are often comorbid, meaning an individual meets criteria for two or more disorders, such as both an anxiety disorder and a depressive disorder simultaneously.

If my friend breaks out in a cold sweat over the idea of giving her presentation in class, does she have social anxiety? If another friend feels sad and doesn't enjoy his favorite things anymore, is he depressed? If your neighbor believes that he is being followed when he leaves the house, is he psychotic? When do feelings or behaviors cross from feeling sadness or being worried into a mental illness? How does someone know if they have a mental illness? Who decides?

If a person's sadness is pervasive and hard to control and he cannot seem to find the energy to do simple tasks, he *may* meet the criteria for a mood disorder. Similarly, if a person's fear of speaking in front of others interferes with her ability to perform to her potential, she *may* meet criteria for an anxiety disorder. The level of a person's delusion *may* be a sign that he is struggling with a psychotic disorder. The psychiatric distinction used for identification of a mental disorder requires that a recognizable group of symptoms or behaviors interfere with a person's functioning in one or more areas of life. In terms of adjustment, one or many coping strategies for confronting challenges in everyday life are failing for the person through no choice of their own.

Mental disorders are diagnosed and treated by *clinical psychologists*, who are doctors with advanced degrees in psychology, and *psychiatrists*, who are doctors with medical degrees. Psychologists and psychiatrists use a classification system, based on a medical model of symptoms and criteria, to determine if an individual can be diagnosed with a certain mental disorder. These clinicians refer to the *Diagnostic and Statistical Manual of Mental Disorders* (5th ed.; *DSM–5*) published by the American Psychiatric Association (2013a) to determine if a person meets the criteria for a given mental disorder and then plan treatment and interventions. Simply reading the list of criterion is not sufficient to make a diagnosis, however, and you, savvy reader of this text, should not attempt to diagnose yourself, your friends, or your family. If you do believe that yourself or someone you care about is struggling with an inability to adjust to the demands of life, reaching out to a professional is always the best choice.

The vignettes of Jake and Mary at the beginning of the chapter are examples of the most frequent of mental disorders—mood disorders and anxiety. Another major category of mental disorders, illustrated earlier by the neighbor example, is thought disorders, which contain elements of psychosis, or a loss of touch with reality. Neurodevelopmental disorders, such as autism and attention deficit disorder (ADD), are also included in the 297 disorders in the *DSM–5*, as are eating disorders and substance use disorders. We'll explore these major categories of mental illness briefly, beginning with the most common.

Anxiety Disorders

Anxiety, or negative anticipation over a future event, is a normal and common reaction to stress and can actually help us achieve our goals. If we are worried about taking a test, for example, we are more likely to study hard for it and get a better grade. But for those who struggle with more intense anxiety, worries are not temporary challenges but overwhelming and debilitating fears. Anxiety reaches the level of a disorder when it becomes a fear, an emotional reaction to a real or perceived threat, and creates behaviors that interfere with getting through the day. Like the example of Mary in the beginning of the chapter, anxiety disorders can make it impossible to succeed in life.

Collectively, anxiety disorders are the most common mental disorders in America today (NIMH, 2016a). Based on the National Comorbidity Survey (2007a), an ongoing national effort to understand the scope of mental illness across the United States, over a 12-month period, 19.1% of Americans meet criteria for a diagnosable anxiety disorder; 31.2% of Americans struggle with an anxiety disorder at some point in their lives (National Comorbidity Survey, 2007b). Think about all the people you know, right now, about one in five of those people are experiencing symptoms of anxiety, and one in three of them have or will experience symptoms in their lifetimes. Many anxiety disorders begin in childhood or adolescence and if they go untreated may persist (American Psychiatric Association, 2013a).

The *DSM–5* breaks down anxiety into 10 different disorders, and all 10 include elements of fear and anxiety, with different presentations of behavioral disturbances (American Psychiatric Association, 2013a). Physical components of anxiety and related disorders can include any or all of the following: accelerated heart rate, difficulty breathing, digestive problems, trembling, sweating, muscle tension, difficulty sleeping, or restlessness. Cognitive symptoms can include distractibility, difficulty focusing, forgetfulness, racing thoughts, or irritability. When struggling with these symptoms, individuals often avoid situations and people that contribute to their anxiety. Some people have panic attacks, which feel like a heart attack, with their heart beating wildly and an inability to think clearly.

Someone who has anxiety when faced with presenting in front of class may struggle with *social anxiety*. Also referred to as social phobia, social anxiety is the most prominent anxiety disorder, present in 6.8% of the population (Kessler, Chiu, Demler, & Walters, 2005). This disorder encompasses fear of being observed and judged by others and often leads to avoiding social situations, having a fear of public speaking, or meeting new people. Other *phobias* are specific, irrational fears of objects or situations, and about 12.5% of Americans struggle with irrational fears of things such as spiders or other animals, blood, needles, heights, storms, or water at some point in their lives (National Comorbidity Survey, 2007b).

When a person worries about something nearly all the time and has trouble controlling their worry, they may meet criteria for *generalized anxiety disorder* (GAD). GAD is another common anxiety disorder and impacts 5.7% of Americans sometime during their lives (National Comorbidity Survey, 2007b). For about 4.7% of Americans, recurrent and unexpected panic attacks begin to rule their lives, and they become overwhelmed with fear of having another panic attack. *Panic attacks* create physical sensations similar to a heart attack with racing heartbeat, trouble breathing, shaking, and are very debilitating in the moment. Being outside of their home, or using public transportation, or fear of open spaces creates a condition called agoraphobia for some individuals who may or may not experience panic attacks when attempting to go out into the world.

Obsessive-compulsive disorders, as well as *post-traumatic stress disorder* (PTSD) and other stress disorders, share physical and cognitive symptoms with anxiety disorders, though the behavioral manifestations of the disorders are different. The category of obsessive-compulsive disorders includes obsessive-compulsive disorder (OCD), body dysmorphic disorder (preoccupation with perceived bodily flaws), hoarding, trichotillomania (hair pulling), and excoriation (skin picking). All of these disorders contain elements of obsessions, which are thoughts, urges, or images that are experienced as uncontrollable, or compulsions, which are repetitive behaviors or mental acts, such as counting, or both. The person struggling with obsessive-compulsive challenges holds their world together through their obsessions or compulsions, and if they are unable to complete their thought process or compulsive action, their anxiety grows and may feel unbearable.

Living through life and death situations, such as violent encounters, war, accidents, or abusive situations, is overwhelming and can result in disorders falling into the trauma and stressor-related category. For each disorder in this group, the individual has been directly exposed to traumatic or

American soldiers are at risk for developing post-traumatic stress disorder, especially after exposure to combat.

stressful events and experiences and recurring and intrusive thoughts, feelings, and behaviors. The most well-known trauma disorder is PTSD, experienced by about 6.8% of Americans (National Comorbidity Survey, 2007b). Those struggling with PTSD often experience involuntary and distressing memories of the traumatic event, recurrent and distressing dreams, and flashbacks when the person actually feels as if the event is happening again. Often attempting to avoid situations that may trigger a reaction, they may also experience shifts in mood, and thinking may become muddled and confused.

Origins of Anxiety Disorders

Approaching an understanding of anxiety disorders from a biopsychosocial perspective, key vulnerabilities contribute to the development of a level of anxiety that becomes untenable (Barlow, 2000). The majority of people who develop anxiety disorders have a heritable vulnerability, based on their genetics. In the more psychological realm, some individuals fail to develop a sense of control over important life events as they grow up and learn fear and helplessness when anticipating future events. Also, specific objects or situations can become the focus of worry and patterns of anxiety develop in response to stimuli.

The thoughts or behaviors of those struggling with obsessions and compulsions are often rewarded, therefore reinforcing and increasing the behaviors. For example, if a new mother becomes obsessed with germs, washes her hands multiple times a day to the point that they become chapped and bleeding, and her baby stays healthy, she may attribute the healthy child to her clean hands and continue to wash them excessively. The reward system actually rewards the obsession or compulsion, for many of the obsessive-compulsive disorders, increasing the likelihood the person will continue to perform in the same manner. Similarly, phobias and worries are often conditioned by the environment and reinforced, continuing patterns.

Mood Disorders

At the beginning of the chapter, we observed Jake, a young man who could not find the energy to live his life. Based on our description, Jake may be diagnosed with a **mood disorder**. The next most common group of mental disorders after anxiety disorders, mood disorders are based in experiences of either a lack of energy and depressed mood, sometimes accompanied by periods of excessive energy and expansive mood.

Depression is present in both major mood diagnoses. More than a simple bad mood, a diagnosis of a major depressive disorder indicates a person feels physical symptoms including low energy, depressed affect, fatigue, changes in weight (loss or gain), and/or trouble sleeping most of the day, most days for 2 weeks or more (American Psychiatric Association, 2013a). Major depression often manifests in thoughts and feelings of worthless or inappropriate guilt; anhedonia (inability to experience pleasure); difficulty in thinking clearly and concentration; and thoughts of death, sometimes with suicidal ideation. These feelings are distinguished from grief and bereavement that follows the death or loss of a loved one. Nearly 17% of Americans meet the criteria for major depressive disorder sometime in their lifetime (National Comorbidity Survey, 2007b). On a worldwide basis, WHO (2014b) reports about 400 million people in the world struggle with depression.

In addition to the symptoms of major depression, some people also experience periods of mania, resulting in a diagnosis of a bipolar disorder. Previously referred to as manic depression, bipolar disorder has a lifetime prevalence of 4.4% (National Comorbidity Survey, 2007b). Globally, more than 60 million people meet criteria for bipolar depression (WHO, 2014c).

A *manic episode* presents as an extreme amount of energy, literally the polar opposite of the low levels of energy felt during depression. This excessive energy can be seen in grandiose thinking (wild and expansive ideas), a sense that sleeping is unnecessary, impulsive decisions often with harmful consequences (e.g., rash spending, bad investments, sexual indiscretions), racing thoughts, and pressured speech. The highest levels of extreme energy are present most of the day, nearly every day for a week or more, unless intervention ends the episode earlier, leading to a diagnosis of bipolar I disorder (American Psychiatric Association, 2013a). For some individuals, the level of energy is somewhat less severe and last 4 days or more, resulting in a diagnosis of hypomania ("under" mania or lesser mania) called bipolar II disorder.

When a person is experiencing either a major depressive episode or a manic episode, they are unable to remember feeling differently that they do in that moment. If they are severely depressed and unable to find the energy to take care of themselves, they do not remember feeling "normal." If they experience mania, they do not remember not having energy to stay up all night and cannot imagine feeling sad or depressed. This cognitive and emotional division in experience contributes to the discouragement and negative emotions described by those struggling with mood disorders.

Origins of Mood Disorders

Sometimes, the first encounter with a major depressive episode can be linked to a specific life event, but the vast majority of individuals who struggle with depression report that the feeling has been with them since childhood. During the course of their lives, symptoms often come unexpectedly, without direct environmental causes, contributing to the somatogenic explanation of these as organic disorders based in imbalances of neurotransmitters in the brain (Khalsa, McCarthy, Sharpless, Barrett, & Barber, 2011). Brain imaging studies demonstrate that structures and functioning in the brain is different when a person is depressed, though the imaging studies do not tell us why this is true (NIMH, 2016a). In addition, family, adoption, and twin studies have all contributed to the theory of a genetic susceptibility to both major depression and bipolar disorder, and geneticists are working to discover specific alleles indicating an individual is at higher risk for developing a mood disorder (Morley, Hall, & Carter, 2004). From a psychogenic perspective, cognitive patterns have been shown to develop, which exacerbate symptoms and increase depression (Beck, Rush, Shaw, & Emery, 1987).

Psychotic Disorders

How do we know if the world around us is real or only just a dream? Philosophers and moviemakers have puzzled over the capacity of the human mind to create its own reality for centuries. One 4th-century BC Chinese parable tells of a man dreaming he is a butterfly and waking to find he is a man; he is then uncertain if he is a butterfly dreaming of being a man or truly a man dreaming of being a butterfly (Chan, n.d.). Grappling with the concept of reality can be difficult for philosophers but a matter of life and death to those struggling with psychosis.

Psychosis occurs when a person loses touch with reality and ceases to know what is real and what is delusion. The person may not realize what is being experienced in his or her mind is not the same as others' experiences. This loss of reality is devastating, and psychotic disorders are often characterized as the most tragic of all mental disorders. One of the most tragic aspects of this disorder is the average of onset—which is just on the cusp of adulthood: The first psychotic break for most individuals happens in their late teens or early 20s (Andreasen, 2000).

The full spectrum of psychotic disorders includes severe cases of bipolar I disorder, when the manic episode crosses into a loss of reality, as well as the schizophrenia and brief psychotic disorder. Literary descriptions contain accounts of what appears to be psychotic processes for many centuries, and interestingly, there appear to be no cultural barriers to psychosis. Schizophrenia spectrum experiences are present in stories from every culture around the globe.

Schizophrenia is the most well-known of the psychotic disorders and affects 1% of Americans (NIMH, 2016d) and 21 million people worldwide (WHO, 2014a). All psychotic disorders affect multiple thought processes and share the presence of one or more of these: delusions (a fixed belief that can not be changed in spite of rational evidence to the contrary), hallucinations (the perception of something that is not present), disorganized thinking and/or speech, disorganized motor movement, and negative symptoms (American Psychiatric Association, 2013a). For someone suffering with psychotic thoughts, their fantasies seem to be fact and their perceptions are distorted and confused. The brain of the person struggling with psychosis misinterprets common stimuli in the environment and creates an altered state of consciousness. Yet no two individuals present these symptoms in the same manner; each person demonstrates a unique constellation of different symptoms and the presence of the disorder is more than the sum of a checklist of symptoms (Andreasen, 2000).

Delusions, hallucinations, and disorganized speech or movement are considered positive symptoms of schizophrenia—not positive in a good sense but rather positive in the fact that they are present, though they should not be. The negative symptoms of schizophrenia are no less tragic to witness and consist of the absence of vital components of life. Avolition, or the lack of will to accomplish tasks or goals, as well as diminished emotional expression, make it very difficult to hold a job, go to school, or be a productive member of society. In considering the diversity of symptoms associated with disorder on the schizophrenia spectrum, the information processing—or thinking—in the brain is dysfunctional and dysregulated (Andreasen, 2000).

Origins of Psychosis

The current theories of etiology of psychotic disorders are as varied as the symptoms. Somatogenic perspectives are currently the most prominent with a neurodevelopmental basis. A correlation has been established between the environment of the fetus before birth, as well as early postnatal environmental factors and later development of schizophrenia, epilepsy, and cerebral palsy (Rehn & Rees, 2005). Linked with these theories are structural differences in brain structures, as well as well-established disruption in neurotransmitters including dopamine, serotonin, glutamate, and gamma-aminobutyric acid. Additionally, psychogenic factors have been identified that contribute but do not cause schizophrenia or psychotic disorders. These factors include psychological stress and trauma (Anderson, Voineskos, Mulsant, George, & McKenzie, 2014), urbanization, and immigration (WHO, 2014a).

Eating Disorders

You notice that your friend, James, never seems to have time to go to lunch with you. He is often in the gym but never seems to eat much. He talks often about building muscles and the size of this body. You are beginning to wonder if James has a problem with eating and how he feels about his body.

While **eating disorders** are more common in women, men also suffer from disordered relationships with food, unhealthy exercise patterns, and/or distorted body image.

Not just about food and eating, eating disorders are complex disorders and are often about control, relationships, depression, and self-concept. Beginning primarily in adolescence, 2.7% of children from 13- to 18-year-olds have diagnosed "severe" eating disorders (Merikangas et al., 2010).

Three major types of eating disorders are included in the *DSM–5* (American Psychiatric Association, 2013a). *Anorexia nervosa* is characterized by restriction in nutritional intake, fear of gaining weight or persistent behavior that interferes with weight gain, and a disturbance in self-perceived weight or body shape. The level of severity of the eating disorder is based on body mass index (BMI) percentiles, based on the WHO standards for thinness in adults, adolescents, and children, with the range of 33 pounds below BMI being extreme. Data from the National Comorbidity Survey found lifetime prevalence at 0.9% for women and 0.3% for men (Hudson, Hiripi, Pope, & Kessler, 2007). Anorexia nervosa has the highest mortality, or death, rate of any psychiatric illness (Millar et al., 2005; Sullivan, 1995).

The second type of eating disorder is *bulimia nervosa*, in which the individual binge eats repeatedly, engages in purging behaviors such as vomiting or excess use of laxatives to compensate for binging, and has a self-concept that is overly influenced by his or her body shape and weight (American Psychiatric Association, 2013a). Some individuals will not engage in binging but will purge after smaller amounts of eating. These binging and inappropriate compensatory behaviors happen, on average, for people struggling with bulimia at least once a week for at least 3 months. Rates of bulimia peak in older adolescence and young adulthood; 1% to 1.5% of young women meet criteria over a 12-month period. Lifetime prevalence has been reported as 1.5% for women and 0.5% for men (Hudson et al., 2007).

The 2013 edition of the *DSM–5* added a diagnosis of *binge eating disorder* (American Psychiatric Association). Recurring episodes of eating more than what most people would eat is characteristic of binge eating in a discrete period of time. Holidays and special occasion overeating is not considered binge eating, so if you overeat at Thanksgiving dinner, you likely do not meet criteria for this disorder. When an individual engages in this behavior, he or she eats more rapidly than normal; often eat until he or she feels uncomfortable; sometimes eats large amounts of food when he or she isn't actually feeling hungry; eat alone due to embarrassment over how much he or she is consuming; and feels disgusted, depressed, or extremely guilty afterward. When binge eating happens, he or she feels very upset and distressed yet feels the behavior is outside of his or her control. With binge eating disorder, compensatory behaviors, such as vomiting, do not occur. More people who are seeking weight loss treatment engage in binge eating behaviors than people in the general population, and the gender ratio is less skewed toward women. Lifetime prevalence for binge eating has been reported at 3.5% of women and 2.0% of men in the United States (Hudson et al., 2007).

Origins of Eating Disorders

More so than other disorders we have discussed, there is a major social component to eating disorders. Values placed on appearance and weight in Western culture have been demonstrated to impact the rate of eating disorders (Mohr & Messina, 2015). Studies have shown that merely being exposed to Western messages while temporarily vacationing or studying in the United States has increased poor body image and the presence of eating disorders for young women from Japan, Singapore, and Iran (Nobakht & Dezhkam, 2000; Ung, 2003). Swanson et al. (2012) explored correlations among immigrants to the United States from Mexico and discovered higher rates of binge eating disorder in those born in the United States with two U.S. born

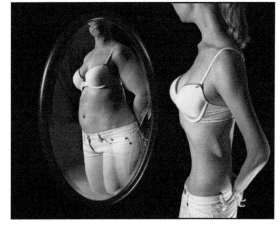

Eating disorders distort how individuals perceive their own bodies.

parents; the presence of English spoken in the home also correlated with higher rates of eating disorders. Globalization has impacted the prevalence of thinness as desirable in women. One example can be found in the Miss World beauty contest. In 2001, the first African woman to win the Miss World contest since its inception in 1950 was Agbani Darego (Onishi, 2002). However, many in Nigeria, her home country, did not find her attractive but rather much too thin.

The concept of vanity as a driver for eating disorders, however, is a limited interpretation, and does not take into account many other biological and psychological contributing factors (Striegel-Moore & Bulik, 2007). From the somatogenic perspective, genetic studies have shown that individuals with a first-degree relative with an eating disorder are more likely to develop an eating disorder, and twin studies have been relatively definitive as to their heritability (Rikani et al., 2013). One of the major neurotransmitters in the brain is serotonin, which serves a primary function in relaying messages and impacts a wide array of human functions, everything from mood to appetite to sleep to thinking and learning. Disruption of the serotonin pathway is present in the brains of individuals struggling with eating disorders both during and following recovery, demonstrating the impact of eating disorders on many aspects of functioning (Kaye, Bailer, Frank, Wagner, & Henry, 2005; Kaye, Frank, et al., 2005). Related to impulse control, eating disorders may alter functioning in the right frontal lobe of the brain (Mohr & Messina, 2015). While researchers are unable to link these correlations directly to causation, the neurological findings can impact potential treatments.

In addition to the cultural factors discussed earlier, psychogenic risk factors for eating disorders are numerous. One major element is distorted body image issues (Mohr & Messina, 2015). Especially prevalent among young women, feelings of dissatisfaction with their bodies and public self-consciousness are highly correlated with eating disorders. College-age women have been shown to be more self-critical of their body than college-age men, and both heterosexual genders make mistakes in understanding what the other finds attractive (Fallon & Rozin, 1985).

The complexity of eating disorders is best understood from a biopsychosocial perspective. Central to this conceptualization is the understanding of the uniqueness of each and every presentation of this—and any—mental disorders. Each person struggling deserves respect and the awareness that mental illness is not a choice but a struggle.

Substance Abuse Disorders and Addictions

Another area of struggle for many individuals revolves around the use of mind-altering substances such as alcohol, recreational and prescription drugs, and even those everyday substances like coffee and cigarettes. Addictions, considered in all forms to be mental disorders, alter the human brain. **Substance-related disorders** include ten different classes, or groups, of drugs including alcohol, cannabis, caffeine, hallucinogens, inhalants, opioids (prescription pain relieving medications), sedatives including hypnotics and anxiolytics (antianxiety medications), stimulants (amphetamine-type substances, cocaine), tobacco, and other or unknown substances (American Psychiatric Association, 2013a).

What these substances all share is activation of the reward circuitry in the brain that is involved in behavior reinforcement and formation of memories. The drugs produce such intense activation of the reward system that other things in life, which are otherwise important when not using the substances, are often ignored. While the actual brain chemicals are different for different types of drugs, they all share this activation of the reward system, creating the experience of a "high"—at least temporarily.

Another critical component to the substance-related disorders is continued use, in spite of negative consequences, as well as a subjective loss of control over the use of the substance over time (Shaffer et al., 2004). In other words, people who drink or do drugs enough to meet criteria for a disorder often continue to use the substances even though they have many problems because of using and consistently report that they can't stop because their use is out of their control. Individuals who meet criteria experience cravings for the substance, some of which change the body and brain permanently. The parts of the brain affected by substance use are those parts responsible for our survival, including decision making, motivation, risk and reward assessment, impulse control, emotion, learning, memory, and stress (National Center on Addiction and Substance Abuse at Columbia University, 2012). Together, these attributes are known as the three Cs of addiction: cravings to compulsions, continued use in spite of negative consequences, and a subjective loss of control (Shaffer et al., 2004).

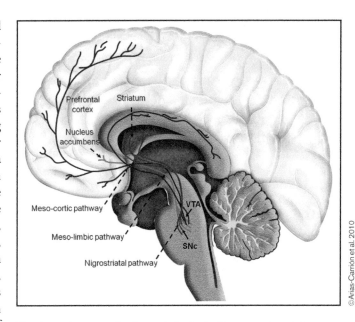

The dopamine reward pathway in the brain. Drugs produce intense activation of this reward system.

Excessive and problematic use of each of the 10 classes of substances can lead to a diagnosis of disorder (American Psychiatric Association, 2013a; see Table 13.1). The potential disorders include substance use disorder, intoxication disorder, or withdrawal disorder. In addition to the presence of the three Cs of addiction, substance use disorders require tolerance, or needing more of the drug to achieve the same level of effect. Tolerance varies extensively among individuals, with some people developing tolerance quickly and others over longer periods of time. Breaking down tolerance further, different parts of the central nervous system become tolerant at different rates, so an individual may become more tolerant with their motor control than their breathing rates, creating confusion over whether someone is intoxicated or not, in a given circumstance.

Intoxication disorders occur when clinically significant behavior or psychological changes occur to a person when using a substance and can apply to all of the substances except tobacco (American Psychiatric Association, 2013a). This might present as someone drinking alcohol excessively who stumbles, slurs their words, and says inappropriate things. Intoxication may occur for a person whose drug use does not meet criteria for a substance use disorder, though over time, repeated intoxication may lead to a disorder. Intoxication is experienced as distortions in perception and thinking, judgment is generally impaired, attention is altered, and motor control is impacted. Acute episodes of intoxication often have different signs than chronic intoxication; individuals who are intoxicated often do not appear as intoxicated as their blood alcohol level would indicate.

Like intoxication disorders, most substances have corresponding *withdrawal disorders* (American Psychiatric Association, 2013a). Unlike intoxication, which can happen without the presence of a substance use diagnosis, withdrawal is a syndrome occurring when the blood and tissue in the human body has built up such a concentration through heavy use of the substance that discontinuing use creates multiple physiological and psychological symptoms. The effects of withdrawal are unique to each substance but create difficulties in everyday functioning and potentially long-term health issues.

In addition to diagnoses of substance use disorders, frequent and prolonged use of substances can create *substance-induced mental disorders* (American Psychiatric Association, 2013a). These are potentially severe and have the potential to impact the central nervous system, sometimes permanently. Substances that are central nervous system depressants, including alcohol, sedatives, hypnotics, and antianxiety drugs, can

Table 13.1 Substance Classes and Possible Diagnoses

Substances by Class and Associated Mental Disorders								
	Psychotic Disorders	Bipolar Disorders	Depressive Disorders	Anxiety Disorders	Obsessive-Compulsive Disorders	Sleep Disorders	Sexual Dysfunction	Delirium	Neuro-cognitive Disorders
Alcohol	X	X	X	X		X	X	X	X
Caffeine				X		X			
Cannabis	X			X		X		X	
Hallucinogens	X	X	X	X				X	
Inhalants	X		X	X				X	X
Opioids			X	X		X	X	X	
Sedatives	X	X	X	X		X	X	X	X
Stimulants	X	X	X	X	X	X	X	X	
Tobacco						X			
Other/ Unknown	X	X	X	X	X	X	X	X	X

Source: Adapted from American Psychiatric Association, 2013.

produce clinically significant depressive disorders during periods of intoxication, while producing equally distressing anxiety conditions during withdrawal from the substances. For stimulants, such as cocaine and amphetamines, prolonged substance use can create substance-induced psychotic disorders during intoxication, with both anxiety and depression symptoms at withdrawal. Marijuana has been linked with development of psychotic disorders, especially in those with predisposition to psychosis (National Institute of Drug Abuse, 2010).

Lifetime prevalence in the American population for any substance use disorder is 35.3% (National Comorbidity Survey, 2007b). Men exhibit higher rates of substance disorders, with lifetime prevalence at 41.8% for men and 29.6% for women. Breaking these numbers down further, alcohol use disorders have a lifetime prevalence of 13.2% in the American population, with about one in four men, or 19.6%, meeting criteria over their lifetimes, and 7.5% of women. Use of the 10 different classes of drugs, including cannabis, hallucinogens, inhalants, opioids, sedatives, and stimulants, has been found to have a lifetime prevalence of 8.0% in the American population, with 4.8% of women and 11.6% of men meeting criteria. As these statistics illustrate, substance use disorders represent a major national health concern and the largest category of lifetime prevalence for any mental illness.

High rates of comorbidity are a complicating factor in the diagnosis and treatment of addictions. *Comorbidity*, as mentioned earlier in the chapter, is the term used to describe two different disorders occurring in the same person—either at the same time or just after one another. Comorbidity implies interactions between the two disorders and impacts the prognosis, or likely outcome, of both. A number of major illnesses are often comorbid with substance use disorders such as HIV, cancer, hepatitis C, and cardiovascular disease (National Institute of Drug Abuse, 2010).

In addition to these major medical illnesses, psychiatric comorbidity is high with all addictions. Depression and anxiety can be the result of using substances as discussed earlier, but for many individuals, depression and anxiety, as well as psychosis, can be happening at the same time, not induced by use of substances but already present for the individual. The changes occurring in the brain with all mental disorders share commonalities in structural and functional disruptions. Individuals struggling with mood and anxiety disorders, for example, are twice as likely to develop a substance use disorder (see Table 13.2). An example of a particularly deadly combination is tobacco addiction and psychiatric disorders. Individuals diagnosed with mental disorders including major depressive disorder, bipolar disorder, psychotic disorders, substance abuse disorders, and PTSD are twice as likely to smoke as other people but also have high rates of smoking cessation (Lasser et al., 2000).

Origins of Addictions

As with all of the mental disorders we have discussed, there is not a single cause for addiction. Rather, a biopsychosocial model with insights into the somatogenic and psychogenic patterns in viewing addiction provides the most thorough and comprehensive explanation currently available. Beginning with the biological, at the genetic level, moderate to high genetic influences on addiction have been identified through classical genetic studies (Agrawal & Lynskey, 2008). These studies have examined the rates of addiction among twins, adoption, and family studies to determine if genes, especially specific genes, may play a role in whether a person becomes as addict. Overall, findings show that there is no single gene but rather multiple genes are present producing cumulative and interactive effects.

In exploring any genetic influences, however, the impact of the environment cannot be minimized. While predisposition to addiction may be hereditary, the ability to obtain substances—drugs or alcohol—is necessary to become addicted. Simply living in a higher density, urban environment versus a rural area has been shown to result in a five-fold increase in genetic effects for teens (Dick, Rose, Viken, Kaprio, & Koskenvuo, 2001). Similarly, greater amounts of time spent with parents reduced the genetic impact and rates on teen's cigarette smoking behavior, suggesting that greater monitoring of behavior lessened smoking and moderated the genetic impact (Dick et al., 2007).

The age when a person begins using substances represents a risk factor for the development of addiction. The critical period of vulnerability for the development of an addiction is adolescence (National Center on Addiction and Substance Abuse at Columbia University, 2012). In 96.5% of cases, addiction begins with substance use before age 21. Risky behavior is, for many teens and young adults, synonymous with being young, and pushing boundaries and rules often involves substance use. Because the adolescent brain is still developing, the impact of frequent use of alcohol and drugs can further impair judgment and interfere with brain development. Teens and young adults with genetic predispositions—relatives with substance use disorders such as alcoholism and drug addiction—are at the greatest risk for developing addiction themselves.

Mental illness, in all of the forms we have discussed in this chapter, represents significant challenges to living everyday life. Adjusting to the impact of mental illness on top of everyday stressors can become so overwhelming that some individuals contemplate escaping the pain through suicide. Thoughts of suicide, or suicidal ideation, as well as actual attempts are the most drastic of choices and the most final solution to the problems that are part of mental illness. See Researching Adjustment: Suicide—The Most Drastic Choice.

| Table 13.2 Major Mental Illnesses and Their Prevalence |

Major Types of Disorders	Includes	Prevalence in the U.S.
Anxiety Disorders	Social anxiety, Phobias, Generalized Anxiety, Panic Disorder, Agoraphobia. RELATED DISORDERS: Obsessive-Compulsive Disorder, Traumatic and Stress disorders	12-month: 19.1% (1 in 5) Lifetime: 31.2% (1 in 3)
Mood Disorders	Major Depressive Disorder, Bipolar disorder	Major Depression: 17% Bipolar Disorder: 4.4%
Psychotic Disorders	Schizophrenia, Brief Psychotic disorder, extreme periods of Bipolar disorder	Schizophrenia: Lifetime:1%
Eating Disorders	Anorexia Nervosa, Bulimia Nervosa, Binge Eating Disorder	Lifetime: Anorexia: Women: 0.9%, Men: 0.3% Bulimia: Women: 1.5%, Men: 0.5% Binge-Eating: Women: 3.5%, Men: 2.0%
Substance Abuse Disorders: Substance Use, Substance Intoxication, or Substance Withdraw	Classes of drugs: alcohol, cannabis, caffeine, hallucinogens, inhalants, opioids, sedatives, stimulants, tobacco, and other/unknown.	Lifetime for Any Substance: Women: 29.6% Men: 41.8% Alcohol: Lifetime in Population: 13.2%: Men: 19.6% (1 in 4) Women: 7.5% Drug Use (cannabis, hallucinogens, inhalants, opioids, sedatives, stimulants) Lifetime in Population: 8.0% Men: 11.6% and Women: 4.8%
Neurodevelopmental: Attention-Deficit Disorders	Attention Deficit Disorder (ADD), Attention Deficit Hyperactivity Disorder (ADHD)	Children 3-17: 7% Children 13-18: 9% (note overlap) Adults: 4.1%
Neurodevelopmental: Autism Spectrum Disorder (ASD)	Previously included Pervasive Developmental Disorder and Aspergers	1 in 68 children

RESEARCHING ADJUSTMENT
Suicide–The Most Drastic Choice

The most extreme example of the need for professional intervention is when a person becomes suicidal. Suicide is ranked as the 10th most common cause of death in the United States (CDC, 2015b). In 2013, there were 41,149 people in the United States who took their own lives, nearly 3 times the rate of homicide at a rate of one death every 13 minutes or 113 deaths a day (CDC, 2015c). Suicide was the second highest cause of death for young people between the ages of 15 and 34. Men are nearly 4 times more likely than women to be successful in their suicide attempts, as they often choose more lethal means, but women attempt suicide more often than men. Suicide is the 7th leading cause of death among men, and the 14th among women. WHO (2015) estimates that more than 800,000 people die globally a year from suicide.

Why do people choose this most drastic of steps? Any attempt at explanation has been shown to require a biopsychosocial approach to understanding (WHO, 2015). Identification of risk and protective factors, elements in a person's life that create increased or decreased likelihood of an outcome respectively, is a first step in both understanding and prevention. Many individuals who attempt or successfully end their own lives have been diagnosed, or meet the criteria, for a mental disorder—most frequently mood disorders and/or substance abuse disorders (Mann, 2002; WHO, 2015). However, the importance of understanding that not all individuals who struggle with mental disorders are suicidal and not all individuals who attempt suicide are mentally ill is very important.

Many factors correlate with suicide ideation, or thoughts of suicide, and attempts (Gunnell, 2015). Having self-harmed or attempted suicide in the past correlates very highly, as does access to the means of a planned suicide attempt. Suicide can occur in clusters, and copycat suicides are a major concern; media representation of suicides can increase their attractiveness to individuals struggling with despair. Stress, combined with a predisposition, has been shown to be a contributor to suicidal ideation and attempts (van Heeringen, 2000). Predisposition, in this theory, is psychological and stems from negative beliefs about oneself and learned helplessness and combines with increased activation of the stress response system. In addition to heightened stress responses, abnormalities in the serotonergic transmitters have been found to contribute to suicidal patterns in thinking and behavior (Pandey, 2013). Clearly, suicidal ideation and attempts are biopsychosocial in nature.

Individuals who choose the most permanent solution to their difficulties are unique, with their own stories and particular combinations of risk factors. While they may not be able to conceive of other choices as they contemplate ending their own lives, other choices do exist, and intervention can make a difference. Education about suicide and all forms of mental illness is crucial to reducing the stigma of seeking help (WHO, 2015). Knowing the signs of someone who is suicidal can help family, friends, and communities to intervene effectively. Reduction in access to means of suicide is an important public health concern, as is the adoption of standards for the reporting of suicides in the media. Protective factors that have shown to reduce suicide attempts include close personal relationships, religious or spiritual beliefs, and the practice of positive self-talk and coping techniques. If you believe a friend or family member is suicidal, reaching out for professional help is the greatest act of caring you can provide.

(Continued)

Reflection Questions

1. As a society, what are steps we can take to lower the staggering statistics around suicide?

2. If you have a friend who is struggling and you are afraid he or she may be suicidal, what should you do? Should you keep his or her secret?

Neurodevelopmental Disorders

While the other major disorders discussed most commonly begin in adolescence or young adulthood, **neurodevelopmental disorders** begin in childhood and impact the development of the human brain. This disruption of development of the brain from conception through childhood creates deficits in functioning and may be seen in physical and motor development as well as school and social interactions. Both *attention deficit disorders*—ADD and *attention deficit/hyperactivity disorder* (ADHD)—as well as *autism* are well-known neurodevelopmental disorders. While these two disorders present in very different ways, both originate in childhood, most commonly before the person enters grade school. Both ADD and ADHD and autism have been found to be heterogeneous, impacting individuals across gender, race, and socioeconomic class.

Attention Deficit Disorders

Difficulties maintaining attention on tasks and overactivity—or hyperactivity—are the two hallmarks of the diagnoses of ADD and ADHD. The *DSM–5* makes a distinction between those people who have trouble with focus, concentration, organization, and follow-through (ADD) and those who have trouble sitting still as well as restless, overly talkative, and unable to quietly play or engage relaxing activities (ADHD; American Psychiatric Association, 2013a). For a diagnosis to be made by a professional, these symptoms must present before age 12 and impact the person's life in two or more settings, such as home, school, or work, or with friends or family or in other activities.

Rates of ADD/ADHD vary by country and even sometimes from study to study; overall rates in the United States are minimally 7% in children ages 3 to 17, as high as 9% in children ages 13 to 18, and 4.1% of adults (Camilleri & Makhoul, 2013; NIMH, 2016b). WHO (2014b) utilizes the term *hyperkinetic disorders* and does not distinguish between ADD and ADHD, with worldwide prevalence at approximately 5% to 6% of the population, though underdiagnosis is believed to be frequent in many countries (Camilleri & Makhoul, 2013; Polanczyk, de Lima, Less-Horta, Biederman, & Rohde, 2007). For individuals struggling with attention difficulties, the average age of onset is 7 years of age, and boys are at 4 times greater risk for developing attention disorders than girls (NIMH, 2016b).

Long before these data were gathered, in 1937, a physician who was treating children for headaches recognized a counterintuitive, or not what you might think, aspect to attention disorders (Sajid, Poor, & Diaz, 2010). Stimulants given to treat headaches actually increased focus in children with behavioral problems. In other words, for children and adults who have difficulty with focus, impulsivity, and overactivity, stimulant medication increases concentration and focus. Double-blind, placebo-controlled studies have found rates of improvement in ADD/ADHD symptoms for every two out of three patients who are treated with short acting stimulant medications (Daughton & Kratochvil, 2009).

Origins of Attention Deficit Disorders

Hundreds of studies have identified genetic components for ADD/ADHD (Banaschewski, Becker, Scherag, Franke, & Coghill, 2010), and heritability has been estimated as high as 76% (Taylor et al., 1998). For a person with ADD/ADHD, parents and siblings are 4 to 5 times more likely to have ADHD than someone from the general population, further supporting a somatogenic, genetic explanation for ADD/ADHD. The expression of these genes typically happens in childhood and early adolescence, creating patterns in neurological development.

Autism Spectrum Disorder

Students of all ages who struggle with ADD/ADHD have difficulty paying attention.

Marty, 7 years old, has trouble making eye contact and rocks back and forth when he is upset. He is fascinated with trains and will focus for hours on the train set his father gave him. He reads any book about trains that he can find and does not appear to care about other things around him. He doesn't like physical contact and has always pulled away from his mother's embrace. Based on these observations, Marty likely meets criteria for a diagnosis of ASD.

The hallmarks of ASD are persistent problems in social communication and interactions, as well as restricted, repetitive patterns of behaviors, interests, or activities (American Psychiatric Association, 2013a). Often, individuals struggling with ASD display difficulty with theory of mind, or understanding that other minds are different from one's own and attribute explanations to other's behaviors. Sometimes, individuals with ASD aren't able to display empathy toward others very well. All symptoms of ASD are on a continuum, with some individuals high functioning and able to take care of themselves, and others at the opposite end, unable to care for themselves or to communicate with others.

Spectrum disorders are syndromes that share the same underlying cause but present with a wide range of severity and intensity. With the publication of the *DSM-5* in 2013, autism was classified as a spectrum disorder and incorporated pervasive developmental disorder, autism, and Asperger's syndrome. Reported rates have steadily increased, perhaps due to increased awareness and new diagnostic criteria, with the Centers for Disease Control and Prevention (CDC; 2015a) estimating 1 in 68 children in the United States as identified with ASD. Five times more boys than girls have been diagnosed with ASD. Worldwide estimates of ASD are at 1 person in 160, though many low- and middle-income countries may not be adequately included (WHO, 2013a).

Origins of Autism Spectrum Disorder

As a neurodevelopmental disorder appearing as early as 18 months of age, ASD explanations are somatogenic. ASD impacts a wide array of functions, and no single gene has been identified as the cause of the spectrum, therefore a polygenetic, or multiple genes, theory is being explored (Hu, 2013). In addition to gene theory, epigenetic, or the interaction between environment and the expression of genes, is another field of research, as are prenatal factors (Williams et al., 2014). Understanding the higher rates of ASD in males raises interesting research questions that are currently being explored.

ASD, like all of the major mental disorders we have discussed, should always be assessed and diagnosed by psychologists and psychiatrists. Labeling friends, families, or people you observe on the street or the bus without professional evaluation promotes stigma and stereotypes. Not every young man who likes to play video games has ASD, just as not every person who stays up one night worrying about an exam has an anxiety disorder. If you or someone you care about does exhibit signs and symptoms of a mental disorder, you can help the most by assisting them to find professional help.

Psychotherapy, along with psychotropic medications, are the most common treatments for mental illness today.

We have talked about major mental illnesses with broad strokes and lots of numbers (see Table 13.2). The reality of mental illness is much more personal for thousands of people who struggle on a daily basis.

Section Two: Treatment of Mental Illness

The way a society explains mental illness, all the way from spiritual to biopsychosocial explanations, affect the ways in which mental illness has been treated throughout history. As a science, the field of psychiatry and clinical psychology builds on knowledge learned over time and reflects these societal explanations. In this section, we will look at the history of treatment of mental illness, looking as far back as asylums from the 15th century and moving forward to the medications and treatments we use today.

Early Treatment: Asylums

The treatment of mental disorders in Western Europe and the United States began with the advent of asylums and the hospitalization of individuals suffering from what would today be considered mental disorders. Dating back to the 15th century, one of the first institutions to begin the housing of mentally ill was The Bethlehem Hospital in London, England (Historic England, 2015). Originally designed to house paupers, Bedlam, as it came to be called, was commissioned in 1247 but by 1407 was housing primarily "lunatics." The term *lunatics* derived from a common myth that behavior was related to the waxing and waning of the moon. The treatment at that time consisted primarily of manacles, locks, and various implements of restraint, carried out by religious monks whose duty was to care for those suffering from "madness." A somatogenic view was taken, and purges, bleeding, and emetics were common.

Public and private asylums were found throughout Europe in the 18th and 19th centuries. The city of Paris also began treatment in a similar fashion; caring for the poor transitioned into caring for the mentally ill with the founding of the Hôpital Général de la Ville de Paris in 1634 (Micale, 1985; Poirier, 2003). Like Bedlam, a wide array of patients included paupers, prostitutes, destitute elderly, disabled, orphans, and abandoned children.

Hospitalization, also referred to as institutionalization, removed care from the family and community, often to the detriment of the patients. Individuals suffering from mental disorders were often viewed as dangerous and violent, and conditions in asylums were focused on containment and restraint, not the improvement of mental health of the individual. This harsh treatment of individuals with mental illness was revolutionized both in England and France in the late 1790s. In England, a Quaker named William Tuke (1732–1822) initiated the York Retreat, where patients were treated like guests and envisioned as a place where the unhappy might find a refuge from difficulties (Bewley, 2008). In about 1797, during the time of the French Revolution, the efforts of early psychiatrists Jean-Baptiste Pussin (1746–1811) and Philippe Pinel (1745–1826) were focused on reformation of the treatment of those with mental disorders (Weiner, 2010b). Taking the chains off of patients and viewing the mentally ill with compassion and care became known as "moral treatment." Asylums became more sanctuaries and less prisonlike for patients.

Settlers of the British colonies brought the concepts of asylums to the New World. The first in the New World, the Philadelphia Hospital, was founded in 1752 and included rooms in the basement for mentally ill patients (U.S. National Library of Medicine, 2006). By 1890, every state in the United States operated at least one mental institution. About the same time as Pussin and Pinel in France, Benjamin Rush (1746–1813), a psychiatrist in Philadelphia, began reformation of treatment conditions and promoted the conceptualization of mental disorders as illnesses, believing mental illness was caused by flow of blood through the brain and that madness was a type of fever (Weiner, 2010a). These attempts to heal and treat mental illness from a medical perspective, a drastic shift from previous treatment, were an important beginning to psychiatric care.

Asylums and state hospitals continued through the turn of the 20th century as the primary care facilities for individuals struggling with mental illness. Soldiers from the Civil War, as well as World War I and World War II, crowded facilities and conditions in U.S. asylums as well as those in Europe. A second wave of moral treatment came about in the United States through the efforts of Dorothea Dix (1802–1887), the Civil War superintendent of army nurses in the mid-1800s (Gollaher, 1993). Dix successfully petitioned the U.S. Congress for lands and funding for humane treatment of indigent and insane persons.

Jacksonville, Illinois, Insane Asylum, circa 1890. For thousands of individuals, insane asylums housed those struggling with mental illness.

Unfortunately, moral and humane treatment did not survive in public institutions due to the overcrowding; care became primarily custodial. Early efforts to release patients into the community to combat the overcrowding were largely unsuccessful through the mid-1930s through the 1950s, with many patients returning shortly after release (Pow, Baumeister, Hawkins, Cohen, & Garand, 2015).

Deinstitutionalization represented another revolution in the care and treatment of mental illness. However, the advent of antipsychotic drugs combined with a movement toward community mental health drastically lowered the hospital populations (Gronfein, 1985). From 1955 to 1980, the population of patients in the United States fell from 559,000 to 154,000 through the movement of deinstitutionalization (Koyanagi, 2007). In 1963, the last bill President John F. Kennedy (1917–1963) signed before his assassination was the Community Mental Health Act, designed to revolutionize the care and treatment of mentally ill and developmentally disabled persons (Rosenberg, 2014). Kennedy believed that moving from "cold mercy of custodial care" to the "open warmth" of communities would change lives for the better. Continuing efforts to improve the community care of individuals with mental disorders focuses on education and community involvement (Murphy & Rigg, 2014).

The types and level of care given to patients in both public and private asylums were driven by explanations of mental illness. Psychogenic and somatogenic basis alternated in popularity and focus throughout hospitalization, moral treatment, and deinstitutionalization revolutions in psychiatric care. On a simultaneous trajectory, both psychogenic and somatogenic explanations have created the most effective options for treatment today.

Psychotherapy: A Psychogenic Approach

Considered the founder of psychotherapy, Sigmund Freud (1856–1939), a Viennese physician, transformed psychogenic explanations at the beginning of the 20th century. Freud proposed that our unconscious mind influenced our actions, and our childhood experiences shaped all of our interactions with ourselves and the world around us. Through his initial work with hypnosis and the treatment of hysteria, Freud and his colleague, Josef Breuer (1842–1925), began an intervention process with patients that developed into psychoanalytic theory and the practice of psychoanalysis (Breger, 2000).

Central to psychoanalytic theory was the presence of the unconscious mind and explanations of the inner life of humans (Schwartz, 1999). The idea of the unconscious

Group therapy offers individuals the benefit of healing alongside others who share similar struggles.

mind was completely revolutionary and has influenced Western philosophy, literature, and art from its beginnings. First proposed by Freud (1899/1955) in his seminal work *The Interpretation of Dreams*, the unconscious mind was proposed to drive behaviors outside of conscious awareness. Freudian theory suggested that some desires are simply too much for the human mind to bear, and therefore, it represses these desires and expresses them through dreams and dysfunctional behaviors (Schwartz, 1999). These unconscious and animalistic desires reside in the id, or the most primitive part of personality, far below the surface of conscious awareness. The id is balanced by the superego, the part of personality that seeks approval and follows societal rules and is somewhat within our awareness. These two opposing parts of personality are balanced by the ego, another aspect of personality that is somewhat within our awareness. When the ego is unable to balance successfully, dysfunction occurs, and the individual may exhibit wild, unacceptable behaviors, or become rigid, overly conscientious and rule following.

The major goal of **psychoanalysis**, a type of talk therapy, is for the patient to become more aware of their unconscious processes, to tame their primitive urges without overcompensating and being driven only by the superego. Insight into the patterns created by childhood would free the individual to understand his or her behavior more fully and lead to clarity in action and resolution of dysfunction. Accomplished through talk therapy, the psychoanalyst guides the analysand, or person undergoing psychoanalysis. The process of psychoanalysis was originally believed to be effective through meeting 5 days a week, usually for many years, to uncover and understand the depths of the individual's experiences, though only a small number of patients are treated this frequently today.

Psychoanalysis was the major method of treatment during the first half of the 20th century in both Europe and the United States, though not the only major theory regarding human behavior to develop at the time. The introduction of behaviorism as a scientific explanation for why and how individuals acted created a new theoretical basis and eventually impacted treatment. With its origins in the writings of John B. Watson (1878–1958), behaviorism proposed that emotions and thoughts could not be observed and, therefore, could not be scientifically studied (Watson, 1913). Behaviors that could be observed could therefore be changed and adapted through behavior modification techniques. These ideas, furthered by B. F. Skinner (1904–1990), brought the concepts of reinforcement, punishment, and schedules of reinforcement into the process of changing dysfunctional behaviors (Skinner, 1998). At the heart of behaviorism is the theory that when a behavior is rewarded, the behavior will increase in frequency and when a behavior is punished, the behavior will decrease in frequency. This approach has been used in numerous therapeutic approaches and has contributed to the formation of cognitive behavioral techniques.

Aaron Beck (1921–) is considered the founder of *cognitive behavioral therapy*. Originally trained in psychoanalysis, Beck was working as a psychiatrist in the 1960s when he designed and carried out experiments with his depressed and anxious patients and found that their thought patterns were the source of their struggles, as opposed to patterns created in childhood (Beck, 2011). Beck designed assessments and interventions to help correct the problematic automatic thoughts and behaviors of individuals through focus on techniques such as thought stopping and positive self-talk. Cognitive behavioral therapy remains one of the most frequently used and accessible methods of therapy for many mental disorders.

About the same time as Beck was developing his recognition and theory of the impact of cognitive processes, Carl Rogers (1902–1987), another psychologist originally trained as a psychoanalyst, developed his theories establishing a humanistic view as central to the treatment of mental illness (Rogers, 1961). When researching why some patients change during the therapeutic process and others do not, Rogers recognized the impact of the relationship between the therapist and the patient. Along with Abraham Maslow (1908–1970) and Rollo May (1909–1994), Rogers explored the patient, or *client* as they popularized the term, as the center of the therapeutic encounter and believed through recognition and understanding of the client as a person, situated in their own world, could change and growth take place. *Client-centered therapy*, unlike behaviorism, operates from the theory that humans possess a drive to fulfill their potential and reach a level of self-actualization, with human growth as its focal point. Humanistic psychology, like psychoanalytic and cognitive behavior therapies, has offered both theory and treatment to clinicians working with those struggling with mental illness.

With the approach of the 21st century, psychologists wished to further understand the effectiveness of these different approaches. What worked, and what didn't work? And, as a scientific field, what could be proven to be effective and thereby help the most people in the most efficient manner? The American Psychological Association formed a task force in 1999 to identify, operationalize, and share the components of **empirically validated therapy** (Norcross, 2011). They discovered that elements of each therapeutic approach had their benefits, but a core set emerged as highly effective, including a therapeutic alliance between the therapist and the client, empathy, positive regard and affirmation, and genuineness. These relational aspects were found to work best when tailored to individual clients and form the basis for successful therapy.

The movement toward therapy that is effective and validated through research could also be seen in the increased outcome studies and exploration of the specific treatments for specific mental disorders (Nathan & Gorman, 2015). Findings have consistently found a combination of therapy and medication to be most effective in the treatment of major mental disorders. Research-based findings allow for clinicians today to take an varied approach to selecting treatment modalities for a specific mental illness. An empirically validated treatment approach allows clinicians to choose from many potential treatments to select the type of therapy that has been scientifically supported as the best practice for a given disorder.

The process of selecting someone to help return to healthy adjustment and to manage mental illness can be daunting. For many individuals, the idea of opening up and sharing deeply personal stories provokes anxiety and concerns. As the research that was previously mentioned has shown, though, psychotherapies can be critical in the recovery and management of life challenges. Finding professional help is something to be tackled one step at a time. See Adjustment in Practice: The Experience of Seeking Professional Help for more information on this.

ADJUSTMENT IN PRACTICE
The Experience of Seeking Professional Help

Experiences in seeking professional help are as different as the many different presentations of disorders. The first step is, naturally, to decide that help is needed. The second step is to decide where to find help. Students have an advantage over others in the population because all colleges and universities offer some type of counseling center where students can turn for an evaluation and visit with a professional. In the broader community, people often reach out

(Continued)

(Continued)

Seeking Professional Help

When to seek professional help for mental illness . . .

- As soon as possible following a traumatic experience
- When symptoms interfere with work, school, or relationships
- When feelings of being overwhelmed last more than weeks or months
- When there seems to be no identifiable cause for the way you are feeling or behaving
- Your reactions to situations are frequently out of proportion to the circumstances

to family or friends for a referral to a mental health provider. Referrals are valuable because they offer a chance to connect with someone who is known to the referral source. When referrals aren't available, some people turn to their health insurance provider to offer names of professionals, whose services are covered by the insurance company. Websites also provide listings of psychiatrists, psychologists, and therapists.

As discussed in the text, the relationship between you and your clinician is critical to the success of your therapy, so finding a person you are comfortable talking with is extremely important. Questions to be asked when looking for a provider should be individualized to the person seeking help, but here are a few common questions to ask providers (adapted from the American Psychological Association, 2016):

1. Are you a licensed provider? How many years have you been in practice?

2. I've been (feeling depressed or anxious, worried about my eating or drinking, etc.) and having problems with (school, relationships, etc.). What experience do you have helping people with these types of problems?

3. What are your areas of expertise? Do you usually work with people my age?

4. What kinds of treatment do you use, and have they been shown to be effective with my kind of problem?

5. What are your fees?

6. What kind of insurance do you accept?

Once a provider has been found, the next step is the first appointment. This appointment can be anxiety-provoking itself, because you will be meeting a brand-new person and talking about your personal issues. The clinician may ask you to complete forms, including a form talking about your personal history, before you meet. When you meet for the first time, it is very likely the clinician will ask you questions about what is bringing you to therapy or treatment at this time in your life. Depending on their approach to treatment, they may ask questions about your family history, or just focus on the current problems you are having. If at any point in the therapy you become uncomfortable or find yourself not confiding in your clinician, you should talk about it and consider finding a different provider. Remember that relationship is a factor in getting effective help.

Most effective therapies will seek to understand the problems or symptoms you are struggling with and seek to alleviate those with treatment. As we have discussed, there are many reasons for the causes of mental illness, and effective treatment seeks to identify causes in order to resolve the problem and improve your functioning. Treatment may include talk therapies, such as interpersonal therapy or cognitive behavioral therapy, and in many cases, medications are important aspects to treatment. As mental illness is complex and biopsychosocial, treatment generally takes multiple meetings with your clinician and can't be fixed in one visit.

Reflection Questions

1. Which type of clinician would you seek out? A psychologist, a psychiatrist, or a master's-level therapist? Why?

2. What information would you want to know about a clinician? What factors are important to you in someone you would share your most personal emotions and thoughts with?

Psychotropic Surgeries and Psychotropic Medications: Somatogenic Approaches

Parallel to these developments in psychologically based interventions were the somatogenic-focused therapies used primarily in asylum and hospital settings. The history of these interventions includes development of psychosurgeries, attempts at directly altering the structures and functioning of the brain to lessen the most challenging of symptoms, and the development and use of psychotropic medications targeting major mental illnesses.

Psychotropic Surgeries

Asylums and hospitals were trying to develop interventions to work directly on the brain simultaneously with development of medications (Whitaker, 2010). The first three techniques to be utilized regularly in the 1930s and early 1940s were *insulin coma therapy*, whereby the patient was injected with a high dose of insulin resulting in a coma and then drawn out of the coma with injections of glucose. Believing this restored the brain circuitry to sanity, the technique was initially well regarded. *Electroconvulsive therapy* (ECT), a second technique and a type of brain stimulation, created a seizure state for the patient through the delivery of electric shocks to the brain and allowed the patient to awake without psychotic or depressed thoughts, though often without short-term memories.

Finally, *lobotomies* were developed from the research of Antonio Egas Moniz (1874–1955), a Nobel Prize–winning Portuguese neurologist (Berrios, 1997). Moniz discovered through the severing of connections between the prefrontal cortex in the brain and the areas below symptoms of psychosis and severe mental illness would disappear. This focus followed the development of insights into localization of specific functions within the brain and the desire to treat symptoms that were resistant to any other known interventions.

The work of Moniz was followed by another young neurosurgeon, Walter Freeman (1895–1972), in the United States (El-Hai, 2005). In an attempt to simplify Moniz's procedure, Freeman developed a technique using an ice pick that was inserted through the eye socket and moved in a back-and-forth motion. Severing the connection between the frontal lobe of the brain and connecting tissue, patients were free of a variety of symptoms; however, they were also free from many rational thought processes and decision-making ability. Many patients relapsed, and many others had to be taught how to control basic bodily functions; approximately one third of the patients died from the procedure. Freeman was credited with performing over 3,500 lobotomies in psychiatric hospitals across the United States over a 40-year period. While initially hailed as a savior of those with mental illness, the barbarity of the procedure, as well as deaths and debilitating outcomes, eventually became public knowledge, and Freeman was eventually banned from performing further surgeries. The attempts of these early neurosurgeons to treat mental illness did not lead to any sustainable methods of surgical intervention. At this point in time, there are no surgical procedures to alleviate symptoms of major mental illnesses. See Researching Adjustment: Brain Stimulation Therapies for more modern and less invasive procedures.

RESEARCHING ADJUSTMENT
Brain Stimulation Therapies

Brain stimulation therapies are less invasive than psychosurgeries but still involve activating or touching the brain directly with magnets, electricity, or implants. These treatments are generally used to treat chronic mental disorders that have not responded to psychotherapy or medication and are least common interventions being used today.

ECT, first developed in 1938, is the oldest and most researched of the brain stimulation therapies. Administered when the person is under general anesthesia, electrodes placed in precise locations pass an electric current through the brain, resulting in a seizure lasting less than a minute. Generally, 6 to 12 treatments are given, though some people have additional follow-up treatments. Following the treatment, the person is usually able to resume normal activities in a short time. One study into its use with treatment-resistant depression found ECT to be effective for 86% of those treated for severe, chronic depression, as well as effective in follow-up treatment (Kellner et al., 2006). Side effects of ECT typically include headache, nausea, and muscle aches. The original form of ECT displayed more memory loss side effects than the more modern targeted versions of ECT.

Instead of the electric current of ECT, repetitive transcranial magnetic stimulation (rTMS) uses a magnetic pulse to activate the brain. Originally developed in 1985, rTMS has been studied as a possible treatment for depression and psychosis in the 1990s. The magnetic pulses are targeted directly to specific brain areas, and the administration does not require anesthesia, making it less intrusive than ECT. Research into the effectiveness of rTMS is ongoing, and no definitive results have been found yet. Side effects have been shown to be less than experienced in electroconvulsive treatments (Spellman et al., 2008) and most frequently included headaches and scalp discomfort (Janicak et al., 2008).

More invasive, two methods of brain stimulation that require insertion of devices that are connected to the brain have been approved by the U.S. Food and Drug Administration (FDA) for treatment of severe mental illness. Vagus nerve stimulation (VNS) involves a device inserted under the skin that sends signals to the cranial vagus nerve that controls messages from the brain to the heart, lungs, and digestive track as well as areas that control mood and sleep. The implantation of the device is completed through surgery and connects through wires to under the skin up to the vagus nerve, located on the left side of the neck. Just approved in 2005, research is ongoing into the effectiveness of VNS with severe, treatment resistant depression and other serious illness.

Finally, deep brain stimulation (DBS) requires brain surgery and is the most invasive treatment. DBS involves the implantation of electrodes on both sides of the brain with each electrode then being connected to its own battery generator implanted in the chest. The FDA approved one type of DBS device in 2008 for the treatment of OCD but under the terms of a humanitarian device exemption to be used only in clinical trial settings (FDA, 2013). Approval was granted to another type of DBS device in 2015 to be used in the treatment of Parkinson's disease (FDA, 2015). Small, early trials have suggested that DBS may be effective with treatment-resistant depression (Mayberg et al., 2005), but a great deal of research needs to be done before usage of this invasive technique, with all of the risks of brain surgery, becomes common.

Reflection Questions

1. Would the possible outcome be worth the physical and emotional costs of the procedure and side effects? This is the type of question many people who are desperate for treatment for various mental and physical illnesses ask themselves. How would you answer? It may be hard to know if you haven't experienced the severity of symptoms that some people face.

2. How much research would you expect before a device requiring brain surgery be used to treat mental illness?

Psychotropic Medications

The path of psychotropic medications, however, has been more successful. Much like the advent of psychoanalysis with the eventual evolution of talk therapy, the ability to utilize medications designed to deliver relief of physical, and eventually mental, symptoms began in Europe at about the turn of the 20th century (Whitaker, 2010) with the discovery of a mechanism of delivery for chemicals to interact and alter specific aspects of cells. Initial success discovered medications to treat syphilis by 1926 and penicillin by 1944—discoveries that remarkably prolonged life and were considered magic bullets that revolutionized medicine.

The actual discovery of psychotropic medications was somewhat less direct, with the first discoveries of antipsychotic medications resulting from observations of the calming effects of medications designed for other purposes (Whitaker, 2010). In the late 1940s in France, anesthetic drugs were being developed to assist in surgeries. In early forms, the relaxing and calming properties of the chemicals led to extraction of a milder form of the drug, chlorpromazine. Marketed in the United States as Thorazine, chlorpromazine became the first antipsychotic medication to be widely used to alleviate symptoms of severe mental illness. Thorazine was followed quickly by medications for the treatment of anxiety and depression. In 1963, the NIMH conducted a 6-week trial of Thorazine and other psychotropic drugs and concluded they were more effective than placebos in treating symptoms of mental illness.

Today, there are five major classes of medications used to treat mental disorders: *antidepressant medications* used in the treatment of depression and anxiety, *antipsychotic medications* used to control psychotic symptoms and disorganized thinking, *mood stabilizers* and anticonvulsant medications used in the treatment of bipolar disorder, *antianxiety medications* used to treat severe anxiety, and stimulant medications to treat ADD/ADHD (National Alliance on Mental Illness, n.d.; Preston, O'Neal, & Talaga, 2013). Within each classification, multiple different medications have been developed, with varying side effects and different mechanisms of action in the brain. Medications are designed to treat symptoms and do not cure the disorder. Psychotropic drugs work very differently for different individuals—even those with the same diagnosis (NIMH, 2016c). For some individuals struggling with mental illness, symptoms are resolved over time and medication and therapy discontinued. For others, especially those with chronic, severe mental illness, taking medication may be a lifelong process.

For the major mental illnesses explored in this chapter, most effective is a combination of both psychotropic medications and efficacious psychotherapy (Nathan & Gorman, 2015). The classes of medications may sound as if they track onto the major mental illnesses—antipsychotics to treat psychosis, for example. However, there are overlaps, and some antidepressants are used to treat anxiety or antipsychotics to treat bipolar depression without psychosis. Similarly, these overlaps can be seen with the types of psychotherapies. Evidence-based psychotherapies such as interpersonal therapy and cognitive behavioral therapy have been shown to effectively treat major mental illness such as depression and anxiety, as well as eating disorders and substance abuse disorders. Many of these therapies have different modalities, such as individual versus group therapy, but share underlying theories. Overall, medications combined with therapy change people's lives for the better and contribute to more effective functioning and quality of life (see Adjustment in Practice: Making a Choice to Try Medication).

ADJUSTMENT IN PRACTICE
Making a Choice to Try Medication

The decision to try a psychotropic medication is very individual (see Table 13.3). Some people worry about long-term effects of medications directed at the brain, and others are in search of a magic pill that will make their troubles go away. Unfortunately, magic pills don't exist, but many psychotropic medications have solid research and offer the possibility of relieving symptoms and increasing coping. All prescription drugs go through processes of clinical trials and are approved by the FDA. Information continues to be gathered about drugs after approval, and visiting the FDA website (www.fda.gov) can provide some of the latest information about medications.

Before you begin taking medications, you should be sure you understand the way the drug will work in your body, including the benefits, the side effects, and the time it will take to experience these. In many cases, side effects occur before the benefits of the medication have a chance to begin working, so patience may be helpful. Here are a few questions you may want to ask your psychiatrist:

1. Why is this medication likely to work for me?

2. When will I experience a benefit from the medication?

3. What are the side effects? Will I experience the side effects or the benefits first? How long do the side effects last?

4. What should I do if I experience unpleasant side effects?

5. How often will we meet to review or change the medication?

6. If I stop the medication, what is likely to happen?

7. Can you provide me with any written information about the medication?

One of the important questions is about stopping the medication. For many of the psychotropic medications, there are very negative side effects for simply discontinuing your medication. Medications should always be discontinued under a physician's care. Similarly, psychotropic medications are prescribed specifically for an individual for their unique set of symptoms and presentation. Taking other people's medications can be dangerous and should be avoided.

Reflection Questions

1. As when discussing brain stimulation therapies, the question of a cost–benefit analysis—are the benefits worth the side effects?—applies equally to medications. Are side effects worth the benefit or elevating mood or quelling anxiety?

2. Does the level of disorder matter to this question? Most clinicians believe that the benefit of antipsychotic medications, which have some of the most serious side effects and primarily impact the symptoms of delusions and hallucinations, are definitely worth the side effects. What do you think? If someone is delusional or hallucinating and out of touch with reality, does it change the cost–benefit analysis?

Table 13.3	Common Psychotropic Medications	
Category	**For Treatment Of**	**Medications**
Antidepressants	Depression and Anxiety	Prozac, Wellbutrin, Zoloft, Paxil, Effexor, Lexapro, Cymbalta
Stimulants	ADD/ADHD	Ritalin, Concerta, Focal, Vyvanse, Adderall, Provigil
Mood Stabilizers	Bipolar Disorder	Lithium, Fluoxetine, Depakote, Lamictal
Anti-Anxiety	Anxiety	Valium, Klonopin, Ativan, Xanax
Anti-Psychotics	Psychosis	Thorazine, Haldol, Seroquel, Cloraril, Risperdal, Zyprexa, Geodon, Abilify

The Future of Mental Health

The impact of mental illness on those suffering and those who love them can be devastating. The NIMH estimates the total costs associated including direct costs of medical and psychiatric services and interventions and the indirect costs in disability support and lost earnings to be in excess of $467 billion annually (Insel, 2015). More than just numbers, the impact of mental illness on individuals and their families cannot be calculated. The stigma associated with mental illness interferes with seeking treatment for many people. While public stigma associated with mental illness dropped through the end of the 20th century, personal stigma remains a major factor for many individuals (Pescosolido, 2013). Internalized stigma, or self-stigma, the fear of being rejected or alienated by others based on our perceptions of other's opinions of us, results in reduced self-esteem and loss of a sense of empowerment and hope as well as has been shown to exacerbate, or worsen, many symptoms and reduce engagement in treatment (Livingston & Boyd, 2010; Lucksted & Drapalski, 2015).

Both public and self-stigma have been recognized as global and national health concerns (WHO, 2015). The most effective interventions to combat stigma have been identified as including education to combat myths around mental health, cognitive techniques to correct negative self-stigmatizing thoughts, and increasing individuals' sense of agency around their own lives and increase empowerment and hope (Yanos, Lucksted, Drapalski, Roe, & Lysaker, 2015).

Further exploration of public conversations and scientific research offer insights into what other possibilities the future of mental health may bring. One of the major trends at this time has to do with increased knowledge and understanding of the human brain. In April 2013, President Barack Obama announced the BRAIN (Brain Research Through Advancing Innovative Neurotechnologies) Initiative, designed to advance our understanding of the human brain (The White House, n.d.). This initiative has created funding for research that has a direct impact on our understanding of how the brain functions and—just as importantly to the topic of mental illness—how it fails to function.

As this chapter has shown, mental disorders are diagnosed on the basis of symptoms and classified in groups based on these symptoms and considered behavioral (Insel, 2012). However, we now understand connections between disorders as never before.

Genetic research has uncovered linkage among autism, ADHD, bipolar disorder, major depression, and schizophrenia (Cross-Disorder Group of the Psychiatric Genomics Consortium, 2013). These findings are contributing to a new manner of thinking about mental disorders and, ultimately, treatment.

Treatment is driven, as we have discussed in this chapter by the prevailing conceptualizations in society of mental illness. At this point in time, mental illness is still defined by some people as a weakness of character, but more and more frequently, mental illness is seen through a scientific lens. This scientific lens calls for exploration from a scientific perspective, and one of the leaders in scientific direction is the NIMH. By defining how we research and study mental disorders, the NIMH will be heavily influencing societal conceptualization of mental illness.

NIMH research is currently exploring an experimental approach to the study of disorders, the *Research Domain Criteria* (RDoC) project (NIMH, n.d.). The RDoC project is truly biopsychosocial in nature and is striving to understand mental illness through multiple dimensions of thought patterns, behavior, genetics, and neurobiological markers and measures (Insel, 2012). Currently, there are five domains exploring negative and positive emotions, cognitive processes, social processes, and arousal/regulatory systems through analysis of genes, molecules, cells, brain circuits, physiology, behaviors, self-reports, and experimental conditions referred to as paradigms (Sanislow, Quinn, & Sypher, 2015). The goal of the project seeks to integrate neuroscience into the array of knowledge concerning mental illness, allowing more effective research to alleviate the suffering of hundreds of thousands of individuals.

Increasing knowledge of the workings of the brain, combined with heightened understanding of the lived experience of mental illness, has the potential to lead us to less suffering and greater knowledge. Our hope is that in a few decades, we will broaden our knowledge base and have effective treatments to improve lives. In the meanwhile, therapeutic outcome-based research is striving to determine the most effective means of treating mental illness with existing tools (Nathan & Gorman, 2015).

Conclusion

Adjustment to the challenges of everyday living can be tough, but for those struggling with mental illness, simple coping and getting by become impossible. Symptoms of mental illness can be overwhelming and interfere with work, school, or social life to the point of dysfunction. Mental illness has been documented for centuries, and various explanations for the causes of mental illness have guided treatment over the ages. Ranging from supernatural to somatogenic to psychogenic, most contemporary psychologists view mental illness from a biopsychosocial perspective, attempting to understand the full array of influences over a person's life and adjustment.

Major mental illnesses strike one in five people in the United States in their lifetimes and include anxiety disorders, mood disorders, thought or psychotic disorders, as well as eating, substance abuse, and neurodevelopmental disorders. All together there are nearly 300 different mental illnesses, but discussing all of these is beyond the scope of this book. All mental disorders are marked by a major impact in one or more areas of everyday life and contain physical, emotional, psychological, and/or behavioral symptoms. Etiologies for the major mental illnesses range from biological reasons such as neurotransmitter imbalances, prenatal environmental factors to genetic and psychological reasons like environmental impact, cultural expectations, trauma, and abuse. There is no single explanation for any mental illness just as there is no simple cure. And the cost to our society and to many individuals is very high. The person struggling with mental illness has to combat stigma as well as the symptoms of the illness, and this internalized stigma impacts the ability to seek and comply with treatment. In more concrete terms, the cost to the workforce and economy for the loss of contributions to our society is in the billions of dollars annually.

Clinicians diagnose and treat individuals struggling with the disorders discussed in this chapter. The history of treatment reflects the changing understanding of our society regarding mental illness from asylums to medications and psychotherapies. Psychotropic medications, discovered accidentally in many cases, target neurotransmitters in the brain and seek to alleviate symptoms, but they cannot cure the disorders. Psychotherapies, especially when used in conjunction with medications, have been shown to significantly improve the lives of those suffering from mental disorders. Today, many psychotherapists use empirically validated therapies, scientifically shown to impact functioning and coping with mental illness.

The future of the treatment and fate of those suffering is impacting by our growing understanding of the brain, its structures and functions. A new system of classifying and studying mental illness is being explored, and our neurological knowledge is expanding by leaps and bounds. Our hope is that the future holds greater knowledge, leading to more effective and helpful treatment.

Review Questions (Section One: Mental Illness)

1. When does everyday sadness or worry become a disorder? What is the criterion?

2. What are supernatural explanations for mental illness? How do these explanations differ from somatogenic and psychogenic explanations? Be able to compare and contrast these explanations.

3. What are the components of a biopsychosocial approach to mental illness? How do previous explanations fit into this model?

4. Complete the grid below for the major mental illnesses discussed in this chapter (anxiety disorders, mood disorders, psychosis/schizophrenia, eating disorders, substance abuse disorders, ADD/ADHD, and autism).

5. What is the cost of mental illness to our society? Discuss financial and intangible costs.

6. What was life like inside hospitals and asylums during the 19th and early 20th centuries? How were those struggling with mental illness treated?

7. Why and when should a person seek professional help for mental illness? Who should they turn to if they need help?

Disorder	Cognitive Symptoms	Emotional or Psychological Symptoms	Physical Symptoms	Behavioral Symptoms	Possible Etiology

Review Questions (Section Two: Treatment of Mental Illness)

1. What are the basic ideas behind psychoanalysis, cognitive behavioral therapy, client-centered therapy, and empirically supported therapy? How do they differ, and what do they share?

2. Describe a lobotomy. Why were these discontinued?

3. How were psychotropic medications discovered? What are the basic classes of these medications?

4. What is the cost of mental illness to the individual and his or her family? Discuss public and internalized stigma.

5. How would the RDoC project explain a person's depression? Or someone's anxiety? What makes this approach unique from other classification systems?

Key Terms

anxiety 271

biopsychosocial model 272

eating disorders 278

empirically validated therapy 291

mental disorder 270

mood disorders 274

neurodevelopmental disorders 274

psychoanalysis 289

psychogenic 271

psychosis 271

schizophrenia 278

somatogenic 271

substance use disorders 274

supernatural 271

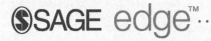

Sharpen your skills with SAGE edge at **edge.sagepub.com/moritsugu**

SAGE edge for students provides a personalized approach to help you accomplish your coursework goals in an easy-to-use learning environment.

Go to **edge.sagepub.com/moritsugu** for additional exercises and web resources. Select Chapter 13, Dysfunction and Maladjustment for chapter-specific resources.

Chapter

14

The Search for Balance and the Future

As a little girl, she would dream of having a house with running water. It seemed such a luxury to have water in the house and available almost as soon as she wanted it. And yet, walking to school through the woods, she did not know when, where, or how this would occur. Her father farmed on land he did not own. He cleared the parcel and grew vegetables on what some later would call a truck farm. The name came from the fact that the produce was taken to the market regularly, on a truck. At this time, the truck was a horse-drawn wagon. Over the roads she would go with her father to deliver the goods. She knew that sometimes the produce was plentiful and the money sufficient. But she also knew that at times there was not enough. And so she lived with her brothers and sisters in the simple house on land not their own, farming and dreaming of times to come.

She did not know that in the span of her life, she would go to high school, learn a trade, and come to know many people who owned their own homes, had running water, and did not worry about what their next meal would be. She would live among those people and be one of them. It might seem magical that the dirt roads she now traveled would become concrete highways or that she would know people who owned cars, lived on roads with sidewalks, and expected their children to go to college. In the space of her generation, she saw her own children go to college, have running water, own homes, drive cars, and make their own comfortable lives. Little did she know as a young girl that her dreams of running water would be realized and that her life would be beyond what she could ever have imagined. It would have amazed her.

. . . .

When we consider all the changes that occurred in the 20th century, it is amazing in so many ways. At the beginning of that century, not everyone had automobiles—in fact, horses were the typical mode of transportation. There were no airplanes, much less ones that flew more than 200 people at near-supersonic speeds to destinations thousands of miles away. We did not have antibiotics. The Chinese abacus and slide rule were the calculators and computers of the time.

The point of the opening story is that there have been dramatic changes over the last century. We are in the beginning years of a new century and can anticipate even greater changes to come. Looking back at the 20th century, it is hard to imagine the magnitude and the swiftness of the alterations in our lives. We are left to wonder what could happen to us in the space of the next 10, 20, 30, or 40 years. And yet, like the young girl in our story, things to come are beyond our imagination. She had an active hand in creating opportunities for herself. She was not passive or merely pushed about by the forces of life and society. She was the actor and narrator of her story, influencing not just the world around her but its meaning to her life.

What does the future hold for us? As we bring this text to a close, we look forward to the future. We have emphasized the active role we play in living our lives, in seeking balance among its many parts. Toward that end, we present two different kinds of challenges to our readers. The first set deals with personal challenges. The psychology literature offers interesting concepts for us to contend with at a personal level. They suggest shifts in how we think about our selves and our world. These will take time and consideration to integrate into our thinking and actions.

The second section presents challenges from the world around us. We offer areas where our changing environments may place new demands on us. As we have come

©iStockphoto.com/Minerva Studio

There have been dramatic changes since the 19th century, including modes of transportation.

to see in this text, it is not just the person but also the context that evolves and impacts who we are and how we think and behave.

The third section explores the challenges of changing technologies and their impact on us socially and personally. The acceleration of change and the growing dependence on these technologies demand new ways of thinking and interacting.

This chapter presents anticipated challenges to adjustment in the days to come. Given that change is a normal part of life, the following sections discuss areas where the challenges to adjustment are likely to occur. The 21st century brings issues to confront, problems to solve, and skills to acquire. The challenges ahead may be guided by a purposeful orientation toward life and a mindful awareness of self.

Personal Challenges of the Future

At a personal level, some of the following ways of framing the world will help us to better understand and deal with our world and our lives. And yet, they are new ways of thinking about the world. Among them are an understanding of person and place as dynamic determinants to behaviors, the balance of thinking about both ourselves and others, and the advantages of not placing ourselves at the center of our considerations.

The Dynamics of Person and Place

Sameroff (2010) described our lives as dynamic and transactional in nature. We do not stand still as passive recipients of information. Rather, the environment influences us and, in turn, we influence the environment. He proposes that our lives are better understood as the result of choices and reactions to environmental opportunity structures. These structures can either encourage or discourage our development. There are times when the lack of these opportunities brings long-lasting and broadly based negative impacts on our lives. For example, learning to read can have profound positive effects or the lack of literacy can have far-reaching negative effects on our lives. Reading is a skill that requires systematic exposure and feedback. Some people do not have optimal circumstances for acquiring this skill.

An illustration of the power of opportunity structures is found in a longitudinal research of 4-year-olds who were followed through high school (Gutman, Sameroff, & Cole, 2003). The study discovered that individuals with low intelligence who lived in opportunity-rich settings with low-risk factors (lacking in negative experiences) did better than those with high intelligence who lived in environments with high-risk and low positive promoting potentials. The environment was "more powerful" than "native intelligence."

When there was a negative (risky) environment, exposure to a positive environment could prevent problems and promote health. These findings fit with our understanding

The yin-yang symbol demonstrates the mutual influence of one part on the other part.

of resilience (Luthar, Cicchetti, & Becker, 2000; Masten, 2011) as discussed in Chapter 3. When faced with adverse conditions, individuals will not thrive. However, these adverse conditions can be counterbalanced by positive personal and community resources such as social skills, intelligence, and support. In the simplest sense, it is like arithmetic where negatives and positives are combined: If the result is negative, there are problems, and if the result is positive, there is thriving.

Sameroff (2010) also emphasized the individual's development of a meaningful world. The power of personal meaning and a coherent world is illustrated in a report linking cultural alienation to risk for suicide among Canadian First Nations youth (Chandler, Lalonde, Sokol, & Hallett, 2003). In turn, this set of studies also demonstrated the positive effects of "preserving and promoting" culture on reducing this risk. When one's basis for understanding life is undermined or devalued, trouble follows. As presented in Chapter 2, a host of research has found purpose and meaning to be positive influences in our lives. They provide us with ways to understand and organize events, and they serve as a protective shield for us in times of change or stress.

The nature of these two factors brings focus to Sameroff's argument that both the individual and the environment are influences in shaping the person. When trying to understand a person, we need to consider both the individual and the environment and remember that the interaction between the two is dynamic. Sameroff's models are dialectical in nature, recognizing the two forces at work. He describes the Asian yin-yang symbol as an excellent example of this dialectic. Light and dark are interwoven, supporting and influencing the other.

In the same way, the individual and the environment balance and influence each other. Even at the individual's biological level, we now recognize an epigenetic process. In epigenetics, the environment influences the expression of the genes. Environmentally, there is the transactional model, where the individual takes an active role in structuring the situation or its meaning. We can stand in the rain, or we can come out of the rain. Most often, it is our choice.

In one manner, our search for balance can be framed in terms of the environment and the individual. We have read chapters dealing specifically with issues of purpose and meaning (Chapter 2) and of context (Chapter 3). In the applied section (Chapters 7 to 13), we have seen the psychological research addressing specific significant situations in our lives and how our reactions may lead to positive or negative outcomes.

For Sameroff (2010), present and future considerations of our lives and the lives of others can best be informed by this complex, interactive perspective. Contrary to our more traditional search for the simplest answers, it is proposed that many factors influence our behaviors, thoughts, and emotions. (The emphasis on simplicity is based on a philosophical stance called Occam's razor, stating that the simplest answer is usually the correct answer.) If we are to understand and apply the science of psychology to our lives and to society, the best existing models employ multiple determinants from both the person *and* the environment, mutually influencing each other. The outcomes of these interactions are both short and long term. They influence the individual and his or her social structures and lead to positive or negative opportunities (Masten & Cicchetti, 2010).

The next time someone raises an issue regarding human behaviors, the challenge is not to think of the person in question or to consider the environmental circumstances but to understand both the person and the environment in transaction with each other.

Agency and Communion

Agency and **communion** provide the second area of personal challenge (Frimer, Walker, Dunlop, Lee, & Riches, 2011). *Agency* is defined as "advancement of the self" (p. 150). *Communion* is defined as "concern for the well-being of others" (p. 150). Others have defined this distinction as the difference between "getting ahead" versus "getting along" (Hogan, 1982) or "self-enhancement" versus "self-transcendence" (Schwartz, 1992). The two approaches appear to be in opposition to each other. At best, there is a tension between the self–other foci.

In studying this seeming contradiction of positions, Frimer and colleagues (2011) compared interviews with award-winning caregivers to interviews with normal people. Matched for demographics (age, social class), the two groups showed differences in their interviews. Award winners were higher in both agency (self and achievement focus) and communion (group and caring focus). The award winners also combined self and community more often. For them, the two were mutually supportive and not contradictory.

In a second study of agency and communion, analyzing the speeches of exemplars of caring, agency was used as a means to achieving community goals (Frimer, Walker, Lee, Riches, & Dunlop, 2012). Self and community were not in conflict but were complementary to each other. One's accomplishments are used to further one's efforts in caring for the community.

From these studies, we see support for a synergistic, reconciliation model for what appear to be opposing motivations—for self and for one's community (Frimer & Walker, 2009). The researchers believe understanding the interdependence of the person and their environment is a sign of personal maturity. "Reconciling" the two is a move to a more complex and a balanced approach. "When this happens, agency breathes life into communion, and communion gives agency a greater purpose" (Frimer & Walker, 2009, p. 1677).

Lack of reconciliation leads to an unbalanced, singular focus on either one's self or one's community responsibilities. This leads to immature values that are not well suited to life. This reconciliation is part of a normal developmental process. Successfully resolving the tension between the self and other focus leads to a more integrated and complex view of the world. This view is adaptive to our adult world tasks. However, such a successful resolution of the conflict is not always found. This may be especially so, given cultural and social pressures to move one way or another and avoid that tension. We might consider what these pressures are and what the goals of such foci are. Just recognizing the two is a first step to resolution of the conflict. Some have termed this resolution in service of the greater good "enlightened self-interest" (Frimer et al., 2011).

These types of considerations might be especially vexing in social or cultural communities that do not have an interdependent orientation. Research has found culture (self-oriented/individualistic versus group-oriented/collectivistic) to mediate the presence of agent motives (Frimer, Schaefer, & Oakes, 2014). At the same time, the self-agentic motive is present in all cultures.

While the research on this topic is contemporary, we are reminded of Adler's theory from the early 20th century. Adler

Mahatma Gandhi is a famous exemplar of caring.

theorized that the primary human motivational system was the individual's striving for superiority or perfection (Adler, 1938/1998). He also theorized that this striving needed to be counterbalanced by concern for one's social group. In similar ways, we can see the interplay of self and community.

This issue of our self and our communities may arise in a variety of ways. Perhaps the lack of integration of agency with community results in what we call "blind ambition." In turn, consideration of such a balance may be what we ultimately look for in our selves, our colleagues, and our leaders.

Personal Perspectives

The third area of personal challenge is maintaining realistic personal perspectives. This area spans all aspects of our lives—from work to relationships to our opinions of others.

For example, people typically underestimate the amount of time it takes them to complete a task. Research has found that individuals who are bad at estimating time to completion have a tendency to focus on the required tasks and to ignore their past task performance (Buehler, Griffin, & Ross, 1994). This leads to optimistic estimates based on the task itself. When asked about past failures to turn in work on time, externally based reasons are given, such as, "If it were not for my car, or my boyfriend, or my dog, I would have gotten it done."

In contrast to this tendency for optimistic self-estimates, we are more likely to believe others will take much longer. We see the problems others can have but ignore the problems we could have. This bias, in favor of our "best" self-potential, disappears if we are reminded to recall our past performances. We typically choose to forget past experiences and do not use them as an estimate of how we will do in the future. However, this process is usually informative.

This problem seems to stem from our difficulty in having a realistic perspective of our own work (Grossmann & Kross, 2014). It is hard to see issues with our own work; we are wiser when dealing with other people's business. We are more willing to acknowledge not knowing something, we ask questions and listen to the answers, and we are willing to compromise or to change what has to be done. On the other hand, when considering something like our own relationship problems, we are less likely to think "wisely" than if dealing with a friend's relationship problem (see Figure 14.1).

Kross and Grossmann (2012) found that stepping back and taking a more distant perspective on issues led to more openness to "diverse viewpoints." Such findings are congruent with earlier studies where a more context–situation focus led to less personal entanglement in solution seeking (Grossmann & Kross, 2010). We have a better perspective on the world when we can transcend our focus on our self (Kross & Grossmann, 2012).

When immersed in a situation so that they saw themselves as personally involved, students were less likely to provide complex thinking (dialectical thinking) and less likely to be intellectually open to more information ("I don't know everything that needs to be known"). When taking a personally detached perspective on the situation, complex thinking and openness to more information increased. In a study of how we talk to ourselves about our problems, simply not using the first person pronoun was sufficient to bring about better distancing from the problem and therefore better performance (Kross et al., 2014).

Our best thinking occurs when we disentangle our "self" from the situation and we view all the facts in a detached manner. The research supports this distancing of self from the problem at hand. We can then open ourselves to the possible solutions and feel less intimidated by the situation.

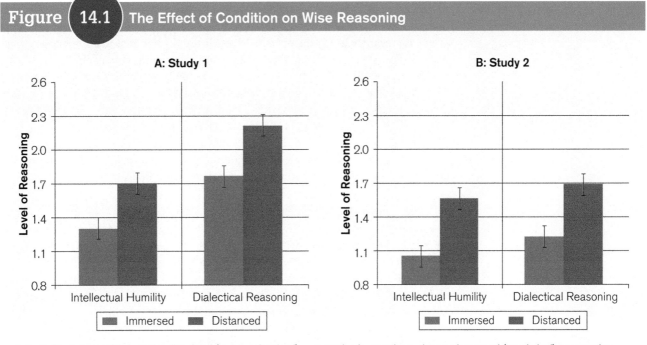

Figure 14.1 The Effect of Condition on Wise Reasoning

In both Study 1 and Study 2, the distanced (non-ego involved) perspective is superior to the ego-immersed (egotistical) perspective. This superiority is in the form of intellectual humility, i.e. openness to other possibilities, and dialectical reasoning, i.e. sophisticated and complex thinking.

Source: Igor Grossmann and Ethan Kross. Exploring Solomon's Paradox. *Psychological Science*. First published on June 10, 2014 doi:10.1177/0956797614535400

The personal challenges presented in this section make up dimensions of wisdom discovered by researchers who have been involved in deriving and studying the elements of wisdom:

> An emerging consensus suggests that three important dimensions of wisdom involve recognizing that the world is in flux and the future is likely to change, recognizing that there are limits associated with one's own knowledge, and possessing a prosocial orientation that promotes the "common good." (Kross & Grossmann, 2012, p. 43)

Rising up to the challenges of these dimensions can benefit us personally by making us wiser and by helping us to contribute to and improve our society.

Societal Challenges of the Future

There will be many challenges to our future. Going forward into the 21st century, these challenges from the changing context in which we live will demand new ways to think about our world and adjust to its demands. The first challenge is the diversity we face as the result of demographic changes and redefinitions of **gender** and sexuality. The second challenge is the accelerating changes occurring in our technological-wired world.

Diversity

There are many ways to think of diversity. By definition, diversity includes any of the dimensions by which an individual may be recognized as different from others. Our considerations of diversity are narrowed to three areas. The first two come from an awareness of shifts in the demographics within the United States. These changes will mean that we need to interact and work with a variety of individuals with whom we may not previously have had contact. This leads to issues in group definitions and assumptions with regard to group membership. Specifically, the numbers in different age groups (called cohorts) are shifting, as are cultural–ethnic grouping proportions.

The second diversity dimension we will examine is gender and **sexual orientation**. These considerations have brought us a better understanding of individual differences in these areas. These are not demographic changes so much as a growing recognition of the many ways in which we define and express ourselves in these areas.

In response to an increasingly diverse culture, we are challenged to appraise the processes that govern our definitions of community and the principles of inclusivity and fairness. Let us begin with the shifts in age and ethnicity.

Demographics of Age and Ethnicity

The population of the United States is shifting. U.S. Census Bureau data show that the country is like no other time in its history. In 1990, the Census estimate of the population was approximately 248 million (http://www.census.gov/popest/data/national/totals/1990s/tables/nat-total.txt). In 2010, the population was estimated to be almost 309 million, and by 2014, the number had risen to almost 319 million. In 2014, the two largest state populations were California with about 38.8 million and Texas with over 26.9 million. In comparison, Canada has a population of approximately 35 million and Australia has 22 million (http://www.geoba.se/population.php?pc=world).

In the United States, millennials (born 1980 to 2004) comprise more than 25% of the population (83 million) and are culturally diverse (44% racial or ethnic minority group membership; U.S. Census Bureau, 2015). The youngest age grouping, those 5 years old and below, are even more diverse, with 50.2% in the ethnic minority designation. For comparison's sake, those over 65 years old number 46.2 million in 2014 with 22% of them racial or ethnic minorities. One can anticipate the shift in population; soon the minorities will be a majority. See Figure 14.2.

The 2015 Census identified five states that held the majority of minorities: Hawaii (77%), Texas (56.5%), the District of Columbia (64%), California (61.5%), and New Mexico (61%; U.S. Census Bureau, 2015). Nevada has not quite reached majority–minority proportions, but it is close (48.5%).

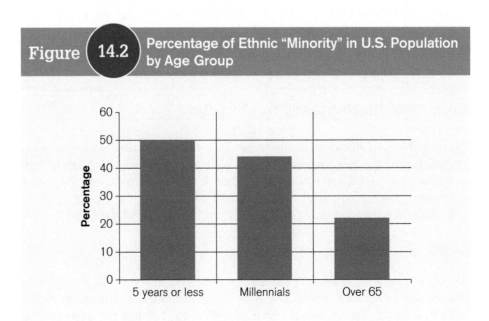

Figure 14.2 Percentage of Ethnic "Minority" in U.S. Population by Age Group

Source: Data from U.S. Census Bureau.

Baby boomers (those born between 1945 and 1964) number 75 million and are out-numbered by the millennials (those born between 1980 and 2004). Yet the United States is on average older than it ever has been and will continue to grow older, given the increased longevity of the baby boomers. By 2029, about 20% of the U.S. population will be over 65 years of age (Colby & Ortman, 2014). The oldest populations reside in Florida (19%) and Maine (18%). Utah (10%) and Alaska (9%) have the smallest proportion of individuals over 65 (U.S. Census Bureau, 2015).

These shifts in demographics are indicative of the ways in which our minority and age grouping contexts will change. We will be living with more diverse cultural and ethnic populations. And we will be living with a higher percentage of older adults.

Historically, both of these groups have been considered oppressed. As their numbers grow larger and their social and political significance increases, we will be called on to adjust to these changing demographics. This will mean challenging the old ways of looking at who has power and influence. Let us now look at another set of social context shifts that require recognition.

Gender and Sexual Orientation

Awareness of gender diversity has grown since the mid-1990s. While this diversification was discussed in Chapter 8, we note that this area of identities has come to be better understood and more openly discussed. Consideration of gender identity raises important questions as to who we are and how we need to be appreciative and respectful of the variations in humanity.

Gender is defined as "the attitudes, feelings, and behaviors that a given culture associates with a person's biological sex" (American Psychological Association, 2011). It is notable that diversity in the area of gender has been documented in many indigenous, Western, and non-Western cultures. In American culture, the general public has come to an increasing awareness and acceptance of these distinctions. However, these designations remain a source of much discussion. We previously dichotomized the gender categories into male or female and based such distinctions on the external physical characteristics of the individual—that is, their physical sex traits. However, these two categories have been expanded to include new gender identity designations. Among these gender categories are the following:

- Transgender—Gender identity is different from assigned sex.
- Genderqueer—Gender identity is not either male or female, possibly a unique category in itself or something that is not an absolute and exclusionary categorical identification like male or female (they see themselves having both qualities).

People often confuse gender and sexual orientation. *Sexual orientation* is defined by "an enduring pattern of emotional, romantic and/or sexual attractions to men, women or both sexes . . . a person's sense of identity (is) based on those attractions, related behaviors and membership in a community of others who share those attractions" (American Psychological Association, 2008). Sexual orientation deals with who arouses us sexually. These preferences appear fairly stable for heterosexuals and male homosexuals, with more variability found for bisexuals and lesbians (Baumeister, 2000; Diamond, 2008; Mock & Eibach, 2011).

The body of research supports female erotic plasticity, which "refers to the extent to which the sex drive can be shaped by social, cultural, and situational factors" (Baumeister, 2004, p. 133). Female sexuality is influenced by environmental and specific relational factors. In a 10-year study of young adults living in a supportive cultural environment (New Zealand), there was variation in sexual attractions over time, with fluidity in attractions, especially among women (Dickson, Paul, & Herbison, 2003). This fluidity among women was found again in a later U.S.-based longitudinal study (Diamond, 2008).

We see a broader array of alternatives for sexual attraction and lifestyles as the result of the sexual revolution of the 1960s and 1970s (Baumeister, 2004). Same-sex couples can and do live in committed relationships and raise children who are adjusted and get along with others (American Psychological Association, 2008). The acceptance of same-sex pairings has reached the point of legal status for same-sex marriages in the United States as ruled by the Supreme Court on *Obergefell v. Hodges* (Liptak, 2015).

Effects of Diversity

One particular concern about diversity is that it can erode our sense of belonging, trust, and concern for each other. Putnam (2007) has argued that a fracturing of the language or demographics within a community may damage its cohesiveness. Cohesiveness can be defined as the ties that bind individuals together and enable community members to feel both connection with and responsibility for others. While this argument has numerous supporters, the data on this idea is mixed (Sturgis, Brunton-Smith, Read, & Allum, 2011; Uslaner, 2012; Wu, Hou, & Schimmele, 2011). One study reports that it depends on how the cohesion question is worded (Ariely, 2014). Another finds that it depends on the geographic unit under study and the opportunities for positive interaction. For example, in small community units where there is support for interactions, there is no lack of cohesion (Kokkonen, Esaiasson, & Gilljam, 2014). Uslaner (2012) believed that it is segregation and not diversification that leads to the lack of trust and social bonding.

Both the Kokkonen et al. (2014) and the Uslaner (2012) findings align with the psychological literature on group contact and the reduction of prejudice and stereotypes (Allport, 1949/1979; Jones, Dovidio, & Vietze, 2013; Katz & Taylor, 1988). In general, we organize our perceptions of people into categories. The categorization can be based on what we see or hear (Rakić, Steffens, & Mummendey, 2011). In turn, this categorization sets up expectations as to the person we have categorized. In broad terms, this can be people we perceive as our group, called the **in-group**, or as "others," those called the **out-group**. This placement as an in-group or out-group member brings with it several outcomes (Dovidio & Gaertner, 2010). Among these are the following:

- The perception of the in-group members as similar in many ways to the perceiver
- The perception of the out-group members as very much alike; they are "all the same"
- The perception of the out-group members as "less human"
- A tendency to approach in-group members and avoid out-group members
- An increased willingness to help other in-group members

These outcomes have important implications for inter-group relationships. In-group membership has clear advantages. The social psychology literature has clearly established the existence of these tendencies over several decades of research.

The general tendency to favor the in-group category and not favor the out-group category is one of the ways that we can react to diversity. Beyond discrimination (treating people differently based on their group membership), some individuals act aggressively toward those they feel to be different (Allport, 1949/1979). While overt acts of discrimination are not publicly condoned in our present-day settings of higher education, they still occur. More common are the subtle and nuanced manifestations of prejudice, described as symbolic, aversive, or implicit.

In **symbolic prejudice** (racism), there is no negativity expressed to individuals. Here, the complaint is to policies (symbols) that try to address contextual advantages that have historically been given to the in-group (Kinder & Sears, 1981; Sears & Henry, 2003). Rather, in symbolic racism, the belief is that all things are now correct and fair and that any discrepancies in outcome are the fault of the individual for not working hard enough or being good enough.

Aversive prejudice is based on an individual's desire not to be prejudiced. He or she is conflicted by his or her desire to be good and yet he or she hold prejudiced beliefs (Gaertner & Dovidio, 1986). An example of this was found in a study by Son Hing, Chung-Yan, Hamilton, and Zanna (2008). In this study, the aversive prejudiced individual did not express prejudiced beliefs but unconsciously had them, which led to nonprejudicial decisions when there were clear environmental signals for a favorable decision. However, when the situation was ambiguous, and a favorable decision was not clearly indicated, the prejudice appeared and a negative decision was given. Therefore, if there is a reason to react negatively to a nonfavored group member, the individual reacted negatively. In contrast, if there was a reason to react negatively to a favored group member, the favored member was given the benefit of the doubt, giving an advantage to the favored group member.

Implicit prejudice is based on learning about the biases from our culture or society. Given these experiences, we tend to associate categories of people in particular ways. Think of "soft men" and "hard women"; they are uncommon pairings. There is an advantage to other types of pairings. At one time, "leaders" and "men" were seen as related and "leaders" and "women" less so. Now we do not overtly notice such discrepancies, but we note such discrepancies can still remain. The prejudgments are often nearly instantaneous and not conscious but exist (Greenwald & Benaji, 1995).

These various types of reactions to groups can be detrimental to the focus of such prejudicial thinking or discrimination. The challenge for the nontargeted groups is to respond in nonprejudicial ways. The values of equality and respect for individual differences call for addressing such challenges.

What are the benefits of diversity? In a study of diverse groups versus high-ability groups trying to solve computational problems, the diverse groups proved superior (Hong & Page, 2004). In a study of publicly traded businesses in France, Germany, Great Britain, and the United States, those with a more diverse board of directors produced over 50% better returns on equity than those without such diversity (Barta, Kleiner, & Neumann, 2012). These outcomes are supported by research showing exposure to multiple cultures increases creativity and cognitive complexity (Leung, Maddux, Galinsky, & Chiu 2008; Maddux & Galinsky, 2009).

How can we deal with diversity in positive and proactive ways? We can become more open to the advantages it brings. We can understand and become self-aware of the normal tendencies to group people into categories of "us" and "them." We can further understand the advantages for people who we feel resemble ourselves and the disadvantages for those we perceive as different. Psychology provides a number of ways to achieve this.

Reducing Reactivity and Increasing Appreciation

We live in a changing, increasingly diverse world. The shifting demographics of ethnicity, culture, and age group concentration, and the broadening acceptance of variations in gender identity, orientation, and gender roles speak to the diversity for which we need to be better prepared to communicate and interact. These changes require us to be educated and prepared to be successful in our future world. With all of the changes related to diversity, there exists the potential for harm in the human tendency toward categorization and perception of diverse others as members of out-groups. Becoming educated about these tendencies can mitigate the negative potential of out-group categorization.

Travel to visit foreign lands opens us to what diversity brings.

As psychological science has begun to provide evidence of the benefits of interactions with others who are different from ourselves, we have basic knowledge to support our positive engagement in attitudes and behavior toward a more inclusive, open, and accepting society. We are challenged to understand and live with the breadth of human experience. This shift to a more open and accepting society places all of us under the challenge of understanding and living with the breadth of human experiences. The following are several strategies that are based on psychological research related to how prejudice can be lessened.

Travel

Travel to visit foreign lands opens us to what diversity brings (Maddux & Galinsky, 2009). This assumes that we engage in understanding those cultures and their differences in worldview. For example, if we go to Japan and eat only at McDonald's, it is hard to say we have come to better understand Japanese cuisine. See Researching Adjustment: Multicultural Experience.

RESEARCHING ADJUSTMENT
Multicultural Experience

Testing the impact of exposure to multicultural materials, a 20-minute video presentation on both American and Chinese cultures (multicultural condition), including aspects of architecture, apparel, and foods, resulted in less expression of stereotypes and less discrimination in hiring judgments for student subjects (Tadmor, Hong, Chao, Wiruchnipawan, & Wang, 2012). In that same study, students asked to write essays on multicultural experiences were more tolerant of ambiguity and less closed-minded. The research program went on to demonstrate this lack of tolerance and closed-mindedness to be the forces behind the forms of prejudice they studied. Quite notably, being asked to reflect on and write about multicultural experiences were less likely to be prejudicial. The authors noted that the comparisons of culture seemed to "unfreeze" thinking about groups.

Reflection Questions

1. What are some positive ways in which exposure to different cultures have opened you to appreciating differences?

2. How could the positive effects of exposure be reversed with ridicule?

Classes

Taking a class on diversity has been shown to change students' obvious and more unconscious prejudices (Rudman, Ashmore, & Gary, 2001). The study suggests that a smaller class that encourages discussion can be helpful. Such classes can inform the student as to the various types of prejudice that exist and provide ways to combat the prejudice. In a longitudinal study of the impact of an ethnic studies class or a cultural awareness workshop in college, Bowman, Brandenberger, Hill, and Lapsley (2011) found such experiences contributed to senior students' prosocial orientation (i.e., willingness to be helpful). In a second analysis of 13-year postcollege follow-up data, the class or workshop still showed an effect on adult volunteering, recognition of racism, and seeking to better understand their world.

Being Happy

Positive emotions broaden awareness of the world, opening individuals to experiences (Fredrickson, 2013). Positive emotions seem to have the tendency to be more inclusive, bringing both in-group and out-group members into one group (Dovidio, Isen, Guerra, Gaertner, & Rust, 1998).

Johnson and Fredrickson (2005) found racial differences in face recognition disappeared when subjects watched a comedy video prior to looking at the faces of different racial groups. This effect was again found when the comedy video was played prior to testing for facial recognition. The laughing aided in both learning and recalling the faces without regard to race.

Researchers found that smiling alone can break the hold of implicit prejudice. Getting people to smile lowered the implicit prejudice measures relating to Blacks (Ito, Chiao, Devine, Lorig, & Cacioppo, 2006). Ito et al. (2006) believed that the facial muscle feedback to the brain caused subjects to think they had positive feelings toward Black people. This feeling generalized to other Blacks. Those who are associated with positive feelings are seen favorably.

Common Goals

An early study of group formation and reintegration found that common goals helped bring people together (Sherif, Harvey, White, Hood, & Sherif, 1954/1961). When groups have to work together to achieve common goals, they come together around that common purpose. This was especially interesting because the subjects in these studies were boys from intact middle-class families. Similar results were found in a classroom setting in a study by Aronson (Aronson, 2004; Aronson & Bridgeman, 1979). Setting up assignments that required cooperation and interdependence among students led to improved relations among the individual students.

These results have been replicated many times since the 1970s. In particular, the importance of interdependence and cooperation has been emphasized (Walker & Crogan, 1998). In a class that required cooperation for success, students came together and interacted. Social activities, such as classroom assignments or tasks that require participation and cooperation by all members and that encourage and reinforce interaction for achieving the group's goals, have been found successful in getting diverse groups together.

Desire to Change

Awareness of one's own biases and the personal desire to change can positively influence such changes. When we are motivated by explicit social norms to act in nonprejudicial ways, we can do it (Plant & Devine, 1998). However, the internal-implicit-automatic prejudices are much harder to change (Devine, Plant, Amodio, Harmon-Jones, & Vance, 2002; Moskowitz & Stone, 2012).

Liking another person who carries a message of nonprejudice and openness can be a powerful incentive to change (Sinclair, Lowery, Hardin, & Colangelo, 2005). In the Sinclair et al. (2005) study, students demonstrated less prejudicial and more open attitudes when they interacted with experimenters who they liked. Context can be

©iStockphoto.com/PeopleImages

When we like people, we are more likely to listen and be open.

powerful for explicit prejudice when we feel the external social normative pressures, but it can also be powerful for implicit prejudice when we like those in our social group and they convey particular attitudes toward prejudice. It can influence our desire to be nonprejudicial.

Contact

Most of the previous actions set up opportunities for contact among diverse groups. In a review of literature spanning decades and numbering in the hundreds, Pettigrew and Tropp (2006) found that intergroup contact led to declines in prejudice. The reduction in prejudicial attitudes seemed to generalize to other groups beyond the initial contacted group.

Allport (1949/1979) believed that four conditions were needed in the intergroup contact: equal status, common goals, cooperation, and support of authorities. Pettigrew and Tropp's (2006) analyses suggested that the four conditions optimized intergroup contact effects. However, they were not imperative to getting some effects. Of the four, support by the authorities seemed most important. While the four conditions are desirable, they are not essential. Contact is believed to reduce anxiety with the other group (Turner, Hewstone, & Voci, 2007), as familiarity gained from the contact would lessen the anxiety of interacting with different groups.

Loving Kindness Meditation

Learning about and then practicing a loving kindness meditation 5 days a week for 6 weeks resulted in less implicit (nonexplicit) prejudicial reactions (Kang, Grey, & Dovidio, 2014). Note that explicit prejudicial attitudes were not affected. It was in the unconscious area that people changed in their stereotypes. This finding reinforces the nature of the mindful act and the dictum that "we become what we practice." In examining possible mechanisms for this change in prejudice, the indications were that the changes had occurred at the emotional level. People felt less stressed when faced with previously negative viewed groups. One could say they were now seen with loving-kindness. Later research reinforced this practice effect. When comparing loving-kindness meditation practice versus discussion, the meditators alone were changed in their loving-kindness reaction to others (Kang, Gray, & Dovidio, 2015).

Declassification, Reclassification, Individuation

Brewer and Miller (1988) believed that we should individualize the individuals we meet. That is, we want to think, feel, and treat others for who they are and not what we expect them to be as a member of a particular group. The previous activities mentioned help to bring substance to our encounters with others. That is why they advocate that in our contacts with others, we interact with them in meaningful ways that can lead to mutually reinforcing consequences. These kinds of encounters help to break down the prejudgments that we automatically make based on our group memberships (race, ethnicity, gender, age, etc.). This authentic and rewarding encounter will open us to who the individual really is. In this manner, we "individuate" and potentially "declassify" people from their categories and possibly "reclassify" them along realistic lines for who they really are.

In a study of individuation or reclassification, just such a reduction in prejudice was found (Gaertner, Mann, Murrell, & Dovidio, 1989). By emphasizing the uniqueness of the person, the favoritism to the in-group was diminished. By emphasizing inclusiveness, the individuals were reclassified as within the in-group. Both accomplish the same thing—a reduction in prejudice and a negative reaction toward a member of a categorized group. Another example of this comes from an intervention that emphasized commonalities among members in a crisis and resulted in decreases in prejudices (Dovidio et al., 2004).

Note that ethnic or racial differences seem to have stronger effects than gender or age effects (Ito & Urland, 2003; Montepare & Opeyo, 2002). Therefore, while we have covered a variety of ways in which diversity can be manifested, there do seem to be differences in the reactions to these various ways of categorizing. Nonetheless, these methods for opening oneself to diversity can prepare us for the changes to come, whatever they may be.

Changing Technologies

What stands out the most for millennials is that they are the first generation to have access to the Internet during their childhood and/or adolescence (The White House, 2014). Another term for this generation, *digital natives*, captures the world as a place full of connectivity through technology with instantaneous communication around the globe, vastly different from the environment in which most of the world's population grew up (Palfrey & Gasser, 2008). Described as a generation both sophisticated and narrow, digital natives have never known a world without the Internet and mobile devices.

A Brief History of Technology

While the history of technology spans centuries, we'll focus on the technologies that are most relevant to our world today—the history of the technology born with the digital natives after 1980 (see Figure 14.3). The digital settlers created the world of the Internet and mobile technologies that they inhabit today, alongside the digital natives and the digital immigrants, who learned computer and mobile technologies as adults (Palfrey & Gasser, 2008). The earliest digital settlers were the first computer scientists.

The first transmission of information dates back to the 1930s when information (or intelligence) intersected with the need to communicate that intelligence over distances. One of the technologies to come out of Germany in the early 1930s, the telex used phone lines to transmit telegraphy signals (Computer History Museum, 2016). Transmission of data over phone lines continued, and in 1949 the modem was introduced as a method of modulating radar signals, a form of number-based data, into sounds and then demodulating them back into the original digital data. By 1958, the world's largest computer covered a half-acre of land and was North America's air defense system, supported by Massachusetts Institute of Technology (MIT) and International Business Machines (IBM; Gribbin, 2011). At this time, the primary task of computers was to compute: to run calculations, find patterns, and sort data.

In 1963, a computer scientist, J. C. R. Licklider, had an idea to connect computers together to share data, and he wrote a memo to his colleagues at the U.S. Defense Advanced Research Projects Agency (DARPA) proposing the Intergalactic Computer Network. In 1969, MIT and DARPA successfully linked computers between Stanford University and University of California, Los Angeles (UCLA). Donald Davies, a British scientist, invented a packet-switching technology at the National Physical Laboratory, allowing communication that would not overpower the computer systems. By 1970, the Arpanet, as it was initially called, linked 13 computers across the United States. Arpanet continued to connect systems and began shortening the name "internetworking" to "Internet."

Late in the 1970s, the advent of bulletin board systems allowed people with access to large computer systems to communicate and share information (Palfrey & Gasser, 2008). Apple Computer was born during this time, bringing the concept of "personal computing" into homes and

Technology spans generations.

Figure 14.3 A Brief Timeline of Technology

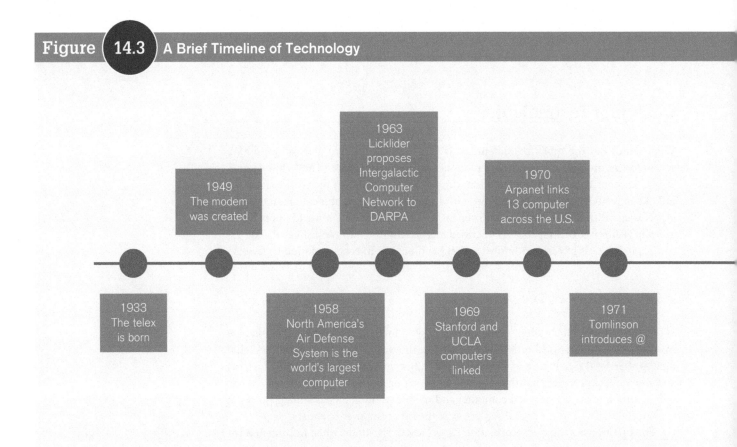

businesses across the country (Rawlinson, 2015). E-mail communications were happening, thanks to the application of the @ symbol to separate user and host names, by a programmer, Ray Tomlinson, in 1971. The Internet refers to the rules and protocols used by computer networks to talk with one another. Tools of the Internet that utilize its architecture include e-mails, some types of messaging, phone and video calling such as Skype, and torrent streaming services.

One of the most significant steps forward was an information management system to allow the transmission of both text and graphics.[1] In 1989, a computer scientist named Tim Berners-Lee, working at the CERN laboratory in Geneva, Switzerland, proposed the World Wide Web as the medium for access to files and pages that are hosted on other computer networks (Pew Research Center, 2014b). On Christmas Day 1990, he released his code for the web free to the world. In less than a decade, the Internet and the World Wide Web transformed communication around the globe, touching lives in countless ways. From education to communication to shopping, the Computer Age was transformed into the Digital Age.

In 1995, Jeff Bezos founded Amazon in Seattle, Washington, transforming the retail industry, starting with books. Originally named BackRub and renamed Google in 1997, Stanford PhD students Larry Page and Sergey Brin revolutionized information searches in the morass of information that had become the web. These two familiar Internet names were joined by Facebook in 2004 and Twitter in 2006.

---

[1]As this brief history demonstrates, there is a difference between the Internet and the web. This distinction can be explained as layers, with the Internet as the foundational layer that the web uses to send files and graphic images from one computer network to another. However, the distinction is not common in everyday conversation, and many individuals taking part in the research we are discussing do not recognize the difference. Therefore, the terms *Internet* and *web* are generally used interchangeably in scholarly research and will be so used in this chapter.

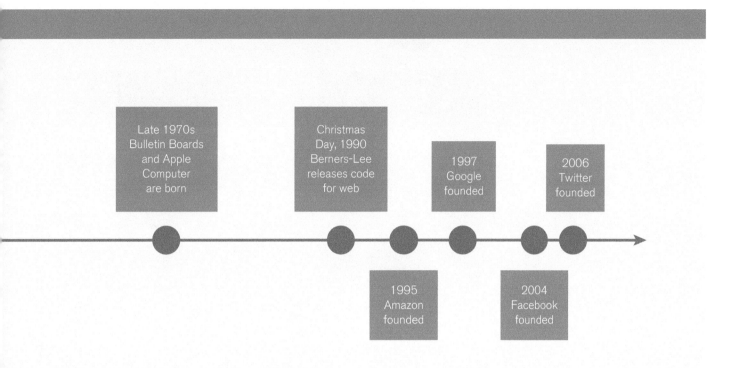

Technology Around the Globe

The International Telecommunication Union (ITU), a specialized agency of the United Nations, tracks global usage of information and communication technologies (ICTs). In 2000, there were 400 million Internet users around the world, with a ratio of 3 to 1 for developed versus developing countries (ITU, 2015). By the end of 2015, 3.2 billion people were using the Internet, with 2 billion from developed countries. A **digital divide** exists globally as well as within the United States between the people who have access to technology and those who do not (see Figure 14.4). In the least developed countries of the world, only 9.5% of the people use the Internet, compared with 82.2% in the developed world. In the United States, 48.5% of the lowest income individuals use the Internet, compared with 94.9% of the wealthiest (ITU, 2015; Pew Research Center, 2015b).

Europe and the Americas have the highest rates of mobile broadband usage, with 78 active subscriptions per 100 people; rates in developing nations are between 41% and 50%, with only the African nations below 20% of the global population with mobile subscriptions (ITU, 2015; Rainie, 2015).

The ability to hold the Internet in the palm of our hand while walking around a college campus is one of the most significant changes to the hardware of the Digital Age. A far cry from the half-acre computer of 1958, the smartphone brings the Internet into the hands of the user. Ninety-two percent of all American adults have mobile subscriptions, with 68% of those using smartphones (Pew Research Center, 2015a). Smartphones, beginning with the iPhone and first sold by Apple in 2007, have altered access to the Internet, providing constant availability of information. As the Pew Research Center (2015a) found, 10% of Americans owning smartphones have no other access to the Internet than their phones, and 15% of U.S. smartphone owners report that they have limited availability to the Internet from other sources.

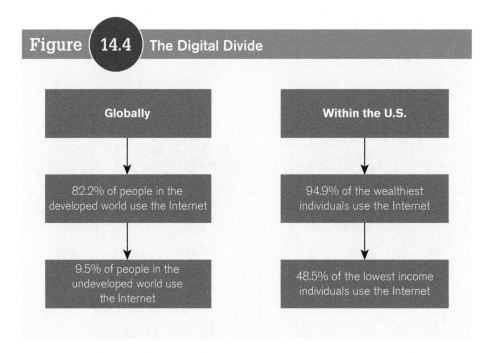

Figure 14.4 The Digital Divide

Globally	Within the U.S.
82.2% of people in the developed world use the Internet	94.9% of the wealthiest individuals use the Internet
9.5% of people in the undeveloped world use the Internet	48.5% of the lowest income individuals use the Internet

What are we doing on our smartphones and high-speed Internet connections? We are texting, using Snapchat, surfing the web, updating our status, sharing ideas, taking and sharing photos, or even occasionally making a phone call. And many of us are dating and entering into both casual and serious romantic relationships. Online dating represents an opportunity to meet others for relationships of various durations, as well as the potential for soul-crushing rejection and carefully crafted deception.

Interpersonal Relationships

Matchmaking, in one form or another, has been part of cultures around the globe for centuries, and the Digital Age brings its unique twist to the process. Differences exist between online dating and off-line conventional dating (Finkel, Eastwick, Karney, Reis, & Sprecher, 2012). Online daters can evaluate many more partners than they may otherwise have a chance to meet in other, more traditional ways. Once they identify a profile that is attractive to them, online daters have the chance to communicate with the other person before actually meeting face to face. Finally, many of the dating websites and apps utilize computer algorithms, promising a good match based on participants' responses to dozens or even hundreds of questions.

These advantages, however, come with detractions as well. The two-dimensionality of the potential partners fails to capture interactive components of attraction and can lead to objectification of others (Finkel et al., 2012). The feeling that someone better is just a click away impedes the willingness to put time into relationships and work through initial awkwardness. While the opportunity to get to know someone through texting and sending e-mails before meeting may foster communication of a certain sort, expectations of a good match may be less realistic than if two people met earlier, as in more traditional connections. Finally, scientifically validated proof of the validity and success of the algorithms used by dating sites does not yet exist. Dating has changed, and as we are seeing in our exploration of technology, there are benefits and drawbacks.

With just 51% of the American public married, a record low, both the goals of dating and the process of meeting potential partners have shifted (Lenhart, 2014). Among individuals responding to a national survey who self-identify as single and seeking a partner, 38% have used online dating. Of these individuals, the reasons for trying online dating are varied, but the majority responded that they believe online dating is a way to meet people who share similar interests and values. Nearly half of those in this study, 46%, report they were seeing someone for a long-term relationship or marriage. One third of online daters stated their schedule made it difficult to meet interesting people through traditional methods. One in four online daters just want to have fun and are not seeking a serious relationship.

Couples of all ages meet online.

The majority of online daters are in their mid-20s to mid-40s, attend or have attended college, and most frequently live in cities or suburbs (Lenhart, 2014). However, older online dating users are increasing (McWilliams & Barrett, 2013). Older users tend to use dating websites (median age of 38), while younger users favor dating apps (median age of 29; Lenhart, 2014). In 2013, about 29% of surveyed Internet users stated they knew at least one couple who was in a long-term relationship or marriage that began through online dating, up from just 15% in 2005. In general, the public supports online dating, with 59% of Internet users endorsing online dating as a good way to meet people, though 32% also endorsed the statement that online dating keeps people from settling down.

Older adults are dating online as well. In 2010, Match.com is reported as listing adults over 50 as their fastest growing demographic (McWilliams & Barrett, 2013). Traditional gender norms in evaluating partners are seen strongly in the middle and later aged online daters; criteria for male online daters in their mid-50s through their mid-70s center on physical attractiveness while women in the same age group focus on abilities. The pressure on women, who are competing with younger women for male attention, has resulted in the creation of youthful images, while men are pressured to create profiles reflecting middle-class masculinity and financial stability.

These traditional values are similar for online daters of all ages and sexual orientations. The male focus on physical attractiveness has been found across age cohorts. Alternatively, the feminine focus is on interpersonal communication (Menkin, Robles, Wiley, & Gonzaga, 2015). Gay men who tended to privilege masculinity more often presented themselves partially clothed and talked about fitness and exercise in their profile descriptions (Miller, 2015).

Sixty-six percent of individuals responding to a national survey who have tried online dating go on a date with someone they met through a dating site or app, and 23% have entered into a long-term relationship or marriage (Lenhart, 2014). Large, national studies have identified 33% of all marriages in the United States as having originated online; in comparisons with marriages beginning off-line, online marriages were slightly less likely to end in separation or divorce and correlated with slightly higher marital satisfaction (Cacioppo, Cacioppo, Gonzaga, Ogburn, & VanderWeele, 2013). Additional studies have demonstrated more success for those individuals seeking casual relationships than more serious ones and slightly higher breakup rates (Paul, 2014). Online dating is changing the dynamics of relationships for Americans.

Risks identified by online daters have included concerns over lies and deceit, sexual risks including sexually transmitted diseases (STDs) and sexual violence, emotional risks, and possibilities of encountering dangerous and untrustworthy people (Couch, Liamputtong, & Pitts, 2012). While these risks also exist in off-line romance, Internet-based relationships lack some of the safeguards that are often found in off-line relationships, such as shared friends, activities, or interests. The majority of people (54%) who reported to the Pew Research Center in a national survey that they dated online have encountered someone who "seriously misrepresented themselves" on their profile; nearly one third (28%) of these individuals have been contacted by someone through the site or app that made them feel uncomfortable or harassed (Lenhart, 2014).

Women rated online dating scenarios as requiring greater self-protective behavior than face-to-face dating scenarios, especially among women who had never dated online (Cali, Coleman, & Campbell, 2013). Online daters often engage in uncertainty reduction strategies to reduce their anxieties, such as verifying the claims made by the other person known as warranting (Gibbs, Ellison, & Lai, 2011). Often, daters will limit their self-disclosure until they are able to sufficiently feel safe that the other party is representing himself or herself accurately. Those who do misrepresent themselves often justify their deceits with unstated rules of engagement, such as portraying themselves in their profiles as they would like to be in the future—an aspirational profile (Ellison, Hancock, & Toma, 2012).

Technology has changed billions of lives around the planet. Information is shared and people communicate with one another in ways barely imagined just 50 years ago. Compared with advances in travel and communication prior to the Computer and Digital Ages, this time frame is a blink of the cursor. But what does it mean for our everyday lives?

Negative and Positive Effects of Today's Technologies

Technology gives us power, but it does not and cannot tell us how to use that power. Thanks to technology, we can instantly communicate across the world, but it still doesn't help us to know what to say.

Jonathan Sacks

Since the popularity of smartphones and constant, ever-present texting, tweeting, and surfing, individuals have an entirely new way to feel socially isolated while in the presence of others (Turkle, 2011). The Digital Age has transformed communication—not just communication from a distance through e-mails and texts but in person. Of the 92% of American adults who have cell phones, 31% say that they never turn their phones off, and 45% report they rarely turn their phones off (Pew Research Center, 2015b).

Eighty-nine percent of these mobile phone users reported that they used their phones during the most recent social gathering they attended, though 82% of the respondents agreed that it inhibited their social interaction (Pew Research Center, 2015c). This constantly buzzing and beeping device in one's pocket has altered how we talk with one another and has been rapidly changing social norms. How will we deal with this cognitive dissonance created by our inability to resist the lure of the phones in our pockets and maintain healthy and happy relationships with others?

Narcissism

Fewer than 10 years after Google became part of the Internet, researchers were asking these questions about the impact of technology on the people using it every day. One of the questions is whether narcissism, or excessive self-interest and self-absorption, has been on the rise among young people. Research on narcissism among college students found significant increases from 2002 to 2007 at twice the rate of previous gains from the 1980s until 2006 (Twenge & Foster, 2008; Twenge, Konrath, Foster, Campbell, & Bushman, 2008; Twenge, Miller, & Campbell, 2014). National samples of high school students have identified goals related to extrinsic values of money, image, and fame as more important than goals related to intrinsic values of self-acceptance, affiliation, and community (Twenge, Campbell, & Freeman, 2012). Students in this study were also less likely to donate to charities, help the environment, or express empathy for others.

Other samples of teens found unrealistically high expectations for income and future jobs (Reynolds, Stewart, Sischo, & MacDonald, 2006). A meta-analysis of samples of college students found significant declines in both empathic concern and perspective taking since 2000 (Konrath, O'Brien, & Hsing, 2011). Empathic concern, or the ability to relate to other people in a manner that fosters cooperation and unity rather than conflict and isolation, is central to healthy interpersonal relationships, as is perspective taking, the ability to step outside of one's self and understand another person's viewpoint.

The most frequent number, or median, of confidants reported in 2004 was 0.

Increasing Isolation

We are relating to one another differently, leaving many people with a feeling of being increasingly alone. Comparing the networks of connections we have to others, people are connecting to fewer individuals (McPherson, Smith-Lovin, & Brashears, 2006). People saying there is no one with whom they discuss important matters nearly tripled from 1985 to 2004; in 1985, the most frequent number of confidants was three other people, but in 2004, the most frequent number of confidants was zero. While an individual study may overestimate individuals' isolation, these smaller and smaller networks demonstrate significant changes in the social life of Americans.

Not only do we have fewer confidants but we are no more willing to express our opinions to people we believe will not agree with us over social media than we are through conventional public or private conversations (Pew Research Center, 2014a). A pre-Internet communication theory—the spiral of silence theory—sets forth the idea that if we believe the people we are talking with will not agree with us, we self-censor and do not express our opinions because we are afraid of ridicule or ostracism (Noelle-Neumann, 1974). While social media has the capacity for anonymity and increased freedom of expression, it has not offered new forums for differing opinions.

Leaving our phones out of sight and on "do not disturb" while attempting to be present for other people in our lives might improve our relationships. Referred to as the **iPhone effect**, the mere presence of a mobile device will alter the quality of communication between two people (Misra, Cheng, Genevie, & Yuan, 2014). Social exchanges between two people were observed in a naturalistic field study, and when a mobile phone was present—either in someone's hand or on the table between them—the quality of their interaction decreased. The empathic concern expressed was significantly greater without the presence of a mobile device.

Negative Self-Perceptions

Not only are relationships with others changing but also the constant stream of connection and information impacts our relationships with ourselves. We craft and mold our presentation to the world through the pictures and selfies we post, the events we chronicle, and the messages we respond to versus those we ignore (Gardner & Davies, 2013). Social media often gives the impression that others are doing better at life and can lead to negative social comparison. Greater Facebook use among young adults correlated with higher rates of negative social comparison, lower self-perceived social competence, and a lower sense of physical attractiveness (de Vries & Kuhne, 2015). Among individuals in this group who rated themselves as happy, this relationship was weaker. Social network sites can be viewed as increasing negative self-perceptions, especially for people who are unhappy. With seemingly unlimited reach, social media has the power to create negative social comparisons.

Internet Addiction

With all of our Internet use, the question of an Internet addiction is a viable concern. The *Diagnostic and Statistical Manual of Mental Disorders* (*DSM–5*; American Psychological Association, 2013a) defines Internet gaming addiction as an area needing further clinical study before inclusion into the manual (American Psychiatric Association, 2013). The idea of a process or behavioral addiction to the Internet is under ongoing investigation (Northrup, Lapierre, Kirk, & Rae, 2015). With so many everyday applications from gaming to dating to shopping to booking travel, the Internet is a compelling companion. While one cannot be addicted to the Internet itself, compulsive processes involved in its use, such as checking e-mails or status updates to the exclusion of other activities, can result in negative outcomes in personal and occupational lives. Behavioral compulsions, such as video gaming, have a similar impact on dopamine pathways in the brain as those of chemical addictions. Additional research may shed light on these possibilities.

Is this constant communication necessary for our happiness? One thing is definite: It is here to stay, and people don't want to give it up. Technologies we enjoy are hard to imagine giving up and are increasingly viewed as essential to daily life (Pew Research Center, 2014b). Forty-six percent of adult Internet users say that the Internet would be hard to impossible to give up, along with 44% stating the same for their cell phones. Translating these numbers to the general population, 39% feel they absolutely need access to the Internet. Sixty-one percent of those who find being online essential identify job-related or other reasons, though about 30% say they find it essential because they enjoy being online. Social media did not bear as well as the more general Internet; just 10% of adults said it would be hard to give up social media. See Adjustment Application: Steps to Healthy Limits in the Use of Technology for tips to limit screen time.

ADJUSTMENT APPLICATION
Steps to Healthy Limits in the Use of Technology

While we do not need to abandon our use of technology, most of us could probably manage a little less screen time. If you ever feel you might benefit from a little less time online or with your phone in your hand, consider following these steps:

1. Set a reasonable goal for how much time you would like to be off-line or without your screen. This might be a few minutes to an hour or more a day. Write down your goal, and post it somewhere you will see it.

2. Let your family and friends know when you are taking a screen break and that you will get back to them later. This way, you won't be tempted to just respond to one more message or phone call.

3. Pick an activity that you would like to do with others, and make plans with your friends or family to have a "screenless" event. Have everyone put phones and computers in a safe location and enjoy your time together.

4. Pick an activity that you want to do just for yourself—without your screen—and set a date to engage without technology. This is most successfully achieved outside of your home: yoga, exercise, a movie, a new book to read at your favorite coffee shop.

5. Keep a journal to record your time without your screen. Write about the experiences and how it feels to be unplugged. Record your successes, and keep working on finding new opportunities.

6. Think about a new habit you would like to add to your life. Many of us use our phones and surf the Internet out of habit; we just pick up the phone or follow a link. To stop our habitual use, we need to replace our bad habit with a new, good habit. Repeat a new habit during the time you might be surfing the net or on your phone.

7. Announce your intentions to your family and friends. Post something online! By publicly stating your intentions, you create accountability for yourself. You can receive support from others and be encouraged in your goals.

8. You may not always succeed every time you try. But try, try, try again if you are serious about increasing your time doing something off-line. When you slip and don't achieve your goal, just try again the next time.

Reflection Questions

1. Do you use the Internet too much? How much time is too much time online? Do you and your friends or family agree on how much time is too much time?

2. Are there aspects of your screen time that are habitual? Can you identify these habitual aspects in order to change them?

3. Even if you don't want to limit your technology time, can you make a list of three things you could do without using technology?

Positive Aspects of the Internet

Is it all gloom and doom? Are we creating future generations that won't know how to hold a conversation to talk intimately to their family and friends? Children and adolescents are being observed as less empathetic and caring about others' feelings (Turkle, 2015; Twenge et al., 2014). Likening middle school students to robots unable to process the emotions of others presents a disturbing picture.

Yet this is not the entire picture. While these concerns have validity, positive aspects of the Internet abound (see Figure 14.5). The majority of Americans find the Internet a boon to their lives. For the 25th anniversary of the World Wide Web, the Pew Research Center (2014b) asked adult Internet users if the Internet has been a good thing or a bad thing. Ninety percent said the Internet has been a good thing for them personally compared with 6% who said it has been a bad thing and 3% who say it has been both. Seventy-six percent of the Internet users responded by saying it has been a good thing for society, 15% that it has been a bad thing, and 8% reporting equally good and bad. Sixty-seven percent of all Internet users, regardless of age or education, believe that communication with family and friends has been strengthened, compared with 18% who believe it has weakened relationships.

Figure 14.5   The Internet: A Good Thing

Positive and Negative Aspects Reported	Percent of Adult Internet Users in the U.S.
The Internet is a good thing in my life.	90% – Yes
	6% – No
	3% – Both good and bad
The Internet is a good thing for society.	76% – Yes
	15% – No
	8% – Both good and bad
The Internet has improved or weakened communication with my family and friends.	67% – Improved
	15% – Weakened

Source: Pew Research Center, 2014b.

Relationships formed online with others are perceived as kind by 76% of Internet users, with just 13% reporting that others were mostly unkind (Pew Research Center, 2014b). When exploring kindness and cruelty with younger users, 18- to 29-year-olds reported higher rates in all categories, with 89% reporting they have been treated kindly by others, 69% endorsing having seen an online group help someone, 44% reporting being treated unkindly or attacked, and 39% reporting having left an online group because it was mean or unpleasant. Younger Internet users, as more frequent Internet users, have a broader range of experiences.

Social scientists debate the presence of narcissism and lack of empathy among adolescents and young adults (Trzesniewski & Donnellan, 2009, 2010; Twenge & Campbell, 2010; Twenge et al., 2008). Statistical exploration of research raises controversy and leaves no definite answer to the character of children, teens, and young adults today. While researchers appear to agree that youth are more cynical and less trusting, with higher education expectations, they do not agree that meaningful changes can be seen in egotism, individualism, and self-esteem. Initial research into the millennial generation has found greater diversity and acceptance of others than in past generations (Gardner & Davies, 2013).

How does the Internet benefit our lives? Young people today embrace what were once marginalized identities with much less fear, finding online support from around the globe. Following a series of suicides among gay teens in 2011, Dan Savage and his partner, Terry Miller, created a YouTube video to reach out to gay and lesbian youth with the following message: It gets better (It Gets Better Project, 2015). The video led to a worldwide movement, with over 50,000 user-created videos viewed more than 50 million times. The It Gets Better Project is just one example of the positive benefits of the Internet.

The opportunity of the creation and fostering of relationships seems endless. Connectivity around the globe offers opportunity for understanding one another as never before. Families and friends can instantly talk and see one another thousands of miles away, literally on the other side of the globe. In 2016, Pope Francis referred to the Internet as a "gift from God," demonstrating his belief that the Internet has more power to build relationship greater than its potential harm (Spadaro, 2016).

What do we need to do to maximize the benefits and minimize the costs of technology to our society? A vital first step is recognizing we have the power to control our use of the technology. While some people pay money to go to camp these days to escape the constant demand for connections (Baek, 2013), we have the ability to

1950s computers

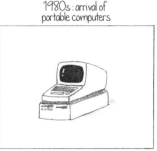
1980s: arrival of portable computers

2000s: cellphones become working computers

2035:?

One example of change is the great shift in the size of our computers over the years.

turn off our phones. Disconnection from the constant stream of information is a personal choice.

We can improve our relationship skills and push ourselves to communicate directly—at least some of the time. Fostering conversations and creating spaces in our lives to talk to one another in person is a choice and our technologically flooded world can still allow us this opportunity (Turkle, 2015). Engage others in conversation. Make eye contact, which creates emotional stability and fuels social connection (Pönkänen, Alhoniemi, Leppänen, & Hietanen, 2011; Senju & Johnson, 2009). Adults and older peers guide young people; opportunities to engage abound. Preteens who attended a 5-day overnight nature camp with no technology were compared with school-based matched controls, and their recognition of nonverbal emotion cues improved significantly (Uhls et al., 2014). Controlling our use of the Internet and reliance on devices is a choice we make in how we live our lives.

What choices will we face in the future? What may come next is still in the imaginations of the pioneers of the next great technologies. And the ways we develop as individuals and a culture are in our hands and the choices we make.

Conclusion

We have reached the end of our text. Looking back, we hope that you have come to see life as an adventure that can be challenging and full of wonders. The alternative is to frame it as full of fearful and bothersome changes and demands that lead to more work and stress. While it can be the latter at times, it is in many ways up to us to determine how we view it and that in this creative act we control what the world is for us in many ways. (See Adjustment in Practice: The Power of the Narrative.)

ADJUSTMENT IN PRACTICE
The Power of the Narrative

One of the authors tells a story of his grandfather who came to this country in the early 20th century. It seems that the grandfather's community wanted to have a dance. This dance was part of the usual list of annual activities that

(Continued)

(Continued)

occurred in the home country. Unfortunately, no one in the community knew the songs that were typically played for this dance. The community was considering canceling the dance since there was no music to dance to. The grandfather, so the story goes, reflected on this problem and decided to make up new songs for the dance. They would be similar to the old songs but new—in honor of the community coming to the new country. The dance was held, the songs were sung, and the community thought the event was a hit. This story has made it through family storytelling now for a little over 100 years.

Stories help us to organize events in our lives, to remember those events, and then to make meaning of our lives. Did this story actually happen exactly as told? Probably not. But it was a good one as it helped the family remember hard times and the ways in which they and their community successfully dealt with the challenges of being in a new country, being without what they used to have, and coping with the dilemmas that ensued. Note that narratives that emphasize "agency" and exploration are related to higher levels of well-being and adjustment (McAdams & McLean, 2013).

McAdams (2013) noted that a more evolved sense of self develops during the adolescent and emerging adulthood years. Here the individual as autobiographical author creates a story of who she or he is. This story serves the mature adult as a framework for purpose in life. These narratives are predictive of our abilities at self-regulation (Cox & McAdams, 2014) and our efforts to contribute to our communities (McAdams & Guo, 2015). Both of these qualities are believed to be valuable to us personally and to our larger society. And so we are really the authors of our story and creators of our life.

Reflection Questions

1. What are some stories you like?

2. What do you find to be helpful stories about family and friends that serve as a guide or as an example of how the world works?

This positive view of the world requires us to be open to these experiences, which is supported by the psychological literature. Individuals who are resilient in the face of adversities were actively engaged in their world and summoned the resources around them to help them to solve the issues that inevitably arise from growth, maturation, and environmental changes in demands on the individual. We read of this throughout the preceding chapters. There is also research to support this kind of openness in our attitudes to the world (Graziano & Ward, 1992; Hair & Graziano, 2003; Shaffer, Harrison, Gregersen, Black, & Ferzandi, 2006; Steel, Schmidt, & Shultz, 2008) and in our flexibility in thinking about and reacting to that world (Cheng, Lau, & Chan, 2014; Genet & Siemer, 2011).

Graziano and colleagues (Graziano & Ward, 1992; Hair & Graziano, 2003) found that openness was related to adolescent academic adjustment to movements to new schools. And Shaffer et al. (2006) discovered openness to be related to personal and work adjustments to new cultures.

Flexibility and adjustment were more strongly correlated when cultural settings emphasized collectivity over individualism (Cheng et al., 2014), but it was clearly influential in an individual's adaptability. Wisdom is based on the ability to see and accept change and the willingness to be open to that change (Grossmann, Na, Varnum, Kitayama, & Nisbett, 2013; Staudinger & Glück, 2011).

Whether we consider the areas of relationships, intimacy, money, school, work, or our aging processes, the mastery of the issues in each area can be supported by the development of attitudes and skills described in this book. Each of these important areas of life can be informed by better understanding of what is going on and what skills can help to resolve particular issues raised. This array of information can be used or ignored. While there are aspects to life and satisfaction that are beyond our control, the potential for influence and change resides within each of us. Openness, flexibility, and wisdom can contribute to our sense of being in charge of our lives.

Besides encouraging the cultivation of attitudes of openness and flexibility, we hope that we have imparted enough to make you curious as to what the rest of psychology might offer now and in the future. While there are many articles referenced here, there will always be more. A curiosity as to what new discoveries are being made will help to keep you current with developments in psychology and its potential applications to your life. When some authors of this text began their career, there was not much known as to why sleep was so beneficial. Now those questions are being answered at the cognitive and physiological levels, but still more work is in development. There were questions as to risk factors and protective factors in children's development. We now know much more about what these factors are. Some of this work is being applied in prenatal, neonate, and early school programs as well as in programs for retention of college students.

The human challenge is to embrace life with courage (May, 1975). Exploration, travel, and curiosity open us to transformative experiences from which we grow. We are faced with finding the balance between security and openness, self and community, and mastery of the familiar and discovery of the new. Our very best wishes go out to you in that adventure.

Review Questions

1. What is an opportunity structure, and why is it important?

2. Define *agency* and *communion*, and discuss how they differ.

3. How is *wisdom* defined in this text? What does it have to do with perspective taking?

4. How is the United States changing in demographics? How does this look for the different age groups?

5. Identify the various ways in which an individual can identify as to gender.

6. What are the advantages of being in an in-group? Of having cohesion?

7. Name three different kinds of present-day prejudice.

8. Explain the digital divide.

9. What are some of the impacts of technology on us?

10. Describe some of the ways that the Internet has been a positive force in present-day society.

Key Terms

agency 307

aversive prejudice 313

cohesiveness 312

communion 307

digital divide 319

digital natives 317

gender 309
genderqueer 311
implicit prejudice 313

in-group 312
iPhone effect 323
out-group 312

sexual orientation 310
symbolic prejudice 312
transgender 311

Sharpen your skills with SAGE edge at **edge.sagepub.com/moritsugu**

SAGE edge for students provides a personalized approach to help you accomplish your coursework goals in an easy-to-use learning environment.

Go to **edge.sagepub.com/moritsugu** for additional exercises and web resources. Select Chapter 14, The Search for Balance and the Future for chapter-specific resources.

Glossary

academic motivation—The intrinsic value, interest, and importance that students attribute to academic schoolwork.

academic self-efficacy—One's confidence to be successful in an academic setting.

accommodation—Changing one's existing organizational framework to allow for new information.

active coping—An action where an individual does something to try to solve or eliminate a stressful situation.

active learning—A teaching methodology that emphasizes the student's participation in the construction of what is to be learned, allowing the student to "create" the knowledge in a way that is personally more involved and meaningful.

acute stressor—A time-limited, discrete, stressful event with a starting and stopping point.

adjustment—The process of coping with the problems of everyday life.

agency—The emphasis a person places on himself or herself and accomplishments.

aging in place—A term that refers to older adults' strong preference to grow old in communities and settings that are familiar to them, where they have control over their daily routines.

altruism—Actions that benefit another person without any expected reward for oneself.

anxiety—Negative anticipation over a future event. Anxiety is a normal and common reaction to stress and can actually help us achieve our goals.

assimilation—Fitting incoming information into one's existing organizational framework.

associative play—A mutual type of parallel play where children are focused on separate activities but comment on each other's play and exchange toys.

assurance—A friendship maintenance behavior that refers to affirming statements made about the friendship.

assuring behavior—A relationship maintenance behavior involving reminding your partner how much you value him or her.

autonomic nervous system—The portion of the nervous system that has traditionally been assumed to be beyond willful control. This system controls bodily functions such as breathing, heart rate, and body temperature.

average life expectancy—The typical number of years a person can expect to live.

aversive prejudice—A form of prejudice in which individuals are sympathetic to racial minorities and believe themselves to be without prejudice while still harboring negative feelings and beliefs about those groups, which affects their attitudes and actions toward minorities.

avoidant coping—Responses that potentially impede or interfere with problem solving such as not thinking about a problem.

banter—The private jokes or stories that exist between us and the close friends in our life.

behavioral economics—Field of study that combines cognitive psychology and microeconomics.

behaviorism—A school of psychology that emphasizes the importance of settings and consequences on the probability of behaviors.

belonging—A sense of community or friendship with others so that the individuals or groups do not feel alone.

biopsychosocial model—The broad view that considers biological (or somatogenic), psychological (or psychogenic), and social explanations in the etiology and treatment of mental illness.

bonding—Attachment to others through regular contact or the formation of friendships.

bridging—Connecting others together, in the form of an individual-to-individual connection, a group-to-individual connection, or a group-to-group connection.

brokerage—Providing linkages between individuals or groups; serving as a bridge that allows others to make contact.

Buddhism—A psychology and a philosophy derived from the life of Buddha and the practices of his followers primarily in countries throughout Asia. As Buddhism was brought to the West, the understanding and practice of mindfulness associated with Buddhism has become a subject of interest and study to Western psychology.

career indecisiveness—Describes a state of high anxiety around making a decision.

career or vocation—Terms to describe a person's lifelong pursuit and ideally represents what one is meant to do with his or her life.

cascading effect—Small changes can lead to bigger effects further in time as the changes impact more and more of the individual's life.

chaining—A special operant conditioning situation where the operant starts as one behavior and is then linked to a sequence of behaviors one at a time until the chain of linked behaviors is the "operant" to be reinforced.

challenge—Refers to a perspective where one tries to discover how the job loss might be an opportunity to grow.

chronic stressors—Ongoing stressful events that may be challenging to interrupt and may be unavoidable.

circumscription—A narrowing process where occupations are eliminated based on the aforementioned factors.

cognitive flexibility—The ability to switch between thinking about two different concepts and to think about multiple concepts simultaneously, which may be influenced by practices of mindfulness.

cognitive–affective complexity—Refers to older adults' ability to have self-awareness and a greater sensitivity to others' perspectives.

commitment—The attitude that it is best to stay involved with the people and events around you rather than to withdraw.

communion—The emphasis a person places on the common good and what can be accomplished for that good.

competent individual—A person who possesses the necessary skills with which to master a given demand or environment.

compromise—The process of giving up your most preferred choices for less compatible choices that are perceived as more accessible.

computer-mediated communication—A friendship maintenance behavior that involves staying in touch with friends electronically.

conditioned response (CR)—A learned reaction to a stimulus.

conditioned stimulus (CR)—A stimulus that elicits a conditioned response after conditioning or learning has occurred.

conformity—The tendency to agree with the group regardless of what one thinks or feels.

contempt—Any behavior that belittles a partner or denigrates one's character.

context—The circumstances or settings that influence behaviors or help individuals to better understand the meaning of what occurs.

control—Making efforts to influence the outcomes (e.g., like going through retraining programs) rather than to give up.

cooperative play—A type of peer interaction where there is a common goal such as playing make-believe or working on a puzzle together.

coping—The voluntary response to stressors that involves "regulation of emotion, cognition, behavior, physiology and the environment in response to stressful events or circumstance" (Compas, Connor-Smith, Saltzman, Thomsen, & Wadsworth, 2001, p. 89).

criticism—A complaint about a behavior that becomes a generalization about the partner (e.g., "you always...").

culture—A set of values, attitudes, feelings, behaviors, and rituals based on a group standard of meaning and reality that provides a way of life to that group, which may be transmitted in a structured and planned manner across generations.

defensiveness—A type of denial, often accompanied by some sarcasm, where one partner attempts to blame the other.

dialectic—Through a process of dialogue, or interchange, finding or advancing truth.

digital divide—The difference between individuals who have grown up with computers and the Internet and those who did not, creating the belief that the technological skill and assumptive world of these two sets of people differs markedly.

digital natives—A generation that has always had personal access to computers and the Internet, has a working knowledge of the technology associated with these digital devices, and assumes this to be a part of their world.

discriminative stimuli—A stimulus that signals emitting a behavior will lead to a given consequence.

durability bias—The expectation that emotions last for a longer time than they really do.

eating disorder—A condition that occurs when a person has a disordered relationship with food, unhealthy exercise patterns, and/or a distorted body image. Examples include anorexia, bulimia, and binge-eating disorders.

ecological psychology—A psychological theory stating that individuals and settings influence each other and that this influence may be best understood by watching these interactions over time.

ecological—A model for understanding the world and a person's interactions with that world. This model assumes multiple determinants to outcomes and that these determinants influence each other.

economic socialization—Social learning about money, what it is, and how to use it.

ego integrity—The capacity to view one's life in the context of larger humanity, which involves coming to terms with the life one has lived.

emotional or self-esteem support—Help through listening, reflecting, or demonstrating empathy. This may help individuals or groups to feel cared for, understood, or otherwise held in regard.

emotion-focused coping—A reaction in response to a stressful event aimed at modifying the emotional impact of the event.

empathy—The ability to relate to others at an emotional level.

empirically validated therapies—therapeutic techniques and practices that have been scientifically studied and shown to be the most effective with specific types of mental illness.

equifinality—A developmental psychopathology concept that states many different beginnings may still lead to the same outcome.

eustress—Positive responses we have to stress, such as growth or finding new opportunities.

existential psychology—A school of psychology that emphasizes the unique qualities of human existence. Among those qualities is an awareness of life and death, the construction of perceptions of the world, and the search for meaning and purpose within that world.

explicit learning—Learning that takes effort and conscious focus.

first-generation college students—A term used for students who are the first ones in their family to go to college.

flexibility—A type of thinking that reflects the ability to adapt to changing circumstances.

flow—A state of being where a person performing an activity is fully immersed in what is happening.

focused attention (FA) meditation—Meditation in which an image, object, word, or phrase is the focus of the meditation practice and where the meditator brings attention continuously back to the focus when distracted by sensations, feelings, or thoughts.

genderqueer—Subscription to a culture and behavior style that is not bound by male or female labels.

gender—The culturally determined set of practices and attitudes used to identify male and female within that society.

general adaptation syndrome (GAS)—A concept authored by Hans Selye that describes a predictable physiological sequence within an organism caused by stress. That sequence is alarm, resistance, and exhaustion.

generativity—Refers to the need to leave a legacy or make a contribution to subsequent generations.

goodness of fit—The organism's suitability to the demands and requirements of the environment.

hardy individuals—Persons able to handle change and stress because they possess a commitment to life, see disruption as a challenge to be mastered, and feel they have the ability to control outcomes.

hassles—Everyday stressors that are not problematic on their own but when accumulated can be very distressful to people.

homophily—The tendency to like or befriend others who are like us.

impermanence—The temporary nature of the material world; the realization that the world is constantly changing.

implicit learning—Learning that is effortless and seems to occur without awareness.

implicit prejudice—A negative orientation to a group that one holds without awareness or intention, which results in automatic and unconscious ways of thinking and behaving.

indegree centrality—A measure of linkage with others. The more connections a person has, the higher his or her indegree centrality will be.

informational support—Help through the provision of knowledge. This knowledge may provide access to resources or facts and skills that can be helpful.

in-group—A social grouping that holds power and determines social norms. Membership in this group brings advantages in the evaluation of performance (more lenient) and the distribution of rewards (more generous).

institutional and personal religion—Two ways of constructing one's religious sense. Institutional religion emphasizes formal, historically derived codes and rules, providing external control over one's behaviors and motivated by social approval. Personal religion is a belief and value system motivated by the individual's need for meaning and being open to change and development in response to that individual's experiences.

instrumental grievers—Describes people who experience loss less emotionally and more cognitively and prefer to act out their grief by creating rituals or memorials.

internalization—Religious beliefs based on personal choices.

intimate partner violence (IPV)—Physical, sexual, or psychological harm by a current or former partner or spouse.

intrinsic and extrinsic orientations—Two ways of making decisions related to religious practice. In intrinsic orientation, decisions are based on a personal quest for religious meaning. In extrinsic orientation, decisions are based on perceived external pressures or expectations.

introjected beliefs—Religious beliefs based on perceptions of social pressure.

intuitive grievers—Describes people who have strong emotional responses to loss and experience significant relief from being able to express those feelings through crying or talking to others

iPhone effect—The increase in communication capabilities and the use of computer-assisted smart devices has increased multitasking and the assumptions of polyconscious capabilities, increasing the mental and physical demands placed on individuals to the point of being unrealistic.

job—Employment frequently seen as a means to an end, or a way to pay the bills.

long-term memory—The fund of knowledge we acquire throughout our lifetime, which is a type of intelligence that is less impacted by aging.

meditation—A disciplined approach to experiencing the world using practices that guide the meditator toward mental habits valued by various cultures and traditions.

mental disorder—A mental health condition that occurs when a recognizable group of symptoms or behaviors interfere with a person's functioning in one or more areas of life; also referred to as psychiatric illness.

mentor—A person with advanced experience and knowledge who is emotionally invested in someone else's development.

microaggressions—Subtle forms of bias or oppression that are brief, commonplace, and daily and include indignities that communicate negative or derogatory slights.

mindfulness meditation—Specific meditation practices that cultivate awareness through the focus of attention on the basic fundamentals of experience: breath, sensations (e.g., sight, sound, smell, taste), emotions, and thoughts.

mindfulness—The act of paying attention, moment to moment, to lived experience by focusing on sensations, feelings, and thoughts.

mirror neurons—Neurons that are activated when an individual acts and when he or she observes the acts, which may set the state for the development of empathy in humans.

Montessori preschool—A type of school, named after Italian physician Maria Montessori, that is designed to promote exploration and discovery, child-selected activities, and the equal promotion of social development and cognitive development.

mood disorder—A condition based in the experience of a lack of energy and depressed mood, sometimes accompanied by periods of excessive energy and expansive mood.

multifinality—A developmental psychopathology concept that states a common beginning may still lead to many possible outcomes.

negative affect reciprocity—A cycle of negative responses to a partner's or spouse's negative emotions.

networking—A relationship maintenance behavior that involves staying connected with the significant others (i.e., family, friends) in your lives.

nonjudgmental awareness—A mindfulness and acceptance of all aspects of one's experiences, even in the face of unpleasant sensations, emotions, or difficult thoughts and experiences.

occupation—Employment that a person might be trained to do that requires a specific type of education or preparation.

old-old—A category of older adults who are in poor physical condition and need help with daily living.

open-monitoring (OM) meditation—When the internal experiences of sensation, feeling, and thought are used as the focus of meditation, during which the meditator learns to become an observer of the flow of experience.

operant conditioning—Also called Skinnerian conditioning, in which a stimulus signals a particular behavior that will result in a predictable consequence, strengthening or weakening the probability of that behavior.

operant—A behavior that acts upon the environment.

out-group—Individuals outside of the preferred in-group. Membership in the out-group brings harsher judgment and less favorable distribution of rewards.

pathways—A particular route or trail that determines the direction taken by an individual.

perpetual problems—Problems that are chronic and reoccurring, often defying resolution.

perspective taking—The recognition that one's own viewpoint may not be shared by others.

positive aging—A general term used to describe behaviors thought to protect a person from the potentially negative effects of aging.

positive mental health—A definition of mental status that emphasizes productivity, happiness, well-being, and a fulfilling life.

positivity—Friendship maintenance actions that make spending time with a friend enjoyable and interesting.

positivity—Relationship maintenance behaviors that bring about pleasant experiences.

pragmatic problem solving—Involves using logic to solve real-world problems and is a function of cognitive skills and experience in the real world.

primary appraisal—The initial part of the assessment of a stressor that determines whether it is a threat to the individual.

problem solving–focused coping—A response intended to make changes to a person's environment in reaction to a stressor.

prosocial behavior—An action that is intended to assist others or act selflessly.

protectors or regulators—A parental role that distances children from money decisions so as not to place a burden on them. The parent serves as controller of money expenditures.

psychoanalysis—A type of talk therapy originated by Sigmund Freud that focuses on gaining insight and awareness into unconscious processes.

psychoeducation—Any of a variety of interventions that emphasize teaching an individual about himself or herself and the skills he or she may require to cope with given situations. These interventions may take the form of books, classes, workshops, or individual training and coaching.

psychogenic—A term used to describe explanations for mental illness that focus on environmental factors such as stress and trauma, as well as dysfunctional, learned associations and distorted perceptions.

psychosis—A condition that occurs when a person loses touch with reality and ceases to know what is real and what is delusion.

punishers—Consequences to a behavior that weaken the likelihood of that behavior occurring again.

purpose in life—A reason for one's existence.

reframing—A new way of seeing a situation that involves accepting alternative perspectives on a given event (e.g., seeing a stressful event as an opportunity to learn about oneself).

reinforcer—A consequence to a behavior that strengthens the likelihood of that behavior occurring again.

rejected aggressive—A term describing children who are impulsive, hyperactive, and inattentive as well as have a high level of conflict in their lives.

rejected withdrawn—A term describing children who are socially awkward and more avoidant of people.

relationship talks—A relationship maintenance behavior involving checking in with your partner to see if everything is okay in the relationship.

religion—A system of values and meaning that influence an individual's understanding of the world and direct a way of behaving in relation to those values and meaning.

respondent conditioning—Another term for classical or Pavlovian conditioning, in which associations are made between an unconditioned and a neutral stimulus until the neutral stimulus elicits the same reaction as the unconditioned stimuli.

routine contact—A friendship maintenance behavior that involves having a regularity of spending actual time together.

rule learning—Learning the probability of events occurring. This is best illustrated in language, where the positioning of nouns, verbs, and other words follow grammatical rules and an individual can anticipate what will happen after learning the rules that govern it.

salutogenic—Health-making qualities of the person or the environment.

scaffolding—The teaching aids that guide the student in the use of a more advanced cognitive framework. The framework should offer the appropriate next step in complexity and sophistication and not overstep a student's conceptual reach.

schedule to the reinforcement—The rule or formula that determines when a reinforcement is to be delivered. Sometimes that rule calls for each behavior to be reinforced, and sometimes the rule requires more than one behavior.

schema—An outline, model, or plan that helps organize information.

school belonging—Defined as students' perceptions that others in the school are on their side and that they matter in the school community.

school climate—Refers to the values, policies, practices, and general expectations of schools.

school resources—A wide category of environmental factors such as the quality of the school building itself, the amount of money spent per pupil, the salaries that teachers make, the technology, and books that are available.

schizophrenia—A thought disorder with psychosis; may include delusions, hallucinations, disorganized thinking/speech, disorganized movements, lack of will, and/or lack of affect.

secondary appraisal—The subsequent part of the stressor assessment process, which factors in the person's expectations of being able to handle the event.

secondary reinforcer—A learned reinforcer, a learned stimulus event that increases the likelihood of the behavior it follows.

self-beliefs—Individual ideas that we have about ourselves within a particular setting such as our ability to do well in sports.

self-disclosure—A relationship maintenance behavior that involves sharing your thoughts and feelings and requires a willingness to be vulnerable.

self-matching—The agreement between sense of self in the present and sense of self in the future.

self-regulation—The skills that allow us to inhibit our impulses and redirect our attention.

sense of coherence—A feeling that the world is understandable and orderly. The three factors that go into this are comprehensibility, manageability, and meaningfulness.

sexual orientation—Romantic or sexual excitation directed to categories of individuals: male, female, or both.

social capital—The value of social connection. This value may be in the form of information, access to others, or willingness to partner with another and is accumulated as the result of social behaviors or social position.

social learning theory—An approach to learning that describes social and cognitive components that influence learning, which includes modeling, imitation, expectations, and vicarious learning.

social networking—A friendship maintenance behavior that refers to involving others in one's friendship.

somatogenic—A term used to describe explanations for mental illness that focus on the body as the causal agent.

spiritual and religious aspirations—A possible sixth personality factor, beyond the standard five personality factors (openness, conscientiousness, extroversion, agreeableness, neurotic). This sixth factor addresses the personal need to go beyond everyday life concerns.

spirituality—A sense of power beyond one's self.

stereotype threat—The knowledge that a stereotype is held about a group to which you belong, which creates anxiety that interferes with performance on a task such as a test.

stonewalling—An action where a person physically leaves a conversation or emotionally shuts down in the middle of a discussion.

stress—The occurrence of a stimulus event, a process of appraisal, and a reaction.

study skills—The competencies that allow for acquiring, recording, organizing, synthesizing, remembering, and using information.

substance use disorder—A condition marked by tolerance to, and excessive and problematic use of, substances including central nervous system depressants and stimulants.

supernatural—A term used to describe occurrences that are beyond scientific knowledge or the laws of nature.

symbolic prejudice—A form of negative evaluation of policies, actions, or individuals based upon a perceived violation of a "principle"; these prejudices are justified as being caused by the principles rather than the individuals involved.

tangible support—Help in the form of direct aid to an individual or group. This may take the form of money, goods, or provision of physical help.

task behavior—A relationship maintenance behavior that involves making the time to be helpful in tangible ways to your partner.

task sharing—A friendship maintenance behavior that refers to the tangible help that we can give to our friends when they are in need.

telomeres—The structures at the end of chromosomes that influence their stability.

terror management theory—The experimental proposition that humans, when confronted with their mortality, reaffirm their existence.

third age—Describes a period of time after middle adulthood, usually around ages 65 to 79, which is a time of personal fulfillment.

transgender—Identifying as belonging to a gender different from the physical gender markers one possesses.

unconditioned response (UCR)—A natural reaction to a stimulus.

unconditioned stimulus (UCS)—A stimulus that naturally elicits an unconditioned response.

understanding behaviors—Relationship maintenance behaviors that involve using words and actions.

values—Personal life directions established by an individual through self-reflection on important life domains such as education, work, and family, which are created in the context of family and culture.

vicarious learning—Learning by observing others, without having to perform the behavior.

visualization—The creation of a focused mental picture, both of the plan for change and the strategies that will be used to overcome obstacles on the path toward achieving a new set of behaviors or a positive, durable habit.

vocational hope—A positive motivational state associated with envisioning a future in which meaningful work is attainable.

work—An all-encompassing term that describes both jobs and occupations.

working memory—Refers to the ability to form new memories, some of which ultimately get rehearsed and embedded into our long-term memory.

young-old—Describes a category of older adults who are in good physical condition and can function independently.

References

ACT. (2008). *2008 retention/completion summary tables.* Retrieved from www.act.org/research/policymakers/pdf/retain_trends.pdf

Adams, K. B., Sanders, S., & Auth, E. A. (2004). Loneliness and depression in independent living retirement communities: Risk and resilience factors. *Aging and Mental Health, 8*(6), 475–485.

Adaval, R., & Wyer, R. S., Jr. (2011). Conscious and nonconscious influences of a price anchor: Effects on willingness to pay for related and unrelated products. *Journal of Marketing Research, 48*(2), 355–365.

Adjust. (1993). In *The New Shorter Oxford English Dictionary.* Oxford, England: Clarendon Press.

Adler, A. (1998). *Social interest: Adler's key to the meaning of life.* London, England: Oneworld Publications. (Original work published 1938)

Agrawal, A., & Lynskey, M. T. (2008). Are there genetic influences on addiction: Evidence from family, adoption and twin studies. *Addiction, 103*(7), 1069–1081.

Aguado, T., Ballesteros, B., & Malik, B. (2003). Cultural diversity and school equity: A model to evaluate and develop educational practices in multicultural education contexts. *Equity & Excellence in Education, 36*(1), 50–63.

Ainsworth, M., Blehar, M., Waters, E., & Wall, S. (1978). *Patterns of attachment.* Hillsdale, NJ: Erlbaum.

Aknin, L. B., Barrington-Leigh, C. P., Dunn, E. W., Helliwell, J. F., Burns, J., Biswas-Diener, R., . . . Norton, M. I. (2013). Prosocial spending and well-being: Cross-cultural evidence for a psychological universal. *Journal of Personality and Social Psychology, 104*(4), 635–652.

Aknin, L. B., Dunn, E. W., Sandstrom, G. M., & Norton, M. I. (2013). Does social connection turn good deeds into good feelings? On the value of putting the "social" into prosocial spending. *International Journal of Happiness and Development, 1*(2), 155–171.

Aknin, L. B., Sandstrom, G. M., Dunn, E. W., & Norton, M. I. (2011). It's the recipient that counts: Spending money on strong social ties leads to greater happiness than spending on weak social ties. *PLoS ONE, 6*(2), e17018.

Aldwin, C. M., Jeong, Y., Igarashi, H., & Spiro, A. (2014). Do hassles and uplifts change with age? Longitudinal findings from the VA Normative Aging Study. *Psychology and Aging, 29*(1), 57–71. doi:10.1037/a0035042

Alexander, C. N., Langer, E. J., Newman, R. I., Chandler, H. M., & Davies, J. L. (1989). Transcendental meditation, mindfulness, and longevity: An experimental study with the elderly. *Journal of Personality and Social Psychology, 57*(6), 950–964.

Allen, T. D., Eby, L. T., Poteet, M. L., Lentz, E., & Lima, L. (2004). Career benefits associated with mentoring for protégée: A meta-analysis. *Journal of Applied Psychology, 89*(1), 127–136.

Allport, G. (1950). *The individual and his religion.* New York, NY: MacMillan.

Allport, G. (1979). *The nature of prejudice.* New York, NY: Basic Books. (Original work published 1949)

Altmaier, E. M., & Hansen, J.-I. C. (Eds.). (2011). *The Oxford hanbook of counseling psychology.* New York, NY: Oxford University Press.

Altman, I., & Taylor, D. (1973). *Social penetration: The development of interpersonal relationships.* New York, NY: Holt, Rinehart and Winston.

Alzheimer's Association. (2015). *What is dementia?* Retrieved from http://www.alz.org/what-is-dementia.asp

Amato, P. R. (2000). The consequences of divorce for adults and children. *Journal of Marriage and Family, 62*(4), 1269–1287.

Amato, P. R., & Cheadle, J. (2005). The long reach of divorce: Divorce and child well-being across three generations. *Journal of Marriage and Family, 67*(1), 191–206.

American Institutes for Research. (2013). Predictors of postsecondary success. Retrieved from http://www.ccrscenter.org/sites/default/files/CCRS%20Center_Predictors%20of%20Postsecondary%20Success_final_0.pdf

American Psychiatric Association. (2013a). *Diagnostic and statistical manual of mental disorders* (5th ed.). Washington, DC: Author.

American Psychiatric Association (2013b). *Internet gaming addiction.* Retrieved from http://www.dsm5.org/Documents/Internet%20Gaming%20Disorder%20Fact%20Sheet.pdf

American Psychological Association. (2006). *Introduction to mentoring: A guide for mentors and mentees.* Washington, DC: Author.

American Psychological Association. (2008). *Answers to your questions: For a better understanding of sexual orientation and homosexuality.* Washington, DC: Author. Retrieved from www.apa.org/topics/lgbt/orientation.pdf

American Psychological Association. (2011). *The guidelines for psychological practice with lesbian, gay, and bisexual clients.* Retrieved from http://www.apa.org/pi/lgbt/resources/guidelines.aspx

American Psychological Association. (2016). *How to choose a psychologist.* Retrieved from http://www.apa.org/helpcenter/choose-therapist.aspx

Anderson, K. K., Voineskos, A., Mulsant, B., George, T. P., & McKenzie, K. (2014). The role of untreated psychosis in neurodegeneration: A review of hypothesized mechanisms of neurotoxicity in first-episode psychosis. *Canadian Journal of Psychiatry, 59*(10), 513–517.

Andreasen, N. C. (2000). Schizophrenia: The fundamental questions. *Brain Research Reviews, 31*(2–3), 106–112.

Ano, G., & Vasconcelles, E. (2005). Religious coping and psychological adjustment to stress: A meta-analysis. *Journal of Clinical Psychology, 61*(4), 461–480.

Ansbacher, H. (1990). Alfred Adler, pioneer in prevention of mental disorders. *Journal of Primary Prevention, 11*, 37–68. doi:10.1007/BF01324860

Antonovsky, A. (1979). *Health, stress and coping.* San Francisco, CA: Jossey-Bass.

Antonovsky, A. (1987). *Unraveling the mystery of health: How people manage stress and stay well.* San Francisco, CA: Jossey-Bass.

Antonovsky, A. (1993). The structure and properties of the sense of coherence scale. *Social Science and Medicine, 36*(6), 725–733.

Antonovsky, A. (1998). The sense of coherence: An historical and future perspective. In H. I. McCubbin, E. A. Thompson, A. I. Thompson, & J. E. Fromer (Eds.), *Stress, coping, and health in families: Sense of coherence and resiliency* (pp. 3–20). Thousand Oaks, CA: Sage.

Archer, J. (2000). Sex differences in aggression between heterosexual partners: A meta-analytic review. *Psychological Bulletin, 126*(5), 651–680.

Arévalo, S., Prado, G., & Amaro, H. (2008). Spirituality, sense of coherence and coping responses in women receiving treatment for alcohol and drug addiction. *Evaluation and Program Planning, 31*(1), 113–123.

Ariely, D. (2010). *Predictably irrational: The hidden forces that shape our decisions.* New York, NY: Harper Perennial.

Ariely, D., Huber, J., & Wertenbroch, K. (2005). When do losses loom larger than gains. *Journal of Marketing Research, 42*(2), 134–138.

Ariely, D., Loewenstein, G., & Prelec, D. (2006). Tom Sawyer and the construction of value. *Journal of Economic Behavior and Organization, 60*, 1–10.

Ariely, G. (2014). Does diversity erode social cohesion? Conceptual and methodological issues. *Political Studies, 62*(3), 573–595. doi:10.1111/1467-9248.12068

Arndt, J., Greenberg, J., Pyszczynski, T., & Solomon, S. (1997). Subliminal exposure to death-related stimuli increases defense of the cultural worldview. *Psychological Science, 8*, 379–385.

Arndt, J., Landau, M. J., Vail, K. E., III, & Vess, M. (2013). An edifice for enduring personal value: A terror management perspective on the human quest for multi-level meaning. In K. Markman, T. Proulx, & M. Lindberg (Eds.), *The psychology of meaning.* Washington, DC: American Psychological Association.

Arnett, J. J. (2000). Emerging adulthood: A theory of development from the late teens through the twenties. *American Psychologist, 55*(5), 469–480. doi:10.1037/0003-066X.55.5.469

Arnett, J. J. (2014). Presidential address: The emergence of emerging adulthood: A personal history. *Emerging Adulthood, 2*(3), 155–162. doi:10.1177/2167696814541096

Arns, M., Heinrich, H., & Strehl, U. (2013). Evaluation of neurofeedback in ADHD: The long and winding road. *Biological Psychology, 95*, 108–115.

Aronson, E. (2004). Reducing hostility and building compassion: Lessons from the jigsaw classroom. In A. G. Miller (Ed.), *The social psychology of good and evil* (pp. 469–488). New York, NY: Guilford.

Aronson, E., & Bridgeman, D. (1979). Jigsaw groups and the desegregated classroom: In pursuit of common goals. *Personality and Social Psychology Bulletin, 5*(4), 438–446. doi:10.1177/014616727900500405

Aronson, J., & Steele, C. M. (2005). Stereotypes and the fragility of academic competence, motivation, and self-concept. In A. J. Elliot & C. S. Dweck (Eds.), *Handbook of competence and motivation* (pp. 436–456). New York, NY: Guilford.

Asch, S. E. (1951). Effects of group pressure upon the modification and distortion of judgment. In H. Guetzkow (Ed.), *Groups, leadership and men.* Pittsburgh, PA: Carnegie Press.

Asch, S. E. (1956). Studies of independence and conformity: I. A minority of one against a unanimous majority. *Psychological Monographs: General and Applied, 70*(9), 1–70.

Aslin, R. N., & Newport, E. L. (2012). Statistical learning: From acquiring specific terms to forming general rules. *Current Directions in Psychological Science, 21*(3), 170–176. doi:10.1177/0963721412436806

Atkins, D. C., Yi, J., Baucom, D. H., & Christensen, A. (2005). Infidelity in couples seeking marital therapy. *Journal of Family Psychology, 19*(3), 470–473.

Awa, W. L., Plaumann, M., & Walter, U. (2010). Burnout prevention: A review of intervention programs. *Patient Education and Counseling, 78*(2), 184–190.

Azar, B. (2011). Oxytocin's other side: Oxytocin has garnered media attention for its potential as a social lubricant and as a treatment for autism and other disorders. *Monitor on Psychology, 42*(3), 40–42.

Azaroff, L. S., Champagne, N. J., Nobrega, S., Shetty, K., & Punnett, L. (2010). Getting to know you: Occupational health researchers investigate employee assistance professionals' approaches to workplace stress. *Journal of Workplace Behavioral Health, 25*(4), 296–319.

Babcock, J. C., Green, C. E., & Robie, C. (2004). Does batterers' treatment work? A meta-analysis of domestic violence treatment. *Clinical Psychology Review, 23*(8), 1023–1053.

Badenes-Ribera, L., Frias-Navarro, D., Bonilla-Campos, A., Pons-Salvador, G., & Monterde-Bort, H. (2015). Intimate partner violence in self-identified lesbians: A meta-analysis of its prevalence. *Sexuality Research and Social Policy, 12*(1), 47–59.

Baek, R. (2013). *At tech-free camps, people pay hundreds to unplug.* All Tech Considered, National Public Radio. Retrieved from http://www.npr.org/sections/alltechconsidered/2013/07/05/198402213/at-tech-free-camps-people-pay-hundreds-to-unplug

Balasch, J. (2010). Aging and infertility: An overview. *Gynecological Endocrinology, 26*(12), 855–860.

Baldwin, T. T., Bedell, M. D., & Johnson, J. L. (1997). The social fabric of a team-based M.B.A. program: Network effects on student satisfaction and performance. *Academic Management Journal, 40*(6), 1369–1397.

Ball, M. M., Perkins, M. M., Hollingsworth, C., Whittington, F. J., & King, S. V. (2009). Pathways to assisted living: The influence of race and class. *Journal of Applied Gerontology, 28*(1), 81–108.

Balogun, J., & Johnson, G. (2004). Organizational restructuring and middle manager sensemaking. *Academy of Management Journal, 47*(4), 523–549.

Balsam, P. D., Fairhurst, S., & Gallistel, C. R. (2006). Pavlovian contingencies and temporal information. *Journal of Experimental Psychology: Animal Behavior Processes, 32*(3), 284–294. doi:10.1037/0097-7403.32.3.284

Banaschewski, T., Becker, K., Scherag, S., Franke, B., & Coghill, D. (2010). Molecular genetics of attention-deficit/hyperactivity disorder: An overview. *European Child & Adolescent Psychiatry, 19*(3), 237–257.

Bandura, A. (1976). Social learning analysis of aggression. In E. Ribes-Inesta, A. Bandura (Eds.), *Analysis of delinquency and aggression.* Oxford, England: Erlbaum.

Bandura, A. (1977a). Self-efficacy: Toward a unifying theory of behavioral change. *Psychology Review, 84*(2), 191–215.

Bandura, A. (1977b). *Social learning theory.* Oxford, England: Prentice Hall.

Bandura, A. (1982). Self-efficacy mechanism in human agency. *American Psychologist, 37*(2), 122–147. doi:10.1037/0003-066X.37.2.122

Bandura, A. (1986). *Social foundations of thought and action: A social cognitive theory.* Englewood Cliffs, NJ: Prentice Hall.

Bandura, A. (1993). Perceived self-efficacy in cognitive development and functioning. *Educational Psychologist, 28*(2), 117–149.

Bandura, A. (2001a). Social cognitive theory: An agentic perspective. In S. T. Fiske (Ed.), *Annual review of psychology* (Vol. 52, pp. 1–26). Palo Alto, CA: Annual Reviews.

Bandura, A. (2001b). Social cognitive theory of mass communication. *Media Psychology, 3*(3), 265–299. doi:10.1207/S1532785XMEP0303_03

Bandura, A. (2006). Going global with social cognitive theory: From prospect to paydirt. In S. I. Donaldson, D. E. Berger, & K. Pezdek (Eds.), *Applied psychology: New frontiers and rewarding careers* (pp. 53–79). Mahwah, NJ: Erlbaum.

Bandura, A. (2011). But what about that gigantic elephant in the room? In R. M. Arkin (Ed.), *Most underappreciated: 50 prominent social psychologists describe their most unloved work* (pp. 51–59). New York, NY: Oxford University Press.

Barbaris, N. (2013). Thirty years of prospect theory in economics: A review and assessment. *Journal of Economic Perspectives, 27,* 173–196.

Bargh, J. A., Gollwitzer, P. M., Lee-Chai, A. Y., Barndollar, K., & Troetschel, R. (2001). The automated will: Nonconscious activation and pursuit of behavioral goals. *Journal of Personality and Social Psychology, 81*(6), 1014–1027.

Barker, R. G. (1965). Explorations in ecological psychology. *American Psychologist, 20*(1), 1–14.

Barker, R. G. (1968). *Ecological psychology: Concepts and methods for studying the environment of human behavior.* Palo Alto, CA: Stanford University Press.

Barlow, D. H. (2000). Unraveling the mysteries of anxiety and its disorders from the perspective of emotion theory. *American Psychologist, 55*(11), 1247–1263.

Barrera, M. (1986). Distinctions between social support concepts, measures, and models. *American Journal of Community Psychology, 14*(4), 413–445.

Barrera, M. S. (2000). Social support research in community psychology. In J. Rappaport & E. Seidman (Eds.), *Handbook of community psychology* (pp. 215–246). New York, NY: Springer.

Barta, T., Kleiner, M., & Neumann, T. (2012, April). Is there a payoff from top-team diversity. *McKinsey Quarterly.* Retrieved from http://www.mckinsey.com/insights/organization/is_there_a_payoff_from_top-team-diversity

Bassuk, S. S., & Manson, J. E. (1985). Epidemiological evidence for the role of physical activity in reducing risk of Type 2 diabetes and cardiovascular disease. *Journal of Applied Physiology, 99*(3), 1193–1204.

Bateson, G. (2000). *Steps to an ecology of mind: Collected essays in anthropology, psychiatry, evolution, and epistemology.* Chicago, IL: University of Chicago Press.

Baumeister, R. F. (1991). *Meanings of life.* New York, NY: Guilford.

Baumeister, R. F. (2000). Gender differences in erotic plasticity: The female sex drive as socially flexible and responsive. *Psychological Bulletin, 126*(3), 347–374. doi:10.1037/0033-2909.126.3.347

Baumeister, R. F. (2004). Gender and erotic plasticity: Sociocultural influences on the sex drive. *Sexual and Relationship Therapy, 19*(2), 133–139. doi:10.1080/14681990410001691343

Baumeister, R. F., Sparks, E. A., Stillman, T. F., & Vohs, K. D. (2008). Free will in consumer behavior: Self-control, ego depletion and choice. *Journal of Consumer Psychology, 18*(1), 4–13. doi:10.1016/j.jcps.2007.10.002

Baumeister, R. F., Vohs, K. D., Aaker, J., & Garbinsky, E. N. (2013). Some key differences between a happy life and a meaningful life. *Journal of Positive Psychology, 8*(6), 505–516.

Baumeister, R. F., Vohs, K. D., DeWall, C. N., & Zhang, L. (2007). How emotion shapes behavior: Feedback, anticipation, and reflection, rather than direct causation. *Personality and Social Psychology Review, 11*(2), 167–203.

Bearman, P., Moody, J., & Stovel, K. (2004). Chains of affection. *American Journal of Sociology, 110*(1), 44–91.

Beck, A. T. (1975). *Cognitive therapy and the emotional disorders.* Madison, CT: International Universities Press.

Beck, A. T. (1997). The past and future of cognitive therapy. *Journal of Psychotherapy Practice & Research, 6*(4), 276–284.

Beck, A. T., Rush, J., Shaw, B. F., & Emery, G. (1987). *Cognitive therapy of depression.* New York, NY: Guilford.

Beck, J. (2011). *Cognitive behavior therapy: Basics and beyond.* New York, NY: Guilford.

Becker, M. W., Alzahabi, R., & Hopwood, C. J. (2013). Media multitasking is associated with symptoms of depression and social anxiety. *Cyberpsychology, Behavior, and Social Networking, 16*(2), 132–135.

Bengtsson, H. (2005). Children's cognitive appraisal of others' distressful and positive experiences. *International Journal of Behavioral Development, 27*(5), 457–466.

Benjamin, L. T., Jr. (2004). A history of clinical psychology as a profession in America (and a glimpse at its future). *Annual Review of Clinical Psychology, 1*(1), 1–30.

Bennett, K. M. (2007). No sissy stuff: Toward a theory of masculinity and emotional expression in older widowed men. *Journal of Aging Studies, 21*(4), 347–356.

Bennett, K. M., Smith, P. T., & Hughes, G. M. (2005). Coping, depressive feelings, and gender differences in late life widowhood. *Aging and Mental Health, 9*(4), 348–353.

Benz, J., Sedensky, M., Tompson, T., & Agiesta, J. (2013). *Working longer: Older Americans' attitudes on work and retirement.* Chicago, IL: NORC Center for Public Affairs Research.

Bergin, A. E. (1991). Values and religious issues in psychotherapy and mental health. *American Psychologist, 46*(4), 394–403.

Berk, L. E. (2006). *Development through the lifespan* (4th ed.). Boston, MA: Allyn & Bacon.

Berk, L. E. (2009). *Development through the lifespan.* Boston, MA: Pearson Education.

Berk, L. E. (2014a). *Exploring human development.* Boston, MA: Allyn & Bacon.

Berk, L. E. (2014b). *Exploring lifespan development.* Upper Saddle River, NJ: Pearson.

Berkman, F., Seeman, T., Albert, M., Blazer, D., Kahn, R., Mohs, R., . . . McClearn, G. (1993). High, usual, and impaired functioning in community dwelling older men and women: Findings from the MacArthur Foundation research network on successful aging. *Journal of Clinical Epidemiology, 46*(10), 1129–1140.

Bernheim, B. D., Garrett, D. M., & Maki, D. M. (2001). Education and saving: The long-term effects of high school financial curriculum mandates. *Journal of Public Economics, 80*(3), 436–467.

Berntson, G. G., Sarter, M., & Cacioppo, J. T. (2003). Ascending visceral regulation of cortical affective information processing. *European Journal of Neuroscience, 18*(8), 2103–2109.

Berrios, G. E. (1997). The origins of psychosurgery: Shaw, Burckhardt, and Moniz. *History of Psychiatry, 8*(29), 61–81.

Berry, J. (2004). An ecological perspective on the development of competence. In R. Sternberg & E. Grigorenko (Eds.), *Culture and competence* (pp. 3–22). Washington, DC: American Psychological Association.

Bertsch, S., & Pesta, B. (2014). Generating active learning. In V. A. Benassi, C. E. Overson, C. M. Hakala, V. A. Benassi, C. E. Overson, & C. M. Hakala (Eds.), *Applying science of learning in education: Infusing psychological science into the curriculum* (pp. 71–77). Washington, DC: Society for the Teaching of Psychology.

Beutler, I., & Dickson, L. (2008). Consumer economic socialization. In J.J. Xiao (Ed.), *Handbook of consumer finance research* (pp. 83–103). New York, NY: Springer.

Bewley, T. (2008). *Madness to mental illness: A history of the Royal College of Psychiatrists.* London, England: The Royal College of Psychiatrists.

Birger, J. (2015). *Date-onomics: How dating became a lopsided numbers game.* New York, NY: Workman Publishing Company.

Bleuler, M. (1974). The offspring of schizophrenics. *Schizophrenia Bulletin, 1*, 93–109.

Blieszner, R., & Roberto, K. A. (2012). Partners and friends in adulthood. In S. K. Whitbourne & M. J. Sliwinski (Eds.), *The Wiley-Blackwell handbook of adulthood and aging* (pp. 381–398). Malden, MA: Wiley-Blackwell.

Block, M., & Zautra, A. (1981). Satisfaction and distress in a community: A test of the effects of life events. *American Journal of Community Psychology, 9*(2), 165–180. doi:10.1007/BF00896365

Blumenthal, J. A., Babyak, M. A., Doraiswamy, P. M., Watkins, L., Hoffman, B., Barbour, K., . . . & Sherwood, A. (2007). Exercise and pharmacotherapy in the treatment of major depressive disorder. *Psychosomatic Medicine, 69*, 587–596.

Blustein, D. L. (2006). *The psychology of working: A new perspective for career development, counseling, and public policy.* New York, NY: Routledge.

Blustein, D. L. (2008). The role of work in psychological health and well-being: A conceptual, historical, and public policy perspective. *American Psychologist, 63*(4), 228.

Board of Governors of the Federal Reserve System. (2013). *2013 Survey of consumer finances.* Retrieved from http://www.federalreserve.gov/econresdata/scf/scfindex.htm

Bolsen, T. (2013). A light bulb goes on: Norms, rhetoric, and actions for the public good. *Political Behavior, 35*(1), 1–20.

Bond, R., & Smith, P. (1996). Culture and conformity: A meta-analysis of studies using Asch's line judgment task. *Psychological Bulletin, 119*(1), 111–137.

Bordia, P., Hohman, E., Jones, L., & Callan, V. (2004). Uncertainty during organizational change: Types, consequences, and management strategies. *Journal of Business and Psychology, 18*(4), 507–532.

Boring, E. (1950). *A history of experimental psychology* (2nd ed.). New York, NY: Prentice Hall.

Boswell, G., Kahana, E., & Dilworth-Anderson, P. (2006). Spirituality and healthy lifestyle behaviors: Stress counterbalancing effects on the well-being older adults. *Journal of Religion and Health, 45*(4), 587–602.

Bowen, K. S., Uchino, B. N., Birmingham, W., Carlisle, M., Smith, T. W., & Light, K. C. (2014). The stress-buffering effects of functional social support on ambulatory blood pressure. *Health Psychology, 33*(11), 1440–1443. doi:10.1037/hea0000005

Bowlby, J. (1969). *Attachment and loss: Vol. 1, Attachment.* New York, NY: Basic Books.

Bowman, N. A., Brandenberger, J. W., Hill, P. L., & Lapsley, D. K. (2011). The long-term impact of college diversity experiences: Well-being and social concerns 13 years after graduation. *Journal of College Student Development, 52*(6), 729–739.

Boyce, C. J., Wood, A. M., Banks, J., Clark, A. E., & Brown, G. D. A. (2013). Money, well-being, and loss aversion: Does an income loss have a greater effect on well-being than an equivalent income gain? *Psychological Science, 24*, 2557–2562.

Boyd, D. (2014). *It's complicated: The social lives of networked teens.* New Haven, CT: Yale University Press.

Bratter, B., & Dennis, H. (2008). *Project renewment: The first retirement model for career women.* New York, NY: Scribner.

Braxton, N., Lang, D., Sales, J., Wingood, G., & DiClemente, R. (2007). The role of spirituality in sustaining the psychological well-being of HIV-positive black women. *Women and Health, 46*(2–3), 113–129.

Breger, L. (2000). *Freud: Darkness in the midst of vision.* Hoboken, NJ: Wiley.

Breiding, M. J., Black, M. C., & Ryan, G. W. (2008). Chronic disease and health risk behaviors associated with intimate partner violence—18 US states/territories, 2005. *Annals of Epidemiology, 18*(7), 538–544.

Breland, K., & Breland, M. (1961). The misbehavior of organisms. *American Psychologist, 16*(11), 681–684.

Brewer, M. B. (1999). The psychology of prejudice: In-group love or out-group hate? *Journal of Social Issues, 55*(3), 429–444.

Brewer, M. B., & Miller, N. (1988). Contact and cooperation: When do they work? In P. A. Katz, D. A. Taylor, P. A. Katz, & D. A. Taylor (Eds.), *Eliminating racism: Profiles in controversy* (pp. 315–326). New York, NY: Plenum.

Brissette, I., Scheier, M. F., & Carver, C. S. (2002). The role of optimism in social network development, coping, and psychological adjustment during a life transition. *Journal of Personality and Social Psychology, 82*(1), 102–111.

Bronfenbrenner, U. (1979). Contexts of child rearing: Problems and prospects. *American Psychologist, 34*(10), 844–850. doi:10.1037/0003-066X.34.10.844

Bronfenbrenner, U. (1993). The ecology of cognitive development: Research models and fugitive findings. In R. H. Wozniak & K. W. Fischer (Eds.), *Development in context: Acting and thinking in specific environments* (pp. 3–44). Hillsdale, NJ: Erlbaum.

Bronk, K. C., Hill, P., Lapsley, D., Talib, N., & Finch, W. H. (2009). Purpose, hope, and life satisfaction in three age groups. *Journal of Positive Psychology, 4*(6), 500–510.

Brooks-Gunn, J. (2003). Do you believe in magic? What we can expect from early childhood intervention programs. *Social Policy Report of the Society for Research in Child Development, 17*(1), 3–14.

Brown, P. C., Roediger, H., & McDaniel, M. A. (2014). *Make it stick: The science of successful learning.* Cambridge, MA: Belknap Press.

Brown, S. D., Lamp, K., Telander, K., & Hacker, J. (2013). Career counseling as prevention. In E. Vera (Ed.), *Oxford handbook of prevention in counseling psychology* (pp. 374–392). New York, NY: Oxford University Press.

Brown, S. D., & Lent, R. (2005). *Career development and counseling: Putting theory and research to work.* Hoboken, NJ: Wiley.

Buechel, E. C., & Morewedge, C. K. (2014). The (relative and absolute) subjective value of money. In E. H. Biljleveld & H. Aarts (Eds.), *The psychological science of money* (pp. 93–120). New York, NY: Springer.

Buehler, R., Griffin, D. W., & Ross, M. (1994). Exploring the "planning fallacy": Why people underestimate their task completion times. *Journal of Personality and Social Psychology, 67*(3), 366–381.

Bukowski, W., Motzoi, C., & Meyer, F. (2009). Friendship as process, function, and outcome. In K. Rubin, W. Bukowski, & B. Laursen (Eds.), *Handbook of peer interactions, relationships, and groups* (pp. 217–231). New York, NY: Guilford.

Bureau of Justice Statistics. (2009). *Female victims of violence.* U.S. Department of Justice, Office of Justice Programs, NCJ 228356. Retrieved from http://www.bjs.gov/content/pub/pdf/fvv.pdf

Burger, J. M. (2009). Replicating Milgram: Would people still obey today? *American Psychologist, 64*(1), 1–11.

Burger, J. M., & Arkin, R. M. (1980). Prediction, control, and learned helplessness. *Journal of Personality and Social Psychology, 38*(3), 482–491.

Burke, B., Martens, A., & Faucher, E. (2010). Two decades of terror management theory: A meta-analysis of mortality salience research. *Personality and Social Psychology Review, 14*, 155–195.

Burns, K. (2009). *The amazing adventures of working girl: Real life career advice you can actually use.* Philadelphia, PA: Running Press.

Burrow, A., & Hill, P. (2013). Derailed by diversity? Purpose buffers the relationship between ethnic composition on trains and passenger negative mood. *Personality and Social Psychology Bulletin, 39*(12), 1610–1619.

Burrow, A., Stanley, M., Sumner, R., & Hill, P. (2014). Purpose in life as a resource for increasing comfort with ethnic diversity. *Personality and Social Psychology Bulletin, 40*(11), 1507–1511.

Burt, R., Kilduff, M., & Tasselli, S. (2013). Social network analysis: Foundations and frontiers on advantage, *Annual Review of Psychology, 64*, 527–547.

Butler, A. C., Chapman, J. E., Forman, E. M., & Beck, A. T. (2006). The empirical status of cognitive behvioral therapy: A review of meta-analyses. *Clinical Psychology Review, 26*(1), 17–31.

Buxton, O. M., Cain, S. W., O'Connor, S. P., Porter, J. H., Duffy, J. F., Wang, W., . . . Shea, S. A. (2012). Adverse metabolic consequences in humans of prolonged sleep restriction combined with circadian disruption. *Science Translational Medicine, 4*, 129ra43. Retrieved from http://stm.sciencemag.org/content/4/129/129ra43.abstract

Caciopp o, J. T., Cacioppo, S., Gonzaga, G. C., Ogburn, E. L., & VanderWeele, T. J. (2013). Marital satisfaction and break-ups differ across on-line and off-line meeting venues. *Proceedings of the National Academy of Sciences, USA, 110*(25), 10135–10140.

Cacioppo, J. T., Hawkley, L. C., Rickett, E. M., & Masi, C. M. (2005). Sociality, spirituality, and meaning making: Chicago health, aging, and social relations study. *Review of General Psychology, 9*(2), 143–155.

Cali, B. E., Coleman, J. M., & Campbell, C. (2013). Stranger danger? Women's self-protection intent and the continuing stigma of online dating. *Cyberpsychology, Behavior & Social Networking, 16*(12), 853–857.

Camara, W., O'Connor, R., Mattern, K., & Hanson, M. (Eds.). (2015). Beyond academics: A holistic framework for enhancing education and workplace success. *ACT Research Report Series, 4*, 1–100. Retrieved from http://www.act.org/content/dam/act/unsecured/documents/RR2015-4-beyond-academics-a-holistic-framework-for-enhancing-education-and-workplace-success.pdf

Camilleri, N., & Makhoul, S. (2013). ADHD: From childhood into adulthood. *Malta Medical Journal*, *25*(1), 2–7.

Cannon, W. (1915). *Bodily changes in pain, hunger, fear, and rage: An account of recent researches into the function of emotional excitement*. New York, NY: Appleton-Century-Crofts.

Cannon, W. (1929). *Bodily changes in pain, hunger, fear, and rage*. New York, NY: Appleton-Century-Crofts.

Carmon, Z., Wertenbroch, K., & Zeelenberg, M. (2003). Option attachment: When deliberating makes choosing feel like losing. *Journal of Consumer Research*, *30*(1), 15–29.

Carter, T. J. (2014). The psychological science of spending money. In E. Bijleved & H. Aarts (Eds.), *The psychological science of money* (pp. 213–242). New York, NY: Springer.

Carter, T. J., & Gilovich, T. (2010). Relative relativity of material and experiential purchases. *Journal of Personality and Social Psychology*, *98*(1), 146–159.

Carter, T. J., & Gilovich, T. (2012). I am what I do, not what I have: The differential centrality of experiential and material purchases to the self. *Journal of Personality and Social Psychology*, *102*(6), 1304–1317.

Carver, C. S., Scheier, M. F., & Weintraub, J. K. (1989). Assessing coping strategies: A theoretically based approach. *Journal of Personality and Social Psychology, 56*(2), 267–283.

Carver, K., Joyner, K., & Udry, J. (2003). National estimates of adolescent romantic relationships. In R. Florsheim (Ed.), *Adolescent romantic relations and sexual behavior: Theory, research, and practical implications* (pp. 23–56). Mahwah, NJ: Erlbaum.

Cedarblad, M., & Hansson, K. (1995). Sense of coherence: A concept influencing health and quality of life in a Swedish psychiatric at-risk group. *Israel Journal of Medical Sciences, 32*(3–4), 194–199.

Ceja, M. (2006). Understanding the role of parents and siblings as information sources in the college choice process of Chicana students. *Journal of College Student Development, 47*(1), 87–104.

Center for the Digital Future. (2009, April). *The 2009 digital future report: Surveying the digital future—Year eight*. Los Angeles, CA: Author.

Center for Hearing and Communication. (2012). *Facts about hearing loss*. Retrieved from www.chchearing.org/about-hearing-loss/facts-about-hearing-loss

Centers for Disease Control and Prevention. (2010a). *The National Intimate Partner and Sexual Violence Survey*. Retrieved from http://www.cdc.gov/violenceprevention/nisvs/index.html

Centers for Disease Control and Prevention. (2010b, June 4). Youth risk behavior surveillance—United States, 2009. *MMWR, 59*(SS-5). Retrieved from http://www.cdc.gov/mmwr/pdf/ss/ss5905.pdf

Centers for Disease Control and Prevention. (2014). *Life expectancies*. Retrieved from http://www.cdc.gov/nchs/fastats/life-expectancy.htm

Centers for Disease Control and Prevention. (2015a). *Facts about ASD*. Retrieved from http://www.cdc.gov/ncbddd/autism/facts.html

Centers for Disease Control and Prevention. (2015b). *Suicide and self-inflicted injury*. Retrieved from http://www.cdc.gov/nchs/fastats/suicide.htm

Centers for Disease Control and Prevention. (2015c). *Suicide facts at a glance*. Retrieved from http://www.cdc.gov/violenceprevention/pdf/suicide-datasheet-a.pdf

Cerasoli, C. P., & Ford, M. T. (2014). Intrinsic motivation, performance, and the mediating role of mastery goal orientation: A test of self-determination theory. *The Journal of Psychology: Interdisciplinary and Applied*, *148*(3), 267–286. doi:10.1080/00223980.2013.783778

Cerasoli, C. P., Nicklin, J. M., & Ford, M. T. (2014). Intrinsic motivation and extrinsic incentives jointly predict performance: A 40-year meta-analysis. *Psychological Bulletin, 140*(4), 980–1008. doi:10.1037/a0035661

Champion, R. (2003). A matter of vocabulary: Performance of low-income African American children the Peabody Picture Vocabulary Test. *Communication Disorders Quarterly, 24*(3), 121–127.

Chan, W. C. (n.d.). The butterfly dream. *The Philosopher, 83*(2). Retrieved from http://www.the-philosopher.co.uk/butter.htm

Chandler, M. J., Lalonde, C. E., Sokol, B. W., & Hallett, D. (2003). Personal persistence, identity development, and suicide: A study of native and non-native North American adolescents. *Monographs of the Society for Research in Child Development, 68*(2, Serial No. 273).

Chandra, A., Mosher, W. D., Copen, C., & Sionean, C. (2011). *Sexual behavior, sexual attraction, and sexual identity in the United States: Data from the 2006–2008 National Survey of Family Growth*. Atlanta, GA: Centers for Disease Control and Prevention.

Chartrand, J. M., Martin, W. F., Robbins, S. B., McAuliffe, G. J., Pickering, J. W., & Calliotte, J. A. (1994). Testing a level versus an interactional view of career indecision. *Journal of Career Assessment, 2*(1), 55–69.

Chaves, A. P., Diemer, M. A., Blustein, D. L., Gallagher, L. A., DeVoy, J. E., Casares, M. T., & Perry, J. C. (2004). Conceptions of work: The view from urban youth. *Journal of Counseling Psychology, 51*(3), 275–286.

Chemers, M., Hu, L., & Garcia, B. (2001, March). Academic self-efficacy and first-year college student performance and adjustment. *Journal of Educational Psychology, 93*(1), 55–64.

Cheng, C., Lau, H., & Chan, M. (2014). Coping flexibility and psychological adjustment to stressful life changes: Meta-analytic review. *Psychological Bulletin, 140*(6), 1582–1607.

Chess, S., & Thomas, A. (1991). Temperament and the concept of goodness of fit. In J. Strelau & A. Angleitner (Eds.), *Explorations in temperament: International perspectives on theory and measurement* (pp. 15–28). New York, NY: Plenum.

Chess, S., & Thomas, A. (1999). *Goodness of fit: Clinical applications from infancy through adult life*. New York, NY: Routledge.

Chima, F. O. (2004). Depression and the workplace: Occupational social work development and intervention. *Employee Assistance Quarterly, 19*(4), 1–20.

Choy, S. (2001). *Students whose parents did not go to college: Postsecondary access, persistence, and attainment* (NCES 2001-126). Washington, DC: U.S. Department of Education, National Center for Education Statistics, Government Printing Office.

Christakis, N., & Fowler, J. (2009). *Connected: The surprising power of our social networks and how they shape our lives.* New York, NY: Little, Brown.

Christenson, S. L., & Thurlow, M. L. (2004). School dropouts: Prevention considerations, interventions, and challenges. *Current Directions in Psychological Science, 13*(1), 36–39.

Christie, C., Jolivette, K., & Nelson, M. (2007). School characteristics related to high school dropout rates. *Remedial and Special Education, 28*(6), 325–339.

Cialdini, R. B., Borden, R. J., Thorne, A., Walker, M. R., Freeman, S., & Sloan, L. R. (1976). *Basking in reflected glory: Three (football) field studies. Journal of Personality and Social Psychology, 34*(3), 366–375.

Cialdini, R., & Goldstein, N. (2004). Social influence: Compliance and conformity. *Annual Review of Psychology, 55,* 591–621.

Cialdini, R. B., Kallgren, C. A., & Reno, R. R. (1991). A focus theory of normative conduct: A theoretical refinement and reevaluation of the role of norms in human behavior, *Advances in Experimental Social Psychology, 24,* 201–234.

Cicchetti, D., & Toth, S. L. (1998). The development of depression in children and adolescents. *American Psychologist, 53*(2), 221–241.

Cicchetti, D., & Toth, S. L. (2009). The past achievements and future promises of developmental psychopathology: The coming of age of a discipline. *Journal of Child Psychology and Psychiatry, 50*(1–2), 16–25.

Clark, C., Martin, R., van Kempen, E., Alfred, T., Head, J., Davies, H. W., . . .Stansfeld, S. A. (2006). Exposure-effect relations between aircraft and road traffic noise exposure at school and reading comprehension. *American Journal of Epidemiology, 163*(1), 27–37.

Clark, R., Anderson, N. B., Clark, V. R., & Williams, D. R. (1999). Racism as a stressor for African Americans: A biopsychosocial model. *American Psychologist, 54*(10), 805–816.

Clark, R. A., Harden, S. L., & Johnson, W. B. (2000). Mentor relationships in clinical psychology doctoral training: Results of a national survey. *Teaching of Psychology, 27*(4), 262–268.

Clark-Stewart, K. A., & Brentano, C. (2006). *Divorce: Causes and consequences.* New Haven, CT: Yale University Press.

Clarke, A. (2006). Coping with interpersonal stress and psychological health among children and adolescents: A meta-analysis. *Journal of Youth and Adolescence, 35*(1), 11–24.

Coan, J. A., Schaefer, H. S., & Davidson, R. J. (2006). Lending a hand social regulation of the neural response to threat. *Psychological science, 17*(12), 1032–1039.

Cohen, S. (2004). Social relations and health. *American Psychologist, 59*(8), 676–684.

Cohen, S., Kamarck, T., & Mermelstein, R. (1983). A global measure of perceived stress. *Journal of Health and Social Behavior, 24*(4), 385–396.

Cohen, S., Mermelstein, R., Kamarck, T., & Hoberman, H. (1985). Measuring the functional components of social support. In I. G. Sarason & B. R. Sarason (Eds.), *Social support: Theory, research, and application* (pp. 73–94). The Hague, Netherlands: Martinus Nijhoff.

Cohen, S., & Wills, T. (1985). Stress, social support, and the buffering hypothesis. *Psychological Bulletin, 98*(2), 310–357.

Colby, S. L., & Ortman, J. M. (2014, May). *The baby boom cohort in the United States: 2012 to 2060: Population estimates and projections.* U.S. Census Bureau. Retrieved from https://www.census.gov/prod/2014pubs/p25-1141.pdf

Colby, S. L., & Ortman, J. M. (2014). Projections of the size and composition of the U.S. population: 2014 to 2060, Current Population Reports (P25–P1143). Washington, DC: U.S. Census Bureau. Retrieved from https://www.census.gov/content/dam/Census/library/publications/2015/demo/p251143.pdf

Cole, S. W., Hawkley, L. C., Arevalo, J. M., & Cacioppo, J. T. (2011). Transcript origin analysis identifies antigen-presenting cells as primary targets of socially regulated gene expression in leukocytes. *Proceedings of the National Academy of Sciences, 108*(7), 3080–3085.

Coleman, R., & Rainwater, L. (1978). *Social standing in America.* New York, NY: Basic Books.

Collins, W. A., & Masden, S. D. (2006). Personal relationships in adolescence and early adulthood. In A. L. Vangelisti & D. Perlman (Eds.), *The Cambridge handbook of personal relationships* (pp. 191–209). New York, NY: Cambridge University Press.

Compas, B. (2006). Psychobiological processes of stress and coping: Implications for resilience in children and adolescents—Comments. *Annals of the New York Academy of Science, 1094*(1), 226–234.

Compas, B., Connor-Smith, J., Saltzman, H., Thomsen, A., & Wadsworth, M. (2001). Coping with stress during childhood and adolescence: Progress, problems, and potential. *Psychological Bulletin, 127*(1), 241–257.

Computer History Museum. (2016). *Timeline of computer history.* Retrieved from http://www.computerhistory.org/timeline/1933

Connell, J. P., Spencer, M. B., & Aber, J. L. (1994). Educational risk and resilience in African-American youth: Context, self, action, and outcomes in school. *Child Development, 65*(2), 493–506.

Connidis, I. A. (2010). *Family ties and aging.* Thousand Oaks, CA: Pine Forge Press.

Connors, D., & Davies, G. (2015). *History of money* (4th ed.). Cardiff: University of Wales Press.

Cooper, M. L. (2002). Alcohol use and risky sexual behavior among college students and youth: Evaluating the evidence. *Journal of Studies on Alcohol, 14*(14), 101–117.

Copeland, W. E., Wolke, D., Angold, A., & Costello, J. (2013). Adult psychiatric outcomes of bullying and being bullied by peers in childhood and adolescence. *Journal of the American Medical Association, 70*(4), 419–426. doi:10.1001/jamapsychiatry.2013.504

Couch, D., Liamputtong, P., & Pitts, M. (2012). What are the real and perceived risks and dangers of online dating?

Perspectives from online daters. *Health, Risk & Society*, *14*(7–8), 697–714.

Cowen, E. L. (1994). The enhancement of psychological wellness: Challenges and opportunities. *American Journal of Community Psychology, 22*(2), 149–179.

Cowen, E. L. (1998). Changing concepts of prevention in mental health. *Journal of Mental Health, 7*(5), 451–461. doi:10.1080/09638239817833

Cox, K., & McAdams, D. P. (2014). Meaning making during high and low point life story episodes predicts emotion regulation two years later: How the past informs the future. *Journal of Research in Personality, 50*(1), 5066–5070.

Craik, F. I. M., & Lockhart, R. S. (1972). Levels of processing: A framework for memory research. *Journal of Verbal Learning and Verbal Behavior, 11*(6), 671–684.

Crandall, C. S., & Stangor, C. (2005). Conformity and prejudice. In J. F. Dovidio, P. Glick, L. A. Rudman, J. F. Dovidio, P. Glick, & L. A. Rudman (Eds.), *On the nature of prejudice: Fifty years after Allport* (pp. 295-309). Malden, MA: Blackwell.

Crofford, L. J. (2007). Violence, stress, and somatic syndromes. *Trauma, Violence, & Abuse, 8*(3), 299–313.

Cross-Disorder Group of the Psychiatric Genomics Consortium. (2013). Identification of risk loci with shared effects on five major psychiatric disorders: A genome-wide analysis. *The Lancet, 381*(9875), 1371–1379.

Crumbaugh, J. C., & Maholick, J. (1964). An experimental study in existentialism: The psychometric approach to Frankl's concept of noogenic neurosis. *Journal of Clinical Psychology, 20*(2), 200–207.

Cruz, J. (2013). *Marriage more than a century of change*. National Center for Family & Marriage Research. Retrieved from http://www.bgsu.edu/content/dam/BGSU/college-of-arts-and-sciences/NCFMR/documents/FP/FP-13-13.pdf

Csikszentmihalyi, M. (1997). *Finding flow: The psychology of engagement with everyday life*. New York, NY: Basic Books.

Csikszentmihalyi, M. (2008). *Flow*. New York, NY: Harper Perennial.

Cunningham, M. (2001). The influence of parental attitudes and behaviors on children's attitudes toward gender and household labor in early adulthood. *Journal of Marriage and Family, 63*(1), 111–122.

Dahlin, L., & Cedarblad, M. (2009). Salutogenesis: Protective factors for individuals brought up in a high-risk environment with regard to the risk for mental or social disorder. *Nordic Journal of Psychiatry, 47*(1), 53–60.

Danes, S. M., & Haberman, H. (2007). Teen financial knowledge, self-efficacy, and behavior: A gendered view. *Financial Counseling and Planning, 18*(2), 48–60.

Daughton, J. M., & Kratochvil, C. J. (2009). Review of ADHD pharmacotherapies: advantages, disadvantages, and clinical pearls. *Journal of the American Academy of Child and Adolescent Psychiatry, 48*(3), 240–248.

Davidson, R. J., & Harrington, A. (2001). *Visions of compassion: Western scientists and Tibetan Buddhists examine human nature*. New York, NY: Oxford University Press.

Davidson, R. J., Kabat-Zinn, J., Schumacher, J., Rosenkranz, M., Muller, D., Santorelli, S. F., . . . Sheridan, J. F. (2003). Alterations in brain and immune function produced by mindfulness meditation. *Psychosomatic Medicine, 65*(4), 564–570.

Davidson, R. J., & Kaszniak, A. W. (2015). Conceptual and methodological issues in research on mindfulness and meditation. *American Psychologist, 70*(7), 581–592.

Davidson, R., & Lutz, A. (2008). Buddha's brain: Neuroplasticity and meditation. *IEEE Signal Processing Magazine, 25*(1), 174–176.

Davis, S. N., & Greenstein, T. N. (2009). Gender ideology: Components, predictors, and consequences. *Annual Review of Sociology, 35*, 87–105.

Day, S. X., & Rounds, J. (1998). Universality of vocational interest structure among racial and ethnic minorities. *American Psychologist, 53*(7), 728–736.

Dean, A., & Lin, N. (1977). The stress-buffering role of social support. *Journal of Nervous and Mental Diseases, 165*(6), 403–417.

Deci, E. L., & Ryan, R. M. (1985). *Intrinsic motivation and self-determination in human behavior*. New York, NY: Plenum.

Deci, E. L., & Ryan, R. M. (2008). Self-determination theory: A macrotheory of human motivation, development, and health. *Canadian Psychology/Psychologie Canadienne, 49*(3), 182–185. doi:10.1037/a0012801

DeGruy, F. V., & Etz, R. S. (2010). Attending to the whole person in the patient-centered medical home: The case for incorporating mental health care, substance abuse care, and health behavior change. *Families, Systems, & Health, 28*(4), 298–307.

DeLongis, A., Coyne, J. C., Dakof, G., Folkman, S., & Lazarus, R. S. (1982). Relationship of daily hassles, uplifts, and major life events to health status. *Health Psychology, 1*(2), 119–136.

DeNavas-Walt, C., Proctor, B. D., & Smith, J. C. (2011, September). Income, poverty, and health insurance coverage in the United States: 2010. *Current Population Reports, U.S. Census Bureau* (P60-239). Washington, DC: Government Printing Office.

Dennis, H., & Fike, K. T. (2012). Retirement planning: New context, process, language, and players. In J. W. Hedge & W. C. Borman (Eds.), *The Oxford handbook of work and aging* (pp. 538–548). New York, NY: Oxford University Press.

Derogatis, L., & Coons, H. (1993). Self-report measures of stress. In L. Goldberger & S. Breznitz (Eds.), *Handbook of stress: Theoretical and clinical aspects* (2nd ed.). New York, NY: Free Press.

Devine, P. G. (1989). Stereotypes and prejudice: Their automatic and controlled components. *Journal of Personality and Social Psychology, 56*(1), 5–18.

Devine, P. G. (2001). Implicit prejudice and stereotyping: How automatic are they: Introduction to the special section. *Journal of Personality and Social Psychology, 81*(5), 757–759.

Devine, P. G., Plant, E. A., Amodio, D. M., Harmon-Jones, E., & Vance, S. L. (2002). The regulation of explicit and implicit race bias: The role of motivations to respond without prejudice. *Journal of Personality and Social Psychology, 82*(5), 835–848. doi:10.1037/0022-3514.82.5.835

de Vries, D. A., & Kuhne, R. (2015). Facebook and self-perception: Individual susceptibility to negative social comparison on Facebook. *Personality and Individual Differences, 86*, 217–221.

DeWitz, S., Woolsey, M., Walsh, W. (2009). College student retention: An exploration of the relationship between self-efficacy beliefs and purpose in life among college students. *Journal of College Student Development, 50*(1), 19–34.

Dhar, R., & Wertenbroch, K. (2000). Consumer choice between hedonic and utilitarian goods. *Journal of Marketing Research, 37*, 60–71.

Diamond, L. M. (2008). Female bisexuality from adolescence to adulthood: Results from a 10-year longitudinal study. *Developmental Psychology, 44*(1), 5–14.

Diamond, L. M., & Savin-Williams, R. (2009). Adolescent sexuality. In R. Lerner & L. Sternberg (Eds.), *Handbook of adolescent psychology* (pp. 479–523). Hoboken, NJ: Wiley.

DiBlasio, F. A. (2000). Decision-based forgiveness treatment in cases of marital infidelity. *Psychotherapy: Theory, Research, Practice, Training, 37*(2), 149–158.

Dick, D. M., Rose, R. J., Viken, R. J., Kaprio, J., & Koskenvuo, M. (2001). Exploring gene–environment interactions: Socioregional moderation of alcohol use. *Journal of Abnormal Psychology, 110*(4), 625–632.

Dick, D. M., Viken, R., Purcell, S., Kaprio, J., Pulkkinen, L., & Rose, R. J. (2007). Parental monitoring moderates the importance of genetic and environmental influences on adolescent smoking. *Journal of Abnormal Psychology, 116*(1), 213–218.

Dickson, N., Paul, C., & Herbison, P. (2003). Same-sex attraction in a birth cohort: Prevalence and persistence in early adulthood. *Social Science & Medicine, 56*(8), 1607–1615.

Diemer, M. A., Mistry, R. S., Wadsworth, M. E., López, I., & Reimers, F. (2013). Best practices in conceptualizing and measuring social class in psychological research. *Analyses of Social Issues and Public Policy, 13*(1), 77–113. doi:10.1111/asap.1200112001

Diener, E., Ng, W., Harter, J., & Arora, R. (2010). Wealth and happiness across the world: Material prosperity predicts life evaluation, whereas psychosocial prosperity predicts positive feeling. *Journal of Personality and Social Psychology, 99*(1), 52–61.

Diener, E., Tay, L., & Oishi, S. (2013). Rising income and the subjective well-being of nations. *Journal of Personality and Social Psychology, 104*(2), 267–276.

DiFonzo, N., & Bordia, P. (2007). Tumor, gossip and urban legends. *Diogenes, 54*(1), 19–35.

Digman, J. M. (1990). Personality structure: Emergence of the five-factor model. *Annual Review of Psychology, 41*, 417–440.

Dimidjian, S., & Segal, Z. V. (2015). Prospects for a clinical science of mindfulness based intervention. *American Psychologist, 70*(7), 593–560.

DiPlacido, J. (1998). Minority stress among lesbians, gay men, and bisexuals. In G. Herek (Ed.), *Stigma and sexual orientation: Understanding prejudice against lesbians, gay men, and bisexuals* (pp. 138–159). Thousand Oaks, CA: Sage.

Dodge, K. A., Coie, J. D., & Lynam, D. (2006). Aggression and antisocial behavior in youth. In N. Eisenberg (Ed.), *Handbook of child psychology: Social, emotional, and personality development* (pp. 719–788). Hoboken, NJ: Wiley.

Dohrenwend, B. (2006). Inventorying stressful life events as risk factors for psychopathology: Toward resolution of the problem of intracategory variability. *Psychological Bulletin, 132*, 477–495.

Doka, K. J., & Martin, T. (2010). *Grieving beyond gender: Understanding the ways men and women mourn.* New York, NY: Routledge.

Dollard, J., Doob, L., Miller, N., Mower, O. H., & Sears, R. (1939). *Frustration and aggression.* New Haven, CT: Yale University Press. doi:10.1037/10022-000

Dollard, J., & Miller, N. E. (1950). *Personality and psychotherapy: An analysis in terms of learning, thinking, and culture.* New York, NY: McGraw-Hill.

Donnay, D. A. C., Morris, M. L., Schaubhut, N. A., & Thompson, R. C. (2005). *Strong Interest Inventory manual: Research, development, and strategies for interpretation.* Mountain View, CA: Consulting Psychology Press.

Dovidio, J. F., & Gaertner, S. L. (2010). Intergroup bias. In S. T. Fiske, D. T. Gilbert, & G. Lindzey (Eds.), *Handbook of social psychology* (Vol. 2, 5th ed., pp. 1084–1121). Hoboken, NJ: Wiley.

Dovidio, J. F., Isen, A. M., Guerra, P., Gaertner, S. L., & Rust, M. (1998). Positive affect, cognition, and the reduction of intergroup bias. In C. Sedikides, J. Schopler, C. A. Insko, C. Sedikides, J. Schopler, & C. A. Insko (Eds.), *Intergroup cognition and intergroup behavior* (pp. 337–366). Mahwah, NJ: Erlbaum.

Dovidio, J. F., Kawakami, K., Johnson, C., Johnson, B., & Howard, A. (1997). On the nature of prejudice: Automatic and controlled processes. *Journal of Experimental Social Psychology, 33*(5), 510–540.

Dovidio, J. F., ten Vergert, M., Stewart, T. L., Gaertner, S. L., Johnson, J. D., Esses, V. M., . . . Pearson, A. R. (2004). Perspective and prejudice: Antecedents and mediating mechanisms. *Personality and Social Psychology Bulletin, 30*(12), 1537–1549.

DuBois, D. L., Portillo, N., Rhodes, J. E., Silverthorn, N., & Valentine, J. C. (2011). How effective are mentoring programs for youth? A systematic assessment of the evidence. *Psychological Science in the Public Interest, 12*, 257–291.

Duckworth, A. L., Peterson, C., Matthews, M. D., & Kelly, D. R. (2007). Grit: Perseverance and passion for long-term goals. *Journal of Personality and Social Psychology, 92*(6), 1087–1101.

Dunkel, C. S., & Sefcek, J. A. (2009). Eriksonian lifespan theory and life history theory: An integration using the example of identity formation. *Review of General Psychology, 13*(1), 13–23. doi:10.1037/a0013687

Dunn, E., & Norton, M. (2014). *Happy money: The science of happier spending.* New York, NY: Simon & Schuster.

Dunn, E. W., Aknin, L. B., & Norton, M. I. (2014). Prosocial spending and happiness: Using money to benefit others pays off. *Current Directions in Psychological Science, 23*(1), 41–47. doi:10.1177/0963721413512503

Dweck, C. S. (2002). Messages that motivate: How praise molds students' beliefs, motivation, and performance (in surprising ways). In J. Aronson (Ed.), *Improving academic achievement: Impact of psychological factors on education* (pp. 37–60). San Diego, CA: Academic Press.

Dweck, C. S. (2006). *Mindset*. New York, NY: Ballantine.

Dweck, C. S. (2007). The perils and promise of praise. *Educational Leadership, 65*(2), 34–39.

Easterlin, R. A. (2003). Explaining happiness. *Proceedings of the National Academy of Sciences, USA, 100*(19), 11176–11183.

Easterlin, R. A., McVey, L. A., Switek, M., Sawangfa, O., & Smith Zweig, J. (2010). The happiness–income paradox revisited. *Proceedings of the National Academy of Sciences, USA, 107*(52), 22463–22468. doi:10.1073/pnas.1015962107

Eby, L. T., Allen, T. D., Hoffman, B. J., Baranik, L. E., Sauer, J. B., Baldwin, S., & Evans, S. (2013). An interdisciplinary meta-analysis of the potential antecedents, correlates, and consequences of protégé perceptions of mentoring. *Psychological Bulletin, 139*(2), 441–476. doi:10.1037/a0029279

Eccles, J., Adler, T., Futterman, R., Goff, S., Kaczala, C., Meece, J., & Midgley, C. (1983). Expectancies, values, and academic behaviors. In J. Spence (Ed.), *Achievement and achievement motives* (pp. 78–147). San Francisco, CA: Freeman.

Eccles, J., & Roeser, R. (2009). Schools, academic motivation, and stage-environment fit. In R. Lerner & L. Sternberg (Eds.), *Handbook of adolescent psychology* (pp. 404–434). Hoboken, NJ: Wiley.

Edwards, B. A., O'Driscoll, D. M., Ali, A., Jordan, A., Trinder, J., & Malhotra, A. (2010). Aging and sleep: Physiology and pathophysiology. *Seminars in Respiratory Critical Care Medicine, 31*(5), 618–633.

Eid, M., & Diener, E. (2001). Rules for experiencing emotions in different cultures: Inter- and intranational differences. *Journal of Personality and Social Psychology, 81*(5), 869–885.

Eisenberg, N. (2003). Prosocial behavior, empathy, and sympathy. In M. Bornstein & L. Davidson (Eds.), *Well-being: Positive development across the life course* (pp. 253–265). Mahwah, NJ: Erlbaum.

Eisenberg, N., Fabes, R. A., Shepard, S. A., Murphy, B. C., Jones, S., & Guthrie, I. K. (1998). Contemporaneous and longitudinal prediction of children's sympathy from dispositional regulation and emotionality. *Developmental Psychology, 34*(5), 910–924.

Eisenberger, N. I. (2012). Broken hearts and broken bones: A neural perspective on the similarities between social and physical pain. *Current Directions in Psychological Science, 21*(1), 42–47.

Eisenberger, N. I., Lieberman, M. D., & Williams, K. D. (2003). Does rejection hurt: An fMRI study of social exclusion. *Science, 302*(5643), 290–292.

Elder, G. H., Jr., & Conger, R. D. (2000). *Children of the land*. Chicago, IL: University of Chicago Press.

El-Hai, J. (2005). *The lobotomist: A maverick medical genius and his tragic quest to rid the world of mental illness*. Hoboken, NJ: Wiley.

Elliott, M. A. (2002). *The culture concept: Writing and difference in the age of realism*. Minneapolis: University of Minnesota Press.

Ellison, N. B., Hancock, J. T., & Toma, C. L. (2012). Profile as promise: A framework for conceptualizing veracity in online dating self-presentations. *New Media & Society, 14*(1), 45–62.

Elwert, F., & Chistakis, N. A. (2006). Widowhood and race. *American Sociological Review, 71*(1), 16–41.

Endler, N. S. (1975). A person-situation interaction model for anxiety. In C. D. Spielberger & I. G. Sarason (Eds.), *Stress and anxiety* (Vol. 1). Washington, DC: Hemisphere Publications.

Eng, P., Rimm, E., Fitzmaurice, G., & Kawachi, I. (2002). Social ties and change in social ties in relation to subsequent total and cause-specific mortality and coronary heart disease incidence in men. *American Journal of Epidemiology, 155*(8), 700–709. doi:10.1093/aje/155.8.700

Engel, G. L. (1980). The clinical application of the biopsychosocial model. *American Journal of Psychiatry, 137*(5), 535–544.

Engle, J., Bermeo, A., & O'Brien, C. (2006). *Straight from the source: What works for first-generation college students*. Washington, DC: The Pell Institute for the Study of Higher Education. Retrieved from http://www.pellinstitute.org/publications.html

Englund, M., Kuo, S., Puig, J., & Collins, W. (2011). Early roots of adult competence: The significance of close relationship. *International Journal of Behavioral Development, 35*(6), 490–496.

Entwisle, D. R., Alexander, K. L., & Olson, L. S. (2005) First grade and educational attainment by age 22: A new story. *American Journal of Sociology, 110*(5), 1458–1502.

Epel, E. S., Blackburn, E. H., Lin, J., Dhabar, F. S., Adler, N. E., Morrow, J. D., & Cawthon, R. M. (2004). Accelerated telomere shortening in response to life stress. *Proceedings of the National Academy of Sciences, USA, 101*(49), 17312–17315.

Epel, E. S., Merkin, S. S., Cawthon, R., Blackburn, E., Adler, N., Pletcher, M., & Seeman, T., (2009). The rate of leukocyte telomere shortening predicts mortality from cardiovascular disease in elderly men: A novel demonstration. *Aging, 1*(1), 81–88.

Erev, I., & Barron, G. (2005). On adaptation, maximization, and reinforcement learning among cognitive strategies. *Psychological Review, 112*(4), 912–931. doi:10.1037/0033-295X.112.4.912

Erikson, E. H. (1950). *Childhood and society*. New York, NY: Norton.

Erikson, E. H. (1993). *Identity, youth and crisis*. New York, NY: Norton. (Original work published 1968)

Eriksson, M., & Lindstrom, B. (2005). Validity of Antonovsky's sense of coherence scale: A systematic review. *Journal of Epidemiology and Community Health, 59*(6), 460–466. doi:10.1136/jech.2003.018085

Eriksson, M., & Lindstrom, B. (2007). Antonovsky's sense of coherence scale and its relation with quality of life: A systematic review. *Journal of Epidemiology and Community Health, 61*(11), 938–944. doi:10.1136/jech.2006.056028

Ershler, W. B., & Keller, E. T. (2000). Age-associated increased interleukin-6 gene expression, late-life diseases, and frailty. *Annual Review of Medicine, 51*, 245–270.

Ersner-Hershfield, H., Garton, T., Ballard, Samanez-Larking, G., & Knutson, B. (2009). Don't stop thinking about tomorrow: Individual differences in future self-continuity account for saving, *Judgment and Decision Making, 4*(4), 280–286.

Ersner-Hershfield, H., Wimmer, G.E., & Knutson, B. (2009). Saving for the future self: Neural measures of future self-continuity predict temporal discounting. *Social Cognition and Affective Neuroscience, 4*, 85–92. doi:10.1093/scan/nsn042

Eschleman, K. J., Bowling, N. A., & Alarcon, G. M. (2010). A meta-analytic examination of hardiness. *International Journal of Stress Management, 17*(4), 277–307.

Espelage, D. L., & Holt, M. K. (2012). Understanding and preventing bullying and sex harassment in school. In K. R. Harris, S. Graham, T. Urdan, S. Graham, J. M. Royer, & M. Zeidner, *APA educational psychology handbook, Vol 2: Individual differences and cultural and contextual factors* (pp. 391–416). Washington, DC: American Psychological Association.

Estes, W. K. (1950). Toward a statistical theory of learning. *Psychological Review, 57*(2), 94–107.

Estes, W. K. (1964). Probability learning. In A. W. Melton (Ed.), *Categories of human learning* (pp. 89–128). New York, NY: Academic Press.

Estes, W. K. (1976). The cognitive side of probability learning. *Psychological Review, 83*(1), 37–64.

Fagundas, C., & Way, B. (2014). Early-life stress and adult inflammation. Current *Directions in Psychological Science, 4*, 277–283.

Fallon, A. E., & Rozin, P. (1985). Sex differences in perceptions of desirable body shape. *Journal of Abnormal Psychology, 94*(1), 102–105.

Fang, R., Landis, B., Zhang, Z., Anderson, M. H., Shaw, J. D., & Kilduff, M. (2015). Integrating personality and social networks: A meta-analysis of personality, network position, and work outcomes in organizations. *Organization Science, 26*(4), 1243–1260. doi:10.1287/orsc.2015.0972

Fedzechkina, M., Jaeger, T., & Newport, E. (2011). Functional biases in language learning: Evidence from word order and case-marking interaction. In L. Carlson, C. Hölscher, & T. Shipley (Eds.), *Proceedings of the 33rd annual conference of the Cognitive Science Society* (pp. 318–323). Austin, TX: Cognitive Science Society.

Field, T., Hernandez-Reif, M., Diego, M., Schanberg, S., & Kuhn, C. (2005). Cortisol decreases and serotonin and dopamine increase following massage therapy. *International Journal of Neuroscience, 115*(10), 1397–1413.

Field, T. M. (1998). Massage therapy effects. *American Psychologist, 53*(12), 1270–1281.

Feldman, M. D., & Moreno-John, G. (2014). Intimate partner violence. In M. D. Feldman, J. F. Christensen, & J. M. Satterfield (Eds.), *Behavioral medicine: A guide for clinical practice* (4th ed., pp. 436–441). New York, NY: McGraw-Hill.

Feldman, R., Weller, A., Sirota, L., & Eidelman, A. I. (2002). Skin-to-skin contact (kangaroo care) promotes self-regulation in premature infants: Sleep-wake cyclicity, arousal modulation, and sustained exploration. *Developmental Psychology, 38*(2), 194–207. doi:10.1037/0012-1649.38.2.194

Felner, R., Jason, L., Moritsugu, J., & Farber, S. (Eds.). (1983). *Preventive psychology: Theory, research and practice.* New York, NY: Pergamon.

Ferrari, P., & Coude, G. (2011). Mirror neurons and imitation from a developmental and evolutionary perspective. In A. Vilian, C. Abry, J. L. Schwartz, & J. Vauclair (Eds.), *Primate communication and human language* (pp. 121–138). Amsterdam, Netherlands: John Benjamins.

Ferster, C. B., & Skinner, B. F. (1957). *Schedules of reinforcement.* East Norwalk, CT: Appleton-Century-Crofts. doi:10.1037/10627-000

Fifer, W., & Moon, C. (1989). Psychobiology of newborn auditory preferences. *Seminars in Perinatology, 13*(5), 430–433.

Finkel, E. J., Eastwick, P. W., Karney, B. R., Reis, H. T., & Sprecher, S. (2012). Online dating: A critical analysis from the perspective of psychological science. *Psychological Science in the Public Interest, 13*(1), 3–66.

Fiske, S. (1998). Stereotyping, prejudice, and discrimination. In D. T. Gilbert & S. T. Fiske (Eds.), *The handbook of social psychology* (4th ed., Vol. 1, pp. 357–441). New York, NY: McGraw-Hill.

Flavell, J. H. (1996). Piaget's legacy. *Psychological Science, 7*(4), 200–203.

Flavin, M. A. (1981). The adjustment of consumption to changing expectations about future income. *Journal of Political Economy, 89*(5), 974–1009.

Folkman, S., Lazarus, R., Dunkel-Schetter, C., DeLongis, A., & Gruen, R. (1986). Dynamics of a stressful encounter: Cognitive appraisal, coping, and encounter outcomes. *Journal of Personality and Social Psychology, 50*(5), 992–1003. doi:10.1037/0022-3514.50.5.992

Foltz, J. L., Cook, S. R., Szilagyi, P. G., Auinger, P., Stewart, P. A., Bucher, S., . . . Baldwin, C. D. (2011). U.S. adolescent nutrition, exercise, and screen time baseline levels prior to national recommendations. *Clinical Pediatrics, 50*(5), 424–433.

Forste, R., & Heaton, T. B. (2004). The divorce generation: Well-being, family attitudes, and socioeconomic consequences of marital disruption. *Journal of Divorce & Remarriage, 41*(1–2), 95–114.

Foster, G. D., Sherman, S., Borradaile, K. E., Grundy, K. M., Vander Veur, S. S., Nachmani, J., . . . Shults, J. (2008). A policy-based school intervention to prevent overweight and obesity. *Pediatrics, 121*(4), e794–e802.

Fouad, N. A., & Byars-Winston, A. (2005). Cultural context of career choice: Meta-analysis of race/ethnicity differences. *The Career Development Quarterly, 53*(3), 223–233.

Fouad, N. A., & Bynner, J. (2008). Work transitions. *American Psychologist, 63*(4), 241–251.

Francis, D., Diorio, J., Liu, D., & Meaney, M. J. (1999). Nongenomic transmission across generations of maternal behavior and stress responses in the rat. *Science, 286*(5442), 1155–1158.

Frankl, V. E. (1985). *Man's search for meaning* (Rev. ed.). New York, NY: Washington Square Press. (Original work published 1959)

Fredrickson, B. (2013). Positive emotions broaden and build. In P. Devine & A. Plant (Eds.), *Advances in experimental social psychology* (Vol. 47, pp. 1–53). Burlington, VT: Academic Press.

Freeman, S., Eddy, S. L., McDonough, M., Smith, M. K., Okoroafor, N., Jordt, H., & Wenderoth, M. P. (2014). Active learning increases student performance in science, engineering, and mathematics. *Proceedings of the National Academy of Sciences, USA, 111*(23), 8410–8415.

Frensch, P. A., & Runger, D. (2003). Implicit learning. *Current Directions in Psychological Science, 12*(1), 13. doi:10.1111/1467-8721.01213

Fretz, B. R., Kluge, N. A., Ossana, S. M., Jones, S. M., & Merikangas, M. W. (1989). Intervention targets for reducing preretirement anxiety and depression. *Journal of Counseling Psychology, 36*(3), 301–307.

Freud, S. (1955). *The interpretation of dreams* (J. Strachey, Trans.). New York, NY: Basic Books. (Original work published 1899)

Freudenberg, N., & Ruglis, J. (2007). Reframing school dropout as a public health issue. *Preventing Chronic Disease, 4*(4), A107.

Friedline, T. L., Elliott, W., & Nam, I. (2011). Predicting savings from adolescence to young adulthood: A propensity score approach. *Journal of the Society for Social Work and Research, 2*(1), 1–22. doi:10.5243/jsswr.2010.13

Friedman, H. S., & Martin, L. (2011). *The longevity project.* New York, NY: Hudson Street Press.

Friend, D. J., Cleary Bradley, R. P., Thatcher, R., & Gottman, J. M. (2011). Typologies of intimate partner violence: Evaluation of a screening instrument for differentiation. *Journal of Family Violence, 26*, 551–563.

Frimer, J. A., Schaefer, N. K., & Oakes, H. (2014). Moral actor, selfish agent. *Journal of Personality and Social Psychology, 106*(5), 790–802. doi:10.1037/a0036040

Frimer, J. A., & Walker, L. J. (2009). Reconciling the self and morality: An empirical model of moral centrality development. *Developmental Psychology, 45*(6), 1669–1681.

Frimer, J. A., Walker, L. J., Dunlop, W. L., Lee, B. H., & Riches, A. (2011). The integration of agency and communion in moral personality: Evidence of enlightened self-interest. *Journal of Personality and Social Psychology, 101*(1), 149–163.

Frimer, J. A., Walker, L. J., Lee, B. H., Riches, A., & Dunlop, W. L. (2012). Hierarchical integration of agency and communion: A study of influential moral figures. *Journal of Personality, 80*(4), 1117–1145. doi-10.1111/j.1467-6494.2012.00764.x

Fritsche, I., Jonas, E., Fischer. P., Koranyi, N., Berger, N., & Fleischmann, B. (2007). Mortality salience and the desire for offspring. *Journal of Experimental Social Psychology, 43*(5), 753–762.

Fulghum, R. (1993). *All I really need to know I learned in kindergarten.* New York, NY: Ballantine.

Furnham, A. (1993). *Reaching for the counter. The new child consumers—Regulation or education? (Risk controversies).* London, England: Social Affairs Unit.

Furnham, A. (2008). *The economic socialization of young people.* London, England: The Social Affairs Unit.

Gaertner, S. L., & Dovidio, J. F. (1986). The aversive form of racism. In J. F. Dovidio & S. L. Gaertner (Eds.), *Prejudice, discrimination, and racism* (pp. 61–86). Orlando, FL: Academic Press.

Gaertner, S. L., Mann, J., Murrell, A., & Dovidio, J. F. (1989). Reducing intergroup bias: The benefits of recategorization. *Journal of Personality and Social Psychology, 57*(2), 239–249.

Gaillot, M. T., & Baumeister, R. F. (2007). The psychology of willpower: Linking blood glucose to self-control. *Personality and Social Psychology Review, 11*, 303–327.

Gallistel, C., & Matzel, L. (2013). The neuroscience of learning: Beyond the Hebbian synapse. *Annual Review of Psychology, 64*, 169–200. doi:10.1146/annurevpsych-113011-143807.

Galvin, A. (2014). Insights about adolescent behavior, plasticity, ad policy from neuroscience research. *Neuron, 83*(2), 262–265.

Gamino, L. A., Easterling, L. W., & Sewell, K. W. (2003). The role of spiritual experience in adapting to bereavement. In G. R. Cox, R. A. Bendiksen, & R. G. Stevenson (Eds.), *Making sense of death: Spiritual, pastoral, and personal aspects of death, dying, and bereavement* (pp. 13–27). Amityville, NY: Baywood.

Garber, C. E., Blissmer, B., Deschenes, M. R., Franklin, B. A., Lamonte, M. J., Lee, I. M., . . . American College of Sports Medicine. (2011). American College of Sports Medicine stand. Quantity and quality of exercise for developing and maintaining cardiorespiratory, musculoskeletal, and neuromotor fitness in apparently healthy adults: Guidance for prescribing exercise. *Medicine and Science in Sports and Exercise, 43*(7), 1334–1359.

Garbinsky, E. N., Klesse, A., & Aaker, J. (2014). Money in the bank: Feeling powerful increases saving. *Journal of Consumer Research, 41*(3), 610–623. doi:10.1086/676965

Garces, E., Thomas, D., & Currie, J. (2000). Long-term effects of head start. *Princeton Publications.* Retrieved from http://www.princeton.edu/~jcurrie/publications/Longer_Term_Effects_HeadSt.pdf

Garcia, J., Kimeldorf, D. J., & Koelling, R. A. (1955). Conditioned aversion to saccharin resulting from exposure to gamma radiation. *Science, 122*(3160), 157–158.

Garcia, J., & Koelling, R. A. (1966). Relation of cue to consequence in avoidance learning. *Psychosomatic Science, 4*(3), 123–124.

Garcia, J., Lasiter, P. S., Bermudez-Rattoni, F., & Deems, D. A. (1985). A general theory of aversion learning. *Annals of the New York Academy of Sciences, 443*, 8–21.

Gardner, H., & Davies, K. (2013). *The app generation: How today's youth navigate identity, intimacy, and imagination in a digital world.* New Haven, CT: Yale University Press.

Garmezy, N. (1987). Stress, competence, and development: Continuities in the study of schizophrenic adults, children vulnerable to psychopathology, and the search for stress-resistant children. *American Journal of Orthopsychiatry, 57*(2), 159–174.

Garmezy, N., & Streitman, S. (1974). Children at risk: The search for the antecedents of schizophrenia: Conceptual models and research methods. *Schizophrenia Bulletin, 8*, 14–90.

Gaylord-Harden, N. K., & Cunningham, J. A. (2009). The impact of racial discrimination and coping strategies on internalizing symptoms in African American youth. *Journal of Youth and Adolescence, 38*(4), 532–543.

Gaylord-Harden, N. K., Elmore, C. A., Campbell, C. L., & Wethington, A. (2011). An examination of the tripartite model of depressive and anxiety symptoms in African American youth: Stressors and coping strategies as common and specific correlates. *Journal of Clinical Child and Adolescent Psychology, 40*(3), 360–374.

Geertz, C. (1984). From the native's point of view. In R. Shweder & R. Levine (Eds.), *Theory: Essays on mind, self and emotion* (pp. 123–136). Cambridge, England: Cambridge University Press.

Genet, J. J., & Siemer, M. (2011). Flexible control in processing affective and non-affective material predicts individual differences in trait resilience. *Cognition and Emotion, 25*(2), 380–388. doi:10.1080/02699931.2010.491647

George, L. K., Ellison, C. G., & Larson, D. B. (2002). Explaining the relationships between religious involvement and health. *Psychological Inquiry, 13*(3), 190–200.

Gettinger, M., & Seibert, J. K. (2002). Contributions of study skills to academic competence. *School Psychology Review, 31*(3), 350–365.

Gibbons, D. (2004). Friendship and advice networks in the context of changing professional values. *Administrative Science Quarterly, 49*, 238–262.

Gibbs, J. L., Ellison, N. B., & Lai, C.-H. (2011). First comes love, then comes Google: An investigation of uncertainty reduction strategies and self-disclosure in online dating. *Communication Research, 38*(1), 70–100.

Giedd, J. N., Blumenthal, J., Jeffries, N. O., Castellanos, F. X., Lui, H., Zijdenbos, A., . . . Rapoport, J. L. (1999). Brain development during childhood and adolescence: A longitudinal MRI study. *Nature Neuroscience, 2*, 861–863.

Gilbert, (2010). *The American class structure in an age of growing inequality* (8th ed.). Thousand Oaks, CA: Sage.

Gillespie, B. J., Frederick, D., Harari, L., & Grov, C. (2015). Homophily, close friendship, and life satisfaction among gay, lesbian, heterosexual, and bisexual men and women. *PLoS ONE, 10*(6), e0128900. doi:10.1371/journal.pone.0128900

Gillium, R., & Ingram, D. (2006). Frequency of attendance at religious services, hypertension, and blood pressure: The Third National Health and Nutrition Examination Survey. *Psychosomatic Medicine, 68*(3), 382–385.

Gioia, D. A., & Chittipeddi, K. (1991). Sensemaking and sensegiving in strategic change initiation. *Strategic Management Journal, 12*(6), 433–448

Glass, S. P. (2002). Couple therapy after the trauma of infidelity. In A. S. Gurman & N. S. Jacobson (Eds.), *Clinical handbook of couple therapy* (pp. 488–507). New York, NY: Guilford.

Gloria, A. M., & Rodriguez, E. R. (2000). Counseling Latino university students: Psychosociocultural issues for consideration. *Journal of Counseling & Development, 78*(2), 145-154.

Goldstein, J. (2002). *One dharma: The emerging Western Buddhism*. New York, NY: HarperCollins.

Gollaher, D. L. (1993). Dorothea Dix and the English origins of the American asylum movement. *Canadian Review of American Studies, 23*(3), 149.

Gómez, A., Dovidio, J. F., Huici, C., Gaertner, S. L., & Cuadrado, I., (2008). The other side of we: When outgroup members express common identity. *Personality and Social Psychology Bulletin, 34*, 1613-1626.

Goodenow, C., & Grady, K. E. (1993). The relationship of school belonging and friends' values to academic motivation among urban adolescent students. *The Journal of Experimental Education, 62*(1), 60–71.

Gordon, V. N. (2007). *The undecided college student: An academic and career advising challenge*. Springfield, IL: Charles C Thomas.

Gortmaker, S. L., Lee, R. M., Cradock, A. L., Sobol, A. M., Duncan, D. T., & Wang, Y. C. (2012). Disparities in youth physical activity in the United States: 2003–2006. *Medicine and Science in Sports and Exercise, 44*(5), 888–893.

Gott, M., & Hinchliff, S. (2003). How important is sex in later life? The views of older people. *Social Science and Medicine, 56*(8), 1617–1628.

Gottesman, I. I. (2001). Psychopathology through a life span-genetic prism. *American Psychologist, 56*(11), 867–878. doi:10.1037/0003-066X.56.11.867

Gottfredson, L. S. (2005). Applying Gottfredson's theory of circumspection and compromise in career guidance and counseling. In S. D. Brown & R. W. Lent (Eds.), *Career development and counseling: Putting theory and research to work* (pp. 71–100). Hoboken, NJ: Wiley.

Gottlieb, B. H. (1981). *Social networks and social support*. Beverly Hills, CA: Sage.

Gottlieb, B. H. (1997). Conceptual and measurement issues in the study of chronic stress. In B. H. Gottlieb (Ed.), *Coping with chronic stress* (pp. 3–37). New York, NY: Plenum.

Gottman, J. M. (1999). *The marriage clinic: A scientifically based marital therapy*. New York, NY: Norton.

Gottman, J. M., & Driver, J. L. (2005). Dysfunctional marital conflict and everyday marital interaction. *Journal of Divorce & Remarriage, 43*(3–4), 63–78.

Gottman, J. M., Driver, J. L., & Tabares, A. (2002). Building the sound marital house: An empirically derived couple therapy. In A. S. Gurman & N. S. Jacobson (Eds.), *Clinical handbook of couple therapy* (pp. 373–399). New York, NY: Guilford.

Gottman, J. M., Levenson, R. W., Gross, J., Frederickson, B. L., McCoy, K., Rosenthal, L., . . . Yoshimoto, D. (2003). Correlates of gay and lesbian couples' relationship satisfaction and relationship dissolution. *Journal of Homosexuality, 45*(1), 23–43.

Graham, S., Munniksma, A., & Juvonen, J. (2014). Psychosocial benefits of cross-ethnic friendships in urban middle schools. *Child Development, 85*(2), 469–483.

Graham, S., Taylor, A., & Ho, A. (2009). Race and ethnicity in peer relations research. In K. Rubin, W. Bukowski, & B. Laursen (Eds.), *Handbook of peer interactions, relationships, and groups* (pp. 394–413). New York, NY: Guilford.

Granovetter, M. (1974). *Getting a job: A study of contacts and careers*. Cambridge, MA: Harvard University Press.

Granovetter, M. S. (1973). The strength of weak ties. *The American Journal of Sociology, 78*(6), 1360–1380. doi:10.1086/225469

Granovetter, M. S. (1983). The strength of weak ties: A network theory revisited. *Sociological Theory, 1*(6), 201–233.

Graziano, W. G., & Ward, D. (1992). Probing the Big Five in adolescence: Personality and adjustment during a developmental transition. *Journal of Personality, 60*(2), 425–440.

Greater Good. (n.d.). *Compassion.* Retrieved from http://greatergood.berkeley.edu/topic/compassion/definition

Green, R.-J., Bettinger, M., & Zacks, E. (1996). Are lesbian couples fused and gay male couples disengaged? Questioning gender straightjackets. In J. Laird & R.-J. Green (Eds.), *Lesbians and gays in couples and families: A handbook for therapists* (pp. 185–230). San Francisco, CA: Jossey-Bass.

Green, R.-J., & Mitchell, V. (2002). Gay and lesbian couples in therapy: Homophobia, relational ambiguity, and social support. In A. S. Gurman & N. S. Jacobson (Eds.), *Clinical handbook of couple therapy* (pp. 546–568). New York, NY: Guilford.

Greenberg, J., Koole, S., & Pyszczynski, T. (Eds.). (2004). *Handbook of experimental existential psychology.* New York, NY: Guilford.

Greenberg, M. T., Weissberg, R. P., O'Brien, M. U., Zins, J. E., Fredericks, L., Resnik, H., & Elias, M. J. (2003). Enhancing school-based prevention and youth development through coordinated social, emotional, and academic learning. *American Psychologist, 58*(6–7), 466–474.

Greenwald, A. G., & Banaji, M. R. (1995). Implicit social cognition: Attitudes, self-esteem, and stereotypes. *Psychological Review, 102*(1), 4–27. doi:10.1037/0033-295X.102.1.4

Greenwald, A. G., Poehlman, T. A., Uhlmann, E. L., & Banaji, M. R. (2009). Understanding and using the Implicit Association Test: III. Meta-analysis of predictive validity. *Journal of Personality and Social Psychology, 97*(1), 17–41.

Grello, C. M., Welsh, D. P., & Harper, M. S. (2006). No strings attached: The nature of casual sex in college students. *Journal of Sex Research, 43*(3), 255–267.

Grello, C. M., Welsh, D. P., Harper, M. S., & Dickson, J. W. (2003). Dating and sexual relationship trajectories and adolescent functioning. *Adolescent and Family Health, 3*(3), 103–111.

Gribbin, A. (2011). A brief history of the Internet. *New Statesman, 140*(5066), 30.

Griskevicius, V., Ackerman, J. M., Cantú, S. M., Delton, A. W., Robertson, T. E., Simpson, J. A., . . . Tybur, J. M. (2013). When the economy falters, do people spend or save? Responses to resource scarcity depend on childhood environments. *Psychological Science, 24*(2) 197–205. doi:10.1177/0956797612

Gronfein, W. (1985). Psychotropic drugs and the origins of deinstitutionalization. *Social Problems, 32*(5), 437–454.

Grossmann, I., & Kross, E. (2010). The impact of culture on adaptive versus maladaptive self-reflection. *Psychological Science, 21,* 1150–1157. doi:10.1177/0956797610376655

Grossmann, I., & Kross, E. (2014). Exploring Solomon's paradox: Self-distancing eliminates the self-other asymmetry in wise reasoning about close relationships in younger and older adults. *Psychological Science, 25*(8), 1571–1580.

Grossmann, I., Na, J., Varnum, M. E. W., Kitayama, S., & Nisbett, R. E. (2013). A route to well-being: Intelligence versus wise reasoning. *Journal of Experimental Psychology: General, 142*(3), 944–953. doi:10.1037/a0029560

Grossman, P., Niemann, L., Schmidt, S., & Walach, H. (2004). Mindfulness-based stress reduction and health benefits: A meta-analysis. *Journal of Psychosomatic Research, 57*(1), 35–43.

Grov, C., Bimbi, D. S., Nanin, J. E., & Parsons, J. T. (2006). Race, ethnicity, gender, and generational factors associated with the coming-out process among gay, lesbian, and bisexual individuals. *Journal of Sex Research, 43*(2), 115–121.

Gudmunson, C. G., & Danes, S. M. (2011). Family financial socialization: Theory and critical review. *Journal of Family and Economic Issues, 32*(4), 644–667.

Gueldner, S. H., Loeb, S., Morris, D., Penrod, J., Bramlett, M., Johnston, L., & Schlotzhauer, P. (2001). A comparison of life satisfaction and mood in nursing home residents and community dwelling elders. *Archives of Psychiatric Nursing, 15*(5), 232–240.

Guiffrida, D. A. (2006). Toward a cultural advancement of Tinto's theory. *Review of Higher Education: Journal of the Association for the Study of Higher Education, 29*(4), 451–472.

Gunnar, M., & Quevedo, K. (2007). The neurobiology of stress and development. *Annual Review of Psychology, 58,* 145–173.

Gunnell, D. (2015). A population health perspective on suicide research and prevention: What we know, what we need to know, and policy priorities. *Crisis: The Journal of Crisis Intervention and Suicide Prevention, 36*(3), 155–160.

Gunter, B., & Furnham, A. (1998). *Children as consumers.* London, England: Routledge.

Gutman, L. M., Sameroff, A. J., & Cole, R. (2003). Academic growth curve trajectories from first to twelfth grades: Effects of multiple social risk and preschool child factors. *Developmental Psychology, 39*(4), 777–790.

Hair, E. C., & Graziano, W. G. (2003). Self-esteem, personality and achievement in high school: A prospective longitudinal study in Texas. *Journal of Personality, 71*(6), 971–994. doi:10.1111/1467-6494.7106004

Hall, C., Lindzey, G., & Campbell, J. (1998). *Theories of personality* (4th ed.). New York, NY: Wiley.

Hall, K. L., Feng, A. X., Moser, R. P., Stokols, D., & Taylor, B. K. (2008). Moving the science of team science forward: Collaboration and creativity. *American Journal of Preventive Medicine, 35* (2 Suppl.), S243–S245.

Hall, P. D. (1999). The effect of meditation on the academic performance of African American college students. *Journal of Black Studies, 29*(3), 408–415.

Halonen, J., & Santrock, J. (1997). *Human adjustment.* New York, NY: Brown & Benchmark.

Hames, J. L., Hagan, C. R., & Joiner, T. E. (2013). Interpersonal processes in depression, *Annual Review of Psychology, 9,* 355–377. doi:10.1146/annurev-clinpsy-050212-185553

Hamid, P. N., Yue, X. D., & Leung, C. M. (2003). Adolescent coping in different Chinese family environments. *Adolescence, 38*(149), 111–130.

Hamilton, L., & Julian, A. M. (2014). The relationship between daily hassles and sexual function in men and women.

Journal of Sex & Marital Therapy, 40(5), 379–395. doi:10. 1080/0092623X.2013.864364

Hamm, J. V. (2000). Do birds of a feather flock together? The variable bases for African American, Asian American, and European American adolescents' selection of similar friends. *Developmental Psychology, 36*(2), 209–219.

Hampton, K., Sessions, L., Her, E. J., & Rainie, L. (2009). *Social isolation and new technology: How the Internet and mobile phones impact Americans' social networks.* Washington, DC: Pew Internet & American Life Project. Retrieved from http://pewinternet.org/Reports/2009/18--Social-Isolation-and-New-Technology/Executive-Summary.aspx?r=1

Hanifan, L. J. (1916, September). The rural school community center. *The Annals of the American Academy of Political and Social Science, 67*, 130–138.

Harbaugh, W., Mayr, U., Burghart, D. (2007). Neural responses to taxation and voluntary giving reveal motives for charitable donations. *Science, 316*, 1622–1625. doi:10.1126/science.1140738

Harlow, H. F. (1958). The nature of love. *American Psychologist, 13*(12), 673–685.

Harrington, A., & Dunne, J. (2015). When mindfulness is therapy: Ethical qualms, historical perspectives. *American Psychologist, 70*(7), 621–631.

Hart, C., Newell, L., & Olsen, S. (2003). Parenting skills and social communicative competence in childhood. In J. O. Greene & B. R. Burleson (Eds.), *Handbook of communication and social interaction skills* (pp. 753–797). Mahwah, NJ: Erlbaum.

Hart, D., Eisenberg, N., & Vallente, C. (2007). Personality change at the intersection of autonomic arousal and stress. *Psychological Science, 18*, 492–497.

Hartup, W. W. (2006). Relationships in early and middle childhood. In A. L. Vangelisti & D. Perlman (Eds.), *Cambridge handbook of personal relationships* (pp. 177–190). New York, NY: Cambridge University Press.

Harvey, S., & Goudvis, A. (2000). *Strategies that work: Teaching comprehension to enhance understanding.* York, ME: Stenhouse.

Hayes, S., & Smith, S. (2005). *Get out of your mind and into your life.* Oakland, CA: New Harbinger.

Hayes, S., Strosahl, K., & Wilson, K. (2012). *Acceptance and commitment therapy: The process and practice of mindful changes.* New York, NY: Guilford.

Hays, P. (2014). *Creating well-being: Four steps to a happier, healthier life.* Washington, DC: APA Books.

Hays, R. B. (1984). The development and maintenance of friendship. *Journal of Social and Personal Relationships, 1*(1), 75–98.

Head Start Bureau. (2008). *Head Start fact sheet.* Retrieved from www.acf.hhs.gov/programs/ohs/about/fy2008.html

Hebb, D. O. (1949). *The organization of behavior.* New York, NY: Wiley.

Heckman, J. J., & Masterov, D. V. (2004). *The productivity argument for investing in young children.* Working Paper 5, Invest in Kids Working Group, Committee for Economic Development. Retrieved from jenni.uchicago.edu/Invest

Hein, G., Engelmann, J., Vollberg, M., & Tobler, P. (2016). How learning shapes the empathic brain. *Proceedings of the National Academy of Sciences, USA, 113*(1), 80–85.

Heine, S. J., Proulx, T., & Vohs, K. D. (2006). The meaning maintenance model: On the coherence of social motivations. *Personality and Social Psychology Review, 10*(2), 88–110.

Heintzelman, S. J., & King, L. A. (2014). Life is pretty meaningful. *American Psychologist, 69*(6), 561–574. doi:10.1037/a0035049

Hendrick, S., & Hendrick, C. (2002). Love. In C. Snyder & S. Lopez (Eds.), *Handbook of positive psychology* (pp. 472–484). New York, NY: Oxford University Press.

Hendry, L. B., & Kloep, M. (2002). *Lifespan development: Resources, challenges and risks.* Andover, United Kingdom: Cengage Learning EMEA.

Heppner, P. P., Heppner, M. J., Lee, D.-G., Wang, Y.-W., Park, H.-J., & Wang, L.-F. (2006). Development and validation of a collectivist coping styles inventory. *Journal of Counseling Psychology, 53*(1), 107–125.

Hernandez, M., & Newcomer, R. (2007). Assisted living and special populations. What do we know about differences in use and potential access barriers? *Gerontologist, 47*(Suppl. 1), 110–117.

Hernandez, P. R., Schultz, P., Estrada, M., Woodcock, A., & Chance, R. C. (2013). Sustaining optimal motivation: A longitudinal analysis of interventions to broaden participation of underrepresented students in STEM. *Journal of Educational Psychology, 105*(1), 89–107. doi:10.1037/a0029691

Hertenstein, M. J., Keltner, D., App, B., Bulleit, B. A., & Jaskolka, A. R. (2006). Touch communicates distinct emotions. *Emotion, 6*(3), 528.

Higgins, E. (1997). Beyond pleasure and pain. *American Psychologist, 52*, 1280–1300.

Hill, P. L., Burrow, A. L., Brandenberger, J. W., Lapsley, D. K., & Quaranto, J. C. (2010). Collegiate purpose orientations and well-being in early and middle adulthood. *Journal of Applied Developmental Psychology, 31*(2), 173–179.

Hill, P. L., & Turiano, N. (2014). Purpose in life as a predictor of mortality across adulthood. *Psychological Science, 25*(7), 1482–1486.

Hill, R. D. (2011). A positive aging framework for guiding geropsychology interventions. *Behavior Therapy, 42*(1), 66–77.

Hill, R. D. (2015). A positive aging framework for counseling older adults. In C. L. Juntunen & J. P. Schwartz (Eds.), *Counseling across the lifespan* (pp. 375–390). Thousand Oaks, CA: Sage.

Hirschberger, G., & Shaham, D. (2012). The impermanence of all things: An existentialist stance on personal and social change. In P. Shaver & M. Mikulincer (Eds.), *Meaning, mortality, and choice: The social psychology of existential concerns* (pp. 111–125). Washington, DC: American Psychological Association.

Historic England. (2015). *From Bethlehem to Bedlam: England's first mental institution.* Retrieved from https://historicengland.org.uk/research/inclusive-heritage/disability-history/1050-1485/from-bethlehem-to-bedlam

Hobfoil, S., & Vaux, A. (1993). Social support: Social resources and social context. In L. Goldberg & S. Breznitz (Eds.), *Handbook of stress: Theoretical and clinical aspects* (pp. 685–705). New York, NY: Free Press.

Hogan, R. (1982). A socioanalytic theory of personality. In M. M. Page (Ed.), *Nebraska symposium on motivation: Vol. 29. Personality: Current theory and research* (pp. 55–89). Lincoln: University of Nebraska Press.

Holbrook, C., Sousa, P., & Hahn-Holbrook, J. (2011). Unconscious vigilance: Worldview defense without adaptations for terror, coalition, or uncertainty management. *Journal of Personality and Social Psychology, 101*(3), 451–466. doi:10.1037/a0024033

Holland, J. (1997). *Making vocational choices: A theory of vocational personalities and work environments*. Odessa, FL: Psychological Assessment Resources.

Holmes, T., & Rahe, R. (1967). The social readjustment rating scale. *Journal of Psychosomatic Research, 11*(2), 213–218. doi:10.1016/0022-3999(67)90010-4

Holt-Lunstad, J., Smith, T. B., Layton, J. B. (2010). Social relationships and mortality risk: A meta-analytic review. *PLoS Medicine, 7*(7), e1000316. doi:10.1371/journal.pmed.1000316

Holtzworth-Munroe, A., Meehan, J., Rehman, U., & Marshall, A. (2002). Intimate partner violence: An introduction for couple therapists. In A. S. Gurman & N. S. Jacobson (Eds.), *Clinical handbook of couple therapy* (pp. 441–465). New York: Guilford.

Hombrados-Mendieta, M. I., Gomez-Jacinto, L., Dominguez-Fuentes, J. M., Garcia-Leiva, P., & Castro-Travé, M. (2012). Types of social support provided by parents, teachers, and classmates during adolescence. *Journal of Community Psychology, 40*(6), 645–664. doi:10.1002/jcop.20523

Hong, L., & Page, S. (2004). Groups of diverse problem solvers can outperform groups of high-ability problem solvers. *Proceedings of the National Academy of Sciences, USA, 101*(46), 16385–16389.

Hong, Y., Chiu, C., Dweck, C., Lin, D., & Wan, W. (1999). Implicit theories, attributions, and coping: A meaning system. *Journal of Personality and Social Psychology, 77*(3), 588–599.

Hu, V. W. (2013). From genes to environment: Using integrative genomics to build a "systems-level" understanding of autism spectrum disorders. *Child Development, 84*(1), 89–103.

Hudson, J. I., Hiripi, E., Pope, H. G., & Kessler, R. C. (2007). The prevalence and correlates of eating disorders in the National Comorbidity Survey Replication. *Biological Psychiatry, 61*(3), 348–358.

Hudson Kam, C. L., & Newport, E. L. (2005). Regularizing unpredictable variation: The roles of adult and child learners in language formation and change. *Language Learning and Development, 1*(2), 151–195.

Hull, C. L. (1943). *Principles of behavior: An introduction to behavior theory*. New York, NY: Appleton-Century-Crofts.

Hutteman, R., Hennecke, M., Orth, U., Reitz, A. K., & Specht, J. (2014). Developmental tasks as a framework to study personality development in adulthood and old age. *European Journal of Personality, 28*, 267–278. doi:10.1002/per.1959. Retrieved from https://www.academia.edu/6603932/Developmental_tasks_as_a_framework_to_study_personality_development_in_adulthood_and_old_age

Iacoboni, M. (2009). Imitation, empathy, and mirror neurons. *Annual Review of Psychology, 60*, 653–670.

IJzerman, H., & Semin, G. R. (2009). The thermometer of social relations: Mapping social proximity on temperature. *Psychological Science, 20*(10), 1214–1220.

Impermanence. (1993). In *The New Shorter Oxford English Dictionary*. Oxford, England: Clarendon Press.

Inagaki, T. K., & Eisenberger, N. I. (2013). Shared neural mechanisms underlying social warmth and physical warmth. *Psychological Science, 24*, 2272–2280.

Inkelas, K. K., & Weisman, J. L. (2003). Different by design: An examination of student outcomes among participants in three types of living-learning programs. *Journal of College Student Development, 44*(3), 335–368.

Insel, T. (2012). *Director's blog: Research Domain Criteria: RDoC*. Retrieved from http://www.nimh.nih.gov/about/director/2012/research-domain-criteria-rdoc.shtml

Insel, T. (2015, May 15). *Director's blog: Mental health awareness month*: By the numbers. Retrieved from http://www.nimh.nih.gov/about/director/2015/mental-health-awareness-month-by-the-numbers.shtml

International Telecommunication Union. (2015). *The world in 2015. ICT: Facts and figures*. Retrieved from http://www.itu.int/en/ITUD/Statistics/Documents/facts/ICTFactsFigures2015.pdf

Inzlicht, M., McGregor, I., Hirsh, J. B., & Nash, K. (2009). Neural markers of religious conviction. *Psychological Science, 20*(3), 385–392. doi:10.1111/j.14679280.2009.02305.x

Iqbal, H., Neal, S., & Vincent, C. (2016). Children's friendships in super-diverse localities: Encounters with social and ethnic difference. *Childhood, 1*–15.

It Gets Better Project. (2015). *About us*. Retrieved from http://www.itgetsbetter.org

Ito, T. A., Chiao, K. W., Devine, P. G., Lorig, T. S., & Cacioppo, J. T. (2006). The influence of facial feedback on race bias as measured with the Implicit Association Test. *Psychological Science, 17*, 256–261.

Ito, T. A., & Urland, G. R. (2003). Race and gender on the brain: Electrocortical measures of attention to the race and gender of multiply categorizable individuals. *Journal of Personality and Social Psychology, 85*(4), 616–626. doi:10.1037/0022-3514.85.4.616

Jahoda, M. (1958). *Current concepts of positive mental health*. New York, NY: Basic Books. Retrieved from https://archive.org/details/currentconceptso00jaho

James, J. B., & Wink, P. (2007). The third age: A rationale for research. In J. B. James & P. Wink (Eds.), *Annual review of genontology and geriatrics* (pp. xix–xxxii). New York, NY: Springer.

James, W. (1884) What is an emotion? *Mind, 9*(34), 188–205.

James, W. (1902). *The varieties of religious experience*. Retrieved from http://www.psywww.com/psyrelig/james/toc.htm

Janicak, P. G., O'Reardon, J. P., Sampson, S. M., Husain, M. M., Lisanby, S. H., Rado, J. T., . . . Demitrack, M. A. (2008).

Transcranial magnetic stimulation in the treatment of major depressive disorder: A comprehensive summary of safety experience from acute exposure, extended exposure, and during reintroduction treatment. *Journal of Clinical Psychiatry, 69*(2), 222–232.

Jayson, S. (2012, January 13–15). Stress. *USA Weekend*.

Ji, C. Y., Chen, T. J., & Working Group on Obesity in China. (2013). Empirical changes in the prevalence of overweight and obesity among Chinese students from 1985 to 2010 and corresponding preventive strategies. *Biomedical and Environmental Sciences, 26*(1), 1–12.

John, D. (1999). Consumer socialization of children: A retrospective look at twenty-five years of research. *Journal of Consumer Research, 26*(3), 183–213.

Johnson, K., & Fredrickson, B. (2005). "We all look the same to me" positive emotions eliminate the own-race bias in face recognition. *Psychological Science, 16*(11), 875–881.

Johnson, S. B., Blum, R. W., & Giedd, J. N. (2009). Adolescent maturity and the brain: The promise and pitfalls of neuroscience research in adolescent health policy. *Journal of Adolescent Health, 45*(3), 215–221.

Johnson, W. B. (2002). The intentional mentor: Strategies and guidelines for the practice of mentoring. *Professional Psychology: Research and Practice, 33*(1), 88–96.

Johnson, W. B. (2007). Student-faculty mentoring outcomes. In T. D. Allen & L. T. Eby (Eds.), *The Blackwell handbook of mentoring: A multiple perspectives approach* (pp. 189–210). Oxford, England: Blackwell. doi:10.1002/9780470691960.ch12

Jones, J. (1996). *Prejudice and racism* (2nd ed.). New York, NY: McGraw-Hill.

Jones, J., Dovidio, J., & Vietze, D. (2013). *The psychology of diversity: Beyond prejudice and racism*. Hoboken, NJ: Wiley.

Jordan, T. E., & Pope, M. L. (2001). Developmental antecedents to adolescents' occupational knowledge: A 17-year prospective study. *Journal of Vocational Behavior, 58*(2), 279–292.

Joshi, P. D., & Fast, N. (2013). Power and reduced temporal discounting. *Psychological Science, 24*(4), 432–438.

Kabat-Zinn, J. (1990). *Full catastrophe living: Using the wisdom of your body and mind to face stress, pain and illness*. New York, NY: Bantam.

Kabat-Zinn, J. (1994). *Wherever you go, there you are*. New York, NY: Hyperion Press.

Kabat-Zinn, J., Lipworth, L., & Burney, R. (1985). The clinical use of mindfulness meditation for the self-regulation of chronic pain. *Journal of Behavioral Medicine, 8*(2), 163–190.

Kahneman, D. (1994). New challenges to the rationality assumption. *Journal of Institutional and Theoretical Economics, 150*(1), 18–36.

Kahneman, D. (2003). Maps of bounded rationality: Psychology for behavioral economics. *The American Economic Review, 93*(5), 1449–1475.

Kahneman, D. (2013). *Thinking, fast and slow*. New York, NY: Macmillan.

Kahneman, D., & Deaton, A. (2010). High income improves evaluation of life but not emotional well-being. *Proceedings of the National Academy of Sciences, USA, 107*(38), 16489–16493. doi:10.1073/pnas.1011492107

Kahneman, D., & Tversky, A. (1979). Prospect theory: An analysis of decision under risk. *Econometrica, 47*(2), 263–291.

Kahneman, D., & Tversky, A. (1984). Choices, values and frames. *American Psychologist, 39*(4), 341–350.

Kalpidou, M., Costin, D., & Morris, J. (2011). The relationship between Facebook and the well-being of undergraduate college students. *Cyberpsychology, Behavior, and Social Networking, 14*(4), 183–189.

Kamiya, J. (1969). Operant control of the EEG alpha rhythm and some of its reported effects on consciousness. In E. Tart (Ed.), *Altered states of consciousness* (pp. 507–517). New York, NY: Wiley.

Kang, S.-M., & Lau, A. S. (2013). Revisiting the out-group advantage in emotion recognition in a multicultural society: Further evidence for the in-group advantage. *Emotion, 13*(2), 203–215.

Kang, Y., Gray, J. R., & Dovidio, J. F. (2014). The nondiscriminating heart: Loving kindness mediation training decreases implicit intergroup bias. *Journal of Experimental Psychology: General, 143*(3), 1306–1313.

Kang, Y., Gray, J. R., & Dovidio, J. F. (2015). The head and the heart: Effects of understanding and experiencing lovingkindness on attitudes toward the self and others. *Mindfulness, 6*(5), 1063–1070. doi:10.1007/s12671-014-0355-6

Kanner, A. D., Coyne, J. C., Schaefer, C., & Lazarus, R. S. (1981). Comparison of two modes of stress measurement: Daily hassles and uplifts versus major life events. *Journal of Behavioral Medicine, 4*(1), 1–39. doi:10.1007/BF00844845

Kashdan, T. B., & McKnight, P. E. (2013). Commitment to a purpose in life: An antidote to the suffering by individuals with social anxiety disorder. *Emotion, 13*(6), 1150–1159. doi-10.1037/a0033278

Kassam, K. S., Morewedge, C. K., Gilbert, D. T., & Wilson, T. D. (2011). Winners love winning and losers love money. *Psychological Science, 20*, 1–5. doi:10.1177/0956797611405681

Kasser, T., & Sheldon, K. (2009). Time happiness as a path toward personal happiness and ethical business practice: Empirical evidence from four studies. *Journal of Business Ethics, 84*(2), 243–255.

Kasser, V. G., & Ryan, R. M. (1999). The relation of psychological needs for autonomy and relatedness to vitality, well-being, and mortality in a nursing home. *Journal of Applied Social Psychology, 29*(5), 935–954.

Katz, P., & Taylor, D. (1988). *Eliminating racism*. New York, NY: Springer.

Kaye, W. H., Bailer, U. F., Frank, G. K., Wagner, A., & Henry, S. E. (2005). Brain imaging of serotonin after recovery from anorexia and bulimia nervosa. *Physiology and Behavior, 86*(1–2), 15–17.

Kaye, W. H., Frank, G. K., Bailer, U. F., Henry, S. E., Meltzer, C. C., Price, J. C., . . . Wagner, A. (2005). Serotonin alterations in anorexia and bulimia nervosa: New insights from imaging studies. *Physiology and Behavior, 85*(1), 73–81.

Kelley, S. S., Borawski, E. A., Flocke, S. A., & Keen, K. J. (2003). The role of sequential and concurrent sexual relationships and the risk of sexually transmitted diseases among adolescents. *Journal of Adolescent Health, 32*(4), 296–305.

Kellner, C. H., Knapp, R. G., Petrides, G., Rummans, T. A., Husain, M. M., Rasmussen, K.,... Fink, M. (2006). Continuation electroconvulsive therapy versus pharmacotherapy for relapse prevention in major depression: a multisite study from CORE. *Archives of General Psychiatry, 63*(12), 1337–1344.

Kelly, A., Conell-Price, J., Covinsky, K., Cenzer, I. S., Chang, A., Boscardin, W. J., & Smith, A. K. (2010). Length of stay for older adults residing in nursing homes at the end of life. *Journal of the American Geriatrics Society, 58*(9), 1701–1706.

Kelly, J. G. (1966). Ecological constraints on mental health services. *American Psychologist, 21*(6), 535–539. doi:10.1037/h0023598

Kelly, J. G. (2006). *Becoming ecological: An expedition into community psychology.* New York, NY: Oxford University Press.

Kelly, J. G. (2010). More thoughts: On the spirit of community psychology. *American Journal of Community Psychology, 45*(3–4), 272–284. doi:10.1007/s10464-010-9305-1

Kelly, J. G., & Chang, J. (2008). Pluralistic inquiry for the history of community psychology. *Journal of Community Psychology, 36*(5), 675–691.

Keltner, D., Haidt, J., & Shiota, M. N. (2006). Social functionalism and the evolution of emotions. In M. Schaller, J. A. Simpson, & D. T. Kenrick (Eds.), *Evolution and social psychology* (pp. 115–142). New York, NY: Psychology Press.

Kendall, P. C. (1978). Anxiety: States, traits—situations? *Journal of Consulting and Clinical Psychology, 46*(2), 280–287. doi:10.1037/0022-006X.46.2.280

Kennedy-Moore, E. (2012, February 26). Growing friendships. *Psychology Today.* Retrieved from http://www.psychology today.com/blog/growing-friendships/201202/childrens-growing-friendships

Kessler, R. C., Berglund, P., Demler, O., Jin, R., Merikangas, K. R., & Walters, E. E. (2005). Lifetime prevalence and age-of-onset distributions of *DSM-IV* disorders in the National Comorbidity Survey Replication. *Archives Of General Psychiatry, 62*(6), 593–602. doi:10.1001/archpsyc.62.6.593

Kessler, R. C., Chiu, W. T., Demler, O., & Walters, E. E. (2005). Prevalence, severity, and comorbidity of twelve-month *DSM–IV* disorders in the National Comorbidity Survey Replication (NCS-R). *Archives of General Psychiatry, 62*(6), 617–627.

Khalsa, S., McCarthy, K. S., Sharpless, B. A., Barrett, M. S., & Barber, J. P. (2011). Beliefs about the causes of depression and treatment preferences. *Journal of Clinical Psychology, 67*(6), 539–549.

Kidd, A. R., III, & Bao, J. (2012). Recent advances in the study of age-related hearing loss: A mini-review. *Genontology, 58*(6), 490–496.

Kim, J., & Hoi, K. S. (2003). Predicting children's academic achievement from early assessment scores: A validity generalization study. *Early Childhood Research Quarterly, 18*(4), 547–566.

Kimmel, H. (1974). Instrumental conditioning of automatically mediated responses in human beings. *American Psychologist, 29*, 325–335.

Kinder, D. R., & Sears, D. O. (1981). Prejudice and politics: Symbolic racism versus racial threats to the good life. *Journal of Personality and Social Psychology, 40*(3), 414–431.

Kluckhohn, C. (1954). Culture and behavior. In G. Lindzey (Ed.), *Handbook of social psychology* (Vol. 2, pp. 921–970). Cambridge, MA: Addison-Wesley

Kobasa, S. C. (1979). Stressful life events, personality and health: An inquiry into hardiness. *Journal of Personality and Social Psychology, 37*(1), 1–11.

Kobasa, S. C. (1982). Commitment and coping in stress resistance among lawyers. *Journal of Personality and Social Psychology, 42*(4), 707–717.

Kobasa, S. C., Maddi, S. R., & Courington, S. (1981). Personality and constitution as mediators of the stress–illness relationship. *Journal of Health and Social Behavior, 22*(4), 368–378.

Kobasa, S. C., Maddi, S. R., & Kahn, S. (1982). Hardiness and health: A prospective study. *Journal of Personality and Social Psychology, 42*(1), 884–890.

Kobasa, S. C., Maddi, S. R., & Puccetti, M. (1982). Personality and exercise as buffers in the stress–illness relationship. *Journal of Behavioral Medicine, 5*(4), 391–404.

Koenig, H. G. (2001). Religion and medicine II: Religion, mental health, and related behaviors. *International Journal of Psychiatry in Medicine, 31*(1), 97–109.

Kogan, S. M., Brody, G. H., & Chen, Y.-F. (2011). Natural mentoring processes deter externalizing problems among rural African American emerging adults: A prospective analysis. *American Journal of Community Psychology, 48*(3–4), 272–283.

Kokkonen, A., Esaiasson, P., & Gilljam, M. (2014). Migration-based ethnic diversity and social trust: A multilevel analysis of how country, neighbourhood and workplace diversity affects social trust in 22 countries. *Scandinavian Political Studies, 37*(3), 263–300. doi:10.1111/1467-9477.12027

Konrath, S. H., O'Brien, E. H., & Hsing, C. (2011). Changes in dispositional empathy in American college students over time: A meta-analysis. *Personality and Social Psychology Review, 15*(2), 180–198.

Koole, S. L., Greenberg, J., & Pyszczynski, T. (2006). Introducing science to the psychology of the soul: Experimental existential psychology. *Current Directions in Psychological Science, 15*(5), 212–216. doi:10.1111/j.14678721.2006.00438.x

Koolhaas, J. M., Bartolomucci, A., Buwalda, B., de Boer, S. F., Flugge, G., Korte, S. M., ... Fuchs, E. (2011). Stress revisited: A critical evaluation of the stress concept. *Neuroscience and Biobehavioral Review, 35*(5), 1291–1301.

Korotkov, D. L. (1998). The sense of coherence: Making sense out of chaos. In P. P. Wong & P. S. Fry (Eds.), *The human quest for meaning: A handbook of psychological research and clinical applications* (pp. 51–70). Mahwah, NJ: Erlbaum.

Kosciw, J. G., Greytak, E. A., Diaz, E. M., & Bartkiewicz, M. J. (2010). *The 2009 National School Climate Survey: The experiences of lesbian, gay, bisexual and transgender youth in our nation's schools.* New York, NY: GLSEN.

Kouvonen, A. M., Väänänen, A., Vahtera, J., Heponiemi, T., Koskinen, A., Cox, S. J., & Kivimäki, M. (2010). Sense of coherence and psychiatric morbidity: A 19-year register-based prospective study. *Journal of Epidemiology and Community Health, 64*(3), 255–261. doi:10.1136/jech.2008.083352

Koyanagi, C. (2007). *Learning from history: Deinstitutionalization of people with mental illness as precursor to long-term care reform.* Retrieved from https://www2.nami.org/Template.cfm?Section=About_the_Issue&Template=/ContentManagement/ContentDisplay.cfm&ContentID=137545

Krause, N. (2008). The social foundation of religious meaning in life. *Research on Aging, 30*(4), 395–427. doi:10.1177/0164027508316619

Krause, N. (2012). Religious involvement, humility, and change in self-related health over time. *Journal of Psychology and Theology, 40*(3), 199–210.

Krishnamoorthy, J. S., Hart, C., & Jelalian, E. (2006). The epidemic of childhood obesity: Review of research and implications for public policy. *Social Policy Report of the Society for Research in Child Development, 20*(2).

Kristeller, J., & Ragpay, L. (2013). *Buddhism: A blend of religion, spirituality, and psychology in APA handbook of psychology, religion, and spirituality* (Vol. 1). Washington, DC: American Psychological Association.

Kross, E., Berman, M. G., Mischel, W., Smith, E. E., & Wager, T. D. (2011). Social rejection shares somatosensory representations with physical pain. *Proceedings of the National Academy of Sciences, USA, 108*(15), 6270–6275.

Kross, E., & Grossmann, I. (2012). Boosting wisdom—Distance from the self enhances wise reasoning, attitudes, and behavior. *Journal of Experimental Psychology: General, 141*(1), 43–48. doi:10.1037/a0024158

Kross, E., Bruehlman-Senecal, E., Park, J., Burson, A., Dougherty, A., Shablack, H., . . . Ayduk, O. (2014). Self-talk as a regulatory mechanism: How you do it matters. *Journal of Personality and Social Psychology, 106*(2), 304–324.

Kuhn, D. (2009). Adolescent thinking. In R. Lerner & L. Steinberg (Eds.), *Handbook of adolescent psychology* (pp. 152–186). Hoboken, NJ: Wiley.

Kumar, R., Seay, N., & Karabenick, S. A. (2015). Immigrant Arab adolescents in ethnic enclaves: Physical and phenomenological contexts of identity negotiation. *Cultural Diversity and Ethnic Minority Psychology, 21*(2), 201–212. doi:10.1037/a0037748

Labouvie-Vief, G. (1985). Logic and self-regulation from youth to maturity: A model. In M. Commons, F. Richards, & C. Armon (Eds.), *Beyond formal operations: Late adolescent and adult cognitive development* (pp. 158–180). New York, NY: Praeger.

Ladd, G. W., Birch, S., & Buhs, E. (1999). Children's social and scholastic lives in kindergarten: Related spheres of influence? *Child Development, 70*(6), 1371–1400.

Laidra, K., Pullmann, H., & Allik, J. (2007). Personality and intelligence testing as predictors of academic achievement: A cross-sectional study from elementary to secondary school. *Personality and Individual Differences, 42*, 441–451.

Lambert, S. M., Masson, P., & Fisch, H. (2006). The male biological clock. *World Journal of Urology, 24*, 611–617.

Lang, P. (1974). Learned control of heart rate in a computer controlled environment. In P. Obrist, A. Black, J. Brener,

& L. DiCara (Eds.), *Cardiovascular psychophysiology* (pp. 392–405). Chicago, IL: Aldine.

Lanza, S. T., Valisenko, S. A., Dziak, J. J., & Butera, N. M. (2015). Trends among U.S. high school seniors in recent marijuana use and associations with other substances: 1976–2013. *Journal of Adolescent Health, 57*(2), 198–204.

Lapan, R. T., Gysbers, N. C., & Petroski, G. F. (2001). Helping seventh graders be safe and successful: A statewide study of the impact of comprehensive guidance and counseling programs. *Journal of Counseling and Development, 79*(3), 320–330.

Lasser, K., Boyd, J. W., Woolhandler, S., Himmelstein, D. U., McCormick, D., & Bor, D. H. (2000). Smoking and mental illness: A population-based prevalence study. *Journal of the American Medical Association, 284*(20), 2606–2610.

Lawrence, A. R., & Schiller Schigelone, A. R. (2002). Reciprocity beyond dyadic community: Aging related communal coping. *Research on Aging, 24*(6), 684–704.

Lawson, D. M. (2003). Incidents, explanation, and treatment of partner violence. *Journal of Counseling and Development, 81*(1), 19–32.

Lazarus, R. S. (1993). From psychological stress to the emotions: A history of changing outlooks. *Annual Review of Psychology, 44*, 1–22.

Lazarus, R. S., & Folkman, S. (1984). *Stress, appraisal, and coping.* New York, NY: Springer.

Leavy, R. (1983). Social support and psychological disorder: A review. *Journal of Community Psychology, 77*(1), 3–21.

Lee, D. L., & Ahn, S. (2011). Racial discrimination and Asian mental health: A meta-analysis. *The Counseling Psychologist, 39*(3), 463–489.

Lee, E. K. O. (2007). Religion and spirituality as predictors of well-being among Chinese American and Korean American older adults. *Journal of Religion, Spirituality & Aging, 19*(3), 77–100.

Lehr, C. A., Johnson, D. R., Bremer, C. D., Cosio, A., & Thompson, M. (2004). *Essential tools: Increasing rates of school completion: Moving from policy and research to practice.* Minneapolis, MN: ICI Publications.

Leiser, D., Sevon, G., & Levy, D. (1990). Children's economic socialization: Summarizing the cross-cultural comparison of ten countries. *Journal of Economic Psychology, 11*(4), 591–614.

Lenhart, A. (2014, April 26). *Dating and mating in the digital age.* Retrieved from http://www.pewinternet.org/2014/04/26/dating-mating-in-the-digital age

Lent, R. W., Brown, S. D., & Hackett, G. (1994). Toward a unifying social cognitive theory of career and academic interest, choice, and performance. *Journal of Vocational Behavior, 45*(1), 79–122.

Leong, F. T. L., Comas-Díaz, L., Nagayama Hall, G. C., McLoyd, V. C., & Trimble, J. E. (2014). *APA handbook of multicultural psychology, Vol. 1: Theory and research.* Washington, DC, US: American Psychological Association. doi:10.1037/14189-000

Lerner, J. V. (1983). The role of temperament in psychosocial adaptation in early adolescents: A test of a "goodness of fit" model. *The Journal of Genetic Psychology: Research and Theory on Human Development, 143*(2), 149–157.

Lerner, R. M. (1991). Changing organism-context relations as the basic process for development: A developmental contextual perspective. *Developmental Psychology, 27,* 27–32.

Lerner, R. M., Lerner, J. V., von Eye, A., Bowers, E. P., & Lewin-Bizan, S. (2011). Individual and contextual bases of thriving in adolescence: A view of the issues. *Journal of Adolescence, 34*(6), 1107–1114. doi:10.1016/j.adolescence.2011.08.001

Leserman, J., & Drossman, D. A. (2007). Relationship of abuse history to functional gastrointestinal disorders and symptoms. *Trauma, Violence, & Abuse, 8*(3), 331–343.

Leung, A. K., Maddux, W. W., Galinsky, A. D., & Chiu, C. Y. (2008). Multicultural experience enhances creativity? The when, and how. *American Psychologist, 63*(6), 169–181.

Levey, S. M. B., Miller, B. F., & deGruy, F. V., III. (2012). Behavioral health integration: An essential element of population-based health care redesign. *Translational Behavioral Medicine, 2*(3), 364–371.

Levine, R. V. (1998). *A geography of time: The temporal misadventures of a social psychologist* (Rev. ed.). New York, NY: Basic Books.

Lewin, K. (2008). *Principles of topological psychology.* Eastford, CT: Martino Fine Books. (Originally work published 1936)

Lewin, K. (2015). *Principles of topological psychology.* Eastford, CT: Martino Fine Books. (Original work published 1936)

Li-Grining, C. P., Votruba-Drzal, E., Maldonado-Carreno, C., & Haas, K. (2010). Children's early approaches to learning and academic trajectories through fifth grade. *Developmental Psychology, 46*(5), 1062–1077.

Lillard, A. (2007) *Montessori: The science behind genius.* New York, NY: Oxford University Press.

Lillard, A., & Else-Quest, N. (2006). Evaluating Montessori education. *Science, 313*(5795), 1893–1894.

Lin, N., Simeone, R., Ensel, W., & Kuo, W. (1979). Social support, stressful life events, and illness: A model and an empirical test. *Journal of Health and Social Behavior, 20*(2), 108–119.

Liptak, A. (2015, June 26). Supreme court ruling makes same-sex marriage right nationwide. *The New York Times.* Retrieved from http://www.nytimes.com/2015/06/27/us/supreme-court-same-sex-marriage.html?_r=0

Livingston, J. D., & Boyd, J. E. (2010). Correlates and consequences of internalized stigma for people living with mental illness: A systematic review and meta-analysis. *Social Science and Medicine, 71*(12), 2150–2161.

Loewenstein, G. (1996). Out of control: Visceral influences on behavior. *Organizational Behavior and Human Decision Processes, 65*(3), 272–292.

Lohoff, F. W. (2010, December). Overview of the genetics of major depressive disorder. *Current Psychiatry Reports, 12*(6), 539–546. doi:10.1007/s11920-010-0150-6

Lopez, J. D. (2005). Race-related stress and sociocultural orientation among Latino students during their transition into a predominately White, highly selective institution. *Journal of Hispanic Higher Education, 4*(4), 354–365.

Love, J. M., Tarullo, L. B., Raikes, J., & Chazan-Cohen, R. (2006) Head Start: What do we know about its effectiveness? What do we need to know? In K. McCartney & D. Phillips (Eds.), *Blackwell Handbook of early childhood development* (pp. 550–575). Malden, MA: Blackwell.

Lucas, R. E., Clark, A. E., Georgellis, Y., & Diener, E. (2004). Unemployment alters the set point for life satisfaction. *Psychological Science, 15*(1), 8–13.

Lucksted, A., & Drapalski, A. L. (2015). Self-stigma regarding mental illness: Definition, impact, and relationship to societal stigma. *Psychiatric Rehabilitation Journal, 38*(2), 99–102.

Lund, D. A., & Caserta, M. S. (2004). Facing life alone: Loss of a significant other in later life. In D. Doda (Ed.), *Living with grief: Loss in later life* (pp. 201–223). Washington, DC: Hospice Foundation of America.

Luo, Y., Hawkley, L. C., Waite, L. J., & Cacioppo, J. T. (2012). Loneliness, health, and mortality in old age: A national longitudinal study. *Social Science & Medicine, 74*(6), 907–914.

Lutgen-Sandvik, P., Namie, G., & Namie, R. (2009). Workplace bullying: Causes, consequences, and corrections. In P. Lutgen-Sandvik & B. D. Sypher (Eds.), *Destructive organizational communication* (pp. 41–89). New York, NY: Routledge.

Luthar, S. S., Cicchetti, D., & Becker, B. (2000). The construct of resilience: A critical evaluation. *Child Development, 71*(3), 543–562.

Lutz, A., Brefczynski-Lewis, J., Johnstone, T., & Davidson, R. J. (2008). Regulation of the neural circuitry of emotion by compassion meditation: Effects of meditative expertise. *PLoS ONE, 3*(3), e1897. doi:10.1371/journal.pone.0001897

Lutz, A., Greischar, L. L., Rawlings, N. B., Ricard, M., & Davidson, R. J. (2004). Long-term meditators self-induce high-amplitude gamma synchrony during mental practice. *Proceedings of the National Academy of Sciences, USA, 101*(46), 16369–16373.

Lutz, A., Jha, A., Dunne, J., & Saron, C. (2015). Investigating the phenomenological matrix of mindfulness-related practices from a neurocognitive perspective. *American Psychologist, 70*(7), 632–658.

Lyons, A. C. (2004). A profile of financially at-risk college students. *The Journal of Consumer Affairs, 38*(1), 56–80.

Maccoby, E. E. (2002). Gender and group process: A developmental perspective. *Current Directions in Psychological Science, 11*(2), 54–58.

Machado, A., & Matos, M. (2014). Male victims of partner violence: Methodological analysis of prevalence studies. *Psicologia & Sociedade, 26*(3), 726–736.

Machell, K. A., Disabato, D. J., & Kashdan, T. B. (2015). Buffering the negative impact of poverty on youth: The power of purpose in life. *Social Indicators Research, 126*(2), 845–861. doi:10.1007/s11205-015-0917-6

MacKenzie, M., & Baumeister, R. (2014). Meaning in life: Nature, needs and myths. In A. Bathyany & P. Russo-Netzer (Eds.), *Meaning in positive and existential psychology.* New York, NY: Springer.

Maddi, S. R. (2002). The story of hardiness: Twenty years of theorizing, research, and practice. *Consulting Psychology Journal: Practice and Research, 54*(3), 175–185. doi:10.1037//1061-4087.54.3.175.

Maddi, S. R. (2006). Hardiness: The courage to grow from stresses. *Journal of Positive Psychology, 1*(3), 160–168. doi:10.1080/17439760600619609

Maddi, S. R., Harvey, R. H., Khoshaba, D. M., Lu, J. L., Persico, M., & Brow, M. (2006). The personality construct of hardiness, III: Relationships with repression, innovativeness, authoritarianism, and performance. *Journal of Personality, 74*(2), 575–597.

Maddi, S. R., & Khoshaba, D. M. (2005). *Resilience at work: How to succeed no matter what life throws at yo*u. New York, NY: AMACOM.

Maddux, W. W., & Galinsky, A. D. (2009). Cultural borders and mental barriers: The relationship between living abroad and creativity. *Journal of Personality and Social Psychology, 96*(5), 1047–1061.

Maitlis, S. (2005). The social processes of organizational sensemaking. *Academy of Management Journal, 48*(1), 21–49.

Mann, J. J. (2002). A current perspective of suicide and attempted suicide. *Annals of Internal Medicine, 136*(4), 302–311.

Manning, W. D., Giordano, P. C., & Longmore, M. A. (2006). Hooking up: The relationship contexts of "nonrelationship" sex. *Journal of Adolescent Research, 21*(5), 459–483.

Markovits, H., Benenson, J., & Dolensky, E. (2001). Evidence that children and adolescents have internal models of peer interactions that are gender differentiated. *Child Development, 72*(3), 879–886.

Markus, H. R., & Kitayama, S. (1991). Culture and the self-implications for cognition, emotion, and motivation. *Psychological Review, 98*(2), 224–253.

Markus, H. R., & Kitayama, S. (2010). Cultures and selves: A cycle of mutual constitution. *Perspectives on Psychological Science, 5*(4), 420–430.

Marshall, H., & Magruder, L. (1960). Relations between parent money education practices and children's knowledge and use of money. *Child Development, 31*(2), 253–284.

Martinez, M., & Klopott, S. (2005). *The link between high school reform and college access and success for low-income and minority youth.* Washington, DC: American Youth Policy Forum and Pathways to College Network. Retrieved from http://www.aypf.org/publications/index.htm

Martin Lohfink, M., & Paulsen, M. B. (2005). Comparing the determinants of persistence for first-generation and continuing-generation students. *Journal of College Student Development, 46*(4), 409–428.

Mashburn, A. J. (2008). Quality of social and physical environments in preschools and children's development of academic, language, and literacy skills. *Applied Developmental Science, 12*(3), 113–127.

Masi, C. M., Chen, H. Y., Hawkley, L. C., & Cacioppo, J. T. (2011). A meta-analysis of interventions to reduce loneliness. *Personality and Social Psychology Review, 15*(3), 219–266

Maslow, A. H. (1943). A theory of human motivation. *Psychological Review, 50*(4), 370-396.

Masten, A. S. (2001). Ordinary magic: Resilience processes in development. *American Psychologist, 56*(3), 227–238.

Masten, A. S. (2006). Developmental psychopathology: Pathways to the future. *International Journal of Behavioral Development, 30*(1), 47–54.

Masten, A. S. (2011). Resilience in children threatened by extreme adversity: Framework for research, practice and

translational synergy. *Development and Psychopathology, 23*(2), 493–506.

Masten, A. S., Best, K. M., & Garmezy, N. (1990). Resilience and development: Contributions from the study of children who overcome adversity. *Development and Psychopathology, 2*(4), 425–444.

Masten, A. S., & Cicchetti, D. (Eds.). (2010). Developmental cascades [Special issue]. *Development and Psychopathology, 22*(3), 491–495.

Masten, A. S., & Coatsworth, J. D. (1995). Competence, resilience, and psychopathology. In D. Cicchetti & D. Cohen (Eds.), *Developmental psychopathology: Vol. 2. Risk, disorder, and adaptation* (pp. 715–752). New York, NY: Wiley.

Masten, A. S., & Tellegen, A. (2012). Resilience in developmental psychopathology: Contributions of the Project Competence Longitudinal Study. *Development and Psychopathology, 24*(2), 345–361.

Master, S. L., Eisenberger, N. I., Taylor, S. E., Naliboff, B. D., Shirinyan, D., & Lieberman, M. D. (2009). A picture's worth: Partner photographs reduce experimentally induced pain. *Psychological Science, 20*(11), 1316–1318.

Masters, R. K. (2012). Uncrossing the U.S. Black-White mortality crossover: The role of cohort forces in life course mortality risk. *Demography, 49*(3), 773–796.

Maton, K. I., Perkins, D. D., Altman, D., Gutierrez, L., Kelly, J. G., Rappaport, J., & Saegert, S. (Eds.). (2006). Community-based interdisciplinary research: Prospects, processes and approaches. *American Journal of Community Psychology, 38*, 1–139.

Maulik P., Eaton W., & Bradshaw C. (2009). The effect of social networks and social support on common mental disorders following specific life events. *Acta Psychiatrica Scandinavica, 122*(2), 118–128. doi:10.1111/j.16000447.2009.01511.x.

May, R. (1960). The emergence of existential psychology. In R. May (Ed.), *Existential psychology.* New York, NY: Random House.

May, R. (1975). *The courage to create.* New York, NY: Norton.

Mayberg, H. S., Lozano, A. M., Voon, V., McNeely, H. E., Seminowicz, D., Hamani, C., . . . Kennedy, S. H. (2005) Deep brain stimulation for treatment-resistant depression. *Neuron, 45*(5), 651–660.

Mays, V. M., Cochran, S. D., & Barnes, N. W. (2007). Race, race-based discrimination, and health outcomes among African Americans. *Annual Review of Psychology, 58*, 201–225.

Mazzeo, S. E., Gow, R. W., & Bulik, C. (2012). Integrative approaches to the prevention of eating disorders and obesity in youth: Progress, pitfalls, and possibilities. In E. Vera (Ed.), *Oxford handbook of prevention in counseling psychology* (pp. 226–249). New York, NY: Oxford University Press.

McAdams, D. P. (2013). The psychological self as actor, agent, and author. *Perspectives on Psychological Science, 8*(3), 272–295.

McAdams, D. P., & Guo, J. (2015). Narrating the generative life. *Psychological Science, 26*(4), 475–483. doi:10.1177/0956797614568318

McAdams, D. P., & McLean, K. C. (2013). Narrative identity. *Current Directions in Psychological Science, 22*(3), 233–238. doi:10.1016/j.jrp.2014.03.004

McCarthy, B. (2002). Sexuality, sexual dysfunction, and couple therapy. In A. S. Gurman & N. S. Jacobson (Eds.), *Clinical handbook of couple therapy* (pp. 629–652). New York, NY: Guilford.

McClelland, D. (1987). *Human motivation.* New York, NY: University of Cambridge.

McCormick, C. M., Kuo, S. I.-C., & Masten, A. S. (2011). Developmental tasks across the lifespan. In K. L. Fingerman, C. A. Berg, J. Smith, & T. C. Antonucci (Eds.), *Handbook of lifespan development* (pp. 117–140). New York, NY: Springer.

McCrae, R. R., & Costa, P. T., Jr. (1987). Validation of the five-factor model of personality across instruments and observers. *Journal of Personality and Social Psychology, 52*(1), 81–90.

McCullough, M. E., Enders, C. K., Brion, S. L., & Jain, A. R. (2005). The varieties of religious development in adulthood: A longitudinal investigation of religion and rational choice. *Journal of Personality and Social Psychology, 89*(1), 78–89.

McEwan, B., & Guerrero, L. K. (2012). Maintenance behavior and relationship quality as predictors of perceived availability of resources in newly formed college friendship networks. *Communication Studies, 63*(4), 421–440.

McMahon, M., & Patton, W. (1997). Gender differences in children and adolescents' perceptions of influences on their career development. *School Counselor, 44*(5), 368–376.

McPherson, M., Smith-Lovin, L., & Brashears, M. E. (2006). Social isolation in America: Changes in core discussion networks over two decades. *American Sociological Review, 71*(3), 353–375.

McQuown, C., & Sterns, H. L. (2015). Facilitating transitions through retirement. In C. Juntunen & J. Schwartz (Eds.), *Counseling across the lifespan* (pp. 391–408). Thousand Oaks, CA: Sage

McWilliams, S., & Barrett, A. E. (2013). Online dating in middle and later life: Gendered expectations and experiences. *Journal of Family Issues, 35*(3), 411–436.

Meaningfulness. (1993). In *The new shorter Oxford English dictionary.* Oxford, England: Clarendon Press.

MedlinePlus. (2016, May 11). *Autoimmune diseases.* Retrieved from http://www.nlm.nih.gov/medlineplus/autoimmune diseases.html

Meichenbaum, D. (1977). *Cognitive behavior modification: An integrative approach.* New York, NY: Plenum.

Menkin, J. A., Robles, T. F., Wiley, J. F., & Gonzaga, G. C. (2015). Online dating across the life span: Users' relationship goals. *Psychology and Aging, 30*(4), 987–993. doi:10.1037/a0039722

Merikangas, K., Jian-Ping, H., Brody, D., Fisher, P., Bourdon, K., & Koretz, D. (2010, January). Prevalence and treatment of mental disorders among US children in the 2001–2004 NHANES. *Pediatrics, 125*(1), 75–81.

Micale, M. S. (1985). The Salpêtrière in the age of Charcot: An institutional perspective on medical history in the late nineteenth century. *Journal of Contemporary History, 20,* 703–731.

Michalik, N. M., Eisenberg, N., Spinrad, T., Ladd, B., Thompson, M., & Valiente, C. (2007). Longitudinal relations among parental emotional expressivity and sympathy and prosocial behavior in adolescence. *Social Development, 16*(2), 286–309.

Milgram, S. (1963). Behavioral study of obedience. *Journal of Abnormal and Social Psychology, 67*(4), 371–378.

Milgram, S. (2009). *Obedience to authority: An experimental view.* New York, NY: Harper Perennial Modern Classics. (Original work published 1974)

Millar, H., Wardell, F., Vyvyan, J., Naji, S., Prescott, G., & Eagles J. (2005). Anorexia nervosa mortality in northeast Scotland, 1965–1999. *The American Journal of Psychiatry, 162*(4), 753–757.

Miller, A. G. (2014). The explanatory value of Milgram's obedience experiments: A contemporary appraisal. *Journal of Social Issues, 70*(3), 558–573.

Miller, B. (2015). "Dude, where's your face?" Self-presentation, self-description, and partner preferences on a social networking application for men who have sex with men: A content analysis. *Sexuality & Culture, 19*(4), 637–658.

Miller, N. E. (1978). Biofeedback and visceral learning. *Annual Review of Psychology, 29,* 373–404.

Miller, N. E., & Dollard, J. (1941). *Social learning and imitation.* New Haven, CT: Yale University Press.

Mineka, S., & Henderson, R. W. (1985). Controllability and predictability in acquired motivation. *Annual Review of Psychology, 36,* 495–529.

Mineka, S., & Kihlstrom, J. F. (1978). Unpredictable and uncontrollable events: A new perspective on experimental neurosis. *Journal of Abnormal Psychology, 87*(2), 256–271. doi:10.1037/0021-843X.87.2.256

Mischel, W., Ayduk, O., Berman, M. G., Casey, B. J., Gotlib, I. H., Jonides, J., . . . Shoda, Y. (2011). "Willpower" over the life span: Decomposing self-regulation. *Social Cognitive and Affective Neuroscience, 6*(2), 252–256.

Misra, S., Cheng, L., Genevie, J., & Yuan, M. (2014). The iPhone effect: The quality of in-person social interactions in the presence of mobile devices. *Environment and Behavior, 124,* 1–24.

Mock, S., & Eibach, S. (2011). Stability and change in sexual orientation identity over a 10-year period in adulthood. *Archive of Sexual Behaviors, 41*(3), 641–648.

Moffitt, T. E., Arseneault, L., Belsky, D., Dickson, N., Hancox, R. J., Harrington, H., . . . Caspi, A. (2011). A gradient of childhood self-control predicts health, wealth, and public safety. *Proceedings of the National Academy of Sciences, USA, 108*(7), 2693–2698. doi:10.1073/pnas.1010076108

Moffitt, T. E., Caspi, A., & Rutter, M. (2006). Measured gene–environment interactions in psychopathology: Concepts, research strategies, and implications for research, intervention, and public understanding of genetics perspectives on psychological science. *Perspectives on Psychological Science, 1*(1), 5–27.

Mohr, C., & Messina, S. (2015). Brain dysfunctions, psychopathologies, and body image distortions: Propositions for a possible common cause. *European Psychologist, 20*(1), 72–81.

Mok, D., Wellman, B., & Carrasco, J. A. (2010). Does distance still matter in the age of the Internet? *Urban Studies, 47*(13), 46–50.

Mokhtari, K., & Reichard, C. (2002). Assessing students' metacognitive awareness of reading strategies. *Journal of Educational Psychology, 94*(2), 249–259.

Moll, J., Krueger, F., Zahn, R., Pardini, M., de Oliveira-Souza, R., & Grafman, J. (2006). Human fronto–mesolimbic networks guide decisions about charitable donation. *Proceedings of the National Academy of Sciences, USA, 103*(42), 15623–15628.

Moller, A., Deci, E. L., & Ryan, R. M. (2006). Choice and ego-depletion: The moderating role of autonomy. *Personality and Social Psychology Bulletin, 32*, 1024–1036.

Money matters on campus: How college students behave financially and plan for the future. (2015). Retrieved from http://moneymatchersoncampus.org/wpcontent/uploads/2013/02/MoneyMatters_WhitePaper_2015_FINAL.pdf

Montepare, J. M. (2006). Body consciousness across the adult years: Variations with actual and subjective age. *Journal of Adult Development, 13*(2), 102–107.

Montepare, J. M., & Opeyo, A. (2002). The relative salience of physiognomic cues in differentiating faces: A methodological tool. *Journal of Nonverbal Behavior, 26*(1), 43–59. doi:10.1023/A:1014470520593

Montgomery, M. J., & Cote, J. (2003). College as a transition to adulthood. In G. R. Adams & M. D. Berzonsky (Eds.), *Blackwell handbook of adolescence* (pp. 149–172). Malden, MA: Blackwell.

Moon, C., Cooper, R. P., & Fifer W. P. (1993). Two-day-olds prefer their native language. *Infant Behavior and Development, 16*(4), 495–500. doi:10.1016/01636383(93)80007-u

Moradi, B., & Yoder, J. D. (2011). The psychology of women. In E. M. Altmaier & J.-I. Hansen (Eds.), *Oxford handbook of counseling psychology* (pp. 346–374). New York, NY: Oxford University Press.

Moreno, A. J., Klute, M. M., & Robinson, J. L. (2008). Relational and individual resources as predictors of empathy in early childhood. *Social Development, 17*(3), 613–637.

Morgan, M., & Vera, E. (2011). Prevention and psychoeducation in counseling psychology. In E. M. Altmaier & J.-I. C. Hansen (Eds.), *The Oxford hanbook of counseling psychology.* New York, NY: Oxford Press. doi:10.1093/oxfordhb/9780195342314.013.0020

Moritsugu, J., Vera, E., Wong, F., & Duffy, K. (2013). *Community psychology* (5th ed.). Boston, MA: Allyn & Bacon.

Morley, K. I., Hall, W. D., & Carter, L. (2004). Genetic screening for susceptibility to depression: Can we and should we? *Australian and New Zealand Journal of Psychiatry, 38*, 73–80.

Moskowitz, G. B., & Stone, J. (2012). The proactive control of stereotype activation-Implicit goals to not stereotype. *Zeitschrift Für Psychologie, 220*(3), 172–179. doi:10.1027/2151-2604/a000110

Murphy, J. W., & Rigg, K. K. (2014). Clarifying the philosophy behind the community mental health act and community-based interventions. *Journal of Community Psychology, 42*(3), 285–298.

Myers, C. B., & Pavel, D. (2011). Underrepresented students in STEM: The transition from undergraduate to graduate programs. *Journal of Diversity in Higher Education, 4*(2), 90–105. doi:10.1037/a0021679

Myers, D., Olsen, R., Seftor, N., Young, J., & Tuttle, C. (2004). *The impacts of regular Upward Bound: Results from the third follow-up data collection.* Washington, DC: U.S. Department of Education, Office of the Under Secretary, Policy and Program Studies Service.

Nathan, P. E., & Gorman, J. M. (2015). *A guide to treatments that work* (4th ed.). New York, NY: Oxford University Press.

National Alliance on Mental Illness. (n.d.) *Major classes of psychotropic medication.* Retrieved from http://www2.nami.org/Content/NavigationMenu/Intranet/Homefront/Major_Classes_Psychotropic_Meds.pdf

National Center for Education Statistics. (2013). *Digest of education statistics 2012.* Washington, DC: U.S. Department of Education.

National Center for Education Statistics. (2015, May). *Annual earnings of young adults* (Figure 2). Washington, DC: Author. Retrieved from http://nces.ed.gov/programs/coe/indicator_cba.asp

National Center on Addiction and Substance Abuse at Columbia University. (2012). *Addiction medicine: Closing the gap between science and practice.* Retrieved from http://www.casacolumbia.org/addiction-research/reports/addiction-medicine

National Comorbidity Survey. (2007a). *12-month prevalence of DSM–IV/WMH-CIDI disorders by sex and cohort.* Retrieved from http://www.hcp.med.harvard.edu/ncs/ftp dir/NCS-R_12-month_Prevalence_Estimates.pdf

National Comorbidity Survey. (2007b). *Lifetime prevalence of DSM–IV/WMH-CIDI disorders by sex and cohort.* Retrieved from http://www.hcp.med.harvard.edu/ncs/ftp dir/NCS-R_Lifetime_Prevalence_Estimates.pdf

National Institute for Occupational Safety and Health. (2009). *Stress at work.* Retrieved from http://www.cdc.gov/niosh/docs/99-101/pdfs/99-101.pdf

National Institute of Drug Abuse. (2010). *Comorbidity: Addiction and other mental illnesses.* Washington, DC: National Institute of Mental Health.

National Institute of Mental Health. (2016a, March). *Anxiety disorders.* Retrieved from http://www.nimh.nih.gov/health/topics/anxiety-disorders/index.shtml

National Institute of Mental Health. (2016b, March). *Attention deficit hyperactivity disorder.* Retrieved from http://www.nimh.nih.gov/health/topics/attention-deficit-hyperactivity-disorder-adhd/index.shtml

National Institute of Mental Health. (2016c, January). *Mental health medications.* Retrieved from http://www.nimh.nih.gov/health/topics/mental-health-medications/mental-health-medications.shtml

National Institute of Mental Health. (2016d, February). *Schizophrenia.* Retrieved from http://www.nimh.nih.gov/health/topics/schizophrenia/index.shtml

National Institute of Mental Health. (n.d.) *Research Domain Criteria.* Retrieved from http://www.nimh.nih.gov/research-priorities/rdoc/index.shtml

National Sleep Foundation. (n.d.). *Healthy sleep tips.* Retrieved from https://sleepfoundation.org/sleep-tools-tips/healthy-sleep-tips

Neal, S., & Vincent, C. (2013). Multiculture, middle class competencies and friendship practices in super-diverse geographies. *Social & Cultural Geography*, *14*(8), 909–929.

Neal, Z. (2015). Making big communities small: Using network science to understand the ecological and behavioral requirements for community social capital. *American Journal of Community Psychology*, *55*(3–4), 369–380. doi:10.1007/s10464-015-9720-4

Neff, K. D., Rude, S. S., & Kirkpatrick, K. (2007). An examination of self-compassion in relation to positive psychological functioning and personality traits. *Journal of Research in Personality*, *41*(4), 908–916.

Newport, F. (2012). Seven in 10 Americans are very or moderately religious. *Gallup*. Retrieved from www.gallup.com/poll/159050

Nix, G. A., Ryan, R. M., Manly, J. B., & Deci, E. L. (1999). Revitalization through self-regulation: The effects of autonomous and controlled motivation on happiness and vitality. *Journal of Experimental Social Psychology*, *35*, 266–284.

Nobakht, M., & Dezhkam, M. (2000). An epidemiological study of eating disorders in Iran. *International Journal of Eating Disorders*, *28*(3), 265–271.

Noelle-Neumann, E. (1974). The spiral of silence: A theory of public opinion. *Journal of Communication*, *24*(2), 43–51.

Norcross, J. C. (2011). *Psychotherapy relationships that work* (2nd ed.). New York, NY: Oxford University Press.

Northrup, J. C., Lapierre, C., Kirk, J., & Rae, C. (2015). The Internet process addiction test: Screening for addictions to processes facilitated by the Internet. *Behavioral Sciences*, *5*(3), 341–352.

NOVA. (1996, October, 26). *The history of money*. Retrieved from http://www.pbs.org/wgbh/nova/ancient/history-money.html

Oakes, J. M., & Rossi, P. H. (2003). The measurement of SES in health research: Current practice and steps toward a new approach. *Social Science and Medicine*, *56*(4), 769–784.

Ohman, A., & Mineka, S. (2001). Fears, phobias, and preparedness: Toward an evolved module of fear and fear learning. *Psychological Review*, *108*(3), 483–522. doi:10.1037/0033-295X.108.3.483

Ogden, C. L., Carroll, M. D., Kit, B. K., & Flegal, K. M. (2014). Prevalence of childhood and adult obesity in the United States, 2011–2012. *Journal of the American Medical Association*, *311*(8), 806–814.

Oishi, S., & Diener, E. (2013). Residents of poor nations have more meaning in life than residents of wealthy nations. *Psychological Science*, *25*, 422–430.

Olds, D. L. (2010). The nurse-family partnership. In B. M. Lester & J. D. Sparrow (Eds.), *Nurturing children and families: Building on the legacy of T. Berry Brazelton* (pp. 192–203). Hoboken, NJ: Wiley.

O'Leary, K., Vivian, D., & Malone, J. (1992). Assessment of physical aggression against women in marriages: The need for multimodal assessment. *Behavioral Assessment*, 14(1), 5-14.

Onishi, N. (2002, October 3). Globalization of beauty makes slimness trendy. *The New York Times*, p. A4.

Oppenheimer, L. (1991). Determinants of action: An organismic and holistic approach. In L. Oppenheimer & J. Valsiner (Eds.), *The origins of action: Interdisciplinary and international perspectives* (pp. 37–63). New York, NY: Springer-Verlag.

Osbourne, J. W. (2012). Psychological effects of the transition to retirement. *Canadian Journal of Counselling and Psychotherapy*, *46*(1), 45–58.

O'Sullivan, G. (2011). The relationship between hope, eustress, self-efficacy, and life satisfaction among undergraduates. *Social Indicators Research*, *101*(1), 155–172.

Oswald, D. L., Clark, E. M., & Kelly, C. M. (2004). Friendship maintenance: An analysis of individual and dyadic behaviors. *Journal of Social and Clinical Psychology*, *23*(3), 413–441.

Owsley, C. (2011). Aging and vision. *Vision Research*, *51*(13), 1610–1622.

Palfrey, J., & Gasser, U. (2008). *Born digital*. New York, NY: Basic Books.

Pandey, G. N. (2013). Biological basis of suicide and suicidal behavior. *Bipolar Disorders*, *15*(5), 524–541.

Pargament, K. I. (1997). *The psychology of religion and coping: Theory, research, practice*. New York, NY: Guilford.

Pargament, K. I. (2002). The bitter and the sweet: An evaluation of the costs and benefits of religiousness. *Psychological Inquiry*, *13*, 168–181.

Pargament, K. I. (2008). *Is religion good for your health? It depends*. Paper presented to the Heritage Foundation, Washington, DC.

Pargament, K. I., Exline, J. J., & Jones, J. (Eds.). (2013). *APA handbook of psychology, religion and spirituality (Vol. 1): Context, theory, and research*. Washington, DC: American Psychological Association.

Pargament, K. I., Mahoney, A., Exline, J. J., Jones, J. W., & Shafranske, E. P. (2013). Envisioning an integrative paradigm for the psychology of religion and spirituality. In K. I. Pargament, J. J. Exline, & J. W. Jones (Eds.), *APA handbook of psychology, religion and spirituality (Vol. 1): Context, theory, and research* (pp. 3–19). Washington, DC: American Psychological Association.

Park, C. L. (2005). Religion as a meaning-making framework in coping with life stress. *Journal of Social Issues*, *61*(4), 707–729. doi:10.1111/j.15404560.2005.00428.x

Park, C. L. (2010). Making sense of the meaning literature: An integrative review of meaning making and its effects on adjustment to stressful life events. *Psychological Bulletin*, *136*(2), 257–301. doi:10.1037/a0018301

Park, C. L., Edmondson, D., & Hale-Smith, A. (2013). Why religion? Meaning as motivation. In K. I. Pargament, J. J. Exline, & J. W. Jones (Eds.), *APA handbook of psychology, religion, and spirituality (Vol. 1): Context, theory, and research* (pp. 157–171). Washington, DC: American Psychological Association.

Parrish, B. P., Zautra, A. J., & Davis, M. C. (2008). The role of positive and negative interpersonal events on daily fatigue in women with fibromyalgia, rheumatoid arthritis, and osteoarthritis. *Health Psychology*, *27*(6), 694–702. doi:10.1037/0278-6133.27.6.694

Parten, M. B. (1932). Social participation among preschool children. *Journal of Abnormal and Social Psychology*, *27*(3), 243–269.

Patrick, K., Calfas, K. J., Norman, G. J., Zabinski, M. F., Sallis, J. F., Rupp, J., . . . Cella, J. (2006). Randomized controlled trial of a primary care and home-based intervention for physical activity and nutrition behaviors: PACE for adolescents. *Archives of Pediatrics and Adolescent Medicine, 160*(2), 128–136.

Patrick, V. M., Chun, H. H., & Macinnis, D. J. (2009). Affective forecasting and self-control: Why anticipating pride wins over anticipating shame in a self-regulation context. *Journal of Consumer Psychology, 19*(3), 537–545.

Paul, A. (2014). Is online better than offline for meeting partners? Depends: Are you looking to marry or to date? *Cyberpsychology, Behavior & Social Networking, 17*(10), 664–667.

Paus, T. (2009). Brain development. In R. Lerner & L. Steinberg (Eds.), *Handbook of adolescent psychology* (pp. 95–115). Hoboken, NJ: Wiley.

Pavlov, I. (1928). *Lectures on conditioned reflexes: Twenty-five years of objective study of higher nervous activity (behaviour) of animals* (2 Vols.). New York, NY: International Publishers. (Original work published 1923)

Pescosolido, B. A. (2013). The public stigma of mental illness: What do we think; what do we know; what can we prove? *Journal of Health and Social Behavior, 54*(1), 1–21.

Pettigrew, T. F., & Tropp, L. R. (2006). A meta-analytic test of intergroup contact theory. *Journal of Personality and Social Psychology, 90*(5), 751–783. doi:10.1037/0022-3514.90.5.751

Pew Research Center. (2014a, August 26). *Social media and the "spiral of silence."* Retrieved from http://www.pewinternet.org/2014/08/26/social-media-and-the-spiral-of-silence

Pew Research Center. (2014b, February 27). *The web at 25 in the U.S.* Retrieved from http://www.pewinternet.org/2015/10/08/social-networking-usage-2005-2015

Pew Research Center. (2015a, April 1). *U.S. smartphone use in 2015.* Pew Research Center. Retrieved from http://www.pewinternet.org/2015/04/01/us-smartphone-use-in-2015

Pew Research Center. (2015b, June 26). *America's Internet Access: 2000–2015.* Retrieved from http://www.pewinternet.org/2015/06/26/americans-internet-access-2000-2015

Pew Research Center. (2015c, August 26). *American's view on mobile etiquette.* Retrieved from http://www.pewinternet.org/2015/08/26/americans-views-on-mobile-etiquette

Piedmont, R. L. (2012). Overview and development of a trait-based measure of numinous constructs: The assessment of spirituality and religious sentiments (APIRES) scale. In L. Miller (Ed.), *The Oxford handbook of psychology and spirituality.* New York, NY: Oxford Press.

Piedmont, R. L., Ciarrochi, J. W., Dy-Liacco, G. S., & Williams, J. E. G. (2009). The empirical and conceptual value of the spiritual transcendence and religious involvement scales for personality research. *Psychology of Religion and Spirituality, 1*(3), 162–179

Piedmont, R. L., & Leach, M. M. (2002). Cross-cultural generalizability of the Spiritual Transcendence Scale in India: Spirituality as a universal aspect of human experience. *American Behavioral Scientist, 45*(12), 1888–1901.

Piedmont, R. L., & Wilkins, T. A. (2013). Spirituality, religiousness, and personality: Theoretical foundations and empirical applications. In K. I. Pargament, J. J. Exline, & J. W. Jones (Eds.), *APA handbook of psychology, religion, and spirituality (Vol. 1): Context, theory, and research* (pp. 173–186). Washington, DC: American Psychological Association. doi:10.1037/14045-009

Pieterse, A. L., Todd, N. R., Neville, H. A., & Carter, R. T. (2012). Perceived racism and mental health among Black American adults: A meta-analytic review. *Journal of Counseling Psychology, 59*(1), 1–9.

Plant, E. A., & Devine, P. G. (1998). Internal and external motivation to respond without prejudice. *Journal of Personality and Social Psychology, 75*(3), 811–832.

Poirier, J. (2003). *The history of neurosciences at La Pitié and La Salpêtrière.* Retrieved from http://www.baillement.com/lettres/histoire-salpetriere-engl.html

Polanczyk, G., de Lima, M. S., Less-Horta, B., Biederman, J., & Rohde, L. A. (2007). The worldwide prevalence of ADHD: A systematic review and metaregression analysis. *American Journal of Psychiatry, 164*(6), 942–948.

Polanin, M., & Vera, E. M. (2013). Bullying prevention and social justice. *Theory into practice, 52*(4), 303–310.

Pong, S. L., & Ju, D. B. (2000). The effects of change in family structure and income on dropping out of middle and high school. *Journal of Family Issues, 21*(2), 147–169.

Pönkänen, L. M., Alhoniemi, A., Leppänen, J. M., & Hietanen, J. K. (2011). Does it make a difference if I have eye contact with you or with your picture? An ERP study. *Scan, 6*(4), 486–494.

Poortinga, W. (2006). Social relations or social capital? Individual and community health effects of bonding social capital. *Social Science and Medicine, 63*(1), 255–270.

Portes, A. (1998). Social capital: Its origins and applications in modern sociology. *Annual Review of Sociology, 24*, 1–24.

Pow, J. L., Baumeister, A. A., Hawkins, M. F., Cohen, A. S., & Garand, J. C. (2015). Deinstitutionalization of American public hospitals for the mentally ill before and after the introduction of antipsychotic medications. *Harvard Review of Psychiatry, 23*(3), 176–187.

Powell, L. H., Shahabi, L., & Thoresen, C. E. (2003). Religion and spirituality: Linkages to physical health. *American Psychologist, 58*, 36–52.

Prelec, D., & Loewenstein, G. (1998). The red and the black: Mental accounting of savings and debt. *Marketing Science, 17*(1), 4–28.

Premack, D. (1959). Toward empirical behavior laws: I. Positive reinforcement. *Psychological Review, 66*(4), 219–233. doi:10.1037/h0040891

Pressley, M., & Afflerbach, P. (1995). *Verbal reports of reading: The nature of constructively responsive reading.* Hillsdale, NJ: Erlbaum.

Pressman, S., Gallagher, M., & Lopez, S. (2013). Is the emotion-health connection a "first-world" problem? *Psychological Science, 24*(4), 544–549.

Preston, J. D., O'Neal, J. H., & Talaga, M. C. (2013). *Handbook of clinical psychopharmacology for therapists.* Oakland, CA: New Harbinger.

Prilleltensky, I., & Prilleltensky, O. (2006). *Promoting well-being: Linking personal, organizational, and community change*. Hoboken, NJ: Wiley.

Procidano, M. (1992). The nature of perceived social support: Findings of meta-analysis studies. In C. Spielberger & J. Butcher (Eds.), *Advances in personality assessment* (Vol. 9, pp. 1–26). Hillsdale, NJ: Erlbaum.

Prokasky, W., & Raskin, D. (1973), *Electrodermal activity in psychological research*. New York, NY: Academic Press.

Proulx, T., Markman, K., & Lindberg, M. (2013). Introduction: The new science of meaning. In K. Markman, T. Proulx, & M. Lindberg (Eds.), *The psychology of meaning*. Washington, DC: American Psychological Association.

Provasnik, S., & Planty, M. (2008). *Community colleges: Special supplement to the 2008 condition of education*. Washington, DC: National Center for Education Statistics.

Putnam, R. D. (1995). Bowling alone: America's declining social capital. *Journal of Democracy, 6*(1), 65–78. doi:10.1353/jod.1995.0002

Putnam, R. D. (2007). E pluribus unum: Diversity and community in the twenty first century: The 2006 Johan Skytte Prize Lecture. *Scandinavian Political Studies, 30*(2), 137–174.

Rahe, R. H., Meyer, M., Smith, M., Kjaer, G., & Holmes, T. (1964). Social stress and illness onset. *Journal of Psychosomatic Research, 8*(1), 35–44.

Rainie, L. (2015, September 22). *Digital divides 2015*. Pew Research Center. Retrieved from http://www.pewinternet .org/2015/09/22/digital-divides-2015

Rakić, T., Steffens, M. C., & Mummendey, A. (2011). Blinded by the accent! The minor role of looks in ethnic categorization. *Journal of Personality and Social Psychology, 100*(1), 16–29.

Ramaswami, A., & Dreher, G. (2007). The benefits associated with workplace mentoring relationships. In T. D. Allen & L. T. Eby (Eds.), *Blackwell handbook of mentoring: A multiple perspectives approach* (pp. 211–231). Malden, MA: Blackwell.

Rando, T. A. (1993). *Treatment of complicated mourning*. Champaign, IL: Research Press.

Rank, M. R., Hirschl, T. A., & Foster, K. A. (2014). *Chasing the American dream: Understanding what shapes our fortunes*. New York, NY: Oxford University Press.

Rasmussen, A., Aber, M. S., & Bhana, A. (2004). Adolescent coping and neighborhood violence: Perceptions, exposure, and urban youths' efforts to deal with danger. *American Journal of Community Psychology, 33*(1–2), 61–75.

Rawes, E. (2015, January 25). The 10 richest cities in America. *The Cheat Sheet, USA Today*. Retrieved from http://www .usatoday.com/story/money/personalfinance/2015/01/25/ cheat-sheet-10-richest-cities/21394881

Rawlinson, N. (2015, October 8). History of Apple: Read about how Apple came to lead the tech industry. *Macworld*. Retrieved from http://www.macworld.co.uk/feature/apple/ history-of-apple-steve-jobs-what-really-happened-mac-computer-1984-3606104

Rehn, A. E., & Rees, S. M. (2005). Investigating the neurodevelopmental hypothesis of schizophrenia. *Clinical and Experimental Pharmacology and Physiology, 32*(9), 687–696.

Reis, H. T., Sheldon, K. M., Gable, S. L., Roscoe, J., & Ryan, R. M. (2000). Daily well being: The role of autonomy, competence, and relatedness. *Personality and Social Psychology Bulletin, 26*(4), 419–435.

Rescorla, R. A. (1968). Probability of shock in the presence and absence of CS in fear conditioning. *Journal of Comparative and Physiological Psychology, 66*(1), 1–5.

Rescorla, R. A. (1988). Pavlovian conditioning: It's not what you think it is. *American Psychologist, 43*(3), 151–160.

Rescorla, R. A., & Wagner, A. R. (1972). A theory of Pavlovian conditioning: Variations in the effectiveness of reinforcement and nonreinforcement. In A. Black & W. F. Prokasy (Eds.), *Classical conditioning: II. Current research and theory* (pp. 64–99). New York, NY: Appleton-Century-Crofts.

Reynolds, J., Stewart, M., Sischo, L., & MacDonald, R. (2006). Have adolescents become too ambitious? High school seniors' educational and occupational plans, 1976 to 2000. *Social Problems, 53*(2), 186–206.

Rican, P., & Janosova, P. (2010). Spirituality as a basic aspect of personality: A cross cultural verification of Piedmont's model. *The International Journal for the Psychology of Religion, 20*(1), 2–13.

Richmond, C. A. M., Ross, N. A., & Egeland, G. M. (2007). Social support and thriving health: A new approach to understanding the health of indigenous Canadians. *American Journal of Public Health, 97*(10), 1827–1833.

Rick, S., Cryder, C., & Loewenstein, G. (2007). Tightwads and spendthrifts. *Journal of Consumer Research, 34*(6), 767–782.

Rideout, V., Foehr, U., & Roberts, D. (2010). *Generation M2: Media in the lives of 8 to 18 year olds*. Menlo Park, CA: Kaiser Family Foundation.

Rigby, K. (2007). *Bullying in schools and what to do about it*. Victoria, Australia: ACER Press.

Rikani, A. A., Choudhry, Z., Choudhry, A. M., Ikram, H., Asghar, M. W., Kajal, D., . . . Mobassarah, N. J. (2013). A critique of the literature on etiology of eating disorders. *Annals of Neurosciences, 20*(4), 157–161.

Rinpoche, S. (1992). *The Tibetan book of living and dying*. New York, NY: HarperCollins.

Rizzolatti, G., & Craighero, L. (2004). The mirror-neuron system. *Annual Review of Neuroscience, 27*(1), 169–192.

Roberts, J. A. (1998). Compulsive buying among college students: An investigation of its antecedents, consequences, and implications for public policy. *The Journal of Consumer Affairs, 32*(2), 295–319.

Robinson, M. D., & Clore, G. L. (2002). Belief and feeling: Evidence for an accessibility model of emotional self-report. *Psychological Bulletin, 128*(6), 934–960.

Rochat, F., & Blass, T. (2014). Milgram's unpublished obedience variation and its historical relevance. *Journal of Social Issues, 70*(3), 456–472. doi:10.1111/josi.12071

Rogers, C. (1961). *On becoming a person*. New York, NY: Houghton Mifflin.

Romberg, A., & Saffron, J. (2010). Statistical learning and language acquisition. *Interdisciplinary Reviews: Cognitive Science, 1*(6), 906–914. doi:10.1002/wcs.78

Romeo, R., & McEwan, B. (2006). Stress and the adolescent brain. *Annals of the New York Academy of Science, 1094*, 202–214.

Root, M. J. (2016). Thriving in a stressful world: A review of hardiness: Turning stressful circumstances into resilient growth. *Journal of Contructivist Psychology, 29*(3), 335–337.

Roscigno, V. J., Tomaskovic-Devey, D., & Crowley, M. (2006). Education and the inequalities of place. *Social Forces, 84*(4), 2121–2145.

Rose, C. A., Monda-Amaya, L. E., & Espelage, D. L. (2010). Bullying perpetration and victimization in special education: A review of the literature. *Remedial and Special Education, 32*(2), 114–130. doi:10.1177/0741932510361247

Rose, G. M., Shoham, A., Kahle, L. R., & Batra, R. (1994). Social values, conformity, and dress. *Journal of Applied Social Psychology, 24*(17), 1501–1519. doi:10.1111/j.1559-1816.1994.tb01560.x

Rosenberg, L. (2014). Advancing on the new frontier of behavioral health. *Journal of Behavioral Health Services & Research, 41*(1), 1–2.

Rottinghaus, P. J., Larson, L. M., & Borgen, F. H. (2003). Theoretical and empirical linkages of self-efficacy and interests. *Journal of Vocational Behavior, 62,* 221–236.

Royal Swedish Academy of Sciences. (2002). *The Sveriges Riksbank prize in economic sciences in memory of Alfred Nobel 2002 (press release).* Retrieved from http://www.nobel prize.org/nobel_prizes/economic-sciences/laureates/2002

Rubin, K. H., Bowker, J., & Gazelle, H. (2010). Social withdrawal in childhood and adolescence: Peer relationships and social competence. In K. H. Rubin & R. J. Coplan (Eds.), *The development of shyness and social withdrawal* (pp. 131–156). New York, NY: Guilford.

Rubin, K. H., Bukowski, W., & Parker, J. G. (2006). Peer interactions, relationships, and groups. In W. Damon, R. M. Lerner, & N. Eisenberg (Eds.), *Handbook of child psychology: Vol. 3, Social, emotional, and personality development* (pp. 571–645). Hoboken, NJ: Wiley.

Rudman, L., Ashmore, R., & Gary, M. (2001). "Unlearning" automatic biases: The malleability of implicit prejudice and stereotypes. *Journal of Personality and Social Psychology, 81*(5), 856–868.

Rutter, M. (1976). Research report: Isle of Wight studies. *Psychological Medicine, 6*(2), 313–332.

Rutter, M. (1987). Psychosocial resilience and protective mechanisms. *American Journal of Orthopsychiatry, 57*(3), 316–331.

Rutter, M. (2012). Resilience as a dynamic concept. *Development and Psychopathology, 24*(2), 335–344.

Ryan, R. M., & Deci, E. L. (2004). Avoiding death or engaging life as accounts of meaning and culture: Comment on Pyszczynski et al. (2004). *Psychological Bulletin, 130*(3), 473–477. doi:10.1037/0033-2909.130.3.473

Ryan, R. M., & Deci, E. L. (2006). Self-regulation and the problem of human autonomy: Does psychology need choice, self-determination, and will? *Journal of Personality, 74*(6), 1557–1585. doi:10.1111/j.14676494.2006.00420.x

Ryan, R. M., & Deci, E. L. (2008). A self-determination theory approach to psychotherapy: The motivational basis for effective change. *Canadian Psychology/Psychologie Canadienne, 49*(3), 186–193. doi:10.1037/a0012753

Ryan, R. M., & Frederick, C. M. (1997). On energy, personality, and health: Subjective vitality as a dynamic reflection of well-being. *Journal of Personality, 65*(3), 529–205.

Ryan, R. M., Rigby, S., & King, K. (1993). Two types of religious internalization and their relations to religious orientations and mental health. *Journal of Personality and Social Psychology, 65*(3), 586–596.

Ryff, C. D., & Singer, B. H. (1998). The contours of positive human health. *Psychological Inquiry, 9,* 1–28.

Saegert, S. C., Adler, N., Bullock, H., Cauce, A. M., Liu, W. M., & Wyche, K. (2006). *Report of the APA Task Force on Socioeconomic Status.* Washington, DC: American Psychological Association.

Sajid, A., Poor, M. C., & Diaz, D. R. (2010). Overview of ADHD. *Annals of the American Psychotherapy Association, 13*(3), 58–59.

Salzberg, S. (1995). *Lovingkindness: The revolutionary art of happiness.* Boston, MA: Shambala.

Sameroff, A. (2010). A unified theory of development: A dialectic integration of nature and nurture. *Child Development, 81*(1), 6–22.

Sameroff, A., & Chandler, M. (1975). Reproductive risk and the continuum of caretaking casualty. In F. D. Horowitz, E. M. Hetherington, S. Scarr-Salapatek, G. M. Siegel (Eds.), *Review of child development research* (pp. 187–244). Chicago, IL: University of Chicago Press.

Sameroff, A. J. (2000). Developmental systems and psychopathology. *Development and Psychopathology, 12,* 297–312.

Sander, T., & Putnam, R. (2010). Still bowling alone? The post-9/11 split. *Journal of Democracy, 21*(1), 9–16.

Sandvik, A. M., Bartone, P. T., Hystad, S. W., Phillips, T. M., Thayer, J. F., & Johnsen, B. H. (2013). Psychological hardiness predicts neuroimmunological responses to stress. *Psychology, Health & Medicine, 18*(6), 705–713.

Sanislow, C. A., Quinn, K. J., & Sypher, I. (2015). NIMH Research Domain Criteria (RDoC). In R. L. Cautin & S. O. Lilienfeld (Eds.), *Encyclopedia of clinical psychology.* Hoboken, NJ: Wiley-Blackwell.

Satir, V. (1983). *Conjoint family therapy.* Palo Alto, CA: Science and Behavior Books.

Satpute, A. B., Mumford, J. A., Naliboff, B. D., & Poldrack, R. A. (2012). Human anterior and posterior hippocampus respond distinctly to state and trait anxiety. *Emotion, 12*(1), 58–68. doi:10.1037/a0026517

Savin-Williams, R. (2005). *The new gay teenager.* Cambridge, MA: Harvard University Press.

Savin-Williams, R. (2007). Girl on girl sexuality. In B. Leadbeater & N. Way (Eds.), *Urban girls revisited: Building strengths* (pp. 301–318). New York: New York University Press.

Schaie, K. W. (1994). The course of adult intellectual development. *American Psychologist, 49*(4), 304–313.

Schlehofer, M., Omoto, A., & Adelman, J. (2008). How do "religion" and "spirituality" differ? Lay definitions among older adults. *Journal for the Scientific Study of Religion, 47*(3), 411–425. doi:10.1111/j.1468-5906.2008.00418.x

Schmeichel, B. J., Vohs, K. D., & Baumeister, R. F. (2003). Intellectual performance and ego depletion: Role of the self in logical reasoning and other information processing. *Journal of Personality and Social Psychology, 85*(1), 33–46.

Schoeneman, T. J. (1984). The mentally ill witch in textbooks of abnormal psychology: Current status and implications of a fallacy. *Professional Psychology: Research and Practice, 15*(3), 299–314.

Schuler, R. (1980). Definition and conceptualization of stress in organizations. *Organizational Behavior and Human Performance, 25*(2), 184–215.

Schunk, D. H., & Pajares, F. (2005). Competence perceptions and academic functioning. In A. J. Andrews & C. S. Dweck (Eds.), *Handbook of competence and motivation* (pp. 85–104). New York, NY: Guilford.

Schwartz, J. (1999). *Cassandra's daughter: A history of psychoanalysis in Europe and America.* New York, NY: Penguin Putnam.

Schwartz, S. H. (1992). Universals in the content and structure of values: Theoretical advances and empirical tests in 20 countries. *Advances in Experimental Social Psychology, 25,* 1–65. doi:10.1016/S0065-2601(08)60281-6

Scully, J. A., Tosi, H., & Banning, K. (2000). Life event checklists: Revisiting the Social Readjustment Rating Scale after 30 years. *Educational and Psychological Measurement, 60*(6), 864–876.

Sears, D. O., & Henry, P. J. (2003). The origins of symbolic racism. Journal of *Personality and Social Psychology, 85*(2), 259–275.

Sedlmeier, P., Eberth, J., Schwarz, M., Zimmermann, D., Haarig, F., Jaeger, S., & Kunze, S. (2012). The psychological effects of meditation: A meta-analysis. *Psychological Bulletin, 138*(6), 1139–1171.

Segerstrom, S. C., & Miller, G. E. (2004). Psychological stress and the human immune system: A meta-analytic study of 30 years of inquiry. *Psychological Bulletin, 130,* 601–630.

Seligman, M. E. P. (1970). On the generality of the laws of learning. *Psychological Review, 77*(5), 406–418.

Seligman, M. E. P. (1971). Phobias and preparedness. *Behavior Therapy, 2*(3), 307–320.

Seligman, M. E. P., & Csikszentmihalyi, M. (2000). Positive psychology: An introduction. *American Psychologist, 55*(1), 5–14. doi:10.1037/0003-066X.55.1.5

Seligman, M. E. P., Steen, T. A., Park, N., & Peterson, C. (2005). Positive psychology progress: Empirical validation of interventions. *American Psychologist, 60*(5), 410–421. doi:10.1037/0003-066X.60.5.410

Selman, R. (1980). *The growth of interpersonal understanding.* New York, NY: Academic Press.

Selye, H. (1955). Stress and disease. *Science, 122*(3171), 625–631.

Selye, H. (1956). *The stress of life.* New York, NY: McGraw-Hill.

Selye, H. (1974). *Stress without distress.* Philadelphia, PA: Lippincott.

Senju, A., & Johnson, M. (2009). The eye contact effect: Mechanisms and development. *Trends in Cognitive Science, 13*(3), 127–143.

Sergeant, J. F., Ekerdt, D. J., & Chapin, R. (2008). Measurement of late life residential relocation: Why are rates for such a manifest event so varied? *Journal of Gerontology, 63*(2), 92–98.

Shaeer, O., & Shaeer, K. (2012). The global online sexual survey: The United States of America in 2011. Chapter 1: Erectile dysfunction among English-speakers. *Journal of Sexual Medicine, 9*(12), 3018–3027.

Shaffer, H. J., LaPlante, D. A., LaBrie, R. A., Kidman, R. C., Donato, A. N., & Stanton, M. V. (2004). Toward a syndrome model of addition: Multiple expressions, common etiology. *Harvard Review of Psychiatry, 12*(6), 367–374.

Shaffer, M. A., Harrison, D. A., Gregersen, H., Black, J. S., & Ferzandi, L. A. (2006). You can take it with you: Individual differences and expatriate effectiveness. *Journal of Applied Psychology, 91*(1), 109–125. doi:10.1037/00219010.91.1.109

Shampanier, K., Mazar, N., & Ariely, D. (2007). How small is zero price? The true value of free. *Marketing Science, 26,* 742–757.

Shanks, D. R. (2010). Learning: From association to cognition. *Annual Review of Psychology, 61,* 273–301. doi:10.1146/annurev.psych.093008.100519

Shapiro, D. H., Jr. (1980). *Meditation: Self-regulation strategy and altered state of consciousness.* New York, NY: Aldine.

Shapiro, S. (2009). Meditation and positive psychology. In *Oxford handbook of positive psychology.* New York, NY: Oxford University Press.

Shaver, P., & Mikulincer, M. (Eds.). *Meaning, mortality, and choice: The social psychology of existential concerns.* Washington, DC: American Psychological Association.

Sheard, M., & Golby, J. (2007). Hardiness and undergraduate academic study: The moderating role of commitment. *Personality and Individual Differences, 43,* 579–588.

Sheldon, K. M., Abad, N., & Hinsch (2011). A two-process view of Facebook use and relatedness need-satisfaction: Disconnection drives use and connection rewards it. *Journal of Personality and Social Psychology, 100*(4), 766–775.

Sheldon, S. B., & Epstein, J. L. (2004). Getting students to school: Using family and community involvement to reduce chronic absenteeism. *School Community Journal, 14,* 39–56.

Shields, A., Cicchetti, D., & Ryan, R. (1994). The development of emotional and behavioral self-regulation and social competence among maltreated school age children. *Development and Psychopathology, 6*(1), 57–75.

Sherif, M., Harvey, O. J., White, B. J., Hood, W. R., & Sherif, C. W. (1954/1961). *Intergroup conflict and cooperation: The Robbers Cave experiment.* Retrieved from http://psychclassics.yorku.ca/Sherif

Shinn, M., & Toohey, S. M. (2003). Community contexts of human welfare. *Annual Review of Psychology, 54,* 427–259. doi:10.1146/annurev.psych.54.101601.145052

Shoda Y., Mischel W., & Peake P. (1990). Predicting adolescent cognitive and self-regulator competencies from preschool delay of gratification: Identifying diagnostic conditions. *Developmental Psychology, 26*(6), 978–986.

Shors, T., Foy, M., Levine, S., & Thompson, R. (1990). Unpredictable and uncontrollable stress impairs neuronal plasticity in the rat hippocampus. *Brain Research Bulletin, 24,* 663-667.

Shrestha, L. B., & Heiser, E. J. (2011). *The changing demographic profile of the United States.* Washington, DC: Congressional

Research Service. Retrieved from http://www.fas.org/sgp/crs/misc/RL32701.pdf

Shrewsbury, V., & Wardle, J. (2008). Socioeconomic status and adiposity in childhood: A systematic review of cross-sectional studies 1990–2005. *Obesity, 16*(2), 275–294.

Shweder, R. (2003). *Why do men barbecue? Recipes for cultural psychology.* Cambridge, MA: Harvard University Press.

Shweder, R., & Sullivan, M. (1993). Cultural psychology: Who needs it? *Annual Review of Psychology, 44,* 497–523.

Silberg, J. L., Maes, H., & Eaves, L. J. (2010). Genetic and environmental influences on the transmission of parental depression to children's depression and conduct disturbance: An extended children of twins study. *Journal of Child Psychology and Psychiatry, 51*(6), 734–744. doi:10.1111/j.1469-7610.2010.02205.x

Silberman, I. (2005). Religion as a meaning system: Implications for the new millennium. *Journal of Social Issues, 61*(4), 641–663.

Silva, A., & Caetano, A. (2013). Daily hassles and uplifts at work: Perceived effects on well-being. In F. Sarracino (Ed.), *The happiness compass: Theories, actions and perspectives for well-being* (pp. 153–175). Hauppauge, NY: Nova Science Publishers.

Simmons, B. L. (2000). *Eustress at work: Accentuating the positive* (Unpublished doctoral dissertation). Oklahoma State University, Stillwater.

Simon, R. (2011, September–October). The mindfulness movement: Do we even need psychotherapy anymore? *Psychotherapy Networker.* Retrieved from https://www.psychotherapynetworker.org/blog/details/635/how-psychotherapy-embraced-the-mindfulness-movement

Sinclair, S., Lowery, B., Hardin, C., & Colangelo, A. (2006). Social tuning of automatic racial attitudes: The role of affiliative motivation. *Journal of Personality and Social Psychology, 89*(4), 583–592.

Skinner, B. F. (1938). *The behavior of organisms: An experimental analysis.* New York, NY: Appleton-Century-Crofts.

Skinner, B. F. (1965). *Science and human behavior.* New York, NY: Macmillan.

Skinner, B. F. (1998). The experimental analysis of operant behavior. In R. W. Reiber & K. Salzinger (Eds.), *Psychology: Theoretical-historical perspectives* (2nd ed., pp. 289–298). Washington, DC: American Psychological Association.

Smits, J. & Otto, M. (2011). *Exercise for mood and anxiety: Proven strategies for overcoming depression and enhancing well-being.* New York, NY: Oxford University Press.

Snyder, C., & Lopez, S. (2009). *The Oxford handbook of positive psychology.* New York, NY: Oxford University Press.

Son Hing, L. S., Chung-Yan, G. A., Hamilton, L. K., & Zanna, M. P. (2008). A two-dimensional model that employs explicit and implicit attitudes to characterize prejudice. *Journal of Personality and Social Psychology, 94*(6), 971–987.

South, S. J., Haynie, D. L., & Bose, S. (2007). Student mobility and dropout. *Social Science Research, 36,* 68–94.

Sowell, E. R., Thompson, P. M., Holmes, C. J., Jernigan, T. L., & Toga, A. W. (1999). In vivo evidence for post-adolescent brain maturation in frontal and striatal regions. *Nature Neuroscience, 2,* 859–861.

Spadaro, A. (2016). *Pope Francis and the Internet culture.* Paper presented at the Search for Meaning Conference Presentation, Seattle University

Spellman, T., McClintock, S. M., Terrace, H., Luber, B., Husain, M. M., & Lisanby, S. H. (2008). Differential effects of high dose magnetic seizure therapy (MST) and electroconvulsive shock (ECS) on cognitive function. *Biological Psychiatry, 63*(12), 1163–1170.

Spielberger, C. D. (1972). Anxiety as an emotional state. In C. D. Spielberger (Ed.), *Anxiety: Current trends in theory and research* (Vol. 1). New York, NY: Academic Press.

Spinrad, T. L., & Eisenberg, N. (2009). Empathy, prosocial behavior, and positive development in schools. In R. Gilman, E. S. Huebner, & M. J. Furlong (Eds.), *Handbook of positive psychology in schools* (pp. 119–129). New York, NY: Routledge.

Spitalnick, J. S., & McNair, L. D. (2005). Couples therapy with gay and lesbian clients: An analysis of important clinical issues. *Journal of Sex and Marital Therapy, 31*(1), 43–56.

Spokane, A. R., & Cruza-Guet, M. C. (2005). Holland's theory of vocational personalities in work environments. In S. D. Brown & R. W. Lent (Eds.), *Career development and counseling: Putting theory and research to work* (pp. 24–41). Hoboken, NJ: Wiley.

Stafford, L. (2011). Measuring relationship maintenance behaviors: Critique and development of the revised relationship maintenance behavior scale. *Journal of Social and Personal Relationships, 28*(2), 278–303.

Stafford, L., & Canary, D. J. (1991). Maintenance strategies and romantic relationship type, gender, and relational characteristics. *Journal of Social and Personal Relationships, 8*(2), 217–242.

Stafford, L., Dainton, M., & Haas, S. (2000). Measuring routine and strategic relational maintenance: Scale revision, sex versus gender roles, and the prediction of relational characteristics. *Communication Monographs, 67*(3), 306–323.

Staudinger, U. M., & Glück, J. (2011). Psychological wisdom research. *Annual Review of Psychology, 62,* 215–241.

Stearns, E., Moller, S., Blau, J., & Potochnick, S. (2007). Staying back and dropping out: The relationship between grade retention and school dropout. *Sociology of Education, 80*(3), 210–240.

Steel, P., Schmidt, J., & Shultz, J. (2008). Refining the relationship between personality and subjective well-being. *Psychological Bulletin, 134*(1), 138–161. doi:10.1037/0033-2909.134.1.138

Steger, M. F. (2012). Experiencing meaning in life: Optimal functioning at the nexus of spirituality, psychopathology, and well-being. In P. T. P. Wong (Ed.), *The human quest for meaning* (2nd ed., pp. 165–184). New York, NY: Routledge.

Steger, M. F., & Frazier, P. (2005). Meaning in life: One link in the chain from religiousness to well-being. *Journal of Counseling Psychology, 52,* 574–582.

Steiner, N. J., Frenette, E. C., Rene, K. M., Brennan, R. T., & Perrin, E. C. (2014). In-school neurofeedback training for ADHD: Sustained improvements from a randomized control trial. *Pediatrics, 133,* 483–492.

Sternberg, R. (2006). A duplex theory of love. In R. Sternberg & K. Weis (Eds.), *The new psychology of love* (pp. 184–199). New Haven, CT: Yale University Press.

Stillwell, R., & Sable, J. (2013). *Public school graduates and dropouts from the common core of data: School year 2009–10. First look (provisional data)*. Washington, DC: National Center for Education Statistics. Retrieved from http://nces .ed.gov/pubs2013/2013309rev.pdf

Stohs, S. J. (2011). The role of free radicals in toxicity and disease. *Journal of Basic and Clinical Physiology and Pharmacology, 6*(3–4), 205–228.

Stokols, D. (2006). Toward a science of transdisciplinary action research. *American Journal of Community Psychology, 38*(1–2), 63–77.

Stokols, D., Hall, K. L., Taylor, B. K., & Moser, R. P. (2008). The science of team science: Overview of the field and introduction. *American Journal of Preventive Medicine, 35*(2 Suppl.), S77–S89.

Stovel, K., & Shaw, L. (2012). Brokerage. *Annual Review of Sociolology, 38*(1), 139–158.

Strahilevitz, M. A., & Loewenstein, G. F. (1998). The effect of ownership history on the valuation of objects. *Journal of Consumer Research, 25*(3), 276–289.

Straus, S. E., Johnson, M. O., Marquez, C., & Feldman, M. D. (2013). Characteristics of successful and failed mentoring relationships: A qualitative study across two academic health centers. *Academic Medicine: Journal of the Association of American Medical Colleges, 88*(1), 82–89. doi:10.1097/ ACM.0b013e31827647a0

Strauss, A. L. (1952). The development and transformation of monetary meanings in the child. *American Sociological Review, 17*, 275–286. doi:10.2307/2088073

Striegel-Moore, R. H., & Bulik, C. M. (2007). Risk factors for eating disorders. *American Psychologist, 62*(3), 181–198.

Stults, C., Javdani, S., Greenbaum, C., Barton, S., Kapadia, F., & Halkitis, P. (2015). Intimate partner violence and victimization among YMSM: The P18 cohort study. *Psychology of Sexual Orientation and Gender Diversity, 2*(2), 152–158.

Sturgis, P., Brunton-Smith, I., Read, S., & Allum, N. (2011). Does ethnic diversity erode trust? Putnam's "hunkering down" thesis reconsidered. *British Journal of Political Science, 41*(1), 57–82.

Substance Abuse and Mental Health Services Administration. (2007). *Results from the 2006 National survey on drug use and health: National findings*. Rockville, MD: SAMHSA Office of Applied Studies.

Sue, D. W. (2010). *Microaggressions in everyday life: Race, gender, and sexual orientation*. Hoboken, NJ: Wiley.

Sue, D. W., Bucceri, J., Lin, A. I., Nadal, K. L., & Torino, G. C. (2007). Racial microaggressions and the Asian American experience. *Cultural Diversity and Ethnic Minority Psychology, 13*(1), 72–81.

Sue, D., Sue, D. W., & Sue, D. (2013). *Understanding abnormal behavior* (10th ed.). Belmont, CA: Wadsworth.

Suhay, E. (2015). Explaining group influence: The role of identity and emotion in political conformity and polarization. *Political Behavior, 37*(1), 221–251. doi:10.1007/s11109-014-9269-1

Sullivan, P. F. (1995). Mortality in anorexia nervosa. *American Journal of Psychiatry, 152*(7), 1073–1074.

Super, D. E., Savickas, M. L., & Super, C. M. (1996). The life span, life space approach to careers. In D. Brown & L. Brooks (Eds.), *Career choice and development* (pp. 121–178). San Francisco, CA: Jossey-Bass.

Swanson, S. A., Saito, N., Borges, G., Benjet, C., Aguilar-Gaxiola, S., Medina-Mora, M. E., & Breslau, J. (2012). Change in binge eating and binge eating disorder associated with migration from Mexico to the U.S. *Journal of Psychiatry Research, 46*(1), 31–37.

Swanson, D. P., Spencer, M. B., Harpalani, V., Durpee, D., Noll, E., Ginzburg, S., & Seaton, G. (2003). Psychosocial development in racially and ethnically diverse youth: Conceptual and methodological challenges in the 21st century. *Development and Psychopathology, 15*(3), 743–771. doi:10.1017/S0954579403000361

Tadmor, C. T., Hong, Y.-Y., Chao, M. M., Wiruchnipawan, F., & Wang, W. (2012). Multicultural experiences reduce intergroup bias through epistemic unfreezing. *Journal of Personality and Social Psychology, 103*(5), 750–772.

Tagaki, E., Silverstein, M., & Crimmins, E. (2007). Intergenerational coresidence of older adults in Japan: Conditions for cultural plasticity. *Journal of Gerontology, 62*(5), 330–339.

Tam, L., & Dholakia, U. (2014). Saving in cycles: How to get people to save more money. *Psychological Science, 25*(2), 531–537. doi:10.1177/0956797613512129

Tang, Y. Y., & Posner, M. I. (2014). Training brain networks and states. *Trends in Cognitive Sciences, 18*(7), 345–350.

Taylor, E., Sergeant, J., Doepfner, M., Gunning, B., Overmeyer, S., Möbius, H. J., & Eisert, H. G. (1998). Clinical guidelines for hyperkinetic disorder. *European Child & Adolescent Psychiatry, 7*(4), 184–200.

Taylor, M. A., & Geldhauser, H. A. (2007). Low-income older workers. In K. S. Shultz & G. A. Adams (Eds.), *Aging and work in the 21st century* (pp. 25–49). Mahwah, NJ: Erlbaum.

Taylor, S. (2011). Social support: A review. In H. Friedman (Ed.), *Oxford handbook of health psychology* (pp.189–214). New York, NY: Oxford Press.

Taylor, S. E., Klein, L. C., Lewis, B. P., Gruenewald, T. L., Gurung, R. A., & Updegraff, J. A. (2000). Biobehavioral responses to stress in females: Tend-and-befriend, not fight or-flight. *Psychological Review, 107*(3), 411–429.

Taylor-Carter, M. A., Cook, K., & Weinberg, C. (1997). Planning and expectations of the retirement experiences. *Educational Gerontology, 23*(3), 273–288.

Thaler, R. (1980). Toward a positive theory of consumer choice. *Journal of Economic Behavior and Organization, 1*(1), 39–60.

Thaler, R. (1990). Anomalies: Savings, fungibility, and mental accounts. *Journal of Economic Perspectives, 4*, 193–205.

Thaler, R. (2008). Mental accounting and consumer choice. *Marketing Science, 27*(1), 15–25.

Therien, J. M., Worwa, C. T., Mattia, F. R., & deRegnier, R.-A. (2004). Altered pathways for auditory discrimination and recognition memory in preterm infants. *Developmental Medical Child Neurology, 46*(12), 816–824.

Thoits, P. (1995). Stress, coping and social support processes: Where are we? What next? [Extra issue]. *Journal of Health and Social Behavior*, 53–79.

Thompson, M., & Phillips, J. (2013). Promoting college retention in first generation college students. In E. Vera (Ed.), *Oxford handbook of prevention in counseling psychology* (pp. 330–346). New York, NY: Oxford University Press.

Timmerman, I. G. H., Emanuels-Zuurveen, E. S., & Emmelkamp, P. M. G. (2000). The Social Support Inventory (SSI): A brief scale to assess perceived adequacy of social support. *Clinical Psychology & Psychotherapy*, *7*(5), 401–410. doi:10.1002/1099-0879(200011)7:5<401::AID-CPP253>3.0.CO;2-I

Tinto, V. (1987). *Leaving college: Rethinking the causes and cures of student attrition* (1st ed.). Chicago, IL: University of Chicago Press.

Tix, A., & Frazier, P. (1998). The use of religious coping during stressful life events: Main effects, moderation, and mediation. *Journal of Consulting and Clinical Psychology*, *66*(2), 411–422.

Torres, J. B., & Solberg, V. S. (2001). Role of self-efficacy, stress, social integration, and family support in Latino college student persistence and health. *Journal of Vocational Behavior*, *59*(1), 53–63.

Tracy, S. J., Alberts, J. K., & Rivera, K. D. (2007, January 31). *How to bust the office bully: Eight tactics for explaining workplace abuse to decision-makers* (Report No. 0701). Retrieved from http://staffombuds.berkeley.edu/sites/default/files/How%20to%20Bust%20the%20Office%20Bully.pdf

Triandis, H. C. (1995). *Individualism & collectivism: New directions in social psychology*. Boulder, CO: Westview Press.

Triandis, H. C. (1996). The psychological measurement of cultural syndromes. *American Psychologist*, *51*(4), 407–415.

Triandis, H. C. (2002). Subjective culture. *Online Readings in Psychology and Culture*, *2*(2). doi:10.9707/2307-0919.1021

Trickett, E. (2009). Community psychology: Individuals and interventions in community context. *Annual Review of Psychology*, *60*, 395–419.

Troiano, R. P., Berrigan, D., Dodd, K. W., Masse, L. C., Tilert, T., & McDowell, M. (2008). Physical activity in the United States measured by accelerometer. *Medicine and Science in Sports and Exercise*, *40*(1), 181–188.

Trzesniewski, K. H., & Donnellan, M. B. (2009). Reevaluating the evidence for increasingly positive self-views among high school students: More evidence for consistency across generations (1976–2006). *Psychological Science*, *20*(7), 920–922.

Trzesniewski, K. H., & Donnellan, M. B. (2010). Rethinking "Generation Me": A study of cohort effects from 1976–2006. *Perspectives on Psychological Science*, *5*(1), 58–75.

Tsabari, O., Tziner, A., & Meir, E. I. (2005). Updated meta-analysis on the relationship between congruence and satisfaction. *Journal of Career Assessment*, *13*(2), 216–232.

Tsai, J. L., Ang, J. Y., Blevine, E., Goernandt, J., Fung, H. H., Jiang, D., . . . Haddouk, L. (2016). Leaders' smiles reflect cultural differences in ideal affect. *Emotion*, 16(2), 183–195.

Tsai, J. L., Louie, J. Y., Chen, E. E., & Uchida, Y. (2007). Learning what feelings to desire: Socialization of ideal affect through children's storybooks. *Personality and Social Psychology Bulletin*, *33*(1), 17–30.

Turkle, S. (2011). *Alone together*. New York, NY: Basic Books.

Turkle, S. (2015). *Reclaiming conversation: The power of talk in the digital age*. New York, NY: Penguin Books.

Turner, R. N., Hewstone, M., & Voci, A. (2007). Reducing explicit and implicit outgroup prejudice via direct and extended contact: The mediating role of self-disclosure and inter- group anxiety. *Journal of Personality and Social Psychology*, *93*(3), 369–388.

Tversky, A., & Kahneman, D. (1981). The framing of decisions and the rationality of choice. *Science*, *211*, 453–458.

Twenge, J. M., & Campbell, W. K. (2010). Birth cohort differences in the monitoring the future dataset and elsewhere: Further evidence for Generation Me: Commentary on Trzesniewski & Donnellan (2010). *Perspectives on Psychological Science*, *5*(1), 81–88.

Twenge, J. M., Campbell, W. K., & Freeman, E. C. (2012). Generational differences in young adults' life goals, concern for others, and civic orientation, 1966–2009. *Journal of Personality and Social Psychology*, *102*(5), 1045–1062.

Twenge, J. M., & Foster, J. D. (2008). Mapping the scale of the narcissism epidemic: Increases in narcissism 2002–2007 within ethnic groups. *Journal of Research in Personality*, *42*(6), 1619–1622.

Twenge, J. M., Konrath, S., Foster, J. D., Campbell, W. K., & Bushman, B. J. (2008). Further evidence of an increase in narcissism among college students. *Journal of Personality*, *76*(4), 919–928.

Twenge, J. M., Konrath, S., Foster, J. D., Keith Campbell, W., & Bushman, B. J. (2008). Egos inflating over time: A cross-temporal meta-analysis of the Narcissistic Personality Inventory. *Journal of Personality*, *76*(4), 875–902.

Twenge, J. M., Miller, J. D., & Campbell, W. K. (2014). The narcissism epidemic: Commentary on modernity and Narcissistic Personality Disorder. *Personality Disorders: Theory, Research, and Treatment*, *5*(2), 227–229.

Uchino, B. N., Bowen, K., Carlisle, M., & Birmingham, W. (2012). Psychological pathways linking social support to health outcomes: A visit with the "ghosts" of research past, present, and future. *Social Science and Medicine*, *74*(7), 949–957.

Uchino, B. N., Cacioppo, J. T., & Kiecolt-Glaser, J. K. (1996). The relationship between social support and physiological processes: A review with emphasis on underlying mechanisms and implications for health. *Psychological Bulletin*, *119*(3), 488–531.

Uhls, Y. T., Michikyan, M., Morris, J., Garcia, D., Garcia, D., Small, G. W., . . . Greenfield, P. M. (2014). Five days at outdoor education camp without screens improves preteen skills with nonverbal emotion cues. *Computers in Human Behavior*, *39*, 387–392.

Umbach, P. D., & Wawrzynski, M. R. (2005). Faculty do matter: The role of college faculty in student learning and engagement. *Research in Higher Education*, *46*(2), 153–183.

Ung, E. K. (2003). Eating disorders in Singapore: A review. *Annals Academy of Medicine Singapore, 32*, 19–24.

United Way. (2008). *Seizing the middle ground: Why middle school creates the pathway to college and the workforce.* Los Angeles, CA: United Way of Greater Los Angeles.

Uno, D., Uchino, B., & Smith, T. (2002). Relationship quality moderates the effect of social support given by close friends on cardiovascular reactivity in women. *International Journal of Behavioral Medicine, 9*(3), 243–262.

U.S. Bureau of Labor Statistics. (2013). *The aging workforces: Challenges for the health care industry.* Retrieved from http://www.dol.gov/odep/pdf/NTAR-AgingWorkforce HealthCare.pdf

U.S. Census Bureau. (2012). *A profile of older Americans 2012: Key indicators of well-being.* Washington, DC: Government Printing Office.

U.S. Census Bureau. (2013). *Statistical abstract of the United States* (132nd ed.). Washington, DC: Government Printing Office.

U.S. Census Bureau. (2015, June 25). *Millennials outnumber baby boomers and are far more diverse.* Retrieved from http://www.census.gov/newsroom/press-releases/2015/cb15-113.html

U.S. Department of Education. (2009). *Digest of education statistics, 2008.* Washington DC: Government Printing Office.

U.S. Department of Education. (2013). *Digest of education statistics, 2012.* Washington, DC: Government Printing Office.

U.S. Department of Education, Office of Postsecondary Education. (2008). *A profile of the federal TRIO programs and child care access means parents in school program.* Washington, DC: Author.

U.S. Department of Health and Human Services. (2011a). *Births: Preliminary data for 2010.* Retrieved from www.cdc.gov/nchs/data/nvsr/nvsr60/nvsr60_02.pdf

U.S. Department of Health and Human Services. (2011b). *The surgeon general's call to action to prevent and decrease overweight and obesity: Overweight children and adolescents.* Retrieved from www.surgeongeneral.gov/library/calls/obesity/fact_adolescents.html

U.S. Department of Health & Human Services and U.S. Department of Agriculture. (2015, December). 2015–2020 dietary guidelines for Americans (8th ed.). Retrieved from http://health.gov/dietaryguidelines/2015/guidelines

U.S. Food and Drug Administration. (2013). *Reclaim DBS therapy for OCD.* Retrieved from http://www.fda.gov/MedicalDevices/ProductsandMedicalProcedures/DeviceApprovalsandClearances/Recently-Approved Devices/ucm125520.htm

U.S. Food and Drug Administration. (2015). *June 2015 PMA approvals.* Retrieved from http://www.fda.gov/medical devices/productsandmedicalprocedures/deviceapproval sandclearances/pmaapprovals/ucm459241.htm

Uslaner, E. M. (2012) *Segregation and mistrust.* Cambridge MA: Cambridge University Press.

U.S. National Library of Medicine. (2006). *Diseases of the mind: Highlights of American psychiatry through 1900: Early psychiatric hospitals and asylums.* Retrieved from https://www.nlm.nih.gov/hmd/diseases/early.html

Valentine, J. C., DuBois, D. L., & Cooper, H. (2004). The relation between self-beliefs and academic achievement: A meta-analytic review. *Educational Psychologist, 39*(2), 111–133.

Valkenburg, P. M., Peter, J., & Schouten, A. P. (2006). Friend networking sites and their relationship to adolescents' well-being and social self-esteem. *CyberPsychology & Behavior, 9*(5), 584–590.

van Dijk, J. (2006). *The network society* (2nd ed.). Thousand Oaks, CA: Sage.

van Heeringen, K. (2000). A stress-diathesis model of suicidal behavior. *Crisis: The Journal of Crisis Intervention and Suicide Prevention, 21*(4), 192.

Vansteenkiste, M., Simons, J., Lens, W., Sheldon, K. M., & Deci, E. L. (2004). Motivating learning, performance, and persistence: The synergistic effects of intrinsic goal contents and autonomy-supportive contexts. *Journal of Personality and Social Psychology, 87*(2), 246–260. doi:10.1037/00223514.87.2.246

Vera, E. M., Vacek, K., Blackmon, S., Coyle, L., Gomez, K., Jorgenson, K., . . . Steele, J. C. (2012). Subjective well-being in urban, ethnically diverse adolescents: The role of stress and coping. *Youth and Society, 44*(3), 331–347.

Vera, E. M., Vacek, K., Coyle, L. D., Stinson, J., Mull, M., Doud, K., . . . Langrehr, K. J. (2011). An examination of culturally relevant stressors, coping, ethnic identity, and subjective well-being in urban, ethnic minority adolescents. *Professional School Counseling, 15*(2), 55–66.

Vohs, K. D., Mead, N. L., & Goode, M. R. (2006). The psychological consequences of money. *Science, 314*, 1154–1156. doi:10.1126/science.1132491

Vohs, K. D., & Faber, R. J. (2007). Spent resources: Self-regulatory resource availability affects impulse buying. *Journal of Consumer Research, 33*(4), 537–547.

von Freymann, J. W. (2002). A practitioner's application of the marketing concept to employee absenteeism and behavioral change programs. *Employee Assistance Quarterly, 17*(3), 61–77.

Vrangalova, S., & Savin-Williams, R. (2008). *Casual sex: A sexual orientation, a context-dependent behavior, or a personal pathology?* Unpublished manuscript, Cornell University, Ithaca, NY.

Vygotsky, L. S. (1978). *Mind in society: The development of higher psychological processes* (M. Cole, V. John-Steiner, S. Scribner, & E. Souberman, Eds. & Trans.). Cambridge, MA: Harvard University Press. (Original work published 1934)

Vygotsky, L. S. (2012). *Thought and language* (Rev. ed.). Cambridge, MA: MIT Press.

Vyncke, V., Peersman, W., Maeseneer, J., & Willems, S. (2012). Measuring the immeasurable? Operationalizing social capital in health research. *Health, 4*(9), 555–566. doi:10.4236/health.2012.49087

Wai, J., Lubinski, D., Benbow, C. P., & Steiger, J. H. (2010). Accomplishment in science, technology, engineering, and mathematics (STEM) and its relation to STEM educational dose: A 25-year longitudinal study. *Journal of Educational Psychology, 102*(4), 860–871. doi:10.1037/a0019454

Walker, I., & Crogan, M. (1998). Academic performance, prejudice, and the jigsaw classroom: New pieces to the puzzle. *Journal of Community & Applied Social Psychology, 8*(6), 381–393.

Walker, M. P. (2009a). The role of sleep in cognition and emotion. *Annals of the New York Academy of Science, 1156*, 168–197. doi:10.1111/j.1749-6632.2009.04416.x.

Walker, M. P. (2009b). The role of slow wave sleep in memory processing. *Journal of Clinical Sleep Medicine, 5*(2 Suppl.), S20–S26. PMCID: PMC2824214 Retrieved from http://www.ncbi.nlm.nih.gov/pmc/articles/PMC2824214

Walsh, K. E., & Berman, J. R. (2004). Sexual dysfunction in the older woman: An overview of the current understanding and management. *Therapy in Practice, 21*(10), 655–675.

Walsh, R. (2011). Lifestyle and mental health. *American Psychologist, 66*(7), 579–592.

Wang, H., & Wellman, B. (2010). Social connectivity in America: Changes in adult friendship network size from 2002 to 2007. *American Behavioral Scientist, 53*(8), 1148–1169.

Warren, J. E., Sauter, D. A., Eisner, F., Wiland, J., Alexander Dresner, M., Wise, R. J. S., . . . Scott, S. K. (2006). Positive emotions preferentially engage an auditory-motor "mirror" system. *The Journal of Neuroscience, 26*(50), 13067–13075.

Wasserman, S., & Faust, K. (1994). *Social network analysis: Methods and applications.* New York, NY: Cambridge University Press.

Watson, J. B. (1913). Psychology as the behaviorist views it. *Psychological Review, 20*(2), 158–177.

Watts, R. (2000). Entering the new millennium: Is individual psychology still relevant. *Journal of Individual Psychology, 56*, 21–30.

Webley, P., & Nyhus, E. K. (2006). Parents' influence on children's future orientation and saving. *Journal of Economic Psychology, 27*(1), 140–164.

Webley, P., & Nyhus, E. K. (2013). Economic socialization, saving and assets in European young adults. *Economics of Education Review, 33*, 19–30. doi:10.1016/j.econedurev.2012.09.001

Weeden, J., & Sabini, J. (2007). Subjective and objective measures of attractiveness and their relation to sexual behavior and sexual attitudes in university students. *Archives of Sexual Behavior, 36*(1), 79–88.

Wehlage, G. (1989). Dropping out: Can schools be expected to prevent it? In L. Weis, E. Farrar, & H. Petrie (Eds.), *Dropouts from school* (pp. 1–19). Albany: State University of New York Press.

Weick, K. (1995). *Sensemaking in organizations.* Thousand Oaks, CA: Sage.

Weick, K., & Quinn, R. (1999). Organizational change and development. *Annual Review of Psychology, 50*(1), 361–386.

Weiner, D. B. (2010a). The madman in the light of reason. Enlightenment psychiatry: Part II. Alienists, treatises, and the psychological approach in the era of Pinel. In E. B. Wallace & J. Gach (Eds.), *History of psychiatry and medical psychology: With an epilogue on psychiatry and the mind-body relation* (pp. 281–304). New York, NY: Springer.

Weiner, D. B. (2010b). Philippe Pinel in the 21st century: The myth and the message. In E. B. Wallace & J. Gach (Eds.), *History of psychiatry and medical psychology: With an epilogue on psychiatry and the mind-body relation* (pp. 305–312). New York, NY: Springer.

Weir, K. (2011). The exercise effect. *Monitor on Psychology, 42*(11), 49–52.

Weiten, W., Dunn, D., & Yost Hammer, E. (2015). *Psychology applied to modern life: Adjustment in the 21st century.* Stamford, CT: Cengage.

Werner, E. E., & Smith, R. S. (2001). *Journeys from childhood to midlife.* Ithaca, NY: Cornell University Press.

Wertheimer, M. (2012). *A brief history of psychology* (5th ed.). New York, NY: Psychology Press.

Wettersten, K. B., Schreurs, A., Munch, J., Faith, C., & Sell, D. (2015). Promoting healthy relationships in young adults. In C. Juntunen & J. Schwartz (Eds.), *Counseling across the lifespan* (pp. 241–258). Thousand Oaks, CA: Sage.

Wheaton, B. (1997). The nature of chronic stress. In B. Gottlieb (Ed.), *Coping with chronic stress* (pp. 43–103). New York, NY: Plenum.

Whitaker, R. (2010). *Anatomy of an epidemic: Magic bullets, psychiatric drugs, and the astonishing rise of mental illness in America.* New York, NY: Crown Publishers.

Whitbourne, S. K., Sneed, J. R., & Sayer, A. (2009). Psychosocial development from college through midlife: A 34-year sequential study. *Developmental Psychology, 45*(5), 1328–1340. doi:10.1037/a0016550

Whitebread, D., Coltman, P., Jameson, H., & Lander, R. (2009). Play, cognition and self-regulation: What exactly are children learning when they learn through play? *Educational and Child Psychology, 26*(2), 40.

The White House. (n.d.). *Brain initiative.* Retrieved from https://www.whitehouse.gov/BRAIN

The White House. (2014). *15 economic facts about millennials.* Retrieved from https://www.whitehouse.gov/sites/default/files/docs/millennials_report.pdf

Whitty, M. T. (2003). Pushing the wrong buttons: Men's and women's attitudes toward on line and off line infidelity. *Cyberpsychology & Behavior, 6*(6), 569–579.

Wiedenfeld, S. A., O'Leary, A., Bandura, A., Brown, S., Levine, S., & Raska, K. (1990). Impact of perceived self-efficacy in coping with stressors on components of the immune system. *Journal of Personality and Social Psychology, 59*(5), 1082–1094. doi:10.1037/0022-3514.59.5.1082

Wigfield, A., Byrnes, J. B., & Eccles, J. (2006). Adolescent development. In P. A. Alexander & P. Winne (Eds.), *Handbook of educational psychology* (pp. 87–113). Mahwah, NJ: Erlbaum.

Wilcox, B. (1981). Social support, life stress, and psychological adjustment: A test of the buffering hypothesis. *American Journal of Community Psychology, 9*(4), 371–386.

Wilkie, S. S., Guenette, J. A., Dominelli, P. B., & Scheel, A. W. (2012). Effects of an aging pulmonary system on expiratory flow limitation and dyspnoea during exercise in healthy women. *European Journal of Applied Physiology, 112*(6), 2195–2204.

Willett, M. (2008). The new model for retirement education and counseling. *Financial Services Review, 17*, 105–130.

Williams, K., Woolfenden, S., Roberts, J., Rodger, S., Bartak, L., & Prior, M. (2014). Autism in context 1: Classification, counting and causes. *Journal of Paediatrics & Child Health, 50*(5), 335–340.

Wilson, T. D., Gilbert, D. T., & Centerbar, D. B. (2003). Making sense: The causes of emotional evanescence. In I. Brocas & J. D. Carillo (Eds.), *The psychology of economic decisions*. Volume 1: Rationality and well-being (pp. 209–233). New York, NY: Oxford University Press.

Wilson, W. J. (1996). *When work disappears*. New York, NY: Knopf.

Wingate, U. (2006). Doing away with "study skills." *Teaching in Higher Education, 11*(4), 457–469.

Wink, P., Ciciolla, L., Dillon, M., & Tracy, A. (2007). Religiousness, spiritual seeking, and personality: Findings from a longitudinal study. *Journal of Personality, 75*(5), 1051–1070.

Wink, P., & Dillon, M. (2002). Religiousness, spirituality, and psychosocial functioning in later adulthood: Findings from a longitudinal study. *Psychology of Religion and Spirituality, 5*, 102–113.

Wolff, T. (2010). *The power of collaborative solutions*. San Francisco, CA: Jossey-Bass.

Wood, S. L., & Bettman, J. (2007). Predicting happiness: How normative feeling rules influence (and even reverse) durability bias. *Journal of Consumer Psychology, 17*(3), 188–201.

World Health Organization. (2001). *World health report: Mental disorders affect one in four people*. Retrieved from http://www.who.int/whr/2001/media_centre/press_release/en

World Health Organization. (2013a). *Autism spectrum disorders and other developmental disorders: From raising awareness to building capacity*. Geneva, Switzerland: Author. Retrieved from http://apps.who.int/iris/bitstream/10665/103312/1/9789241506618_eng.pdf

World Health Organization. (2013b). *Obesity and overweight*. Retrieved from www.who.int/medicentre/factsheets/fs311/en

World Health Organization. (2014a). *The ICD-10 classification of mental and behavioural disorders: Clinical descriptions and diagnostic guidelines*. New York, NY: Author.

World Health Organization. (2014b). *Mental health fact sheet*. Retrieved from http://www.who.int/mediacentre/factsheets/fs396/en

World Health Organization. (2014c). *Schizophrenia fact sheet*. Retrieved from http://www.who.int/mediacentre/factsheets/fs397/en

World Health Organization. (2014d). *World health statistics*. Retrieved from http://www.who.int/mediacentre/news/releases/2014/world-health-statistics-2014/en

World Health Organization. (2015). *World Health Organization's report on preventing suicide*. Retrieved from http://www.cdc.gov/violenceprevention/suicide/who-report.html

Wu, Z., Hou, F., & Schimmele, C. M. (2011). Racial diversity and sense of belonging in urban neighborhoods. *City & Community, 10*(4), 373–392.

Wulff, D. (1997). *Psychology of religion: Classic and contemporary views* (2nd ed.). Hoboken, NJ: Wiley.

Wyckoff, S., & Birbaumer, N. (2014). Neurofeedback and brain–computer interfaces. In D. I. Mostofsky (Ed.), *The handbook of behavioral medicine* (pp. 275–312). Hoboken, NJ: Wiley-Blackwell.

Wysocki, D. K., & Childers, C. D. (2011). Let my fingers do the talking: Sexting and infidelity in cyberspace. *Sexuality & Culture: An Interdisciplinary Quarterly, 15*(3), 217–239.

Xie, L., Kang, H., Xu, O., Chen, M., Liao, Y., Thiyagarajan, M., . . . Nedergaard, M. (2013, October 18). Sleep drives metabolite clearance from the adult brain. *Science, 342*(6156), 373–377. doi:10.1126/science.1241224

Yalom, I. D. (1980). *Existential psychotherapy*. New York, NY: Basic Books.

Yang, C. Y., Boen, C., Gerken, K., Li, T., Schorpp, K., & Mullan Harris, K. (2016). Social relationships and physiological determinants of longevity across the human lifespan. *Proceedings of the National Academy of Sciences, USA, 113*(3), 578–583. doi:10.1073/pnas.151108511

Yanos, P. T., Lucksted, A., Drapalski, A. L., Roe, D., & Lysaker, P. (2015). Interventions targeting mental health self-stigma: A review and comparison. *Psychiatric Rehabilitation Journal, 38*(2), 171–178.

Yeager, D. S., Henderson, M. D., Paunesku, D., Walton, G. M., D'Mello, S., Spitzer, B. J., & Duckworth, A. L. (2014). Boring but important: A self-transcendent purpose for learning fosters academic self-regulation. *Journal of Personality and Social Psychology, 107*(4), 559–580. doi:10.1037/a0037637

Zajacova, A., Lynch, S., & Espenshade, T. (2005, September). Self-efficacy, stress, and academic success in college. *Research in Higher Education, 46*(6), 677–706. doi:10.1007/s11162-004-4139-z

Zautra, A. (2003). *Emotions, stress, and health*. New York, NY: Oxford University Press.

Zautra, A. J., Affleck, G. G., Tennen, H., Reich, J. W., & Davis, M. C. (2005). Dynamic approaches to emotions and stress in everyday life: Bolger and Zuckerman reloaded with positive as well as negative affects. *Journal of Personality, 73*(6), 1511–1538. doi:10.1111/j.0022-3506.2005.00357.x

Zimmerman, B. J. (2000). Self-efficacy: An essential motive to learn. *Contemporary Educational Psychology, 25*(1), 82–91.

Zimmerman, B. J. (2002). Becoming a self-regulated learner: An overview. *Theory into practice, 41*(2), 64–70.

Zimmerman, M. A., Bingenheimer, J. B., & Notaro, P. C. (2002). Natural mentors and adolescent resiliency: A study with urban youth. *American Journal of Community Psychology, 30*(2), 221–243. doi:10.1023/A:1014632911622

Zinnbauer, B., Pargament, K., Cole, B., Rye, M., Butler, E., Belavich, T., . . .Kadar, J. (1997). Religion and spirituality: Unfuzzying the fuzzy. *Journal for the Scientific Study of Religion, 36*(4), 549–564. doi:10.2307/1387689

○ Index

Aaker, J., 31, 236
   see also Baumeister, R. F.
Abad, N., 155
Aber, J. L., 54
Aber, M. S., 120
Abnormal factors, 7–8
Abusive behaviors, 170–172
Academic hardiness, 34–35
Academic mentoring, 47
Academic motivation, 184, 184 (table), 196
Academic self-efficacy, 184, 184 (table), 195, 196, 198
Academic success, 183–185, 184 (table), 187–190
Acceptance
   see Mindfulness; Nonjudgmental awareness
Accommodation, 83
Ackerman, J. M.
   see Griskevicius, V.
Acquaintances, 51
ACT, 193
Active behaviors, 259
Active coping, 120–121, 121 (table), 123
Active learning, 70, 84 (figure), 84–85
Active listening, 165
Acute stressors, 113
Adams, K. B., 263
Adaval, R., 228
ADD/ADHD
   see Attention deficit disorders
ADDHealth study, 161
Addictive behaviors, 169, 274, 280–283, 282 (table),
   284 (table), 324
Adelman, J., 35
Adjust, 6
Adjustment
   biofeedback, 12–13
   definitions, 5–11
   goodness of fit, 6–7
   individual characteristics, 6–11
   lack of problems, 7–8
   mind-body interaction, 9–13
   positive life experiences, 8–9, 10 (table)
   sleep-memory connections, 11–12
   typical questions, 6 (table)
Adjustment in Practice
   avoidance learning, 75
   bullying, 185–186
   choice conditions, 41
   compassion, 152
   five-factor model (FFM) of personality, 37
   Head Start program, 182–183
   healthy technology usage, 324–325
   Holland's theory, 217

in-groups versus out-groups, 57–58
loneliness, 254–255
loving-kindness meditation (LKM), 102–103
meditation exercise, 93
mentoring, 199
microaggressions, 123
mindfullness practice, 100–101
myths of good relationships, 165
narratives and stories, 327–328
personal values, 105–106
Premack principle, 77
Present–Future Similarity Test, 235–236
psychotropic medications, 296–297, 298 (table)
seeking professional help, 291–293, 292 (figure)
self-control, 78–79
sleep-memory connections, 11–12
Adler, A., 308
Adler, Alfred, 21, 307–308
Adler, N. E.
   see Epel, E. S.; Saegert, S. C.
Adler, T.
   see Eccles, J.
Admirable qualities, 9, 10 (table)
Adolescence
   addictive behaviors, 283
   career and vocational interest assessment, 207, 213–214
   cognitive changes, 250
   coping strategies and styles, 120, 122, 123
   dating relationships, 161–162
   friendships, 143–145
   higher education programs, 194–195
   Internet impacts, 326–327
   narratives and stories, 328
   obesity rates, 131–132
   perceived work opportunities, 211
   physical activity/exercise, 133–134
   purpose in life, 32, 33 (figure)
   resiliency, 65 (table)
   same-sex versus opposite-sex attraction, 160–161
   savings patterns, 234
   school dropout rate, 191
   social support impacts, 48, 49 (figure)
   substance abuse, 134–135
   suicidal behaviors, 285
   see also Romantic relationships
Adrenaline, 113, 127
Adultery, 168–170
Adulthood
   altruistic behavior, 153
   bullying, 186
   cognitive changes, 249–251, 255 (table)
   friendships, 147–148, 148 (figure)

life tasks, 16–17, 17 (table)
narratives and stories, 328
obesity rates, 131–132
online dating, 321
physical activity/exercise, 133–134
physical changes, 246–249, 247 (table)
purpose in life, 33
resiliency, 65 (table)
savings patterns, 234
sexual activity, 166
social support impacts, 49 (figure), 253–254, 255 (table)
socioemotional changes, 251–255, 255 (table)
substance abuse, 134–135
Adversity, 128, 306
Affairs, 168–170
Affiliation, 66
Affleck, G. G., 18
Afflerbach, P., 196
African Americans
college enrollment trends and graduation rates, 195 (figure)
committed partnerships, 162–163
coping strategies and styles, 120, 122, 123
friendships, 143, 144
higher education programs, 194
implicit prejudice, 315
learning community interventions, 200
life expectancies, 245
microaggressions, 122
obesity rates, 131–132
spousal loss, 261
substance abuse, 134–135
Agency, 307–308
Age-related changes
see Aging
Aggressive behaviors, 170–172
Agiesta, J., 256
Aging
adjusting to loss, 260–262
aging in place, 263–265
cognitive changes, 249–251, 255 (table)
financial planning, 257–258, 258 (figure)
life expectancies, 244–246, 245 (figure), 256
living situations, 263–265
loneliness, 253, 254–255
physical changes, 246–249, 247 (table)
retirement, 210–211, 256–258, 263–265
role redefinition, 257
socioemotional changes, 251–255, 255 (table)
spiritual and religious beliefs and activities, 261, 262 (table)
successful aging, 258–259
third age, 256
Agoraphobia, 275, 284 (table)
Agrawal, A., 283
Aguado, T., 187
Aguilar-Gaxiola, S.
see Swanson, S. A.
Ahn, S., 122
Ainsworth, M., 140
Aknin, L. B., 239
Alarcon, G. M., 34
Alaska, 311

Albert, M.
see Berkman, F.
Alberts, J. K., 186
Alcohol consumption, 280, 281, 282 (table)
see Substance abuse
Aldwin, C. M., 19
Alexander, C. N., 97
Alexander Dresner, M.
see Warren, J. E.
Alexander, K. L., 191
Alfred, T.
see Clark, C.
Alhoniemi, A., 327
Ali, A.
see Edwards, B. A.
Alienation, 30
Allen, T. D., 47
see also Eby, L. T.
Allik, J., 188
Allport, G., 36, 57, 58, 312, 316
Allport, Gordon, 36
Allum, N., 312
Altmaier, E. M., 9
Altman, D.
see Maton, K. I.
Altman, I., 175
Altruism, 33, 141–142, 150, 152–153
Alzahabi, R., 130
Alzheimer's Association, 251
Amaro, H., 38
Amato, P. R., 172, 174
Amazon, 318
American College of Sports Medicine
see Garber, C. E.
American Institutes for Research, 5
American Psychiatric Association, 274, 275, 276, 277, 279, 280, 281, 282 (table), 286, 287, 324
American Psychological Association, 47, 48, 291, 292, 311, 312, 324
Amodio, D. M., 315
Amphetamines, 280, 282
Anderson, K. K., 278
Anderson, M. H.
see Fang, R.
Anderson, N. B., 113
Andreasen, N. C., 277, 278
Anger, 107, 127, 165
Ang, J. Y.
see Tsai, J. L.
Angold, A., 185
Ano, G., 38
Anorexia nervosa, 279, 284 (table)
Ansbacher, H., 21
Anterior cingulate cortex (ACC), 38, 39 (figure)
Antianxiety medications, 280, 281, 296, 298 (table)
Anticipation, 19–20, 231, 239
Anticonvulsant medications, 296
Antidepressant medications, 296, 298 (table)
Antipsychotic medications, 296, 298 (table)
Antisocial personality disorder, 172
Antonovsky, A., 20, 32

Anxiety/anxiety disorders
    bullying, 185
    career indecisiveness, 208
    characteristics, 271, 274, 282 (table), 284 (table)
    developmental origins, 276
    ending relationships, 174
    exercise benefits, 126
    intimate partner violence (IPV), 172
    multitasking effects, 130
    nursing home residents, 265
    onset, 7
    physical and cognitive symptoms, 275–276
    prevalence, 274–275, 284 (table)
    psychotropic medications, 280, 281, 296, 298 (table)
    stress reactions, 117, 127
    substance-induced mental disorders, 282, 283
App, B., 124
Apple Computer, 317
Archer, J., 170
Arevalo, J. M., 154
Arévalo, S., 38
Ariely, D., 228, 230, 232
Ariely, G., 312
Arkin, R. M., 30
Arndt, J., 30, 31
Arnett, J. J., 65, 147, 207
Arns, M., 13
Aronson, E., 315
Aronson, J., 187
Arora, R., 237
Arpanet, 317
Arseneault, L.
    see Moffitt, T. E.
Asch, S. E., 56, 57
Asghar, M. W.
    see Rikani, A. A.
Ashmore, R., 314
Asians/Asian Americans
    committed partnerships, 163
    coping strategies and styles, 122, 123–124
    friendships, 144
    microaggressions, 122
    obesity rates, 131
Aslin, R. N., 82
ASPIRES (assessment of spiritual and religious sentiments), 37–38
Assimilation, 83, 194
Assisted living situations, 253
Associative play, 141
Assurance/assuring behaviors, 149, 150 (table), 175 (table), 176
Asylums, 288–289, 293
Atkins, D. C., 168
At-risk populations, 63 (table), 63–64
Attention deficit disorders, 274, 284 (table), 286–287, 296, 298 (table)
Auinger, P.
    see Foltz, J. L.
Austin, Texas, 238 (table)
Australia, 310
Auth, E. A., 263
Authority, 57

Autism spectrum disorder (ASD), 274, 284 (table), 287
Automatic savings, 236
Autonomic nervous system, 12
Autonomy, 40
Average life expectancy, 244
Aversive prejudice, 313
Avoidance learning, 75, 104, 107, 154
Avoidant coping, 120–121, 121 (table), 123
Awa, W. L., 220
Ayduk, O.
    see Kross, E.; Mischel, W.
Azar, B., 124
Azaroff, L. S., 219

Babcock, J. C., 171
Baby boomers, 311
BackRub, 318
Badenes-Ribera, L., 171
Bad stress, 127
Baek, R., 327
Bailer, U. F., 280
    see also Kaye, W. H.
Balasch, J., 246
Baldwin, C. D.
    see Foltz, J. L.
Baldwin, S.
    see Eby, L. T.
Baldwin, T. T., 50
Ballard, K., 234, 235
Ballesteros, B., 187
Ball, M. M., 264
Balogun, J., 20
Balsam, P. D., 76
Banaji, M. R., 58, 71, 313
Banaschewski, T., 287
Bandura, A., 62, 74, 80, 81, 82, 184, 215, 225
    see also Wiedenfeld, S. A.
Bandura, Albert, 70
Banking services, 232–234
Banks, J., 237
    see also Boyce, C. J.
Banning, K., 114
Banter, 149, 150 (table)
Bao, J., 248
Baranik, L. E.
    see Eby, L. T.
Barbaris, N., 30
Barber, J. P., 277
Bargh, J. A., 30
Barker, R. G., 7, 53, 55
Barlow, D. H., 276
Barndollar, K., 30
Barnes, N. W., 122
Barrera, M. S., 48, 124
Barrett, A. E., 321
Barrett, M. S., 277
Barrington-Leigh, C. P., 239
Barron, G., 77
Bartak, L.
    see Williams, Katrina
Barta, T., 313

Bartkiewicz, M. J., 185
Bartolomucci, A.
  see Koolhaas, J. M.
Bartone, P. T.
  see Sandvik, A. M.
Barton, S.
  see Stults, C.
Bassuk, S. S., 133
Bateson, G., 128
Batra, R., 57
Baucom, D. H., 168
  see also Atkins, D. C.
Baumeister, A. A., 289
Baumeister, R. F., 30, 31, 40, 230, 231, 239, 311, 312
Bearman, P., 52
Beck, Aaron, 290
Beck, A. T., 80, 129, 277
Becker, B., 63, 306
  see also Luthar, S. S.
Becker, K., 287
Becker, M. W., 130
Beck, J., 290
Bedell, M. D., 50
Bedlam, 288
Behavior acquisition, 71–72
Behavioral economics, 224, 228–229
Behavioral settings
  conformity influences, 56–57
  cultural influences, 59 (table), 59–60
  developmental demands and capabilities, 62
  discriminative stimuli, 55–56, 73
  ecological psychology, 53–55
  environmental contexts, 53
  obedience to authority, 57
  shaping, 78
  see also Consequences
Behavior-consequence relationships, 74–77
Behaviorism, 55, 290
Behavior modification, 272
Belavich, T.
  see Zinnbauer, B.
Belongingness, 48, 184 (table), 185, 189, 195
Belsky, D.
  see Moffitt, T. E.
Benbow, C. P., 213
Benenson, J., 142
Bengtsson, H., 153
Benjamin, L. T., Jr., 94
Benjet, C.
  see Swanson, S. A.
Bennett, K. M., 260, 261
Benz, J., 256
Bereavement support, 261–262, 262 (table)
Berger, N.
  see Fritsche, I.
Bergin, A. E., 36, 38
Berglund, P.
  see Kessler, R. C.
Berk, L. E., 131, 133, 134, 140, 141, 148, 150, 153, 154, 155, 161, 174, 181, 183, 184, 193, 207, 244, 245, 246, 247, 248, 250, 251, 252, 253, 256, 260, 261, 263, 264

Berkman, F., 259
Berman, J. R., 166
Berman, M. G., 174
  see also Kross, E.; Mischel, W.
Bermeo, A., 194
  see also Engle, J.
Bermudez-Rattoni, F., 71
Berners-Lee, Tim, 318
Bernheim, B. D., 234
Berntson, G. G., 52
Berrigan, D.
  see Troiano, R. P.
Berrios, G. E., 293
Berry, J., 58
Bertsch, S., 84
Best, K. M., 63
Bethlehem Hospital, 288
Bettinger, M., 167
Bettman, J., 231, 239
Beutler, I., 226
Bewley, T., 288
Bezos, Jeff, 318
Bhana, A., 120
Biederman, J., 286
Bimbi, D. S., 161
Binge eating disorder, 279, 284 (table)
Bingenheimer, J. B., 47
Biofeedback, 12–13
Biological aging, 246
Biological predispositions, 71–72
Biopsychosocial model, 272, 273 (figure), 276, 280, 283, 285
Bipolar disorder, 172, 276–277, 278, 282 (table), 284 (table), 296, 298 (table)
Birbaumer, N., 12
Birch, S., 140
Birger, J., 162
Birmingham, W., 48
  see also Bowen, K. S.
Biswas-Diener, R.
  see Aknin, L. B.
Black Americans
  see African Americans
Blackburn, E. H.
  see Epel, E. S.
Black, J. S., 328
  see also Shaffer, M. A.
Black, M. C., 171
Blackmon, S.
  see Vera, E. M.
Blass, T., 57
Blau, J., 191
Blazer, D.
  see Berkman, F.
Blehar, M., 140
Bleuler, M., 63
Blevine, E.
  see Tsai, J. L.
Blieszner, R., 147
Blindness, 248
Blissmer, B.
  see Garber, C. E.

Block, M., 18
Bloodletting, 272
Blumenthal, J. A., 126
Blumenthal, Jon
    see Giedd, J. N.
Blum, R. W., 62
Blustein, D. L., 206, 210, 211
    see Chaves, A. P.
Board of Governors of the Federal Reserve System, 258
Bodily humors, 272
Body dysmorphic disorder, 275
Body mass index (BMI), 279
Boen, C.
    see Yang, C. Y.
Bolsen, T., 57
Bonding, 52
Bond, R., 57, 59
Bone density decline, 247
Bonilla-Campos, A., 171
Borawski, E. A., 161
Borden, R. J.
    see Cialdini, R. B.
Borderline personality disorder, 172
Bor, D. H.
    see Lasser, K.
Bordia, P., 20
Borgen, F. H., 215
Borges, G.
    see Swanson, S. A.
Boring, E., 94
Borradaile, K. E.
    see Foster, G. D.
Boscardin, W. J.
    see Kelly, A.
Bose, S., 191
Boston, Massachusetts, 238 (table)
Boswell, G., 38
Bourdon, K.
    see Merikangas, K. R.
Bowen, K. S., 48, 50
Bowers, E. P., 7
Bowker, J., 154
Bowlby, J., 140
Bowling, N. A., 34
Bowman, N. A., 315
Boyce, C. J., 237, 238
Boyd, D., 146
Boyd, J. E., 298
Boyd, J. W.
    see Lasser, K.
Bradshaw, C., 48
BRAIN (Brain Research Through Advancing Innovative
        Neurotechnologies) Initiative, 298
Brain research
    see Neurological research
Brain stimulation therapies, 293, 294–295
Bramlett, M.
    see Gueldner, S. H.
Brandenberger, J. W., 33, 315
    see also Hill, P. L.
Brashears, M. E., 323

Bratter, B., 257
Braxton, N., 38
Breakups, 172–174
Brefczynski-Lewis, J., 102
Breger, L., 289
Breiding, M. J., 171
Breland, K., 71
Breland, M., 71
Bremer, C. D., 191
Brennan, R. T., 13
Brentano, C., 172
Breslau, J.
    see Swanson, S. A.
Breuer, Josef, 289
Brewer, M. B., 57, 58, 316
Bridgeman, D., 315
Bridge retirement, 256
Bridging, 52
Brief psychotic disorder, 278, 284 (table)
Brin, Sergey, 318
Brion, S. L., 37
Brissette, I., 124
Brody, D.
    see Merikangas, K. R.
Brody, G. H., 47
    see also Kogan, S. M.
Broken hearts, 174
Brokerage, 50–51
Bronfenbrenner's ecological model,
        8 (figure)
Bronfenbrenner, U., 7, 8 (figure)
Bronk, K. C., 32
Brooklyn, New York, 238 (table)
Brooks-Gunn, J., 183
Brow, M.
    see Maddi, S. R.
Brown, G. D. A., 237
    see also Boyce, C. J.
Brown, P. C., 84
Brown, S. D., 206, 213, 214, 215, 216
    see also Lent, R. W.
Brown, Shirley
    see Wiedenfeld, S. A.
Bruehlman-Senecal, E.
    see Kross, E.
Brunton-Smith, I., 312
Bucceri, J., 122
Bucher, S.
    see Foltz, J. L.
Buddhism, 94–95
    see also Mindfulness
Buechel, E. C., 228
Buehler, R., 308
Buffering theory, 124
Buhs, E., 140
Bukowski, W., 140, 141
Bulik, C. M., 131, 280
    see also Mazzeo, S. E.
Bulimia nervosa, 279, 284 (table)
Bulleit, B. A., 124
Bulletin board systems, 317

Bullock, H.
see Saegert, S. C.
Bullying, 152, 153, 185–186, 189
Bureau of Justice Statistics, 170
Burger, J. M., 30, 57
Burghart, D., 239
see also Harbaugh, W.
Burke, B., 30
Burney, R., 96
Burnout, 220
Burns, J.
see Aknin, L. B.
Burns, K., 199
Burrow, A. L., 33
see also Hill, P. L.
Burson, A.
see Kross, E.
Burt, R., 51
Bushman, B. J., 322
see also Twenge, J. M.
Butera, N. M., 134
Butler, A. C., 80
Butler, E.
see Zinnbauer, B.
Buwalda, B.
see Koolhaas, J. M.
Buxton, O. M., 11
Buying skills
see Money
Byars-Winston, A., 211
Bynner, J., 207, 209, 211
Byrnes, J. B., 186
Bystanders, 186

Cacioppo, J. T., 31, 36, 48, 52, 154, 254, 315, 321
see also Ito, T. A.; Masi, C. M.; Uchino, B. N.
Cacioppo, S., 321
Caetano, A., 19
Caffeine, 280, 282 (table)
Cain, S. W.
see Buxton, O. M.
Calfas, K. J.
see Patrick, K.
Cali, B. E., 322
California, 310
Callan, V., 20
Calliotte, J. A.
see Chartrand, J. M.
Camara, W., 5
Camilleri, N., 286
Campbell, Catherine, 322
Campbell, Cynthia L., 117
Campbell, J., 99
Campbell, W. K., 322, 326
see also Twenge, J. M.
Canada, 310
Canary, D. J., 175
Cannabis, 280, 282, 282 (table)
Cannon, W., 10
Cantú, S. M.
see Griskevicius, V.

Care, 15, 15 (table)
CareerCast, 218
Careers
contextual influences, 211, 213–214
counseling services, 208–209
definition, 206
employee assistance programs (EAPs), 219–220
first job, 209
flow, 218
fundamental human needs, 206–207, 210
importance, 206–207
indecisiveness, 208–209
life span salience, 207–211
meaningful work, 205
midcareer period, 210
retirement, 210–211
rewards and risks, 218–220
science, technology, engineering, and mathematics (STEM)
programs, 212 (figure), 212–213
stress levels, 218–219
theory of occupational circumscription and compromise,
214–215
Caregiver relationships, 140
Carlisle, M., 48
see also Bowen, K. S.
Carmon, Z., 232
Carrasco, J. A., 146
Carroll, M. D., 131
Carter, L., 277
Carter, R. T., 122
Carter, T. J., 239
Carver, C. S., 120, 124
Carver, K., 161
Casares, M. T.
see Chaves, A. P.
Cascading effect, 17, 62, 64–65
Caserta, M. S., 260, 261
Casey, B. J.
see Mischel, W.
Caspi, A., 61
2011.see Moffitt, T. E.
Castellanos, F. X.
see Giedd, J. N.
Castro-Travé, M., 50
Casual sexual arrangements, 161–162
Cataclysmic situations, 33–34
Cataracts, 248
Cauce, A. M.
see Saegert, S. C.
Cawthon, R. M.
see Epel, E. S.
Cedarblad, M., 32
Ceja, M., 193
Cella, J.
see Patrick, K.
Cell phones, 319, 322, 323
Centerbar, D. B., 231
Center for Hearing and Communication, 247
Center for the Digital Future, 146
Centers for Disease Control and Prevention (CDC), 134, 170,
244, 284, 287

Cenzer, I. S.
   see Kelly, A.
Cerasoli, C. P., 40
CERN laboratory, 318
Chaining, 76
Challenge as personal quality, 34, 210
Champagne, N. J., 219
Champion, R., 189
Chance, R. C., 213
Chandler, H. M., 97
Chandler, M. J., 64, 306
Chandra, A., 161
Chang, A.
   see Kelly, A.
Change processes
   comprehensibility, 20
   developmental stages, 13–17, 15 (table)
   existential hardiness, 33–35
   health risks, 29–30
   impermance, 29
   individual perceptions, 18–20
   interdisciplinary approaches, 20–21,
      21 (figure)
   mindfullness-based practices, 106, 107–108
   planned versus unplanned change, 19–20
   positive versus negative events, 18–19,
      19 (figure), 34, 63–65
   prejudicial attitudes, 315–316
   psychoeducation, 20
   societal change, 17–18
   work transitions, 207–211
   see also Aging
Chang, J., 56
Chan, M., 328
   see also Cheng, C.
Chan, W. C., 277
Chao, M. M., 314
Chapin, R., 263
Chapman, J. E., 80
Characterological violence, 171
Chartrand, J. M., 208
Chaves, A. P., 231
Chazan-Cohen, R., 182
Cheadle, J., 172
Cheating/cheaters, 168–170
Chemers, M., 81
Chen, E. E., 59
Cheng, C., 328, 329
Cheng, L., 323
Chen, H. Y., 154, 254
   see also Masi, C. M.
Chen, M.
   see Xie, L.
Chen, T. J., 131
Chen, Y.-F., 47
   see also Kogan, S. M.
Chess, S., 6, 7
Chiao, K. W., 315
   see also Ito, T. A.
Child-centered preschools, 181
Childers, C. D., 168

Childhood
   altruistic behavior, 153
   divorce impacts, 172–173
   early childhood education, 181–183
   friendships, 141–143, 142 (table)
   mental disorders, 284 (table)
   money understanding, 225–226
   neurodevelopmental disorders, 283, 284 (table), 286–287
   obesity rates, 131–132
   perceived work opportunities, 211
   physical activity/exercise, 133–134
   rejection and loneliness, 153–154
   savings patterns, 234
   school experiences, 180–181
   self-regulation skills, 181–182
   sexual orientation, 160–161
   substance abuse, 134–135
Chima, F. O., 219
Chistakis, N. A., 261
Chittipeddi, K., 19
Chiu, C. Y., 74, 313
Chiu, W. T., 275
Chlorpromazine, 296
Choice, 40, 41
Choudhry, A. M.
   see Rikani, A. A.
Choudhry, Z.
   see Rikani, A. A.
Choy, S., 193
Christakis, N., 51, 52, 151
Christensen, A., 168
   see also Atkins, D. C.
Christenson, S. L., 191
Christie, C., 191
Chronic stress/stressors, 10, 113, 122
Chung-Yan, G. A., 313
Chun, H. H., 230
Cialdini, R. B., 57, 72
Ciarrochi, J. W., 37
Cicchetti, D., 17, 60, 62, 63, 306
   see also Luthar, S. S.
Ciciolla, L., 37
Cigarette smoking, 283
   see Substance abuse
Circumscription, 214–215
Clark, A. E., 206, 237
   see also Boyce, C. J.
Clark, C., 190
Clarke, A., 121
Clark, E. M., 149
Clark, Richard A., 47
Clark, Rodney, 113
Clark-Stewart, K. A., 172
Clark, V. R., 113
Classes/workshops, 314–315
Classical conditioning, 70–72, 75–76
Class system, 227–228
   see also Social class
Cleary Bradley, R. P., 171
Client-centered therapy, 291
Clinical psychology, 21, 21 (figure)

Clore, G. L., 231
Closed-mindedness, 314
Coan, J. A., 125
Coatsworth, J. D., 9
Cocaine, 280, 282
Cochran, S. D., 122
Coghill, D., 287
Cognitive–affective complexity, 250, 255 (table)
Cognitive behavioral therapy, 79–80, 254, 290, 296
Cognitive development, 83–84
Cognitive flexibility, 97
Cognitive psychology, 239
Cohen, A. S., 289
Cohen, S., 48, 50, 115, 117
Coherence, 20, 32
Cohesiveness, 312
Coie, J. D., 154
Coinage, 225
Colangelo, A., 315
    see also Sinclair, S.
Colby, S. L., 17, 311
Cole, B.
    see Zinnbauer, B.
Coleman, J. M., 322
Coleman, R., 227
Cole, R., 305
Cole, S. W., 154
Collective efficacy, 81–82
Collectivist coping styles, 123
Collectivistic cultures, 59 (table), 59–60, 307, 329
College experience
    career and vocational interest, 207, 208
    challenges, 192–193
    dropout rate, 193
    enrollment trends and graduation rates, 195 (figure)
    first-generation college students, 193–195, 199, 200
    mentoring, 198–200
    money management, 224
    study skills, 195, 196, 197 (figure), 198, 198 (table)
    success factors, 193–194
    TRIO programs, 194–195, 199
Collins, W. A., 16, 147
Coltman, P., 181
Comas-Díaz, L., 60
Commitment
    healthy relationships, 165, 166 (figure)
    individual hardiness, 34
    involuntary job loss, 210
    positive behavioral change, 107–108
    purpose in life, 28
Committed partnerships, 162–163, 163 (figure)
Common goals, 315
Communion, 307–308
Community contexts
    cultural influences, 58–60, 59 (table)
    developmental demands and capabilities, 60–63
    mentoring, 47–48, 62–63
    resiliency, 63–65, 64 (table), 65 (table)
    situational/contextual influences, 53–58, 60–61, 66
    socialization process, 65–66
    social support, 48–53, 49 (figure), 51 (figure)

Community Mental Health Act (1963), 289
Community psychology, 20, 21 (figure)
Comorbidity, 282–283
Companionate love, 166 (figure)
Companionship, 253–254, 260
Compas, B., 113, 119, 120
Compassion, 20, 97, 101–103, 107, 140, 151–152
Competence, 15, 15 (table)
Competency-building communities, 9
Competent individuals, 9
Comprehensibility, 20
Compromise, 214–215
Computer Age, 318
Computer History Museum, 317
Computer-mediated communication, 149, 150 (table)
Computer systems technology, 317–318
Conditioned response (CR), 70–71, 71 (figure), 72
Conditioned stimulus (CS), 70–71, 71 (figure), 72, 76
Conell-Price, J.
    see Kelly, A.
Confidants, 323
Conformity, 56–57
Conger, R. D., 185, 190
Connell, J. P., 54
Connidis, I. A., 260
Connors, D., 225
Connor-Smith, J., 119
    see also Compas, B.
Consequences, 72, 74–77
Consummate love, 166 (figure)
Contempt, 164, 173
Context, 6–7
Contextual influences
    conformity, 56–57
    discriminative stimuli, 55–56
    environmental contexts, 53
    obedience to authority, 57
Control
    academic success, 196
    age-related changes, 253, 255 (table)
    individual hardiness, 34
    involuntary job loss, 210
Controllable stressors, 121–122
Cook, K., 258
Cook, S. R.
    see Foltz, J. L.
Coons, H., 117
Cooperative learning, 315
Cooperative play, 141
Cooper, H., 184
Cooper, M. L., 134
Cooper, R. P., 65
Copeland, W. E., 185
Copen, C., 161
Coping skills
    controllable versus uncontrollable stressors, 121–122
    dysfunctional coping skills, 271
    individual hardiness, 34
    occupation-related stress, 219–220
    personal experiences, 112
    spousal loss, 260–262, 262 (table)

strategies and styles, 119–121, 121 (table)
stress processes, 117
Cortisol, 113, 117, 125, 127, 128
Cosio, A., 191
Costa, P. T., Jr., 37
Costello, J., 185
Costin, D., 145
Cost of living calculations, 238 (table)
Cote, J., 193
Couch, D., 321
Coude, G., 151
Counseling services
  career indecisiveness, 208–209
  couples counseling, 168–170
  interdisciplinary approaches, 20–21, 21 (figure)
  minority populations, 213
  occupation-related stress, 219–220
Courington, S., 33
Covinsky, K.
  see Kelly, A.
Cowen, E. L., 8, 9
Cox, K., 328
Cox, S. J.
  see Kouvonen, A. M.
Coyle, L. D.
  see Vera, E. M.
Coyne, J. C., 19, 113
Cradock, A. L.
  see Gortmaker, S. L.
Craighero, L., 102
Craik, F. I. M., 84
Crandall, C. S., 57
Credit cards, 232–234
Crimmins, E., 263
Criticism, 164, 173
Crofford, L. J., 171
Crogan, M., 315
Cross-cultural friendships, 144–145
Cross-Disorder Group of the Psychiatric Genomics
  Consortium, 299
Cross-ethnic friendships, 143, 144–145
Cross-gender friendships, 147, 148 (figure)
Crowley, M., 191
Crumbaugh, J. C., 32
Cruza-Guet, M. C., 217
Cruz, J., 162, 163
Cryder, C., 232
  see also Rick, S.
Csikszentmihalyi, M., 7, 8, 9, 15–16, 40, 218
Cuadrado, I., 122
Cultural awareness, 314–315
Cultural influences, 306
Culturally-related stressors, 122–124
Culturally-relevant coping, 123–124
Culture
  collectivist versus individualist cultures, 59 (table),
    59–60, 307, 329
  cultural complexes, 60
  definition, 58
  social networks, 52
Cunningham, J. A., 123

Cunningham, M., 211
Curiosity, 329
Currency
  see Money
Current versus future self, 234–235, 235 (figure)
Currie, J., 182
  see also Garces, E.

Dahlin, L., 32
Dainton, M., 176
Dakof, G., 113
Danes, S. M., 225, 226
Darego, Agbani, 280
DARPA
  see U.S. Defense Advanced Research Projects Agency
    (DARPA)
Data transmission, 317
Dating relationships, 160–161
Dating websites, 320
Daughton, J. M., 286
Davidson, R. J., 20, 97, 102, 125
Davies, Donald, 317
Davies, G., 225
Davies, H. W.
  see Clark, C.
Davies, J. L., 97
Davies, K., 323
Davis, M. C., 18, 19
Davis, S. N., 211
Day, S. X., 217
Dean, A., 124
Death
  fear of death, 30–31
  grieving process, 260–262, 262 (table)
  socioemotional changes, 252
  spiritual and religious beliefs and activities, 261
Deaton, A., 237, 238
de Boer, S. F.
  see Koolhaas, J. M.
Deci, E. L., 31, 40
  see also Vansteenkiste, M.
Decision-making processes, 259
Declassification, 316
Deems, D. A., 71
Deep brain stimulation (DBS), 295
Defensiveness, 164, 173
DeGruy, F. V., III, 135
Deinstitutionalization, 289
Delayed gratification, 234–235
Deliberative decision-making, 229, 230–231
de Lima, M. S., 286
Delirium, 282 (table)
DeLongis, A., 11, 113
Delton, A. W.
  see Griskevicius, V.
Delusions, 277–278
Demitrack, M. A.
  see Janicak, P. G.
Demler, O., 275
  see Kessler, R. C.
DeNavas-Walt, C., 227

Dennis, H., 257, 258
Denver, Colorado, 238 (table)
de Oliveira-Souza, R.
    see Moll, J.
Depression
    brain stimulation therapies, 294–295
    bullying, 185
    casual sexual arrangements, 162
    characteristics, 271
    ending relationships, 174
    exercise benefits, 126
    genetic research, 277
    intimate partner violence (IPV), 171, 172
    job loss impacts, 206
    multitasking effects, 130
    nursing home residents, 265
    older adulthood, 211
    onset, 7
    psychotropic medications, 296, 298 (table)
    reframing skills, 129
    social support impacts, 124
    spiritual and religious beliefs and activities, 38, 261
    spousal loss, 261–262
    stress reactions, 117, 127
    substance-induced mental disorders, 282, 283
    see also Mood disorders
deRegnier, R.-A., 65
Derogatis, L., 117
Derogatory slurs, 122
Deschenes, M. R.
    see Garber, C. E.
Determination of worth, 231–232
Developmental demands and capabilities, 60–63
Developmental psychology, 20, 21 (figure)
Developmental psychopathology, 60–63, 62 (figure)
Developmental tasks of adulthood, 16–17, 17 (table)
Devine, P. G., 58, 71, 315
    see also Ito, T. A.
DeVoy, J. E.
    see Chaves, A. P.
de Vries, D. A., 323
DeWall, C. N., 239
Dewey, John, 94
DeWitz, S., 33
Dezhkam, M., 279
Dhabar, F. S.
    see Epel, E. S.
Dhar, R., 231
Dholakia, U., 236
Diagnostic and Statistical Manual of Mental Disorders (DSM-5),
    274, 275, 279, 286, 287, 324
Dialectic, 83
Dialectical reasoning, 308, 309 (figure)
Diamond, L. M., 160, 161, 311
Diaz, D. R., 286
Diaz, E. M., 185
DiBlasio, F. A., 168, 169, 170
Dick, D. M., 283
Dickson, J. W., 161
    see also Grello, C. M.
Dickson, L., 226

Dickson, N., 311
    see Moffitt, T. E.
DiClemente, R., 38
Diego, M., 125
Diemer, M. A., 227
    see Chaves, A. P.
Diener, E., 33, 206, 231, 237, 238
Diet and nutrition, 131–132, 132 (figure)
Difficult experiences, 104
DiFonzo, N., 20
Digital Age, 318–322
    see also Technology
Digital divide, 319, 320 (figure)
Digital immigrants, 317
Digital natives, 317
Digital settlers, 317
Digman, J. M., 37
Dillon, M., 37, 261
Dilworth-Anderson, P., 38
Dimidjian, S., 90, 101
Diorio, J., 125
DiPlacido, J., 167
Disabato, D. J., 32
Discriminative stimuli, 55–56, 72, 73
Disease, susceptibility to, 247, 247 (table)
Disengagement, 53
Disorganized speech/movement, 278
Distorted body image, 280
Distorted thinking, 271, 278, 296
District of Columbia, 310
Diversity
    acceptance and tolerance, 313–316
    benefits, 313
    community impact, 312–313
    demographic shifts, 310 (figure), 310–311
    friendships, 143, 144–145
    gender identity and sexual orientation, 311–312
    purpose in life, 33
    societal challenges, 17, 309–310
Divorce, 162, 172–174
Dix, Dorothea, 289
D'Mello, S.
    see Yeager, D. S.
Dodd, K. W.
    see Troiano, R. P.
Dodge, K. A., 154
Doepfner, M.
    see Taylor, E.
Dohrenwend, B., 29
Doka, K. J., 260
Dolensky, E., 142
Dollard, J., 20, 79
Domestic violence, 170–172
Dominelli, P. B., 246
Dominguez-Fuentes, J. M., 50
Donato, A. N.
    see Shaffer, H. J.
Donnay, D. A. C., 216
Donnellan, M. B., 326
Doob, L., 20
Dormant social or psychological potentiality mobilization, 259

Doud, K.
see Vera, E. M.
Dougherty, A.
see Kross, E.
Dovidio, J. F., 58, 122, 312, 313, 315, 316
Drapalski, A. L., 298
Dreher, G., 198
Driver, J. L., 163, 164, 165
Dropout rates, 191–192, 193
Drossman, D. A., 171
Drugs
see Substance abuse
DuBois, D. L., 47, 63, 184
Duckworth, A. L., 35, 188
see Yeager, D. S.
Duffy, J. F.
see Buxton, O. M.
Duffy, K., 21
Dukka, 98
Duncan, D. T.
see Gortmaker, S. L.
Dunkel, C. S., 14
Dunkel-Schetter, C., 11
Dunlop, W. L., 307
see also Frimer, J. A.
Dunn, D., 5
Dunne, J., 92, 95
see also Lutz, A.
Dunn, E. W., 239
see Aknin, L. B.
Durability bias, 231, 239
Durpee, D.
see Swanson, D. P.
Dweck, C. S., 74, 187
Dy-Liacco, G. S., 37
Dysfunctional behaviors, 271, 277–278, 290
Dziak, J. J., 134

Eagles J.
see Millar, H.
Early adulthood
altruistic behavior, 153
cognitive changes, 249–250, 255 (table)
excessive self-interest, 322
friendships, 147
Internet impacts, 326–327
life tasks, 17 (table)
median income by education, 192 (figure)
narratives and stories, 328
online dating, 321
physical changes, 246, 247 (table)
purpose in life, 33
resiliency, 65 (table)
savings patterns, 234
school dropout rate, 191–192
sexual activity, 166
sexual fluidity, 311
social support impacts, 49 (figure)
socioemotional changes, 252, 255 (table)
substance abuse, 134–135
suicidal behaviors, 285

Early childhood education, 181–183
Easterling, L. W., 261
Easterlin, R. A., 238
Eastwick, P. W., 320
see also Finkel, E. J.
Eating disorders, 274, 278–280, 284 (table)
Eaton, W., 48
Eaves, L. J., 7
Eberth, J.
see Sedlmeier, P.
Eby, L. T., 47, 48
Eccles, J., 184, 185, 186, 189, 190
Ecological model, 7, 8 (figure)
Ecological psychology, 53–55
Economics, 21, 21 (figure)
Economic socialization, 234
Economic stress, 209, 226
Eddy, S. L.
see Freeman, S.
Edmondson, D., 39
Edwards, B. A., 248
Efficacy, 81–82
Effortful learning, 82–83
Effort-success relationship, 74–75, 187–188
Egeland, G. M., 124
Ego, 290
Ego depletion, 230–231
Ego integrity, 252–253
Eibach, S., 311
Eidelman, A. I., 125
Eid, M., 231
Eisenberger, N. I., 66, 174
see also Master, S. L.
Eisenberg, N., 64, 152, 153
see also Michalik, N. M.
Eisert, H. G.
see Taylor, E.
Eisner, F.
see Warren, J. E.
Ekerdt, D. J., 263
Elder, G. H., Jr., 185, 190
Electroconvulsive therapy (ECT), 293, 294
El-Hai, J., 294
Elias, M. J.
see Greenberg, M. T.
Elliott, M. A., 60
Elliott, W., 234
see also Friedline, T. L.
Ellison, C. G., 38
see also George, L. K.
Ellison, N. B., 322
Elmore, C. A., 117
Else-Quest, N., 181
Elwert, F., 261
E-mail communications, 318, 322
see also Technology
Emanuels-Zuurveen, E. S., 48
Emery, G., 277
Emmelkamp, P. M. G., 48
Emotional support, 48, 50, 124
Emotion-focused coping, 119–120, 121 (table), 123

Emotions
    attachment theory, 231–232
    behaviorism, 290
    breakups, 173, 174
    cognitive changes, 250
    decision-making processes, 229–230
    disciplined thoughts, 98–99
    diversity acceptance, 315
    dysfunctional behaviors, 271
    grieving process, 260–262, 262 (table)
    infidelity, 168–169
    material goods, 231
    negative emotions, 163
    positive emotions, 52, 163, 175, 239, 315
    relationship maintenance, 175
    socioemotional changes, 250–255, 255 (table)
Empathy, 97, 101–102, 140, 141–142, 150–151, 326
Empirically validated therapy, 291
Employee assistance programs (EAPs), 219–220
Empty love, 166 (figure)
Empty nest syndrome, 252
Enders, C. K., 37
Ending relationships, 172–174
Endler, N. S., 53
Endorphins, 126
Engel, George, 272
Engel, G. L., 272
Engelmann, J., 72
England, 288
Engle, J., 194, 195
Englund, M., 16
Eng, P., 48
Ensel, W., 48
Entitlement-motivated affairs, 169
Entwisle, D. R., 191
Environmental influences, 46–47, 305–306
Environmental stressors, 10–11
Epel, E. S., 10, 113, 246
Epigenetics, 61, 306
Epstein, J. L., 191
Equanimity, 102
Equifinality, 61
Erev, I., 77
Erikson, E. H., 14, 15, 16, 65, 143, 248, 252, 253
Erikson's theory of psychosocial development,
    14–17, 15 (table)
Eriksson, M., 32
Ershler, W. B., 10
Ersner-Hershfield, H., 234, 235
Esaiasson, P., 312
    see also Kokkonen, A.
Eschleman, K. J., 34
Espelage, D. L., 185
Espenshade, T., 81
Esses, V. M.
    see Dovidio, J. F.
Estes, W. K., 77
Estrada, M., 213
Ethnic populations
    career decisions, 208
    college dropout rate, 193
    college enrollment trends and graduation rates, 195 (figure)
    coping strategies and styles, 120, 122, 123–124
    demographic shifts, 310 (figure), 310–311
    friendships, 143, 144, 144–145
    higher education programs, 194
    learning community interventions, 200
    life expectancies, 245
    mentoring, 198–199
    microaggressions, 122
    money management, 224
    obesity rates, 131
    science, technology, engineering, and
        mathematics (STEM) programs, 212–213
    spiritual and religious beliefs and activities, 261
    work aspirations and expectations, 211, 213
Etz, R. S., 135
Eustress, 128
Evans, S.
    see Eby, L. T.
Evidence-based psychotherapies, 296
Excessive self-interest, 322
Excoriation, 275
Executive functioning, 250, 255 (table)
Exercise, 34, 126, 133–134
Existential hardiness, 33–35
Existential psychology, 28–31
Exline, J. J., 35, 36
    see also Pargament, K. I.
Experimental existential psychology, 30–31
Explicit learning, 70, 82–83
Explicit prejudice, 316
Extramarital sexual relationships, 168–170
Extreme energy, 277
    see also Mood disorders
Extrinsic motivation, 40
Extrinsic religious orientation, 36
Extrinsic values, 322

Faber, R. J., 230, 231
Fabes, R. A.
    see Eisenberg, N.
Facebook, 130, 145, 155, 318, 323
Facial recognition, 315
Fagundas, C., 10
Fairhurst, S., 76
Faith, C., 149
    see also Wettersten, K. B.
Fallon, A. E., 280
Family relationships, 253–254
    see also Aging; Relationships
Fang, R., 50
Farber, S., 21
Fast, N., 236
Fatuous love, 166 (figure)
Faucher, E., 30
Faust, K., 50
Fear, 171, 271
    see also Anxiety/anxiety disorders
Fear of death, 30–31
Fechner, Gustav, 94
Fedzechkina, M., 82

Feedback
    discriminative stimuli, 73
    regularities, 77
    reinforcers, 74, 77
    shaping, 78
    social media, 145
Feldman, M. D., 47, 170
Feldman, R., 125
Felner, R., 21
Female erotic plasticity, 311–312
Feng, A. X., 20
Ferrari, P., 151
Ferster, C. B., 76, 77
Ferzandi, L. A., 328
    see also Shaffer, M. A.
Fidelity, 15, 15 (table)
Field, T. M., 125
Fifer, W. P., 65
Fight-or-flight reaction, 10, 127
Fike, K. T., 258
Financial planning, 257–258, 258 (figure)
Finch, W. H., 32
Finkel, E. J., 320
Fink, M.
    see Kellner, C. H.
First friendships, 141
First-generation college students, 189–190,
    193–195, 199, 200
First job, 209
Fischer, P.
    see Fritsche, I.
Fisch, H., 246
Fisher, P.
    see Merikangas, K. R.
Fiske, S., 229
Fitzmaurice, G., 48
Five-factor theory of personality, 36–38
Fixed-interval reinforcement schedules, 76 (figure)
Flavell, J. H., 83
Flavin, M. A., 234
Flegal, K. M., 131
Fleischmann, B.
    see Fritsche, I.
Flexibility, 259, 329
Flocke, S. A., 161
Florida, 311
Flow, 218
Flugge, G.
    see Koolhaas, J. M.
Fluid intelligence, 251
Focused attention (FA) meditation, 92
Focused breathing, 125
Foehr, U., 130
Folkman, S., 11, 113, 117, 119, 120
Foltz, J. L., 131
Ford, M. T., 40
Forgetfulness, 251
Formal religions, 35
Forman, E. M., 80
Forste, R., 174
Forward conditioning, 71

Foster, G. D., 132
Foster, J. D., 322
    see also Twenge, J. M.
Foster, K. A., 227
Fouad, N. A., 207, 209, 211
Fowler, J., 51, 52, 151
Foy, M., 30
France, 288
Francis, D., 125
Francis (Pope), 326
Franke, B., 287
Frank, G. K., 280
    see also Kaye, W. H.
Franklin, B. A.
    see Garber, C. E.
Frankl, V. E., 29
Frankl, Victor, 28, 29
Frazier, P., 35, 38, 39
Frederick, C. M., 40
Frederick, D., 147
    see also Gillespie, B. J.
Fredericks, L.
    see Greenberg, M. T.
Fredrickson, B. L., 315
    see also Gottman, J. M.
Free, concept of, 230
Freeman, E. C., 322
Freeman, S., 84
    see Cialdini, R. B.
Freeman, Walter, 294
Free will, 40
Frenette, E. C., 13
Frensch, P. A., 82
Fretz, B. R., 258
Freudenberg, N., 191
Freudian psychology, 99, 289–290
Freud, S., 290
Freud, Sigmund, 99, 205, 289
Frias-Navarro, D., 171
Friedline, T. L., 234
Friedman, H. S., 211
Friend, D. J., 171
Friendships
    adolescence, 143–145
    adulthood, 147–148, 148 (figure)
    care and maintenance, 148–150, 150 (table)
    childhood, 141–143, 142 (table)
    first friendships, 141
    importance, 140–141
    Internet use, 145–146, 146 (figure)
    similarities, 144–145
    social media impacts, 145–147
Friends with benefits, 161–162
Frimer, J. A., 307
Fritsche, I., 31
Frontal lobe injuries, 172
Fuchs, E.
    see Koolhaas, J. M.
Fulghum, R., 180
Functional magnetic resonance imaging (fMRI),
    96, 125

Fundamental human needs, 206–207, 210
Fung, H. H.
   see Tsai, J. L.
Furnham, A., 226
Futterman, R.
   see Eccles, J.
Future challenges
   personal level, 305–309, 309 (figure)
   societal change, 309–317
Future-self connection, 236
   see also Present–Future Similarity Test

Gable, S. L., 40
Gaertner, S. L., 122, 312, 313, 315, 316
   see also Dovidio, J. F.
Gaillot, M. T., 230
Galinsky, A. D., 313, 314
Gallagher, L. A.
   see Chaves, A. P.
Gallagher, M., 11
Gallistel, C. R., 76, 82
Gallup News Service, 261
Galvin, A., 62, 65
Gaming addictions, 324
Gamino, L. A., 261
Garand, J. C., 289
Garber, C. E., 133
Garbinsky, E. N., 31, 236
   see also Baumeister, R. F.
Garces, E., 182, 183
Garcia, B., 81
Garcia, D.
   see Uhls, Y. T.
Garcia, J., 71
Garcia-Leiva, P., 50
Gardner, H., 323
Garmezy, N., 63
Garrett, D. M., 234
Garton, T., 234, 235
Gary, M., 314
Gasser, U., 317
Gay and lesbian relationships, 166–168, 321
Gaylord-Harden, N. K., 117, 123
Gazelle, H., 154
Geertz, C., 60
Geldhauser, H. A., 257
Gender
   adjusting to loss, 260–262
   aggressive behaviors, 170–172
   career decisions, 208
   casual sexual arrangements, 162
   committed partnerships, 162–163, 163 (figure)
   definition, 311
   eating disorders, 279, 280
   friendships, 143, 147, 148 (figure)
   identity and sexual orientation, 311–312
   infidelity, 168–169
   intimate partner violence (IPV), 170–172
   life expectancies, 245, 260
   mental disorders, 284 (table)
   microaggressions, 122

   money management, 224
   neurodevelopmental disorders, 286–287
   obesity rates, 131–132
   online dating, 321–322
   physical activity/exercise, 133
   reproductive capacity decline, 246, 247, 247 (table)
   retirement planning, 257
   same-sex relationships, 166–168, 321
   school dropout rate, 191
   science, technology, engineering, and mathematics (STEM)
      programs, 212 (figure), 212–213
   sexual fluidity, 311
   societal challenges, 309
   socioemotional changes, 252
   spiritual and religious beliefs and activities, 261
   stress reactions, 117
   substance use disorders, 282
   suicidal behaviors, 285
   work aspirations and expectations, 211, 213, 215
Genderqueer, 311
Gender-specific individual treatment (GSIT), 172
General adaptation syndrome (GAS), 10, 117
Generalized anxiety disorder (GAD), 7, 275, 284 (table)
Generation effect, 84
Generativity, 14, 252, 255 (table), 257
Genetic influences, 61
Genet, J. J., 328
Genevie, J., 323
Gene X environment interaction, 61
George, L. K., 38
Georgellis, Y., 206
George, T. P., 278
Gerken, K.
   see Yang, C. Y.
Gettinger, M., 196, 198
Gibbons, D., 50
Gibbs, J. L., 322
Giedd, J. N., 62, 250
Gilbert, D. T., 227, 229, 231
Gillespie, B. J., 147, 148
Gillium, R., 38
Gilljam, M., 312
   see also Kokkonen, A.
Gilovich, T., 239
Ginzburg, S.
   see Swanson, D. P.
Gioia, D. A., 19
Giordano, P. C., 161
   see also Manning, W. D.
Glass, S. P., 168, 169, 170
Global Measure of Perceived Stress, 115–116
Gloria, A. M., 199
Glück, J., 329
Goals, 104, 107–108, 184, 215
Goernandt, J.
   see Tsai, J. L.
Goff, S.
   see Eccles, J.
Golby, J., 34
Gold standard, 225
Goldstein, J., 29

Goldstein, N., 57
Gollaher, D. L., 289
Gollwitzer, P. M., 30
Gómez, A., 122
Gomez-Jacinto, L., 50
Gomez, K.
    see Vera, E. M.
Gonzaga, G. C., 321
Goode, M. R., 229
Goodenow, C., 184, 185
Goodness of fit, 6–7
Good stress, 127–129
Good study skills, 196
Google, 220, 318
Gordon, V. N., 207
Gorman, J. M., 291, 296, 299
Gortmaker, S. L., 133
Gotlib, I. H.
    see Mischel, W.
Gottesman, I. I., 7
Gottfredson, L. S., 214–215
Gottfredson's theory, 214–215
Gottlieb, B. H., 48, 113
Gott, M., 166
Gottman, J. M., 163, 164, 165, 166, 171, 173, 177
Goudvis, A., 198
Gow, R. W., 131
    see also Mazzeo, S. E.
Grady, K. E., 184, 185
Grafman, J.
    see Moll, J.
Graham, S., 140, 143
Granovetter, M. S., 51
Gray, J. R., 316
Graziano, W. G., 328
Greater Good, 152
Greenbaum, C.
    see Stults, C.
Greenberg, J., 30, 31
Greenberg, M. T., 153
Green, C. E., 171
Greenfield, P. M.
    see Uhls, Y. T.
Green, R.-J., 167
Greenstein, T. N., 211
Greenwald, A. G., 58, 71, 313
Gregersen, H., 328
    see also Shaffer, M. A.
Greischar, L. L., 97
Grello, C. M., 161, 162
Greytak, E. A., 185
Gribbin, A., 317
Grieving process, 260–262, 262 (table)
Griffin, D. W., 308
Griskevicius, V., 226
Grit, 34–35
Gronfein, W., 289
Gross domestic product (GDP), 239
Gross, J.
    see Gottman, J. M.
Grossmann, I., 308, 309, 329

Grossman, P., 125
Group membership, 50–51, 57–58, 72, 312–313, 315–316
Group-oriented cultures, 59, 307
Group pressure, 57
Grov, C., 147, 161
    see also Gillespie, B. J.
Gruenewald, T. L.
    see Taylor, S. E.
Gruen, R., 11
Grundy, K. M.
    see Foster, G. D.
Gudmunson, C. G., 225, 226
Gueldner, S. H., 265
Guenette, J. A., 246
Guerra, P., 315
Guerrero, L. K., 149, 150
Guiffrida, D. A., 194
Gunnar, M., 11
Gunnell, D., 285
Gunning, B.
    see Taylor, E.
Gunter, B., 226
Guo, J., 328
Gurung, R. A.
    see Taylor, S. E.
Guthrie, I. K.
    see Eisenberg, N.
Gutierrez, L.
    see Maton, K. I.
Gutman, L. M., 305
Gysbers, N. C., 213

Haarig, F.
    see Sedlmeier, P.
Haas, K., 140
Haas, S., 176
Haberman, H., 226
Habits, 107
Hacker, J., 213
    see also Brown, S. D.
Hackett, G., 215
    see also Lent, R. W.
Haddouk, L.
    see Tsai, J. L.
Hagan, C. R., 7
Hahn-Holbrook, J., 31
Haidt, J., 151
Hair, E. C., 328
Hale-Smith, A., 39
Halkitis, P.
    see Stults, C.
Hall, C., 99
Hallett, D., 306
Hall, K. L., 20
Hall, P. D., 97
Hallucinations, 278
Hallucinogens, 280, 282, 282 (table)
Hall, W. D., 277
Halonen, J., 5
Hamani, C.
    see Mayberg, H. S.

Hames, J. L., 7
Hamid, P. N., 124
Hamilton, L. D., 19
Hamilton, L. K., 313
Hamm, J. V., 144
Hampton, K., 146
Hancock, J. T., 322
Hancox, R. J.
    see Moffitt, T. E.
Hanifan, L. J., 52
Hansen, J.-I. C., 9
Hanson, M., 5
Hansson, K., 32
Happiness
    characteristics, 31–32
    diversity acceptance, 315
    income-happiness relationship, 237 (figure),
        237–239
    social networks, 51–52
    spiritual and religious beliefs and activities, 38
Harari, L., 147
    see also Gillespie, B. J.
Harassment
    see Bullying
Harbaugh, W., 239
Harden, S. L., 47
Hardin, C., 315
    see also Sinclair, S.
Hardiness, 33–35, 34–35
Hardy individuals, 33
Harlow, H. F., 66
Harmon-Jones, E., 315
Harpalani, V.
    see Swanson, D. P.
Harper, M. S., 161, 162
    see also Grello, C. M.
Harrington, A., 20, 95
Harrington, H.
    see Moffitt, T. E.
Harris, Dan, 126
Harrison, D. A., 328
    see also Shaffer, M. A.
Hart, Chantelle, 132
Hart, Craig H., 181
Hart, D., 64
Harter, J., 237
Hartup, W. W., 141, 142
Harvey, O. J., 315
Harvey, R. H.
    see Maddi, S. R.
Harvey, S., 198
Hassles, 113
Hawaii, 310
Hawkins, M. F., 289
Hawkley, L. C., 31, 154, 254
    see also Cacioppo, J. T.; Masi, C. M.
Hayes, S., 103, 104
Haynie, D. L., 191
Hays, P., 124, 125, 126, 127, 129, 218
Hays, R. B., 149
Head injuries, 172

Head, J.
    see Clark, C.
Head Start Bureau, 182
Head Start program, 182–183
Health and well-being
    age-related changes, 246–249, 246–255, 247 (table), 255 (table)
    broken hearts, 174
    change impacts, 29–30
    diet and nutrition, 131–132, 132 (figure)
    friendships, 140–143, 145
    habits, 107
    income-happiness relationship, 237 (figure), 237–239
    intimate partner violence (IPV), 170–172
    loneliness, 154
    meaningful work, 206
    meditation effects, 125
    physical activity/exercise, 34, 126, 133–134
    positive characteristics, 9
    positive versus negative change events, 18–19
    purpose and meaning in life, 31
    sense of coherence, 32
    social media impacts, 145
    social support impacts, 48, 49 (figure), 50, 124, 254
    spiritual and religious beliefs and activities, 38–39
    substance abuse, 134–135
Healthy aging, 254
Healthy eating, 131–132, 132 (figure)
Healthy intimate relationships, 163–165
Healthy sleep tips, 11–12
Healthy stress management strategies
    exercise, 126
    meditation, 125–126
    physical touch, 124–125
    self-help activities, 126
    social support, 124
Hearing changes, 247, 247 (table), 248
Heaton, T. B., 174
Hebb, D. O., 73
Hebb's rule, 73–74
Heckman, J. J., 183
Heine, S. J., 39
Hein, G., 72
Heinrich, H., 13
Heintzelman, S. J., 31, 33
Heiser, E. J., 244
Helliwell, J. F.
    see Aknin, L. B.
Helplessness, 171
Henderson, M. D.
    see Yeager, D. S.
Henderson, R. W., 30
Hendrick, C., 165
Hendrick, S., 165
Hendry, L. B., 211
Hennecke, M., 16
    see also Hutteman, R.
Henry, P. J., 312
Henry, S. E., 280
    see also Kaye, W. H.
Heponiemi, T.
    see Kouvonen, A. M.

Heppner, M. J.
    see Heppner, M. J.
Heppner, P. P., 123
Heraclitus, 13, 29
Herbison, P., 311
Her, E. J., 146
    see also Hampton, K.
Hernandez, M., 264
Hernandez, P. R., 213
Hernandez-Reif, M., 125
Hertenstein, M. J., 124
Heterosexism, 160–161, 167
Heterosexual friendships, 147, 148 (figure)
Hewstone, M., 316
Hietanen, J. K., 327
Higgins, E., 232, 239
High-achieving students, 196
Higher education experience, 192–193
High-risk populations, 63 (table), 63–64
High School Transcript Study (HSTS), 212 (figure)
Hill, P. L., 32, 33, 315
Hill, R. D., 244, 245, 253, 256, 257, 258, 259, 260
Himmelstein, D. U.
    see Lasser, K.
Hinchliff, S., 166
Hinsch, C., 155
Hippocrates, 272
Hiripi, E., 279
    see also Hudson, J. I.
Hirschberger, G., 30
Hirschl, T. A., 227
Hirsh, J. B., 38
    see also Inzlicht, M.
Historic England, 288
Ho, A., 143
    see also Graham, S.
Hoarding, 275
Hoberman, H., 48
Hobfoil, S., 123
Hoffman, B. J.
    see Eby, L. T.
Hogan, R., 307
Hohman, E., 20
Hoi, K. S., 188
Holbrook, C., 31
Holland, J., 208
Holland's theory, 208, 214, 216–217
Hollingsworth, C., 264
Holmes, C. J., 62
    see also Sowell, E. R.
Holmes, T., 18, 29, 113, 114
Holt-Lunstad, J., 48
Holt, M. K., 185
Holtzworth-Munroe, A., 170, 171, 172
Hombrados-Mendieta, M. I., 50
Homophily, 52
Homophobia, 161, 167
Homophobic microaggressions, 122
Homosexual friendships, 147, 148 (figure)
Honesty, 169
Hong, L., 313

Hong, Y.-Y., 74, 314
Hood, W. R., 315
Hooking up, 161–162
Hope, 15, 15 (table)
Hôpital Général de la Ville de Paris, 288
Hopwood, C. J., 130
Hospitalization, 288, 293
Hou, F., 312
Housing arrangements, 263–265
Howard, A., 58
Hsing, C., 323
Huber, J., 232
Hudson, J. I., 279
Hudson Kam, C. L., 82
Hugging, 125
Hughes, G. M., 260
Huici, C., 122
Hu, L., 81
Hull, C. L., 79
Human development stages, 14–17, 15 (table)
Human experiences
    see Life experiences
Humanistic psychology, 291
Humors, bodily, 272
Husain, M. M.
    see Janicak, P. G.; Kellner, C. H.; Spellman, T.
Husserl, Edmund, 94
Hutteman, R., 16, 17 (table)
Hu, V. W., 287
Hyperkinetic disorders, 286
Hypnotics, 280, 281
Hystad, S. W.
    see Sandvik, A. M.

Iacoboni, M., 151
Id, 290
Identity changes, 252, 255 (table)
Identity-context relationship, 54–55
Igarashi, H., 19
IJzerman, H., 66
Ikram, H.
    see Rikani, A. A.
Illegal drugs
    see Substance abuse
Imitation, 80, 151
Immune response decline, 246, 247 (table)
Impermanence, 28, 29–30
Implicit learning, 70, 82–83
Implicit prejudice, 313, 315–316
Impulsive behaviors, 174, 230–231
Inactivity
    see Physical activity
Inagaki, T. K., 66
Income-happiness relationship, 237 (figure), 237–239
Indegree centrality, 50
Independent retirement living, 263
Individual-environmental balance, 305–306
Individual hardiness, 33–35
Individualistic cultures, 59 (table), 59–60, 307, 329
Individuation, 316
Industry, 14

Infatuation, 166 (figure)
Infidelity, 168–170
Informational support, 48, 50
Information and communication technologies (ICTs), 319
Information influence, 56
Ingram, D., 38
In-groups, 50–51, 57–58, 312, 315–316
Inhalants, 280, 282, 282 (table)
Inkelas, K. K., 199
Insel, T., 273, 298, 299
Insight meditation, 106
Instagram, 130
Institute of Education Sciences, 212 (figure)
Institutionalization, 288
Institutional religion, 35, 40
Instrumental grievers, 260, 262, 262 (table)
Instrumental support, 48
Insulin coma therapy, 293
Insults, 122
Intellectual humility, 308
Intelligence/intelligence testing, 187–189
Interactive behavior, 163
Interactive ecological model, 54–55
Intergalactic Computer Network, 317
Intergroup contact, 316
Internalization, 36
Internalized stigma, 298
International Business Machines (IBM), 317
International Classification of Mental and Behavioural Disorders, Tenth Revision (ICD-10), 273
International Telecommunication Union (ITU), 319
Internet
    addictive behaviors, 324
    global usage, 319–320, 320 (figure)
    historical perspective, 317–318
    negative impacts, 322–324
    online dating, 320–322
    positive impacts, 325–327, 326 (figure)
    social media impacts, 145–146, 146 (figure), 323
Interpersonal relationships, 320–322
Interpersonal therapy, 296
Interval schedules, 76 (figure), 77
Intimacy, 14, 165, 166 (figure)
Intimate partner violence (IPV), 170–172
Intimate relationships
    early adulthood, 147
    healthy relationships, 163–165
    psychosocial development, 14
    sexuality, 165–166
Intoxication disorder, 281
Intrinsic motivation, 40
Intrinsic religious orientation, 36
Intrinsic values, 322
Introjected beliefs, 36
Intuitive grievers, 260, 262, 262 (table)
Involuntary job loss, 209–210, 256
Involuntary work transitions, 209
Inzlicht, M., 38, 39
iPhone effect, 323
iPhones, 319
Iqbal, H., 145

Irrational fears, 275
    see also Anxiety/anxiety disorders
Isen, A. M., 315
Isolation, 154–155, 194, 200, 254, 263, 323
It Gets Better Project, 326
Ito, T. A., 315, 316

Jaeger, S.
    see Sedlmeier, P.
Jaeger, T., 82
Jahoda, M., 8, 9
Jain, A. R., 37
James, J. B., 256
Jameson, H., 181
James, W., 35, 52, 94
James, William, 35, 36, 40, 52, 94, 95
Janicak, P. G., 295
Janosova, P., 37
Jaskolka, A. R., 124
Jason, L., 21
Javdani, S.
    see Stults, C.
Jayson, S., 126
Jealousy, 172
Jeffries, N. O.
    see Giedd, J. N.
Jelalian, E., 132
Jeong, Y., 19
Jernigan, T. L., 62
    see also Sowell, E. R.
Jha, A., 92
    see also Lutz, A.
Jiang, D.
    see Tsai, J. L.
Jian-Ping, H.
    see Merikangas, K. R.
Ji, C. Y., 131
Jin, R.
    see Kessler, R. C.
Job loss, 206, 209–210, 256
Jobs
    career indecisiveness, 208–209
    contextual influences, 211, 213–214
    definition, 205
    employee assistance programs (EAPs), 219–220
    first job, 209
    flow, 218
    fundamental human needs, 206–207, 210
    importance, 206–207
    life span salience, 207–211
    meaningful work, 205
    midcareer period, 210
    retirement, 210–211
    rewards and risks, 218–220
    science, technology, engineering, and mathematics (STEM) programs, 212 (figure), 212–213
    stress levels, 218–219
    theory of occupational circumscription and compromise, 214–215
John, D., 226

Johnsen, B. H.
  see Sandvik, A. M.
Johnson, B., 58
Johnson, C., 58
Johnson, D. R., 191
Johnson, G., 20
Johnson, J. D.
  see Dovidio, J. F.
Johnson, J. L., 50
Johnson, K., 315
Johnson, M. H., 327
Johnson, M. O., 47
Johnson, S. B., 62
Johnson, W. B., 47, 48
Johnstone, T., 102
Johnston, L.
  see Gueldner, S. H.
Joiner, T. E., 7
Jolivette, K., 191
Jonas, E.
  see Fritsche, I.
Jones, J., 58, 312
Jones, J. W., 35, 36
  see also Pargament, K. I.
Jones, L., 20
Jones, S.
  see Eisenberg, N.
Jones, S. M., 258
Jonides, J.
  see Mischel, W.
Jordan, A.
  see Edwards, B. A.
Jordan, T. E., 208
Jordt, H.
  see Freeman, S.
Jorgenson, K.
  see Vera, E. M.
Joshi, P. D., 236
Joyner, K., 161
  see also Carver, K.
Ju, D. B., 191
Julian, A. M., 19
Juvenal, 13
Juvonen, J., 140
  see also Graham, S.

Kabat-Zinn, J., 96, 125
  see also Davidson, R. J.
Kaczala, C.
  see Eccles, J.
Kadar, J.
  see Zinnbauer, B.
Kahana, E., 38
Kahle, L. R., 57
Kahneman, D., 30, 228, 229, 237, 238
Kahneman, Daniel, 228
Kahn, R.
  see Berkman, F.
Kahn, S., 33
Kajal, D.
  see Rikani, A. A.

Kallgren, C. A., 57
Kalpidou, M., 145
Kamarck, T., 48, 115
  see also Cohen, S.
Kamiya, J., 12
Kang, H.
  see Xie, L.
Kang, S.-M., 60
Kang, Y., 316
K'an-k'ai, 123
Kanner, A. D., 19, 113
Kapadia, F.
  see Stults, C.
Kaprio, J., 283
  see also Dick, D. M.
Karabenick, S. A., 55
Karney, B. R., 320
  see also Finkel, E. J.
Kashdan, T. B., 32
Kassam, K. S., 229
Kasser, T., 239
Kasser, V. G., 40
Kaszniak, A. W., 97
Katz, P., 312
Kawachi, I., 48
Kawakami, K., 58
Kaye, W. H., 280
Keen, K. J., 161
Keller, E. T., 10
Kelley, S. S., 161
Kellner, C. H., 294
Kelly, A., 265
Kelly, C. M., 149
Kelly, D. R., 35, 188
Kelly, J. G., 7, 20, 56
  see Maton, K. I.
Keltner, D., 124, 151
Kendall, P. C., 53
Kennedy, John F., 289
Kennedy-Moore, E., 142 (table)
Kennedy, S. H.
  see Mayberg, H. S.
Kessler, R. C., 7, 275, 279
  see also Hudson, J. I.
Khalsa, S., 277
Khoshaba, D. M., 209
  see also Maddi, S. R.
Kidd, A. R., III, 248
Kidman, R. C.
  see Shaffer, H. J.
Kiecolt-Glaser, J. K., 48
  see also Uchino, B. N.
Kihlstrom, J. F., 30
Kilduff, M., 51
  see Fang, R.
Kimeldorf, D. J., 71
  see also Garcia, J.
Kim, J., 188
Kimmel, H., 12
Kinder, D. R., 312
Kindergarten, 181

King, K., 36
King, L. A., 31, 33
King, S. V., 264
Kirk, J., 324
Kirkpatrick, K., 103
Kitayama, S., 46, 59, 329
Kit, B. K., 131
Kivimäki, M.
    see Kouvonen, A. M.
Kjaer, G., 113
Kleiner, M., 313
Klein, L. C.
    see Taylor, S. E.
Klesse, A., 236
Kloep, M., 211
Klopott, S., 193
Kluckhohn, C., 58
Kluge, N. A., 258
Klute, M. M., 150
Knapp, R. G.
    see Kellner, C. H.
Knutson, B., 234, 235
Kobasa, S. C., 33, 34
Koelling, R. A., 71
    see also Garcia, J.
Koenig, H. G., 38
Kogan, S. M., 47
Kokkonen, A., 312
Konrath, S. H., 322, 323
    see also Twenge, J. M.
Koole, S. L., 30, 31
Koolhaas, J. M., 20
Koranyi, N.
    see Fritsche, I.
Koretz, D.
    see Merikangas, K. R.
Korotkov, D. L., 39
Korte, S. M.
    see Koolhaas, J. M.
Kosciw, J. G., 185
Koskenvuo, M., 283
Koskinen, A.
    see Kouvonen, A. M.
Kouvonen, A. M., 32
Koyanagi, C., 289
Kratochvil, C. J., 286
Krause, N., 39, 253
Krishnamoorthy, J. S., 132
Kristeller, J., 94, 95
Kross, E., 174, 308, 309
Krueger, F.
    see Moll, J.
Kuhn, C., 125
Kuhn, D., 250
Kuhne, R., 323
Kumar, R., 55
Kunze, S.
    see Sedlmeier, P.
Kuo, S. I.-C., 16, 65
    see also McCormick, C. M.
Kuo, W., 48

Labouvie-Vief, G., 250
LaBrie, R. A.
    see Shaffer, H. J.
Ladd, B.
    see Michalik, N. M.
Ladd, G. W., 140
Lai, C.-H., 322
Laidra, K., 188
Lalonde, C. E., 306
Lambert, S. M., 246
Lamonte, M. J.
    see Garber, C. E.
Lamp, K., 213
    see also Brown, S. D.
Landau, M. J., 30
Lander, R., 181
Landis, B.
    see Fang, R.
Lang, D., 38
Langer, E. J., 97
Lang, P., 12
Langrehr, K. J.
    see Vera, E. M.
Language learning, 65, 82, 83
Lanza, S. T., 134
Lapan, R. T., 213
Lapierre, C., 324
LaPlante, D. A.
    see Shaffer, H. J.
Lapsley, D. K., 32, 33, 315
    see also Hill, P. L.
Larson, D. B., 38
    see also George, L. K.
Larson, L. M., 215
Lasiter, P. S., 71
Lasser, K., 283
Latinas/Latinos
    coping strategies and styles, 120
    friendships, 143
    learning community interventions, 200
    money management, 224
Lau, A. S., 60
Lau, H., 328
    see also Cheng, C.
Lawrence, A. R., 264
Lawson, D. M., 172
Layton, J. B., 48
Lazarus, R. S., 11, 19, 113, 117, 119, 120
Leach, M. M., 37
Learned reinforcers, 225–226
Learning, 20, 21 (figure)
Learning communities, 200
Learning probabilities, 82
Learning schedules, 76 (figure)
Leavy, R., 48
Lee, B. H., 307
    see also Frimer, J. A.
Lee-Chai, A. Y., 30
Lee, D.-G.
    see Heppner, M. J.
Lee, D. L., 122

Lee, E. K. O., 38
Lee, I. M.
  see Garber, C. E.
Lee, R. M.
  see Gortmaker, S. L.
Legacies, 252, 255 (table)
Lehr, C. A., 191
Leiser, D., 226, 231
Lenhart, A., 320, 321
Lens, W., 40
  see also Vansteenkiste, M.
Lent, R. W., 206, 215, 216
Lentz, E., 47
Leong, F. T. L., 60
Leppänen, J. M., 327
Lerner, J. V., 7
Lerner, R. M., 7, 15
Lesbian relationships, 166–168
Leserman, J., 171
Less-Horta, B., 286
Leung, A. K., 313
Leung, C. M., 124
Levenson, R. W.
  see Gottman, J. M.
Levey, S. M. B., 135
Levine, R. V., 60
Levine, S., 30
  see Wiedenfeld, S. A.
Levy, D., 226
  see also Leiser, D.
Lewin-Bizan, S., 7
Lewin, K., 21, 60
Lewin, Kurt, 53
Lewis, B. P.
  see Taylor, S. E.
LGBT (lesbian, gay, bisexual, and transgender) population,
    166–168, 321, 326
Liamputtong, P., 321
Liao, Y.
  see Xie, L.
Licklider, J. C. R., 317
Lieberman, M. D., 174
  see Master, S. L.
Life event measures, 114–115 (table)
Life expectancies, 244–246, 245 (figure), 256, 260
Life experiences
  acceptance and tolerance, 313–315
  aging, 251, 260
  cognitive development, 70, 72, 75, 83
  contextual influences, 55–56, 61–62
  loss of loved ones, 260–262
  mentoring, 48
  money management, 226, 232–233, 239
  negative life experiences, 18–19, 19 (figure), 104
  positive life experiences, 8–9, 10 (table), 18–19, 19 (figure)
  prejudicial attitudes, 313
  resiliency, 63–65, 64 (table), 328
  social learning theory, 80, 82–83
  spiritual and religious beliefs and activities, 35, 36
  see also Childhood; Friendships; Mental illness/mental
      disorders; Mindfulness; School; Stress

Life tasks, 16–17, 17 (table)
Light, K. C.
  see Bowen, K. S.
Li-Grining, C. P., 140
Liking, 166 (figure)
Lillard, A., 181
Lima, L., 47
Lin, A. I., 122
Lin, D., 74
Lindberg, M., 31
Lindstrom, B., 32
Lindzey, G., 99
Lin, J.
  see Epel, E. S.
Lin, N., 48, 124
Liptak, A., 312
Lipworth, L., 96
Lisanby, S. H.
  see Janicak, P. G.; Spellman, T.
Li, T.
  see Yang, C. Y.
Liu, D., 125
Liu, W. M.
  see Saegert, S. C.
Living situations, 263–265
Livingston, J. D., 298
Loans, 233
Lobotomies, 293–294
Locke, John, 13
Lockhart, R. S., 84
Loeb, S.
  see Gueldner, S. H.
Loewenstein, G. F., 228, 229, 232
  see also Rick, S.
Lohoff, F. W., 7
London, England, 288
Loneliness
  causal factors, 153–155
  friendships, 143
  nursing home residents, 265
  older adulthood, 253, 254–255, 263
  social networks, 51, 52
  spousal loss, 260–261
Longmore, M. A., 161
  see also Manning, W. D.
Long-term memory, 251, 255 (table)
López, I., 227
Lopez, J. D., 122
Lopez, S., 9, 11
Lorig, T. S., 315
  see also Ito, T. A.
Los Angeles, California, 238 (table)
Loss, 260–262, 262 (table)
Louie, J. Y., 59
Love, 15, 15 (table), 160, 166 (figure)
Love, J. M., 182
Loving-kindness meditation (LKM),
    102–103, 316
Low-achieving students, 196
Lowery, B., 315
  see also Sinclair, S.

Lozano, A. M.
    see Mayberg, H. S.
Luber, B.
    see Spellman, T.
Lubinski, D., 213
Lucas, R. E., 206
Lucksted, A., 298
Lui, H.
    see Giedd, J. N.
Lu, J. L.
    see Maddi, S. R.
Lunatics, 288
Lund, D. A., 260, 261
Luo, Y., 254
Lutgen-Sandvik, P., 186
Luthar, S. S., 63, 65, 306
Lutz, A., 92, 97, 102, 108
Lynam, D., 154
Lynch, S., 81
Lynskey, M. T., 283
Lyons, A. C., 232
Lysaker, P., 298

Maccoby, E. E., 143
MacDonald, R., 323
Machado, A., 170
Machell, K. A., 32
Macinnis, D. J., 230
MacKenzie, M., 40
Macular degeneration, 248
Maddi, S. R., 33, 34, 209
Maddux, W. W., 313, 314
Madness, 272
Maeseneer, J., 52
Maes, H., 7
Magruder, L., 226
Maholick, J., 32
Mahoney, A., 35, 36
Maine, 311
Maitlis, S., 19
Major depressive disorders, 276
Majority–minority populations, 310–311
Makhoul, S., 286
Maki, D. M., 234
Maladaptive social cognitions, 254
Maladjustment, 271
Maldonado-Carreno, C., 140
Malhotra, A.
    see Edwards, B. A.
Malik, B., 187
Malone, J., 172
Manhattan, New York, 238 (table)
Mania/manic depression, 276–277, 278
Manly, J. B., 40
Manning, W. D., 161, 162
Mann, Jeffrey, 316
Mann, J. John, 285
Manson, J. E., 133
Marijuana, 282
Marijuana use, 134
Markman, K., 31

Markovits, H., 142
Markus, H. R., 46, 59
Marquez, C., 47
Marriage, 162–163, 163 (figure)
Marshall, A., 170
    see also Holtzworth-Munroe, A.
Marshall, H., 226
Martens, A., 30
Martinez, M., 193
Martin, L., 211
Martin Lohfink, M., 193
Martin, R.
    see Clark, C.
Martin, T., 260
Martin, W. F.
    see Chartrand, J. M.
Masden, S. D., 147
Mashburn, A. J., 182
Masi, C. M., 31, 154, 254
    see also Cacioppo, J. T.
Maslow, Abraham, 291
Maslow, A. H., 206
Massachusetts Institute of Technology (MIT), 317
Massage therapy, 125
Masse, L. C.
    see Troiano, R. P.
Masson, P., 246
Masten, A. S., 9, 16, 17, 62, 63, 64, 64 (table), 65, 306
    see also McCormick, C. M.
Masterov, D. V., 183
Master, S. L., 174
Masters, R. K., 245
Mastery and expertise, 250, 251
Mastery-oriented goals, 184
Match.com, 321
Matchmaking, 320
    see also Interpersonal relationships
Mathematics and Science Assessments, 212 (figure)
Maton, K. I., 20
Matos, M., 170
Mattern, K., 5
Matthews, M. D., 35, 188
Mattia, F. R., 65
Maturation process, 65–66
Matzel, L., 82
Maulik, P., 48
Mayberg, H. S., 295
May, R., 28–29, 329
May, Rollo, 28, 29, 291
Mayr, U., 239
    see also Harbaugh, W.
Mays, V. M., 122
Mazar, N., 230
Mazzeo, S. E., 131, 132
McAdams, D. P., 328
McAuliffe, G. J.
    see Chartrand, J. M.
McCarthy, B., 166
McCarthy, K. S., 277
McClearn, G.
    see Berkman, F.

McClelland, D., 66
McClintock, S. M.
 see Spellman, T.
McCormick, C. M., 16, 65
McCormick, D.
 see Lasser, K.
McCoy, K.
 see Gottman, J. M.
McCrae, R. R., 37
McCullough, M. E., 37
McDaniel, M. A., 84
McDonough, M.
 see Freeman, S.
McDowell, M.
 see Troiano, R. P.
McEwan, B., 113, 149, 150
McGregor, I., 38
 see also Inzlicht, M.
McKenzie, K., 278
McKnight, P. E., 32
McLean, K. C., 328
McLoyd, V. C., 60
McMahon, M., 208
McNair, L. D., 167
McNeely, H. E.
 see Mayberg, H. S.
McPherson, M., 323
McQuown, C., 256
McVey, L. A., 238
McWilliams, S., 321
Mead, N. L., 229
Meaney, M. J., 125
Meaning in life/meaningfulness
 existential perspective, 28–29
 fear of death, 30–31
 importance, 31–32, 40, 306
 personal change, 306
 sense of coherence, 32
 spiritual and religious beliefs and activities, 35, 39–40
Median income by education, 192 (figure)
Medina-Mora, M. E.
 see Swanson, S. A.
Meditation
 basic concepts and characteristics, 91–93
 current research assessment tools, 98
 loving-kindness meditation (LKM), 102–103, 316
 practice exercise, 93
 scientific research background, 92–93, 96 (figure), 96–97
 as stress management strategy, 125–126
MedlinePlus, 127
Meece, J.
 see Eccles, J.
Meehan, J., 170
 see also Holtzworth-Munroe, A.
Meichenbaum, D., 80
Meir, E. I., 217
Meltzer, C. C.
 see Kaye, W. H.
Memorials, 260, 262, 262 (table)
Memory processes, 11–12
Menkin, J. A., 321

Mental disorder treatment approaches
 asylums, 288–289, 293
 brain stimulation therapies, 293, 294–295
 future outlook, 298–300
 psychoanalysis, 272, 289–293
 psychotropic medications, 295–297, 298 (table)
 psychotropic surgeries, 293–294
 seeking professional help, 291–293, 292 (figure)
Mental health
 definition, 8–9
 job loss impacts, 206
 meaningful work, 206
 older adulthood, 211
 sense of coherence, 32
 social support impacts, 48
 spiritual and religious beliefs and activities, 36, 261
 stress reactions, 117
Mental illness/mental disorders
 addictive behaviors, 280–283, 284 (table)
 anxiety disorders, 274–276, 282 (table), 284 (table)
 biopsychosocial model, 272, 273 (figure), 276, 280, 283, 285
 categories, 274, 299
 causal factors, 271–272
 definition, 270–271
 diagnostic criteria, 273–274
 eating disorders, 278–280, 284 (table)
 future outlook, 298–300
 genetic research, 272, 276, 277, 280, 283, 299
 historical perspective, 271–272
 intimate partner violence (IPV), 172
 mood disorders, 276–277, 284 (table)
 neurodevelopmental disorders, 283, 284 (table), 286–287
 onset, 7
 personal and public stigma, 298
 prevalence, 273, 276, 279, 280, 286, 299
 psychotic disorders, 277–278, 284 (table)
 substance use disorders, 280–283, 282 (table), 284 (table)
 suicidal behaviors, 283, 284–286
 treatment approaches, 287–289
Mentors/mentoring, 47–48, 62–63, 194, 198–200, 210
Merikangas, K. R., 279
 see also Kessler, R. C.
Merikangas, M. W., 258
Merkin, S. S.
 see Epel, E. S.
Mermelstein, R., 48, 115
 see also Cohen, S.
Messina, S., 279, 280
Metacognitive Awareness of Reading Strategies Inventory
 (MARSI), 197 (figure)
Metal coins, 225
Meyer, F., 140
Meyer, M., 113
Micale, M. S., 288
Michalik, N. M., 153
Michikyan, M.
 see Uhls, Y. T.
Microaggressions, 122–123
Microassaults, 122
Microinsults, 122
Microinvalidations, 122

Midcareer period, 210
Middle adulthood
    cognitive changes, 250, 255 (table)
    life tasks, 17 (table)
    narratives and stories, 328
    online dating, 321
    physical changes, 247, 247 (table)
    resiliency, 65 (table)
    savings patterns, 234
    sexual activity, 166
    social support impacts, 49 (figure)
    socioemotional changes, 252, 255 (table)
Midgley, C.
    see Eccles, J.
Mikulincer, M., 30
Milgram, S., 57
Millar, H., 279
Millennial generation, 310, 310 (figure), 311, 317, 326
Miller, A. G., 57
Miller, Benjamin F., 135
Miller, Brandon, 321
Miller, G. E., 10
Miller, J. D., 322
    see also Twenge, J. M.
Miller, N. E., 12, 20, 79
Miller, Norman, 316
Miller, Terry, 326
Mind-body interaction, 9–13
Mindfulness
    acceptance and action, 103–104, 106–108
    benefits, 90
    compassion, 101–103, 107
    current research assessment tools, 98
    definition, 91
    disciplined thoughts, 98–99
    historical perspectives, 94–95, 95 (figure)
    nonjudgmental awareness, 99, 104, 106–107
    positive mental states, 98
    scientific research background, 92–93, 96 (figure),
        96–97, 108
    self-regulation, 99–101
    stress reduction programs, 220
Mindfulness-Based Stress Reduction (MBSR), 96
Mindfulness meditation, 92, 95 (figure), 96
Mindlessness, 91
Mineka, S., 30, 71
Minority populations
    college dropout rate, 193
    college enrollment trends and graduation rates,
        195 (figure)
    coping strategies and styles, 120, 122, 123–124
    demographic shifts, 310 (figure), 310–311
    friendships, 143, 144, 144–145
    higher education programs, 194, 199
    learning community interventions, 200
    life expectancies, 245
    mentoring, 198–199
    microaggressions, 122
    obesity rates, 131–132
    science, technology, engineering, and mathematics (STEM)
        programs, 212–213
    spiritual and religious beliefs and activities, 261
    substance abuse, 134–135
    work aspirations and expectations, 211, 213
Mirror neurons, 102, 151
Mischel, W., 62, 174
    see also Kross, E.
Misra, S., 323
Miss World beauty contest, 280
Mistry, R. S., 227
Mitchell, V., 167
Mobassarah, N. J.
    see Rikani, A. A.
Mobile devices, 319, 322, 323
Möbius, H. J.
    see Taylor, E.
Mock, S., 311
Modeling, 80–81
Modern Western psychology, 94
Moffitt, T. E., 13, 61
Mohr, C., 279, 280
Mohs, R.
    see Berkman, F.
Mok, D., 146
Mokhtari, K., 197 (figure)
Moller, A., 40
Moller, S., 191
Moll, J., 239
Monda-Amaya, L. E., 185
Money
    buying behavior and skills, 230–232
    comparison evaluations, 228–229, 230
    credit card use, 232–234
    decision-making processes, 229, 230–232
    determination of worth, 231–232
    developmental progressions, 226
    everyday happiness relationship, 237 (figure), 237–239
    historical perspective, 225
    influencing factors, 229
    learned reinforcers, 225–226
    powerfulness, 236
    psychological perspectives, 224, 228
    retirement planning, 257–258, 258 (figure)
    savings patterns and practices, 234–236
    ten richest cities in America, 238 (table)
"Money matters on campus", 224, 232
Moniz, Antonio Egas, 293–294
Monkey mind, 98
Montepare, J. M., 249, 316
Monterde-Bort, H., 171
Montessori, Maria, 181
Montessori preschools, 181
Montgomery, M. J., 193
Mood disorders, 274, 276–277, 283, 284 (table)
Moody, J., 52
Moon, C., 65
Moradi, B., 171
Moral treatment approach, 288–289
Moreno, A. J., 150
Moreno-John, G., 170
Morewedge, C. K., 228, 229
Morgan, M., 21

Moritsugu, J., 21
Morley, K. I., 277
Morris, D.
    see Gueldner, S. H.
Morris, Jessica, 145
Morris, Jordan
    see Uhls, Y. T.
Morris, M. L., 216
Morrow, J. D.
    see Epel, E. S.
Mortality/mortality salience, 30–31
Moser, R. P., 20
Mosher, W. D., 161
Moskowitz, G. B., 315
Motivation, 40, 184, 184 (table), 196
Motzoi, C., 140
Mower, O. H., 20
Mullan Harris, K.
    see Yang, C. Y.
Muller, D.
    see Davidson, R. J.
Mull, M.
    see Vera, E. M.
Mulsant, B., 278
Multicultural experiences, 314
Multifinality, 61
Mumford, J. A., 53
Mummendey, A., 312
Munch, J., 149
    see also Wettersten, K. B.
Munniksma, A., 140
    see also Graham, S.
Murphy, B. C.
    see Eisenberg, N.
Murphy, J. W., 289
Murrell, A., 316
Myers, C. B., 212, 213
Myers, D., 195

Nachmani, J.
    see Foster, G. D.
Nadal, K. L., 122
Nagayama Hall, G. C., 60
Na, J., 329
Naji, S.
    see Millar, H.
Naliboff, B. D., 53
    see Master, S. L.
Nam, I., 234
    see also Friedline, T. L.
Namie, G., 186
Namie, R., 186
Nanin, J. E., 161
Narcissism, 322–323, 326
Narratives, 327–328
Nash, K., 38
    see also Inzlicht, M.
Nathan, P. E., 291, 296, 299
National Alliance on Mental Illness, 296
National Assessment of Educational Progress (NAEP),
    212 (figure)

National Career Development Association, 208
National Center for Education Statistics (NCES),
    191, 192 (figure), 193, 207, 212 (figure)
National Center for Family and Marriage Research, 162
National Center on Addiction and Substance Abuse at Columbia
    University, 281, 283
National Comorbidity Survey, 274, 275, 276, 279, 282
National Institute for Occupational Safety and
    Health (NIOSH), 219
National Institute of Drug Abuse, 282
National Institute of Mental Health (NIMH), 273, 274, 277, 278,
    286, 296, 298, 299
National Institutes of Health (NIH), 273
National Physical Laboratory, 317
National Science Foundation, 212
National Sleep Foundation, 12
National Survey of Family Growth, 161
Neal, S., 144, 145
Neal, Z., 52
Nedergaard, M.
    see Xie, L.
Need for relatedness, 206–207, 211
Need for self-fulfillment, 206, 210–211
Need for survival, 206, 210
Neff, K. D., 103
Negative affect reciprocity, 163–164
Negative beliefs and expectations, 187
Negative change, 18–19, 19 (figure), 61
Negative consequences, 75
Negative emotions, 163
Negative environments, 305–306
Negative self-perceptions, 323
Negative versus positive change events, 18–19, 19 (figure),
    34, 63–65
    see also Resilience
Nelson, M., 191
Networking, 175 (table), 176
Networking rules, 51–52
Neumann, T., 313
Neurodevelopmental disorders, 274, 282 (table), 284 (table),
    286–287
Neurological research
    age-related changes, 249–250
    brain functions, 298–299
    broken hearts, 174
    current versus future self, 235, 235 (figure)
    depressive disorders, 277
    developmental demands and capabilities, 62
    eating disorders, 280
    learning types, 83
    maturation process, 65–66
    mindfullness-based practices, 96–97, 102
    neurodevelopmental disorders, 287
    physical touch studies, 125
    psychotic disorders, 278
    situational anxiety, 53
    spiritual and religious beliefs and activities, 38, 39 (figure)
Neurons, 102, 151
Neurotransmitter disruptions, 277, 278, 280, 285
Neutral stimulus (NS), 70–71
Nevada, 310

Neville, H. A., 122
Newcomer, R., 264
Newell, L., 181
    see also Hart, Craig H.
Newman, R. I., 97
New Mexico, 310
Newport, E. L., 82
Newport, F., 261
New Shorter Oxford English Dictionary, 32
New York City, 238 (table)
Ng, W., 237
Nicklin, J. M., 40
Niemann, L., 125
Nisbett, R. E., 329
Nix, G. A., 40
Nobakht, M., 279
Nobel Prize, 228
Nobrega, S., 219
Noelle-Neumann, E., 323
Noll, E.
    see Swanson, D. P.
Nondating sexual partnerships, 161–162
    see also Romantic relationships
Nonfavored groups, 312–313
Nonjudgmental awareness, 99, 104, 106–107
Nonprejudice, 315–316
Norcross, J. C., 291
Norman, G. J.
    see Patrick, K.
Normative influence, 56
Norms, 78, 231, 315–316
Northrup, J. C., 324
Norton, M. I., 239
    see also Aknin, L. B.
Notaro, P. C., 47
NOVA, 225
Nursing homes, 264–265
Nutrition, 131–132, 132 (figure)
Nyhus, E. K., 226, 234

Oakes, H., 307
Oakes, J. M., 227
Obama, Barack, 298
Obedience to authority, 57
Obergefell v. Hodges (2015), 312
Obesity rates, 131
O'Brien, C., 195
    see also Engle, J.
O'Brien, E. H., 323
O'Brien, M. U.
    see Greenberg, M. T.
Observational learning, 80–81
Obsessive-compulsive disorder (OCD), 275, 282 (table),
    284 (table)
    see also Anxiety/anxiety disorders
Obstacles, 108, 129
    see also Reframing skills
Occam's razor, 306
Occupational circumscription, 214–215
Occupational Information Network (O*Net), 208
Occupational mentoring, 47

Occupations
    career indecisiveness, 208–209
    contextual influences, 211, 213–214
    definition, 205–206
    employee assistance programs (EAPs), 219–220
    first job, 209
    flow, 218
    fundamental human needs, 206–207, 210
    importance, 206–207
    life span salience, 207–211
    meaningful work, 205
    midcareer period, 210
    retirement, 210–211
    rewards and risks, 218–220
    science, technology, engineering, and mathematics (STEM)
        programs, 212 (figure), 212–213
    stress levels, 218–219
    theory of occupational circumscription and compromise,
        214–215
O'Connor, R., 5
O'Connor, S. P.
    see Buxton, O. M.
O'Driscoll, D. M.
    see Edwards, B. A.
Office of Postsecondary Education, 194
Off-line cheating, 168–170
Off-line conventional dating, 320
Ogburn, E. L., 321
Ogden, C. L., 131
Ohman, A., 71
Oishi, S., 33, 237
    see also Diener, E.
Okoroafor, N.
    see Freeman, S.
Older adulthood
    aging in place, 263–265
    cognitive changes, 251, 255 (table)
    demographic shifts, 310, 310 (figure), 311
    life tasks, 17 (table)
    living situations, 263–265
    loneliness, 253, 254–255
    online dating, 321
    physical changes, 247 (table), 248–249
    residential retirement communities, 263, 264–265
    retirement, 210–211
    sexual activity, 166
    social support impacts, 49 (figure), 253–254, 255 (table)
    socioemotional changes, 252–253, 255 (table)
    see also Aging
Old-old adults, 248
Olds, D. L., 171
O'Leary, A.
    see Wiedenfeld, S. A.
O'Leary, K., 172
Olsen, R., 195
    see also Myers, D.
Olsen, S., 181
    see also Hart, Craig H.
Olson, L. S., 191
Omoto, A., 35
O'Neal, J. H., 296

Onishi, N., 280
Online cheating, 168–169
Online dating, 320–322
Open-mindedness, 314, 315–316, 328–329
Open-monitoring (OM) meditation, 92
Operant conditioning, 72–73, 75, 76
Operants, 72, 73
Opeyo, A., 316
Opioids, 280, 282, 282 (table)
Oppenheimer, L., 215
Opportunity structures, 305–306
Opposite-sex attraction, 160–161
Optimism, 124
O'Reardon, J. P
    see Janicak, P. G.
Orth, U., 16
    see also Hutteman, R.
Ortman, J. M., 17, 311
Osbourne, J. W., 252, 257
Ossana, S. M., 258
Ostracism, 30
O'Sullivan, G., 128
Oswald, D. L., 149
Otto, M. W., 126
Outcome expectations, 215
Out-groups, 57–58, 312, 313, 315
Overmeyer, S.
    see Taylor, E.
Overweight populations, 131
Owsley, C., 247, 248
Oxytocin, 124, 125

PACE (Patient Centered Assessment and Counseling for Exercise
        and Nutrition), 133
Page, Larry, 318
Page, S., 313
Painful experiences, 104
Pajares, F., 184
Palfrey, J., 317
Pandey, G. N., 285
Panic disorders, 185, 275, 284 (table)
Paper money, 225
Parallel play, 141
Pardini, M.
    see Moll, J.
Parental involvement, 54–55, 153, 225–226
Pargament, K. I., 35, 36, 38, 39
    see also Zinnbauer, B.
Paris, France, 288
Park, C. L., 39
Parker, J. G., 141
Park, H.-J.
    see Heppner, M. J.
Park, J.
    see Kross, E.
Park, N., 8
Parrish, B. P., 19
Parsons, J. T., 161
Parten, M. B., 141
Passion, 165, 166 (figure)
Passive learning, 84

Pathways, 7
Patrick, K., 133
Patrick, V. M., 230
Patton, W., 208
Paul, A., 321
Paul, C., 311
Paulsen, M. B., 193
Paunesku, D.
    see Yeager, D. S.
Paus, T., 249, 250
Pavel, D., 212, 213
Pavlov, I., 70
Pavlovian conditioning, 70–72, 71 (figure), 79, 80, 225
Pavlov, Ivan, 70
Peake, P., 62
Pearson, A. R.
    see Dovidio, J. F.
Peer mentoring, 200
Peer relationships, 141–143, 142 (table), 153–155
Peersman, W., 52
Penrod, J.
    see Gueldner, S. H.
Perceived collective efficacy, 81–82
Perceived self-efficacy, 81
Perceived stress, 117
Performance-oriented goals, 184
Perkins, D. D.
    see Maton, K. I.
Perkins, M. M., 264
Perpetual problems, 164
Perrin, E. C., 13
Perry, J. C.
    see Chaves, A. P.
Persico, M.
    see Maddi, S. R.
Personal challenges
    agency and communion, 307–308
    individual-environmental balance, 305–306
    realistic perspectives, 308–309, 309 (figure)
Personal computer systems, 317–318
Personal control, 253, 255 (table)
Personality, 20, 21 (figure)
Personality theory, 36–38, 208, 216 (figure), 216–217
Personal qualities, 64–65, 65 (table)
Personal religion, 35, 40
Personal stigma, 298
Personal values, 103, 104–108
Person by situation interactions, 53
Person–environment fit theory, 208, 214, 216–217
Perspective-taking ability, 141–142, 154, 250
    see also Empathy
Pescosolido, B. A., 298
Pesta, B., 84
Peter, J., 145
Peterson, C., 8, 35, 188
Petrides, G.
    see Kellner, C. H.
Petroski, G. F., 213
Pettigrew, T. F., 316
Pew Research Center, 318, 319, 321, 322, 323, 324, 325
Phased retirement, 256

Philadelphia Hospital, 288
Phillips, J., 193, 194, 195, 200
Phillips, T. M.
    see Sandvik, A. M.
Physical activity, 34, 126, 133–134
Physical aggression, 170–172
Physical appearance changes, 247 (table), 247–249
Physical health
    age-related changes, 246–249, 247 (table),
        255 (table)
    broken hearts, 174
    loneliness, 154
    social support impacts, 48, 49 (figure), 50, 124
    see also Health and well-being
Physical pain, 174
Physical touch, 124–125
Physiological reactivity, 34
Piagetian theory, 83
Piaget, Jean, 83
Pickering, J. W.
    see Chartrand, J. M.
Piedmont, R. L., 36, 37, 38
Pieterse, A. L., 122
Pinel, Philippe, 288
Pitts, M., 321
Place–behavior interactions, 53–55
Planned versus unplanned change, 19–20
Plant, E. A., 315
Planty, M., 193
Plaumann, M., 220
Play, 141, 181
Pleasurable expectations, 231
Pletcher, M.
    see Epel, E. S.
Poehlman, T. A., 71
Poirier, J., 288
Polanczyk, G., 286
Polanin, M., 185, 186
Poldrack, R. A., 53
Pong, S. L., 191
Pönkänen, L. M., 327
Pons-Salvador, G., 171
Poor, M. C., 286
Poortinga, W., 52
Pope, H. G., 279
    see also Hudson, J. I.
Pope, M. L., 208
Population estimates, 310, 310 (figure)
Porter, J. H.
    see Buxton, O. M.
Portes, A., 52
Portillo, N., 47
    see also DuBois, D. L.
Positive aging, 258–259
Positive change, 18–19, 19 (figure), 107, 128
Positive emotions, 52, 163, 175, 239, 315
Positive environments, 305–306
Positive feedback, 145
Positive life experiences, 8–9, 10 (table)
Positive mental health, 8–9
Positive psychology, 9, 10 (table), 15–16

Positive versus negative change events, 18–19, 19 (figure),
    34, 63–65
    see also Resilience
Positivity, 149, 150 (table), 154, 165, 175, 175 (table)
Positron-emission tomography (PET), 96
Posner, M. I., 97
Post-traumatic stress disorder (PTSD), 275, 276
Poteet, M. L., 47
Potochnick, S., 191
Powell, L. H., 38
Pow, J. L., 289
Prado, G., 38
Pragmatic problem solving, 250, 255 (table)
Predictability, 19–20, 30
Predictable outcomes, 75–76, 117
Predictors of divorce, 173
Prefrontal cortex, 250, 293–294
Prejudice, 312–317
Prelec, D., 228, 232
Premack, D., 77
Premack principle, 77
Preparedness, 71–72
Presbycusis, 247
Preschools, 181
Prescott, G.
    see Millar, H.
Prescription drug use, 134–135
Present-future self-matching, 234–235
Present–Future Similarity Test, 235–236
Pressley, M., 196
Pressman, S., 11
Preston, J. D., 296
Prevention and promotion programs, 21
Price, J. C.
    see Kaye, W. H.
Prilleltensky, I., 21
Prilleltensky, O., 21
Primary appraisal, 117, 118 (figure)
Prior, M.
    see Williams, Katrina
Proactive behaviors, 259
Probability learning, 82
Problems, lack of, 7–8
Problem solving-focused coping, 120, 121 (table), 123
Processing speed, 250, 251, 255 (table)
Procidano, M., 48
Proctor, B. D., 227
Professional hugging, 125
Prokasky, W., 12
Prosocial behavior, 32–33, 33 (figure), 150, 152–153, 309, 315
Protective factors, 32–33
Protectors, 226
Proulx, T., 31, 39
Provasnik, S., 193
Psychoanalysis, 272, 289–293
Psychoeducation, 20
Psychogenic etiologies
    addictive behaviors, 283
    basic concepts, 272
    eating disorders, 280
    mental illness treatments, 289–291

mood disorders, 277
    psychotic disorders, 278
Psychological abuse, 170–172
Psychological health
    job loss impacts, 206
    meaningful work, 206
    sense of coherence, 32
    social support impacts, 48
    spiritual and religious beliefs and activities, 36
    stress reactions, 117
Psychology, history of, 94
Psychology of working, 206
Psychopathology, 7–8
Psychopharmaceuticals, 126, 271
Psychosis/psychotic disorders
    characteristics and etiology, 277–278
    diagnostic criteria, 274
    personal experiences, 271
    prevalence, 284 (table)
    psychotropic medications, 296, 298 (table)
    substance-induced mental disorders, 282, 282 (table), 283
Psychosocial development stages, 14–17, 15 (table)
Psychotherapy, 289–293
Psychotropic medications, 295–297, 298 (table)
Psychotropic surgeries, 293–295
Public stigma, 298
Puccetti, M., 33
Puig, J., 16
Pulkkinen, L.
    see Dick, D. M.
Pull factors, 191
Pullmann, H., 188
Punishers, 74, 75, 78–79
Punishment, 74–75, 77, 78–79
Punnett, L., 219
Purcell, S.
    see Dick, D. M.
Purging
    see Binge eating disorder
Purpose, 15, 15 (table)
Purpose in life
    existential perspective, 28–29
    fear of death, 30–31
    importance, 31–32, 33 (figure), 40
    protective factors, 32–33
    spiritual and religious beliefs and activities, 35–40
Push factors, 191
Pussin, Jean-Baptiste, 288
Putnam, R. D., 52, 53, 312
Pyszczynski, T., 30, 31

Quaranto, J. C., 33
    see also Hill, P. L.
Queens, New York, 238 (table)
Quevedo, K., 11
Quinn, K. J., 299
Quinn, R., 20

Racial diversity, 310–311
    see also Ethnic populations; Minority populations
Racism, 122, 213, 312–313

Radical acceptance, 104
Rado, J. T.
    see Janicak, P. G.
Rae, C., 324
Ragpay, L., 94, 95
Rahe, R. H., 18, 29, 113, 114
Raikes, J., 182
Rainie, L., 146, 319
    see also Hampton, K.
Rainwater, L., 227
Rakic, T., 312
Ramaswami, A., 198
Random outcomes, 75–76
Rando, T. A., 261
Rank, M. R., 227
Rapoport, J. L.
    see Giedd, J. N.
Rappaport, J.
    see Maton, K. I.
Raska, K.
    see Wiedenfeld, S. A.
Raskin, D., 12
Rasmussen, A., 120
Rasmussen, K.
    see Kellner, C. H.
Rawes, E., 238 (table)
Rawlings, N. B., 97
Rawlinson, N., 318
Reading skills, 197 (figure)
Read, S., 312
Realistic personal perspectives, 308–309, 309 (figure)
Reclassification, 316
Reduction in force [RIF] programs, 256
Rees, S. M., 278
Reframing skills, 128–129
Regularity, 77
Regular savings, 236
Regulators, 226
Rehman, U., 170
    see also Holtzworth-Munroe, A.
Rehn, A. E., 278
Reichard, C., 197 (figure)
Reich, J. W., 18
Reimers, F., 227
Reinforcement theory, 74–79
Reinforcers, 74, 75, 77–79
Reis, H. T., 40, 320
    see also Finkel, E. J.
Reitz, A. K., 16
    see also Hutteman, R.
Rejected aggressive children, 154
Rejected children, 153–154
Relatedness, need for, 206–207, 211
Relationships
    formation and maintenance, 150–154
    friendships, 140–150
    importance, 140, 155
    Internet impacts, 326–327
    online dating, 320–322
    social media impacts, 145–147
    social support impacts, 253, 255 (table)

success predictors, 175 (table), 175–176
  see also Aging; Romantic relationships
Relationship talks, 175 (table), 175–176
Relationship violence, 170–172
Religion/religious beliefs
  adjusting to loss, 261, 262 (table)
  altruistic behavior, 153
  basic concepts, 35–36
  five-factor model (FFM) of personality, 36–38
  intrinsic and extrinsic orientations, 36
  neurological research, 38, 39 (figure)
  purpose in life, 28
  social support, 253
Religious aspirations, 37
Rene, K. M., 13
Reno, R. R., 57
Repetitive behaviors, 275, 287
Repetitive transcranial magnetic stimulation (rTMS), 294–295
Reproductive capacity decline, 246, 247, 247 (table)
Rescorla, R. A., 72, 74, 75, 76
Research Domain Criteria (RDoC) project, 299
Researching Adjustment
  academic hardiness/grit, 34–35
  biofeedback, 12–13
  brain reactivity-religious belief correlations, 38
  Erikson's theory of psychosocial development, 14–15
  friendship patterns, 144–145
  gene X environment interaction, 61
  Hebb's rule, 73–74
  identity-context relationship, 54–55
  intelligence testing, 188–189
  involuntary job loss, 209–210
  monetary influences, 229
  multicultural experiences, 314
  older adulthood, 248–249
  positive psychology, 15–16
  predictors of divorce, 173
  retirement communities/nursing homes, 264–265
  school dropouts, 191–192
  science, technology, engineering, and mathematics (STEM)
      programs, 212 (figure), 212–213
  social class, 227–228
  social media multitasking, 130
  stress measures, 114–115 (table), 115–116
  suicidal behaviors, 284–286
  TRIO programs, 194–195
Residential retirement communities, 263, 264–265
Resilience, 63–65, 64 (table), 65 (table), 210, 213, 306, 328
Resnik, H.
  see Greenberg, M. T.
Respondent conditioning, 72
Response inhibition, 250, 255 (table)
Retirement, 210–211, 256–258, 263–265
Reynolds, J., 323
Rhodes, J. E., 47
  see also DuBois, D. L.
RIASEC personality model, 208, 216, 216 (figure), 217
Rican, P., 37
Ricard, M., 97
Riches, A., 307
  see also Frimer, J. A.

Richmond, C. A. M., 124
Rickett, E. M., 31
  see Cacioppo, J. T.
Rick, S., 232
Rideout, V., 130
Rigby, K., 185
Rigby, S., 36
Rigg, K. K., 289
Rikani, A. A., 280
Rimm, E., 48
Rinpoche, S., 29
Risk factors, 63 (table), 63–64
Risky behaviors, 134, 283, 321–322
Ritual behaviors, 55, 260, 262, 262 (table)
Rivera, K. D., 186
Rizzolatti, G., 102
Robbins, S. B.
  see Chartrand, J. M.
Roberto, K. A., 147
Roberts, D., 130
Roberts, Jacqueline
  see Williams, Katrina
Roberts, James A., 232
Robertson, T. E.
  see Griskevicius, V.
Robie, C., 171
Robinson, J. L., 150
Robinson, M. D., 231
Robles, T. F., 321
Rochat, F., 57
Rodger, S.
  see Williams, Katrina
Rodriguez, E. R., 199
Roe, D., 298
Roediger, H., 84
Roeser, R., 184, 185, 189, 190
Rogers, C., 291
Rogers, Carl, 290–291
Rohde, L. A., 286
Role model behavior, 153, 171, 198–199, 225–226
  see also Mentors/mentoring
Role redefinition, 257
Romantic relationships
  casual sexual arrangements, 161–162
  committed partnerships, 162–163, 163 (figure)
  early adulthood, 147
  ending relationships, 172–174
  gay and lesbian relationships, 166–168, 321
  healthy intimate relationships, 163–165
  infidelity, 168–170
  intimate partner violence (IPV), 170–172
  maintenance behaviors, 175 (table), 175–176
  romantic love, 166 (figure)
Romberg, A., 82
Romeo, R., 113
Ronald E. McNair Post-baccalaureate Achievement Program, 194
Root, M. J., 34
Roscigno, V. J., 191
Roscoe, J., 40
Rose, C. A., 185
Rose, G. M., 57

Rosenberg, L., 289
Rosenkranz, M.
    see Davidson, R. J.
Rosenthal, L.
    see Gottman, J. M.
Rose, R. J., 283
    see also Dick, D. M.
Rossi, P. H., 227
Ross, M., 308
Ross, N. A., 124
Rottinghaus, P. J., 215
Rounds, J., 217
Routine contact, 149, 150 (table)
Royal Swedish Academy of Sciences, 228
Rozin, P., 280
Rubin, K. H., 141, 154
Rude, S. S., 103
Rudman, L., 314
Ruglis, J., 191
Rule learning, 82
Rummans, T. A.
    see Kellner, C. H.
Runger, D., 82
Rupp, J.
    see Patrick, K.
Rush, Benjamin, 288–289
Rush, J., 277
Rust, M., 315
Rutter, M., 61, 63
Ryan, G. W., 171
Ryan, R. M., 31, 36, 40, 62
Rye, M.
    see Zinnbauer, B.
Ryff, C. D., 31

Sabini, J., 162
Sable, J., 191
Sacks, Jonathan, 322
Sadness, 260, 271
Saegert, S. C., 227
    see Maton, K. I.
Saffron, J., 82
Saito, N.
    see Swanson, S. A.
Sajid, A., 286
Sales, J., 38
Sallis, J. F.
    see Patrick, K.
Saltzman, H., 119
    see also Compas, B.
Salutogenesis, 32
Salutogenic understanding, 20
Salzberg, S., 103
Samanez-Larking, G., 234, 235
Same-ethnicity friendships, 143
Same-gender friendships, 147, 148 (figure)
Sameroff, A. J., 17, 61, 64, 305, 306
Same-sex attraction, 160–161
Same-sex relationships, 166–168, 312, 321
Sampson, S. M.
    see Janicak, P. G.

Sanders, S., 263
Sander, T., 53
San Diego, California, 238 (table)
Sandstrom, G. M., 239
Sandvik, A. M., 34
San Francisco, California, 238 (table)
Sanislow, C. A., 299
San Jose, California, 238 (table)
Santorelli, S. F.
    see Davidson, R. J.
Santrock, J., 5
Saron, C., 92
    see also Lutz, A.
Sarter, M., 52
Satir, V., 128
Satpute, A. B., 53
Sauer, J. B.
    see Eby, L. T.
Sauter, D. A.
    see Warren, J. E.
Savage, Dan, 326
Savickas, M. L., 207
Savings, 234–236, 257–258, 258 (figure)
Savin-Williams, R., 160, 161
Sawangfa, O., 238
Sayer, A., 14
    see also Whitbourne, S. K.
Scaffolding, 84
Schaefer, C., 19, 113
Schaefer, H. S., 125
Schaefer, N. K., 307
Schaie, K. W., 250, 251
Schanberg, S., 125
Schaubhut, N. A., 216
Schedule to the reinforcement, 76
Scheel, A. W., 246
Scheier, M. F., 120, 124
    see also Carver, C. S.
Schema, 82, 83
Scherag, S., 287
Schiller Schigelone, A. R., 264
Schimmele, C. M., 312
Schizophrenia, 278, 284 (table)
Schlehofer, M., 35
Schlotzhauer, P.
    see Gueldner, S. H.
Schmeichel, B. J., 230
Schmidt, J., 328
Schmidt, S., 125
Schoeneman, T. J., 272
School
    academic success factors, 183–185, 184 (table), 187–190
    belongingness, 184 (table), 185, 189, 195
    bullying, 185–186, 189
    dropout rate, 191–192
    early childhood education, 181–183
    educational climate, 184 (table), 189–190
    importance, 180–181
    size and resources, 184 (table), 190
    see also College experience
School Nutrition Policy Initiative (SNPI), 132

School success
    see Academic success
Schorpp, K.
    see Yang, C. Y.
Schouten, A. P., 145
Schreurs, A., 149
    see also Wettersten, K. B.
Schuler, R., 20
Schultz, P., 213
Schumacher, J.
    see Davidson, R. J.
Schunk, D. H., 184
Schwartz, J., 289, 290
Schwartz, S. H., 307
Schwarz, M.
    see Sedlmeier, P.
Science, technology, engineering, and mathematics (STEM)
        programs, 84, 199, 212 (figure), 212–213
Scott, S. K.
    see Warren, J. E.
Scully, J. A., 114
Search Inside Yourself program, 220
Sears, D. O., 312
Sears, R., 20
Seaton, G.
    see Swanson, D. P.
Seattle, Washington, 238 (table)
Seay, N., 55
Secondary appraisal, 117, 118 (figure)
Secondary reinforcers, 225
Sedatives, 280, 281, 282, 282 (table)
Sedensky, M., 256
Sedlmeier, P., 93, 108
Seeking professional help, 291–293, 292 (figure)
Seeman, T.
    see Berkman, F.; Epel, E. S.
Sefcek, J. A., 14
Seftor, N., 195
    see also Myers, D.
Segal, Z. V., 90, 101
Segerstrom, S. C., 10
Seibert, J. K., 196, 198
Self-absorption, 322
Self-awareness skills, 250
Self-beliefs, 184, 184 (table), 187–188
Self-censorship, 323
Self-compassion, 101, 102, 103, 107
Self-concept, 214
Self-control, 78–79, 230–231
Self-determination theory (SDT), 40
Self-disclosure, 175, 175 (table), 322
Self-distraction, 120, 121
Self-efficacy, 81, 184, 184 (table), 195, 196, 198, 215–216
Self-esteem
    casual sexual arrangements, 162
    Internet impacts, 326
    intimate partner violence (IPV), 171
    mental disorders, 298
    social media impacts, 145, 323
    social support impacts, 48
Self-fulfillment, 206, 210–211

Self-help activities, 126
Self-identification, 58
Self-interest, 322
Self-matching, 234–235
Self-motivation, 40
Self-oriented cultures, 307
Self-other model, 307–308
Self-regulation, 62, 99–101, 181–182, 198, 230–231, 328
Self-restraint, 230–231
Self-stigma, 298
Self-transcendence, 34–35
Seligman, M. E. P, 7, 8, 9, 16, 72
Sell, D., 149
    see also Wettersten, K. B.
Selman, R., 141, 142, 142 (table), 150
Selye, H., 10, 117, 127, 128
Semin, G. R., 66
Seminowicz, D.
    see Mayberg, H. S.
Senior services, 265
Senju, A., 327
Sense of coherence, 20, 32
Sense of control, 196, 253, 255 (table)
Sergeant, J. A.
    see Taylor, E.
Sergeant, J. F., 263
Serotonin, 280, 285
Sessions, L., 146
    see also Hampton, K.
Settings
    see Behavioral settings
Severed relationships, 172–174
Sevon, G., 226
    see also Leiser, D.
Sewell, K. W., 261
Sexual activity, 134, 247
Sexual attraction, 311–312
Sexual contact network, 52
Sexual dysfunction, 282 (table)
Sexual experimentation, 161–162
Sexuality, 165–166, 311–312
Sexually transmitted diseases (STDs), 134, 321
Sexual orientation
    childhood, 160–161
    definition, 311
    friendships, 147, 148 (figure)
    microaggressions, 122
    societal challenges, 310
Sexual violence, 321
Shablack, H.
    see Kross, E.
Shaeer, K., 247
Shaeer, O., 247
Shaffer, H. J., 281
Shaffer, M. A., 328
Shafranske, E. P., 35
    see also Pargament, K. I.
Shahabi, L., 38
    see also Powell, L. H.
Shaham, D., 30
Shampanier, K., 230

Shanks, D. R., 83
Shaping, 78
Shapiro, D. H., Jr., 92
Shapiro, S., 90, 97, 101
Sharpless, B. A., 277
Shaver, P., 30
Shaw, B. F., 277
Shaw, George Bernard, 244
Shaw, J. D.
   see Fang, R.
Shaw, L., 50
Sheard, M., 34
Shea, S. A.
   see Buxton, O. M.
Sheldon, K. M., 40, 155, 239
   see also Vansteenkiste, M.
Sheldon, S. B., 191
Shepard, S. A.
   see Eisenberg, N.
Sheridan, J. F.
   see Davidson, R. J.
Sherif, C. W., 315
Sherif, M., 315
Sherman, S.
   see Foster, G. D.
Shetty, K., 219
Shields, A., 62
Shinn, M., 46, 53
Shiota, M. N., 151
Shirinyan, D.
   see Master, S. L.
Shoda, Y., 62
   see Mischel, W.
Shoham, A., 57
Shors, T., 30
Short-term memory, 251
Shrestha, L. B., 244
Shrewsbury, V., 132
Shui-chi tzu-an, 123
Shults, J.
   see Foster, G. D.
Shultz, J., 328
Shweder, R., 60
Siddhartha Gautama, 94–95
Siemer, M., 328
Silberg, J. L., 7
Silberman, I., 39
Silva, A., 19
Silverstein, M., 263
Silverthorn, N., 47
   see also DuBois, D. L.
Simeone, R., 48
Similarity, 144–145
Simmons, B. L., 128
Simmons, Russell, 126
Simon, R., 125
Simons, J., 40
   see also Vansteenkiste, M.
Simpson, J. A.
   see Griskevicius, V.
Sinclair, S., 315

Singer, B. H., 31
Sionean, C., 161
Sirota, L., 125
Sischo, L., 323
Situational anxiety, 53
Situational violence, 171
Skinner, B. F., 55, 70, 72, 76, 77, 225, 290
Skinnerian conditioning, 72, 79–80, 225
Skype, 318
Sleep, 11–12
Sleep disorders, 282 (table)
Sleep pattern changes, 247 (table), 248
Sloan, L. R.
   see Cialdini, R. B.
Small, G. W.
   see Uhls, Y. T.
Smartphones, 319–320
Smith, A. K.
   see Kelly, A.
Smith, E. E., 174
   see also Kross, E.
Smith, J. C., 227
Smith-Lovin, L., 323
Smith, M., 113
Smith, M. K.
   see Freeman, S.
Smith, P. B., 57, 59
Smith, P. T., 260
Smith, R. S., 63, 64, 65 (table)
Smith, S., 104
Smith, T. B., 48
Smith, T. W., 50
   see also Bowen, K. S.
Smith, Vernon, 228
Smith Zweig, J., 238
Smits, J. A. J., 126
Smoking, 283
   see Substance abuse
Snapchat, 320
Sneed, J. R., 14
   see also Whitbourne, S. K.
Snyder, C., 9
Sobol, A. M.
   see Gortmaker, S. L.
Social anxiety, 32, 275, 284 (table)
Social capital, 48, 52–53
Social class, 144–145, 213, 226, 227–228, 234
Social cognitive career theory (SCCT), 215–216
Social cognitive theory, 184, 215
Social–companionate support, 48
Social constructivist theory, 272
Social disengagement, 53
Social–emotional learning (SEL) programs, 153
Social interactions, 16–17, 31, 50–52, 51 (figure), 254, 265
Social isolation, 154, 263
Socialization process, 65–66
Social learning theory, 62, 70, 80
Social media
   friendships, 145–147
   infidelity, 168–169
   Internet impact, 145–146, 146 (figure), 323

loneliness intervention, 154–155
multitasking effects, 130
Social networks
academic environments, 188
basic concepts, 50–52
diversity, 144
friendship maintenance behavior, 149, 150 (table)
mentoring, 48
negative self-perceptions, 323
sample networks, 51 (figure)
Social norms, 78, 231, 315–316
Social penetration theory, 175
Social psychology, 20, 21 (figure)
Social Readjustment Rating Scale, 114–115 (table)
Social relationships
see Friendships
Social support
age-related changes, 49 (figure), 253–254
change processes, 34
characteristics, 48, 50
divorce impacts, 174
grieving process, 261–262, 262 (table)
physical impacts, 48, 49 (figure), 124
research background, 48
social capital, 48, 52–53
social networks, 48, 50–52, 51 (figure)
spiritual and religious beliefs and activities, 39
as stress management strategy, 124
Social withdrawal, 265
Societal challenges
diversity, 17, 309–317
technology, 17–18, 317–327
Socioeconomic status (SES), 132, 172, 208, 211, 213, 245
Socioemotional changes, 251–255, 255 (table)
Sociology, 21, 21 (figure)
Sokol, B. W., 306
Solberg, V. S., 81
Solomon, S., 31
Somatogenic etiologies
addictive disorders, 283
basic concepts, 272
eating disorders, 280
mental illness treatments, 288, 289, 293–297, 298 (table)
mood disorders, 277
neurodevelopmental disorders, 287
psychotic disorders, 278
Somatovisceral feedback, 52
Son Hing, L. S., 313
Sousa, P., 31
South, S. J., 191
Sowell, E. R., 62, 65
Spadaro, A., 326
Sparks, E. A., 231
Specht, J., 16
see also Hutteman, R.
Spellman, T., 295
Spencer, M. B., 54
see Swanson, D. P.
Spielberger, C. D., 53
Spinrad, T. L., 152
see Michalik, N. M.

Spiral of silence theory, 323
Spiritual aspirations, 37
Spirituality
adjusting to loss, 261, 262 (table)
basic concepts, 35–36
five-factor model (FFM) of personality, 36–38
intrinsic and extrinsic orientations, 36
neurological research, 38, 39 (figure)
purpose in life, 28
see also Buddhism
Spiro, A., 19
Spitalnick, J. S., 167
Spitzer, B. J.
see Yeager, D. S.
Spokane, A. R., 217
Spousal loss, 260–261
Sprecher, S., 320
see also Finkel, E. J.
Stafford, L., 175, 176
Stanford University, 317, 318
Stangor, C., 57
Stanley, M., 33
Stansfeld, S. A.
see Clark, C.
Stanton, M. V.
see Shaffer, H. J.
State hospitals, 288–289
State populations, 310–311
Statistical learning, 82
Staudinger, U. M., 329
Stearns, E., 191
Steele, C. M., 187
Steele, J. C.
see Vera, E. M.
Steel, P., 328
Steen, T. A., 8
Steffens, M. C., 312
Steger, M. F., 31, 35, 39
Steiger, J. H., 213
Steiner, N. J., 13
STEM careers
see Science, technology, engineering, and mathematics (STEM) programs
Stereotypes/stereotyping
diverse populations, 312–313
microaggressions, 122
retirement, 256
stereotype threats, 184 (table), 187
theory of occupational circumscription and compromise, 214–215
work aspirations and expectations, 211, 213
Sternberg, R., 165, 166 (figure)
Sterns, H. L., 256
Stewart, M., 323
Stewart, P. A.
see Foltz, J. L.
Stewart, T. L.
see Dovidio, J. F.
Stillman, T. F., 231
Stillwell, R., 191
Stimulants, 280, 282, 282 (table), 286, 296, 298 (table)

Stinson, J.
  see Vera, E. M.
Stohs, S. J., 246
Stokols, D., 20
Stone, J., 315
Stonewalling, 164, 173
Stovel, K., 50, 52
Strahilevitz, M. A., 232
Strategy of visualization, 108
Strauss, A. L., 226
Straus, S. E., 47
Strehl, U., 13
Streitman, S., 63
Stress
  age-related changes, 249
  anxiety disorders, 275–276, 284 (table)
  change processes, 18
  components, 112–113
  diet and nutrition, 131–132, 132 (figure)
  employee assistance programs (EAPs), 219–220
  fight-or-flight reaction, 10
  good stress versus bad stress, 126–129
  healthy stress management strategies, 124–126
  individual hardiness, 34
  intimate partner violence (IPV), 172
  measurement approaches, 114–115 (table), 115–116,
    119 (table)
  mindfullness-based practices, 96, 96 (figure), 99–101
  occupation-related stress, 218–220
  physical activity/exercise, 126, 133–134
  physiological consequences, 113, 127, 154
  social media multitasking, 130
  social support impacts, 48, 49 (figure), 50
  spiritual and religious beliefs and activities, 38
  stressors, 10–11, 29–30, 113, 121–124, 260
  stress processes, 117, 118 (figure)
  stress reactions, 117, 119, 119 (table)
  substance abuse, 134–135
  suicidal behaviors, 285
  see also Mental illness/mental disorders
Stressors
  categories, 113
  controllable versus uncontrollable stressors, 121–122
  culturally-related stressors, 122–124
  environmental stressors, 10–11
  life changes, 29–30
  spousal loss, 260–261
Striegel-Moore, R. H., 280
Strong Interest Inventory, 208, 216
Strosahl, K., 103
Student-to-teacher ratios, 190
Study skills
  college success factors, 196, 197 (figure), 198, 198 (table)
  higher education programs, 195
Stults, C., 171, 172
Sturgis, P., 312
Substance abuse, 134–135, 172, 206
Substance Abuse and Mental Health Services
    Administration, 134
Substance-induced mental disorders, 281–282
Substance use disorders, 274, 280–283, 282 (table), 284 (table)

Success-effort relationship, 74–75, 187–188
Successful aging, 258–259
Successful intimate relationships, 163–165
Successful retirement, 256–258
Sue, David, 7
Sue, Derald Wing, 7, 122
Sue, Diane M., 7
Suhay, E., 57
Suicidal behaviors, 283, 284–286, 306, 326
Sullivan, M., 60
Sullivan, P. F., 279
Sumner, R., 33
Super, C. M., 207
Super, D. E., 207
Superego, 290
Supernatural etiologies, 271–272
Survival, need for, 206, 210
Susceptibility to disease, 247, 247 (table)
Swanson, D. P., 54, 55
Swanson, S. A., 279
Switek, M., 238
Symbolic prejudice, 312–313
Sypher, I., 299
Szilagyi, P. G.
  see Foltz, J. L.

Tabares, A., 165
Tadmor, C. T., 314
Tagaki, E., 263
Talaga, M. C., 296
Talent Search, 194
Talib, N., 32
Talks, relationship, 175 (table), 175–176
Talk therapy, 125, 271, 272, 290
Tam, L., 236
Tangible support, 48, 50
Tang, Y. Y., 97
Tarullo, L. B., 182
Task behavior, 175 (table), 176
Task sharing, 149, 150 (table)
Tasselli, S., 51
Tay, L., 237
  see also Diener, E.
Taylor, A., 143
  see also Graham, S.
Taylor, B. K., 20
Taylor-Carter, M. A., 258
Taylor, D., 175, 312
Taylor, E., 287
Taylor, M. A., 257
Taylor, S. E., 48, 50
  see also Master, S. L.
Teacher beliefs and expectations, 184 (table), 186–187, 189
Teachers' encouragement and praise, 184 (table), 187–188
Technology
  friendships, 145–147, 146 (figure)
  healthy usage limits, 324–325
  historical perspective, 317–318, 318–319 (figure)
  infidelity, 168–169
  interpersonal relationships, 320–322
  loneliness intervention, 154–155

negative impacts, 322–324
positive impacts, 325–327, 326 (figure)
social media multitasking, 130
societal challenges, 17–18, 317–327
see also Internet
Teenagers
see Adolescence
Telander, K., 213
see also Brown, S. D.
Tellegen, A., 9
Telomeres, 10, 246
Temperature sensitivity, 247 (table), 248
Tennen, H., 18
Ten richest cities in America, 238 (table)
ten Vergert, M.
see Dovidio, J. F.
Terrace, H.
see Spellman, T.
Terror management theory, 30–31
Texas, 310
Text messages, 320, 322
Thaler, R., 228, 234
Thales of Miletus, 13
Thatcher, R., 171
Thayer, J. F.
see Sandvik, A. M.
Theory of occupational circumscription and compromise,
    214–215
Theory of person–environment fit, 208, 214, 216–217
Theory of psychosocial development, 14–17, 15 (table)
Theory of student departure, 193–194
Therapy, couples, 168–170
Therien, J. M., 65
The White House, 298, 317
Third age, 256
Thiyagarajan, M.
see Xie, L.
Thoits, P., 48, 50
Thomas, A., 6, 7
Thomas, D., 182
see also Garces, E.
Thompson, Marilyn
see Michalik, N. M.
Thompson, Megan, 191
Thompson, Mindi N., 193, 194, 195, 200
Thompson, P. M., 62
see also Sowell, E. R.
Thompson, R. C., 216
Thompson, R. F., 30
Thomsen, A., 119
see also Compas, B.
Thorazine, 296
Thoresen, C. E., 38
see also Powell, L. H.
Thorne, A.
see Cialdini, R. B.
Thought control, 98–99
Three Cs of addiction, 281
Thurlow, M. L., 191
Tilert, T.
see Troiano, R. P.

Timing considerations, 76 (figure), 76–77
Timmerman, I. G. H., 48
Tinto, V., 193–194
Tix, A., 38
Tobacco use, 280, 282 (table), 283
see Substance abuse
Tobler, P., 72
Todd, N. R., 122
Toga, A. W., 62
see also Sowell, E. R.
Tolerance, 281, 313–316
Toma, C. L., 322
Tomaskovic-Devey, D., 191
Tomlinson, Ray, 318
Tompson, T., 256
Toohey, S. M., 46, 53
Torino, G. C., 122
Torrent streaming services, 318
Torres, J. B., 81
Tosi, H., 114
Toth, S. L., 60, 62
Touch, 124–125
Touch therapy, 125
Tracy, A., 37
Tracy, S. J., 186
Transgender, 311
Trauma-related disorders, 275–276, 284 (table)
Travel, 314
Triandis, H. C., 58, 59
Trichotillomania, 275
Trickett, E., 53
Trimble, J. E., 60
Trinder, J.
see Edwards, B. A.
TRIO programs, 194–195, 199
Troetschel, R., 30
Troiano, R. P., 133
Tropp, L. R., 316
Trust, 169
Trzesniewski, K. H., 326
Tsabari, O., 217
Tsai, J. L., 59
Tuke, William, 288
Turiano, N., 32
Turkle, S., 322, 325, 327
Turner, R. N., 316
Tuttle, C., 195
see also Myers, D.
Tversky, A., 30, 228
Twenge, J. M., 322, 325, 326
Twitter, 145, 318
Tybur, J. M.
see Griskevicius, V.
Tziner, A., 217

Uchida, Y., 59
Uchino, B. N., 48, 50
see also Bowen, K. S.
Udry, J., 161
see also Carver, K.
Uhlmann, E. L., 71

Uhls, Y. T., 327
Umbach, P. D., 187, 190
Uncertainty, 31, 34, 56, 322
Unconditioned response (UCR), 70–71, 71 (figure), 72
Unconditioned stimulus (UCS), 70–71, 71 (figure), 72, 76
Unconscious mind, 289–290
Uncontrollable stressors, 121–122
Understanding behaviors, 175 (table), 176
Ung, E. K., 279
United Kingdom, 144–145
United Way, 190
University of California, Los Angeles (UCLA), 317
Uno, D., 50
Unplanned versus planned change, 19–20
Unprotected sex, 134
Unsuccessful intimate relationships, 163–165
Updegraff, J. A.
    see Taylor, S. E.
Upward Bound, 194, 195
Urland, G. R., 316
U.S. Bureau of Labor Statistics, 256
U.S. Census Bureau, 172, 212, 247, 260, 310, 311
U.S. Defense Advanced Research Projects Agency (DARPA), 317
U.S. Department of Agriculture, 131, 135
U.S. Department of Education, 192, 193, 194, 212 (figure)
U.S. Department of Health and Human Services, 131, 132, 133, 135, 245, 248, 263
U.S. Food and Drug Administration, 295, 297
Uslaner, E. M., 312
U.S. National Library of Medicine, 288
Utah, 311

Väänänen, A.
    see Kouvonen, A. M.
Vacek, K.
    see Vera, E. M.
Vagus nerve, 125, 295
Vagus nerve stimulation (VNS), 295
Vahtera, J.
    see Kouvonen, A. M.
Vail, K. E., III, 30
Valentine, J. C., 47, 184
    see also DuBois, D. L.
Valiente, C.
    see Michalik, N. M.
Valisenko, S. A., 134
Valkenburg, P. M., 145
Vallente, C., 64
Values, 95, 103, 104–108, 322
Vance, S. L., 315
Vander Veur, S. S.
    see Foster, G. D.
VanderWeele, T. J., 321
van Dijk, J., 146
van Heeringen, K., 285
van Kempen, E.
    see Clark, C.
Vansteenkiste, M., 40, 41
Variable-interval reinforcement schedules, 76 (figure)
Varnum, M. E. W., 329
Vasconcelles, E., 38

Vaux, A., 123
Venting, 120
Vera, E. M., 21, 120, 122, 185, 186
"Very old" population, 245
Vess, M., 30
Veterans Upward Bound, 194
Vicarious learning, 81, 153
Vietze, D., 312
Viken, R. J., 283
    see also Dick, D. M.
Vincent, C., 144, 145
Violence against women, 170–172, 321
Vipassana, 106
Virtuous qualities, 9, 10 (table)
Vision changes, 247, 247 (table), 248
Visualization, 108
Vivian, D., 172
Vocational development
    characteristics, 205
    decision-making process, 208, 214–217
    demographic factors, 211, 213–214
    life span salience, 211
    personality assessments, 208–209, 216 (figure), 216–217
    theoretical perspectives, 214–217
Vocational hope, 214
Vocation, definition of, 206
Voci, A., 316
Vohs, K. D., 31, 39, 229, 230, 231, 239
    see also Baumeister, R. F.
Voineskos, A., 278
Vollberg, M., 72
Voluntary work transitions, 209, 256
Volunteering opportunities, 210–211, 256, 262
von Eye, A., 7
von Freymann, J. W., 219
Voon, V.
    see Mayberg, H. S.
Votruba-Drzal, E., 140
Vrangalova, S., 161
Vygotsky, Lev, 83–84
Vygotsky, L. S., 83
Vyncke, V., 52
Vyvyan, J.
    see Millar, H.

Wadsworth, M. E., 119, 227
    see also Compas, B.
Wager, T. D., 174
    see also Kross, E.
Wagner, Angela, 280
    see also Kaye, W. H.
Wagner, A. R., 72, 74, 75, 76
Wai, J., 213
Waite, L. J., 254
Walach, H., 125
Walker, I., 315
Walker, L. J., 307
    see also Frimer, J. A.
Walker, M. P., 11
Walker, M. R.
    see Cialdini, R. B.

Wall, S., 140
Walsh, K. E., 166
Walsh, R., 126
Walsh, W., 33
Walters, E. E., 275
    see Kessler, R. C.
Walter, U., 220
Walton, G. M.
    see Yeager, D. S.
Wang, H., 146, 146 (figure)
Wang, L.-F.
    see Heppner, M. J.
Wang, W., 314
    see Buxton, O. M.
Wang, Y. C.
    see Gortmaker, S. L.
Wang, Y.-W.
    see Heppner, M. J.
Wan, W., 74
Ward, D., 328
Wardell, F.
    see Millar, H.
Wardle, J., 132
Warren, J. E., 52
Washington, D.C., 238 (table)
Wasserman, S., 50
Waters, E., 140
Watson, J. B., 290
Watson, John B., 290
Watts, R., 21
Wawrzynski, M. R., 187, 190
Way, B., 10
Webley, P., 226, 234
Weeden, J., 162
Wehlage, G., 185
Weick, K., 19, 20
Weinberg, C., 258
Weiner, D. B., 288, 289
Weintraub, J. K., 120
    see also Carver, C. S.
Weir, K., 126
Weisman, J. L., 199
Weissberg, R. P.
    see Greenberg, M. T.
Weiten, W., 5
Well-being
    see Health and well-being
Weller, A., 125
Wellman, B., 146, 146 (figure)
Welsh, D. P., 161, 162
    see also Grello, C. M.
Wenderoth, M. P.
    see Freeman, S.
Werner, E. E., 63, 64, 65 (table)
Wertenbroch, K., 231, 232
Wertheimer, M., 94
Wertheimer, Max, 94
Western psychology, 94, 98–99
Wethington, A., 117
Wettersten, K. B., 149
Wheaton, B., 113

Whitaker, R., 293, 295, 296
Whitbourne, S. K., 14
White, B. J., 315
Whitebread, D., 181
White House, 298, 317
Whittington, F. J., 264
Whitty, M. T., 169
Widowhood, 260–261
Wiedenfeld, S. A., 81
Wigfield, A., 186
Wiland, J.
    see Warren, J. E.
Wilcox, B., 124
Wiley, J. F., 321
Wilkie, S. S., 246
Wilkins, T. A., 36, 37, 38
Will, 15, 15 (table)
Willems, S., 52
Willett, M., 258
Williams, D. R., 113
Williams, J. E. G., 37
Williams, Katrina, 287
Williams, Kipling D., 174
Wills, T., 48
Wilson, K., 103
Wilson, T. D., 229, 231
Wilson, W. J., 206
Wimmer, G.E., 234
Wingate, U., 196
Wingood, G., 38
Wink, P., 37, 256, 261
Wiruchnipawan, F., 314
Wisdom, 15, 15 (table), 309, 329
Wisdom traditions, 92
Wise, R. J. S.
    see Warren, J. E.
Witchcraft, 272
Withdrawal disorder, 281
Withdrawn children, 154
Wolff, T., 36
Wolke, D., 185
Wong, F., 21
Wood, A. M., 237
    see also Boyce, C. J.
Woodcock, A., 213
Wood, S. L., 231, 239
Woolfenden, S.
    see Williams, Katrina
Woolhandler, S.
    see Lasser, K.
Woolsey, M., 33
Work
    career indecisiveness, 208–209
    contextual influences, 211, 213–214
    definition, 206
    employee assistance programs (EAPs),
        219–220
    first job, 209
    flow, 218
    fundamental human needs, 206–207, 210
    importance, 206–207

life span salience, 207–211
meaningful work, 205
midcareer period, 210
older adulthood, 256
retirement, 210–211
rewards and risks, 218–220
science, technology, engineering, and mathematics (STEM)
 programs, 212 (figure), 212–213
stress levels, 218–219
theory of occupational circumscription and compromise,
 214–215
Working Group on Obesity in China, 131
Working memory, 251, 255 (table)
Workplace bullying, 186
Workshops/classes, 314–315
World Health Organization (WHO), 131, 245, 273, 276, 278, 279,
 285, 286, 287, 298
World Wide Web, 318, 325
Worth, determination of, 231–232
Worwa, C. T., 65
Wulff, D., 35
Wundt, Wilhelm, 94
Wu, Z., 312
Wyche, K.
 see Saegert, S. C.
Wyckoff, S., 12
Wyer, R. S., Jr., 228
Wysocki, D. K., 168

Xie, L., 11
Xu, O.
 see Xie, L.

Yalom, I. D., 29
Yalom, Irvin, 28
Yang, C. Y., 48
Yanos, P. T., 298
Yeager, D. S., 33, 34–35

Yi, J., 168
 see also Atkins, D. C.
Yoder, J. D., 171
York Retreat, 288
Yoshimoto, D.
 see Gottman, J. M.
Yost Hammer, E., 5
Young adults
 see Early adulthood
Young, J., 195
 see also Myers, D.
Young-old adults, 248
Youth mentoring programs, 47
Youth Risk Behavioral Surveillance Data, 134
YouTube, 326
Yuan, M., 323
Yue, X. D., 124

Zabinski, M. F.
 see Patrick, K.
Zacks, E., 167
Zahn, R.
 see Moll, J.
Zajacova, A., 81
Zanna, M. P., 313
Zautra, A. J., 18, 19
Zeelenberg, M., 232
Zhang, L., 239
Zhang, Z.
 see Fang, R.
Zijdenbos, A.
 see Giedd, J. N.
Zimmerman, B. J., 47, 81, 196
Zimmermann, D.
 see Sedlmeier, P.
Zinnbauer, B., 35
Zins, J. E.
 see Greenberg, M. T.